THE ROUTLEDGE HANDBOOK OF EPISTEMIC CONTEXTUALISM

Epistemic contextualism is a recent and hotly debated topic in philosophy. Contextualists argue that the language we use to attribute knowledge can only be properly understood relative to a specified context. How much can our knowledge depend on context? Is there a limit, and if so, where does it lie? What is the relationship between epistemic contextualism and fundamental topics in philosophy such as objectivity, truth, and relativism?

The Routledge Handbook of Epistemic Contextualism is an outstanding reference source to the key topics, problems, and debates in this exciting subject and is the first collection of its kind. Comprising thirty-seven chapters by a team of international contributors, the *Handbook* is divided into eight parts:

- Data and motivations for contextualism
- Methodological issues
- Epistemological implications
- Doing without contextualism
- Relativism and disagreement
- Semantic implementations
- Contextualism outside 'knows'
- Foundational linguistic issues

Within these sections central issues, debates, and problems are examined, including contextualism and thought experiments and paradoxes such as the Gettier problem and the lottery paradox; semantics and pragmatics; the relationship between contextualism, relativism and disagreement; and contextualism about related topics like ethical judgments and modality.

The Routledge Handbook of Epistemic Contextualism is essential reading for students and researchers of epistemology and philosophy of language. It will also be very useful for those in related fields such as linguistics and philosophy of mind.

Jonathan Jenkins Ichikawa is Associate Professor of Philosophy at the University of British Columbia, Canada. His research focuses on issues in epistemology, philosophy of mind, and philosophy of language. He is the co-author, with Benjamin Jarvis, of *The Rules of Thought* (2013), and the author of *Contextualising Knowledge: Epistemology and Semantics* (2017).

ROUTLEDGE HANDBOOKS IN PHILOSOPHY

Routledge Handbooks in Philosophy are state-of-the-art surveys of emerging, newly refreshed, and important fields in philosophy, providing accessible yet thorough assessments of key problems, themes, thinkers, and recent developments in research.

All chapters for each volume are specially commissioned, and written by leading scholars in the field. Carefully edited and organized, *Routledge Handbooks in Philosophy* provide indispensable reference tools for students and researchers seeking a comprehensive overview of new and exciting topics in philosophy. They are also valuable teaching resources as accompaniments to textbooks, anthologies, and research-orientated publications.

Recently published:

The Routledge Handbook of Embodied Cognition
Edited by Lawrence Shapiro

The Routledge Handbook of Philosophy of Well-Being
Edited by Guy Fletcher

The Routledge Handbook of Philosophy of Imagination
Edited by Amy Kind

The Routledge Handbook of the Stoic Tradition
Edited by John Sellars

The Routledge Handbook of Philosophy of Information
Edited by Luciano Floridi

The Routledge Handbook of the Philosophy of Biodiversity
Edited by Justin Garson, Anya Plutynski, and Sahotra Sarkar

The Routledge Handbook of Philosophy of the Social Mind
Edited by Julian Kiverstein

The Routledge Handbook of Philosophy of Empathy
Edited by Heidi Maibom

The Routledge Handbook of Epistemic Contextualism
Edited by Jonathan Jenkins Ichikawa

The Routledge Handbook of Epistemic Injustice
Edited by Ian James Kidd, José Medina and Gaile Pohlhaus

The Routledge Handbook of Philosophy of Pain
Edited by Jennifer Corns

The Routledge Handbook of Brentano and the Brentano School
Edited by Uriah Kriegel

The Routledge Handbook of Metaethics
Edited by Tristram McPherson and David Plunkett

The Routledge Handbook of Philosophy of Memory
Edited by Sven Bernecker and Kourken Michaelian

The Routledge Handbook of Evolution and Philosophy
Edited by Richard Joyce

The Routledge Handbook of Mechanisms and Mechanical Philosophy
Edited by Stuart Glennan and Phyllis Illari

THE ROUTLEDGE HANDBOOK OF EPISTEMIC CONTEXTUALISM

Edited by Jonathan Jenkins Ichikawa

LONDON AND NEW YORK

First published 2017
By Routledge
2 Park Square, Milton Park, Abingdon, Oxon, OX14 4RN

and by Routledge
711 Third Avenue, New York, NY 10017

Routledge is an imprint of the Taylor & Francis Group, an informa business

© 2017 selection and editorial matter, Jonathan Jenkins Ichikawa; individual chapters, the contributors

The right of Jonathan Jenkins Ichikawa to be identified as the author of the editorial material, and of the authors for their individual chapters, has been asserted in accordance with sections 77 and 78 of the Copyright, Designs and Patents Act 1988.

All rights reserved. No part of this book may be reprinted or reproduced or utilised in any form or by any electronic, mechanical, or other means, now known or hereafter invented, including photocopying and recording, or in any information storage or retrieval system, without permission in writing from the publishers.

Trademark notice: Product or corporate names may be trademarks or registered trademarks, and are used only for identification and explanation without intent to infringe.

British Library Cataloguing-in-Publication Data
A catalogue record for this book is available from the British Library

Library of Congress Cataloging-in-Publication Data
Names: Ichikawa, Jonathan Jenkins., editor.
Title: The Routledge handbook of epistemic contextualism / edited by Jonathan Jenkins Ichikawa.
Description: 1 [edition]. | New York : Routledge, 2017. | Series: Routledge handbooks in philosophy | Includes bibliographical references and index.
Identifiers: LCCN 2016043135 | ISBN 9781138818392 (hardback : alk. paper) | ISBN 9781315745275 (e-book)
Subjects: LCSH: Contextualism (Philosophy) | Knowledge, Theory of. | Context (Linguistics)
Classification: LCC B809.14 .R68 2017 | DDC 121—dc23
LC record available at https://lccn.loc.gov/2016043135

ISBN: 978-1-138-81839-2 (hbk)
ISBN: 978-1-315-74527-5 (ebk)

Typeset in Bembo
by Apex CoVantage, LLC

Printed and bound in Great Britain by
TJ International Ltd, Padstow, Cornwall

CONTENTS

Notes on contributors   *ix*
Acknowledgements   *xiv*

    Introduction: what is epistemic contextualism?   1
    Jonathan Jenkins Ichikawa

PART I
Data and motivations   **11**

 1 The variability of 'knows': an opinionated overview   13
    Crispin Wright

 2 The intuitive basis for contextualism   32
    Geoff Pynn

 3 Epistemic contextualism and linguistic behavior   44
    Wesley Buckwalter

 4 Feminism and contextualism   57
    Evelyn Brister

PART II
Methodological issues   **69**

 5 Epistemic contextualism and conceptual ethics   71
    E. Diaz-Leon

Contents

6　Does contextualism hinge on a methodological dispute?　81
Jie Gao, Mikkel Gerken and Stephen B. Ryan

7　The psychological context of contextualism　94
Jennifer Nagel and Julia Jael Smith

8　What are we doing when we theorize about context sensitivity?　105
Derek Ball

PART III
Epistemological implications　**119**

9　Epistemic contextualism and the shifting the question objection　121
Brian Montgomery

10　Skepticism and contextualism　131
Michael J. Hannon

11　Contextualism and fallibilism　145
Keith DeRose

12　Contextualism and closure　156
Maria Lasonen-Aarnio

13　Lotteries and prefaces　168
Matthew A. Benton

14　Contextualism and knowledge norms　177
Alex Worsnip

15　Contextualism and Gettier cases　190
John Greco

PART IV
Doing without contextualism　**203**

16　'Knowledge' and pragmatics　205
Patrick Rysiew

17　Loose use and belief variation　218
Wayne A. Davis

18　Semantic minimalism and speech act pluralism applied to 'knows'　230
Herman Cappelen

Contents

19 Interest-relative invariantism   240
Brian Weatherson

PART V
Relativism and disagreement   **255**

20 The disagreement challenge to contextualism   257
Justin Khoo

21 On disagreement   272
Torfinn Thomesen Huvenes

22 Contextualism, relativism, and the problem of lost disagreement   282
Elke Brendel

23 Epistemological implications of relativism   292
J. Adam Carter

PART VI
Semantic implementations   **303**

24 The semantic error problem for epistemic contextualism   305
Patrick Greenough and Dirk Kindermann

25 Conversational kinematics   321
Robin McKenna

26 'Knowledge' and quantifiers   332
Nathan R. Cockram

27 Gradability and knowledge   348
Michael Blome-Tillmann

PART VII
Contextualism outside 'knows'   **359**

28 Moral contextualism and epistemic contextualism: similarities
and differences   361
Berit Brogaard

29 Contextualism about epistemic reasons   375
Daniel Fogal and Kurt Sylvan

Contents

30 Contextualism about epistemic modals 388
J.L. Dowell

31 Contextualism about belief ascriptions 400
Roger Clarke

32 Counterfactuals and knowledge 411
Karen S. Lewis

33 Contextualism about foundations 425
Daniel Greco

PART VIII
Foundational linguistic issues **439**

34 The semantics-pragmatics distinction and context-sensitivity 441
Maite Ezcurdia

35 The mind-independence of contexts for knowledge attributions 455
Giovanni Mion and Christopher Gauker

36 Index, context, and the content of knowledge 465
Brian Rabern

37 Contextualism in epistemology and relevance theory 480
Mark Jary and Robert J. Stainton

Index *493*

CONTRIBUTORS

Derek Ball is a Lecturer in Philosophy at the University of St Andrews. His professional interests range widely across philosophy of mind, philosophy of language, metaphysics, epistemology, and cognitive science.

Matthew A. Benton is an Assistant Professor of Philosophy at Seattle Pacific University. Prior to that he held postdoctoral research fellowships at the University of Notre Dame and the University of Oxford. His research is mainly in epistemology and related areas in philosophy of language and philosophy of religion.

Michael Blome-Tillmann is an Associate Professor of Philosophy and William Dawson Scholar at McGill University. His research is primarily in the areas of epistemology and philosophy of language. He is the author of *Knowledge and Presuppositions* (OUP, 2014).

Elke Brendel is a Professor of Philosophy at the University of Bonn, Germany. Her research focuses on logic, epistemology, philosophy of language, and philosophical methodology. She has worked on logical and semantic paradoxes and is particularly interested in the semantics of disagreement.

Evelyn Brister is an Associate Professor of Philosophy at Rochester Institute of Technology. Her work examines the effect of epistemic practices on science policy decisions. In addition to work on feminism, skepticism, and contextualism, she has written on interdisciplinarity, climate ethics, and science education.

Berit Brogaard is Professor of Philosophy at University of Miami. Her areas of research include philosophy of perception, philosophy of emotions, and philosophy of language. She is the author of *Transient Truths* (OUP, 2012), *On Romantic Love* (OUP, 2015), and *The Superhuman Mind* (Penguin, 2015).

Wesley Buckwalter is a Banting Fellow in the Department of Philosophy at the University of Waterloo. He studies a wide range of categories and concepts in philosophy and cognitive science, including knowledge, belief, delusion, action, ability, assertion, obligation, and bias.

Contributors

Herman Cappelen is a Professor of Philosophy at the Universities of Oslo and St Andrews. He works on philosophy of language, philosophical methodology, and related issues in metaphysics, philosophy of mind, and epistemology.

J. Adam Carter is a Lecturer in Philosophy at the University of Glasgow, working mainly in epistemology, and increasingly on topics at the intersection of epistemology and the philosophy of mind and cognitive science, value theory, bioethics, and the philosophy of language.

Roger Clarke is a Lecturer in Philosophy at Queen's University Belfast, working mainly in epistemology. Belief is nearer to his heart than other objects of philosophical investigation. Additional research interests include formal epistemology and free will/moral responsibility.

Nathan R. Cockram is a Ph.D. student at the University of British Columbia. His interests mostly lie in and around epistemology. Outside of philosophy, he is also an avid angler.

Wayne A. Davis is Professor of Philosophy at Georgetown University. He works mainly on the foundations of semantics and pragmatics, publishing *Implicature* (CUP, 1998), *Meaning, Expression, and Thought* (CUP, 2003), *Irregular Negatives, Implicatures, and Idioms* (Springer, 2016), and other books and articles. He received his Ph.D. from Princeton University and is Editor of *Philosophical Studies*.

Keith DeRose is the Allison Foundation Professor of Philosophy at Yale University. He works mainly in epistemology, philosophy of language, and philosophy of religion. He has authored *The Case for Contextualism* (OUP, 2009) and *The Appearance of Ignorance* (OUP, 2017). He received his Ph.D. from UCLA and taught at New York University and Rice University before coming to Yale.

E. Diaz-Leon is a Ramon y Cajal Researcher at the University of Barcelona. Prior to that she was an Assistant and then Associate Professor at the University of Manitoba. She works mainly in philosophy of mind and language, feminist philosophy, and philosophy of race. She has worked on the nature of consciousness and phenomenal concepts, and her current work focuses on the nature of gender, race, and sexual orientation. She has additional research interests in metaphysics and epistemology.

J. L. Dowell is an Associate Professor at Syracuse University. She has published in metaphysics, philosophy of language, philosophy of mind, philosophical methodology, and metaethics. In 2014, she won the Marc Sanders Prize in Metaethics. Currently, she is working on a book on deontic modals, under contract with Oxford University Press.

Maite Ezcurdia is a Research Fellow at the Instituto de Investigaciones Filosóficas of the National Autonomous University of Mexico (UNAM). Her research interests lie primarily in philosophy of language, philosophy of mind, and cognitive science, and, secondarily, in epistemology. She is especially interested in semantics, reference, knowledge of language, and the connections between thought and language, self-thoughts, and perception.

Daniel Fogal is a Postdoctoral Research Fellow at Uppsala University. He works on a range of issues in epistemology, ethics, and philosophy of language. He also has research interests in metaphysics and early modern philosophy.

Contributors

Jie Gao (Ph.D. Edinburgh, 2016) works primarily in epistemology and related areas such as the philosophy of mind and formal epistemology. Her current research focuses on a number of issues concerning the relation between knowledge, doxastic attitudes, and practical factors.

Christopher Gauker is the Professor for Theoretical Philosophy at the University of Salzburg, Austria. He works primarily in the philosophy of language, philosophy of mind, and philosophical logic. He is the author of *Words without Meaning* (MIT, 2003), *Conditionals in Context* (MIT, 2005), and *Words and Images: An Essay on the Origin of Ideas* (OUP, 2011).

Mikkel Gerken (Ph.D. UCLA, 2007) works in epistemology and related areas such as the philosophy of mind, science, and language. His interests also include cognitive science and philosophical methodology. Gerken is the author of two books: *Epistemic Reasoning and the Mental* (Palgrave, 2013) and *On Folk Epistemology* (OUP, forthcoming).

Daniel Greco is an Assistant Professor of Philosophy at Yale University. His research is mainly in epistemology, though he also has secondary interests in the philosophy of mind, metaethics, and the philosophy of science, especially as they relate to epistemology.

John Greco holds the Leonard and Elizabeth Eslick Chair in Philosophy at Saint Louis University. He has published on a variety of topics in epistemology, including Gettier cases and contextualism.

Patrick Greenough is a Senior Lecturer in the Department of Philosophy at the University of St Andrews. He has a particular interest in vagueness, the liar paradox, and skepticism.

Michael J. Hannon is a Bader Postdoctoral Fellow at Queen's University, Canada. His main areas of research are epistemology, philosophy of language, and cognitive science. He is especially interested in how epistemic language ('knows', 'understands', etc.) contributes to human survival and flourishing.

Torfinn Thomesen Huvenes is a Senior Lecturer in Philosophy at Umeå University in Sweden. His main areas of research are philosophy of language and epistemology, with a particular emphasis on issues concerning disagreement.

Jonathan Jenkins Ichikawa is an Associate Professor of Philosophy at the University of British Columbia. His research focuses on issues in epistemology, philosophy of mind, and philosophy of language. He is the co-author, with Benjamin Jarvis, of *The Rules of Thought* (OUP, 2013), and the author of *Contextualising Knowledge: Epistemology and Semantics* (OUP, 2017).

Mark Jary is a Reader in English Language and Linguistics at the University of Roehampton, London. His work centres on linguistic mood and its contribution to utterance meaning. He is the author of *Assertion* (Palgrave, 2010) and co-author, with Mikhail Kissine, of *Imperatives* (CUP, 2014).

Justin Khoo is an Assistant Professor of Philosophy at MIT. He works primarily in philosophy of language and has written on modals, conditionals, disagreement, and moral and political discourse.

Contributors

Dirk Kindermann is an Assistant Professor at the University of Graz and a postdoctoral researcher on the FWF project "The Fragmented Mind". His main research interests are in the philosophy of language and its intersection with epistemology and philosophy of mind.

Maria Lasonen-Aarnio is an Associate Professor at the University of Michigan. Her research is primarily in epistemology, as well as related topics in philosophy of mind, language, and metaphysics. Lately she has started thinking about normativity and rationality more generally, across the theoretical and practical domains.

Karen S. Lewis is an Assistant Professor of Philosophy at Barnard College, Columbia University. Her research interests are primarily in philosophy of language and philosophical linguistics. She has written on dynamic semantics, pragmatics, anaphora, conditionals, and context-sensitivity.

Robin McKenna is a Postdoctoral Fellow at the University of Vienna. His main areas of research are epistemology, philosophy of language, and metaethics, but he is increasingly interested in the philosophy of science, social metaphysics, and feminist philosophy. He is currently working on a book arguing that knowledge is a social kind.

Giovanni Mion is an Assistant Professor at Istanbul Technical University. His research is mainly focused on epistemic contextualism and philosophy of language. He is also interested in the use of formal tools to investigate traditional philosophical problems and to interpret the work of past philosophers.

Brian Montgomery is a Visiting Assistant Professor at the University of Texas-El Paso. His research focusses mainly on the intersection between epistemology and the philosophy of language. He also holds research interest in metametaphysics, the philosophy of science, and the philosophy of sex and love.

Jennifer Nagel is an Associate Professor of Philosophy at the University of Toronto. Much of her recent work focuses on natural instincts about knowledge and the question of exactly what these instincts can tell us about knowledge itself.

Geoff Pynn is an Associate Professor of Philosophy at Northern Illinois University. His research focuses on epistemology and philosophy of language.

Brian Rabern is a Lecturer in Philosophy at the University of Edinburgh. His research interests centre around philosophy of language, philosophical logic, and formal semantics.

Stephen B. Ryan is a Teaching Assistant in Philosophy at the University of Edinburgh. His research interests lie primarily in epistemology and philosophical methodology, with particular focus on the roles of thought experiments and intuitive judgments.

Patrick Rysiew is a Professor of Philosophy at the University of Victoria. His primary research interests are in epistemology, including its points of intersection with certain issues in the philosophies of language and mind.

Contributors

Julia Jael Smith is a doctoral student in philosophy at the University of Toronto. Her primary areas of interest are epistemology and ethics. Her current research focuses on epistemic rationality, evidence, and disagreement.

Robert J. Stainton is a Distinguished University Professor of Philosophy at the University of Western Ontario. In linguistics, his primary focus is presently Theoretical and Clinical Pragmatics. In philosophy, he writes on philosophy of language and mind, but occasionally dabbles in history of philosophy of language.

Kurt Sylvan is an Assistant Professor of Philosophy at the University of Southampton. His primary research interests concern the nature of reasons, rationality, and normativity in epistemology and ethics, and he has secondary interests in the philosophy and cognitive science of perception, metaphysics, and axiology.

Brian Weatherson is the Marshall M. Weinberg Professor of Philosophy at the University of Michigan, Ann Arbor, and Professorial Fellow at Arché, University of St Andrews. He works primarily in epistemology, philosophy of language, and ethics.

Alex Worsnip is an Assistant Professor of Philosophy at the University of North Carolina at Chapel Hill. His work focuses on questions about rationality and normativity, both in epistemology and in the theory of practical reason, as well as related topics in philosophy of language and mind.

Crispin Wright, FBA, FAAAS, is a Professor of Philosophy at New York University and Professor of Philosophical Research at the University of Stirling where he leads the John Templeton Foundation funded project, Knowledge Beyond Natural Science. He has published extensively on topics in the philosophy of language and epistemology, and was the founder and first director of the Arché research centre at St Andrews.

ACKNOWLEDGEMENTS

I am grateful to the Routledge team for making this project a reality; thanks particularly to Tony Bruce for getting the ball rolling and for invaluable advice and support along the way, and to Adam Johnson for shepherding me and the authors through the details.

Nathan Cockram and Marc Hewitt each served as research assistants in preparing this volume; they both saved me many headaches throughout the preparation, and I'm grateful to them for their dedication and diligence.

Thanks to Ernest Sosa for first introducing me to contextualism and for being so careful about use and mention.

Thanks to all five referees who read the original proposal for this volume. I'm particularly grateful to the four referees who gave insightful and relevant comments; I believe the volume is much stronger than it would otherwise have been due to their feedback and suggestions.

I'm grateful also to Janice Dowell, Jennifer Lackey, Brian Weatherson, and others, for leadership and advice.

Thanks always to Carrie Jenkins for constant support, insight, and counsel.

Especial thanks to all the authors for writing such clear and incisive pieces, in tolerable proximity to the deadlines. My first time editing wasn't as huge a nightmare as I'd feared it might be.

INTRODUCTION
What is epistemic contextualism?

Jonathan Jenkins Ichikawa

The existence of epistemic contextualism refutes the tired complaint that there is nothing new in philosophy. Epistemological questions about the possibility, the nature, and the extent of human knowledge are as old as philosophy itself; seeking insight by placing these questions alongside more distinctively *semantic* questions about the language we use to *talk* about knowledge is an innovation of the twentieth century. It wasn't until the late twentieth century, once semanticists and philosophers of language created a formal apparatus for representing indexicals, that contextualism was even articulable.[1] Many contemporary epistemologists now hold that these linguistic questions have critical epistemological implications.

To an approximation, contextualism about "knows" is the idea that the word "knows" is context-sensitive – its contributions to the meaning of a sentence vary according to the conversational context in which the sentence is produced.[2] Here are some examples of uncontroversially context-sensitive words in English:

- "I"
- "she"
- "here"

There is a sense in which the word "I" has a stable meaning in English – one can look up that meaning in a dictionary. But there is another sense in which it means radically different things, depending on who is speaking. For example, when I use the word "I", it means me – Jonathan. When Donald Trump uses the word "I", it refers to a very different person – Donald Trump. In the same way, one utterance of a sentence like "it often rains here" may express a true proposition about Vancouver, while another might express a false proposition about Death Valley.

Most theorists – though not all – think the list of context-sensitive terms extends much further, encompassing *modals* (words like "must", "might", "necessarily", and "probably"), *quantifiers* ("everyone", "somewhere", "most"), and *gradable adjectives* ("tall", "wealthy", "hot"). The literature on epistemic contextualism tends to assume that these terms are context-sensitive.[3] The epistemic contextualist holds that "knows", too, belongs on the list. The content expressed by a sentence involving "knows", according to a contextualist, depends on particular kinds of features of the conversational context in which it is produced.

A simple toy model of contextualism may illustrate the shape of the view. Suppose there are two different "kinds" of knowledge – ordinary, low-standards knowledge (KL) and extraordinary, high-standards knowledge (KH). Maybe lots of KL is relatively easy to obtain; when I am in a cooperating epistemic environment and trust my senses and the testimony of the people around me, I end up with lots of KL, without having to think much about it at all. But suppose that KH is a weightier and dearer epistemic achievement. Sure, I can *KL* that it's raining just by using my eyes and ears. But to *KH* that it's raining, I'd have to do much more. Maybe I'd need to *prove* that my eyes and ears are trustworthy. Maybe I'd need special evidence that *ensures* that no one is deceiving me into thinking that it's raining. Maybe I'd need to derive the fact that it's raining from self-evident or a priori principles. We can leave the details of the demand as schematic; the important thing for our toy case is that KH is pretty difficult to come by.

In distinguishing KL and KH, I'm making an epistemological posit – I'm saying that there are two different epistemic states, with particular kinds of features. This isn't to say anything about any words, so thus far, the toy view I'm sketching isn't a kind of contextualism. It becomes one when we add this linguistic stipulation: the English word "knows", we'll suppose, has a stable linguistic meaning – just as indexicals like "she" do. But it also encodes a kind of context-sensitivity: sometimes "knows" picks out KL, and other times it picks out KH, and the conversational context determines which is which.[4] When the word "knows" is used in a context in which we're just interested in who is keeping track of which information, it expresses KL; when it's used in a philosophical context in which we're wondering whether anybody can really be sure of anything, it expresses KH. Just as "I" might mean me or it might mean Donald Trump, depending on who's talking, so, too, for "knows": it might mean KL or it might mean KH, depending on the epistemic features of the conversation.

A view like this would have certain advantages. In particular, it would allow for a treatment of skepticism that is concessive to ordinary intuitions. It is puzzling that, when thinking about the ultimate justifications for our beliefs, we are inclined to admit that e.g. there's no way to know whether we're the victims of radical skeptical scenarios. (After all if we *were* brains in vats, wouldn't things appear just the same as they actually do?) On the other hand, it is very counter-intuitive to draw the conclusion that I don't know such quotidian facts as that it's raining or that my dog is sitting beside me. But it's also very natural to suppose such knowledge facts *must* go together. If I can't even know whether I'm a brain in a vat, how could I possibly know whether it's raining?

Our toy contextualism can accept all of these intuitions by interpreting them as concerning different "knowledge" states. It will hold that I KL both that it's raining and that I'm not a brain in a vat, but that I don't KH whether it's raining, or whether I'm a brain in a vat. It remains consistent with a "closure" principle for both KL and KH – if I KL/KH that it's raining, then I must be able to KL/KH that I'm not a brain in a vat.[5]

This toy contextualism is just that: a toy. No contemporary contextualist argues that there are simply two candidate referents for "knows" – real contextualists tend to hold either that there are many different "knowledge" relations out there, or (more often) that the hidden syntax of knowledge ascriptions takes an additional argument place that can be filled by a variety of different parameters.[6] I've given no attention to whether there are linguistic considerations in favor of the thesis that "knows" can refer to either KH or to KL. And we haven't considered *how* context influences the content of knowledge ascriptions. It is also not straightforward how to connect the linguistic questions that define contextualism to more traditional questions in epistemology. Contextualism, after all, is first and foremost a view about a particular verb, viz., "knows". Few twenty-first-century epistemologists would accept that traditional questions in epistemology are primarily about this or any other word. Whether a suitable development of a more sophisticated version of contextualism will ultimately enjoy motivation or plausibility is deeply controversial;

Introduction

many of the chapters in this volume take up one or more of these and related questions. I'll give an overview to the volume below. First, however, it will be helpful to make a very important distinction explicit. Discussions of epistemic contextualism have frequently fomented confusion by conflating *use* and *mention*.

Contextualism, use, and mention

In the abstract, the distinction between use and mention is simple. To *use* a word is to employ it, for instance in a spoken or written sentence, to talk about what it stands for. To *mention* a word is to talk or write *about* that word. Most sentences aren't about words, so the words in sentences are typically used, not mentioned. For example, the sentence "it is rainy in Vancouver today" is not about any words. It says something about the weather, not about language. It *uses* "rainy", "Vancouver", and a few other words, but it doesn't mention them. These sentences *mention* words:

- This city is called "Vancouver" in honor of an English Naval Captain.
- "Rainy" is an example of a context-sensitive gradable adjective.
- "Vancouver" is longer than "rainy".

A standard convention – and one employed in this book – will be to designate the mention of words by enclosing them in quotation marks.

Discussions of context-sensitivity require careful treatment of use and mention. When I was a small child, tracking the context-sensitivity of words like "tomorrow" was a significant intellectual achievement.[7] When I was three, I thought that with the passage of time, tomorrow and each subsequent day would become today. But when I became a man, I put childish things away. Now I see that today and tomorrow are each simply days, but the English words "today" and "tomorrow" refer to different days, depending on the context of utterance. Tomorrow will never become today – no Tuesday will ever become a Monday – but I will shortly enter into a conversational context in which tomorrow (Tuesday) is the referent of the word "today".

Just as it'd be a use–mention confusion to say that tomorrow will become today, or that I will become you when you start talking, or that everybody shrinks when I restrict my attention to a smaller group of people (or to a group of smaller people), so, too, would it be a confusion to describe contextualism as the view that people stop knowing when the context changes, or that knowledge depends on context, or that it's harder to know when the stakes are high.

Unfortunately, some discussions of contextualism have led to confusion by failing to make this distinction clear. The most notorious example is David Lewis's (1996) articulation of contextualism. Lewis's form of contextualism is a kind of relevant alternatives approach – a descendant of the kind of suggestion offered in Stine (1976). According to Lewis, which alternatives are 'relevant' for the purpose of a knowledge ascription depends in part on the *attention* of the speakers; if one is thinking about the possibility of being a brain in a vat, then that is a relevant possibility that must be ruled out for a knowledge ascription to be true; but if one is ignoring such possibilities, knowledge ascriptions do not require evidence against them.

As Lewis points out, insofar as epistemological projects often involve attention to skeptical scenarios, knowledge ascriptions in such distinctively epistemological contexts will typically be rather strong. There is probably something right about this,[8] but Lewis's own bald statements to this effect are rather misleading. Lewis writes:

> Do some epistemology. Let your fantasies rip. Find uneliminated possibilities of error everywhere. Now that you are attending to them, just as I told you to, you are no

longer ignoring them, properly or otherwise. So you have landed in a context with an enormously rich domain of potential counter-examples to ascriptions of knowledge. In such an extraordinary context, with such a rich domain, it never can happen (well, hardly ever) that an ascription of knowledge is true. Not an ascription of knowledge to yourself (either to your present self or to your earlier self, untainted by epistemology); and not an ascription of knowledge to others. That is how epistemology destroys knowledge. But it does so only temporarily. The pastime of epistemology does not plunge us forevermore into its special context. We can still do a lot of proper ignoring, a lot of knowing, and a lot of true ascribing of knowledge to ourselves and others, the rest of the time.

. . . Unless this investigation of ours was an altogether atypical sample of epistemology, it will be inevitable that epistemology must destroy knowledge. That is how knowledge is elusive. Examine it, and straightway it vanishes.

(1996, pp. 559–60)

I find little fault in the first half of this quotation. (A stickler might prefer the use of quotation marks to signify mention of "knows", but I'm happy to read "knowledge ascription" as something like "sentence applying the word 'knows'".) Where Lewis runs into trouble is in his transition to talk of "destroying knowledge". If one starts to take skeptical possibilities seriously, thus moving into a conversational context where "knows" expresses a stronger relation that does not obtain, there is no literal sense in which one has "destroyed" knowledge.

Go back to the toy model, where a token of "knows" refers to the ubiquitous KL in contexts that ignore skeptical possibilities, and to the rare KH in context in which skeptical possibilities are considered. You KL that it's raining but you don't KH whether it's raining. If you start in a non-skeptical context where "knows" is used to refer to KL, then your sentence "I know that it's raining" will be true. Then you start thinking about brains in vats, thus generating a skeptical context. Now "I know that it's raining" will be false if you say it. But this isn't because knowledge is destroyed. Nothing has been destroyed – you still have KL, and you never had KH. Knowledge hasn't vanished. (In no context is "knowledge has vanished" true.) You've just moved into a context where certain sentences express logically stronger propositions than they used to.

Lewis admits at the end of his chapter that he is writing loosely; strictly speaking, he ought to have been careful to distinguish use and mention. His attitude seems to have been that the precision wouldn't have been worth the effort.[9] I think that Lewis underestimates the importance of keeping this distinction clear. This is particularly true in light of some of the twenty-first-century alternatives to contextualism that have since emerged. (There *are* views that say that considering skeptical possibilities destroy knowledge, but they're not typically contextualist ones; see the discussion of Chapter 19 below.) Throughout this volume, we will endeavor to keep this distinction as clear as possible. Sometimes the price will be a somewhat cumbersome semantic ascent. I have tried to convince the authors that this price is worth paying; I hope readers will also be convinced.

Overview of the volume

This volume commissions thirty-seven original chapters on contextualism and related topics. All are newly written for this volume, although in many cases, indicated within the chapters, they are based on previous works or bodies of work. The aim is to give the reader a clear idea of the current state of the literature around "knows" contextualism – what it is, in what ways it might be supported or denied, how it is developed, with what alternatives it competes, and how it fits in

Introduction

with more foundational linguistic questions. Most researchers on contextualism, including most of the authors for this book, divide into two categories: those who have approached questions about contextualism primarily from the *epistemological* side, and those who have done so from the *linguistic* side. One of my aims in this volume has been to integrate these discussions more thoroughly than has often happened organically in the literature to date.

The volume is divided into eight parts. In the remainder of this introduction, I'll set out the central questions for each, and give a brief overview as to the contents of each chapter. The division of parts is inevitably somewhat artificial, and many chapters contain material of relevance to the themes of various parts. I'll draw some of those connections in the outline below.

Part I: Data and motivations

Contextualism is a linguistic thesis about certain bits of natural language. Although it may have significant payoffs in epistemological theorizing, if it is to be taken seriously as a description of linguistic reality, it must be grounded at least partly in linguistic considerations. Part I of the book considers these considerations. What kinds of motivations are there, or could there be, for contextualism? What is the most important kind of data, and how can and should we go about collecting it?

In Chapter 1, Crispin Wright gives a broad overview of many of the kinds of phenomena that have motivated contextualists, as well as other "variabilists". This discussion will set the stage for much of the volume, anticipating the exploration of contextualism's alternatives in Parts IV and V. Geoff Pynn (Chapter 2) and Wesley Buckwalter (Chapter 3) each consider the importance of ordinary speakers' intuitions in evaluating contextualism, but they offer competing interpretations of some of the data. Evelyn Brister's contribution in Chapter 4 approaches contextualism from a different angle, bringing feminist approaches in the philosophy of science to bear on our epistemic and linguistic questions.

Part I is concerned primarily with the *prima facie* case for contextualism – its focus is on the degree to which considerations often taken to motivate contextualism can get off the ground. More involved dialectical considerations for and against contextualism will be considered elsewhere in the volume – especially in Parts IV and VI. Descriptions of those parts follow.

Part II: Methodological issues

Part II of the volume foregrounds methodological questions that were near the surface in Part I. What *kinds* of considerations are relevant for the debate about contextualism, and why? E. Diaz-Leon's Chapter 5 relates contextualism to the normative, arguing that language and meaning are tied up with how we *should* use terms as well as how we *do*. (This piece also connects importantly to the discussions of disagreement and relativism in Part V.) In Chapter 6, Mikkel Gerken, Jie Gao, and Stephen B. Ryan suggest that debates about the truth of contextualism and those about the methodology for discerning it are tied importantly together. Jennifer Nagel and Julia Jael Smith (Chapter 7) canvass psychological data on knowledge, belief, and mental state attribution, arguing that some of the attraction to contextualism might be explicable on psychologistic, rather than semantic, grounds.

In Chapter 8, Derek Ball introduces a central methodological question to which authors in other Parts will also return: just what is it, ultimately, for something to be context-sensitive? I gestured at indexicals and other apparent examples above, but, especially when it comes to cases like "knows" where things are less clear, a handful of clear cases isn't enough to delineate the subject matter, or what is at stake behind the question. Ball argues that the question is ultimately

5

tied up in an even larger methodological question: just what *is* semantics, and what is it for? Ball's contribution connects closely with other contributions elsewhere in the volume – particularly Chapters 18 and 34.

Part III: Epistemological implications

Although contextualism is a linguistic thesis, to be adjudicated on linguistic grounds, it is no accident that much of its development and consideration has happened in epistemology. Part III canvasses the connections between contextualism and epistemic matters. What are the costs and benefits of contextualism to epistemological theorizing?

Once we keep clear use and mention, it's not *entirely* obvious that there should be *any* connection between contextualism and epistemology. This line of thought is taken up by Brian Montgomery in Chapter 9. As Montgomery observes, contextualism does seem at least to have significant methodological implications for epistemology, so it is proper for epistemologists to consider and attend to it.

Chapters 10–15 consider, in turn, the application of contextualism to various matters of traditional epistemological concern. In some cases, authors argue that contextualism provides a satisfactory resolution of an epistemological puzzle, e.g. Michael J. Hannon on skepticism (Chapter 10) and Keith DeRose on fallibilism (Chapter 11), while in other cases, authors will point to challenges or unresolved questions about the integration of contextualism and epistemological theorizing, e.g. Maria Lasonen-Aarnio on closure (Chapter 12), Matthew A. Benton on lotteries and prefaces (Chapter 13), Alex Worsnip on knowledge norms (Chapter 14), and John Greco on Gettier cases (Chapter 15).

Of course, the degree to which these chapters point to advantages or disadvantages of contextualism depends in part on how non-contextualist options fare. Examining competitors is the project of Parts IV and V.

Part IV: Doing without contextualism

Assuming (perhaps *pace* Chapter 3) that there really are puzzling patterns of intuitions concerning knowledge ascriptions, there are various choices. Grant for the purpose of argument that it is intuitive that I know that it's raining, but that it's also intuitive that I don't know whether I'm a brain in a vat. (Set aside the possibility of allowing the "abominable conjunction" of these two intuitions.[10]) One choice is to be a contextualist – each intuition is correct, but they are intuitions about distinct "knowledge" states. Another choice is relativism, which is the topic of Part V. Three remaining choices are:

A   Univocal low standards. There's just one "knowledge" state, and contrary to some skeptical intuitions, I know the negation of skeptical scenarios. (The "Moorean" stance.)

B   Univocal high standards. There's just one "knowledge" state, and it is demanding. In fact, contrary to some ordinary intuitions, I don't know much at all. (The skeptical stance.)

C   Univocal, yet shifty. There's just one "knowledge" state, but it varies in how demanding it is. Both intuitions tend to be true because the facts about knowledge tend to change.

One challenge for A-type strategies is to explain why it is, if we know skeptical scenarios not to obtain, that so many of us feel intuitively as if we don't.[11] One common strategy along these lines is to attribute the intuitive repugnance of e.g. "I know that I'm not a brain in a vat" or "I know that my lottery ticket will lose," not to its falsity, but to its *pragmatic infelicity*. Some things would sound bad or improper to say, even though they are true, because they're too likely to mislead the hearer into thinking something false. If I have already finished the manuscript, it would be misleading in most contexts if I were to say, "by next Christmas I will have finished the manuscript". This would be misleading, even though it is true. Patrick Rysiew (Chapter 16) applies a strategy of this kind in defense of an A-style univocal approach to "knows".

The more skeptical way, corresponding to B, is to hold that the one and only standard for knowledge is a high standard that is rarely met. Instead of explaining away the *skeptical* intuitions, an invariantist of this sort needs to explain away the *non-skeptical* ones. If I don't know where my car is (after all, it might have been stolen in the past hour), why is it so natural in many contexts for me to say I do know where it is (after all, I parked it myself, only an hour ago)? Wayne A. Davis (Chapter 17) offers, in defense of this sort of a skeptical invariantism, a treatment of many knowledge ascriptions as cases of "loose use". Saying that I know where my car is, according to Davis, is a pragmatically fine, albeit imprecise, way to use a literal falsehood to convey a truth. Davis also emphasizes that some apparent disagreements about knowledge can be attributed straightforwardly to a difference in the speakers' beliefs.

Herman Cappelen articulates a different kind of defense of a skeptical invariantism in his (Chapter 18) contribution. He develops past work on semantic minimalism and speech-act pluralism to give a general strategy for denying the context-sensitivity of terms, consistent with the facts about divergent usages. According to Cappelen's speech-act pluralism, utterances of sentences like knowledge ascriptions amount to the assertion of many different propositions – and although the proposition *semantically expressed* may be false, other asserted propositions may well be true.

The other central invariantist strategy is to hold that there is only one knowledge relation, but whether it obtains depends on certain surprising features of the subject. Brian Weatherson (Chapter 19) offers an explication and defense of this sort of view. On this kind of approach – what is sometimes called a "subject-sensitive" or "interest-relative" approach to knowledge, whether a subject knows that p may depend on how important to the subject the question whether p is, or on which skeptical possibilities one is considering or ignoring. For example, one might hold that so long as I'm ignoring the possibility that my car is stolen, I may know where it is, but the act of considering a possible theft constitutively undermines my knowledge. Or perhaps, I know where my car is, so long as the question isn't too important, but if the stakes go up, I lose my knowledge.

This view has a certain superficial resemblance to contextualism, but the view itself is deeply separate. Contextualism is a view about *language*; this kind of interest-relativity is a view about the nature of knowledge itself. Relatedly, the family of views considered in Chapter 19 suggests that the *subject's* practical interests are relevant for determining whether one counts as knowing; the *speaker's* practical interests are irrelevant. (If I make a knowledge ascription about you, an "interest-relative invariantist" like Weatherson will hold that *your* interests, not mine, are relevant to whether the ascription is true. Contextualists will hold that *my* interests are relevant because they influence the content of my sentence.[12]) This sort of invariantism, unlike contextualism, *is* a view on which knowledge may be "elusive", vanishing upon examination.[13]

Part V: Relativism and disagreement

Another major competitor to contextualism is *relativism*. Relativists agree with contextualists that there are shifty patterns of intuitions about knowledge ascriptions for which accounting is needed; they disagree with contextualists as to which context is relevant for locating the linguistic flexibility. Where contextualists locate the work that is to be done in the context of utterance, relativists turn instead to the context of *assessment*. Relativism has it that holding fixed my state, the weather, and the features of my context when I utter a sentence like "I know that it's raining in Vancouver," isn't enough to determine whether what I've said is true. It may be true relative to some contexts of assessment, and false relative to others. For example, if two groups of people overhear my utterance, one might think the proposition I expressed is true, and another might think it false – and both might be right.

Until rather recently, few analytic philosophers would have thought this possibility even coherent. But recent work, especially that of John MacFarlane, has brought relativism forward as a serious candidate view, both for "knows" and for other terms.[14] Relativism is introduced in this volume in Chapter 1, where it receives some attention and evaluation; Part V considers relativism in a more focused way. In Chapter 20, Justin Khoo articulates the disagreement challenge to contextualism, which is widely considered to be a – or *the* – central advantage of relativism over contextualism. Torfinn Thomesen Huvenes (Chapter 21) considers foundational questions about the nature of disagreement, with attention to whether it will sustain the challenge. Elke Brendel (Chapter 22) argues that both contextualism and relativism face a challenge related to disagreement, while J. Adam Carter (Chapter 23) considers more broadly the epistemic implications of relativism.

Part VI: Semantic implementations

Because it is a linguistic thesis, contextualism is answerable to semantic considerations.

Perhaps the most influential challenge contextualists have faced is the call for a semantic implementation of contextualism. How, from the point of view of a compositional semantics, does the kind of context-sensitivity the contextualist cites work? Opponents of contextualism have argued that "knows" seems to behave unlike paradigmatic instances of context-sensitive language, such as indexicals, gradable adjectives, and quantifiers; they have also argued that contextualism is committed to the untenable idea that ordinary speakers make systematic errors concerning the context-sensitivity of "knows".[15] Proponents have attempted to meet these challenges or find new models. Patrick Greenough and Dirk Kindermann (Chapter 24) explain and consider this challenge to contextualism, and argue that it is not dispositive. However, Robin McKenna (Chapter 25) argues that a serious challenge for semantic implementations of contextualism remains unsolved, and expresses pessimism about its resolution – he suggests that the project of explaining contextualism in terms of the dynamics of conversation should be abandoned; if McKenna is right, contextualism will need to be implemented in a very different way.

Nathan R. Cockram (Chapter 26) and Michael Blome-Tillmann (Chapter 27) attempt to rebut the idea that "knows" patterns are importantly unlike other context-sensitive terms. Cockram exploits the analogy between knowledge ascriptions and quantifiers and modals; Blome-Tillmann argues that knowledge ascriptions are more similar to sentences involving gradable adjectives than many have argued. Each offers a defense of contextualism along these grounds.

Part VII: contextualism outside "knows"

Most of this book is focused on contextualism about "knows". But contextualism itself is a general framework, potentially applicable in a variety of areas. This section takes up contextualist debates in other fields, with an eye towards connecting them to the case of "knows". In what respects are the prospects for contextualism in other fields stronger or weaker than in epistemology? What lessons from the debates in one area might benefit the debates in another?

Berit Brogaard (Chapter 28) draws explicit connections between epistemic contextualism and contextualism about *moral* vocabulary. Daniel Fogal and Kurt Sylvan (Chapter 29) apply a

Introduction

contextualist framework to discourse about epistemic reasons, and J. L. Dowell (Chapter 30) gives a sophisticated defense of contextualism about epistemic modals. Roger Clarke (Chapter 31) and Karen S. Lewis (Chapter 32) each apply a framework similar to a contextualist relevant-alternatives approach to knowledge – Clarke applies it to belief ascriptions, and Lewis to counterfactual conditionals. Daniel Greco (Chapter 33) develops a form of contextualism about epistemic foundations.

Part VIII: Foundational linguistic issues

This final section takes up deeper questions about the semantic project that defines contextualism, examining some of the assumptions made throughout the literature and earlier in the volume. For example, (as Chapter 16 made clear) the very idea of contextualism seems to presuppose some kind of clear distinction between semantics and pragmatics; in what exactly might any such distinction consist? This question has been broached already in Chapter 8, but we return to it with further focus here. Maite Ezcurdia (Chapter 34) offers a theoretical distinction between semantics and pragmatics, along with a suggestion for what kind of methodology is best-suited for determining whether a term like "knows" is context-sensitive.

Another foundational question concerns the nature and determinants of semantic context itself. Contextualists say that contexts determine various semantic features, but just what sort of a thing *is* a context? In Chapter 35, Giovanni Mion and Christopher Gauker argue that, contrary to widespread assumptions, conversational contexts are mind-independent. This, they argue, has significant consequences for contextualism. Their project is related to that of Chapter 25.

Brian Rabern's (Chapter 36) contribution offers formal frameworks for various approaches to knowledge, including the contextualist approach whereby "knows" is a context-sensitive intensional operator. Rabern also offers models for some of the competing theories discussed above, thereby connecting some of the more purely epistemological work on contextualism to formal semantics.

Finally, Mark Jary and Robert J. Stainton (Chapter 37) consider the relationship between contextualism and relevance theory. They identify a challenge for contextualism: it is empirically implausible as a semantic thesis, but insufficiently powerful as a merely pragmatic one. According to Jary and Stainton, relevance theory offers a way out: one can literally state a range of things with "know", even though it is not a context-sensitive term.

Acknowledgements

I am grateful to Wesley Buckwalter, Wayne Davis, Maite Ezcurdia, Patrick Greenough, Abby Jaques, Carrie Jenkins, Robin McKenna, Ginger Schultheis, and Rob Stainton for helpful comments on drafts of this introduction.

Notes

1 Kaplan (1989, presented in 1977) was particularly important in laying the semantic groundwork on which contextualism relies. Epistemic contextualism developed as a reasonably natural implementation of "relevant alternatives" approaches to knowledge. See especially Stine (1976). More explicit early commitments to contextualism were Cohen (1988), DeRose (1995), and Lewis (1996).
2 The term "contextualism" has sometimes been used differently in epistemology. See e.g. Williams (2001). In this Introduction, I reserve the term for its distinctively linguistic sense. This seems to be the general convention in contemporary philosophy. Chapter 4 discusses this terminological question further, and uses "context" in a broader sense.
3 Chapter 18 outlines some of the pressure against this assumption.

4 A more linguistically plausible alternative to this toy view would be that "knows" is *ambiguous* between KL and KH, the way that "match" is ambiguous between a device for starting fires and a compatible partnership. Ambiguity contrasts with context-sensitivity; there are two separate meanings attached to the sound "match", not one context-sensitive meaning. If there really were just two different knowledge states, the idea that "knows" is ambiguous would be more plausible than that it's context-sensitive. That's part of why this is just a toy model. (For more on the distinction between context-sensitivity and ambiguity, see Chapter 37).

5 I believe that Stine (1976) was the first to point out this advantage for this kind of package of views.

6 This is one reason the suggestion that contextualism requires that "knows" pick out different relations in different contexts is only an approximation; one might hold instead that "knows" univocally expresses a polyadic relation, with an argument place for something like an "epistemic standard" provided by context.

7 My mother's diary attributes this utterance to three-year-old Jonathan: "It's hard to understand but tomorrow will be 'today' and the next day will be 'today'. So we're going to new church today and EVERYDAY is today. It's hard to understand though."

8 It is debatable to what degree Lewis is right to assume that epistemological contexts are inevitably skeptical ones. See Ichikawa (2017, §6.3).

9 "It would have been tiresome, but it could have been done. . . . If you want to hear my story told that way, you probably know enough to do the job for yourself. If you can, then my informal presentation has been enough" (pp. 566–7). See also e.g. Cohen (1998, p. 292, fn. 10).

10 DeRose (1995, pp. 27–8).

11 Another challenge, not taken up in detail in this volume, is to explain *how* it is that we can know skeptical scenarios not to obtain. For a reasonably representative essay, see e.g. Sosa (1999).

12 Contextualists often deny that the practical interests of the subject are relevant, but contextualism itself does not carry any such commitment, and some contextualists have explicitly held that both subject interests and speaker interests are relevant. See Ichikawa (2017, §1.9).

13 A different strategy, related closely to interest-relative invariantism, would have a change in salience or stakes contribute *causally*, rather than *constitutively*, to the loss of knowledge. For example, when the stakes go up, subjects' confidence goes down below the point at which they could have knowledge. Such a view arguably could explain the shifty intuitions without positing a change in epistemic standards. See Nagel (2010). See also Chapter 7.

14 See e.g. MacFarlane (2014).

15 Schiffer (1996) was particularly influential on this score.

References

Cohen, Stewart (1988). How to Be a Fallibilist. *Philosophical Perspectives* 2: 91–123.

Cohen, Stewart (1998). Contextualist Solutions to Epistemological Problems: Scepticism, Gettier, and the Lottery. *Australasian Journal of Philosophy* 76 (2): 289–306.

DeRose, Keith (1995). Solving the Skeptical Problem. *Philosophical Review* 104 (1): 1–52.

Ichikawa, Jonathan (2017). *Contextualising Knowledge*. Oxford: Oxford University Press.

Kaplan, David (1989). "Demonstratives," in Almog, J., Perry, J. and Wettstein, H. (eds.), *Themes from Kaplan*. Oxford: Oxford University Press. pp. 481–563.

Lewis, David (1996). "Elusive Knowledge." *Australasian Journal of Philosophy* 74: 549–67. Reprinted in Lewis (1999): 418–45.

MacFarlane, John (2014). *Assessment Sensitivity: Relative Truth and Its Applications*. Oxford: Oxford University Press.

Nagel, Jennifer (2010). Epistemic Anxiety and Adaptive Invariantism. *Philosophical Perspectives* 24 (1): 407–35.

Schiffer, Stephen (1996). Contextualist Solutions to Scepticism. *Proceedings of the Aristotelian Society* 96 (1): 317–33.

Sosa, Ernest (1999). "How to Defeat Opposition to Moore." *Philosophical Perspectives* 13: 141–53.

Stine, Gail C (1976). "Skepticism, Relevant Alternatives, and Deductive Closure." *Philosophical Studies* 29: 249–61.

Williams, Michael (2001). "Contextualism, Externalism and Epistemic Standards." *Philosophical Studies* 103: 1–23.

PART I

Data and motivations

1

THE VARIABILITY OF 'KNOWS'

An opinionated overview

Crispin Wright

I The variabilist reaction against traditional epistemology

It is fair to say that from the time of the *Theaetetus* until relatively recently, theorists of knowledge tended to conceive their central task as being to explain in what knowledge consists; more exactly, to explain what further conditions need to be satisfied by a true belief if it is to count as knowledgeable. The widely accepted failure of the post-Gettier debates to execute this task convincingly has motivated a very different tendency in mainstream contemporary epistemology. This, influentially promoted by Timothy Williamson in particular, is *epistemic primitivism*: to concede that knowledge is, as Williamson puts it, 'prime' – that it is a fundamental, irreducible cognitive relation. Knowledge, on the primitivist view, is a basic epistemological kind, and to know is to be in a basic, *sui generis* attitudinal state. There can therefore be no correct analysis of it in terms of other, supposedly constitutive or more fundamental cognitive states (true belief + X). The post-Gettier "X knows that P if and only if . . ." cottage industry was doomed to disappointment for this reason. To the contrary, it is in terms of knowledge that other epistemic notions – justification, evidence, warranted assertion and rational action – are to be understood.[1]

This primitivism, however, still shares three traditional assumptions with the reductionism it is set against. They can be wrapped together as the compound idea that knowledge is a unique, objective, purely cognitive type of state – hence something at which the aspiration of reductive analysis could be sensibly (even if mis-) directed. If we unpack that, however, we find the following three distinct thoughts. First, ascriptions of knowledge, that X knows that P, are *contentually invariant* as far as the semantic contribution of 'knows' is concerned. More specifically, once the referent of 'X', the identity of the proposition that P and the time reference associated with 'knows' are settled, the result is a unique proposition, the same for any competent thinker who considers it. Second – although this would normally be taken to be entailed by the first point – this unique proposition has one and the same truth-value, no matter who asserts or assesses it. Third, this truth-value is determined purely by the cognitive achievements of the subject, irrespective of what else, other than that part of her total information relevant to the judgement that P is true of X. In particular, such aspects as X's (or anyone else's) *interest* in whether P, is true, or *what is at stake* for her in its truth, or the range and specifics of counter-possibilities to P that occur, or are *salient*, to X – in short: such, as they are often described, 'non-traditional' or as I shall say *pragmatic* factors – have no bearing on the matter.

13

The striking recent tendency that provides the subject matter of this chapter is the rejection of one or more of these traditional assumptions in favour of one or another form of *variabilism*: broadly, the notion that whether an ascription of knowledge may correctly be regarded as true may depend on pragmatic factors that pertain to the circumstances of the ascriber, or to those of a third party assessing the ascription, or on pragmatic aspects of the circumstances of the ascribee. Although well short of a consensus, a considerable body of opinion has been developed that agrees that *some* form of epistemic variabilism is called for if justice is to be done to the actual employment of 'knows' and its cognates. In what follows, I will review some of the principal considerations that are taken to support that view, critically compare and assess some of the resulting variabilist proposals and recommend a conclusion both about them and about the prospects for primitivism.

II Three types of consideration suggestive of variability

(i) Hume remarked long ago on the contrast between the potency of skeptical doubts, at least in their subtler forms, when developed in the philosophical study and their apparent fatuity when considered in the pub over beer and backgammon.[2] We may of course address the tension by proposing that one or the other – study or pub – response has to be misconceived; but then we remain in a state of cognitive dissonance until we have given a convincing account of which. No need, however, for such an account if "One normally knows that one has two hands" is false in the study but true in the pub – either because the semantic value of 'knows' is context-sensitive (and the context shifts in relevant respects as one moves from the study to the pub), or because the truth-value of the single proposition expressed by tokenings of that sentence in both locations is not absolute or because *we* change in relevant pragmatic respects as we move from the study to the pub.

(ii) John Hawthorne and others have emphasised problems generated by our ordinary practices of knowledge-ascription for the principle of the closure of knowledge across known entailment.[3] A range of cases exists where one might naturally self-ascribe knowledge of a premise of what one knows is a trivially valid entailment but might then hesitate to self-ascribe knowledge of its conclusion. Some of the most striking are so-called lottery cases. Suppose you buy a ticket in next week's UK National Lottery (the first prize has built up to about £50 million). You are under no illusions about the odds and sensibly expect (truly, let's suppose) that you will not win. But, despite this true belief's being overwhelmingly strongly justified, there are powerful reasons for denying that it is, strictly, knowledgeable. For one thing, if it is knowledgeable, then your buying the ticket is irrational – but that seems a harsh verdict; indeed if the scale of the prize and the odds suitably combine, the expected utility may actually rationalise the purchase. Moreover having bought a ticket, you will have, if you *know* that it won't win, no reason not to tear it up. But actually, once having bought a ticket, tearing it up would seem irrational so long as you have every reason to think that the lottery is fair.

Suppose it agreed that, for such reasons, you don't strictly know that you won't win the lottery. On the other hand, there are plenty of things that in ordinary contexts you would take yourself to know – for instance, that you won't be able to afford to buy a new Maserati next week or to retire at the end of the current academic year – that entail that you won't win the lottery. And in general there are plenty of things we would ordinarily be regarded as in position to know about our future circumstances in all kinds of respects (indeed, had better know if knowledge is the basis of rational practical reasoning to conclusions about what to do) that, in turn, entail that we won't be the subject of various forms of unlikely happenstance – even in cases, like lotteries, where it is sure that someone will be – which, once contemplated, we will be inclined to acknowledge that we don't strictly *know* will not occur.

The variability of 'knows'

There is the option of regarding such cases as actually challenging the validity of closure, of course. But that is a hard row to hoe.[4] Variability offers a different recourse. Perhaps the very act of bringing to mind the conclusion of an entailment of relevant kind 'ups the ante' in some way. Maybe the correctness of your self-ascription of knowledge that you will not be able to afford to retire at the end of the current academic year is originally relativised to a range of salient counter-possibilities which do not include lottery wins and which you *are* a position to rule out — and maybe this range enlarges with the purchase of the ticket.

(iii) Perhaps the dominant motivation towards variabilism, however, springs from a range of putative linguistic 'intuitions' concerning proprieties of knowledge-ascription provoked, at least among many of the philosophers who think about them, by imaginary cases of a kind first put forward by Stewart Cohen and Keith DeRose.[5] We can illustrate by reference to a version of DeRose's famous Bank Case. Suppose it is Friday afternoon, and Ashley and Bobbie are considering whether to bank their salary cheques. There are long queues at all the bank counters. Ashley recalls being at the bank on a Saturday morning two weeks ago and says, "Let's come back tomorrow. **I know the bank will be open tomorrow morning**." Suppose that the bank will indeed be open on the Saturday morning.

Case 1 (*Low stakes*): Suppose that there is no particular reason to ensure that the cheques are banked sooner rather than later — say, by the following Monday. Then
Invited intuition: Ashley's recollection of Saturday morning opening two weeks ago suffices for her to speak truly.

Contrast that scenario with

Case 2 (*High stakes*): The couple's mortgage lender will foreclose unless the cheques are in the account by Monday to service their monthly repayment. Ashley and Bobbie know this. Bobbie says, "But what if the bank has changed its opening hours? Or what if the Saturday morning opening was some kind of one-off promotion?" Ashley says, "You're right. **I suppose I don't really *know* that the bank will be open tomorrow** (even though I am pretty confident that it will). We had better join the queue."
Invited intuition: Again, Ashley speaks truly. Too much is at stake to take the risk of e.g. a change in banking hours.

So the suggested conclusion is that "I know the bank will be open tomorrow" uttered by Ashley is true in Case 1 and false in Case 2 even though all that is different between the two are the costs to Ashley and Bobbie of Ashley's being wrong. Only the pragmatic factors have changed. Everything that might be mentioned in a traditional account of knowledge — as we would naturally say, all Ashley's relevant evidence or information — remains the same.

Two further cases may seem to prompt another important conclusion:

Case 3 (*Unknowing high stakes*): The couple's mortgage lender will indeed foreclose unless the cheques are in the account by Monday to service their monthly repayment but Ashley and Bobbie are unaware of this (they habitually leave what looks like circular mail from the mortgage company unopened and have missed the reminder). The dialogue proceeds as first described above, with Ashley asserting, "**I know the bank will be open tomorrow morning**."
Invited intuition: This time, Ashley speaks falsely.

Compare that with

Case 4 (*Unknowing low stakes*): Ashley and Bobbie actually have no good reason to ensure that the cheques are banked before Monday but, misremembering the notice from the mortgage company, they *falsely* believe that Monday will be too late. The dialogue proceeds as in Case 2. *Invited intuition*: This time Ashley's disclaimer, "**I suppose I don't really know that the bank will be open tomorrow**" is false.

The suggested conclusion from Cases 3 and 4 is this: when changes in pragmatic factors convert a true knowledge-ascription into a false one, or vice versa, it is *actual* changes that matter, rather than thinkers' impressions of what changes in such factors may have taken place.

III The varieties of variabilism

We have already, in effect, noted that the space of theoretical options here must include at least three quite different kinds of proposals: one for each of the traditional assumptions distinguished in section I. First, there is the option of maintaining that although knowledge-ascriptions are contentually invariant (in the sense there specified), the proposition thereby expressed may take different truth-values in different circumstances, depending on variation in the pragmatic factors applying to its subject, X. This is the thesis, proposed separately by Stanley and Hawthorne,[6] that is most often termed *interest-relative invariantism* (IRI).[7] The details of a proposal of this kind will naturally depend on just what kinds of pragmatic factor are deemed relevant – saliences seemed to be the germane factor for the issue about closure; but variation in stakes is what seems germane in the various scenarios in the Bank Case. IRI allows, apparently, that a pair of subjects may both truly believe that P on the basis of the same evidence or cognitive achievements yet one knows that P, and the other fails to know that P if they suitably differ in pragmatic respects. I'll come back to this.

Second, there is the option of maintaining that the variability in truth-value of knowledge-ascriptions across the kinds of situation illustrated is actually a product of variation in *content*. The specific version of this proposal made by DeRose and Cohen is standardly termed *ascriber contextualism* (henceforward simply 'contextualism'). In its original and basic form, this view holds that the (level of) cognitive achievement that is required of X by the truth of an utterance of "X knows that P" varies as a function of pragmatic aspects – needs, stakes, saliences – *of the speaker*. Thus, in an example like the Bank Case, variation in pragmatic aspects of a *self*-ascriber across actual, or hypothetical, cases may result in (actual or hypothetical) tokenings of "I know that P" demanding different – more or less exigent – levels of cognitive achievement if they are to count as true. The truth-conditions, hence content, of tokens of such an ascription can vary, even though the only differences in their respective contexts of utterance pertain to the situation of the speaker in purely pragmatic respects.

The third option – that of *knowledge-relativism*, fashioned on the model of assessment-sensitivity as developed by John MacFarlane[8] – shifts the location of the pragmatic factors once again, this time to anyone who evaluates a knowledge-ascription, whether or not they are its original author. So a single token of "X knows that P" may properly be assigned different truth-values in differing contexts of assessment, whether or not distinct assessors are involved, depending on the situation in pragmatic respects of the assessor. Thus, Ashley may again quite correctly return different verdicts on a self-ascription of knowledge that the bank will open on the Saturday in the two contexts described. A smooth account of Hume's observation is likewise in prospect if the knowledge relativist can make a convincing case that travel between the philosophical study and the pub is apt to change the context of assessment in some relevant respect; a relativistic treatment of lottery cases will require a similar story concerning the potential effects of explicit consideration of certain of a statement's consequences. But I shall not here consider in any detail how such an account might run.

It will not have escaped the attention of the alert reader that the three types of variabilist views distinguished exhibit disagreement in two dimensions. Agreeing that the truth-value of a knowledge-ascription may vary as an effect of variation in non-traditional pragmatic factors, they disagree about the *location* – subject, ascriber or assessor – of the relevant factors; but they also disagree about the *semantic significance* of such variation. For both knowledge-relativism and interest-relative invariantism, variation in pragmatic factors is of no semantic significance at all; rather, one and the same proposition gets to vary in truth-value in tandem with variation in the pragmatic characteristics of the subject or assessors of that proposition. For knowledge contextualism, by contrast, at least in its classic form, it is the proposition expressed by a particular knowledge-ascription that varies in a fashion sensitive to the pragmatic factors. Ashley's tokens of "I know the bank will be open tomorrow morning" express different propositions in the low-stakes and high-stakes scenarios outlined. Thus, conceptual space exists for three further types of views that are the duals in these two dimensions of the three distinguished. There is, first, scope for a kind of contextualism – an instance of *non-indexical* contextualism[9] – that agrees with classical contextualism on the matter of location but disagrees on the matter of semantic significance. On this view, Ashley's two imaginary tokens of "I know the bank will be open tomorrow morning" express the same proposition in the low- and high-stakes scenarios, but this proposition takes a different truth-value as a function of the difference in what is at stake for the ascriber – Ashley – in those scenarios. Second, there is scope for a view which, like classical contextualism, regards ascriptions of knowledge as varying in their content (truth-conditions) as a function of variation in pragmatic characteristics but holds, like interest-relative invariantism, that the relevant characteristics are those not of the ascriber but of the subject, or subjects, to whom knowledge is ascribed. On such a view, a predicate of the form " . . . knows that P" will vary in its satisfaction-conditions rather as e.g. " . . . is sharp enough" so varies depending on whether it is being applied to a bread knife or a surgical scalpel. And finally, there is scope for an example of the view that *content itself* is, locally, assessment-sensitive: that what proposition is expressed by a token knowledge-ascription is itself a function of pragmatic characteristics of an assessor of it, with assessment-sensitivity of truth-value merely a consequence of such assessment-relativity of what is said.[10] I do not know if anyone has ever seriously proposed a view of either of these two latter kinds for the semantics of 'knows' but in any case neither will feature further in the discussion to follow. However, in view of the difficulties, to be touched on below, that classical contextualists have encountered in trying to make good the claim that 'knows' is indeed semantically context-sensitive, its non-indexical counterpart presents as worthy of serious consideration. We'll touch on it from time to time below.

IV The location question

So, *whose* standards (saliences, interests, etc.) count? The cases considered to this point involve *self*-ascriptions of knowledge. So they have the subject of the knowledge-ascription coincide with both the ascriber and an assessor. They therefore can suggest, at most, that we should be receptive to *some* sort of variabilism. They are powerless to motivate one rather than another of the variabilist views. Can we find some crucial experiments?

Here is a simple kind of case that has seemed to contextualists to favour their view over IRI:

Case 5 (*High stakes ascriber, low-stakes subject*): Ashley and Bobbie are situated as in Case 2. They ask Chris, another customer who is leaving the building, whether the bank will be open tomorrow.

Chris says "Yes, I happen to know it will – I was in here a couple of weeks ago on a Saturday." Ashley says to Bobbie *sotto voce*, "Hmm. **That person doesn't know any better than we do**. We had better join the queue."

Invited intuition: Ashley speaks truly even though – as we may suppose – there is nothing at stake for Chris, the subject, in whether the bank will open on the Saturday or not. Here, it seems the interests that count are those of the ascriber, even when the subject is someone else whose interests are different (and less urgent).

The significance of this kind of case is prima facie countered, however, by the following simple case that may seem to point back towards IRI:

Case 6 (*Low-stakes ascriber, high-stakes subject*): Ashley, Bobbie and Chris are again situated as in Case 5. Chris is puzzled that Ashley and Bobbie have joined the queue again notwithstanding the advice they were just given about a Saturday opening and asks them about this. They explain their concern about the risk of foreclosure of their mortgage. Chris says, "OK, I understand now. I guess you guys had better not assume that the bank *will* be open tomorrow."

Invited intuition: Chris speaks truly. But since "You know that P but had better not assume that P" is some kind of conceptual solecism, Chris's remark is presumably a commitment to "**You do not know that the bank will be open tomorrow**."[11]

So, neither contextualism nor IRI does well in all the cases – in fact they do just as well and badly as each other: well enough in cases where subject and ascriber are identified, but badly in various kinds of cases where they are distinct – which are of course the crucial cases. This might encourage the thought that *both* have the location issue wrong, and one might therefore wonder whether knowledge-relativism promises an overall better ride. And indeed we can very simply modify Case 5 to get one that seems to favour knowledge-relativism over contextualism *and* IRI:

Case 5★: Ashley and Bobbie are dithering in the foyer and then merely overhear Chris (in a phone conversation) say, "Look, I don't need to wait here now. My partner, Denny, was here a couple of weeks ago on a Saturday and can vouch that this bank will be open tomorrow." Ashley remarks, *sotto voce*, "We can't rely on that; **that Denny doesn't know any better than we do**."

Invited intuition: Ashley speaks truly.

However while knowledge-relativism may possibly best explain some intuitions in cases like this where subject, ascriber and assessor are all distinct, it faces the basic problem that it must coincide in its predictions with contextualism in any case where ascriber and assessor are one. So any two-agent problem cases for contextualism, like Case 6, are problems for relativism, too.

These conflicting intuitions present a potential paradox if we think that they do, near enough, show that there is *some* kind of relativity to pragmatic factors in the offing. How can that be so if the intuitions also suggest that each of the possible hypotheses about location is open to counterexample?

V Attempts to explain away the hard cases

Maybe (some of) the intuitions are misleading and should be explained away rather than accommodated. What might contextualism (and knowledge-relativism) say to explain away Case 6, where the intuition is that the correctness/incorrectness of the knowledge-ascription is determined by the subject's relatively high standards, rather than the ascriber's/assessor's relatively low ones?

The variability of 'knows'

We should flag one tempting but futile tactic of explanation: that Ashley's and Bobbie's relatively high stakes and standards have an adverse effect on their confidence. It might be suggested that they do indeed not know that the bank will be open on that Saturday, as Chris's remark implies, but this is not because, as IRI would have it, the question is properly assessed by reference to their own high standards, but rather because they don't believe – or anyway *sufficiently confidently believe* – that the bank will then be open.

This suggestion has three problems. First, there is no general prohibition on the idea of a relatively diffident belief being knowledgeable. (Think of the schoolteacher's encouraging remark to a hesitant pupil: "Come on, Jonny: you *do* know the answer to this.") Second, there is anyway no need to make it a feature of the example that Ashley be in any significant degree of doubt that the bank will be open on that Saturday (and indeed I explicitly refrained from doing so, as the reader may care to check). Finally, Case 3 – involving low ascriber stakes, but *ignorant* high subject stakes – may be adapted to refurbish the objection as follows:

Case 7 Ashley and Bobbie are situated as in Case 3 – the risk of foreclosure if the cheques are not banked by Monday is real, but they are unaware of this. They ask Chris, another customer who is leaving the building, whether the bank will be open tomorrow. Chris says, "Yes, I happen to know it will – I was in here a couple of weeks ago on a Saturday." Ashley says to Bobbie, "Great. Let's get out of this and go get a coffee." Asked to explain why Ashley and Bobby have left the queue, Chris would doubtless say, "**Because they now know that the bank will be open tomorrow.**"

Invited intuition: Chris speaks falsely. Given Ashley's and Bobbie's – the subjects' – actual high stakes, they are in no position to acquire knowledge by testimony from Chris, even though Chris's low-stakes self-ascription is unexceptionable.

There is, however, another response that at least one leading contextualist has offered to this kind of case that is potentially something of a game-changer. Keith DeRose observes[12] that in taking patterns of conversation like those illustrated by Cases 6 and 7 to constitute prima facie counterexamples to contextualism, we are implicitly taking it for granted that the mechanism whereby the context of a token knowledge-ascription contrives to set the standards for its truth is simply by identifying them with the standards of the ascriber: that "X knows that P" as uttered by Y is true just if X's relevant epistemic situation, replicated by Y but without change in the pragmatic aspects of Y's situation, would suffice for the truth of "Y knows that P". DeRose points out that there is absolutely no reason why that has to be the only kind of case. It is very familiar that in a wide range of examples – 'impure indexicals' like some personal pronouns, demonstratives and gradable adjectives – the semantic values of context-sensitive expressions featuring in particular utterances are settled as a function, in part, of the intentions of the utterer. It is therefore open to the contextualist to allow a similar role for the intentions of the author of a knowledge-ascription in determining the standard of epistemic achievement to be applied in fixing its truth-conditions. This can of course be the standard she would (take herself to) have to meet in order to satisfy the relevant ascription. But it need not be. In certain contexts – like those of Cases 6 and 7 – an ascriber may instead set a standard that defers to the needs, interest or saliences of the subject. In such a case, IRI and contextualism will coincide in their predictions of the truth-conditions of the knowledge-ascription.

I described this 'flexible contextualist' manoeuvre as a potential game-changer. It is, of course, merely *ad hoc* unless a principled and comprehensive account is provided of the conditions under which relevant variations in a speaker's intentions can be expected, enabling empirically testable predictions of variable truth-conditions. DeRose expends some effort in that direction, to not implausible effect. His basic suggestion is that knowledge-ascriptions may be harnessed to two quite different kinds of project: whether X knows that P may be of interest because one wishes to rate X as a potential *source of information*; but it may also be of interest in the context of assessing X's performance as a *rational agent*. In the former type of case one will naturally impose standards on X's claim to knowledge appropriate to one's own needs and interests. (Just this is what seems to be happening in the high-stakes ascriber, low-stakes subject cases reviewed.) But in the latter type of case, when the focus shifts to what it is rational for X to do, it may well be (one's conception of) X's needs and interests that determine what level of cognitive achievement it is reasonable to demand if X is to be credited with the knowledge that P. And this seems to be the driver for the (invited) intuitions operative in the low-stakes ascriber, high-stakes subject cases like 6 and 7.

I have no space here to consider further whether the flexible contextualist manoeuvre can be developed so as to deliver fully satisfyingly on its initial promise. However two points are worth emphasis. The first is that an exactly analogous flexibility on the location question is, obviously, available to knowledge-relativism. Whatever potential shifts of interest are offered to explain variations in the location of standards from the point of view of a knowledge-ascriber, they will be available also to explain such variations from the perspective of a knowledge-ascription assessor. Flexibility thus offers no prospect of an advantage for contextualism over relativism. Second, there is no analogous move open to IRI, which is stuck with the idea that the standards for the truth of a knowledge-ascription are inflexibly set as a function of the needs, interests or saliences of its subject. If IRI is to restore dialectical parity after (and presuming the success of) the flexible contextualist manoeuvre, it must therefore explain away cases, like Case 5, where the location seems to go with an ascriber (or assessor), rather than the subject, as some kind of linguistic mistake. What are the prospects?

It is important to take the full measure of the challenge. Any presumed *knowledgeable* ascription of knowledge to a third party entails – by closure and factivity – an ascription of the same knowledge to oneself. And of course if IRI is right, and one's standards are relatively high, one may not have that knowledge. In that case, one won't be in position to ascribe it to a third party either, whatever their standards. There is therefore, in general, no difficulty for IRI in explaining our *reluctance to ascribe* knowledge in such cases. That, however, is not the relevant *explanandum*. What the defender of IRI has to explain – what the high-stakes ascriber, low-stakes subject examples are meant to illustrate – is a readiness of high-stakes ascribers to (falsely) *deny* knowledge that P to a relevant low-stakes subject. (Thus Ashley: "That person doesn't know any better than we do.")

It would take us too far afield to pursue the details of all the responses that defenders of IRI have offered to this challenge.[13] Suppose, however, that it proves that IRI has no good account to offer of the patterns of knowledge-ascription and denial that we seem to apply in certain high-stakes ascriber, low-stakes subject cases. How damaging is that? Jason Stanley[14] contends that contextualism has an exactly matching set of problems as soon as we consider the relevant *self-ascription* by the low-stakes subject. Thus in Case 5 above, the subject – Chris – affirms that "I happen to know that it [the bank] will [be open tomorrow]" and, from a contextualist point of view, this self-ascription ought to be (absent any detail in the example suggesting the contrary) in perfect order: a true knowledge-ascription made by a low-stakes ascriber on adequate evidence. Yet is that not (a truth-conditional equivalent of) the very claim that Ashley, in a high-stakes context, correctly – by contextualist lights – contradicts?

Non-indexical contextualism will accept that consequence: Ashley and Chris are, in their respective contexts, perfectly correctly endorsing incompatible claims. But historically contextualists have shown no stomach for this near-enough[15] relativistic stance. Rather here is a place where the putative context-sensitivity of 'knows' is made to do some serious theoretical work. When Chris affirms "I happen to know [that the bank will be open tomorrow]" and Ashley

The variability of 'knows'

affirms "That person [Chris] doesn't know any better than we do [that the bank will be open tomorrow]", the contradiction is finessed by the shift in the semantic value of 'know' engineered by the differing standards operative in their two contexts.

We'll return to this shortly.

VI Ugly conjunctions

We have so far been concerned with the challenge to the different variabilist views to capture and explain not just some but all the pragmatically variable patterns of use of 'knows' and its cognates that, according to the 'intuitions', competent speakers seem to find acceptable. And at this point, provided they are prepared to go 'flexible', and thus steal the cases that otherwise favour IRI, contextualism and relativism seem to be tied in the lead. But there is also an obverse challenge: to avoid predicting uses to be acceptable which are apt to impress as anything but. How do the different theories fare on this?

IRI imposes a condition on knowledge-ascriptions as follows:

> X knows that P at t is true only if X's belief at t that P is based on cognitive accomplishments that meet standards appropriate to X's practical interests (or whatever) at t,

and consequently appears to do very badly. Suppose X fails this condition — his practical interests are such that it is vitally important at t for him to be right about whether or not P, and he does at t truly believe that P, but does so on the basis of evidence that, though probative to a degree, impresses us as too slight to confer on him knowledge that P. Then IRI seems to treat as on an equal footing either of two remedies: X can either improve his evidence, or he can work on his practical interests in such a way that much less is at stake whether he is right about P or not. He can grow his evidence to meet the standards for knowledge imposed by his practical interests at t, or he can so modify his practical interests as to shrink, as it were, the standards of knowledge that P requires. Suppose he takes the latter course. Then a situation may arise at a later time, t*, when we can truly affirm an 'ugly conjunction' like:

> X didn't (have enough evidence to) know P at t but does at t*and has exactly the same body of P-relevant evidence at t* as at t.

Such a remark seems drastically foreign to the concept of knowledge we actually have. It seems absurd to suppose that a thinker can acquire knowledge without further investigation simply because his practical interests happen to change so as to reduce the importance of the matter at hand. Another potential kind of ugly conjunction is the synchronic case for different subjects:

> X knows that P but Y does not, and X and Y have exactly the same body of P-relevant evidence

when affirmed purely because X and Y have sufficiently different practical interests. IRI, as we noted earlier, must seemingly allow that instances of such a conjunction can be true.[16]

So far, so bad for IRI. But does contextualism escape any analogue of these problems for its competitor? Certainly, there can be no commitment to either form of ugly conjunction so long as we are concerned with cases where the relevant standards are set as those of an ascriber distinct from X and Y. In that case the same verdict must be returned about X at t and at t*, or about X and Y, simply because some single set of standards is in play. But what if the context is one

21

where contextualism has gone *flexible*, availing itself of the licence to defer to standards set by the (changing) pragmatic characteristics of the subject(s)? In that case, *non-indexical* contextualism, at least, can offer no evident barrier to the assertibility in suitable circumstances of either type of ugly conjunction. So much is simply the price of the flexibility it appropriates to accommodate the cases that seemed to favour IRI.

Regular (indexical) flexible contextualism, by contrast, stands to suffer a commitment only to the metalinguistic counterparts:

> "X doesn't (have enough evidence to) know P" was true at t but "X does (have enough evidence to) know P" is true at t* and X has exactly the same body of P-relevant evidence at t* as at t;
> "X knows that P" and "Y does not know that P" are both true and X and Y have exactly the same body of P-relevant evidence.

These are spared 'ugliness' by the postulated shifts in the semantic values of the occurrences of 'know' which are the trademark of the classical contextualist view and block disquotation. Nevertheless, they are unquestionably extremely strange to an English ear.

Does knowledge-relativism fare better with these potential snags? Again, the interesting question concerns a flexible relativism, one with the resources to handle cases where the pragmatic features of its subject determine the standards that a correct knowledge-ascription has to meet. And of course for the relativist, as for the non-indexical contextualist, there are no complications occasioned by shifts in the semantic value of 'knows'. We know to expect that relativism will coincide in its predictions with non-indexical contextualism in all scenarios where knowledge is ascribed in the indicative mood and where there is no contrast between the ascriber and an assessor. It is therefore no more than the price paid for the flexibility to copy the verdicts of IRI in cases that reflect well on the latter that relativism, like non-indexical contextualism, will sanction certain cases, both synchronic and diachronic, of ugly conjunctions.

So, here is the scorecard.

IRI is, seemingly, encumbered by a commitment to the assertibility, in suitable circumstances, of both forms of ugly conjunction.

However, commitments of this kind are not, as is sometimes assumed, a distinctive problem for that particular form of variabilism.

Non-indexical contextualism and *relativism* both share that commitment provided they avail themselves of the option of 'flexibility'. And, of course, if they do not so avail themselves, the IRI-favourable cases stand as counterexamples to their proposals.

Classical (flexible) contextualism is committed only to metalinguistic versions of ugly conjunctions. That is not as bad only provided (i) the metalinguistic versions are not as ugly and (ii) their disquotation is indeed blocked, i.e. provided 'knows' is indeed context-sensitive.

VII Is there any good reason to think that 'knows' is context-sensitive?

When utterances of the same type-sentence in different contexts appear to be able to take differing truth-values, context-sensitivity – that is, sensitivity of the content expressed to features of the utterance-context – is plausibly the most natural explanation. So, anyway, it must have seemed to the original authors of contextualism when first reflecting on the apparent variability of 'knows', but that was before the rival invariantist kinds of explanations considered here entered the scene. Can evidence be mustered to restore the presumption that context-sensitivity is at the root of the variability phenomena, and so give classical contextualism an edge?

The variability of 'knows'

The literature on the matter is complex, extensive and inconclusive; it is fair to say that there are no uncontroversial, or even generally agreed upon, criteria for (non-) context-sensitivity.[17] Jason Stanley argues persuasively[18] that the alleged context-sensitivity of 'knows' is not felicitously assimilated to that of any of gradable adjectives ('rich', 'tall'), pronouns ('I', 'you', 'this') or quantificational determiners ('all', 'many', 'some'). Schaffer and Szabo grant this but suggest instead a comparison with so called A-quantifiers ('always', 'somewhere').[19] Still, there is no reason in any case why a bone fide context-sensitive expression should behave exactly like context-sensitive expressions of other kinds. Is there any *general* reason to think that 'knows' and its cognates are context-sensitive, whether or not their behaviour sustains close comparison with that of other, uncontroversially context-sensitive expressions?

Here is a natural litmus. If 'S' contains context-sensitives, then distinct tokens of 'S' in different mouths may have different truth-conditions. So distinct token questions, "S?" in the mouths of different questioners may have different conditions for affirmative answers. Hence, if 'knows' and its cognates are context-sensitive, it should be possible to design a pair of conversational contexts within which a pair of tokens of the question, "Does X know that P" presented simultaneously to a single agent – the *questionee* – can respectively properly deserve prima facie conflicting answers. Why simultaneously? Because 'knows' *is* of course context-sensitive, at least to the extent of admitting of significant tense and X, the subject, may know different things at different times. (We needn't require strict simultaneity though. It will be enough to ensure that both the questionee's and [if distinct] the subjects' information-states are relevantly unaltered throughout the interval when the two questions are put.) Why a single questionee? Because, again, we want to ensure that if different answers are appropriate to the distinct token questions, they are so because of variations in pragmatic factors determined by their respective conversational contexts, rather than variations in the information of the questionee.

Call this the *forked-tongue test*. It's pretty crude – for instance, it won't distinguish context-sensitivity from simple ambiguity. Still, its credentials as at least a necessary condition for context-sensitivity seem good. Let's construct a simple illustration. Suppose Ashley and Bobbie are wondering whether to duck out of the queues at the bank and go to get coffee and cake. Chris meanwhile, standing nearby, is on the phone to Denny. Bobbie overhears Chris say, "Yes, my dear, there is. There is a Caffè Nero just two minutes away where they serve excellent coffee and *torta di cioccolata*." Bobbie says, "Excuse me, but did you say that there is a nice coffee shop just two minutes away." Chris replies, "Ah. Actually, no. I mean: I did say that, but I was talking to my partner about a location downtown."

Thus, "just two minutes away" passes the test. It was the context of Denny's question, rather than Bobbie's, that set the reference of "just two minutes way" in Chris's original remark. When Bobbie puts a token of essentially the same type-question, the reference shifts and the correct answer changes.

Can we get a similar result with 'know'? Let's try to construct an analogously shaped case, but where the questioners' respective contexts differ in respect of the stakes they have in the truth of the answer.

In Case 8, Ashley and Bobbie are dithering in the foyer of the bank as before. They talk about the risk of foreclosure and Bobbie says, "Look, we had better ask someone." Chris and Denny, standing near the back of one of the queues, happen to overhear their conversation. Denny is also perturbed by the length of the queues and says to Chris, "Do you know if the bank will be open tomorrow? We could come back then if it will, but I'd rather not leave it till Monday since I have a hairdresser's appointment on Monday morning and am meeting Stacy for coffee and a chat in the afternoon." Chris, recalling the Saturday morning visit of two weeks earlier says, "It's OK. I happen to know the bank will be open tomorrow. I'll drive you over after breakfast." Ashley,

23

overhearing, says, "Excuse me, but did you say that you know the bank will be open tomorrow?" Chris, mindful of Ashley and Bobbie's overheard priorities, replies, "Ah. Actually, no. I mean, I did use those words, but I was talking to Denny here, who has less at stake than you guys."

Case-hardened contextualists may find this dialogue unexceptionable, but I would suggest that Denny, Ashley and Bobbie might reasonably be baffled by Chris's last reply. It is also striking that, if the dialogue *is* regarded as unexceptionable, it should remain so if all play with 'know' is dropped and the operative question is rephrased as simply, "Will the bank be open tomorrow?" But in that case the explanation of the acceptability of Chris's final remark will presumably have nothing to do with context-sensitivity in the operative question. So it looks as though the contextualist faces a choice between admitting that 'know' fails the forked-tongue test in this instance or insisting that it passes but that this fact has no significance for its putative context-sensitivity.

VIII Is there any good reason to think that 'knows' is *not* context-sensitive?

The consideration that has proved perhaps the most influential in this regard in the recent debates, and indeed has provided the prime motivation for knowledge relativism, is provided by ostensible patterns of *correction and retraction* that our knowledge-talk seems to exhibit. Here's a toy example of the relevant kind. Chris and Denny have gone away for the weekend and have left Ashley and Bobbie the keys for the use of their car:

Ashley: Do you know where their car is parked?
Bobbie: Yes, I do — Chris texted me that they left it in the multi-storey lot as usual after badminton on Friday.
Ashley: But, as you very well know, there have been several car thefts in the neighbourhood recently. We should have gone to get it earlier. What if it's been stolen?
Bobbie: I wasn't reckoning with that. OK, I guess I don't *know* that it is in the multi-storey lot — we had better go and check.

Here, the reader is intended to understand, Ashley's second question doesn't change Bobbie's epistemic situation — it doesn't give her any more evidence. But it does persuade her that it is appropriate to impose more demanding standards of evidence on her answer than she started out doing — and she now disavows the knowledge she originally claimed.

Now, the crucial point for the opponent of contextualism is the suggestion that this disavowal is to be understood as a *retraction*. Consider this continuation of the dialogue:

Ashley: Was your first answer, about knowing where the car is, true when you originally gave it, before I raised the possibility of the car being stolen?

and two possible responses:

Bobbie: *Either* (a) Sure, but I could not truly repeat the words I used, once I was reminded of the recent incidence of car-theft.
            Or (b) No; as I just said, I wasn't thinking about the possibility of the car being stolen. I shouldn't have claimed to know that it is in the multi-storey lot.

The relativist's idea is that contextualism ought to predict that answer (a) can be acceptable. For if the content of a knowledge-ascription is relative to standards set by the context of ascription, then suitable changes in that context may be expected to go along with a shift in content consistent

The variability of 'knows'

with tokens of a single type-ascription being respectively true in an original context but false in a later context. But in fact answer (a) is, on the face of it, simply bizarre, and the natural answer, in context, is answer (b), which notably not merely supplants but critiques and retracts the original. That is evidence, it is alleged, that the content of the knowledge claim has not shifted in response to the change of standards, but has remained invariant throughout.[20]

Note that the contextualist can of course allow Bobbie to affirm not merely that she doesn't know now where the car is but that she *didn't know* when she made her first answer. That is because the referent of 'know', even as used in that past-tense claim, will – according to contextualism – have shifted to some high-standards knowledge relation in response to Ashley's invoking the possibility of theft, whereas Bobbie's original claim will have involved some different, low-standards relation. So contextualism can actually predict what *sounds like* a retraction: "I didn't know that P". What, the critic will charge, it cannot predict is agents' willingness to treat such remarks *as* retractions – their refusal to stand by the different thing that, according to contextualism, they originally said.

Challenged to explain that refusal, some contextualists[21] have taken recourse to the idea – usually captioned (by their critics) as 'semantic blindness' – that ordinary speakers are ignorant of the context-sensitivity of 'know' and its cognates and so are prepared in certain respects to (mis)use this family of expressions to talk misguidedly as if they were not context-sensitive. It can be said in mitigation of such a move that a kind of semantic blindness was anyway part of the epistemic contextualist package from the start: after all, the contextualist has to allow that her thesis is controversial – that it is not just straight-off evident to us that 'knows' is a context-sensitive term.[22] Still, it is one thing to maintain that we are ignorant about the gist of the correct semantic theory for an expression in common parlance, and another to hold that we systematically use that expression in ways that conflict with that theory; that is, that we systematically *mis*use it. It is, at least until more is said, rank bad methodology for proponents of a theory whose whole project is systematically to describe and explain aspects of our linguistic practice, to fall back too readily on the idea that aspects of that practice which fail to accord with the theory may be discounted as misuses.[23] At the least, contextualism needs to show how a prediction of the recalcitrant aspects of our practice may be elicited from its own theoretical resources. If no such account is forthcoming, the retraction data, *provided they are solid*, must constitute a serious strike against the view.

IX But are the retraction data solid?

It is, however, a further question whether our patterns of apparent retraction of knowledge claims really *do* provide the powerful argument for relativism that its supporters, notably MacFarlane, have urged. I'll canvass two doubts.

To begin with, there are issues about what exactly should count as the manifestation in practice of the relevant kind of retraction. Do we, in response to changes in pragmatic factors, really retract former ascriptions of knowledge in exactly the sense that relativism needs? A moment ago we already noted an important distinction in this connection. Consider this dialogue:

Ashley (on a fast moving train):   Look, there is a cougar!
Bobbie: Where? I don't see it.
Ashley: Just there, crouching by those rocks.
Bobbie: I still don't see it.
Ashley: Oh, I am sorry. I see now that it was just a cat-shaped shadow on the rocks. *There wasn't a cougar.*

25

Here Ashley's last speech is a retraction in anyone's book: she is denying, using appropriately changed context-sensitive language, exactly the thing she originally said. But to accomplish this, it suffices merely to change the tense of the original and negate it. Whereas under the aegis of contextualism about 'knows' group ability, corresponding moves do *not* suffice for retraction of a knowledge-ascription, as we observed. Contextualism allows that Bobbie may perfectly properly admit, in response to Ashley's canvassing the possibility of car-theft, both that she does not know where the car is and *did not know when first asked*. The latter admission is not a retraction of the original claim, since – according to contextualism – it concerns a different, high-standards knowledge relation. Accordingly, the relativist needs to point to clear evidence in our linguistic practice that the disposition to retract knowledge claims when the stakes are raised goes deeper than the apparent denial involved in merely changing the tense and negating the result. Speakers will have to be reliably and regularly disposed to say things that distinguish what they are doing from such merely apparent retractions that contextualism can take in stride.

What kinds of sayings would manifest that distinction? Bobbie was presented above as doing something of the needed sort by saying, "I wasn't thinking about the possibility of the car being stolen. *I shouldn't have claimed to know that it is in the multi-storey lot.*" But that is exactly *not* what he should say on the assumption of knowledge-relativism. Relativism allows that the earlier claim, in the lower-standards context then current, can have been perfectly appropriate – indeed, from the standpoint of that context, true. So if that were the form that retractions of knowledge claims were generally to assume, the fact would be at odds with rather than advantageous to relativism. What is wanted, it seems, is a form of repudiation which is neither a simple denial, modulo any needed changes in tense, etc., nor a repudiation of the propriety of one's making the earlier claim in its original context.

The salient remaining possibility is something along the lines of "What I said before is false." So, let the relativist contention be that we are characteristically prone to retractions on this model of former knowledge-ascriptions when pragmatic factors suitably change. Unfortunately, even this pattern of retraction, should it be prevalent, is too coarse to be unpredictable by contextualism. The reason it is so is because in order to give what passes as an appropriate disquotational specification of what was said by some utterance in a previous context – "What he said before by S was that P" – it is not necessary, or indeed possible, to adjust *every* kind of context-sensitive expression that S may have contained. To be sure, if Ashley says, "Right now, I am going crazy waiting in this queue," then in order to specify what she said we'll need to shift pronouns and tenses and temporal adverbs in routine ways: what Ashley said was that, *at that time, she was* going crazy waiting in *that* queue. But this does not apply in general to, for instance, gradable adjectives nor, so the contextualist may contend, to 'knows' and its cognates. If an inexperienced hospital theatre orderly asserts, "This scalpel is very sharp," intending roughly that you could easily cut yourself if handling it carelessly, he may quite properly be reported to an expert surgeon as having said that *that particular scalpel is very sharp*, even when the context set by conversation with the surgeon is understood as one in which the notion of an instrument's sharpness is high standards – for instance, is tied to its suitability for refined neurosurgery. And in such a context, the orderly may have to accept a reprimand and allow that "What I said – *viz.* that that scalpel is very sharp – was false." In short, where some kinds of context-sensitive language are involved, admissible ways of specifying what was said are not guaranteed to deliver an actual content previously asserted rather than a counterpart spawned by differences between the original context of use and the context of the specification.

Of course it's usually easy enough to disambiguate in such cases if the conversational participants find it important to do so. The hospital orderly may (perhaps unwisely) protest that all he meant was that the scalpel had enough of a fine edge to be dangerous if handled carelessly.

The variability of 'knows'

Perhaps therefore the relativist argument should be that we don't go in for such disambiguation where knowledge claims are concerned but, as it were, *simply* retract. But is that true? With "sharp" now annexed to high (neurosurgical) standards, the orderly has to have recourse to other language to explain what he originally meant to say. If that is allowed to constitute sticking by his former claim, then we surely will want to say something similarly exculpatory about the credentials of our erstwhile epistemic situation and an associated knowledge claim even as we feel obliged to revoke the latter purely because of pressure of elevated standards.

It is, accordingly, open to question whether relativists have succeeded in tabling a notion of retraction with each of the needed features (a) that we do go in for retraction of knowledge claims under changes of pragmatic parameters of context, (b) that relativism predicts this and (c) that contextualism cannot predict as much.

The second doubt about the alleged pro-relativistic significance that our patterns of retraction of knowledge claims supposedly carry concerns the *extent* of the phenomenon. Relativism predicts that two contexts of assessment, c_1 and c_2, differing only in the values of pragmatic parameters, may be such that one mandates an endorsement of a knowledge-ascription and another its repudiation. The examples so far considered have tended to focus on one direction: where a knowledge-ascription is made in a relatively low-standards context and then, apparently, retracted as the stakes rise, or certain error-possibilities become salient, or whatever the relevant kind of change is proposed to be. What about the converse direction? Does our practice pattern as relativism should expect?

Let's try an example:

Case 9 begins exactly as Case 2. It is Friday afternoon, and Ashley and Bobbie have arrived at the bank to deposit their salary cheques. However there are long queues at all the bank counters. Ashley recalls being at the bank on a Saturday morning two weeks ago and says, "Let's come back tomorrow. **I know the bank will be open tomorrow morning**." Suppose that the bank will indeed be open on the Saturday morning. However the couple's mortgage lender has written to say the company will foreclose unless the cheques are in the account by Monday to service the monthly repayment, and Ashley and Bobbie are mindful of this. Bobbie says, "But what if the bank has changed its opening hours? Or what if the Saturday morning opening was some kind of one-off promotion?" Ashley says, "You're right. **I suppose I don't really *know* that the bank will be open tomorrow** (even though I am pretty confident that it will). We had better join the queue."
Invited intuition: Ashley correctly retracts her original claim. There is too much at stake to take the risk of e.g. a change in banking hours.

But now let's run the example on. Let it so happen that Eli, who is the manager of the local branch of Ashley and Bobbie's mortgage company, is also waiting in one of the queues and overhears their conversation. Remembering "that nice young couple" and taking pity on them, Eli comes across and says, "Don't worry, guys. Just between us, there is a degree of bluff about these 'final reminder' notices. We never actually foreclose without first making every effort to conduct an interview with the borrowers. It will be absolutely fine if this month's payment is serviced by the end of next week." Ashley and Bobbie are mightily relieved and Ashley says, "Aha. **So actually I *did* know that the bank will be open tomorrow**! Let's go and get a coffee and come back then."

Relativism predicts that Ashley's last emboldened remark is perfectly in order – indeed it expresses a commitment: the context after Eli's intervention is once again low stakes, so low standards, so Ashley's knowledge claim is now mandated by the original evidence, and the

27

intermediate knowledge denial should be retracted. But while relief and the decision to get a coffee are reasonable enough, Ashley's last remark is actually utterly bizarre.

This is a crucial issue for knowledge-relativism. I have no space here to pursue it in detail, but I conjecture that there are actually no clear cases where, moving from a high- to a low-standards context, and *mindful of the fact*, we are content, without acquiring any further relevant evidence, simply to retract a former knowledge-disclaimer and to affirm its contradictory. Where P was the proposition of which knowledge was denied, we may well say things like, "Well, I guess it's reasonable now if we take it that P" or "We can now probably safely assume that P". But the claim to now *know* that P will simply invite the challenge to re-confront the error-possibilities made salient in the previous high-standards context. And when the changes involved in the context shift are wholly pragmatic, we will tend to regard ourselves as, strictly, no better placed, epistemically, to discount those possibilities than we were before. For example, Ashley should not now after conversation with Eli, any more than earlier, want to claim *knowledge* that the Saturday opening of two weeks ago was not a one-off promotion.

The qualification "mindful of the fact" is crucial. No doubt it may happen that, forgetting altogether about a previous high-standards situation, we may in a new, relaxed context be prepared to make knowledge claims that contradict earlier disclaimers. But these claims will properly rank as *retractions* only if we recall the previous context and what we said then. And if we do that, recollection of the error possibilities that drove the early disclaimers is still likely to inhibit our outright claiming the relevant bits of knowledge even if it no longer seems urgent to reckon with those possibilities. Relativism, by contrast, predicts that there is now a mandate for such claims and that any such inhibitions about them conflict with the correct semantics for 'knows'.[24]

X Conclusion

Variabilism, in all its stripes, is motivated by an *appearance*: that the language game of knowledge-ascriptions and denials incorporates a dependence of their truth-values on pragmatics – on interests, or saliences or stakes. Each of the four theoretical proposals here considered, albeit offering very different accounts of the nature of the dependence involved, takes this appearance to be veridical. If, as has been the general tendency of the foregoing discussion, none of these accounts is satisfactory – if each under-predicts (fails to predict some uses) or over-predicts (predicts uses with which we are uncomfortable) – the natural conclusion is that the appearance is *not* veridical: that our discourse involving 'knows' and its cognates is subject to no genuine pragmatics-sensitive variability of truth-conditions.

If we draw that conclusion, two possibilities remain. One, of course, is invariantism. But invariantism must come to a view about where the invariant threshold for knowledge falls, and, wherever it is placed, it will have to be acknowledged that a significant body of our knowledge claims, or knowledge disclaimers, are false, and an explanation will therefore be owing of why so much of our linguistic practice with 'knows' and its cognates falls into error. Invariantists have not been slow to respond to this challenge.[25] I here record the opinion, for which I have no space to argue, that to date their efforts have been unpromising.

The other possibility is a view concerning 'knows' and its cognates that stands in comparison with what deflationists about truth say about 'true'. For the deflationist about truth, very familiarly, it is a metaphysical mistake to ask after the character of the property that 'true' expresses. The proper use of the word is accountable, rather, not to the nature of an assumed referent in the realm of properties, but to the service of certain practical purposes – notably indirect endorsement and generalisation – that it enables us to accomplish. Correspondingly, a deflationism about knowledge will discharge the idea that there is any determinate epistemic relation or – in

The variability of 'knows'

deference to contextualism – family of relations that the proper use of 'knows' serves to record and whose character determines the truth-conditions of knowledge-ascriptions. Rather the use of the word needs to be understood by reference to the practical purposes – notably, for example, as DeRose observed, the accreditation of potential informants and the appraisal of agents' rational performance – that it enables us to accomplish. The variability phenomena surface as one or another of these purposes comes to the fore in a particular pragmatic context. But is a metaphysical mistake to project these phenomena onto the putative nature of an assumed referent, or referents, as IRI and contextualism attempt to do, and seek to explain them thereby.

Relativism doesn't make *that* mistake. Someone who holds that "X knows that P" is assessment-sensitive has already discharged the realism about the knowledge relation that deflationism would counsel us against. But if the suggestion of the preceding section about the asymmetries between our apparent retractions of knowledge-ascriptions and apparent retractions of knowledge-denials are correct, then the concept of knowledge we actually have betrays an (inflationary) invariantist tendency which relativism simply misdescribes. Of course it is open to a relativist to acknowledge this, and to present relativism as reformist. That proposal, however, stands in need of an argument that any purpose would be served by reform. The essence of the case for deflationism about 'knows' is twofold: negatively, that the combination of our tendency to allow the standards for its application to inflate indefinitely while unwilling to accept, with the skeptic, that it never applies, betrays a concept with certain inbuilt tensions and no determinate reference; positively, that the word nevertheless supplies the valuable resources that the variability phenomena reflect. The first part of that might suggest the desirability of reform, but that is compensated for by the second.

Such a general conception of knowledge – or better, of the function of 'knows' – is nothing new,[26] although the present suggestion, that its correctness is the principal lesson which the variability phenomena have to teach us, may be so. If it is correct, the idea that knowledge should come first in analytical epistemology could not be further from the truth. Knowledge – the presumed substantive referent of 'knows' – comes nowhere. But I must defer the further exploration of this form of deflationism to another time.[27]

Notes

1 This second aspect – Williamson's "Knowledge First" programme – is of course strictly independent of and additional to the primitivism.

2 "The *intense* view of these manifold contradictions and imperfections in human reason has so wrought upon me, and heated my brain, that I am ready to reject all belief and reasoning, and can look upon no opinion even as more probable or likely than another. . . . Most fortunately it happens, that since reason is incapable of dispelling these clouds, nature herself suffices to that purpose, and cures me of this philosophical melancholy and delirium . . . I dine, I play a game of backgammon, I converse, and am merry with my friends; and when after three or four hours' amusement, I wou'd return to these speculations, they appear so cold, and strain'd, and ridiculous, that I cannot find in my heart to enter into them any farther" *Treatise* I, IV, 7 (Hume 1738, pp. 268–9).

3 Hawthorne (2004), Dretske (2005).

4 See Hawthorne (2005). See also ch. 12 of this volume.

5 Cohen (1986), DeRose (1992).

6 Hawthorne (2004), Stanley (2005); see also Fantl and McGrath (2007). See ch. 19.

7 Or sometimes: subject-sensitive invariantism.

8 MacFarlane (2005) and (2014). See Part V.

9 As MacFarlane terms it.

10 For experimentation with a version of this kind of view, see Cappelen (2008). Weatherson (2009) makes an interesting application of it to address certain puzzles with indicative conditionals.

11 This is different from – but perhaps not quite as clean-cut as – Stanley's (2005) tactic which is to develop examples where a low-stakes ascriber does not know that the subject is high stakes. For instance, suppose Chris does not notice Ashley and Bobbie join the queue. But Denny, Chris's partner, who has overheard the exchange, does and nudges Chris with a quizzical glance in their direction. Chris says, "Oh, I guess they must have remembered some reason why they can't come back tomorrow – after all, **they now know that the bank will be open then.**" This time, we are supposed to have the intuition that the knowledge-ascription is false.

12 See DeRose (2009), ch. 7.

13 John Hawthorne (2004, ch. 4 at pages 162–6) attempts to enlist the help of what he calls the "psychological literature on heuristics and biases". Hawthorne's idea is that one lesson of this literature is that the becoming salient of a certain risk in a high-stakes situation (e.g. that of the bank's changing its opening hours) characteristically leads us to overestimate its probability in general and hence to project our own ignorance onto subjects in low-stakes situations, too. DeRose (2009, ch. 7, section 3) counters that the phenomenon to be explained – high-stakes agents' denial of knowledge to low-stakes subjects – extends to cases where the former take it that they *do* nevertheless know the proposition in question (because they take themselves to meet the elevated standards demanded by their high-stakes context). That seems right, but I do not see that Hawthorne needed the "projection of ignorance" component in his proposal in any case; a tendency to overestimation of the probabilities of salient sources of error would seem sufficient to do the work he wants on its own. The objection remains, however, that if an overestimation of the risk of a certain source of error underlies a high-stakes ascriber's denial of knowledge to himself, the good standing of that denial is already compromised – whereas IRI requires precisely that the high-stakes context should validate it.

14 Stanley (2005), ch. 7.

15 Non-indexical contextualism allows speakers of the same proposition in distinct contexts to speak truly and falsely, respectively. That may seem relativistic enough for most people's money, but it stops short of the contention, essential to MacFarlane's understanding of relativism, that a single speaking of a proposition may take distinct truth-values as assessed in different contexts.

16 If evidence, too, were an interest-relative notion, then a possible direction of defence for IRI against these ugly-conjunctive commitments would be to try to make the case that variation in the interests of a subject sufficient to make the difference between her knowing that P and failing to do so must also affect what evidence she possesses, thus undercutting the assumption that evidence may remain constant for a subject at different times or for distinct subjects when their interests differ. Stanley canvasses this suggestion (2005, p. 181). It misses the nub of the difficulty, however, because there will presumably be cases where the relevant evidence is known with certainty and hence must be reckoned to be in common no matter what the practical interests of the subjects or subject at different times.

17 For discussion, see Cappelen and Hawthorne (2009), ch. 2.

18 Stanley (2005), ch. 3.

19 Schaffer and Szabo (2013). Their proposal deserves a properly detailed discussion. I believe the comparison is flawed but I have no space to enlarge on that here.

20 See ch. 20.

21 See, e.g. Cohen (2001).

22 See ch. 24.

23 Cf. Baker (2012).

24 This objection should be contrasted with another made by Montminy (2009). His contention is that when *in a high-standards context* we disclaim knowledge that P, we will also judge that we will be wrong to reclaim knowledge that P in a subsequent low-standards context, even though – he allows – that is what we will do once such a context is entered into, and relativism says we will be right to do so. I agree with the first part of that – namely, that we will take a dim view, while in the high-standards context, of the envisaged subsequent reclamation, and that since relativism says that there is nothing wrong with the subsequent reclamation, there is here a tension between something we are inclined to think and what relativism thinks we ought to think. But, unless I misread Montminy, I'm saying something different and stronger as well: namely, that we *won't actually make a retraction* of the previous knowledge-denial when we get into the low-standards context.

Knowledge-relativism, in other words, mispredicts not just aspects of our attitudes to our practice with 'knows' but our practice itself. (MacFarlane responds to Montminy in section 8.6 of his 2014 book, see especially pp. 198 and following. His response does not engage the objection made here.)

25 See, e.g. Williamson (2005). See chs. 7, 16 and 17.

The variability of 'knows'

26 The germ is famously present in Austin (1946, pp. 97–103) where a view is outlined on which utterances of the form "I know that such-and-such" serve a *performative* rather than a descriptive function, and the function of "I know" is in effect to offer a *promise* of truth, on the basis of which others are entitled to act, form beliefs or claim to know, in turn. Austin's ideas receive a thoroughgoing, sympathetic development in Lawlor (2013), though I do not know how far she would welcome the deflationism prefigured here.

27 I am grateful to Jonathan Jenkins Ichikawa for giving me the opportunity to write up and publish this material, the principal ideas in which were generated in graduate classes at New York University in 2005 and further refined at seminars at the Arché research center at St Andrews that took place as part of the AHRC-funded *Contextualism and Relativism* project (2006–9). Thanks to those involved on those occasions and to Filippo Ferrari, Patrick Greenough, Jonathan Jenkins Ichikawa, Carrie Ichikawa Jenkins and Giacomo Melis for more recent helpful discussion.

References

Austin, J.L. (1946) "Other Minds", *Proceedings of the Aristotelian Society*, Supplementary Volume 20: 148–187.

Baker, C. (2012) "Indexical Contextualism and the Challenges from Disagreement", *Philosophical Studies* 157(1): 107–123.

Cappelen, H. (2008) "Content Relativism and Semantic Blindness", in Garcia-Carpintero, M. and Kolbel, M. (eds.), *Relative Truth*, pp. 265–286. Oxford: Oxford University Press.

Cappelen, H. and Hawthorne, J. (2009) *Relativism and Monadic Truth*. Oxford: Oxford University Press.

Cohen, S. (1986) "Knowledge and Context", *The Journal of Philosophy* 83: 574–583.

———. (2001) "Contextualism Defended: Comments on Richard Feldman's 'Skeptical Problems, Contextualist Solutions'", *Philosophical Studies* 103: 87–98.

DeRose, K. (1992) "Contextualism and Knowledge Attributions", *Philosophy and Phenomenological Research* 52: 913–929.

———. (2009) *The Case for Contextualism: Knowledge, Skepticism, and Context: Vol. 1*. Oxford: The Clarendon Press.

Dretske, F. (2005) "The Case Against Closure", in Steup, M. and Sosa, E. (eds.), *Contemporary Debates in Epistemology*, pp. 27–40. Malden, MA: Wiley Blackwell.

Fantl, J. and McGrath, M. (2007) "Knowledge and the Purely Epistemic: In Favor of Pragmatic Encroachment", *Philosophy and Phenomenological Research* 75(3): 558–589.

Hawthorne, J. (2004) *Knowledge and Lotteries*. Oxford: Oxford University Press.

———. (2005) "The Case for Closure," in Steup, M. and Sosa, E. (eds.), *Contemporary Debates in Epistemology*. Malden, MA: Wiley Blackwell.

Hume, D. (1738) *A Treatise of Human Nature* (ed. L. Selby Bigge 1888). Oxford: The Clarendon Press.

Lawlor, K. (2013) *Assurance: An Austinian View of Knowledge and Knowledge Claims*. Oxford: Oxford University Press.

MacFarlane, J. (2005) "The Assessment Sensitivity of Knowledge Attributions", *Oxford Studies in Epistemology* 1: 197–233.

———. (2014) *Assessment Sensitivity: Relative Truth and Its Applications*. Oxford: Oxford University Press.

Montminy, M. (2009) "Contextualism, Relativism and Ordinary Speakers' Judgments", *Philosophical Studies* 143(3): 341–356.

Schaffer, J. and Szabo, Z. (2013) "Epistemic Comparativism: A Contextualist Semantics for Knowledge Ascriptions", *Philosophical Studies* 168(2): 491–543.

Stanley, J. (2005) *Knowledge and Practical Interests*. Oxford: Oxford University Press.

Weatherson, B. (2009) "Conditionals and Indexical Relativism", *Synthese* 166: 333–357.

Williamson, T. (2005) "Contextualism, Subject-Sensitive Invariantism and Knowledge of Knowledge", *The Philosophical Quarterly* 55(2019): 213–235.

2

THE INTUITIVE BASIS FOR CONTEXTUALISM

Geoff Pynn

Francois follows climate science closely, and on this basis she believes, correctly, that the earth's mean temperature will continue to rise over the next century. Does she *know* this? Many would say that she does. Her belief is based on her accurate understanding of the scientific consensus, and we typically treat scientific expertise as a source of knowledge. On the other hand, you might deny that she knows that the temperature will continue to rise, even if you agree that this is likely. After all, climate scientists themselves readily acknowledge that their predictions are not entirely certain. So while Francois may be justified in her belief, she doesn't really *know*. Which answer is right, then? Does Francois know? Or not? Contextualists think that which answer is correct depends, in part, on the context in which the question is asked. Whether Francois can truly claim to know depends on her context's "epistemic standard," which determines how strong her epistemic position must be in order for her to count as knowing in that context – how much evidence she needs, which alternatives she needs to be able to rule out, how reliable her belief-forming mechanisms need to be, and so on. So according to the contextualist, Francois can truly claim to know that the temperature will continue to rise in a context where the epistemic standard is relatively relaxed, but not in a context where the epistemic standard is particularly demanding.

This chapter outlines the intuitive argument for contextualism. To a substantial degree, my presentation follows that of Keith DeRose, who has done more than any other contextualist to develop the argument (see especially DeRose 1992, 2005, 2009 [ch. 2]). The overall shape of the argument is an inference to the best explanation: contextualism, it is claimed, is part of the best explanation for the variability in epistemic standards exhibited by our ordinary knowledge talk. The argument is "intuitive" in that it relies upon intuitive judgments about ordinary knowledge claims. The contents of these judgments furnish the data that contextualism explains. By calling the judgments "intuitive," I mean two things: first, they are more-or-less non-inferential and cognitively effortless; second, they are generated by intellectual reflection or imagination, rather than perception (Nagel 2007, Nado and Johnson 2014). When I say that something "intuitively seems" to be the case, I mean that we (I and, hopefully, the reader) are inclined to make an intuitive judgment that it is the case. When I say that an intuitive judgment is "accepted" or that we "defer to" an intuition or intuitive judgment, I mean that we accept that the judgment's content is true.

The intuitive basis for contextualism

Low–High pairs and the intuitions they elicit

The case for contextualism starts with the observation that we apply different epistemic standards in different contexts when making and evaluating knowledge claims. This observation will not be news to anyone who has been exposed to radical skeptical arguments. When well-constructed and successfully deployed, such arguments lead us temporarily to apply much higher epistemic standards than we ordinarily do, and hence to conclude that we don't know much. Still, as Hume pointed out, even skeptics regard themselves as knowers once the skeptical spell has been lifted: "[T]he first and most trivial event in life will put to flight all their doubts and scruples, and leave them the same, in every point of action and speculation, with the philosophers of every other sect, or with those who never concerned themselves in any philosophical researches" (Hume 1999, 207). One can see the debate over radical skepticism as a debate about which epistemic standard is correct: the very high standard introduced by the skeptic, or the more manageable one in place once our doubts and scruples have been put to flight. Contextualists claim to be able to resolve, or dissolve, this debate: different standards apply in different contexts, so neither one is "correct" *tout court* (see chapter 10). But the contextualist resolution might appear ad hoc. Couldn't nearly *any* philosophical dispute be "resolved" by stipulating that some term at the heart of the dispute has a meaning that varies with context? To avoid this charge, we need independent reason to accept that contextualism is true.

Contextualists argue that shifts in epistemic standards like those triggered by a skeptic's intervention are ubiquitous in ordinary conversations. They present us with pairs of imaginary vignettes to illustrate this variability. In the "Low" vignette, a speaker in some mundane situation claims that a subject knows some proposition. In the "High" vignette, a speaker in a different situation claims that the same subject doesn't know that same proposition. When the vignettes are well constructed, both the positive knowledge claim in the Low case and the negative knowledge claim in the High case seem true. I'll call such cases Low-High pairs. Here is a well-known Low-High pair from Keith DeRose:

> *Low Bank Case.* My wife and I are driving home on a Friday afternoon. We plan to stop at the bank on the way home to deposit our paychecks. But as we drive past the bank, we notice that the lines inside are very long, as they often are on Friday afternoons. Although we generally like to deposit our paychecks as soon as possible, it is not especially important in this case that they be deposited right away, so I suggest that we drive straight home and deposit our paychecks on Saturday morning. My wife says, "Maybe the bank won't be open tomorrow. Lots of banks are closed on Saturdays." I reply, "No, I know it'll be open. I was just there two weeks ago on Saturday. It's open until noon."

> *High Bank Case.* My wife and I drive past the bank on a Friday afternoon, as in [Low Bank Case], and notice the long lines. I again suggest that we deposit our paychecks on Saturday morning, explaining that I was at the bank on Saturday morning only two weeks ago and discovered that it was open until noon. But in this case, we have just written a very large and very important check. If our paychecks are not deposited into our checking account before Monday morning, the important check we wrote will bounce, leaving us in a *very* bad situation. And, of course, the bank is not open on Sunday. My wife reminds me of these facts. She then says, "Banks do change their hours. Do you know the bank will be open tomorrow?" Remaining as confident as I was before that the bank will be open then, still, I reply, "Well, no, I don't know. I'd better go in and check."

> *(DeRose 1992, 913; DeRose 2009, 1–2)*

In Low, it doesn't matter very much whether Keith is right about the bank's hours, and no hypotheses about how he could be wrong has been raised. In High, it matters a lot whether he is right, and a particular hypothesis about how he might be wrong ("Banks do change their hours") has been raised. What leads Keith to deny that he knows in High is not an argument for philosophical skepticism, but his awareness of the ordinary ways he could go wrong, and the exigencies of everyday life.

The intuitive argument for contextualism doesn't rest upon any *particular* Low-High pair such as the Bank Cases or Stuart Cohen's equally well-known Airport Cases (Cohen 1999). Such cases are rather meant to illustrate a pervasive variability in our ordinary knowledge talk, which contextualism (it is argued) best explains. Nonetheless, it simplifies matters to present the argument as if a particular pair of cases were essential to it. There should be no danger in this, provided we bear in mind that the contrast between the Bank Cases is meant to be representative of a ubiquitous phenomenon. So construed, the key claim in the case for contextualism is:

Truth. Keith's claim to know in Low and his claim not to know in High are both true.

Truth, in turn, is underwritten by two intuitive judgments.

First, considered from the perspective of the context in which it was made, each claim seems true. As DeRose puts it, contextualists "appeal to how we, competent speakers, intuitively evaluate the truth-values of particular claims that are made (or are imagined to have been made) in particular situations" (2009, 49). Imagine yourself in each conversation, and ask whether the claim Keith makes in that conversation is true (assuming, of course, that the bank *will* in fact be open); the contextualist thinks that you'll find yourself answering, "Yes." Second, each claim is intuitively appropriate. A claim can be (and seem) true without being (or seeming) appropriate. Asked by a friend who's run out of gas if there is a filling station nearby, I claim that there is one around the corner, without revealing that I know that it has been closed for months. My claim is true but misleading, and hence improper. However, the propriety of a claim is evidence for its truth, since it is generally improper to make a false claim. Not always: hyperbolic and other figurative claims can be proper though false ("It took me a million years to get through Husserl's *Logical Investigations!*"). Nonetheless, such cases are exceptional, and neither of Keith's claims seems at all figurative (*pace* Schaffer 2004 and Hazlett 2007).

It's important to see that neither of these intuitions constitutes a judgment about what Keith *knows* or *doesn't know*. For a contextualist, the question of what a subject knows is different from the question of what knowledge claims are true of her. To say that Keith knows would be to claim, in effect, that he meets the epistemic standards in place in our present context. The case for contextualism does *not* rest on an intuitive judgment that Keith meets or doesn't meet the epistemic standards in place in the context of a philosophical discussion about knowledge or knowledge claims. Rather, it rests on the judgment that Keith's knowledge claims, as made in their imagined contexts, are true. Contextualists typically refrain from issuing or endorsing any first-order judgments about whether the characters in their vignettes know or don't know. DeRose, for example, says that his intuitions about the "object-level question" of whether the characters in his story know "would be far more wavering and uncertain than are my intuitions that the claims made in the cases are true" (2009, 49). Similarly, when arguing for contextualism using his Airport Cases, Stewart Cohen is concerned with whether the speakers use the word "know" correctly, and whether they speak truly, and not with whether the subject of their knowledge attributions knows (1999, 58ff.).

The intuitions are also not judgments about the *sentences* that Keith has uttered. Standard contextualism does treat both sentences as true with respect to their context of utterance. And contextualists are not always careful about distinguishing the truth of a sentence from the truth of a claim made by uttering the sentence (though see Stainton 2010 and Pynn 2015). This is partly because contextualists typically presuppose that what Keith *claims* in each case just *is* the content encoded by the sentence he utters with respect to its context. If a claim's content and truth-value are identified with the content and truth-value of the sentence uttered in making the claim, then Truth implies that the sentences Keith utters in both cases are true. But the intuitive judgments at play in the argument concern the truth and propriety of Keith's claims, and not the sentences he utters in making them.[1]

By and large, contextualists and their opponents have agreed that Keith's claims are intuitively proper and true; controversy has concerned how to accommodate these intuitions, not what they are. Recently, however, work in "experimental philosophy" has been used to raise doubts about the intuitions themselves. Citing surveys designed to elicit judgments about Low-High pairs, Jonathan Schaffer and Joshua Knobe assert that "people simply do not have the intuitions they were purported to have," suggesting that "the whole contextualism debate was founded on a myth" (2012, 675). Chapter 3 discusses this issue in more detail. Two brief responses are worth making.

First, some of the data cited by Schaffer and Knobe is neutral with respect to the intuitive judgments just canvassed (see DeRose 2011 for discussion). Two of the surveys ask subjects about whether various characters in Low-High pairs *know*, rather than whether speakers who claim to know speak truly. A third study (Buckwalter 2010) asked subjects whether the speaker in a Low case who claims to know speaks truly, but then, in a departure from contextualist Low-High pairs, asked whether a speaker in a High-like case who *also* claims to know speaks truly. Only the fourth study (Feltz and Zarpentine 2010) involved a survey in which the bank cases were presented more or less as originally constructed. In Feltz and Zarpentine's study, the average level of agreement that the claims made in High and Low were true was around four on a seven-point Likert scale. While this result does not confirm the contextualist's claims about the intuitions, neither does it disconfirm them; it is neutral.

Second, more recent work than that cited by Schaffer and Knobe suggests that the intuition of truth in Low and High is, in fact, widely shared. Hansen and Chemla (2013) "confirmed DeRose's prediction that speakers would find both 'I know that p' in the Low context and 'I don't know that P' in the High context true" (203). And Buckwalter (2014) designed a new survey where speakers were asked about the truth of knowledge attributions and denials made in various Low and High cases, and found that subjects "generally judged everything true across the board" (156).[2] In light of this subsequent work, we have reason to doubt Schaffer and Knobe's assertion that contextualism is founded on an intuitive myth. Nonetheless, the empirical adequacy of the standard contextualist claim about our intuitive judgments is a subject of lively and ongoing debate; see chapter 3 for a more detailed and sympathetic discussion of this line of criticism.

Why the intuitions should be trusted

Deferring to the intuitive judgments gives us strong reason to accept Truth. But why defer to the intuitions to begin with? Why think that the *seeming* truth and propriety of his claims indicates that they *are* proper and true? This question points towards the vast controversy over the role of intuitions in philosophy; see Pust (2016) for an introduction to this literature.

It is a widely accepted philosophical practice to afford the contents of our intuitive judgments a default level of evidential significance. The practice is not to treat intuitive judgments as infallible or issuing from some faculty of rational intuition, but simply to treat acceptance of their contents as a desideratum when tallying the pros and cons of a philosophical view. When the balance of reasons tips in favor of a view, despite its conflict with some intuitive judgments, standard practice tells us to "bite the bullet" and dismiss the problematic intuitions. Yet even when biting the bullet, we are encouraged to provide an explanation for the wayward intuitions. Fairly powerful reasons are required to conclude that things are not how they intuitively seem, and we may remain dissatisfied with a bullet-biting view until we have been told why things intuitively but wrongly seemed as they did. Employing this standard practice in the present context, the intuitions that Keith's utterances are both proper and true ought to be taken at face value. And to take them at face value is to endorse Truth. If we are to reject them, we are owed an explanation as to why we had them to begin with.

Of course, to describe this practice is not to justify it. Controversy surrounds all general defenses of reliance on intuition in philosophy. A more manageable strategy here may be to pursue a narrower defense. Jennifer Nagel argues that "epistemic evaluations of particular cases" of the sort frequently discussed by epistemologists (e.g., intuitive judgments about Gettier's cases, Carl Ginet's fake barn country, Lawrence Bonjour's Truetemp case) are exercises of our capacity to attribute mental states to other people (Nagel 2007, 2012). Though our "mind-reading" ability is susceptible to error, it is nonetheless generally accurate. If Nagel is right about the source of our intuitive epistemic evaluations, then we can be confident in treating them as evidentially significant (if defeasible). But Nagel's defense of epistemic intuitions, even if successful, may not establish the significance of the contextualist intuitions about Low-High pairs, because the latter may not count as epistemic intuitions; they concern the truth and propriety of knowledge claims, and not whether the subjects of those claims know.

Since the intuitions concern claims made by uttering sentences, we may wish to treat them as linguistic intuitions. Linguists treat the intuitive judgments of competent speakers about certain features of their language as an important source of evidence about those features of the language. The standard rationale for treating such intuitions as evidence is that linguistic competence relies on tacit knowledge of the rules governing the language (Chomsky 1986). On the assumption that a linguistic intuition is the product of a speaker's tacit knowledge of the rules governing their language, we have good reason to accept it. While there is substantial controversy over the adequacy of this traditional rationale (see, e.g., Devitt 2006), it seems undeniable that competent speakers of a language possess at least some degree of epistemic authority concerning many features of their language. If the intuitive judgments of truth and propriety in Low-High pairs are linguistic intuitions, then they have a prima facie claim to deference, on pain of undermining a principle source of evidence in linguistics.

However, just as it is not clear that the intuitions are epistemic, it's also not clear that they are best characterized as linguistic, either. They don't concern the properties of words or sentences, but the claims made by uttering sentences in particular contexts. The competence required to determine what claim is being made by a speaker who utters a particular sentence involves a substantial degree of extra-linguistic knowledge, as does that required to form an accurate judgment about whether a claim is true or conversationally proper. Suppose that Mary utters, "Sharon is by the bank." Linguistic competence alone won't enable you to know whether she is claiming that Sharon is waiting by a financial institution, or that Sharon is down by the riverbank, much less whether Mary's claim is proper or true. Similarly, tacit knowledge of the syntactic and semantic features of the linguistic expressions he uses doesn't suffice for us to know what Keith claims by uttering, "Well, no, I don't know," much less to form a judgment as to whether his claim is true or proper. Intuitions of truth and propriety rest in part upon empirical knowledge of how speakers in various circumstances use particular English sentences, together with our capacity to imaginatively occupy the circumstances described in the case.

But even if the intuitions do not rest entirely upon tacit linguistic knowledge, their being the product of our competence as users of English gives us good reason to treat them with respect.

The intuitive basis for contextualism

Fluent speakers possess practical expertise concerning how to use their language. They are in a position to know what sentences speakers tend to utter in various situations, what speakers typically mean to claim by uttering what they do, and which claims are appropriate to make under which circumstances. The intuitive judgments of competent speakers about the truth and propriety of claims made using their language thus deserve deference for the same reason that the judgments of anyone with practical expertise in any particular area do: expertise in a practice gives you reliable (though not infallible) intuitions about how the practice works. When a chef who has been making mayonnaise for years tells you that you're adding the oil to your emulsion too quickly, you ought to listen. A seasoned jazz musician can tell you, without appeal to theory, whether a given note will sound awkward at a particular moment in an improvised sequence. Similarly, given sufficient background information, a fluent speaker of English can tell you whether a claim made using English in a particular circumstance would be proper, and whether it would be true.[3]

Contextualism and its invariantist rivals

The rest of the intuitive argument for contextualism is devoted to showing that contextualism is better able than its rivals to accommodate and explain Truth. Keith's claims are "surface-contradictory." Making what is implicit in the uttered sentences explicit, the two claims are:

(L) I know [that the bank will] be open.
(H) I don't know [that the bank will be open].

Going by their surface grammar, (L) and (H) are contradictories. So how could both claims be true? We assume that the bank will be open, and that Keith believes this in both cases. Keith has no evidence against the bank's being open in High that he lacks in Low. His epistemic position with respect to the proposition that the bank will be open is the same in both cases. How, then, can he truly claim (L) in Low, but truly claim (H) in High? Contextualism provides a simple answer: whether Keith can truly claim to know something varies with the epistemic standard in the context in which he makes the claim. Since the standard in Low is relatively low, while the standard in High is relatively high, his epistemic position is strong enough for him to count as knowing in Low, but not for him to count as knowing in High.

Invariantists hold that the epistemic standards governing the truth of a knowledge claim are fixed across contexts, and so cannot agree that (L) and (H) are both true owing to a variation in the epistemic standards across the contexts of utterance. Traditionally, invariantists have attempted to block the intuitive inference to Truth by providing alternative explanations for the intuitions that support it. In more recent years, clever versions of invariantism have been developed that accept Truth, and propose ways to explain it, rather than biting the bullet.

Traditional invariantists hold that one of Keith's claims is false. *Skeptical* invariantists hold that the standard is very demanding, and hence that Keith's claim to know in Low is false. *Moderate* invariantists hold that the standard is more relaxed, and hence that Keith's claim not to know in High is false. In either case, one intuition of truth must go. Invariantists have nonetheless been keen to accommodate both intuitions of propriety. This leads to two challenges. The first is to explain how the false claim is nonetheless proper. Let's call this *the propriety challenge*. The second is to explain the wayward intuition of truth. Let's call this *the truth challenge*.

A common strategy for meeting the propriety challenge focuses on the pragmatic effects of knowledge claims (see chapter 16). False claims can pragmatically convey truths, and in virtue of this may be conversationally proper, despite being false. Jessica Brown (2006) offers a pragmatic answer to the propriety challenge on behalf of moderate invariantism. If Keith were to claim that he knows in the High case, his assertion would, though true, be irrelevant, because the conversationally relevant issue is not whether he knows, but whether he is in an especially strong epistemic position. So he falsely claims that he doesn't know, conveying the conversationally relevant truth that he is not in an especially strong epistemic position (for other proposals in this vein see Rysiew 2001 and 2007, Black 2005, Hazlett 2007, and Pritchard 2010). Skeptical invariantists have made parallel proposals. Jonathan Schaffer (2004) treats ordinary knowledge claims as hyperbole, arguing that such hyperbolic falsehoods convey that the speaker can eliminate the possibilities of error relevant in the context of utterance. Wayne Davis (2007) offers a different kind of pragmatic skeptical account of the propriety of Low knowledge claims, arguing that they are examples of "loose use," proper for the same reason that it can be proper to claim, falsely, that a jar with only a few coffee grounds left is empty (see chapter 17).

Though promising as an answer to the propriety challenge, the pragmatic approach faces a significant hurdle in meeting the truth challenge. There are no uncontroversial examples of false claims that seem true in virtue of being proper. The central cases of false-but-proper claims – examples involving figurative speech – do not produce an intuition of truth. And though Davis is surely right that it is often proper to call a coffee jar with a couple of beans in it empty, some (the present author included) hold that this is, in part, because such claims are often true: the standards for emptiness fluctuate with context. If this approach is correct, Davis's proposal treating ordinary knowledge claims as instances of loose use may amount to a version of contextualism, rather than a competitor. It is common for invariantists who recognize the limitations of the pragmatic approach to attempt to meet the truth challenge with an error theory of some kind. Timothy Williamson, for example, suggests that repeated exposure to unusual skeptical possibilities can produce an "illusion of epistemic danger" (Williamson 2005; see also Vogel 1990). High-context speakers, under the sway of such an illusion, may be led to underestimate the strength of their epistemic positions. More recently, Mikkel Gerken (2013) has developed a theory of "epistemic focal bias," which may produce false impressions of knowledge and non-knowledge. There is some tension between the error-theoretic approach to the truth challenge and pragmatic resolutions of the propriety challenge. A claim that results from an error may *seem* proper, but once the error is uncovered, we generally change our minds about its propriety. It is not clear that invariantists can endorse the intuition of propriety while rejecting the intuition of truth (though see Pynn 2014 for an attempt to do both).

Other invariantists accept Truth. One prominent strategy is to offer a psychological explanation for the falsehood of Keith's claim in High. Kent Bach argues that in a High context a speaker's "threshold for (confidently) believing" goes up, so that she "demands more evidence than knowledge requires" before she is willing to form a confident belief (Bach 2005, 77). Jennifer Nagel (2008, 2010a, 2010b) relies on an array of psychological studies to argue that subjects in high-stakes situations require more information before forming settled beliefs, and so tend to refrain from forming settled beliefs on the basis of information that low-stakes subjects treat as sufficient for settled belief. Because high stakes decrease a subject's "need for closure," Keith will be less inclined to form a settled belief about the bank's hours in High than he was in Low. The Bach–Nagel strategy is then to say that Keith doesn't have a settled belief that the bank will be open in High. Since knowledge requires belief, Keith doesn't know in High, and his claim in High is true (see chapter 7).

Another invariantist strategy for accommodating Truth is to argue that the epistemic position required for knowing varies with the subject's practical situation. Proponents of *interest-relative* or *sensitive* invariantism say that whether a subject's epistemic position is strong enough to know that P depends upon the practical significance for her of the question of whether P is true (see chapter 19). On this picture, when the costs of being wrong about P are high, you need to be in

The intuitive basis for contextualism

a stronger epistemic position to know that P than you do when the costs of being wrong are low. Sensitive invariantism predicts that (L) and (H) are both true: since the practical stakes are higher for Keith in High than they are in Low, a stronger epistemic position is required for him to know in High than in Low. This approach rests on a claim known as *anti-intellectualism* or *impurism*; namely, that the epistemic requirements for knowing vary with the subject's practical situation. Anti-intellectualism is controversial, though it has able defenders, and its capacity to enable invariantists to accommodate our intuitions about Low-High pairs is a significant consideration in its favor (see Stanley 2005 and Fantl and McGrath 2009 for major defenses of interest-relative invariantism and impurism, respectively; see also Hawthorne 2004).

Taking one of these approaches enables invariantists to avoid the propriety and truth challenges. But the challenges re-emerge when we make a slight alteration to the structure of a Low-High pair. The bank cases involve first-person knowledge ascriptions made in different scenarios. This makes room for positing some variation in Keith's psychological state or practical situation between the Low and High scenarios, which explains how (L) and (H) can both be true, even though contextualism is false. But we can also construct Low-High pairs where the surface-contradictory claims concern a third party. Such "third-person" cases elicit the same intuitive judgments as the original Bank Cases, but there is no room to posit a difference in the third-party subject's mental states or situation to account for the truth of two surface-contradictory claims. DeRose's Thelma and Louise Cases are designed for just this purpose (DeRose 2009, 4–5; Cohen 1999's Airport Cases also have this structure). Thelma, Louise, and Lena are co-workers. All three saw their colleague John's hat in the hallway and overheard a conversation whose participants presupposed that he was in his office. All three believe that John was in, though they did not actually see him:

> *Low Thelma.* On her way home, Thelma stops at the local tavern to collect on a small bet concerning whether John would be in that day. After her tavern-mates pay up, they ask her whether Lena knows that John was in, since she also had a small bet going on the question. "Yes," Thelma answers, "Lena knows that John was in."

> *High Louise.* Louise is stopped by the police on her way home. They are investigating a serious crime, and need to verify whether John was at work today. They have no reason to doubt that he was, but need Louise's testimony to be sure. She demurs, pointing out that he may have left his hat on the hook the previous day, and that her co-workers who thought he was in may have been mistaken. After all, she points out, she didn't actually see him. So while she believes he was in, she says, she doesn't know. They follow up by asking whether Lena could testify to John's whereabouts. No, Louise answers, she didn't see him either: "Lena doesn't know that John was in."

Thelma and Louise's claims about Lena both seem proper and true when considered against the backdrop of their contexts of utterance. These intuitions, in turn, underwrite:

> *Truth★.* Thelma's claim that Lena knows in Low and Louise's claim that Lena doesn't know in High are both true.

Contextualism accommodates and explains Truth★ in precisely the same way it did Truth. But assuming that Thelma and Louise are speaking simultaneously, Lena's confidence level and practical circumstances must be the same in each case. So we cannot posit a psychological or practical difference to accommodate and explain Truth★. Bach and Nagel both appeal to error theories to handle such third-person cases, chalking the intuitive truth of claims like Lena's up to a kind of error (Bach 2005, 76–77; Nagel 2010b). Stanley takes a somewhat different tack, suggesting that in considering whether Lena knows, Louise is actually concerned with whether Lena would know if she were in Louise's situation. Since she wouldn't, Louise claims that Lena doesn't know; according to Stanley (2005) this is "a perfectly intuitive explanation of the intuitions" (102). That may be, though to the extent that an explanation's simplicity and unity counts in its favor, contextualism is preferable to either of these approaches.

Cross-contextual intuitions: trouble for contextualism?

Insofar as a view's capacity to explain how the contents of our intuitive judgments are true contributes to its superiority over rivals, contextualism so far appears superior to invariantism. However, opponents of contextualism have argued that there are also intuitive judgments at odds with contextualism. These problematic intuitions primarily concern various forms of disagreement, and cross-contextual assessments (see chapter 20). For example, imagine the conversation in High Louise continuing:

> *High Louise, Con't.* The police point out that Thelma was overheard in the tavern claiming that Lena knows that John was in, and ask her what she thinks of that. "No, Thelma's claim was false," Louise replies. "Lena doesn't know."
>
> *(cf. McKenna 2014, 726)*

According to contextualism, Thelma's claim was true. Assuming that Louise's assessment of Thelma's claim is intuitively correct, we appear to have an intuition whose content contextualists must reject. A number of theorists have argued that such assessments furnish intuitive evidence against contextualism (e.g., MacFarlane 2005, 202–203; Stanley 2005, 52; Williamson 2005, 220; Brogaard 2008, 411).

Note that if this case provides evidence against contextualism, it also provides evidence against moderate and sensitive invariantism, at least on the assumption that those views treat Thelma's claim in Low as true. Skeptical invariantists may regard the datum as a point in favor of their own view. However, skeptical invariantists already reject many ordinary intuitions of truth; on their view, ordinary positive knowledge claims are almost *always* false, despite our persistent everyday intuitions to the contrary. So even granting that the case is an intuitive cost for contextualism as compared to skeptical invariantism, it hardly tips the intuitive balance in skeptical invariantism's favor.

We may question the degree to which such cases are intuitively problematic for contextualism. Prominent Low-High pairs are designed to capture what ordinary speakers would say in relevantly similar circumstances. By contrast, it is not clear that an ordinary speaker in circumstances like Louise's would say, "Thelma's claim was false." Provided she were aware of the casual nature of Thelma's tavern conversation, it would be at least as natural for her to say, "Thelma was only speaking loosely," or even, "She didn't really mean that Lena *knows for sure.*" Neither of these assessments would conflict with contextualism; indeed, either of them would provide some indirect confirmation that different standards are operative in each context. Of course, Louise *could* say that Thelma's claim was false, and to the extent that such an assessment would be intuitively correct, this is a fair point against contextualism. But if it is not what Thelma most naturally *would* say, the point is not especially threatening, especially given the intuitive costs already borne by invariantism.[4]

Such cross-contextual assessments play an important role in motivating a newer competitor to contextualism, known as *relativism* about knowledge attributions (see chapters 25 and 26). According to the relativist, the truth-conditions of a knowledge claim vary not with the context of utterance, but the context of assessment (see MacFarlane 2005, Rysiew 2011, and MacFarlane 2014 [ch. 8]). Relativists can treat Thelma's claim as true relative to her own context of

The intuitive basis for contextualism

assessment, but false relative to Lena's. So relativism can accommodate *both* the intuitive truth of Thelma's knowledge attribution *and* the intuitive truth of Lena's assessment of Thelma's knowledge attribution as false. There may be intuitive costs associated with relativism as well, however. According to the relativist, Thelma's claim was true as assessed in Thelma's context of utterance, but it seems doubtful that Lena would be prepared to grant this. Montminy (2009) argues that the relativist must impute to ordinary speakers a kind of semantic error in their cross-contextual judgments. But relativism is an important emerging paradigm in philosophical semantics, and the question of whether contextualism or relativism better accommodates and explains our intuitions about knowledge claims remains open.

Notes

1 To see the difference, it may be helpful to focus on the actual sentence that features in the High Bank Case: "Well, no, I don't know." Speaking for myself, I have no intuition whatsoever about whether that *sentence* is true. I am inclined to say that it is neither true nor false, because it is semantically incomplete, since it has no element corresponding to *what* Keith is claiming not to know.

2 Consistent with his earlier study, Buckwalter's respondents also judged that speakers who claim not to know in Low cases and speakers who claim to know in High cases were speaking truly. This wrinkle leads Buckwalter to suggest that all of the responses were "largely driven by accommodation"; i.e., the conversational rule-schema David Lewis (1979) posited to the effect that speakers ought, so far as possible, to assign semantic values to utterances that permit them to be interpreted as true. Contextualists should welcome Buckwalter's suggestion. If the reason that subjects so readily interpret "know"-involving utterances as true is that they are tacitly adhering to a rule of accommodation for such utterances, then we have a further piece of "intuitive" evidence for contextualism: the more semantically invariant a term, the more resistant we should be to accommodating a variety of "surface-contradictory" utterances involving the term.

3 DeRose suggests that the correct semantic theory of a term is correct partly *in virtue of* the fact that we have the semantic intuitions about the term that we do, together with other facts about our usage of the term (2009, 66–67). He concludes that ordinary usage facts indicating that a term is context-sensitive are thus "some of the best possible type of evidence you could ask for" to conclude that the term is, in fact, context-sensitive. Against this, Cappelen and Lepore argue that intuitions of the sort we have been discussing – intuitions about truth and propriety generated by what they call "minimal pairs" – provide *no* evidence that a term is semantically context-sensitive (2005, 17). Their target is specifically the view that the word "know" should be categorized as an indexical term. (Indeed, as speech-act pluralists, they agree with contextualists that the same sentence can be used to make claims with different contents in different contexts.) Though the claim that "know" is an indexical term has sometimes been thought to be constitutive of contextualism, contextualists are free to reject indexicalism about "know." See Stainton (2010), Pynn (2015), and chapter 37 for further discussion of these issues.

4 See also DeRose's considerations in favor of the "methodology of the straightforward," on which the "simple positive and negative claims speakers make utilizing the piece of language being studied" receive greater weight than "more complex matters, like what metalinguistic claims speakers will make and how they tend to judge how the content of one claim compares with another" (2009, 153).

Bibliography

Bach, K. (2005). "The Emperor's New 'Knows'." In Preyer, G. and Peter, G., editors, *Contextualism in Philosophy: Knowledge, Meaning, and Truth*, pages 51–90. Oxford: Oxford University Press.

Black, T. (2005). "Classical Invariantism, Relevance and Warranted Assertibility Manoeuvres." *The Philosophical Quarterly*, 55(19):328–336.

Brogaard, B. (2008). "In Defense of a Perspectival Semantics for 'Know'." *Australasian Journal of Philosophy*, 86(3):439–459.

Brown, J. (2006). "Contextualism and Warranted Assertibility Manoeuvres." *Philosophical Studies*, 130:407–435.

Buckwalter, W. (2010). "Knowledge Isn't Closed on Saturday: A Study in Ordinary Language." *Review of Philosophy and Psychology*, 1(3):395–406.

Buckwalter, W. (2014). "The Mystery of Stakes and Error in Ascriber Intuitions." In Beebe, J., editor, *Advances in Experimental Epistemology*, pages 145-174. London: Continuum.

Cappelen, H. and Lepore, E. (2005). *Insensitive Semantics: A Defense of Semantic Minimalism and Speech Act Pluralism.* Malden, MA: Blackwell Publishing.

Chomsky, N. (1986). *Knowledge of Language: Its Nature, Origin, and Use.* New York: Praeger Publishers.

Cohen, S. (1999). "Contextualism, Skepticism, and the Structure of Reasons." *Philosophical Perspectives*, 13:57–89.

Davis, W. (2007). "Knowledge Claims and Context: Loose Use." *Philosophical Studies*, 132:395–438.

DeRose, K. (1992). "Contextualism and Knowledge Attributions." *Philosophy and Phenomenological Research*, 52:913–929.

DeRose, K. (2005). "The Ordinary Language Basis for Contextualism, and the New Invariantism." *The Philosophical Quarterly*, 55:172–198.

DeRose, K. (2009). *The Case for Contextualism.* Oxford: Oxford University Press.

DeRose, K. (2011). "Contextualism, Contrastivism, and X-Phi Surveys." *Philosophical Studies*, 156:81–110.

Devitt, M. (2006). "Intuitions in Linguistics." *British Journal for the Philosophy of Science*, 57(3):481–513.

Fantl, J. and McGrath, M. (2009). *Knowledge in an Uncertain World.* Oxford: Oxford University Press.

Feltz, A. and Zarpentine, C. (2010). "Do You Know More When It Matters Less?" *Philosophical Psychology*, 23:683–706.

Gerken, M. (2013). "Epistemic Focal Bias." *Australasian Journal of Philosophy*, 91(1):41–61.

Hansen, N. and Chemla, E. (2013). "Experimenting on Contextualism." *Mind and Language*, 28(3):286–321.

Hawthorne, J. (2004). *Knowledge and Lotteries.* Oxford: Oxford University Press.

Hazlett, A. (2007). "Grice's Razor." *Metaphilosophy*, 38(5):669–690.

Hume, D. (1999). *An Enquiry Concerning Human Understanding.* T. D. Beauchamp, ed. Oxford: Oxford University Press.

Lewis, D. (1979). "Scorekeeping in a Language Game." *Journal of Philosophical Logic*, 8:339–359.

MacFarlane, J. (2005). "The Assessment Sensitivity of Knowledge Attributions." *Oxford Studies in Epistemology*, 1:197–234.

MacFarlane, J. (2014). *Assessment Sensitivity: Relative Truth and Its Applications.* Oxford: Oxford University Press.

McKenna, R. (2014). "Shifting Targets and Disagreements." *Australasian Journal of Philosophy*, 92(4):725–742.

Montminy, M. (2009). "Contextualism, Relativism and Ordinary Speakers' Judgments." *Philosophical Studies*, 143(3):341–356.

Nado, J. and Johnson, M. (2014). "Moderate Intuitionism: A Metasemantic Account." In Booth, A. R. and Rowbottom D., editors, *Intuitions.* Oxford: Oxford University Press, 68–90.

Nagel, J. (2007). "Epistemic Intuitions." *Philosophy Compass*, 2:792–819.

Nagel, J. (2008). "Knowledge Ascriptions and the Psychological Consequences of Changing Stakes." *Australasian Journal of Philosophy*, 86(2):279–294.

Nagel, J. (2010a). "Knowledge Ascriptions and the Psychological Consequences of Thinking About Error." *The Philosophical Quarterly*, 60(239):286–306.

Nagel, J. (2010b). "Epistemic Anxiety and Adaptive Invariantism." *Philosophical Perspectives*, 24:407–435.

Nagel, J. (2012). "Intuitions and Experiments: A Defense of the Case Method in Epistemology." *Philosophy and Phenomenological Research,* 85(3):495–527.

Pritchard, D. (2010). "Contextualism, Skepticism, and Warranted Assertability Manoeuvres." In Campbell, J. C., O'Rourke, M., and Silverstein, H., editors, *Knowledge and Skepticism*, pages 85–103. Cambridge, MA: MIT Press.

Pust, J. (2016). "Intuition." *The Stanford Encyclopedia of Philosophy* (Spring 2016 Edition). E. N. Zalta, ed. http://plato.stanford.edu/archives/spr2016/entries/intuition/

Pynn, G. (2014). "Unassertability and the Illusion of Ignorance." *Episteme*, 11(2):125–143.

Pynn, G. (2015). "Pragmatic Contextualism." *Metaphilosophy*, 46(1):26–51.

Rysiew, P. (2001). "The Context-Sensitivity of Knowledge Attributions." *Noûs*, 35:477–514.

Rysiew, P. (2007). "Speaking of Knowing." *Noûs*, 41(4):627–662.

Rysiew, P. (2011). "Relativism and Contextualism." In Hales, S. D., editor, *A Companion to Relativism*, pages 286–305. Malden, MA: Blackwell.

Schaffer, J. (2004). "Skepticism, Contextualism, and Discrimination." *Philosophy and Phenomenological Research*, 69(1):138–155.

Schaffer, J. and Knobe, J. (2012). "Contrastive Knowledge Surveyed." *Noûs*, 46(4):675–708.

Stainton, R. J. (2010). "Contextualism in Epistemology and the Context Sensitivity of 'Knows'." In O'Rourke, M. and Silverstein, H., editors, *Knowledge and Skepticism*, pages 113–139. Cambridge, MA: MIT Press.

Stanley, J. (2005). *Knowledge and Practical Interests*. Oxford: Oxford University Press.

Vogel, J. (1990). "Are There Counterexamples to the Closure Principle?" In Roth, M. and Ross, G., editors, *Doubting: Contemporary Perspectives on Skepticism*, pages 13–27. Dordrecht: Kluwer.

Williamson, T. (2005). "Contextualism, Subject-Sensitive Invariantism and Knowledge of Knowledge." *The Philosophical Quarterly*, 55(219):213–223.

3

EPISTEMIC CONTEXTUALISM AND LINGUISTIC BEHAVIOR

Wesley Buckwalter

Introduction

Epistemic contextualism is the linguistic theory that the word "knows" is context-sensitive (Lewis 1996; DeRose 2009; Cohen 2013). The theory states that the standards that are required in order to truthfully say a person knows a proposition are set by and shift according to the contexts in which that statement is made. This view is primarily motivated by claims about the linguistic behavior of competent speakers. More specifically, epistemic contextualism is motivated by the claim that it offers the best explanation of observable facts about the use of "knows" in certain cases. According to this theory, for example, people truthfully say both "I know the bank is open tomorrow" and "I do not know the bank is open tomorrow" when the standards required in order to "know" shift between those contexts. Many things could potentially shift standards between contexts. Two specific contextual features are often discussed. One feature involves practical consequences; for example, whether the stakes associated with the bank being closed for the ascriber are low or high. Another feature involves error salience; for example, whether or not uneliminated possibilities of error are made apparent to the ascriber. Contextualists claim that competent speakers behave in these ways, and that the fact that they do this is "evidence of the very best type that one can have for concluding that any piece of ordinary language is context-sensitive" (DeRose 2005: 172; see also Pynn, this volume).

This chapter reviews evidence in experimental cognitive science for epistemic contextualism in linguistic behavior, focusing on three questions. First, have experimental observations confirmed that the behavioral patterns motivating epistemic contextualism in ordinary language are real? Second, does the existence of these behavioral patterns constitute a sufficient reason to accept epistemic contextualism as an explanation of them over other explanations? Third, does epistemic contextualism explain specific linguistic behaviors involving skepticism any better than other theories do, given what has been discovered about the psychological origins of skepticism in cognitive science?

To anticipate the answers to these questions, first, experimental evidence for epistemic contextualism is mixed. Many studies have found evidence that is inconsistent with the motivation for epistemic contextualism, while other studies have found evidence consistent with it. Second, while evidence has been found that is consistent with epistemic contextualism, these results are also equally well explained both by psychological features that do not provide any evidence for contextualism and by rival theories of "knowledge" that are inconsistent with contextualism. Third, experimental research on the origins of skepticism suggests that the theory of epistemic contextualism does not explain certain skeptical patterns observed in ordinary language any better than rivals do. I conclude that despite over thirty years of theoretical developments in philosophy and five years of experimental testing in cognitive science, epistemic contextualism remains underdetermined by existing experimental evidence, yielding little motivation to accept it as an account of our actual linguistic practices.

Mixed linguistic evidence

Epistemic contextualism is primarily motivated by empirical claims about the linguistic behavior of competent speakers in certain situations. One claim is that we find a knowledge-ascribing sentence (e.g. "S knows that p") and its denial (e.g. "S does not know that p") to both be true when the evidential standards set by the context in which they are made shift from low to high. A second claim is that we find the same knowledge-ascribing sentence (e.g. "S knows that p") to be true when the evidential standards set by the context are low and false when the evidential standards set by the context are high. The motivation for contextualism is that the theory can explain these behaviors. But do competent speakers actually behave in these ways? This section reviews studies that have found mixed experimental evidence regarding the motivation for epistemic contextualism in linguistic behavior.

Several studies have detected patterns of responses that challenge the motivation for epistemic contextualism (Buckwalter 2010, 2014; Feltz and Zarpentine 2010; see also May, Sinnott-Armstrong, Hull, and Zimmerman 2010). They have done so by examining stimuli identified by contextualists as the best thought experiments for testing the view that "knows" is a context-sensitive expression (though see DeRose 2011 for criticism). In one experiment for instance, Feltz and Zarpentine (2010: Experiment 1) presented participants with one of two bank cases manipulating the context in which a knowledge sentence was made. One story featured low practical consequences and error salience:

> Hannah and her wife Sarah are driving home on a Friday afternoon. They plan to stop at the bank on the way home to deposit their paychecks. It is not important that they do so, as they have no impending bills. But as they drive past the bank, they notice that the lines inside are very long, as they often are on Friday afternoons. Realizing that it isn't very important that their paychecks are deposited right away, Hannah says, 'I know the bank will be open tomorrow, since I was there just two weeks ago on Saturday morning. So we can deposit our paychecks tomorrow morning.'
>
> *(Feltz and Zarpentine 2010: 703)*

The other story featured high practical consequences and error salience:

> Hannah and her wife Sarah are driving home on a Friday afternoon. They plan to stop at the bank on the way home to deposit their paychecks. Since they have an impending bill coming due, and very little in their account, it is very important that they deposit their paychecks by Saturday. Hannah notes that she was at the bank two weeks before on a Saturday morning, and it was open. But, as Sarah points out, banks do change their hours. Hannah says, 'I guess you're right. I don't know that the bank will be open tomorrow.'
>
> *(Feltz and Zarpentine 2010)*

Participants in both conditions were instructed to "Assume that the bank really will be open tomorrow." Participants in the low context condition were then asked how strongly they agreed or disagreed that "When Hannah says, 'I know the bank will be open tomorrow,' what she says is true." Alternatively, participants in the high context condition were asked how strongly they agreed or disagreed that "When Hannah says, 'I don't know the bank will be open tomorrow,' what she says is true." Participants evaluated these statements on a seven-item agreement scale, where "1" was anchored with "strongly agree", "4" anchored with "neutral", and "7" with "strongly disagree".

Researchers found that participants were ambivalent about the truth of both knowledge sentences. The mean response was 3.74 in high context (or 4.26 after this score was reverse-coded to approximate knowledge ascription) and 3.68 in low context. Contextualism is motivated by the claim that competent speakers find these kinds of knowledge-ascribing and knowledge-denying sentences to both be true. In actuality, participants did not display this tendency. Participants remained neutral about the truth of both of these sentences. They reacted to these sentences using the neutral midpoint of the scale, or at about the level of chance. Researchers replicate this same basic pattern of results across a series of different cover stories.

Researchers have also found evidence that does not support contextualism when examining evaluations of the same knowledge-ascribing sentence across different contexts (Buckwalter 2010). In this study by Buckwalter, participants were presented with three variations on the bank case above. The first case, *Bank*, involved a situation in which practical consequences and error salience were low. The second case, *High Stakes*, involved an adaptation in which error salience was low and practical consequences were high (e.g. "Bruno has written a very large check, and if the money from his pay is not deposited by Monday, it will bounce, leaving Bruno in a very bad situation with his creditors," p. 401). The third case, *High Salience*, involved low practical consequences and high error salience in which a character challenges a speaker's claim (e.g. "Sylvie says, 'Banks are typically closed on Saturday. Maybe this bank won't be open tomorrow either. Banks can always change their hours; I remember that this bank used to have different hours'"). Participants were then instructed: "On a scale of 1 to 5, circle how much you agree or disagree that Bruno's assertion, 'I know the bank will be open on Saturday' is true."

Participants tended to agree that Bruno's knowledge statement was true in all three cases. The mean in Bank was 3.83. The mean in High Stakes was 3.71. The mean in High Salience was 3.64. All three means were significantly greater than the midpoint of this scale, or greater than chance. Contextualism is motivated by the idea that the knowledge-ascribing sentence is more likely to be true in High Stakes or High Salience than in Bank. In actuality, participants did not display this tendency. Participants tended to think that Bruno spoke truthfully in all three cases, despite the changes in context.

Researchers have also found evidence that challenges contextualism when directly asking participants to evaluate evidential standards across contexts (Turri 2016: Experiment 4). In one study, for instance, participants were presented with cases involving either low practical consequences and error salience or high practical consequences and error salience similar to those used in prior research. However, instead of making a claim about knowledge, both stories end with a character asking a question about the standards of evidence required to know:

> Jane continues, "This actually raises a more general question I've been considering. On a scale of 1 to 10, with 10 being the highest, how strong must your evidence be in order to know that the bank is open tomorrow?"
>
> *(p. 11)*

Participants were then instructed to enter a value from one to ten in the following sentence, "Knowing requires evidence that rates _____ on the scale."

Context did not significantly impact people's answers about the evidential standards. The mean response was 8.6 in high context and 8.3 in low context. Contextualism is motivated by the idea that the evidence required to truthfully say someone knows something increases as the context shifts from low to high. In actuality, participants did not display this tendency. Participants selected the same standard of evidence in both low and high context. In other words, ordinary speakers did not acknowledge any shifting evidentiary standards across these contexts.

Lastly, researchers have also found evidence unfavorable to contextualism in related judgments about knowledge ascription (May, Sinnott-Armstrong, Hull, and Zimmerman 2010). In these studies, participants were presented with one of four bank cases that independently varied both practical consequences and error salience. In all four cases, the protagonist claims to know the bank will be open. Participants were then asked to agree or disagree with the statement that the protagonist knows that the bank will be open. They found that participants tended to agree that the protagonist knew in each case. Researchers also found a small main effect whereby overall agreement with the ascription was less pronounced when the stakes were high than low. This study is different from the studies above in that it collects judgments about knowledge ascription (i.e. "Hannah knows") rather than assessments of the truth-value of knowledge-ascribing sentences (i.e. "the expression 'Hannah knows' is true"). As a result of this, some have argued that these findings "have no tendency to jeopardize the kinds of intuitions generally used to support standard forms of contextualism" (DeRose 2011:83). That said, to the extent these judgments are regularly related in ordinary practice, the results do not instill much confidence in the motivation for the theory.

While this body of evidence challenges the motivation offered for epistemic contextualism, there are also limitations to this evidence. On the one hand, subtle features of the stimuli or probing could be obscuring contextualist friendly results yet to be discovered. Perhaps the particular manipulations used involving stakes or error salience were insufficient to effectively shift the conversational context that, in turn, is supposed to affect our evaluations (see Schaffer and Knobe 2012). Moreover, it could be that there are other, more effective factors that shift contextual standards of evidence beyond error salience or practical consequence yet to be discovered. On the other hand, it is important not to underestimate the significance of the present evidence. People said knowledge sentences were true in contexts where they were supposed to find them false and did not say they were true in contexts where they were supposed to do that. Neither did judgments about the amount of evidence required to "know" provide any reason to think evidential standards shifted across low and high conversational contexts. If other factors beyond error salience or practical consequences shift evidentiary standards, then the burden clearly falls on contextualists to identify and characterize them.

Despite the initial evidence detected by several independent teams of researchers challenging the motivations of epistemic contextualism, some researchers have found evidence that the motivation for it is real (Hansen and Chemla 2013). These researchers conducted a complex within-subjects experiment designed to test whether shifts in conversational context impact the standards of evaluation of several types of sentences. They studied whether there were contextualist patterns detectable for "knows". As an interesting point of comparison, they also studied whether there were contextual effects for other sorts of words such as something being "green" or "beige". To do this, researchers manipulated four factors. The first factor was the *Type of Scenario*: Knowledge, Color, or Miscellaneous. Participants in the Knowledge condition saw stories and evaluated sentences about "knows" (e.g. "I know the bank will be open tomorrow"). Participants in the Color condition saw stories and evaluated sentences about color terms like "beige" or "green" (e.g. "The walls in our apartment are beige"). Participants in the Miscellaneous condition saw stories and evaluated sentences about disparate items (e.g. "There is milk in the refrigerator"). The second factor was *Cover Story*. Researchers devised four cover stories within the Knowledge condition, four cover stories within the Color condition, and two cover stories within the Miscellaneous condition. This resulted in ten basic cover stories. The third factor was *Context*. The Context factor manipulated whether the salience of error possibilities was low or high. The fourth factor was *Polarity*. The Polarity factor manipulated whether or not the protagonist in each cover story made a positive or a negative claim about "knowledge", "color", or the "miscellaneous" item involved in that particular story.

This resulted in forty conditions (ten basic cover stories, each of which could have a low or high context, and each of which featured a statement with positive or negative polarity). Forty participants were each given all forty conditions presented in four set orders or "blocks". After seeing each one of these forty cases, researchers asked participants to rate whether or not what the protagonist in the story said about the presence or absence of "knowledge", "color", or the "miscellaneous" item was true. Participants could answer on a number line ranging from "false" to "true" in which values of 0 to 100% were possible.

Researchers found evidence supporting the existence of shifting contextual standards in the Knowledge, Color, and Miscellaneous conditions. Collapsing across all the cover stories within these conditions, there was a significant interaction effect between Context and Polarity for each type of sentence. Participants were more likely to think that positive statements (e.g. "I know the bank will be open tomorrow" or "The walls in our apartment are beige") were true when the context was low than when it was high. And they were more likely to think that negative statements (e.g. "I don't know the bank will be open tomorrow" or "The walls in our apartment aren't beige") were true when the context was high than when it was low. These results are visualized in Figure 3.1.

Results confirm that people say that these knowledge-ascribing sentences are true in low contexts and knowledge-denying sentences are true in high contexts. Incidentally, researchers also found evidence of similar patterns for color terms and other miscellaneous items in ordinary language. However, some aspects of this experiment also question how strongly the results support epistemic contextualism. First, there was a three-way interaction effect between Type of Scenario, Context, and Polarity. The contextual effects for "knows" were weak in comparison to those readily exhibited for color terms or other miscellaneous items in the study, like being "beige". Second, despite the small interaction effect between Context and Parity in Knowledge conditions, participants also simply agreed that knowledge sentences were true

		Knowledge	Color	Miscellaneous
⊕	Low			
	High			
	Statistical diff.	$F(1, 38) = 24, p < .001$	$F(1, 38) = 41, p < .001$	$F(1, 38) = 55, p < .001$
⊖	Low			
	High			
	Statistical diff.	$F(1, 38) = 4.6, p = .05$	$F(1, 38) = 38, p < .001$	$F(1, 38) = 38, p < .001$
	Stat. interaction	$F(1, 38) = 17, p < .001$	$F(1, 38) = 49, p < .001$	$F(1, 38) = 61, p < .001$

Figure 3.1 Mean scores to the dependent variable collapsing across all cover stories in Knowledge, Color, or Miscellaneous conditions. Positive Polarity is indicated by "+", negative by "−". Context is indicated by "Low" and "High". Reprinted from Hansen and Chemla (2013) with permission.

across the board. Overall, the general tendency was to answer that knowledge-ascribing sentences were still true even in high standards contexts and that knowledge-denying sentences were still true in low standards contexts. This begins to question the unique role of context in these matters over and above the presence of simple agreement bias or default trust in testimony that might occur regardless of shifting standards (see Hansen and Chemla 2013: 309; Turri 2016, for discussion). Third, the contextual effects observed for "knows" could be due to task demands of the experiment (though see Hansen 2014). The results reported in Figure 3.1 represent within-subjects comparisons in which participants saw all versions of each cover story. However, researchers obtained different results when they reanalyzed the data at a time-point in which each participant had only seen one version of each cover story. When participants had only seen one version of each story, contextual effects in Color and Miscellaneous were found, but contextual effects in Knowledge were not found. This suggests that the contextual pattern detected for "knows" may be the result of ordering and exposure to other items in the experiment.

Lastly, some researchers have found evidence that supports contextualism in related judgments about knowledge ascription (Alexander, Gonnerman, and Waterman 2014; see also Buckwalter and Schaffer 2015; Waterman, Gonnerman, Yan, and Alexander in press, for replication and cross-cultural variation). These researchers presented participants with two vignettes developed by Nagel (2010) varying the salience of error possibilities about seeing a red object. Here is the *Low Context* case:

> John A. Doe is in a furniture store. He is looking at a bright red table under normal lighting conditions. He believes the table is red.
>
> *(Nagel 2010: 287)*

The *High Context* case included the low context story and the following addition:

> However, a white table under red lighting conditions would look exactly the same to him, and he has not checked whether the lighting is normal, or whether there might be a red spotlight shining on the table.
>
> *(Nagel 2010)*

Alexander, Gonnerman, and Waterman then asked participants whether they agreed or disagreed with the claim that John knows that the table is red. Participants answered on a six-item agreement scale with "1" anchored "strongly disagree" and "6" anchored "strongly agree". They found a large effect between these conditions. Although participants tended to attribute knowledge in both conditions, this tendency was much more pronounced in Low Context (mean response of 5.5) than High Context (mean response of 3.8).

These results are also friendly to contextualism, with three important caveats. First, as noted above, the result technically does not directly test epistemic contextualism because it measures rates of knowledge ascription rather than evaluation of the truth of knowledge-ascribing sentences. But again, to the extent these judgments are closely related, the results are consistent with contextualist claims. Second, despite the large effect of condition on responses, knowledge was attributed in Low and High Context across the board. Third, the experimental and control conditions are not minimally matched pairs. It is possible that wording effects concerning the quality of the initial evidence (e.g. "he has not checked") or large differences in length (i.e. a difference of thirty-seven words) and complexity of stimuli impact responses in unforeseen ways orthogonally to manipulating the contextual standard.

Underdetermined by evidence

Although support for epistemic contextualism is mixed, some ordinary language practices consistent with the motivation for epistemic contextualism have been found. These findings constitute evidence that the motivation for it is real. But does this evidence provide a good reason to accept contextualism over rival theories?

Confirmation of empirical predictions does not always constitute good evidence to accept one theory over a rival theory. One example of this from the history of science is illustrative. Ancient theories of Copernican and Ptolemaic astronomy are rival theories of celestial bodies. Before the invention of the telescope however, these rival theories both successfully predicted the positions of planets and many stars as seen by the naked eye (Kuhn 1962:68). The observable facts collected up until that point supported both rivals. Thus there was little reason to accept the Copernican theory over the Ptolemaic theory until the invention of the telescope allowed for observations of a domain in which these theories made different predictions.

Supposing some behaviors said to motivate epistemic contextualism in ordinary language can be empirically confirmed, the question now becomes whether or not this provides a sufficient reason to prefer epistemic contextualism to rival invariantist theories denying that evidentiary standards are set or shift due to conversational context. Like the case of Ptolemaic and Copernican astronomy, theory choice would be underdetermined if the claims epistemic contextualism makes about linguistic practices can also be explained even if epistemic contextualism was false. In that case, confirming the empirical predictions of epistemic contextualism would not provide a sufficient reason to accept it over invariantism. Researchers have confirmed that this is in fact the case, by showing that the predictions of epistemic contextualism can be found even if contextualism is false.

One recent study examined whether or not epistemic contextualism can explain patterns of responses in classic bank cases any better than rival theories can (Turri 2016: Experiment 1; see also Dinges 2015, for discussion). Participants were presented with one of two closely matched bank case vignettes. One case was a low stakes low error salience variant in which a protagonist Keith attributes knowledge to himself that the bank will be open tomorrow. The other was a high stakes high error salience variant in which Keith denies that he knows the bank will be open. After seeing one of these two cases, participants were asked to rate their agreement with a series of test items, such as that "It's true that the bank is open tomorrow," "Keith believes that the bank is open tomorrow," "Keith has good evidence that the bank is open tomorrow," "Keith should come back tomorrow morning instead," and "When Keith said, 'I [do/don't] know,' what he said was true," respectively (p. 4).

The result was that predictions made by epistemic contextualism were true. Participants in the low stakes condition tended to agree that Keith truthfully said he knew in the low stakes case. Participants in the high stakes condition also tended to agree that Keith truthfully said he did not know. However, large differences were found in the way participants evaluated the other epistemic details of the cases. More specifically, participants were much more likely to agree that it was true the bank was open tomorrow, that Keith had good evidence for this, believed this, and should act in a way that makes sense given the bank is open in the low stakes case than in the high stakes case.

These results are consistent with epistemic contextualism but do not give us a good reason to accept it. Most philosophers agree that knowledge requires justified true belief. So it is perhaps unsurprising that competent speakers evaluate "knowledge" expressions differently as judgments concerning the quality of the evidence a protagonist has, what a protagonist believes, or what is likely to be true, each fluctuate between stories. If these things fluctuate between stories, then

Contextualism and linguistic behavior

there is no need to postulate the existence of shifting standards to explain "knowledge" judgments in low and high cases. Such judgments can easily be explained even if contextualism is false by more traditional theories of knowledge.

Patterns of responses are also equally well explained by rival theories that postulate a connection between knowledge and action (see Hawthorne and Stanley 2008; Fantl and McGrath 2009; Turri and Buckwalter Forthcoming). If truthfully saying a person "knows" something depends partially on whether they can act on a belief, and actionability is being evaluated differently between stories, then there is no need to posit the existence of shifting standards to explain why "knowledge" judgments fluctuate between cases. In short, this evidence suggests that many things are actually not being held fixed when we psychologically process these thought experiments and make judgments about them. The fact that other variables shift during the process of evaluation undermines the motivation for epistemic contextualism. The fact that this happens also questions the support for contextualism offered elsewhere in the experimental literature that does not control for the possibility of other shifting epistemic variables.

Researchers have also demonstrated that some contextualist friendly intuitions are the result of confounds in contextualist thought experiments and experimental stimuli. When constructing test cases, contextualists continually insist that the best evidence for their view comes from comparing judgments about knowledge-ascribing sentences in low contexts and knowledge-denying sentences in high contexts (DeRose 2005: 173; 2009: 50; 2011: 86). But one hypothesis is that our reactions to such sentences reflect basic aspects of the psychology of self-attribution that have nothing to do with contextual standards. More specifically, it could be that participants find knowledge-ascribing and knowledge-denying sentences true despite low or high contexts simply because we tend to defer to what other people say about the state of their own knowledge. If participants evaluate these sentences on the basis of deference, then the fact that people find knowledge-ascribing and denying sentences true in different contexts does not provide good evidence for the existence of shifting contextual standards. The same pattern of responses could just as well be explained by deference even if epistemic contextualism is false.

To test whether or not deference confounds contextualist thought experiments, a separate group of participants was presented with one of two simple bank case variations (Turri 2016: Experiment 2). Both variations featured identical low stakes contexts in which the salience of error was low. The only difference between them was that in one case the protagonist self-attributed knowledge to himself that the bank will be open, while in the other case the protagonist self-denied that knowledge. After seeing one of these cases, participants were then asked the same questions as in the prior experiment. The result was that "knowledge" judgments were highly deferential. Participants in the self-ascription condition tended to agree that the protagonist truthfully said he knew in the low standards case. And participants in the self-denial condition also tended to agree that the protagonist spoke truthfully when he said he did not know that. In other words, the exact pattern of results used to motivate epistemic contextualism can be obtained in the same bank cases where no shifts in stakes or error salience occurred. Subsequent experiments further revealed that contextualist patterns in low and high cases disappeared when steps were taken to control for deference (Turri 2016: Experiment 3; see also Hansen and Chemla 2013; Buckwalter 2014, for evidence of this).

These findings strongly suggest that responses in classic bank cases taken to motivate contextualism are associated with features that have nothing to do with shifting contextual standards. Some contextualists have argued that the pressure to accommodate utterances is itself a factor that can shift contextual standards (Lewis 1979; DeRose 2011: 88). The present results do not rule out this possibility. However, the propensity to defer to what people say about their own mental states can also explain these patterns regardless of the presence of context-sensitive terms. Indeed it is a far simpler explanation than the positing of context-sensitive linguistic expressions. In any event, the fact that people tend to find these knowledge-ascribing and denying sentences true provides no unique motivation for contextualism over other psychological explanations. This also raises the possibility that the construction of contextualist-friendly thought experiments, and in turn, the intuitions motivating the theory, have been confounded by this psychological tendency from the start.

Doubtful theoretical advantage

When theory choice between rival theories is underdetermined, the evidence does not provide sufficient reason to select one theory over another. However, some philosophers of science have argued that we can still have good reasons to prefer one theory to another when this happens. For example, we might prefer one theory to another because that theory is simpler, more explanatory, or more cohesive with other theories we accept (Quine 1955; Laudan and Leplin 1991). In the present case, observations of linguistic behavior do not sufficiently motivate epistemic contextualism. But perhaps there are other reasons why one might accept the theory over rivals.

Some philosophers have argued that contextualism is preferable to rival theories because it provides theoretical solutions to skeptical problems like brain-in-the-vat (BIV) scenarios or the lottery paradox (Lewis 1996; Cohen 1998; Hannon this volume; see also Benton this volume). According to this solution, shifting evidential standards set by conversational context explain why one can truthfully say one knows something in everyday contexts, and truthfully deny one knows something when error possibilities in BIV or lottery odds become salient. This itself, of course, is not evidence that the theory is true. With respect to skepticism, for example, Keith DeRose writes that the contextualist solution would be "unmotivated and ad hoc" without an independent reason to think evidentiary standards do shift in non-philosophical usage (DeRose 2002: 169; see also Rysiew 2011 for discussion). It is doubtful that the relevant shifts in non-philosophical talk have been adequately shown. Nonetheless, the ability to offer solutions to theoretical puzzles that rival theories potentially cannot is one incentive to accept it over those rivals.

Research in experimental cognitive science suggests that contextualism does not explain skepticism any better than rival theories do (Turri 2014; Turri and Friedman 2014). With respect to lottery problems, for instance, research suggests that skeptical judgments are probably not the product of shifting contexts involving the salience of error. In illustrating this point, researchers devised two lottery thought experiments in which high error possibilities were salient (Turri and Friedman 2014: Experiment 5). The cases differed only in one small respect. One version involved the chances of winning a formal lottery, while the other involved the chances of finding a lucky combination of numbers:

> Abigail is talking with her neighbor, Stan, who is a statistician. Stan hands Abigail a bill and says, "Here is the ten dollars I owe you." Abigail looks at the bill and sees that its serial number is 5-0-6-7-4-1-6-9-8-2. Stan continues, "I made an interesting calculation. That serial number is just as likely to be Brad Pitt's mobile phone number as it is to win this week's lottery." Abigail answers, "That combination [will not win this week's lottery/is not Brad Pitt's mobile number]." And Abigail was exactly right: that combination [was a loser/it was not Brad Pitt's number].
>
> *(Turri and Friedman 2014: 61–62)*

When researchers presented these cases to hundreds of participants, they found that people were more likely to agree that Abigail knows the combination was not Brad Pitt's number than it was

Contextualism and linguistic behavior

a loser in the lottery. These results support the assumption that people are skeptical about formal lottery cases. However, the results do not support the idea that this skepticism is explained by shifting evidential standards. People were more skeptical about formal lotteries than informal ones in conversational contexts with identical error salience. On the basis of this observation, Turri and Friedman suggest that lottery intuitions are, at least in part, due to formulaic responses, habituation, or familiarity with formal lotteries specifically. While researchers continue to investigate what factors might underlie formulaic expressions about formal lotteries, the results indicate that intuitions are probably not explained by shifting evidential standards any better than rival theories explain them.

Related research on error salience and the origins of skeptical judgments more generally suggests that skepticism could be the result of several different types of cognitive biases involving "epistemic egocentrism" (Nagel 2010), "focal bias" (Gerken 2013), or the "source-content bias" (Turri 2014). According to the source-content bias theory, for example, the appeal of skepticism results from considering a particular combination of claims. More specifically, the theory postulates that classical skeptical arguments prey on negative claims made on the basis of inferential sources of evidence. Researchers demonstrated this bias exists in the following experiment (Turri 2014: Experiment 1). The experiment independently manipulated whether the *Source* of a belief was perceptual or inferential. It also manipulated whether the *Content* of the belief involved a positive claim about something being present or a negative claim about something being absent. The four resulting cases were as follows:

> Michelle has visited the city zoo every day for the past ten years. Her favorite exhibit is The Big Cat Exhibit. Over thousands of observations, the animal in this exhibit has always been a jaguar. Today [Michelle must stay home and can't visit the zoo because she sprained her ankle. While relaxing on the couch/when Michelle left home to visit the zoo, she almost sprained her ankle. While looking at the animal in the exhibit], Michelle thinks, "The animal in the Big Cat Exhibit today is [a jaguar/not a leopard]." And she is right: it is [a jaguar/not a leopard].
>
> *(Turri 2014: 313)*

Participants were then asked to indicate whether Michelle "knows" or "only believes" that the animal is a jaguar or not a leopard, respectively.

Participants were much more likely to deny knowledge both when a source was inferential rather than perceptual and when the claim was negative rather than positive. Moreover, a large interaction effect was found whereby participants were much more likely to deny knowledge in negative inferential cases than in positive inferential cases. In other words, participants were especially prone to embrace skepticism about negative inferential claims. These results are visualized in Figure 3.2.

The source-content bias may begin to explain why it appears to us that one can truthfully say one knows something in everyday contexts and deny this in extremely skeptical contexts. More specifically, it could be that we are likely to find certain utterances such as "I don't know I'm not a brain in a vat," to be truthful because they are negative and inferential, while we are also likely to view other utterances, such as "I know that I have hands," to be truthful because they are positive and perceptual. In that case, there would be no need to posit shifting standards to explain why those utterances both seem truthful to us. Assuming that biased judgments are less likely to be true than un-biased ones, this hypothesis may also begin to provide an alternative philosophical response to skepticism than epistemic contextualism does. According to this hypothesis, certain knowledge-denying sentences paradigmatic of extreme skepticism such as "I don't know I'm

53

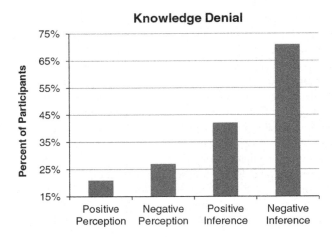

Figure 3.2 Rates of knowledge denial across conditions. Reprinted from Turri (2014) with permission.

not a brain in a vat" are likely false because they are the product of bias. Researchers continue to investigate the interaction between these factors and the degree to which this can satisfactorily explain a variety of different skeptical reactions (for critical discussion, see Gerken Forthcoming). For present purposes, however, the availability of alternative theories strongly questions the idea that contextualism offers a unique theoretical advantage regarding skepticism.

Conclusion

Epistemic contextualism is a linguistic theory that is answerable to observable facts about linguistic behavior. The debate over this theory is well into its third decade without clear experimental evidence that the motivation for it is real or compelling. Many researchers have found evidence that challenges these motivations. Some researchers have found evidence that supports them. However, these results can also be explained even if contextualism is false. For example, it has been demonstrated that shifting between contexts influences other epistemic variables that can explain "knowledge" judgments. There are confounds in thought experiment construction which yield contextualist friendly intuitions that may have nothing to do with shifting standards. Moreover, it is doubtful that epistemic contextualism has other decisive theoretical advantages, such as being uniquely positioned to explain skeptical judgments in ordinary language. This body of evidence significantly questions the motivation for the theory and does not provide a good reason to accept it as an account of our linguistic practices.

In the case of Copernican and Ptolemaic astronomy, theory choice was eventually made possible by the advancements of scientific instruments, allowing for new observations in which the theories made rival predictions. Moving forward, a similar solution may aid theory selection in epistemology. The main instruments used thus far have involved intuition, introspection, and social observation. Testing in experimental cognitive science can improve upon these instruments. In several cases, this approach has already begun to do so by providing growing evidence for invariantist theories in ordinary language (Pinillos 2012; Powell, Horne, Pinillos, and Holyoak 2015; Turri, Buckwalter, and Rose 2016; Turri and Buckwalter Forthcoming). However such testing has not produced compelling evidence for contextualism. This leads one to wonder how long research programs in epistemic contextualism can continue before practitioners deliver clear and concrete experimental evidence that the patterns of linguistic behavior that motivate it are real and cannot be explained in psychological terms or by other theories inconsistent with contextualism.

Acknowledgements

For helpful feedback I thank James Beebe, Nathan Cockram, Mikkel Gerken, Michael Hannon, Jonathan Jenkins Ichikawa, Robert Stanton, and John Turri. This research was supported by a Banting Fellowship awarded through the Social Sciences and Humanities Research Council of Canada.

References

Alexander, Joshua, Gonnerman, Chad, and Waterman, John (2014), 'Salience and Epistemic Egocentrism: An Empirical Study', in James Beebe (ed.), *Advances in Experimental Epistemology* (London: Bloomsbury), 97–118.

Benton, Matthew A. (this volume), 'Lotteries and Prefaces', in Jonathan Ichikawa (ed.), *The Routledge Handbook of Epistemic Contextualism* (London and New York: Routledge).

Buckwalter, Wesley (2010), 'Knowledge Isn't Closed on Saturday: A Study in Ordinary Language', *Review of Philosophy and Psychology*, 1 (3), 395–406.

——— (2014), 'The Mystery of Stakes and Error in Ascriber Intuitions', in James Beebe (ed.), *Advances in Experimental Epistemology* (London: Bloomsbury), 145–174.

Buckwalter, Wesley and Schaffer, Jonathan (2015), 'Knowledge, Stakes, and Mistakes', *Nous*, 49 (2), 201–34.

Cohen, Stewart (1998), 'Contextualist Solutions to Epistemological Problems: Scepticism, Gettier, and the Lottery', *Australasian Journal of Philosophy*, 76 (2), 289–306.

——— (2013), 'Contextualism Defended', in Matthias Steup, John Turri, and Ernest Sosa (eds.), *Contemporary Debates in Epistemology* (2; Malden, MA: Wiley-Blackwell), 69–75.

DeRose, Keith (2002), 'Assertion, Knowledge, and Context', *The Philosophical Review*, 111 (2), 167–203.

——— (2005), 'The Ordinary Language Basis for Contextualism and the New Invariantism', *The Philosophical Quarterly*, 55 (219), 172–98.

——— (2009), *The Case for Contextualism* (Oxford: Oxford University Press).

——— (2011), 'Contextualism, Contrastivism, and X-Phi Surveys', *Philosophical Studies*, 156 (1), 81–110.

Dinges, Alexander (2015), 'Epistemic Invariantism and Contextualist Intuitions', *Episteme*, FirstView, 1–14.

Fantl, Jeremy and McGrath, Matthew (2009), *Knowledge in an Uncertain World* (Oxford: Oxford University Press).

Feltz, Adam and Zarpentine, Chris (2010), 'Do You Know More When It Matters Less?', *Philosophical Psychology*, 23 (5), 683–706.

Gerken, Mikkel (2013), 'Epistemic Focal Bias', *Australasian Journal of Philosophy*, 91 (1), 41–61.

——— (forthcoming), *On Folk Epistemology* (Oxford: Oxford University Press).

Hannon, Michael (this volume), 'Contextualism and Skepticism', in Jonathan Ichikawa (ed.), *The Routledge Handbook of Epistemic Contextualism* (London and New York: Routledge).

Hansen, Nat (2014), 'Contrasting Cases', in James Beebe (ed.), *Advances in Experimental Epistemology* (London: Bloomsbury), 71–95.

Hansen, Nat and Chemla, Emmanuel (2013), 'Experimenting on Contextualism', *Mind and Language*, 28 (3), 286–321.

Hawthorne, John and Stanley, Jason (2008), 'Knowledge and Action', *Journal of Philosophy*, 105 (10), 571.

Kuhn, Thomas (1962), *The Structure of Scientific Revolutions*, 2 vols. (2; Chicago: The University of Chicago Press).

Laudan, Larry and Leplin, Jarrett (1991), 'Empirical Equivalence and Underdetermination', *Journal of Philosophy*, 88, 449–72.

Lewis, David (1979), 'Scorekeeping in a Language Game', *Journal of Philosophical Logic*, 8 (1), 339–59.

——— (1996), 'Elusive Knowledge', *Australasian Journal of Philosophy*, 74 (4), 549–67.

May, Joshua, Sinnott-Armstrong, Walter, Hull, Jay G., and Zimmerman, Aaron (2010), 'Practical Interests, Relevant Alternatives, and Knowledge Attributions: An Empirical Study', *Review of Philosophy and Psychology*, 1 (2), 265–73.

Nagel, Jennifer (2010), 'Knowledge Ascriptions and the Psychological Consequences of Thinking About Error', *The Philosophical Quarterly,* 60 (239), 286–306.

Pinillos, N Ángel (2012), 'Knowledge, Experiments and Practical Interests', in Jessica Brown and MIkkel Gerken (eds.), *New Essays On Knowledge Ascriptions* (Oxford: Oxford University Press), 192–219.

Powell, Derek, Horne, Zachary, Pinillos, Ángel, and Holyoak, Keith (2015), 'A Bayesian Framework for Knowledge Attribution: Evidence from Semantic Integration', *Cognition,* 139, 92–104.

Quine, Willard Van (1955), 'Posits and Reality', *The Ways of Paradox and Other Essays* (Cambridge, MA: Harvard University Press), 246–254.

Rysiew, Patrick (2011), 'Contextualism', *Stanford Encylopedia of Philosophy.* (Winter 2016 Edition), Edward N. Zalta (ed.), forthcoming URL = <https://plato.stanford.edu/archives/win2016/entries/contextualism-epistemology/>.

Schaffer, Jonathan and Knobe, Joshua (2012), 'Contrastive Knowledge Surveyed', *Nous,* 46 (4), 675–708.

Turri, John (2014), 'Skeptical Appeal: The Source-Content Bias', *Cognitive Science,* 38 (5), 307–24.

————— (2016), 'Epistemic Contextualism: An Idle Hypothesis', *Australasian Journal of Philosophy,* 1–16.

Turri, John and Buckwalter, Wesley (Forthcoming), 'Descartes's Schism, Locke's Reunion: Completing the Pragmatic Turn in Epistemology', *American Philosophical Quarterly.*

Turri, John, Buckwalter, Wesley, and Rose, David (2016), 'Actionability Judgments Cause Knowledge Judgments' *Thought: A Journal of Philosophy,* 5, 212–222.

Turri, John and Friedman, Ori (2014), 'Winners and Losers in the Folk Epistemology of Lotteries', in J R Beebe (ed.), *Advances in Experimental Epistemology* (London: Bloomsbury), 45–70.

Waterman, John, Gonnerman, Chad, Yan, Karen, and Alexander, Joshua (in press), 'Knowledge, Certainty, and Skepticism: A Cross-Cultural Study', in E McCready, et al. (eds.), *Epistemology for the Rest of the World* (Oxford: Oxford University Press).

4

FEMINISM AND CONTEXTUALISM

Evelyn Brister

Feminist theory is often associated with social and political philosophy and questions of justice, but epistemology is also a fundamental concern to feminists because feminist claims depend on knowledge of the natural and social world and on knowledge of moral duties and constraints. Feminist claims require accounts of the relation between knowledge and politics and also accounts of the practices and norms that govern how knowledge is produced, evaluated, and circulated. Feminist epistemology keeps social relations in sight while investigating questions about knowledge and knowledge-making practices that are relevant to the goal of cultivating social equality.[1] Contextualist epistemology, with its emphasis on the social and practical context of justification, knowledge attribution, and so on, would thus seem to have much in common with feminist epistemology.

This chapter has two purposes. First, I examine how contextualism is suited to feminist epistemic aims, and I take stock of feminist engagements with epistemic contextualism. Second, I will argue that feminist epistemology provides arguments that can both deepen and strengthen contextualist views and also shed light on internal debates among contextualists. So, just as epistemology is of fundamental importance to feminist theory, I'll argue that feminist theory can play an important role in certain areas of epistemology.

Feminist epistemologists have talked about "context" and "contextualism" since at least the early 1990s and in ways that don't always map neatly onto how those terms are generally used today. For this reason, and to highlight the various connections between feminist epistemology, feminist philosophy of science, and contextualism, I'll use the term "contextualist" in a somewhat broader sense than many of the other essays in this volume. So in addition to the by now standard meaning of epistemic contextualism – where it refers to a theory of knowledge attribution, as in the work of Keith DeRose (1995) and others – I'll also refer to contextualism as a theory of justification, perhaps best exemplified in the work of Michael Williams (1991, 2001). But more than that, I'll also argue that the leading alternative to contextualism – the subject-sensitive or interest-relative invariantism (IRI) of Jason Stanley, John Hawthorne, and Jeremy Fantl and Matthew McGrath – is actually also contextual in the broad sense valued by feminist epistemologists. That is, Stanley and other "sensitive" invariantists argue that knowledge attribution depends on more than just epistemic factors: it also depends on practical features of an inquirer's situation. Contextualists and sensitive invariantists can thus agree that there are cases where the truth of the statement "S knows that p" depends on more than just the subject's evidence, or reasons, or other epistemic factors (where they disagree is

57

on what, exactly, this "more" is). Two people can have exactly the same evidence for p, but, depending on the context or situation, perhaps only one of them can truthfully be said "to know p." As I'll note below, this broad recognition of the importance of context – shared by epistemic contextualists, sensitive invariantists, and defenders of contextualist theories of justification – provides a rich but not entirely unproblematic set of resources for feminist epistemology.

Feminist epistemology has two characteristic features. First, it investigates the social production of knowledge by examining how knowers, knowledge claims, and epistemic practices are socially situated, paying special attention to categories of social identity, such as gender, where they make an epistemic difference (Tanesini 1999). Second, it is broadly naturalistic in order to account for empirical findings concerning social and biological categories (Grasswick 2013). While these features are not universal across all feminist epistemology, they are characteristic in that they emerge out of concerns for how gender categories shape how and by whom knowledge claims are made. This last point is also what makes feminist epistemology *feminist*: while social epistemology is also concerned with social institutions and processes, feminist epistemology is grounded in a concern for how gender, in particular, and power, in general, operates in social contexts.

This means that feminist epistemologists typically reject a conception of epistemology as focused exclusively on questions about interchangeable individual knowers. In this sense it is often opposed to individualistic epistemology: for example, the kind of epistemology that aims to give necessary and sufficient conditions for S knows that p. Rather, feminist epistemology has prioritized issues relating to the epistemic interdependence of subjects, such as trust and credibility, and questions concerning the epistemic relevance of social identity and social power, for instance in testimonial interactions. Feminist epistemology doubts that individualist epistemology can address the questions that are particularly relevant for knowers who are excluded from knowledge-making institutions, who are treated as less credible, whose rational capabilities are in doubt, and who are otherwise treated differently as knowing subjects. The suspicion is not just that individualist epistemology is incomplete, in that it has not yet fully explained how social interactions are relevant to knowing, but that it is pernicious, because it treats individual knowing subjects as all alike, an ideal that loses sight of the epistemic problems that matter to real people in the non-ideal situations that are the rule, not the exception.

As a result, the relationship between feminist epistemology and epistemic contextualism is complicated and conflicted. Feminist epistemology has interests and motivations that may diverge from those of epistemic contextualism. On the one hand, epistemic contextualism has its origin in the concerns of individualist epistemology. For example, some versions of contextualism are centrally concerned with skepticism. But Cartesian skepticism, with its solipsistic implications, is exemplary of the paradoxes that arise out of the assumptions of individualist epistemology. Feminists and social epistemologists, whose starting point is how categories of social identity affect knowledge production, may view the problem of skepticism as neither pressing nor even particularly relevant.[2] On the other hand, however, because contextualism highlights the epistemic importance of context, and because context may include social relations, contextualism does allow for the concerns of feminist epistemology to come into view. Thus, in spite of the apparent distance between the concerns of contextualists and the concerns of feminist epistemologists, they may contribute useful insight and criticism to each other.

Feminism, contextualism, and justification

By paying close attention to social categories and to assumptions of gender essentialism, feminist epistemologists have developed an acute sensitivity to how social contexts affect belief and action. Thus, according to feminist epistemologists, knowers are differently situated in the world by having different perspectives that are due to their different bodies and experiences, different social roles, different interests, different access to testimonial evidence, and different relations to other knowers. Feminist epistemology's attention to situated knowledge is more particular than a general interest in inquiry as social. When feminist epistemologists point to situated knowing, they are indicating not just that inquiry is a social process, but that social location or social identity makes a difference in inquiry. Within feminist epistemology there are multiple approaches to the situatedness of knowers, and most, perhaps all, of these explicitly reject epistemic relativism or the claim, as Elizabeth Anderson (2015) puts it, that "perspectives can only be judged in their own terms." While these approaches recognize the role of context in addressing a range of epistemic questions, including knowledge ascriptions and standards of justification, the contextualism defended by feminist epistemologists is typically a broader sense than that proposed by contextualists such as Keith DeRose (1995, 2009), David Lewis (1979, 1996), and Michael Williams (1991, 2001). While DeRose, Lewis, and Williams focus on relatively narrow issues concerning knowledge-attribution or epistemic justification, feminist epistemologists frequently emphasize the moral and political factors that both motivate epistemological inquiry and operate within particular contexts. For example, Peg O'Connor (2012) defends a position called "felted contextualism" that she presents as an alternative to absolutism and relativism in moral epistemology. José Medina (2013) has developed a view called "polyphonic contextualism" which addresses how agents are unjustly excluded from certain discursive contexts.

Another broadly contextualist account that is motivated, in part, by feminist interests is Helen Longino's (1990) account of scientific reasoning: what she calls "contextual empiricism." In *Science as Social Knowledge*, Longino develops contextual empiricism as an account of the conditions ascribing scientific knowledge in particular. Her view is empiricist rather than holist in that it takes experience as the primary source of justification for knowledge claims, and it is contextualist rather than absolutist in that the standards of justification are relative to a social context (1990: 186). Here Longino takes the context of scientific knowledge production to include verifiable empirical statements, value assumptions that may not be empirically verifiable, and social norms for justificatory practices.

In her later book *The Fate of Knowledge* (2004), Longino explicitly invokes contextualism as a theory of justification, citing Annis (1978) and Cohen (1987) as providing the sort of epistemic theory that supports her account of science as socially produced knowledge: "To be justified is to be able to meet objections in a way that satisfies the practices and norms of one's group" (2004: 105). A contextualist theory of justification and Longino's social account of scientific reasoning overlap in that both spotlight the justificatory norms that arise out of a community's practices of challenge and response. For Longino, this means that standards of scientific justification (such as what kind of and how much observational evidence is required to support a particular hypothesis) are at least partly the product of a social context and cannot be established as a priori necessary rules for weighing empirical evidence. A contextualist theory of justification, as opposed, for example, to standard foundationalism or coherentism, can account for the intersubjective justificatory practices of scientists in the production of new knowledge claims (2004: 81–82). At the same time, contextualism fulfills Longino's need to present a normative alternative to purely descriptive, and hence relative, sociological accounts of scientists' cognitive and discursive behavior.

In her article "Contextualism in Feminist Epistemology and Philosophy of Science" (2011), Kristina Rolin argues that Michael Williams' (2001) version of epistemic contextualism can support Longino's contextual empiricism against significant objections raised by feminist philosophers of science. According to Rolin, Williams' account of contextualist justification is more sophisticated than the earlier accounts cited by Longino, and his particular version anticipates and defends against three objections: (1) that contextual empiricism implies dogmatism, (2) that it lacks justification itself, and (3) that it endorses value relativism (Rolin 2011). Here I will discuss the importance of the response to the first two of these objections and will later consider the third (that contextual empiricism is relativist). By showing how a contextualist theory of justification can insulate Longino's account against these two objections – namely, that it implies dogmatism and is not itself justified – Rolin shows how to extend an epistemological theory beyond its original purpose. This is good both for Longino's contextual empiricism and for contextualism itself – which, as I noted earlier, has over the years referred to a variety of different positions. As Robin McKenna (2015) has recently noted, "While contextualism has increased in sophistication over the past decade, the point of the view has perhaps become lost in the process" (500). This leads McKenna to then recommend that contextualists address the question "How does contextualism in our sense relate to broader forms of contextualism?" (500). Here, the question addressed is how a contextualist theory of justification (namely, Williams' version) relates to a contextualist theory of scientific rationality (Longino's contextual empiricism).

Rolin shows how to expand a contextualist epistemology to promote a contextualist philosophy of science. So, for example, Sharon Crasnow has criticized Longino's contextual empiricism for being unable to resolve disputes over epistemic standards – with the result that such standards can only then be accepted dogmatically (2003: 136). Rolin responds to this objection by arguing that, in Williams' contextualism, the notion of epistemic responsibility *does* provide grounds for adjudicating such standards. According to Rolin and Williams, while we make assumptions, in particular contexts, about the relevant epistemic standards, these assumptions function as default entitlements: this means that they are still subject to appropriate challenges, provided that a challenger is prepared to provide reasons to question the truth or reliability of the standard (Rolin 2011: 38).

Solomon and Richardson (2005) raise a second objection to Longino's contextual empiricism: that her social account of scientific objectivity rests on four norms of social epistemic practice that are still in need of naturalistic justification – for instance by showing their presence in historical episodes of scientific advancement. Here, too, Rolin draws on Williams' (2001) version of epistemic contextualism to support Longino's account. Rather than requiring a naturalistic justification, Rolin argues that it is enough that Longino's social account of objectivity can draw support from Williams' contextualist theory of justification. On Williams' account, the criteria for epistemic responsibility require that (1) justificatory norms be public so that challenges to a default assumption be heard, (2) that both the challenger and the claimant follow the contextual standards for an appropriate challenge, and (3) that appropriate challenges require a response regardless of the social identity of the person presenting them. These correspond to three of Longino's epistemic norms for objective scientific communities (Rolin 2011: 40). The fourth such norm, that appropriate challenges receive a response (or uptake of criticism, as Longino calls it), follows from Williams' notion of a defense commitment (Rolin 2011: 40).

These two challenges to Longino's account have come from philosophers of science whose work supports feminist commitments. Even so, it can be argued that their challenges operate at a sufficiently high level of abstraction so as to distance them from any particular concerns about gender, race, and marginalized social identity. What this shows, then, is that Longino's account of scientific objectivity – one that shows how sexist scientific theories may be mistakenly endorsed as objective, and can critique such theories on those grounds – can be supported by a contextualist theory of justification. This raises a further question: How tight is the connection between epistemic contextualism and specifically feminist epistemological concerns?

On the one hand, it is no accident that contextualism – rather than some other theory of justification – is well-suited to support an account of scientific objectivity that is motivated by feminist criticisms of science. As Rolin points out, Crasnow's objection to Longino's account hinges on assuming that standards of argumentation are either fixed or entirely relative, while contextualism provides a more nuanced explanation of how these standards are anchored to particular discursive contexts. For the contextualist, standards of argumentation are social, as feminist epistemological approaches must be (Grasswick and Webb 2002). Moreover, the structure of Williams' (2001) account can be tied to particular practices in scientific communities, and these are practices that are tied to democratic deliberation (Intemann 2011). And, as Miranda Fricker (2008) notes, Williams' contextualist theory of justification provides an account of how knowers with shifting, socially situated epistemic needs for good information and reliable informants manage to interact with each other to produce knowledge. This kind of contextualism can be called upon whenever feminist epistemology requires a theory that recognizes the practical needs of real knowers engaged in social interactions.

On the other hand, a contextualist account of justification may still be insufficient for the theoretical needs of some feminist epistemologists. Where there are problems that cannot be settled by a theory of justification, this kind of contextualism is largely irrelevant; even where it is relevant, it may yet be insufficiently developed. Rolin, for example, expresses a wish for a more refined account of epistemic responsibility which would analyze "what counts as an appropriate challenge in actual scientific debates, how the burden of proof shifts in these debates, and how relations of power influence these practices" (2011: 42). Without such refinements, there is the lingering concern that a contextualist theory of justification opens the door to epistemic relativism – and relativism is anathema to most feminists, as I explain below. So, while a contextualist theory of justification can lend support to Longino's feminist account of scientific objectivity, some feminist epistemologists remain unconvinced that it lives up to its billing.

Feminism, contextualism, and relativism

I'll now return to the third objection to Longino's contextual empiricism: that it implies a kind of relativism with respect to moral and social values. The objection to Longino's account of socially produced objectivity is that it is regrettably neutral with respect to how feminist (or sexist) values may legitimately influence the evaluation of scientific knowledge claims (Intemann 2008, 2011). Namely, the charge is that while the account promotes diversity of moral and social values in science as a resource for critical discussion, it does not privilege any particular moral and social values over others. Feminists, however, are positively committed to political and social equality and opposed to illiberal views (e.g. misogyny and racism). Thus, coupled with the understanding that values influence not only the formulation and application of scientific theories but also the interpretation and analysis of evidence, sexist values will produce bad science. Some feminist epistemologists see Longino's account of scientific objectivity as being "too evenhanded vis-a-vis moral and social values" (Rolin 2011: 33). Hicks (2011) argues, further, that Longino's view is committed to "actively cultivating" critical beliefs, including critical moral and social views, even if that means promoting anti-feminist (i.e. sexist and racist) values (337).

This concern with relativism has been named "the bias paradox" (Antony 1993). It arises for accounts of objectivity or justification that allow that epistemological views are perspectival. As Deborah Heikes (2004) puts the question it raises: "if there are no unbiased, impartial standards available for evaluating epistemic views, how is it that we can make any principled distinctions among various subjective perspectives?" (318). According to Antony, theories such as Longino's (and Williams') "inevitably leave themselves without resources for making the needed normative distinctions because they deprive themselves of any conceptual tools for distinguishing the grounds of a statement's truth from the explanation of a statement's acceptance" (1993: 115). The dilemma posed by the bias paradox is that if all knowledge is socially situated and incomplete, then there is no external or secure position from which to opt for some values over others or to validate the privilege held by some knowers in certain situations, and yet some feminist epistemologists (including standpoint theorists and some critics of Longino) do hold both theses.

Rolin (2006) diagnoses the source of the bias paradox as an unwitting and unwise acceptance of a foundationalist theory of justification. She argues that adopting a contextualist theory of justification, such as Williams', resolves the bias paradox by providing grounds whereby some values act as default commitments and are justified in particular contexts, though they are not *absolutely* justified and may be challenged and, perhaps, revised. Williams (2007) defends his form of contextualism against the charge of relativism on the grounds that the objection depends on a false choice between the view that epistemic systems are equally valid and the view that epistemic standards must be absolute. He argues that while "epistemology cannot offer guarantees" that "there will be neutral epistemic principles for determining who is right and who is wrong," the contextualist conception of justification describes a way forward in disagreements about epistemic standards that accurately describes how fallible, contingent, and dependent on hard work and "ingenuity" inquiry is (111).

To return to the charge that Longino's account of scientific objectivity is impartial when it should be partial – partial toward inclusive, democratic, and pro-science values – Rolin invokes a contextualist theory of justification to defend Longino:

> In Williams' contextualism, value judgments are subjected to the default and challenge structure of justification in the same way as scientific theories, hypotheses, pieces of empirical evidence, and standards of argumentation. This means that some value judgments are likely to lose their justification because they will be met with an appropriate challenge.
>
> *(2011: 40)*

In other words, sexist value judgments can be challenged in the same way as any other judgment. As part of the process of challenging these judgments we may appeal to grounds that indicate the superiority of feminist over sexist values, but this is a local process that occurs in particular contexts of inquiry and is not stipulated by epistemologists. While contextualism identifies the desire for stable, external validation of certain moral and social values as unnecessary, this has remained a sticking point for feminist epistemologists who do not trust that an open-ended process of inquiry will yield consistent socially progressive results.

Similarly, Nancy Daukas has argued against contextualism for not adequately preventing relativism (2002). Daukas' concern is that, if standards of justification are context-relative, then it is possible that in some contexts knowledge claims could be justified in the absence of empirical support. There might, for instance, be a standard of justification which grants the right of epistemic assessment to a patriarchal authority or one which uses only consistency with religious doctrine as a standard of justification (Daukas 2011: 55). Therefore, a claim that is not justified in a scientific context in 2016 would not be attributed as "knowledge" in that context, but a claimant could be attributed to "know" that claim in a context where different standards of justification hold. Moreover, Daukas argues that variability in context creates relativism between contexts:

> Contextualism implies that when a feminist (or any other) epistemologist critiques a particular theory of knowledge, her critique may simply illustrate how the conventions

defining 'knowledge' in the critic's 'home' context of inquiry differ from those of the 'target' context of inquiry. So semantic contextualism precludes the possibility of a vantage point from which to argue that one theory offers a more accurate, more insightful, more empirically adequate analysis of epistemic practices and attitudes than does another.

(2011: 56)

Thus, Daukas' concern is that contextualism amounts to relativism. Like Intemann, she is particularly concerned that assumptions held in the context of inquiry could stymie transformative criticism from outside that context because different contexts may prioritize different goals of inquiry and develop different standards of justification.

Daukas characterizes her view as "invariantist," holding "that truth-conditions on knowledge claims are stable, and so do not vary contextually" (2011: 54). It is not clear whether she would hold that her argument against contextualism would also hold against sensitive invariantists such as Stanley. So, while nominally opposed to the epistemic contextualism of DeRose and others – Stanley is adamant that there is a *"univocal knowledge relation"* (2005: 86, emphasis added) – Stanley's position is *broadly* contextual in that it treats the knowledge relation as "sensitive to the subject's practical situation at the putative time of knowing" (2005: 86). In other words, while the meaning of "knowledge" does not change with the context (knowledge doesn't come in a range of degrees or strengths), it is harder to truthfully attribute knowledge when the stakes are high for the subject. As a result, according to Stanley, knowledge attribution does depend on practical contextual factors and not just on the quality or quantity of one's evidence.

The relevance of Stanley's interest-relative invariantism to the specific needs and interests of feminist epistemology deserves further attention. In *How Propaganda Works* (2015), he identifies and develops the political relevance of his views on philosophy of language and epistemology, arguing "that flawed ideologies rob groups of knowledge of their own mental states by systematically concealing their interests from them" and by serving as "impediments to democratic deliberation" (5). More generally, he notes that his argument for interest-relative invariantism (2005) was an attempt to "connect practical notions with epistemic ones":

I argued that having more at stake in decisions made knowledge harder to acquire. So, for example, poor citizens who would benefit greatly from the extra spending derived from modest tax increases on wealthy citizens, as well as their advocates, would have a considerably higher bar for knowledge. If so, their claims would be taken less seriously. Since knowledge was required for action, poor citizens would also have a higher epistemic bar for political action.

(Stanley 2015: xvii–xviii)

If knowledge is interest relative and stake dependent, as Stanley argues, then this needs to be recognized for practical and political reasons: otherwise, we won't fully appreciate the "obstacles in the way of oppressed groups trying to ameliorate their oppression" (2015: 254). Since IRI pays attention to the different stakes that agents and attributors have in knowledge claims, it would be an interesting project to test some of the thought experiments used by Stanley by setting them in realistic settings where social identities and social locations make a difference to the stakes of knowers.[3] Such an investigation by feminist epistemologists would show another route through which social power hinders or promotes agents' ability to know and, therefore, to achieve their other aims.

Feminism, contextualism, and skepticism

One of contextualism's strengths is that it promises a response to skepticism. This is certainly how DeRose (1995) presents the position, but it is also a feature of Williams' (2007) contextualist approach to justification. Despite their differences – DeRose is providing a theory of knowledge attribution, while Williams is offering a theory of justification – they agree that contextual factors are relevant in setting the terms of epistemic success and in finding a way around the problem of skepticism. They disagree, however, in exactly how to, finally, put skepticism behind us.

So, in ordinary contexts, standards of justification or knowledge attribution are suited to the type of inquiry at hand, and justification and knowledge are possible in those ordinary contexts, provided that the relevant contextual standards are met. But while Williams argues that "we need not answer a skeptical challenge to a belief unless there is good reason to doubt the belief" (2007: 93) and doubts, furthermore, that skepticism is capable of offering such genuinely "good reasons," DeRose has argued that the skeptic *can* change the standards of knowledge attribution and thereby undermine the intuition that we know quite a lot of things. Thus, according to DeRose, there are some contexts where, as a result of skeptical maneuvers, we don't actually know, for example, that we have two hands.

From DeRose's perspective, the skeptic's challenge to the possibility of knowledge is neither meaningless nor irrelevant: in fact, in contexts where skeptical doubts have been raised, the skeptic's challenge successfully prevents our having knowledge and, therefore, prevents our acting on the basis of knowing that one statement is true rather than another. DeRose's response to the skeptic is then to isolate the special context where skeptical challenges are relevant from the contexts where we do have ordinary standards for knowledge. Apparently, everyone wins: we're right to claim "knowledge" in ordinary contexts while the skeptic is right to say "we don't have knowledge" in contexts where skeptical doubts are on the table. Unfortunately, this is an unstable truce. DeRose's approach makes it appear that the epistemic standards in ordinary contexts are inferior and second rate compared to the high standards that the skeptic insists upon (Brister 2009, Daukas 2002). But that's not clearly correct: we don't think that orthopedic surgeons are doing their job better, or aiming for higher standards, if they first convince themselves that hands do, in fact, exist. More than that, any sense of victory over the skeptic is short-lived: once we grant that skeptical doubts are valid in certain contexts, and once we grant the skeptic the privilege of insisting on "higher" standards wherever she pleases, the meddling skeptic could show up in any conversational context, change the standards, and sink our inquiry. We would no longer be able to respond to a justificatory challenge in the ordinary way, by presenting more and better evidence to support our claim. Once the skeptic is on the scene, no *amount* of new evidence would allow us to proceed; no new *type* of evidence would save us, either.

I have diagnosed the problem here as an arbitrary deployment of epistemic power (Brister 2009). On DeRose's approach, the skeptic need not understand the standards of justification in a context or the reasons for them. The skeptic need not care what is at stake and, at least on some contextualist accounts, the skeptic need not earn entry into an epistemic community. We are entitled to say that the skeptic's move to expand skeptical contexts is unfair because it summarily puts epistemic agents on the defensive. Indeed, it undermines their epistemic agency, denying them any grounds from which they could launch a defense.

This diagnosis of the skeptic's power move urges that we recognize that skeptical standards for justification are not "higher" or more rigorous than ordinary standards. Indeed, skeptical contexts require less from a philosophical skeptic than they would of an agent skeptical about particular claims, and they are epistemically more conservative because they prevent critical inquiry from developing. The skeptic has the option of undermining some forms of inquiry while permitting justificatory standards in other conversational contexts to stand. The skeptical move is not incisive, it is the blunt tool of a bully who has the option to choose which inquiries to silence.[4]

This response may seem overwrought if we consider proper skeptical contexts to be confined to philosophy classrooms and journal pages. However, the similarity between the moves of a philosophical skeptic and that of a denialist might put these concerns in a more concrete context. A skeptic, in the everyday sense, doubts the veracity or relevance of some particular piece of evidence ("I'm skeptical that you ate all your spinach"); a philosophical skeptic doubts the possibility of the existence of any evidence at all ("I'm skeptical that I have two hands"). Similarly, a vaccination skeptic might question the quality of studies that show no correlation between the MMR vaccine and autism. These are particular, localized doubts. In theory, they could be put to rest by more or better or a different kind of evidence. On the other hand, climate denialists have raised doubts that any scientific evidence could, even in theory, demonstrate the existence of climate change. From their perspective it appears that there is, in principle, no evidence that could support climate change – just as, for philosophical skeptics, it appears that there is no evidence that could support my having two hands. Likewise, racism denialists blame poverty or anti-Christian sentiment for recent fatal violence against blacks in Ferguson, Missouri, and Charleston, South Carolina, while denying the relevance of any evidence that demonstrates racism (Heer 2015). The result of this kind of skeptical denialism has been to change the conversational context from action-oriented inquiry ("How shall we mitigate climate change?", "How shall we address racially-motivated violence?") to a conversation that requires, first, settling the existence of climate change or the existence of racism inside a skeptical context that denies the relevance of the empirical evidence identifying these phenomena. The climate science community considers the denialist strategy to be specifically designed to sideline inquiry away from practical goals and to engage scientists in a quixotic conversation about standards of justification, such as what counts as scientific consensus and whether there is a scientific conspiracy (Oreskes and Conway 2010). This skeptical epistemic strategy can be diagnosed as serving the interests of those who benefit from a status quo.

Connections and gaps between feminist epistemology and contextualism

Feminist epistemology has a distinctive contribution to make in evaluating motives to adopt a contextualist epistemology. In particular, feminist epistemology attends to differences in how subjects are socially situated and the implications situatedness has for their claims to know. While it seems likely that the texture of social difference should be relevant to the concept of "context" proposed by epistemic contextualists like Keith DeRose, no feminist epistemologist has yet made a positive connection with DeRose's contextualism explicit. Instead, Rolin (2011) has dismissed the relevance of "high standards" contexts to feminist concerns (34), and Brister (2009) has argued that the distinction between skeptical and ordinary contexts is artificial and pernicious. However, Williams' contextualist theory of justification offers resources that are a good fit with the concerns of feminist theorists, especially in philosophy of science, where care is taken to draw out practical implications of justificatory norms and practices for institutional arrangements.

Another interesting question is where to place Stanley's interest-relative invariantism in this debate. While, as I noted above, his approach is anti-contextual (in the narrow sense), it does recognize the significance of contextual factors, such as stakes, in a broader sense. In addition, because Stanley's target is contextual accounts of knowledge attribution specifically, it appears compatible with a contextualist theory of justification or justification attribution. Finally, more recently, Stanley has made it clear that IRI can shed light on the obstacles facing oppressed and marginal groups, which suggests that it, too, is broadly compatible with feminist epistemological approaches (including the work of Miranda Fricker, whom he frequently cites in his (2015)).

We can see here how contextualism and feminist epistemology can be mutually supportive: contextualism can provide a general epistemic framework for defending feminist values and goals, while feminist epistemology can shed light on some of the overlooked factors (such as power relations) that operate in particular contexts. In addition to encouraging epistemic contextualists to consider how situatedness affects knowing, I would urge feminist epistemologists to continue to engage with classical epistemological problems, like the problem of skepticism, and the evolution of contemporary approaches to such problems. Feminist perspectives on philosophical problems remind us that there are real, practical consequences to epistemological theories and that working out such theories can be mapped to the ways that individuals and groups can better know and intervene in their worlds.

Notes

1 While feminist theory has focused primarily on gender, in recent decades feminists have widely acknowledged that their concern is with unequal social relations and marginalized social identities more generally, including race and sexuality, and with how social identities intersect. Feminist theory is thus concerned not only with gender categories; it theorizes social power relations more generally.
2 For instance, Sharyn Clough (2003) argues that relativism is a central issue for feminist epistemology but that "global skepticism is a nonstarter," and so "we no longer have any motivation for continuing the epistemological debate about how best to address skepticism" (103).
3 Sripada and Stanley (2012) have tested these thought experiments to check our invariantist intuitions; it's a separate question whether and how stakes are related to social identity.
4 It's worth noting here that Williams' contextual theory of justification uses a different strategy against the skeptic: Williams takes a "diagnostic" approach that shifts the burden of proof on to the skeptic to *show* that skeptical doubts and arguments are relevant in a particular context. Williams is doubtful that the skeptic can successfully shoulder this burden but, in any case, this approach blocks the skeptic from *automatically* changing the standards operating in a particular context.

References

Anderson, Elizabeth. 2015. "Feminist Epistemology and Philosophy of Science." In *The Stanford Encyclopedia of Philosophy*, Edward Zalta (ed.), http://plato.stanford.edu/entries/feminism-epistemology/.
Annis, David. 1978. "A Contextualist Theory of Epistemic Justification." *American Philosophical Quarterly* 15 (3): 213–219.
Antony, Louise. 1993. "Quine as Feminist: The Radical Import of Naturalized Epistemology." In *A Mind of One's Own: Feminist Essays on Reason and Objectivity*, Louise Antony and Charlotte Witt (eds.), 185–225. Boulder: Westview Press.
Brister, Evelyn. 2009. "Feminist Epistemology, Contextualism, and Philosophical Skepticism." *Metaphilosophy* 40 (5): 671–688.
Clough, Sharyn. 2003. *Beyond Epistemology: A Pragmatist Approach to Feminist Science Studies*. Lanham, MD: Rowman & Littlefield.
Cohen, Stewart. 1987. "Knowledge, Context, and Social Standards." *Synthese* 73 (1): 3–26.
Crasnow, Sharon. 2003. "Can Science Be Objective?: Feminism, Relativism, and Objectivity." In *Scrutinizing Feminist Epistemology: An Examination of Gender in Science*, Cassandra L. Pinnick, Noretta Koertge, and Robert F. Almeder (eds.), 130–141. New Brunswick: Rutgers University Press.
Daukas, Nancy. 2002. "Skepticism, Contextualism, and the Epistemic 'Ordinary'." *Philosophical Forum* 31 (1): 63–79.
———. 2011. "A Virtue-Theoretic Approach to Pluralism in Feminist Epistemology." In *Feminist Epistemology and Philosophy of Science: Power in Knowledge*, Heidi E. Grasswick (ed.), 45–67. Dordrecht: Springer.
DeRose, Keith. 1995. "Solving the Skeptical Problem." *Philosophical Review* 104: 1–52.
———. 2009. *The Case for Contextualism: Knowledge, Skepticism and Context*. Oxford: Clarendon.
Fricker, Miranda. 2008. "Scepticism and the Genealogy of Knowledge: Situating Epistemology in Time." *Philosophical Papers* 37 (1): 27–50.

Grasswick, Heidi. 2013. "Feminist Social Epistemology." In *The Stanford Encyclopedia of Philosophy,* Edward Zalta (ed.), http://plato.stanford.edu/entries/feminist-social-epistemology/.

Grasswick, Heidi E. and Mark Owen Webb. 2002. "Feminist Epistemology as Social Epistemology." *Social Epistemology* 16 (3): 185–196.

Heer, Jeet. 2015. "National Review's Racism Denial, Then and Now." *New Republic,* June 19. https://newrepublic.com/article/122095/national-reviews-racism-denial-then-and-now.

Heikes, Deborah. 2004. "The Bias Paradox: Why It's Not Just for Feminists Anymore." *Synthese* 138 (3): 315–335.

Hicks, Daniel. 2011. "Is Longino's Conception of Objectivity Feminist?" *Hypatia* 26 (2): 333–351.

Intemann, Kristen. 2008. "Increasing the Number of Feminist Scientists: Why Feminist Aims Are Not Served by the Underdetermination Thesis." *Science & Education* 17 (10): 1065–1079.

———. 2011. "Diversity and Dissent in Science: Does Democracy Always Serve Feminist Aims?" In *Feminist Epistemology and Philosophy of Science: Power in Knowledge,* Heidi E. Grasswick (ed.), 111–132. Dordrecht: Springer.

Lewis, David. 1979. "Scorekeeping in a Language Game." *Journal of Philosophical Logic* 8: 339–359.

———. 1996. "Elusive Knowledge." *Australasian Journal of Philosophy* 74: 549–567.

Longino, Helen. 1990. *Science as Social Knowledge.* Princeton: Princeton University Press.

———. 2004. *The Fate of Knowledge.* Princeton: Princeton University Press.

McKenna, Robin. 2015. "Contextualism in Epistemology." *Analysis* 75 (3): 489–503.

Medina, José. 2013. *The Epistemology of Resistance: Gender and Racial Oppression, Epistemic Injustice, and Resistant Imaginations.* Oxford: Oxford University Press.

O'Connor, Peg. 2012. *Morality and Our Complicated Form of Life: Feminist Wittgensteinian Metaethics.* University Park, PA: Pennsylvania State University Press.

Oreskes, Naomi and Erik M. Conway. 2010. *Merchants of Doubt.* New York: Bloomsbury.

Rolin, Kristina. 2006. "The Bias Paradox in Feminist Standpoint Epistemology." *Episteme* 3 (1–2): 125–136.

———. 2011. "Contextualism in Feminist Epistemology and Philosophy of Science." In *Feminist Epistemology and Philosophy of Science: Power in Knowledge,* Heidi E. Grasswick (ed.), 25–44. Dordrecht: Springer.

Solomon, Miriam, and Alan Richardson. 2005. "A Critical Context for Longino's Critical Contextual Empiricism." *Studies in the History and Philosophy of Science* 36: 211–222.

Sripada, Chandra and Jason Stanley. 2012. "Empirical Tests of Interest-Relative Invariantism." *Episteme* 9: 3–26.

Stanley, Jason. 2005. *Knowledge and Practical Interests.* Oxford: Oxford University Press.

———. 2015. *How Propaganda Works.* Princeton: Princeton University Press.

Tanesini, Alessandra. 1999. *An Introduction to Feminist Epistemologies.* Oxford: Blackwell.

Williams, Michael. 1991. *Unnatural Doubts: Epistemological Realism and the Basis of Scepticism.* Oxford: Blackwell.

———. 2001. *Problems of Knowledge: A Critical Introduction to Epistemology.* New York: Oxford University Press.

———. 2007. "Why (Wittgensteinian) Contextualism Is Not Relativism." *Episteme* 4 (1): 93–114.

PART II

Methodological issues

5

EPISTEMIC CONTEXTUALISM AND CONCEPTUAL ETHICS

E. Diaz-Leon

1 Introduction

What does "knowledge" mean? What should "knowledge" mean? This chapter is about the connection between these two questions. In particular, I will argue that *if* we endorse a certain view about the meaning of "knowledge", namely, epistemic contextualism, according to which the meaning of "knowledge" varies from context to context depending on the standards of the speaker, *then* it seems plausible to say that when we utter sentences of the form "S knows that p", we are not only saying something about whether S knows that p (according to our standards), but we are also communicating information about the way the term "knows" *should* be used. I will also argue that discussions about how the term "knows" should be used are discussions that are worth having, since they are connected with important issues of practical significance.

In order to make a case for these claims, in what follows I aim to develop and defend a certain view about the meaning of knowledge ascriptions according to which when we make knowledge ascriptions of the form "S knows that p", we are expressing two kinds of contents: first, we are *saying* something about whether S satisfies the standards that are needed in order to know that p, and second, we are *implicating* something about what "knowledge" means; that is, we are implicating some *metalinguistic* information about whether the term "knowledge" should be associated with those standards. More specifically, I would like to explore the following combination of views:

(i) Attributor contextualism about phrases of the form "S knows that p", and
(ii) A metalinguistic analysis of (the appearance of) disagreements in pairs of utterances of the form "S knows that p" and "S doesn't know that p" (for the same subject S and the same proposition p).

Let me explain these two views a bit more slowly. *Attributor contextualism* is the view according to which utterances of the form "S knows that p" can vary in meaning from context to context (for the same subject S and the same proposition p), due to certain features of the speaker that can vary from context to context.[1] If attributor contextualism is the correct view about the meaning of "knowledge", then two utterances of the form "S knows that p" and "S doesn't know that p" can be true at the same time (for the same subject S and the same proposition p), if they are uttered by different speakers in different contexts, where different standards are at issue. However, these two utterances still seem to give rise to an appearance of disagreement; that is, we still have the intuition that they disagree with each other. How can we account for this intuition, if we endorse attributor contextualism? The metalinguistic analysis tries to account for the intuition of disagreement as follows: according to this view, the disagreement cannot be explained in terms of the propositions that are *semantically expressed* by the utterances (since according to attributor contextualism those propositions can be compatible; that is, they can both be true, if the sentences are uttered at different contexts), but rather in terms of the propositions that are *pragmatically conveyed*, which are actually about the way we should use the term "knows", and which can indeed contradict each other (i.e. one utterance conveys the claim that "knows" should be used in a certain way and the other utterance denies that very same claim).[2] This combination of views has been suggested by David Plunkett and Tim Sundell (2013), who have developed the thesis in great detail for evaluative and normative terms in general. In this chapter, I want to explore the prospects of the view regarding epistemic terms in particular.

As a way of motivation, Plunkett and Sundell argue that this combination of views can be used in order to block an influential argument against (attributor) contextualism. They say:

> [T]he sort of argument that is our focus . . . is the argument from (a) the premise that an exchange between two speakers expresses a genuine disagreement to (b) the thesis that those speakers mean the same things by the words they use in that exchange. This is a common type of argument in metaethical theorizing about the meanings of our moral or ethical terms. Indeed, it plays a central role quite generally in debates about the meanings of normative and evaluative terms – terms (moral, ethical, aesthetic, epistemological, etc.) whose meaning at least partly involves matters of what one *should* do, think, or feel, or, respectively, about what is *better* or *worse*.
>
> *(2013: 2–3)*

Plunkett and Sundell's main focus is on moral, ethical and aesthetic terms. In this chapter, I would like to extend their account to epistemological terms. First of all, I would like to offer some reasons for the claim that epistemological terms are also normative or evaluative terms; that is, they have to do with what one *ought* to do, or what is better or worse. In my view, to say that S's belief that p is justified (given evidence e) is to say that S *ought* to have that belief (given evidence e).[3] To say that S's belief that p is more justified than S's belief that q (given evidence e) is to say that the belief that p is *better* than the belief that q. If so, then it seems that epistemological terms are normative in the relevant sense; that is, terms such as "justified" are predicates that ascribe evaluative properties that have to do with which beliefs are better than others, or which beliefs we ought to form. Hence, they are similar to other normative terms such as "good" or "right" or "beautiful", which also ascribe evaluative properties to actions or individuals, and have to do with what we ought to do or feel.

2 Normative terms, disagreement and the metalinguistic reply

As we have seen, Plunkett and Sundell want to argue that the fact that two speakers express a genuine disagreement does not entail that their utterances express incompatible propositions. They argue that a (genuine) disagreement could be explained also at the pragmatic level; that is, in terms of the information pragmatically conveyed by the speakers' utterances, in addition to the information that is semantically expressed (which might be compatible after all). In particular, they want to argue that many alleged disagreements involving evaluative terms are genuine

Contextualism and conceptual ethics

disagreements precisely because the speakers express incompatible propositions about the way that very evaluative term *should* be used, but where these propositions are conveyed pragmatically rather than semantically.[4]

In order to show that this is a familiar phenomenon, they first discuss an example (drawing from Barker 2002) of a sentence that is uttered in order to express a metalinguistic claim about the way a certain word is used, where this information is conveyed pragmatically.[5]

Imagine the following conversation between Alice, who is a visitor, and utters (1), and Dana, who is a local, and utters (2):

(1) What counts as tall around here?
(2) Calliope is tall.

Plunkett and Sundell argue that in this conversation, (2) semantically expresses a proposition about Calliope's height, but pragmatically conveys information about what the standards of tallness are in that context. That is, it seems clear that the utterer of (2) is conveying the information that the term "tall" in that context applies to individuals who are at least as tall as Calliope in response to question (1). But this does not seem to be the literal content of (2), so if the speaker can get this content across, it must be because of a pragmatic mechanism. So (2) pragmatically conveys a metalinguistic proposition about the way "tall" is used in that context.

Second, Plunkett and Sundell argue that this pragmatic strategy can also be applied to cases of disagreement. For instance, imagine that a third subject, Ellen, utters (3) as a response to (2) above:

(3) No, Calliope is not tall.

Whereas this utterance semantically expresses a proposition about Calliope's height, it also pragmatically conveys information about the standards that are at issue in that context. In this case, (2) and (3) exhibit genuine disagreement at the pragmatic level; that is, a metalinguistic dispute about how the term "tall" is used in that context, and more in particular, whether it applies to people who are at least as tall as Calliope or not.

As Plunkett and Sundell explain, in this case it seems that (2) and (3) actually express incompatible contents also at the semantic level, assuming that the objective standards for tallness are fixed in the context, and are common for both speakers. In this case, either Dana or Ellen is saying something false (i.e. either it is the case that Calliope counts as tall given the standards that are at issue in that context, or it isn't).[6] But they are also expressing a genuine disagreement about what they take to be the standards at place in the context, by means of a pragmatic mechanism.

However, Plunkett and Sundell argue that there can also be cases of disagreement where the semantic contents are actually compatible but the information pragmatically conveyed by the utterances is not. For example, imagine that two subjects, Bo and Lauren, are making curry together (and want to make it spicy enough for the relevant purposes, say, in order to satisfy their guests), and they both taste it. Bo utters (4), and Lauren responds by uttering (5):

(4) This is spicy!
(5) No, this is not spicy!

According to Plunkett and Sundell, (4) and (5) semantically express propositions that are compatible; namely, something like "this has (or doesn't have) the disposition to cause a certain experience in people like me" (i.e. Bo is saying that the curry has the disposition to cause a certain

73

experience in people like her, and Lauren is saying that the curry doesn't have the disposition to cause that same experience in people like her, both of which claims can be true at the same time). But (4) and (5) also pragmatically convey incompatible propositions; namely, (4) somehow conveys the information that the curry is the way it *should* be (given their purposes; that is, it is sufficiently spicy to please their guests), whereas (5) conveys the information that it is not the way it should be (i.e. it is not sufficiently spicy to please their guests). More in particular, (4) and (5) pragmatically convey information about which standards of spiciness should be associated with the word "spicy". That is, Bo and Lauren disagree about which should be the threshold for spiciness: Bo believes that they should use "spicy" so that the curry they are actually tasting is above the bar, whereas Lauren believes that they should use "spicy" so that the curry they are tasting is below the bar.

Why do they care about the way we should use the word "spicy"? Why is this metalinguistic dispute a dispute that is worth having? According to Plunkett and Sundell, this dispute matters because how we use the word "spicy" has important practical consequences. In particular, if we think that we should apply the word "spicy" to the curry we are making, that means that we believe that we *should not* add more spices, whereas if we believe that we should not apply the word "spicy" to it, we believe that we *should* add more spices to it (assuming that we both have the desire to make it spicy enough so that our guests are pleased).

In this case, (4) and (5) express a genuine disagreement about what the meaning of "spicy" should be. More precisely, there is a disagreement about what the *content* of the term should be (while they both keep the *character* fixed).[7]

3 Epistemic contextualism, disagreement and the metalinguistic reply

Our central question in this section is the following: can we apply a similar analysis in order to explain the appearance of disagreements concerning claims about knowledge? This question is especially pressing, given that similar arguments going from the appearance of disagreement to the expression of incompatible contents are also used in discussions about the meaning of "knowledge". For instance, Mark Richard (2004) says:

> Suppose a confrontation between a skeptic with high standards, and Moore, who has low standards. The skeptic says
>
> [6] You don't know that you have hands.
>
> Contextualism tells us that the content . . . of 'knows' in the skeptic's context is determined by the standards that his context provides. Since he, unlike Moore, has high standards, Moore and the claim that he has hands just don't make the cut. The skeptic's utterance of [6] is true: that is, Moore doesn't know that he has hands.
>   Of course, when Moore utters
>
> [7] I know that I have hands
>
> the standards in his context are the relevant standards, and so, given his low standards, he speaks truly. So Moore knows that he has hands after all. But how can that be? Didn't the skeptic just establish that Moore doesn't know that he has hands? Well, says the contextualist, what the skeptic said was true. But since 'know' is contextually sensitive, [7] doesn't say the same thing, when Moore uses it, as does

Contextualism and conceptual ethics

[8] You know that you have hands

when the skeptic uses it. So there is nothing contradictory about the skeptic's being able to use [6] truly while Moore can so use [7]. One feels that something is awry. One wants to say that when the skeptic and Moore argue with each other, they disagree about whether Moore knows that he has hands.

(2004: 215–216)

Richard's argument is exactly the kind of argument that Plunkett and Sundell criticize; that is, it infers that (6) and (7) must express incompatible semantic contents, given that there is an appearance of disagreement. Therefore, Richard argues, (attributor) contextualism about "knowledge" seems to be in trouble because it has (or could have) the counter-intuitive consequence that (6) and (7) do not actually express incompatible propositions, since they are uttered by different speakers, and therefore the standards of justification that are at issue in each case are different.

However, it could be argued that this inference is not correct because we can also apply here the kind of metalinguistic analysis proposed by Plunkett and Sundell. In particular, we could respond as follows: Moore and the skeptic (might) express compatible propositions at the semantic level, but they still express a genuine disagreement. In particular, their disagreement can be explained at the pragmatic level. That is, when the skeptic utters (6), she is expressing the proposition that Moore does not satisfy certain (very high) standards of justification, whereas when Moore utters (7), he is expressing the proposition that he does satisfy certain lower standards of justification. These two propositions are compatible. But the skeptic is also conveying the information that "knows" *should* be used in a way so that one would count as knowing a proposition only when one satisfies certain very high standards, whereas Moore is also conveying the information that "knows" *should not* be used in that way. These two propositions are obviously incompatible, and this is what explains the appearance of disagreement.

In the remainder of this section, I want to examine the conditional claim that *if* one believes that Plunkett and Sundell's metalinguistic analysis of disagreement involving moral, ethical and aesthetic terms is plausible, *then* one should also believe that the metalinguistic analysis of disagreements involving *epistemological* terms is also plausible. I will pose a problem for this conditional, and I will attempt to solve the worry. In addition, in the next section I will discuss two possible objections to the metalinguistic reply in general, and I will argue that the advocate of the metalinguistic reply can respond to those objections satisfactorily. I will then conclude that the metalinguistic account regarding epistemological terms is a plausible claim that we do not seem to have obvious reasons to doubt and deserves to be taken seriously.

But before we do this, a caveat is in order. Here I will focus on versions of epistemic contextualism that do entail that at the semantic level, the propositions expressed by a pair of utterances like (6) and (7) can be true at the same time. Not all versions of attributor contextualism have this consequence: for instance, DeRose (2009) argues that his version of contextualism doesn't have that consequence, and this is how he responds to Richard's argument above. But my discussion is restricted to versions of contextualism according to which the semantic contents that are literally expressed are compatible, and therefore we need to explain the appearance of disagreement in an alternative way, such as in terms of the metalinguistic account. For example, we can focus on versions of epistemic contextualism that endorse what Jason Stanley (2005) has called the *intention-based* view. That is, he explains that according to this version of attributor contextualism, the content of an utterance of "S knows that p" is determined by the beliefs and intentions of the speaker, since these are the relevant features of the speaker that determine the different contents from context to context.[8]

If so, then it clearly follows that in the conversation between Moore and the skeptic above, Moore's utterance (7) and the skeptic's utterance (6) express semantic contents that can be true at the same time, for they have different beliefs about which standards of justification are relevant; that is, according to the skeptic we should impose high standards whereas according to Moore we should impose lower standards. Hence, if we assume a version of contextualism that endorses the intention-based view, these different beliefs will yield different standards for their respective utterances of "knows", and therefore they will mean different things by the predicate "knows that Moore has hands". Therefore, the disagreement cannot be explained at the semantic level.[9] Could it be explained at the pragmatic level; that is, in terms of claims to the effect that "knows" should be used in this or that way, given our purposes at hand?

Now, in order to defend this view, an advocate of the metalinguistic analysis would have to argue that a dispute concerning how to use the term "knows" is worth having. And for this, one would have to argue that how to use "knows" has important practical consequences. This is crucial because, as Plunkett and Sundell emphasize, in order to make the metalinguistic strategy more intuitive it would be helpful if we can show that the metalinguistic dispute that the speakers are supposed to engage in (at the pragmatic level) is a dispute worth having. Otherwise, why should we believe that the speakers would even bother to convey such complicated metalinguistic contents by means of pragmatic mechanisms? For instance, in the case of the dispute about whether the curry is spicy, the metalinguistic dispute is worth having because it has clear practical consequences regarding whether they should add more spices to the curry or not.

However, one could worry that in the case of "knowledge", it is not clear that anything practical follows from the different views on how to use the phrase "knows that p". No matter whether one is a skeptic or not, we will still trust that we have two hands, and we will go on with our lives using our hands in the standard way, no matter whether we believe that we know that we have hands or not. That is, our different views about how to use "knows that p" and which different standards of justification should be applied seem to make no difference to our actions.

This seems initially plausible. But as Alexis Burgess and David Plunkett (2013a,b) have argued, discussions about how to use a term (i.e. what they call *conceptual ethics*) are important not only because of what follows from a practical or instrumental point of view, but also because of what would follow from a moral, political or theoretical point of view. That is to say, in some cases, it can be argued that using a term in one way rather than another is preferable due to certain moral or political considerations. In my view it is possible to make a case along these lines regarding how we should use the term "knows". For instance, an anti-skeptic could argue that using "knows" in the way the skeptic advocates is problematic for ethical and political reasons. For example, it could be argued that it is a non-efficient way of conducting research about politically significant matters. Or it could be argued that it is a dangerous way of using the term in a medical context. As Sally Haslanger (1999) has argued, when I claim that I know a proposition, I am claiming that I have certain epistemic authority, and that I can give that authority to others (465). If this is right, then we can explain why it makes sense to engage in a dispute about how "knows" should be used: the subjects in the dispute might have different views about which standards of justification give rise to that authority. That is to say, there could be a dispute about which standards of justification (to be associated with the term "knowledge") are more worthy of the special authority that is typically associated with the term "knowledge". And this would give us some reasons to favor some views about which standards are relevant (relative to our purposes at hand) rather than others.

In addition, Burgess and Plunkett also emphasize that disputes about how we should use a term could be useful, given theoretical reasons. For instance it could be argued that one way of using the term carves nature at its joints better than another (that is to say, there are two possible candidate concepts, one of which carves nature at its joints better than the other, and for this reason associating the term with the former concept is preferable to associating it with the latter, less joint-carving one). Or it could be argued that one way of using a term is more illuminating, or has more explanatory or predictive power, than another. In this way, one could argue that the dispute between the skeptic and the Moorean is about how "knows" *should* be used, in order to have the most theoretically useful concept (given some purposes).

Therefore, we can conclude that *if* one finds plausible the idea that disagreements involving moral, ethical and aesthetic terms can (sometimes) be explained in virtue of a metalinguistic dispute, precisely because these are disputes that are *worth having*, then one should also find plausible the idea that disagreements involving epistemological terms can also be explained in the same way, since these disputes are also worth having (at least in some cases).

4 Two objections

To finish, I would like to discuss two possible objections against the general view that disagreements about normative terms can be explained in terms of a metalinguistic dispute at the pragmatic level. The first objection goes as follows: why should we believe that the disagreement that is pragmatically conveyed is actually about how we should use the word, and not directly about how we should *act* (beyond our use of that word)? As we have seen, Plunkett and Sundell argue that it is plausible to endorse the metalinguistic analysis in some cases, precisely because discussions about how we should use a word are relevant due to their connection to discussions about what we should *do* (e.g. whether we should add more spices to the curry). But then perhaps we should say that what is pragmatically conveyed is just a disagreement about what we should do, rather than a disagreement about how we should use the term (that is somehow connected with a further disagreement about how we should act non-linguistically). Why shouldn't we just say that what is pragmatically conveyed is this second non-linguistic disagreement, which we need to appeal to anyway in order to make the existence of a metalinguistic disagreement at all plausible?

As Plunkett and Sundell admit, the metalinguistic strategy might seem counterintuitive. When ordinary speakers utter pairs of sentences like (4–5) or (6–7), it is not transparent to them that they are conveying different views about how one should use the word (rather, what seems more intuitive to the speakers is that they are having a disagreement about first-order matters; namely, whether the curry is in fact spicy, or whether Moore in fact knows that he has two hands). In response, Plunkett and Sundell argue that it is a bit less counterintuitive to say that the speakers are somehow conveying information about how we should act (in addition to the first-order information), and that the metalinguistic strategy can at least vindicate *these* intuitions, because claims about how we should use the corresponding term are connected to claims about how we should act in other ways, as we saw above. But if so, the same worry arises again: why do we need to express a *metalinguistic* disagreement at all, over and above a disagreement about how we should act, which does seem a bit more intuitive?

I think this is an important worry. But one could respond as follows: Plunkett and Sundell argue that debates about how to use a term are important because in many cases the word already plays a certain *functional role* in our community (contingently connected to the meaning of the term), and it is assumed that whichever concept turns out to be expressed by that word *deserves* to play that functional role. For example, a word can be attached to certain values and stereotypes (even if these are not part of the meaning of the term). Then, the question of how we should use the word becomes very relevant, because this is connected to the question of which concept we should associate with that word, and in order to decide this we need to decide which concept (among several candidates) should be attached to those values and stereotypes, which is clearly a significant question. In cases like this, it seems plausible to say that disagreements involving those terms can be explained by means of the metalinguistic strategy. For in these cases, disputes about how to use that very word will become very significant, and therefore these metalinguistic disputes themselves are disputes that are worth having, be it by means of pragmatic or semantic mechanisms. In my view it is clear that the term "knowledge" plays a very important functional role.[10] Hence the question of which concept should be associated with this word is very important, and worth talking about.

The second objection goes as follows: the metalinguistic strategy can explain the appearance of disagreement between pairs of utterances, but what about the appearance of disagreement between pairs of *thoughts*? For example, someone could argue that if the skeptic *believes* that Moore doesn't know that he has hands, whereas the non-skeptic believes that Moore does know that he has hands, they are disagreeing, regardless of whether they utter the corresponding sentences or not. But if so, how can we explain this appearance of disagreement?

The advocate of the metalinguistic strategy could just say that the appearance of disagreement is due to a mistake, based on the intuition that there would be a disagreement *if* the subjects were to utter the corresponding sentences (since they would probably pragmatically convey incompatible metalinguistic propositions), and this intuition is what explains the (misleading) appearance of disagreement at the level of thoughts.

But in my view, we could also say that in many cases there will also be a disagreement at the level of thoughts. In particular, as we have seen, Plunkett and Sundell have argued that in cases of metalinguistic disputes the subjects usually have important disagreements about which concepts should play certain important functional roles, and about certain moral, political, theoretical or instrumental issues that are connected with that dispute. Hence, in the case of two subjects entertaining different contents, involving different concepts, it seems likely that these subjects will have opposing beliefs regarding which concept should play the relevant functional role, and also with respect to some of the corresponding normative issues.

5 Conclusion

In this chapter I have explored the view according to which conversations where one party utters a sentence of the form "S knows that p" and another utters "S doesn't know that p" can involve genuine disagreement, even if the content of "knows" is fixed by appeal to the different standards of justification that the speakers have in mind. In cases like these, even if the semantic contents that are literally expressed are compatible (i.e. it can be true both that S satisfies low epistemic standards with respect to p and that S doesn't satisfy high epistemic standards with respect to p), the speakers are nonetheless communicating incompatible propositions at the pragmatic level. That is, in addition to what they are literally saying, they are also communicating information about how the word "knows" should be used (i.e. one is pragmatically conveying the claim that "knows" should be associated with low standards whereas the other is pragmatically conveying the claim that "knows" should be associated with high standards). I have also argued that these disputes are disputes that are worth having because many terms are culturally associated with certain values and stereotypes, so that it is important to discuss which concept (out of several candidates) deserves to be associated with those values and stereotypes.[11] And in particular, when it comes to discussions about how we should use the term "knowledge", it could be argued that they are significant because they are connected with considerations of several types, including instrumental, moral, political and theoretical factors that might be relevant in order to determine whether using "knowledge" with higher or lower standards of justification is more or less beneficial.[12]

Contextualism and conceptual ethics

Notes

1 The distinction between attributor contextualism and other forms of contextualism was introduced by DeRose (1992), and further elaborated by Stanley (2005) and DeRose (2009), among many others.
2 See the chapters in Part V of this volume for related discussion.
3 I am not claiming that to say that S's belief that p is justified is to say that S ought to believe that p all things considered. I am just claiming that to say that S is justified in believing that p, given e, is to say that S has a *pro-tanto* reason to believe that p, given e, which could nonetheless be trumped by other reasons (i.e. other epistemological or moral or instrumental reasons that S might have against believing that p). For further discussion on the connection between epistemological "oughts" and other kinds of "oughts", see Diaz-Leon (2016).
4 This is just one possible strategy in order to block the inference from (a) to (b) above, but there are others. See López de Sa (2008) for an interesting alternative account of disagreement. In this chapter my main aim is to focus on the metalinguistic analysis. See also chapters 20, 21 and 22 of this volume for further discussion of the question of disagreement.
5 The following example is slightly modified from Barker (2002: 1–2), as quoted in Plunkett and Sundell (2013: 14).
6 I am ignoring the possibility that the term is vague and Calliope is a borderline case, for the sake of simplicity.
7 I am assuming here the familiar distinction between *character* and *content* introduced by Kaplan (1989). As Plunkett and Sundell explain, we could also have metalinguistic disputes about the character of a term (or the meaning of the term more generally, when it is not a context-sensitive term). But it is also possible to have disputes about the content; that is, about what the relevant standards should be, assuming we keep fixed the character of a context-sensitive term, as in the case of "spicy".
8 According to Stanley, this is a standard version of contextualism (which he will reject). He says: "On a standard version of context-sensitive expressions, their semantic contents, relative to a context, are determined by facts about the intentions of the speaker using that expression" (2005: 25).
9 I do not want to imply here that the metalinguistic reply is plausible only when the semantic contents that are literally expressed are compatible. In principle, it is also possible to argue that in other kinds of cases, there could also be some metalinguistic information that is conveyed pragmatically. As we saw above in the discussion about utterances (2–3), here we seem to have a case where the utterances express semantic contents that are incompatible (because they involve the same standards for "tallness"), but they also pragmatically convey opposing metalinguistic claims about the way "tallness" is *actually* used in that context (Plunkett 2015 calls this a *descriptive* metalinguistic dispute). One could also have cases where the semantic contents are incompatible (i.e. there is genuine disagreement at the semantic level), and in addition the utterances pragmatically convey opposing metalinguistic claims about the way the term *should* be used (Plunkett 2015 calls this a *normative* metalinguistic dispute).
10 For example, Haslanger (1999), following Austin (1970), distinguishes between the *locutionary* and the *illocutionary* force of a knowledge attribution, and she argues that claims to the effect that I know a certain proposition might have illocutionary effects that are very significant. Then, the question of which concept of knowledge deserves to have those illocutionary effects is a very significant question. See also Fassio and McKenna (2015) for further discussion about the functional role of knowledge ascriptions.
11 Chalmers (2011) makes a similar point.
12 I have presented this material at the FARBEK Pilot Workshop at the University of Barcelona, and the Philosophy Colloquium at the University of Valencia. I am grateful to the audiences in those occasions for very helpful feedback. Extra thanks are due to the following, for useful comments and discussion: Delia Belleri, Cristina Borgoni, Josep Corbi, Patrick Greenough, Tobies Grimaltos, Dan López de Sa, Aidan McGlynn, Daniel Morgan, Carlos Moya, Sven Rosenkranz, Moritz Schulz, Jordi Valor and Crispin Wright. I am also indebted to Nathan Cockram and Jonathan Ichikawa for excellent editorial comments. This research has been supported by grants RYC-10900-2012 and FFI2013-45968-P (Spanish Government).

References

Austin, J.L. (1970) "Other Minds", in J.O. Urmson & G.J. Warnock (eds.) *Philosophical Papers* (2nd edition), Oxford: Oxford University Press: 76–116.
Barker, C. (2002) "The Dynamics of Vagueness", *Linguistics and Philosophy* 25: 1–36.

Burgess, A. & Plunkett, D. (2013a) "Conceptual Ethics I", *Philosophy Compass* 8 (12): 1091–101.
Burgess, A. & Plunkett, D. (2013b) "Conceptual Ethics II", *Philosophy Compass* 8 (12): 1102–10.
Chalmers, D. (2011) "Verbal Disputes", *Philosophical Review* 120 (4): 515–66.
DeRose, K. (1992) "Contextualism and Knowledge Attributions", *Philosophy and Phenomenological Research* 52 (4): 913–29.
DeRose, K. (2009) *The Case for Contextualism*, Oxford: Oxford University Press.
Diaz-Leon, E. (2016) "Norms of Judgement, Naturalism, and Normativism about Content", *Philosophical Explorations* 19 (1): 48–58.
Fassio, D. & McKenna, R. (2015) "Revisionary Epistemology", *Inquiry* 58 (7–8): 755–79.
Haslanger, S. (1999) "What Knowledge Is and What It Ought to Be: Feminist Values and Normative Epistemology", *Philosophical Perspectives* 13: 459–80.
Kaplan, D. (1989) "Demonstratives", in J. Almog, J. Perry & H. Wettstein (eds.) *Themes From Kaplan*, Oxford: Oxford University Press: 481–563.
López de Sa, D. (2008) "Presuppositions of Commonality: An Indexical Relativist Account of Disagreement", in M. García-Carpintero & M. Kölbel (eds.) *Relative Truth*, Oxford: Oxford University Press: 297–308.
Plunkett, D. (2015) "Which Concepts Should We Use?: Metalinguistic Negotiations and The Methodology of Philosophy", *Inquiry* 58 (7–8): 828–74.
Plunkett, D. & Sundell, T. (2013) "Disagreement and the Semantics of Normative and Evaluative Terms", *Philosophers' Imprint* 13 (23): 1–37.
Richard, M. (2004) "Contextualism and Relativism", *Philosophical Studies* 119 (1): 215–42.
Stanley, J. (2005) *Knowledge and Practical Interests*, Oxford: Oxford University Press.

6

DOES CONTEXTUALISM HINGE ON A METHODOLOGICAL DISPUTE?

Jie Gao, Mikkel Gerken and Stephen B. Ryan

1 Introduction

Epistemic contextualism (henceforth: *contextualism*) is, roughly, the semantic thesis that the truth-conditional contribution of "knows" varies with variations in the context of utterance. Contextualism has been surrounded by methodological disputes as long as it has existed. In fact, a large number of the debates that characterize contemporary meta-epistemology resemble the methodological disputes over contextualism. We think that this is no mere accident. Rather, the nature of and motivation for contextualism naturally raise methodological questions. What is the proper relationship between epistemology and philosophy of language? What is the role of intuitive judgments in epistemological theorizing? What is the proper response when our epistemological theories are incongruous with our folk epistemology?

In this chapter, we aim to simultaneously provide an overview of some of the methodological debates surrounding contextualism and consider whether they are, in effect, based on an underlying methodological dispute. We proceed as follows: in Section 2, we articulate two questions that our discussion will address. In Section 3, we consider case-based motivations of contextualism and DeRose's "methodology of the straightforward." In Section 4, we consider the methodology that consists in modeling a contextualist semantics of "knows" on other context-sensitive linguistic phenomena. In Section 5, we consider attempts to motivate contextualism by appeal to imagined conceptual genealogies or functional roles. In Section 6, we discuss the challenges from experimental philosophy from a methodological perspective. In Section 7, we conclude by revisiting the question as to whether the debates over the case for contextualism are based on a methodological dispute.

2 Contextualism and methodological disputes

As mentioned, contextualism has since its earliest developments been surrounded by disputes of a methodological character. For example, its attempt to "dissolve" skeptical paradoxes was motivated by meta-epistemological considerations such as considerations about the aims of epistemology (DeRose 1995, 1999, 2004; Lewis 1996; Cohen 1999, 2005). However, the contextualist approach was countered with meta-epistemological criticism (Schiffer 1996, 2004). For example, critics questioned whether a semantic thesis is apt to solve epistemological problems (Kornblith 2000; Sosa 2000).

Naturally, contextualists have responded to these methodologically oriented criticisms. But very often the methodological and the substantive issues have been addressed in unison. This raises the question as to whether contextualists "have a distinctive methodology" or, more specifically, whether there are any methodological doctrines that underlie the dispute between contextualists and their opponents. This broad quandary is reflected in our title. But to begin to address this grand issue, we will articulate it a manner that is a bit more conspicuous (and admittedly less grand) as two distinct but interrelated meta-methodological questions:

Q1 *Is there a distinctive methodological doctrine or set of methodological doctrines that is centrally invoked by all epistemic contextualists?*

Q2 *Does the substantive dispute concerning the truth of contextualism depend on underlying methodological disputes?*

Q1 and Q2 are logically independent. Some doctrine could be common to all contextualists without explaining the dispute between contextualists and their opponents – perhaps because the doctrine is also accepted by the majority of the opponents. On the other hand, it might be that whereas contextualism is motivated by various distinct methodologies, opponents to contextualism are in each case in disagreement with the methodology in question.

By structuring the discussion around these two meta-methodological questions, we hope to advance the debates by gaining some clarity on the various aspects of contextualist methodology. We also seek to advance the debate by providing preliminary and qualified answers to the two questions. Roughly, we will answer Q1 by a qualified "no" and Q2 by a qualified "yes." There is no single methodology or set of methodological doctrines that is *distinctive* of contextualism in the sense that all contextualists centrally invoke it. Nevertheless, we will suggest that each of the disputes between contextualists and invariantists tend to be characterized by considerable methodological disputes about what epistemology is or how to motivate an epistemological theory.

Of course, these are complex and preliminary answers. One reason why the questions do not admit of simple and conclusive answers is the noted one that both contextualists and their opponents tend to discuss methodological considerations in tandem with first-order substantive epistemological questions. So, while many contextualist writings contain meditations on matters methodological, the key methodological commitments of contextualists must be articulated by juxtaposing these remarks with critical reflections on the contextualists' *practice*. That is, the contextualist methodologies may to some extent be arrived at by "backward engineering" from considerations on how contextualists go about arguing for the view, responding to criticism and so forth.

In consequence, we will consider three modes of motivation in turn: the method of cases (Section 3), the appeal to linguistic analogies (Section 4) and the appeal to conceptual analogies and functional roles (Section 5). We will then consider the methodological debates arising from experimental philosophy (Section 6) and conclude by answering Q1 and Q2 (Section 7). An advantage of this *modus operandi* is that it will also serve as an overview of the dominant methodological approaches of various contextualists.

3 The method of cases and the methodology of the straightforward

The most prominent way of motivating contextualism is by appeal to case pairs with the following structure: every factor that epistemologists have traditionally taken to be a partial determiner of whether knowledge-ascribing sentences are true is held fixed, but aspects of the speaker's conversational context vary between the cases (DeRose 1995, 2009; Cohen 1999). These factors

Does contextualism hinge on a methodological dispute?

may involve what is at stake, or what error-possibilities are salient, or both. For example, DeRose's bank cases involve the case LOW in which there is a first-person knowledge ascription in a conversational context where little is at stake and which does not mention any alternative to the complement clause of the knowledge ascription. This is contrasted with a case, HIGH, in which there is a first-person knowledge denial in a high-stakes case with a conversationally salient alternative (DeRose 1995, 2009: 1ff).

DeRose claims that ordinary speakers deem the knowledge ascription true in LOW and that they also deem the knowledge denial true in HIGH. He claims that "where the contextualist's cases are well chosen, those are fairly strong intuitions about the cases, at least where each case is considered individually" (DeRose 2009: 49; see also DeRose 2005). Thus, the motivation by cases involves appealing to our intuitive judgments about knowledge ascriptions in isolation and to assumptions about "how speakers in fact, and with propriety, use the claims in question" (DeRose 2009: 50). According to DeRose (2009),

> This 'methodology of the straightforward', as we may call it, takes very seriously the simple positive and negative claims speakers make utilizing the piece of language being studied, and puts a very high priority on making those natural and appropriate straightforward uses come out true, at least when that use is not based on some false belief the speaker has about some underlying matter of fact. Relatively little emphasis is then put on somewhat more complex matters, like what metalinguistic claims speakers will make and how they tend to judge how the content of one claim compares with another (e.g. whether one claim contradicts another).
>
> *(153)*

DeRose is cautious to mention that his attraction to the methodology of the straightforward requires that "its favoring of simple data is not taken too far" (2009: 153). Yet the methodology of the straightforward may be criticized. For example, it may be challenged on empirical grounds whether ordinary speakers in fact speak in this manner. We will consider this line of criticism in Section 6. However, the methodology of the straightforward may also be criticized from a more reflective standpoint. For example, it might be questioned whether it is reasonable to consider the positive and negative knowledge ascriptions in isolation. In many cases, comparative judgments allow us to see flaws in our initial judgments. The idea that it is methodologically more sound to reflect on comparative judgments than to rely on intuitive judgments in isolation is related to one of the most tenacious substantive problems for contextualism – namely, the problem of disagreement: If Ali in HIGH utters "S knows that p" and Adam in HIGH utters "S does not know that p" they appear to disagree and, indeed, to contradict each other (MacFarlane 2014). Importantly, this appearance does not appear to go away on reflection, as one would expect if it were simply due to the two knowledge ascriptions expressing different propositions (Rysiew 2001; see DeRose 2009 for a response). But critics argue that it is methodologically more sound to rely on reflective judgments about both utterances than on intuitive judgments about the utterances in isolation (Nagel 2010; Gerken 2012, forthcoming: ch. 3).

Consequently, non-skeptical invariantists attempt to cast doubt on the reliability of the intuitive judgment that the knowledge denial is true. One strategy consists in arguing that the utterance in HIGH is false but felicitous in virtue of pragmatically conveying something true or appropriate (Dretske 1981; Rysiew 2001; Brown 2006; Bach 2008, 2010; Hazlett 2009; Pritchard 2010). Another response, which reflects the idea that we should rely on *reflective comparative judgments* rather than on *intuitive isolated judgments*, consists in postulating that the intuitive judgments in HIGH are false due to a cognitive bias (Nagel 2008, 2010; Gerken 2012, 2013; Turri 2015).

We will not here canvass the legitimacy of these strategies. What we want to highlight is how they reflect an important methodological alternative to the methodology of the straightforward. Critics of contextualism tend to argue that contextualists' reliance on intuitive judgments about cases in isolation is methodologically suspect because more reflective comparative judgments are a better basis for epistemological theorizing. Contextualists may respond that such an approach may just amount to presupposing non-skeptical invariantism and diverge from how "knows" is actually used. To this, invariantists may respond that our ordinary talk reflects the pragmatic or psychological effects that they postulate. So, the methodological discussion and substantive arguments are often interwoven. Thus, the methodology of the straightforward and the invariantist alternative may reasonably be said to underlie the substantive debates about the plausibility of contextualism.

However, it is important to recognize that contextualists do not rely *exclusively* on the methodology of the straightforward. For example, DeRose (1995, 2009), Lewis (1996), Cohen (1999), and Blome-Tillmann (2009, 2014) all argue that it is a theoretical advantage of contextualism that it can (dis)solve skeptical problems. Nevertheless, we think that the methodology of the straightforward is primary in two important senses. First, contextualism is a semantic thesis about the truth conditions of "knows," and in consequence it must be given a linguistic (use-based) motivation. Second, since we do not want to (dis)solve skeptical paradoxes by a *false* semantic theory, the putative ability to resolve skeptical paradoxes is secondary to independently motivating the semantic theory.

Finally, we want to acknowledge approaches to LOW-HIGH cases that rely less on intuitive judgments. Several contextualists argue that contextualism provides the best answer to a question raised by commitment to non-skeptical fallibilism (Lewis 1996; Cohen 1999; Blome-Tillmann 2014; see Brown 2013 for discussion): how good an epistemic position must S be in for it to be true to assert that S knows that *p*? The contextualist argues that there is a reason why invariantists have failed to answer this question. The reason, according to contextualism, is that the required epistemic position depends on the conversational context. *Given* this answer, reflection on the LOW-HIGH cases may be seen as augmenting this theoretical move rather than as providing self-standing "data" that a theory must account for. So, while the methodology of the straightforward remains a prominent contextualist methodology underlying the appeal to LOW-HIGH case pairs, it may not be *required* in appeals to such cases in motivating contextualism. In fact, some contextualists do not seem to rely on it. If the methodology of the straightforward is merely prominent but not always relied upon, we should answer Q1 in the negative. On this note, let's consider a *prima facie* distinct methodological approach.

4 Linguistic analogies

An important line of motivation for contextualism has gone via linguistic analogies to other areas of language. A number of linguistic analogs have been suggested (see Part VI of this volume), but here we will only briskly discuss two prominent candidates: gradable adjectives and universal domain restriction (see Cohen 1999; DeRose 2009 for the former and Lewis 1996 for the latter).

Cohen presents the analogy with gradable adjectives as follows:

> Many, if not most, predicates in natural language are such that the truth-value of sentences containing them depends on contextually determined standards, e.g. 'flat', 'bald', 'rich', 'happy', 'sad'. . . . These are all predicates that can be satisfied to varying degrees and that can also be satisfied simpliciter. So, e.g., we can talk about one surface being flatter than another and we can talk about a surface being flat simpliciter. For predicates of this kind, context will determine the degree to which the predicate must be satisfied

Does contextualism hinge on a methodological dispute?

in order for the predicate to apply simpliciter. So the context will determine how flat a surface must be in order to be flat.

(1999: 60)

Thus, Cohen and other contextualists suggest that gradable adjectives such as "flat" or "rich" provide a semantic model for "knows." Just as conversational context determines how much money it takes for the sentence "S is rich" to be true, conversational context is said to partly determine how much justification it takes for the sentence "S knows that *p*" to be true. If the analogy with gradable adjectives holds, the fact that a class of terms exhibit a semantic structure similar to that postulated for "knows" may help to embed contextualism in existing semantic frameworks. This, in turn, may serve as a potential response to the objection that the contextualist semantics for "knows" is an epistemological invention with no parallels in natural language.

Quantifier domain restriction provides another candidate linguistic analogy for "knows." This approach most naturally takes place in a *relevant alternatives* framework according to which S knows that *p* only if S can rule out every relevant alternative to *p*. The term "every" is context-sensitive insofar as the domain of its application is partly determined by conversational context. When Lewis (1996) says "all the glasses are empty," he refers to all the glasses at the table, not all the glasses in the bar, and much less all the glasses in the world. By analogy, the term "knows" is said to be context-sensitive insofar as the size of the set of alternative possibilities that is *relevant* is partly determined by conversational context. In Lewis' memorable phrase: "S *knows* that *p* iff S's evidence eliminates every possibility in which not-*p* – Psst! – except for those possibilities that we are properly ignoring" (Lewis 1996: 554; emphasis in original; see Blome-Tillmann 2009, 2012, 2014; Ichikawa 2011 for developments).

The opposition takes several forms. From a methodological perspective, one brand of invariantist opposition to contextualism "plays along" and adopts the methodological assumptions underlying the appeal to linguistic analogies. Such anti-contextualists seek to argue that there are important asymmetries between "knows" and the linguistic models that contextualists invoke. Stanley – an interest-relative invariantist – argues that "knows" is not gradable (Stanley 2005; see Blome-Tillmann 2014 or ch. 27 of this volume for a response). Similarly, some opponents of contextualism argue that there are linguistic differences between the behavior of "knows" and other forms of quantified domain restriction. For example, Stanley argues that the standards for "knows" are more easily raised than lowered whereas the domain restriction on many quantifiers does not exhibit a similar asymmetry (2005: 65). But since those are arguments postulating linguistic disanalogies, they are not at odds with the basic methodology of considering linguistic analogies. An example of a non-invariantist who is also seeking to beat contextualists on their own linguistic turf is MacFarlane (2014), who serves up a bowl of linguistic data to argue that relativism is superior to contextualism. We take it that the opponents of contextualism who engage in disputes over the linguistic data *accept* that such data are methodologically appropriate for epistemological theorizing.

Another line of opposition, however, is characterized by resistance to the idea that linguistic analogies are methodologically appropriate for epistemological theorizing. Sometimes this line of resistance is articulated as the charge that contextualists are changing the topic or, in Kornblith's (2000) gloss, "evading epistemology." One version of this response does not object to contextualism or its motivation. Rather, it consists in holding that an account of the truth-conditions of the term "knows" does not tell us anything of epistemological substance (for a contextualist response to such worries, see DeRose 2009).

A related complaint pertains to the contextualist (dis)solution of skeptical paradoxes (Feldman 1999, 2001, 2004; Klein 2000, 2015; Kornblith 2000; Sosa 2000, 2007; Conee 2005; Bach 2010). According to this complaint, the contextualist solution is too concessive insofar as we want an account of how "S knows that p" is true in a skeptical context. Contextualists are seen as shying away from the desired solution to the skeptical paradox that consists in indicating which premise is false in favor of a semantic dissolution. Of course, such complaints have been met with responses by contextualists – most elegantly by Lewis, who argues that this sort of complaint is methodologically misguided because it presupposes that the skeptical paradox has a solution that may be asserted (Lewis 1996; see Blome-Tillmann 2014 for a development that is designed to be less concessive to skepticism).

How do these considerations bear on our two methodological questions? With regard to Q1, the question as to whether there is a specific methodology that is centrally invoked by all contextualists, the considerations suggest that it should be answered in the negative. After all, the arguments from linguistic analogies are at least independent from the arguments from cases and *vice versa*. With regard to Q2, the answer is less clear. On the one hand, one strand of resistance to arguments from linguistic analogies is overtly methodological insofar as it consists in holding that such arguments are irrelevant for the purpose of *epistemological theorizing*. On the other hand, another strand of opposition appears to accept the methodology but seeks to beat contextualists on their own terms. However, this latter group may differ methodologically in how they assess the linguistic evidence. For example, contextualists may regard "knows" as a *species* of a gradable term with some distinctive features, whereas opponents take these features to suggest that "knows" is not a gradable term at all. So, the cases of linguistic analogy are to a significant extent shaped and influenced by underlying methodological disagreements.

5 Conceptual genealogies and functional roles

Another way of motivating contextualism appeals to assumptions about the social functional roles of "knows" in order to reach conclusions about its semantics. This broad approach is often – although not invariably – inspired by Craig.

Craig (1986, 1990, 2007) pursues what he calls a conceptual *synthesis*, which differs from a conceptual *analysis* in that it does not pursue necessary and sufficient conditions for the application of the concept of knowledge. Rather, a conceptual synthesis characterizes the concept of knowledge via "practical explication" of the *social functions* of knowledge ascriptions. Craig does so via a genealogical methodology which he characterizes as follows:

> We take some prima facie plausible hypothesis about what the concept of knowledge does for us, what its role in our life might be, and then ask what a concept having that role would be like, what conditions would govern its application.
>
> *(1990: 2)*

According to Craig, the conceptual synthesis is genealogical and has two stages. The first stage accounts for how an ancestor to the concept of knowledge came about in what Craig (1990) labels an "epistemic state of nature." Kusch (2009, 2011) labels this precursor the concept of "protoknowledge." The epistemic state of nature is an imaginary early, social community of language-using humans who cooperate and therefore need to depend on each other as informants. Hence, these humans need a concept to identify reliable informants, and Craig suggests that the concept of protoknowledge serves this function (1990: 11). According to Craig the features of a good informant are the following:

(1) He should be accessible to me here and now.
(2) He should be recognizable by me as someone likely to be right about p.

Does contextualism hinge on a methodological dispute?

(3) He should be as likely to be right about *p* as my concerns require.
(4) Channels of communication between me and him should be open.

(1990: 85)

These features are highly contextualized. But they characterize a concept that is very different from our present concept of knowledge. Consequently, the second stage of Craig's genealogy postulates a "process of objectivisation" during which the contextual aspects of the precursor concept are replaced with objective ones. The end-result is our concept of knowledge. For example, the requirement, (3), that the protoknower should be as likely to be right about *p* as the inquirer's concerns require is said to be "objectivized away." Indeed it is replaced with a reliability requirement according to which a knower must be: "someone with a very high degree of reliability, someone who is very likely to be right – for he must be acceptable even to a very demanding inquirer" (Craig 1990: 91).

Contemporary theorists adopt select ideas of Craig's proposal to motivate varieties of contextualism (Greco 2007, 2012; Henderson 2009, 2011; Hannon 2013, 2015; McKenna 2013, 2014). It should be noted, however, that many of these theorists part ways with Craig's specific genealogical approach in favor of a broader appeal to the functional roles of knowledge ascriptions. However, the key idea that the function of knowledge ascriptions serve to flag reliable informants continues to figure centrally.

For example, Henderson's (2009, 2011) "gate-keeping contextualism" appeals to Craig's idea that knowledge ascriptions serve the central function of gate-keeping sources in a social epistemic community. Crucially, Henderson assumes that the *semantics* constitutive of the concept turns on this function:

> To say that a concept arose with "a constitutive eye to" the demands of successful practice, and that what makes for success there is central to the "core conception" of the concept, is to say that the semantics constitutive of the concept turn on what makes for such success . . .

(2011: 86)

Given such an assumption and the further assumption that it is a contextual matter whether it is reasonable to certify S as a good source of information, contextualism may be motivated by genealogical considerations. Various theorists have pursued variations of this line of reasoning. For example, Greco argues that it is "the relevant practical reasoning environment" which determines the context in question and therefore the context may be that of the attributor, the subject, or someone else (2008: 433). Henderson (2011) emphasizes that since a potential source is assessed for general purposes, there is some stability to the contextual variance. Likewise, Hannon (2015) seeks to "stabilize" the content of knowledge ascriptions so as to allow for a restricted contextual variance with practical factors. Because space dictates that we set aside differences between the proponents of this broad strategy, we will restrict our more critical assessment to Craig's approach (but see Gerken 2015, forthcoming).

The genealogical approach is often rejected on the grounds that Craig's genealogy and imaginary "epistemic state of nature" are overly speculative and empirically unconstrained (Gelfert 2011; Kelp 2011; Kornblith 2011; Beebe 2012). This way of objecting to Craig's methodology is especially damaging to appeals to it in motivating contextualism. After all, contextualism purports to be a semantics of *our* term "knowledge." So, if the genealogy is at odds with the best empirical theories of conceptual development, why should we think it bears on our concept of knowledge and, by extension, on the semantics of "knowledge"?

87

This line of objection questions the genealogical methodology and its capacity to motivate contextualism. As such, it exemplifies how the debate between contextualists and invariantists reflects a debate about philosophical methodology. This suggests an affirmative answer to Q2, the question as to whether the dispute between contextualists and invariantists hinges on a methodological dispute. On the other hand, opponents to contextualism do not *have* to reject the genealogical method. Indeed, invariantists may challenge the genealogical motivation of contextualism on Craigian grounds. For example, it may be noted that Craig only claims that the *ancestor* concept is heavily contextualized, not that our present day *objectivized* concept is (Gerken forthcoming). If so, invariantists may accept Craig's genealogical considerations by arguing that they do not on reflection motivate contextualism. Thus, invariantist criticism is, at least in principle, compatible with genealogical methodology. So, on balance the debates over genealogical motivations of contextualism suggest a more guarded answer to Q2: while the dispute between contextualists and invariantists often reflects an underlying methodological dispute, it need not do so.

With regard to Q1, the question as to whether contextualism has a distinctive methodology or set of principles in common, the discussion suggests a negative answer. After all, Craig's conceptual synthesis and genealogical method is a highly unorthodox and distinctive alternative to existing methodologies. So, since the genealogical method is a novel way to motivate contextualism, contextualists are not committed to a particular methodology. Moreover, the fact that contextualists often appeal to functional role without invoking genealogies provides evidence for a plurality of contextualist methods.

6 The challenge from experimental philosophy

As discussed in Section 3, a prominent way of motivating contextualism includes an empirical claim concerning ordinary linguistic practice. As DeRose puts it: "what ordinary speakers will count as 'knowledge' in some non-philosophical contexts they will deny is such in others" (2009: 47). One type of challenge to contextualism deploys experimental techniques to scrutinize this specific claim. Another type of challenge targets more general reliance on intuitive judgments concerning cases in support of this empirical claim. We will consider these challenges in reverse order.

Part of the support for the contextualist's empirical claim stems from intuitive judgments about cases. Some experimental philosophers challenge this line of support by arguing that any epistemically significant reliance on intuitive judgments is illegitimate. They cite several grounds for this assessment. For example, some argue that intuitive judgments are unreliable (Weinberg *et al.* 2001; Nichols *et al.* 2003). Likewise, experiments are taken to suggest that they exhibit sensitivity to irrelevant factors (Alexander and Weinberg 2014). It is also suggested that they are not susceptible to systematic error-detection and correction (Weinberg 2007; cf. Swain *et al.* 2008, but see Wright 2010 for a response). Such challenges are general, targeting not just contextualism but the traditional method of cases in general (see Knobe and Nichols 2008; Knobe *et al.* 2012; and Deutsch 2015 for helpful opinionated surveys). But there are also experimental challenges more specific to contextualism to which we now turn.

More in keeping with the "positive program" of experimental philosophy, the contextualists' empirical claim that ordinary linguistic practice with knowledge ascriptions varies with conversational context may be experimentally investigated. Several studies involving presentation of case pairs to non-philosophers failed to find support for a practical factor (stakes) effect (Buckwalter 2010, 2014; Feltz and Zarpentine 2010; May *et al.* 2010; and see Pinillos and Simpson 2014 for criticism). Consequently, Schaffer and Knobe raise the following concern:

Does contextualism hinge on a methodological dispute?

Strikingly, the results suggest that people simply do not have the intuitions they were purported to have. Looking at this recent evidence, it is easy to come away with the feeling that the whole contextualism debate was founded on a myth.

(2012: 675)

In reply, contextualists might invoke generic worries about experimental studies, such as worries concerning sampling bias (DeRose 2011). It might also be objected that the linguistic practice involved in producing survey responses is not appropriately representative of ordinary linguistic practice (Kauppinen 2007; Cullen 2010). One way to flesh out this worry is to distinguish *within-case* knowledge ascriptions (ascriptions made when in an actual case) from *about-case* knowledge ascriptions (ascriptions made when merely considering a description of a case) (cf. Gerken forthcoming: ch 2, following Fodor 1964, but see Saxe 2006). The relevant studies may measure about-case judgments, while the contextualist's empirical claim concerns within-case judgments.

Another generic worry about experimental technique concerns survey design. Pinillos and Simpson (2014) suggest that the studies producing null results lacked statistical power. Moreover, the formulations of the prompts used in these studies have been challenged. For instance, DeRose (2011) suggests that the details of prompts diverge too much from the best case for contextualism (but see Buckwalter 2014). Relatedly, though more broadly, differences in intuitive judgments may reflect nothing more than differences in how implicit background details of prompts are "filled in" by respondents (Sosa 2009, 2010). As both contextualists and invariantists have argued, stipulating details of a case is not always sufficient to eliminate this possibility (DeRose 2011; Rysiew 2011; Dinges 2016). Thus, respondents are presented with a non-trivial cognitive task, their completion of which remains opaque to experimenters. The worry, then, is that failure to ensure that participants consider the appropriate questions may threaten the reliability of such surveys.

Subsequent empirical work has begun to address these worries. Concerning the salient alternatives effect, Schaffer and Knobe (2012) presented respondents with prompts including salient alternatives that were more "vivid" (i.e. more salient). Their findings indicate a statistically significant salient alternatives effect on knowledge ascriptions (Buckwalter 2014; Buckwalter and Schaffer 2015). Further evidence for a salient alternatives effect is provided by experimental studies by Nagel and colleagues (Nagel 2010; Nagel *et al.* 2013). Their results have also been replicated (Alexander *et al.* 2014). Concerning the stakes effect, the picture is murkier. Taken together, various empirical studies (Pinillos 2012; Sripada and Stanley 2012; Hansen and Chemla 2013; Pinillos and Simpson 2014; Shin 2014) provide inconclusive but non-negligible evidence of a *practical factor* effect on knowledge ascriptions as distinct from a simple stakes effect. Although variance of stakes generates an effect in some studies, evidence suggests that it does so due to a connection to action (e.g. Buckwalter 2014; Shin 2014; Turri and Buckwalter *forthcoming*). This reinforces the impression of a complex practical factor effect that is driven by many moving parts rather than simply by stakes alone.

How does the debate over experimental philosophy reflect upon our two questions? As for Q1, the question as to whether contextualists centrally invoke a distinctive methodology, the debates suggest a negative answer. Some contextualists embrace experimental philosophy and seek to promote contextualism experimentally. For example, Schaffer and Knobe (2012) motivate a contrastivist version of contextualism (though Gerken and Beebe 2016 provide empirical evidence to the contrary). Other contextualists argue that experimental findings ought to have little impact on the assessment of contextualism (DeRose 2011). Likewise, some invariantists seek to compromise contextualism experimentally or by appeal to findings in psychology (Nagel 2008, 2010; Gerken 2012). But other invariantists are critics of experimental philosophy (Sosa 2007;

Brown 2012). So, contextualists and their invariantist opponents do not divide neatly into pro or con about experimental philosophy.

The ramifications of the experimental philosophy debates are less clear for Q2 – the question as to whether disputes about contextualism reflect methodological disputes. A hasty glance at the debates might suggest that experimental philosophers argue against the motivation for contextualism, whereas contextualists respond by questioning the significance of experimental work. But even our cursory overview reveals that such an impression is inaccurate. As noted, both contextualists and invariantists use experimental data to argue for and against contextualism, respectively. Likewise, both contextualists and invariantists have questioned whether experimental work should significantly impact epistemological theorizing. Furthermore, some apparent methodological common ground exists between some strands of contextualism and some strands of experimental philosophy – namely, the methodology of the straightforward. Recall that DeRose (2009) argues that the intuitive judgments should be prioritized by putting "a very high priority" on making them come out true; in contrast, comparative judgments to the effect that knowledge ascriptions in LOW and HIGH are contradictory should be given "relatively little emphasis" (for criticism, see Hansen 2014; Gerken forthcoming). Likewise, proponents of experimental philosophy's *negative program* appear to sometimes presuppose that laymen's intuitive judgments provide strong reasons to reject conflicting theoretical claims.

In consequence, the debates surrounding experimentalist challenges do not indicate a clear answer to Q2. They clearly raise a number of methodological disputes between contextualists and their opponents but without dividing them along neat methodological lines.

7 Concluding remarks

Let us sum up how the discussion of the various methodological strands bears on our guiding questions, Q1 and Q2.

Q1 is the question as to whether central methodological doctrines are centrally invoked by all epistemic contextualists. We take the diversity of the methodologies surveyed above to suggest that this question should be answered in the negative. For example, the appeal to an imagined genealogy is methodologically very far from arguments from linguistic analogies. Likewise, one might accept an experimental motivation for contextualism and reject the traditional method of cases as methodologically problematic. Consequently, we answer Q1 in the negative: *There is no distinctive methodological doctrine or set of methodological doctrines that is centrally invoked by all epistemic contextualists.*

Our discussion suggests a more qualified and reserved answer to Q2, the question as to whether the dispute about contextualism depends on underlying methodological disputes. In each case, we have seen examples of contextualists and their opponents who argue within a commonly presupposed methodology. On the other hand, we have also seen multiple and prominent examples of methodological differences that lie at the bottom of the first-order dispute. So, on balance, we are inclined to answer Q2 in a highly qualified affirmative: *The substantive dispute about the truth of contextualism very frequently, although not invariably, reflects an underlying methodological dispute.*

This concludes our very selective discussion. Both the first-order debates about contextualism and the meta-epistemological debates about proper methodology are bound to go on. We have sought to exemplify that each of these two levels of debate may benefit from considering it explicitly in relation to the other. Contextualism about "knows" is a fruitful case for meta-epistemology. Meta-epistemology may directly inform the first-order debates about the plausibility of contextualism.[1]

Does contextualism hinge on a methodological dispute?

Note

1 The authors contributed equally. Thanks to Daniel Greco and Jonathan Jenkins Ichikawa for helpful comment on previous drafts.

Literature

Alexander, J., Gonnerman, C. and Waterman, J. (2014) Salience and Epistemic Egocentrism: An Empirical Study. In Beebe, J. (ed.) *Advances in Experimental Philosophy*. London: Continuum: 97–117.

Alexander, J. and Weinberg, J. M. (2014) The "Unreliability" of Epistemic Intuitions. In Machery, E. and O'Neill, E. (eds.) *Current Controversies in Experimental Philosophy*. New York: Routledge: 128–145.

Bach, K. (2008). Applying Pragmatics to Epistemology. *Philosophical Issues* 18: 68–88.

Bach, K. (2010). Knowledge In and Out of Context. In Campbell, J. K., O'Rourke, M. and Silverstein, H. S. (eds.) *Knowledge and Skepticism*. Cambridge, MA: MIT Press: 137–163.

Beebe, J. (2012). Social Functions of Knowledge Attributions. In Brown, J. and Gerken, M. (eds.) *Knowledge Ascriptions*. Oxford: Oxford University Press: 220–242.

Blome-Tillmann, M. (2009). Knowledge and Presuppositions. *Mind* 118(470): 241–294.

Blome-Tillmann, M. (2012). Presuppositional Epistemic Contextualism and the Problem of Known Presuppositions. In Brown, J. and Gerken, M. (eds.) *Knowledge Ascriptions*. Oxford: Oxford University Press: 104–119.

Blome-Tillmann, M. (2014). *Knowledge and Presuppositions*. Oxford: Oxford University Press.

Brown, J. (2006). Contextualism and Warranted Assertibility Maneuvers. *Philosophical Studies* 130: 407–435.

Brown, J. (2012). Words, Concepts and Epistemology. In Brown, J. and Gerken, M. (eds.) *Knowledge Ascription*. Oxford: Oxford University Press: 31–54.

Brown, J. (2013). Experimental Philosophy, Contextualism and SSI. *Philosophy and Phenomenological Research* 86(2): 233–261.

Brown, J. and Gerken, M. (2012). *Knowledge Ascriptions*. Oxford: Oxford University Press.

Buckwalter, W. (2010). Knowledge Isn't Closed on Saturday: A Study in Ordinary Language. *Review of Philosophy and Psychology* 1(3): 395–406.

Buckwalter, W. (2014). The Mystery of Stakes and Error in Ascriber Intuitions. In Beebe, J. (ed.) *Advances in Experimental Epistemology*. London: Bloomsbury: 145–174.

Buckwalter, W. and Schaffer, J. (2015). Knowledge, Stakes, and Mistakes. *Noûs* 49(2): 201–234.

Cohen, S. (1999). Contextualism, Skepticism, and the Structure of Reasons. *Philosophical Perspectives* 13: 57–89.

Cohen, S. (2005). Contextualism Defended, & Contextualism Defended Some More. In Steup, M. and Sosa, E. (eds.) *Contemporary Debates in Epistemology*. Oxford: Blackwell: 52–62, 67–71.

Conee, E. (2005). Contextualism Contested, & Contextualism Contested Some More. In Steup, M. and Sosa, E. (eds.) *Contemporary Debates in Epistemology*. Oxford: Blackwell: 47–56, 62–66.

Craig, E. (1986). The Practical Explication of Knowledge. *Proceedings of the Aristotelian Society* 87: 211–226.

Craig, E. (1990). *Knowledge and the State of Nature*. Oxford: Clarendon Press.

Craig, E. (2007). Genealogies and the state of nature. In Thomas, A. (ed.) *Bernard Williams*. Cambridge: Cambridge University Press: 181–200.

Cullen, S. (2010). Survey-driven Romanticism. *Review of Philosophy and Psychology* 1: 275–296.

DeRose, K. (1995). Solving the Skeptical Problem. *Philosophical Review* 104(1): 1–52.

DeRose, K. (1999). Contextualism: An Explanation and Defense. In Greco, J. and Sosa, E. (eds.) *The Blackwell Guide to Epistemology*. Oxford: Blackwell: 185–203.

DeRose, K. (2004). Sosa, Safety, Sensitivity, and Skeptical Hypotheses. In Greco, J. (ed.) *Ernest Sosa and His Critics*. Oxford: Blackwell: 22–41.

DeRose, K. (2005). The Ordinary Language Basis for Contextualism, and the New Invariantism. *Philosophical Quarterly* 55(219): 172–198.

DeRose, K. (2009). *The Case for Contextualism*. New York: Oxford University Press.

DeRose, K. (2011). Contextualism, Contrastivism, and X-Phi Surveys. *Philosophical Studies* 156: 81–110.

Deutsch, M. (2015). Introduction. In Deutsch, M. (ed.) *The Myth of the Intuitive: Experimental Philosophy and Philosophical Method*. Cambridge, MA: MIT Press: ix–xx.

Dinges, A. (2016). Epistemic Invariantism and Contextualist Intuitions. *Episteme* 13(2): 219–232.

Dretske, F. (1981). The Pragmatic Dimension of Knowledge. *Philosophical Studies* 40: 363–378.

Feldman, R. (1999). Contextualism and Skepticism. *Philosophical Perspectives 13: Epistemology*: 91–114.

Feldman, R. (2001). Skeptical Problems, Contextualist Solutions. *Philosophical Studies* 103: 61–85. (A revised version of Feldman 1999.)

Feldman, R. (2004). Comments on DeRose's "Single Scoreboard Semantics". *Philosophical Studies* 119(1–2): 23–33.

Feltz, A. and Zarpentine, C. (2010). Do You Know More When It Matters Less? Philosophical Psychology 23(5): 683–706.

Fodor, J. (1964). On Knowing What We Would Say. *Philosophical Review* 73(2): 198–212.

Gelfert, A. (2011). Steps to an Ecology of Knowledge: Continuity and Change in the Genealogy of Knowledge. *Episteme* 8(1): 67–82.

Gerken, M. (Forthcoming). On Folk Epistemology. How we think and talk about knowledge. Oxfrod: Oxford University Press.

Gerken, M. (2012). On the Cognitive Bases of Knowledge Ascriptions. In Brown, J. and Gerken, M. (eds.) *Knowledge Ascriptions*. Oxford: Oxford University Press: 140–170.

Gerken, M. (2013). Epistemic Focal Bias. *Australasian Journal of Philosophy* 91(1): 41–61.

Gerken, M. (2015). The Roles of Knowledge Ascriptions in Epistemic Assessment. *European Journal of Philosophy* 23(1): 141–161.

Gerken, M. and Beebe, J. (2016). Knowledge In and Out of Contrast. *Noûs* 50(1): 133–164.

Greco, J. (2007). The Nature of Ability and the Purpose of Knowledge. *Philosophical Issues*, 17(1): 57–69.

Greco, J. (2008). What's Wrong with Contextualism? *The Philosophical Quarterly* 58(232): 416–436.

Greco, J. (2012). A (Different) Virtue Epistemology. *Philosophy and Phenomenological Research* 85(1): 1–26.

Hannon, M. (2013). The Practical Origins of Epistemic Contextualism. *Erkenntnis* 78(4): 899–919.

Hannon, M. (2015). Stabilizing Knowledge. *Pacific Philosophical Quarterly* 96(1): 116–139.

Hansen, N. (2014). Contrasting Cases. In Beebe, J. (ed.) *Advances in Experimental Epistemology*. London: Bloomsbury: 71–95.

Hansen, N. and Chemla, E. (2013). Experimenting on Contextualism. *Mind and Language* 28(3): 286–321.

Hazlett, A. (2009). Knowledge and Conversation. *Philosophy and Phenomenological Research* 78(3): 591–620.

Henderson, D. (2009). Motivated Contextualism. *Philosophical Studies* 142(1): 119–131.

Henderson, D. (2011). Gate-Keeping Contextualism. *Episteme* 8(1): 83–98.

Ichikawa, J. (2011). Quantifiers and Epistemic Contextualism. *Philosophical Studies* 155(3): 383–398.

Kauppinen, A. (2007). The Rise and Fall of Experimental Philosophy. *Philosophical Explorations* 10(2): 95–118.

Kelp, C. (2011). What's the Point of 'Knowledge' Anyway? *Episteme* 8(1): 53–66.

Klein, P. (2000). Contextualism and the Real Nature of Academic Skepticism. *Philosophical Issues* 10: 108–116.

Klein, P. (2015). Skepticism. In Zalta, E. (ed.) *The Stanford Encyclopedia of Philosophy* (Summer 2015 Edition), URL: <http://plato.stanford.edu/archives/sum2015/entries/skepticism/>.

Knobe, J., Buckwalter, W., Nichols, S., Robbins, P., Sarkissian, H. and Sommers, T. (2012) Experimental Philosophy. *Annual Review of Psychology* 63: 81–99.

Knobe, J. and Nichols, S. (2008) An Experimental Philosophy Manifesto. In Knobe, J. and Nichols, S. (eds.) *Experimental Philosophy*. New York: Oxford University Press: 3–14.

Kornblith, H. (2000). The Contextualist Evasion of Epistemology. *Noûs* 34(s1): 24–32.

Kornblith, H. (2011). Why Should We Care about the Concept of Knowledge? *Episteme* 8(1): 38–52.

Kusch, M. (2009). Testimony and the Value of Knowledge. In Pritchard, D., Haddock, A. and Millar, A. (eds.) *Epistemic Value*. Oxford: Oxford University Press: 60–94.

Kusch, M. (2011). Knowledge and Certainties in the Epistemic State of Nature. *Episteme* 8(1): 6–23.

Lewis, D. (1996). Elusive Knowledge. *The Australian Journal of Philosophy* 74: 549–567.

MacFarlane, J. (2014). *Assessment Sensitivity: Relative Truth and Its Applications*. Oxford: Oxford University Press.

McKenna, R. (2013). 'Knowledge' Ascriptions, Social Roles and Semantics. *Episteme* 10(4): 335–350.

McKenna, R. (2014). Normative Scorekeeping. *Synthese* 191(3): 607–625.

May, J., Sinnot-Armstrong, W., Hull, J. G. and Zimmerman, A. (2010). Practical Interests, Relevant Alternatives, and Knowledge Attributions: An Empirical Study. *Review of Philosophy and Psychology* 1(2): 265–273.

Nagel, J. (2008). Knowledge Ascriptions and the Psychological Consequences of Changing Stakes. *Australasian Journal of Philosophy* 86: 279–94.

Nagel, J. (2010). Knowledge Ascriptions and the Psychological Consequences of Thinking about Error. *Philosophical Quarterly* 60(239): 286–306.

Nagel, J., San Juan, V. and Mar, R. (2013). Lay Denial of Knowledge for Justified True Beliefs. *Cognition* 129: 652–661.

Nichols, S., Stich, S. and Weinberg, J. M. (2003) Metaskepticism: Meditations in Ethno-Epistemology. In Luper, S. (ed.) *The Skeptics: Contemporary Essays*. Aldershot: Ashgate Publishing: 227–247.

Pinillos, Á. (2012). Knowledge, Experiments, and Practical Interests. In Brown, J. and Gerken, M. (eds.) *Knowledge Ascriptions*. Oxford: Oxford University Press: 192–220.

Pinillos, Á. and Simpson, S. (2014). Experimental Evidence Supporting Anti-Intellectualism About Knowledge. In Beebe, J. (ed.) *Advances in Experimental Epistemology*. London: Bloomsbury: 9–44.

Pritchard, D. (2010). Contextualism and Warranted Assertability Maneuvers. In Campbell, J., O'Rourke, M. and Silverstein, H. (eds.) *Knowledge and Skepticism*. Cambridge, MA: MIT Press: 85–104.

Rysiew, P. (2001). The Context-Sensitivity of Knowledge Attributions. *Noûs* 35: 477–514.

Rysiew, P. (2011). Surveys, Intuitions, Knowledge Attributions. *Philosophical Studies* 156(1): 111–120.

Saxe, R. (2006). Why and How to Study Theory of Mind with fMRI. *Brain Research* 1079(1): 57–65.

Schaffer, J. and Knobe, J. (2012). Contrastive Knowledge Surveyed. *Noûs* 46(4): 675–708.

Schiffer, S. (1996). Contextualism Solutions to Skepticism. *Proceedings of the Aristotelian Society* 96: 317–333.

Schiffer, S. (2004). Skepticism and the Vagaries of Justified Belief. *Philosophical Studies* 103: 161–84.

Shin, J. (2014). Time Constraints and Pragmatic Encroachment on Knowledge. *Episteme* 11(2): 157–180.

Sosa, E. (2000). Skepticism and Contextualism. *Noûs* 34(s1): 1–18.

Sosa, E. (2007). Experimental Philosophy and Philosophical Intuition. *Philosophical Studies* 132(1): 99–107.

Sosa, E. (2009). A Defense of the Use of Intuitions in Philosophy. In Murphy, D. and Bishop, M. (eds.) *Stich and His Critics*. Chichester: Wiley-Blackwell: 101–112.

Sosa, E. (2010). Intuitions and Meaning Divergence. *Philosophical Psychology* 23(4): 419–426.

Sripada, C. and Stanley, J. (2012). Empirical Tests of Interest-Relative Invariantism. *Episteme* 9: 3–26.

Stanley, J. (2005). *Knowledge and Practical Interests*. Oxford: Oxford University Press.

Swain, S., Alexander, J. and Weinberg, J. (2008). The Instability of Philosophical Intuitions: Running Hot and Cold on True-Temp. *Philosophy and Phenomenological Research* 76(1): 138–155.

Turri, J. (2015). Skeptical Appeal: The Source-Content Bias. *Cognitive Science* 38(5): 307–324.

Turri, J. and Buckwalter, W. (forthcoming). Descartes's Schism, Locke's Reunion: Completing the Pragmatic Turn in Epistemology. American Philosophical Quarterly.

Weinberg, J. M. (2007). How to Challenge Intuitions Empirically without Risking Skepticism. *Midwest Studies in Philosophy* XXXI: 318–343.

Weinberg, J. M., Nichols, S. and Stich, S. (2001). Normativity and Epistemic Intuitions. *Philosophical Topics* 29(1&2): 429–460.

Wright, J. C. (2010). On Intuitional Stability: The Clear, the Strong, and the Paradigmatic. *Cognition* 115(3): 419–503.

7

THE PSYCHOLOGICAL CONTEXT
OF CONTEXTUALISM

Jennifer Nagel and Julia Jael Smith

1 Introduction

Philosophy is not the only discipline concerned with shifting epistemic intuitions. Psychology also studies intuitive impressions of knowledge, often with an eye to the ways in which these intuitive impressions can shift as circumstances change. Cognitive and social psychologists explore factors figuring prominently in the contrasting cases motivating contextualism, including rising and falling practical stakes, heightened self-consciousness, and worries about the possibility of error. In some cases, these factors are taken to distort perceptions of knowledge in the attributor, causing the impression of a shift in knowledge where no real shift in knowledge has occurred. In other cases, these factors are taken to have an impact on the subject's actual possession of knowledge, for example by raising or lowering the subject's confidence. Where attributor perceptions of knowledge march in step with variations in the subject's knowledge, there is no reason to consider a shift in perceptions mistaken, but such shifts may risk being misunderstood by theorists who are unaware of the subtle ways in which contextual circumstances change a subject's cognition. If the key claim of contextualism is that statements of the form "S knows that p" can express propositions differing in truth value for subjects matched on traditional epistemic factors (such as confidence and accuracy), philosophers need to be aware of the subtle ways in which these traditional epistemic factors can change, and be instinctively registered as changing, in response to changing circumstances. Equally, philosophers who are sympathetic to contextualism will want to know how it might be psychologically possible for us to deploy shifting standards in evaluating others.

This chapter reviews psychological work relevant to the attainment and perception of knowledge for subjects and attributors in shifting circumstances and discusses the upshot of this work for epistemic contextualism. One major body of relevant research is dual process theory, according to which there are two broad types of judgment, intuitive and reflective. Section 2 outlines the contrast between these modes of thought, highlighting features of the contrast that matter to the production and perception of knowledge in changing circumstances. Beyond this basic binary division, there are more finely graded divisions between more and less effortful ways of thinking. Because the cases motivating contextualism often contrast subjects who seem to need more or less information in order to make up their minds, epistemologists can benefit from reviewing the recent literature on variations in information search, as we do in Section 3. People make up their minds in various ways, sometimes deciding on the basis of a glance or a single evidential cue, sometimes after extended evidence collection. This section looks at the factors governing search termination, and in particular, at factors affecting the relationship between subjects' confidence and their information search behavior. The perspective of the attributor of knowledge is examined more closely in Section 4. Ordinary people track states of knowledge and belief intuitively, but imperfectly. This section gives a quick overview of empirical work on mindreading, or the capacity to attribute mental states, and then takes a closer look at the most-studied imperfection in mindreading, the bias of epistemic egocentrism. Epistemic egocentrism is a natural limitation in our evaluation of more naïve subjects. This robust bias in perspective-taking inclines us to project certain features of our own predicament onto others, even when we are well aware on reflection that this is inappropriate. It is possible that the bias of epistemic egocentrism explains some of the asymmetries in patterns of intuition motivating contextualism; Section 5 will examine this possibility, while also reviewing other ways in which epistemologists have tried to use psychological research to explain, and in some cases explain away, the intuitions motivating contextualism. A brief concluding section summarizes our findings and discusses questions for future research.

2 Dual process theory

Over the past forty years, a number of originally independent research programs in several branches of psychology have converged on the idea that there is a significant divide between two core ways of making judgments. Following Jonathan Evans and Keith Stanovich (2013), we will label these intuitive (or Type 1) and reflective (or Type 2) thinking. A cluster of characteristics is associated with each side of the contrast: intuition is said to be unconscious, low-effort, rapid, and holistic, while reflection is conscious, effortful, slow, and analytic (Evans, 2008). It is now increasingly accepted that the key difference between these two modes of thought is whether key processing occurs in working memory, which is always consciously accessible (Evans & Stanovich, 2013; Carruthers, 2015). To take examples commonly used to illustrate this contrast, the intuitive process of face recognition happens on the basis of geometrical calculations that are not consciously available; the reflective process of mental multiplication of two-digit numbers happens on the result of conscious sequential digit-by-digit operations. Because working memory has a limited capacity, when it is burdened with another task (such as reciting the alphabet backwards), intuitive tasks are relatively unimpaired but reflective tasks become very difficult.

The reflective mode of thought is engaged in hypothetical thinking, high-stakes thinking, and almost all exercises of negation (Strack & Deutsch, 2004; Evans, 2008). So, for example, in order to evaluate the truth value of the proposition "it is not the case that the Pope has just died," a sequence of thoughts is necessary: one needs to entertain the embedded positive proposition about the Pope's death, and then negate it. A question about the name of the current Pope, by contrast, would for someone with the relevant background knowledge simply bring an answer to mind without consciously accessible sequential thought. Some propositions involve operations which demand reflective cognition: "it is not the case that this is a cleverly disguised mule," for example, can only be judged reflectively. Other propositions ("this is a zebra") may be judged either intuitively or reflectively, depending on one's circumstances and motivations.

Ordinarily, shifts between intuitive and reflective thought are automatic and silent: we do not typically decide to think reflectively, or focus on which way we are thinking at any given time. Once a person has entered the reflective mode of thought and consciously entertained a particular content (for example, a scenario involving a painted mule), it will however take some time for this content to fade from working memory, and it will remain active as an input to one's thinking on any related question (Carruthers, 2015). As Section 4 of this chapter will explore in more detail, related questions could include not only one's own judgments about the animal, but also one's representation and evaluation of the judgments of others. The person who is now thinking reflectively about possible painted mules will go back to making naïve intuitive judgments about zebras (and about others' judgments about zebras) only when that possibility fades from working memory, and not at will.

The line between knowledge and ignorance seems to run orthogonal to the line between intuitive and reflective thought. Both automatic exercises of face recognition and effortful exercises of mental arithmetic are ordinarily seen as issuing in knowledge, but either type of process can also occasionally lead to error or mere belief. It's not obvious that intuitive judgments are generally made to a lower standard than reflective ones, or that they have any lesser claim to knowledge: indeed, given that reflective judgments are typically composed of sequences of intuitive judgments (for example, a sequence of intuitive digit-by-digit manipulations in reflective arithmetical thinking), the epistemic quality of reflective judgments presumably depends on the quality of underlying intuitive judgments. A switch from intuitive to reflective judgment may however bring with it a demand for different evidential resources to settle a question; the consequences of this point for contextualism will be examined in Section 5.

3 Search termination

The binary contrast between intuitive and reflective thought is not the only type of variability in judgment. Within the domain of reflective thought, we may engage in more or less extensive searching and weighing of evidence. In theory, we might continue searching and weighing evidence indefinitely on any given question, never reaching an answer. In practice, we need to stop at some point, typically without conscious deliberation about where that point will be. Indeed, if we always needed to preselect a stopping point before making up our minds on any given question, we'd be trapped in a regress of thinking about how hard we needed to think. Cognitive effort is, fortunately, governed by an array of instinctive mechanisms. Unsurprisingly, these mechanisms are broadly adaptive, reflecting the costs and benefits of evidence acquisition and accuracy (Payne, Bettman, & Johnson, 1993). We also seek more evidence when we are made to feel self-conscious about our choices, and when we anticipate needing to justify them to others (Lerner & Tetlock, 1999). Changes in perceived stakes have a natural impact on confidence, so high-stakes subjects need more evidence to make up their minds (Hausmann & Läge, 2008). Many theories about the relationship between confidence and knowledge have been developed, but it is fairly uncontroversial that, at a minimum, a subject needs to have made up her mind about p in order to know that p, and there is an objective psychological fact of the matter as to whether the subject has made up her mind on any given point. Some theorists – notably Keith DeRose (2009) – hold that the possession of knowledge may require higher levels of confidence than mere belief. Subjects with perceived high stakes also adopt (and are also instinctively expected to adopt) more elaborate and effortful decision-making strategies (McAllister, Mitchell, & Beach, 1979). Given that one's confidence and one's way of weighing evidence are traditional factors in knowledge, the contrasting high-stakes and low-stakes subjects in the scenarios taken to motivate contextualism are not typically matched on traditional factors, even when it is specified that they have the same evidence set in mind when making a judgment.

The relationship between stakes and evidence collection can be measured in several different ways. One influential research program describes evidence collection as driven by "variable confidence thresholds": depending on our environment, we will require a higher or lower degree of confirmation from our evidence in order to make up our minds; where decision problems have proved difficult, we come to require higher confidence in order to settle a question. According to this program, the level at which these confidence thresholds are set is something we ordinarily learn in decision environments, alongside our learning about environmental features. In a climate where accurate decisions can be made with fairly minimal search, we learn to stop searching for information fairly rapidly; where more exhaustive search is required for accuracy, we start to need much more confidence to make up our minds and call off the hunt for evidence (Lee, Newell, & Vandekerckhove, 2014). Empirical research into threshold-setting is carried out in controlled laboratory conditions where participants make hundreds of consecutive judgments, often with feedback on accuracy, and with evidence artificially manipulated to require various levels of evidence search to achieve accuracy in various batches of these judgments. It is an interesting and open question what works in practice as a "decision environment" for setting a confidence threshold, for the purpose of intuitive evaluation of epistemological scenarios. Taking as a baseline a friendly decision environment (a normal zoo, where the task is animal identification), merely imagining a hostile decision environment (a zoo run by practical jokers) may be sufficient to trigger a higher threshold and the craving for additional evidence. In any event, shifting confidence thresholds are part of the invisible psychological baggage of judgment: it is easy to see the overt cues on which judgments are made, and these are typically spelled out in the contrasting scenarios we are invited to evaluate, but we are also moved by inner factors controlling our sensitivity to those cues. Because confidence is a traditional factor determining whether someone should count as knowing, when epistemologists are deciding whether contrasting characters in epistemological scenarios are well matched on traditional factors, variable confidence thresholds should be taken into account.

4 Mindreading and egocentric bias

Intuitions about the presence and absence of knowledge feature prominently in our everyday social navigation: verbs meaning "know" appear in all natural languages, and the capacity to recognize knowledge in others develops early and is used often (Bartsch & Wellman, 1995; Goddard, 2010). Commonly labelled our "mindreading" capacity, the intuitive ability to attribute states of knowledge, belief, and desire is active not only in live encounters with other agents, but also in watching videos and reading scenarios about them: indeed, mindreading works the same way – and shows the same limitations – across these various platforms (Saxe, 2006). There is nothing peculiarly philosophical about having an impression that an agent in a story has or lacks knowledge; indeed, the pattern of intuitions taken to motivate contextualism can also be detected in undergraduates without philosophical training (Nagel, Juan, & Mar, 2013). Mentioning a possibility of error ("sometimes clocks are broken") very significantly tips an audience towards using "thinks" rather than "knows" in describing an agent's state of mind (for example, towards describing someone who glances at a clock as having just a belief, rather than knowledge, about the current time, even when it is stipulated that the clock is accurate).

Mindreading is an intuitive capacity in the sense that it performs calculations that are not consciously available to the mind reader: we watch another person move her hand towards an object, and we instinctively see her as knowing that the object is there, and as wanting it. In attributing those mental states we rely on some subtle combination of perceptible cues in the person's posture and orientation towards the scene; likewise, when we read a story about a person who is making a decision or statement, we register various features of his described predicament, actions, and assertions as relevant to whether he possesses knowledge or mere belief. To the extent that the line between knowledge and belief is drawn intuitively, even in highly novel cases, we have limited introspective access to the rules we follow in drawing this line. If it were introspectively obvious why we saw any given case as involving knowledge, we would not have such lively controversies over the reasons why we see shifting attributions in response to various pairs of cases – for example, over whether we are really responding to stakes, or to the salience of error possibilities. To discover what aspects of a scenario matter to knowledge attribution, it seems we have to experiment with a great variety of cases in which various factors are manipulated systematically. We also have to be alert to the limits of our powers of stipulation: we need to be cautious, for example, about taking the traditional factor of confidence to be set as equal across a pair of contrasting cases just by a stipulation that the subject in the second case is as confident as the subject in the first. If our intuitive attributions of confidence are naturally driven by behavioral cues such as whether the individual is seeking further evidence on a question, then we may instinctively register the searching agent as less confident than the settled agent, even if it has been stipulated that they are equally confident.

A further difficulty in relying on intuitive evidence is that intuitive mechanisms have various natural limitations: given the boundless variety of ways in which states like knowledge can be manifested, our mechanisms for the intuitive detection of knowledge need to make certain assumptions and take certain shortcuts. Just as our visual mechanisms can be tricked by various patterns of cues to depth, magnitude, and motion, producing visual illusions, so, too, our mind-reading mechanisms are subject to structurally similar limits, producing cognitive illusions. The deepest bias in mental state attribution is to assume one's own frame of mind as a default for others: known most generally as "epistemic egocentrism," this bias affects both children and adults (Royzman, Cassidy, & Baron, 2003; Birch & Bloom, 2004). There is an asymmetry in this bias: it impairs our evaluation of others who are seen as more naïve, but not our evaluation of others who are seen as better positioned than we are. The bias persists even in the face of forewarnings and incentives to cancel it, and even when we are explicitly aware that the agent we are evaluating does not share our privileged knowledge or concerns. The existence of this bias should raise concerns about the accuracy of our responses to ignorant high-stakes cases, for example, where it is stipulated that the naïve agent is in a life-or-death situation but unaware of this fact. Egocentric bias would incline us to expect such an agent to take more care or collect more evidence than his low-stakes counterpart, before making up his mind.

Epistemic intuitions are ordinarily generated to help us interact with other agents, making sense of their actions and assertions. It makes sense that epistemic intuitions can be elicited only by imagining the target agent as acting or asserting something: the question "does Smith know where his car is?" invites contemplation of a scenario in which Smith needs to drive somewhere, or a scenario in which he is asked about his car. Even if knowledge is a standing state of a subject that persists through sleep and inactivity, if we try to restrict ourselves to imagining Smith as silent and inactive, perhaps deeply asleep, it is hard to generate an intuitive answer to the question of whether he now knows where his car is. The need to imagine a concrete situation may raise problems for our readings of contrasting cases in which we evaluate what speakers say about an absent third party whose strength of epistemic position is supposed to be held fixed across the contrast. Keith DeRose's (2009) Lena cases may provide an example of this kind of difficulty. The cases concern an office worker (Lena), who has a modest amount of evidence that her co-worker (John) was at the office today: she has seen his hat on a hook in the hallway, and she has overheard a conversation suggesting he was present. Lena's epistemic situation is later evaluated by a colleague (Thelma) in a low-stakes barroom conversation about John's whereabouts, and by another colleague (Louise) in an interrogation with the police about a serious crime. When we think about Louise's predicament, as she is being questioned by the police about what Lena knows, she would naturally anticipate that a positive answer – "yes, Lena knows whether John was there" – would lead the police to interrogate Lena. In her low-stakes conversation, Thelma wouldn't need to imagine Lena under interrogation: she could instead ask herself about what Lena would be likely to say if she were also present in the casual barroom. If these contrasting cases naturally trigger us to imagine different types of scenario across the contrast – Lena being questioned by police in one case, Lena engaged in casual conversation in the other – then our evaluation of the knowledge attributions will be a function of our assessment of Lena's resources to make up her mind in those different scenarios. If we stipulate that in both cases Lena is not in fact considering the question of John's whereabouts at the moment, this does not ensure that we will imagine her walking along with her mind on other matters as we try to assess the propriety of various claims about what she knows. We may need to imagine her as acting or asserting something relevant to a proposition in order to get an intuitive sense of whether she knows it; if so, then we need to be careful about what attributors would naturally imagine her as doing or saying, when evaluating her from different perspectives.

5 Applications of psychological research to epistemic contextualism

Philosophers debating the merits of contextualism have engaged with psychological work in a variety of ways. To illustrate their differences, it will be useful to consider a case, drawn from Jonathan Vogel (1990). Smith accurately remembers having parked his car in the lot an hour ago; does Smith know that his car is parked in the lot? It seems natural to say that he does know. But when we make salient an alternative possibility – that many cars are stolen each day, and that Smith's car could have been stolen in the past hour – it seems natural to judge that Smith doesn't know that his car is parked in the lot. In this case nothing about Smith's epistemic position changes when the alternative possibility is introduced in the voice of the narrator, and yet mentioning the possibility of error affects the reader's intuition about whether he possesses knowledge. In general, we tend to think that a subject has less of a claim to knowledge when possible alternatives to the key proposition are mentioned.

Timothy Williamson (2005) and John Hawthorne (2004a, 2004b) have both argued that a form of bias known as the *availability heuristic* interferes with our ability to make an accurate judgment in cases in which alternative possibilities are mentioned. The availability heuristic is a phenomenon whereby we overestimate the likelihood of events that can be easily imagined and recalled (Tversky & Kahneman, 1973). When we are judging whether a subject has knowledge and alternative possibilities are mentioned, we overestimate the likelihood of these possibilities, which causes us to mistakenly judge that the subject lacks knowledge. However, the availability heuristic explanation is problematic for a number of reasons. The availability heuristic leads us to judge probabilities on the basis of ease (or difficulty) of recall or imagination, but it does not always inflate these probabilities: discussion of easy-to-imagine scenarios makes them seem more likely, but discussion of hard-to-imagine scenarios makes them seem less likely (Sherman, 1985). It is not clear that the problematic scenarios mentioned by epistemologists invariably count as easy to imagine, in the relevant sense. It is also not clear that a single explicit mention of any alternative possibility is enough to activate the availability heuristic; indeed, some research suggests that while extended exposure to a type of scenario (such as repeated media reports of airplane crashes) will increase one's estimation of its likelihood, a single mention of a scenario (for example, a novel situation involving tricky lighting) will have the opposite effect (Oppenheimer, 2004). Meanwhile, reliance on the heuristic is attenuated or cancelled if we are forewarned of it (Schwarz, 1998) or in conditions where we expect to have to defend our judgments to others (Lerner & Tetlock, 1999); it is unclear how so fragile a bias could continue to produce the intuitions driving skepticism and contextualism for forewarned participants in an epistemology seminar room. Lastly, even if it were the case that availability bias operated as

Williamson and Hawthorne propose, a more detailed explanation is still needed for why over-estimating the probability of alternative possibilities would make us more hesitant to ascribe knowledge (Nagel, 2010).

The bias of epistemic egocentrism has been offered as another explanation of the shift. Applied to the car case, if we are egocentrically evaluating Smith as if what is salient to us is also salient to him, we will mistakenly evaluate him as though he were also concerned about the possibility of auto theft. If we are imagining Smith as being actively worried about the possibility of theft, we will expect him to secure some evidence that tells against that possibility before arriving at the judgment that his car is parked in the lot after all. When Smith fails to collect this evidence, we see his judgment that his car is parked in the lot as being made too hastily or carelessly to count as knowledge. On this picture, provided that Smith can in fact know that his car is in the lot, our evaluation that Smith lacks knowledge is in error, since it is based on a representation of Smith's mental states that is the natural product of a mental state attribution bias, a representation that would not in fact fit the real mental states of a person who occupied the position Smith is described as occupying in the scenario (Nagel, 2010).

If the egocentrism hypothesis is correct, we should find that describing the subject as aware of the possibility of error, that it may not greatly alter how willing we are to attribute knowledge to him. If egocentrism already causes us to misjudge Smith as being concerned with auto theft, adding to the story that Smith is aware of the possibility of auto theft shouldn't change our assessment of what he knows. If the egocentrism hypothesis is correct, we should also find that if the subject is described as entertaining the possibility that he is wrong, this makes little difference to how willing we are to attribute knowledge to him. If egocentrism already causes us to misjudge Smith as being concerned with auto theft, adding to the story that Smith is in fact entertaining the possibility that his car may have been stolen should again not affect our assessment of what he knows. Alexander, Gonnerman, and Waterman (2014) test these two predictions, finding, as expected, no significant difference between participants' willingness to attribute knowledge in the relevant types of case. In addition, they observe a modest correlation between the degree to which participants saw subjects as sharing their concerns, and the degree to which participants denied that the subject possessed knowledge – again confirming that the effects of epistemic egocentrism are at play in accounting for our tendency to judge that subjects fail to possess knowledge in the relevant cases.

These findings offer some additional support for the egocentrism hypothesis. However, some lingering concerns with this line of explanation remain. First, in Alexander, Gonnerman, and Waterman's results, there is only a modest correlation between the degree to which subjects were seen as sharing the attributor's concerns and knowledge denials. This suggests that egocentric bias is only a part of the explanation for why we are inclined to deny knowledge when alternative possibilities are made salient, and that there are other factors at play that contribute to this particular pattern of intuitions. More problematic is the fact that, if the egocentrism hypothesis is correct, then we should judge subjects in the relevant cases not only as failing to know, but also as failing to be justified in their beliefs. If we judge Smith's belief as falling short of knowledge because we (mistakenly) believe he has formed it hastily or carelessly, it seems to follow that we should also see his belief as being unjustified for the very same reason. However, this prediction is not borne out: in cases where the possibility of error is mentioned, people typically perceive a subject as possessing justified true belief but not knowledge (Nagel et al., 2013).

A third psychological explanation involving variations in cognitive effort may provide a better way forward. Simple and familiar problems are typically handled intuitively, whereas complex problems – such as those including new situations, hypothetical scenarios, or involving a negated phrase – demand reflective thought, and more extensive evidence search. The routine judgment

Psychological context of contextualism

that Smith makes when he utters "I know my car is parked in the lot" on the basis of his memory of having parked it there twenty minutes ago would be arrived at heuristically, using a "low" strategy. Before the possibility of error is mentioned, an attributor who is seeing Smith's circumstances accurately will also most naturally judge that Smith knows his car is parked in the lot through a low cognitive strategy.

Descriptions of agents' situations that mention the possibility of error, on the other hand, characteristically contain the hallmark features that precipitate a higher cognitive strategy: the presence of a hypothetical alternative; an unfamiliar problem; often, too, the presence of negation. So it is quite plausible that the mention of the possibility of car theft causes the attributor to shift into a more effortful mode of thought – more effortful than the one used by the subject himself. We may indeed be saddled with this mode of thought as long as the problematic theft scenario remains active in working memory for us. When we are actively conscious of the possibility of auto theft, it is natural to feel that if we were in Smith's position, we could not know that the car is parked in the lot without collecting evidence that would rule out the possibility that it has been stolen. Now, when we are asked to evaluate whether *Smith* knows that his car is parked in the lot, we conclude that Smith doesn't know, because we use our higher threshold as a benchmark for evaluating Smith's reasoning (Nagel, 2011). Unlike the egocentrism hypothesis, the dual process explanation does not require that we think of Smith as actually engaging in more effortful thinking. It merely requires that we sanction Smith for failing to collect more evidence, or for failing to think harder about the situation, without seeing him as actually sharing our concerns. On this picture, we judge that Smith lacks knowledge because we believe that he has not collected the quantity of evidence that is necessary for knowledge in his circumstances; but importantly, we are still able to judge Smith's belief as justified, since we can still represent him as forming his belief through a low cognitive strategy which is perfectly natural for him given his circumstances. When we think about whether his failure to collect additional evidence might affect the justification of his belief, we can recognize that he had no special reason to think that additional evidence collection could be appropriate in this situation.

Drawing on many of the same resources from the psychological literature, Mikkel Gerken provides an alternate explanation for our tendency to deny knowledge when alternative possibilities are mentioned (Gerken, 2013; Gerken & Beebe, 2014). Gerken's *epistemic focal bias* account relies on two underlying principles: (i) normally, an agent processes a salient alternative possibility to a subject's knowledge that *p* as epistemically relevant, and (ii) normally, attributors form judgments about a subject's claim to knowledge on the basis of a prima facie reason that constitutes a limited amount of the total evidence (Gerken, 2013). The first principle is supported by the general phenomenon of *focal bias*: typically, we tend to give judgments that place undue weight on what occupies our focus, because we typically process what is salient to us even when what happens to be salient is irrelevant to the task at hand (Gigerenzer & Todd, 2000; Stanovich, 2009). The second "satisficing" principle is an epistemological specification of a more general observation prevalent in the psychological literature (H. A. Simon, 1955; H. Simon, 1990; Evans, 2008; Stanovich, 2009); namely, that we conserve cognitive effort in arriving at judgments by settling them on a basis of a prima facie reason before we have processed all the evidence. Given these two principles, it is possible to explain the shift in our intuitions about a subject's knowledge that occurs when a possible alternative is mentioned as a product of a bias that occurs when a contextually salient alternative possibility is in fact epistemically irrelevant.

On this account, when we are told that Smith's car could have been stolen in the past twenty minutes, we regard this information as epistemically relevant due to (i). Moreover, that Smith's car could have been stolen in the past twenty minutes without Smith's knowing it counts as a prima facie reason to think that Smith doesn't know that his car is parked in the lot. Given this prima facie reason, in accordance with (ii), we judge that Smith fails to possess knowledge. However, this conclusion is incorrect if the information that Smith's car could have been stolen is not epistemically relevant – as certain invariantists would maintain.

Unlike contextualists, advocates of the variable cognitive effort explanation and the epistemic focal bias explanation take the introduction of a salient alternative to be a red herring that is not in fact a relevant consideration when it comes to whether the subject is rightly said to know. On the variable cognitive effort model, introducing the salient alternative can change the attributor's frame of mind in a way that will make it harder for her to see the naïve subject as knowing: she is right that if Smith started to think about the possibility that his car had just been stolen, he would have to collect more evidence before making a judgment about its current location, but mistaken to evaluate Smith as if he shared her higher standard for evidence collection. On the epistemic focal bias model, the salient alternative is simply a distraction: neither Smith nor the attributor should contemplate the possibility of recent theft, in this case, and it would be a mistake to do so, either in thinking about the location of the car or in thinking about what Smith knows.

Both hypotheses provide psychological explanations that allow the strict invariantist to explain the patterns of intuition that have often been taken to support contextualism. But both hypotheses also require further epistemological commitments to complete the invariantist's argument. For example, the proponent of the epistemic focal bias account must supply a convincing story about why contextually relevant alternatives are not always epistemically relevant, and further details about what constitutes an epistemically relevant alternative. The invariantist proponent of the dual process explanation must provide a more complete story about when judgments formed through more and less effortful cognitive strategies constitute knowledge.

Although psychological explanations provide a promising framework for strict invariantists to explain the linguistic data that are often taken to support contextualism, these explanations could also admit of interpretations that are consistent with a contextualist's theoretical commitments. Consider the dual process explanation, for example. The contextualist might claim that cases in which we use higher cognitive strategies correspond to higher-standards contexts for knowledge attributions, while cases in which we use lower cognitive strategies correspond to lower-standards contexts for knowledge attributions, and that both kinds of contexts allow for true attributions of knowledge.

Nevertheless, psychological explanations of our intuitions about knowledge ascriptions in cases involving the possibility of error arguably undermine contextualists' arguments for the context-sensitivity of "knows" that rely on these patterns of intuition. For if psychological explanations of these patterns reveal that the intuitive data are prima facie equally compatible with both invariantism and contextualism, the burden of proof is on the contextualist to show why the context-sensitivity of "knows" is still the best explanation for this data, given that positing context-sensitivity here also demands a more elaborate semantics.

6 Conclusion and questions for future research

Thought experiments involve an interplay between what is explicitly stated in the scenario and the resources we apply to them. There would be no interest in asking a question at the end of a scenario which simply prompted one to repeat back one of the scenario's explicit stipulations; we enjoy a sense of discovery in our responses partly because we cannot always tell in advance how our intuitive mechanisms will respond. Epistemological scenarios don't need to stipulate overtly whether someone judges intuitively or reflectively, or what their evidence search termination points or confidence threshold would be; we have intuitive functions that do this work for us, automatically and silently. It is easy to overlook the significance of these silent factors when we

Psychological context of contextualism

are diagnosing the significance of our intuitive reactions to particular cases; however, it is important to take them into account when we are figuring out what these cases are telling us about our knowledge-ascribing practices, and (perhaps indirectly) about knowledge itself.

According to contextualists, our use of "knows" is governed by an appreciation of the target's "strength of epistemic position" (to use Keith DeRose's expression for the traditional factors of evidence, confidence, and the like), as measured against whatever epistemic standard is operative in the relevant conversational context. Our grasp of both of these notions can be improved by studying natural variations in judgment and evidence collection on the one hand, and natural variations and limitations in epistemic assessment on the other. To the extent that contextualism is motivated by patterns in ordinary language, exploring the psychological underpinnings of these patterns can help us see whether contextualism is the right way to explain them.[1]

Note

1 For helpful comments on an earlier draft of this chapter, we would like to thank Nathan Cockram, Jonathan Ichikawa, and Micah Smith. We would also like to acknowledge the support of the Social Sciences and Humanities Research Council of Canada.

References

Alexander, J., Gonnerman, C., & Waterman, J. (2014). Salience and epistemic egocentrism: An empirical study. In J. R. Beebe (Ed.), *Advances in Experimental Epistemology* (pp. 97–118). New York: Bloomsbury.

Bartsch, K., & Wellman, H. M. (1995). *Children Talk about the Mind.* New York: Oxford University Press.

Birch, S., & Bloom, P. (2004). Understanding children's and adults' limitations in mental state reasoning. *Trends in Cognitive Sciences, 8*(6), 255–260.

Carruthers, P. (2015). *The Centered Mind: What the Science of Working Memory Shows Us about the Nature of Human Thought.* Oxford: Oxford University Press.

DeRose, K. (2009). *The Case for Contextualism: Knowledge, Skepticism, and Context* (Volume 1). New York: Oxford University Press.

Evans, J. (2008). Dual-processing accounts of reasoning, judgment, and social cognition. *Annual Review of Psychology, 59*, 255–278.

Evans, J., & Stanovich, K. (2013). Dual-process theories of higher cognition advancing the debate. *Perspectives on Psychological Science, 8*(3), 223–241.

Gerken, M. (2013). Epistemic focal bias. *Australasian Journal of Philosophy, 91*(1), 41–61.

Gerken, M., & Beebe, J. R. (2014). Knowledge in and out of contrast. *Noûs, 49*(2), n/a–n/a.

Gigerenzer, G., & Todd, P. M. (2000). *Simple Heuristics that Make Us Smart.* New York: Oxford University Press.

Goddard, C. (2010). Universals and variation in the lexicon of mental state concepts. In B. Malt & P. Wolff (Eds.), *Words and the Mind* (pp. 72–93). New York: Oxford University Press.

Hausmann, D., & Lage, D. (2008). Sequential evidence accumulation in decision making: The individual desired level of confidence can explain the extent of information acquisition. *Judgment and Decision Making, 3*(3), 229–243.

Hawthorne, J. (2004a). *Knowledge and Lotteries.* New York: Oxford University Press.

Hawthorne, J. (2004b). Replies. *Philosophical Issues, 14*, 510–523.

Lee, M. D., Newell, B. R., & Vandekerckhove, J. (2014). Modeling the adaptation of search termination in human decision making. *Decision, 1*(4), 223–251.

Lerner, J. S., & Tetlock, P. E. (1999). Accounting for the effects of accountability. *Psychological Bulletin, 125*(2), 255–275.

McAllister, D. W., Mitchell, T. R., & Beach, L. R. (1979). Contingency-model for the selection of decision strategies – Empirical-test of the effects of significance, accountability, and reversibility. *Organizational Behavior and Human Performance, 24*(2), 228–244.

Nagel, J. (2010). Knowledge ascriptions and the psychological consequences of thinking about error. *Philosophical Quarterly, 60*(239), 286–306.

Nagel, J. (2011). The psychological basis of the Harman-Vogel paradox. *Philosophers' Imprint, 11*(5), 1–28.

Nagel, J., Juan, V. S., & Mar, R. A. (2013). Lay denial of knowledge for justified true beliefs. *Cognition*, *129*(3), 652–661.

Oppenheimer, D. (2004). Spontaneous discounting of availability in frequency judgment tasks. *Psychological Science*.

Payne, J. W., Bettman, J. R., & Johnson, E. J. (1993). *The Adaptive Decision Maker*. New York: Cambridge University Press.

Royzman, E. B., Cassidy, K. W., & Baron, J. (2003). "I know, you know": Epistemic egocentrism in children and adults. *Review of General Psychology*, *7*(1), 38–65.

Saxe, R. (2006). Why and how to study Theory of Mind with fMRI. *Brain Research*, *1079*(1), 57–65.

Schwarz, N. (1998). Accessible content and accessibility experiences: The interplay of declarative and experiential information in judgment. *Personality and Social Psychology Review*, *2*(2), 87.

Sherman, S. (1985). Imagining can heighten or lower the perceived likelihood of contracting a disease: The mediating effect of ease of imagery. *Personality Social Psychology Bulletin*, *11*(1), 118–127.

Simon, H. (1990). *Reason in Human Affairs* (1st edition). Stanford, CA: Stanford University Press.

Simon, H. A. (1955). A behavioral model of rational choice. *The Quarterly Journal of Economics*, *69*(1), 99–118.

Stanovich, K. (2009). Distinguishing the reflective, algorithmic, and autonomous minds: Is it time for a Tri-Process Theory? In J. Evans & K. Frankish (Eds.), *In Two Minds: Dual Process and Beyond*. Oxford: Oxford University Press, 55–88.

Strack, F., & Deutsch, R. (2004). Reflective and impulsive determinants of social behavior. *Personality and Social Psychology Review*, *8*(3), 220–247.

Tversky, A., & Kahneman, D. (1973). Availability: A heuristic for judging frequency and probability. *Cognitive Psychology*, *5*(2), 207–232.

Vogel, J. (1990). Are there counterexamples to the closure principle? In M. Roth & G. Ross (Eds.), *Doubting: Contemporary Perspectives on Skepticism* (pp. 13–27). Dordrecht: Kluwer.

Williamson, T. (2005). Contextualism, subject-sensitive invariantism and knowledge of knowledge. *Philosophical Quarterly*, *55*(219), 213–235.

8

WHAT ARE WE DOING WHEN WE THEORIZE ABOUT CONTEXT SENSITIVITY?

Derek Ball

It is as widely agreed as anything in philosophy that some words – "I", "she", "that" – are context sensitive, and it is as controversial as anything in philosophy whether some other words are – "knows" prominent among them. But what are we agreeing to when we agree that "I" is context sensitive, and what are we disagreeing about when we disagree whether "knows" is?

We all know an answer to this question: "I" is (and "knows" might be) context sensitive as a matter of its *meaning*; it is *semantically* context sensitive. But in the absence of further explanation, "semantics" and "meaning" are little more than labels for the problem: what does it mean to say that a word is semantically context sensitive?

Various kinds of answers to this and related questions appear in the literature: some rely on some pre-theoretical understanding of meaning – for example, what is said by an utterance of a sentence – claiming that a sentence is context sensitive just in case what is said by utterances of it varies depending on the situation in which the utterances are made; others say linguistics (hence semantics) is a branch of psychology, concerned with the operation of some bit of the human brain, so that the claim that a word is context sensitive must be capturing some sort of psychological fact; according to others, semantics aims at characterizing certain linguistic conventions (and is thus perhaps closer to a branch of sociology), so that the claim that a word is context sensitive must be capturing some conventional fact; and of course there are other possibilities. This chapter surveys a range of views about the aim of semantics and the nature of semantic fact, with an eye toward some relevant disputes about the nature of context and context sensitivity. I begin by setting out some presuppositions of the discussion; subsequent sections focus on the various views of semantics and their consequences for our take on context sensitivity.

1 Ground clearing

In order to keep this chapter to a reasonable length, I will focus on one kind of semantic framework in which the titular question can be posed: the framework of the "model theoretic" tradition,[1] according to which a semantic theory assigns semantic values – typically set-theoretic entities such as functions – to atomic expressions, and describes composition rules by which the semantic values of complex expressions can be determined on the basis of the semantic values of their component expressions and their syntactic structure. Work on context sensitivity in this tradition takes its cue from the treatment of context in Lewis (1970), Montague (1974a, 1974c),

105

and Kaplan (1977): contexts are ordered tuples consisting of (something like, perhaps *inter alia*) a world, time, and speaker;[2] and semantic values – or at least, one kind of semantic value, which we will call *characters* – are functions from contexts to entities of some other kind – for example, the character of a sentence might be a function from contexts to functions from worlds to truth-values.[3] (Because it is possible to be misled by terminology, let me reiterate that I am using "character" and "context" to pick out set-theoretic entities.)

My attention to theories of this kind is mostly for expository convenience; the questions we will consider would arise for most other frameworks that try to treat context sensitivity. But this sort of framework makes certain questions particularly natural and easy to ask. No one thinks that there is an interesting association in the world, independent of the theoretical activity of linguists and philosophers, between the word "I" (say) and a certain function. Functions are theorists' tools; semanticists are using them to represent something about language.[4] But what are they representing?

We can ask this question about semantic theorizing in general, and also about particular aspects of a semantic theory. The treatment of context sensitivity that we have just sketched has two main moving parts: the description of an ordered tuple (the context) with elements of certain kinds, and the assignment of characters as the semantic values of expressions. Our key questions will be about the representational role of each of these:

> **Context Representation:** What do the elements of context represent? What does it mean when we include a particular parameter (location, say) in the context?
>
> **Character Representation:** What does the assignment of a particular character to an expression represent about that expression?

These are the questions that I will sketch some answers to in what follows.[5]

2 The Meaning Perspective

What phenomenon does a semantic theory aim to represent or characterize? We have already noted that there are a variety of possible answers to this question. I want to begin with a relatively straightforward one. Prior to systematic semantic theorizing, we have various semantic concepts: meaning, reference, what is said (by a person or by an utterance), truth, and so forth. The *Meaning Perspective* has it that the job of a semantic theory is to systematize and explain facts about meaning in some pre-theoretical sense – for example, facts about what is said, or about the information communicated by an utterance, or about the truth and falsity of utterances. For example, Larson and Segal claim that facts about the "actual meanings that [. . .] expressions have", such as the fact that "The English sentence *Camels have humps* means that camels have humps" are "the primary data that we would want any semantic theory to account for" (1995: 2). And it is clear that Kaplan (e.g., 1977: 492–4) takes facts about reference and what is said by utterances to be among the facts that semantic theory must explain. (Kaplan introduces the term "content" as a synonym for "what is said" [1977: 500].)

A few clarifications are in order. First, the idea need not be that we are just systematizing our pre-theoretic judgments about some class of semantic phenomena. Plausibly, we should allow that our judgments can be revised in light of theory (for example, in the way judgments about what is said can be revised once one is aware of pragmatic phenomena such as implicature). Moreover, we should want more than a systematization of some data; good semantic theories *explain*. Second, on most conceptions of semantics, the idea is not that we explain *all* of the semantic facts. Rather, at least to a first approximation, we take for granted the semantic facts about atomic expressions, and use them (along with composition rules and syntactic structure) to explain semantic facts about

Theorize about context sensitivity

complex expressions such as sentences. Third, we have already mentioned other approaches to semantics, according to which semantics aims to describe facts about psychology, or about social convention. The proponent of the Meaning Perspective need not deny that facts about meaning in her preferred sense are ultimately psychological (or sociological, etc.) in nature; for example, she might claim that meaning facts are ultimately grounded in (or reducible to, or supervenient on) psychological facts, but still maintain that semantics is its own special science, for nearly all practical purposes independent of psychology (in much the way the study of economics is for all practical purposes independent of physics, even though [at least on a physicalist worldview] facts about economics are ultimately a matter of physics).

To fix ideas, let's suppose (with Kaplan) that our theory is designed to make predictions about what is said by utterances of sentences. ("I began my investigation by asking what is said when a speaker points at someone and says, 'He is suspicious'" [Kaplan 1977: 489].) The observation that motivates Kaplan's theorizing about context sensitivity is that what is said by one and the same sentence varies depending on the situation in which it is uttered. When I utter "I am hungry", what is said is that Derek is hungry; when Jonathan utters the same sentence, what is said is that he is hungry. In order to make predictions about what is said by an utterance of a sentence, we need more information about that utterance: in the case at hand, information about who made it. Let us call a situation in which an utterance might take place – either actual, located in space and time, or possible, the kind of thing that would be located in space and time if it were actual – a *concrete situation*. To a first approximation, contexts represent concrete situations. Following Kaplan (1977: 522–3, 546), we should distinguish sentences-in-contexts (or "occurrences") from utterances: utterances are speech acts, events that take place in space and time, while sentences-in-contexts are formal entities – something like an ordered pair of a sentence and a context. The natural (from the Meaning Perspective) idea that we are exploring is that sentences-in-contexts represent possible utterances.[6]

Let's try to fill in the details. We are considering approaches to semantics on which the semantic values of sentences are mathematical objects. One standard assumption is that what is said by a sentence in a context is represented by a function from indices – usually thought of as a possible world, or a tuple consisting of a possible world and other parameters – to truth-values; on the assumption that the index is just a world, it will be the function that maps a world to truth just in case what is said by the sentence in the context is true at that world, and to falsity otherwise. So the character of a sentence will be a function from contexts to functions from indices to truth-values. Context is an ordered tuple. We need this tuple to give us enough information to generate our representation of what is said. The question then is: what values can we assign to elements of the context to ensure that this is possible? In order to answer this question, we will have to say more about how our representations of what is said work.

3 Character and context from the Meaning Perspective

Our representations of what is said are functions from indices to truth-values. We will also assign functions (from indices to other entities) to sub-sentential expressions. All such functions from indices to other entities are known as *intensions*. The result of applying an intension to an index is an *extension*. The extension of a sentence is standardly assumed to be a truth-value; the extension of a proper name might be an individual. A fairly standard assumption is that the intension of a sentence and its extension at a given index are determined in a systematic way – in the jargon, *compositionally* – by the intensions of its sub-sentential components, their extensions at that index, and the sentence's syntactic structure (though see the discussion of monsters in Section 6 below).[7] (These components may include elements that are syntactically realized but unpronounced, and we will use the term "expression" to include these elements.)

107

We can take the syntactic structure as given. Since an intension, given an index, determines an extension, what we will need from context is enough information to determine the intensions of context-sensitive expressions. And in fact, it is typically assumed that we need less than this; on standard theories, the members of context are *extensions*: a speaker, time, world, and so forth. An intension determines an extension (given an index), but it is not typically the case that an extension determines an intension. (For example, if intensions are functions from worlds to truth-values, there are many intensions that map the actual world to Truth.) But context-sensitive expressions are usually held to be a special case. Intensions are needed to make sense of the behavior of expressions in modal contexts, "belief" contexts, and the like. But familiar context-sensitive words are rigid designators: they are, or at least seem to be, unaffected by modal contexts. So it makes sense to give them constant intensions: functions that map every index to the same value. For example, the intension of "I" at a particular context in which I am the speaker might be the function that maps every index to Derek. If we assume that the intensions of context-sensitive expressions are all constant functions, then we can determine intensions on the basis of extensions: if the extension of a context-sensitive expression is e, its intension will be a constant function from indices to e.

With this in mind, there is a simple way to ensure that we have the information we need: we can simply let the members of context be the extensions of context-sensitive words. For example, if we are only interested in "I" and "that", the context might be an ordered pair $< a_c, t_c >$, where a_c is a speaker (i.e., the extension of "I") and t_c is an object (the extension of "that").[8] Call this the *Simple Strategy*.

The Simple Strategy is advocated explicitly by David Lewis (1970: 24, 62–5) and David Braun (1996: 161). And it may seem an attractive view from the Meaning Perspective. After all, the Meaning Perspective has it that our objective is to capture facts about some pre-theoretic notion of meaning such as what is said. In the case of context-insensitive words, it is not part of the job of semantics to explain how atomic expressions get their intensions and extensions. Why should the situation be any different with respect to context-sensitive vocabulary? We will return to some possible answers to this question momentarily; first, let's see how the Simple Strategy can be developed.

Character, on the Simple Strategy, is a function that maps contexts to constant intensions (which map every world to a particular parameter of the context); for example, the character of "I" will be a function from contexts to functions from worlds to the first member of the context. Formally, we can write:

(1) $[\![I]\!] = [\lambda c.[\lambda i.a_c]]$

(2) $[\![I]\!]^{c,i} = [\![I]\!] (c)(i) = a_c$

(Where $[\lambda c.[\lambda i.a_c]]$ is the function that maps every context c to a constant function from indices to the first member of c.)

Formally, the Simple Strategy is as simple as the name suggests. But what are we representing by describing contexts and assigning characters of this kind? The Meaning Perspective has it that we are representing facts about possible situations in which utterances might take place, and facts about sentences that enable us to make predictions about what would be said by utterances of those sentences in those possible situations. But the Simple Strategist's context will end up being a long and (depending on what context-sensitive expressions there turn out to be) diverse sequence of entities. In what sense does this represent a possible situation?

There is a straightforward way to represent a concrete situation – by giving us enough information to pick it out of the space of possibilities. This is the notion of context familiar from Lewis (1980: 28–9) and others: an ordered triple consisting of a speaker, time, and world; that is, $< a, t, w >$.[9] (Location, time, and world would work just as well for most purposes, but we will assume that the first parameter picks out an agent.) Call this the *straightforward context*. It is clear that the context as appealed to in the Simple Strategy is not the straightforward context. (If we had only a few context-sensitive expressions – just "I" or "here", "now", and "actual" – the Simple Strategy's context would just be the straightforward context. But even "that" makes things more complicated.) The Simple Strategy's context represents a speech situation indirectly by including the semantic values that various context-sensitive expressions would have in that context. Each member of the sequence corresponds to a particular type of context-sensitive expression; for example, the first member might correspond to "I", the second to "that", and so on.

This, then, is the Simple Strategy's answer to the Context Representation question:

> **Context Representation (Meaning Perspective/Simple Strategy)** Context represents a concrete situation by giving the extensions that context-sensitive expressions would have if uttered in that situation. Each parameter in the context corresponds to a particular context-sensitive expression in the language.

On the Simple Strategy, characters are trivial: they only point us to a particular member (the first, say, or the fourteenth) of the context. This works because we are assigning particular values to the parameters of contexts in a systematic way, depending on facts about the concrete situation that we are trying to represent. There is an interesting question here: why do we assign particular values to the parameters of the context that corresponds to a particular concrete situation? To answer this question would be in effect to give a metasemantic theory for context-sensitive expressions: an interesting project, but not one that the Simple Strategist needs to undertake as long as she can somehow give extensions for the expressions under study in a range of relevant cases.

The Simple Strategy will assign some expressions constant characters – functions that map every context to the same intension – and other expressions variable characters. If an expression is assigned a variable character, then that indicates that its contribution to what is said depends on the concrete situation in which it is used. And because intensions are a particular way of representing what is said, and characters are functions from contexts to intensions, characters are defined in terms of our representation of what is said. But characters themselves are doing little work; they serve only as formal devices to retrieve information from context. Simplifying somewhat to put the point bluntly:

> **Character Representation (Meaning Perspective/Simple Strategy)** Characters have no representational significance.

Now I want to turn to two objections to the Simple Strategy. The first objection is empirical: there are data that seem to be a matter of meaning in a pre-theoretical sense that the Simple Strategy just does not explain. The simplest sort of data has to do with infelicity. Suppose I gesture at my favorite chair and say, "He is comfortable", intending to refer to the chair (and not, for example, to make a deferred reference to a person who had been sitting there). Something has clearly gone wrong, and though one could argue about exactly what it is, it seems to be a matter of meaning of the sort that one might want a semantic theory to capture. Or, to take a subtler sort of example, Nunberg (1993: 34) points out that although "that" and "it" are in some respects very similar, it makes sense to say, upon seeing the face of a certain baseball player, "That's my favorite team," but much less sense to say, "It's my favorite team." Why?

The Simple Strategy has no resources to answer these questions. On the Simple Strategy, context delivers intensions and extensions for context-sensitive expressions, but does not explain how or why these expressions get the intensions and extensions they do. It therefore can offer no account of whether and when these expressions might have no intensions and extensions (or of what else might be going on, if the examples are problematic for some other reason). Note that the objection isn't that the Simple Strategy gets things wrong – one could set up contexts to deliver the right predictions here.[10] Rather, it is that the Simple Strategy is incomplete. Explanatory work is needed that the Simple Strategy is not well equipped to tackle.

The second objection to the Simple Strategy, due originally to Cresswell (1973: 111), trades on the fact that it is an open question exactly which words are context sensitive. If very many (or perhaps even all) expressions are context sensitive, contexts will become unwieldy; perhaps, if we aim to treat all possible context sensitivity in natural language, the list will become infinite. So the Simple Strategy threatens to make the task of stating a semantic theory difficult or impossible.[11]

David Lewis (1980) took Cresswell's objection to motivate a shift to the straightforward notion of context, and this clearly requires a corresponding shift in the view of character. Accepting the straightforward notion of context delivers a correspondingly straightforward answer to the Context Representation question:

> **Context Representation (Straightforward)** Context represents a concrete situation by giving information that would enable one to pick it out in the space of possible concrete situations.

As Lewis points out, if facts about a concrete situation determine semantic facts, and straightforward context gives us enough information to pick out a concrete situation, then straightforward context should give us enough information to determine semantic facts – we just need to engineer characters that can do the work.

What would such characters represent? One possibility is that they are representing facts about how an expression's contribution to what is said is determined. But this raises a question: more or less every expression contributes something to what is said, and (plausibly) in every case this is determined by facts about the concrete situation. So what is special about "I" and its ilk? Why do we assign proper names (say) constant characters, rather than characters that represent the metasemantic facts about how their contribution to what is said is determined (so that, for example, the character of "Derek" might be something like $[\lambda c.\lambda i.$ the object at the end of the causal chain that leads to a_c's use of "Derek" at t_c in $w_c]$)?[12]

One possible answer is that characters represent another pre-theoretic notion of meaning, one on which different uses of "I" have the same meaning even when they make different contributions to what is said. Although it is plausible that there is such a sense, it is not clear that it is precisely enough delineated to bear serious theoretical weight. (Do all tokens of "that" have the same meaning in this sense? Do they have the same meaning as tokens of "this"? If not, in what does the difference consist? What of unpronounced expressions, such as (on one view) restrictions on quantifier domains?) There seems to be a need for further theoretical work. A natural place to start is Kaplan's thought that character is a "semantical rule" (1977: 520). But there are different ways that this idea might be developed. We turn to these in the next section.

4 The Rules Perspective: psychology

Rules and rule following are extremely difficult and controversial issues in philosophy, especially in the context of semantics, and we cannot discuss most of the deep questions here. Instead, the aim will be to sketch some conceptions of semantics on which something worth thinking of as a kind of rule enters into the picture, and to discuss some ways these views might relate to controversies about context sensitivity and its representation.

Theorize about context sensitivity

The first type of view has it that semantics aims to capture something about the psychology of language users. On the most prominent version of this style of view (associated with Chomsky and his followers [e.g., Chomsky 1986: ch. 4]) the project is to capture what is represented in or by a certain psychological mechanism – to use Chomsky's technical term, what is *cognized*. In the case of syntax, the traditional view has it that what is cognized is rules, which recursively determine the grammatical sentences of the language. The natural extension to semantics would have it that what is cognized is rules that compositionally determine the semantic facts about sentences (e.g., Larson & Segal 1995: 9–12; Borg 2004: ch. 2).

There are a variety of ways of developing this kind of view. One strategy is to build on the Meaning Perspective. We often can come to know what is said by utterances in various circumstances. One task would be to characterize the psychological mechanism by which we do this. On the hypothesis that this mechanism works in a broadly computational way, the task would be to characterize the representations that are implicated in the functioning of this mechanism.

Another strategy would be to regard the project of characterizing certain mental representations as supplanting, rather than supplementing, the Meaning Perspective. On this view, pretheoretical notions of meaning are to be viewed with skepticism, as riddled with unclarity and imprecision of a sort that makes them unsuitable for serious theorizing. What is cognized is seen as a more tractable replacement for these notions. Exactly what sort of thing it is that speakers cognize should be treated as an empirical question. One hypothesis, naturally suggested by the psychological focus, is that semantics gives rules associating linguistic expressions with concepts (Jackendoff 2002). Another attitude is that we should remain agnostic on this question until more evidence is in (Yalcin 2014).

What might characters look like on this kind of view? The details may depend to some extent on exactly what we want to represent and how we want to represent it. To keep discussion manageable, I will focus on the view that we aim to represent the mental representations underlying our ability to determine what is said. Suppose we begin by assuming that we are working with the straightforward context. Now we might state the character of "I" in precisely the same way as before. But we are now thinking of this character as doing some representational work: speakers know that when someone uses "I" they are speaking of themselves, and the character of "I" represents this knowledge. This gives an answer to the Character Representation question:

> **Character Representation (Rules Perspective-Psychology)** Characters are a theoretical representation of the mental representations that underlie speakers' linguistic competence.

The contrast between the Simple Strategy and the psychological version of the Rules Perspective now under consideration is easier to see with context-sensitive expressions that do not relate in a simple way to an element of the straightforward context. Suppose that the referent of "that" is determined by speaker intentions. We want to describe what speakers know in virtue of which they can extract a word's contribution to what is said from a concrete situation. So the character of "that" might be something like:

(3) $[\![\text{that}]\!] = [\lambda c.[\lambda i. \text{ the object of } a_c\text{'s referential intention in } c]]$

We are now in a position to begin to answer the empirical argument presented at the end of the previous section. Consider the case where I attempt to use "he" to pick out an inanimate object.

Now it is a rule, which competent speakers cognize, that "he" cannot be used in this way. Suppose we decide that the consequence of such misuse is that nothing is said. We can represent this knowledge by making the character of "he" a partial function – i.e., a function that maps contexts in which the speaker-intended object is a human male to intensions, and that fails to map contexts in which the speaker-intended object is not a human male to anything at all. Formally, we can write (using the λ-notation as in Heim & Kratzer 1998: 34–5):

(4) ⟦he⟧ = [λc : the object of a_c's referential intention in c is a human male .[λi. the object of a_c's referential intention in c]]

What of Nunberg's observation that "that" allows deferred reference – i.e., in the case of a demonstrative, reference to something other than the demonstrated object, such as using a demonstrated player to refer to a team – but "it" does not? Nunberg suggests that demonstrated objects play a special role in the semantics of some context-sensitive expressions. For example, "that" picks out an object that is related in some intended way to a demonstrated object; demonstrated objects become "pointers to interpretations" (1993: 38). "It", on the other hand, has no use for a demonstration; as Nunberg points out, "You cannot point at one of the glasses of wine sitting before you at the table and say: 'Now *it's* what I call a good burgundy'" (34). Instead, "it" picks out an "object that is simply salient in the context or in the consciousness of participants" (33). The idea that "it" allows deferred reference therefore makes no sense, since there is no demonstrated object for reference to be deferred from.

Now one way to write down a Nunberg-style character for "that" would be:

(5) ⟦that⟧ = [λc.[λi. the object that stands in the relation that a_c intends to the object demonstrated by a_c]]

But this downplays the special role of demonstrated objects in Nunberg's system. For Nunberg, interpretation of context-sensitive expressions is a two-stage process: first, one must identify the features of the concrete situation that are pointers to interpretations, and then one must develop interpretations on the basis of these pointers. A perspicuous representation of what speakers know would separate these two processes, and the obvious way to do this is to make demonstrated objects parameters of the context that can be appealed to in specifying characters. (This would be particularly appropriate if we adopt the Chomskian hypothesis that there is a mental module or faculty dedicated to language, and the identification of demonstrata is an input to this faculty, not performed by the faculty itself.) For example, letting a context c be an ordered quadruple $< a_c, t_c, w_c, o_c >$, where a_c, t_c, and w_c are as before, and o_c is a demonstrated object:

(6) ⟦that⟧ = [λc.[λi. the object that stands in the relation that a_c intends to o_c]]

We have now developed the context beyond the straightforward context, but not in the direction advocated in the Simple Strategy. The context now provides whatever information the rules we are using characters to represent require. Because the aim is to give a better representation of the rules, call this the *Revealing Strategy*:

Context Representation (Rules Perspective-Revealing Strategy) Context represents a concrete situation by specifying those features of it that speakers need to use in applying linguistic rules.

Theorize about context sensitivity

5 The Rules Perspective: sociology

So far, we have been discussing views of semantics on which semantics aims to characterize facts about the minds of language users. Following Chomsky, some proponents of this style of view draw a sharp contrast with views of language that emphasize social aspects. But a number of theorists have sought to develop the view that language is a social matter – perhaps none more clearly than David Lewis (1983). On Lewis's view, the aim of semantics is to characterize certain social conventions. The semanticist must describe a mapping between sentences and propositions which is such that a speaker s generally makes an assertion using a sentence just in case that sentence is mapped to a proposition s believes, and when s hears an assertion made using a sentence, she generally comes to believe the proposition which that sentence is mapped to, and such that these facts are conventional.

It is a difficult question (and one that we cannot consider here) whether the characters of subsentential expressions play any representational role in Lewis's system (see Yalcin 2014: 39–42). But the characters of sentences can play a role in characterizing conventions (though, as Lewis [1980] in effect points out, this is not the only way the conventions could be described). Suppose for the sake of simplicity that an index is just a world. Then the convention might be: if a sentence S has character c, then one must utter S in a concrete situation represented by context u only if one believes the proposition represented by c(u), and if someone utters S in a concrete situation represented by u, one should believe c(u).

On this view, rules are thought of as describing conventions (rather than as describing the contents of certain mental representations). And this gives another possible answer to the Character Representation question:

Character Representation (Rules Perspective-Sociology) Characters represent social conventions.

6 Context-shifting, indices, and contexts of assessment

Our discussion throughout has tended to assume that contexts are in the business of representing concrete situations, and the discussion has proceeded as though we are thinking of this as a situation in which the expression we are considering might be uttered. But I have been deliberately vague in my "official" statements of answers to the Context Representation question because there are several factors that may complicate this picture.

First, a number of theorists have claimed that character and context also play a compositional role, because there are what Kaplan called "monsters": operators on character that shift the context at which expressions in their scope are evaluated. The idea would be that in addition to expressions like "It is necessary that", which have as their extensions functions from intensions to truth-values, there are expressions that have as their extensions functions from *characters* to truth-values. For example, Kaplan considers (but rejects) the possibility of an operator with the following semantics:

(7) $[\![\text{In some contexts it is the case that}]\!]^{c,i} = [\lambda s : s$ is the character of a sentence. $\exists c'.s(c')$
$(i^{c'}) = 1]$ (where $i^{c'}$ is the index determined by c'; see below for further discussion)

For example, an utterance by me of "In some contexts it is the case that I am hungry" would be true if and only if the agent of some context (not necessarily me) is hungry at the world of that context – i.e., if someone in some world is hungry.

113

It is debatable whether there are (or could be) monsters in English – Kaplan (1977: 510–2) claims that there could not be (though see Santorio 2012; Rabern 2013) – but a number of theorists have argued that there are monsters in other natural languages (Schlenker 2003). If there really are operators on character, it is unclear what we should regard contexts as representing. One possible view is that they play a hybrid role: when we begin evaluating an expression, context represents a concrete situation (i.e., that in which we are considering the expression as being uttered), but as we work through the compositional semantics of the expression, it can come to represent something different (perhaps an aspect of our psychological processing) as it is shifted by operators.

This leaves our answer to the Context Representation question muddled. But as Stalnaker (2014: 214–6) points out, there is an alternative. One can instead insist that context represents a concrete situation. This is in effect to stipulate a representational convention that makes monsters impossible. But one can capture the allegedly monstrous data by building further parameters into the *index*. We can then give the expressions whose interpretations are allegedly shifted by monsters constant characters, functions that map every context to an intension that points to the relevant parameter of the index. For example, we might let indices i be pairs of a world w_i and a speaker s_i, and define a shiftable "I" as follows:

(8) $[\![I_{shiftable}]\!]^{c,i} = s_i$

Then we could introduce an operator "In some indices it is the case that" which shifts "$I_{shiftable}$" in the way that "In some contexts it is the case that" shifted "I":

(9) $[\![$In some indices it is the case that$]\!]^{c,i} = [\lambda s : s$ is the intension of a sentence. $\exists i'.s(i') = 1]$

This would deliver the result that "In some indices it is the case that $I_{shiftable}$ am hungry" is true if and only if someone in some world is hungry, much like "In some contexts it is the case that I am hungry" purports to do. This gives us a mechanism that can make sense of seemingly monstrous data, even while we insist that contexts cannot shift (since the representational role of context is such that context shifting makes little sense).

Does this amount to a vindication of Kaplan's prohibition on monsters? Care is needed, because one of Kaplan's aims was to bar operators that shift the contribution of indexicals to what is said. But if we let the semantic value of "I" be index-sensitive, then it is not clear that intensions are good representations of what is said. (For example, if it is plausible that if I utter "I am hungry," what I am saying is something about me. But it is not clear how to make sense of this if "I" is understood as "$I_{shiftable}$", since the intension of "$I_{shiftable}$ am hungry" has nothing to do with me in particular; it can be evaluated at any speaker.)

We started out with the idea that contexts represent concrete situations, and it is natural to think that when we are trying to evaluate an actual utterance we should look to the context that represents the concrete situation in which it was made. Monsters would complicate this picture. But some theorists have found reasons to think that it needed to be complicated anyway. Perhaps the best theory of communication requires that we look not to the concrete situation, but to the way the participants in the conversation take things to be. (This is one of the key themes in Stalnaker's work on context sensitivity; see especially Stalnaker [1999]. The views of context that we have discussed so far could be modified or developed to reflect this Stalnakerian view; I leave this as an exercise to the reader.) Or perhaps some of the phenomena that we want to model depend not only on facts about the concrete situation of use, but also on facts about something else.

Theorize about context sensitivity

Perhaps the most notable recent proposal of this kind is the *relativist* view that we must take into account not only a context in which a sentence might be uttered, but also a context in which it might be assessed. This view can be developed in two ways. First, it might be that some expressions depend on a context of assessment for their intensions. For example, considering the example of a televangelist who says, "Jesus loves you" to an audience widely spread in space and possibly also time (Egan 2009), Cappelen (2008) maintains that what is said depends not only on the concrete situation in which the sentence is uttered, but also on the concrete situation in which the sentence is heard and interpreted (since this determines the contribution of "you"). If this is correct, then we should see contexts as representing at least two distinct concrete situations. (Whether we do this by letting characters be functions from two contexts to intensions or by maintaining a single context but adding more parameters looks like a technical matter of little interest as long as we are clear on what we are representing.)

The second way of developing a relativist view relies on a role of context that we have so far ignored. When we assess the truth of an utterance, we need both a context and an index. And when we evaluate utterances, we typically begin with an index that corresponds closely to the context. For example, on the assumption that an index is just a world, when we evaluate whether an utterance is true, we will begin by letting the index be the world of the context.

So at least in many cases, context determines the index at which we evaluate utterances. But it may be that the concrete situation of utterance does not include facts that are relevant to some evaluations. (For example, suppose that the future is open and I say "There will be a sea battle tomorrow." It is compatible with all of the facts about the concrete situation of utterance that there will be a sea battle, and also compatible with all of the facts about the concrete situation of utterance that there will not be. But it may make sense in evaluating the utterance later to take into account the later facts.) And it may be that our judgments about when it is appropriate to agree and disagree with what other speakers say, and to retract our own utterances, are best modeled by a system that takes into account features of the concrete situation in which an utterance is assessed (and not just the concrete situation in which it was made).

This is the second way a relativist view might be developed: by letting features of the index be initialized by the context of assessment. For example, suppose we assume that intensions represent what is said, but let indices be pairs of a world and a speaker $< w_i, s_i >$; and suppose that our representation of what is said by an utterance of (10) is a function from indices to truth-values that maps i to truth just in case chili tastes good to s_i in w_i:

(10) Chili is tasty.

The question then is: when we evaluate an utterance of (10) for truth, what index do we use? For example, suppose that I am evaluating Jonathan's assertion of (10), and that Jonathan loves chili and I hate it. Then I can evaluate what Jonathan said at <the actual world, Jonathan>, in which case I should regard it as true, or at <the actual world, Derek>, in which case I should regard it as false. The relativist claims that the latter proposal better fits our actual practice (e.g., because I might regard myself as disagreeing with Jonathan, and might want to argue with him) (Mac-Farlane 2014). If that is right, then we will need to build information representing the concrete situation of assessment into context.

How does this change our proposed answers to the Context Representation question? We could, if we were interested in being fully explicit, state relativist and non-relativist versions of each of the possibilities described above; however, for the purposes of this chapter, it is enough if we keep in mind that a complete theory that maintains that contexts are representing concrete situations must describe not only how they do this, but what situations are represented.

7 Conclusion

One's views about context and character will depend on what we take the task of semantics to be. What is a semantic theory a theory of, and how does it represent its target?

Although some of the questions discussed in this chapter have been debated in some detail (if not in quite these terms) in the literature on epistemic contextualism, others have barely been broached. Do contextualist views give an easy victory to the skeptic (a worry discussed in DeRose [2004])? The answer will depend, in part, on what we take context to represent; for example, views that take context to represent how the conversational participants take things to be may fare differently than views that take context to represent the actual facts about the situation in which the conversation is taking place. Do contextualists have a problem about semantic ignorance and error (as Schiffer [1996] and many others contend)? The answer will depend on what we take characters to represent; semantic ignorance manifests quite differently for views that aim to characterize rules represented by speakers than in views that aim to characterize a social convention, or that aim to make predictions about what is said. Attention to the titular question of this chapter may not resolve these debates, but it is crucial to understanding what is at stake.[13]

Notes

1 The scare quotes are because it is not clear that models play a very substantial role in natural language semantics; see Glanzberg (2014) for discussion.

2 Kaplan (1977) does not explicitly endorse this view of context. In his formal system, he simply stipulates that there is a set of contexts C, but says nothing about the nature of the members of C except that for each c in C, c_A is the agent of c, c_T is the time of c, etc., and that A, T, etc. "may be thought of as functions applying to contexts" (552), so that (e.g.) c_A is the result of applying A to c. The view that contexts are tuples seems a natural fit with the bulk of Kaplan's commitments, so I will proceed with that view in discussion.

3 The sorts of questions that are the focus of this chapter could equally well be posed with respect to Lewis (1980)-style "constant but complicated" semantic values; I focus on a Kaplan-style system because of its familiarity in philosophical discussions of context sensitivity.

4 On one view, attributed to Montague by Thomason (1974: 2), languages are just mathematical entities. Perhaps a proponent of this view would claim that the association between "I" and a certain function does exist independently of the activities of theorists; it is, in effect, just a mathematical fact, no more dependent on theoretical activity (and no more in the business of representing something about language use) than the fact that 2 + 2 = 4. Although I do not deny that this thought is worth taking seriously, I find it hard to relate it to the practice of semantic theorizing with which I am familiar. I therefore set it aside.

5 Considerations of space prevent me from discussing several relevant issues (despite the fact that they are probably essential to understanding context sensitivity, and are among the areas where the most interesting recent work on issues related to context sensitivity has taken place): notable among them, the extent of context sensitivity in natural language (most of the discussion will focus on pronouns, and we will generally assume a fairly standard list of context-sensitive expressions), binding and anaphora (our attention will exclusively be directed at so-called *deictic* uses; i.e., uses "whose interpretations are not drawn from the immediate linguistic context" [Nunberg 1993: 12]), and the role of logic in semantic theory (something that played a crucial role in Kaplan's thinking about context sensitivity, but [as far as I know] very little role in debates about epistemic contextualism).

6 Is this natural idea undermined by the fact that we can evaluate sentences at contexts that represent concrete situations in which no utterance is taking place? Perhaps, but there is much to be discussed; exactly how we regard such contexts will turn on our answers to the questions about the target of semantic theorizing and the representational role of context that are among the topics of the rest of this chapter. Those worried about this detail may take the idea under discussion to be that *at least some* sentences-in-contexts represent possible utterances.

7 I have said that intensions are our representations of what is said, and I am here assuming that those same intensions play a compositional role. But what plays a compositional role need not be identical to the representation of what is said, even on the Meaning Perspective; on some views, the representation of

what is said can be determined from (but is not identical to) compositional semantic value. See Ninan (2010) and Rabern (2012) for discussion. For the sake of ease of discussion, I set this complication aside.

8 Things will need to be more complicated to handle repeated uses of the same context-sensitive word, as in "That is not identical to that". Lewis (1970: 62–3) suggests a technical solution (which he attributes to Kaplan); other approaches might see this as a case of context shifting mid-sentence.

9 See Liao (2012) for doubts about the adequacy of this representation of context.

10 Perhaps the simplest move would be to adopt a representational convention that allowed gappy contexts – contexts that include no extension for certain context-sensitive expressions. See Braun (2005: esp. 621–2 n. 6) for a related idea applied to the use of tuples to represent structured propositions.

11 Cresswell-style objections may not be fatal to the deployment of the Simple Strategy in limited ways. If we are interested in developing a theory that explains some particular linguistic phenomenon, rather than in capturing the full range of context sensitivity in language, the Simple Strategy may be a useful tool that enables us to abstract away from distracting factors. Neale (2004: 96) calls this style of use of the Simple Strategy *methodological anchoring*.

12 The presupposition of the question – that we assign (or should assign) constant characters to names – can be doubted; see Recanati (1993: ch. 8).

13 I am grateful to Brian Rabern and Jonathan Jenkins Ichikawa for very helpful comments, and to Matthew Cameron and Ephraim Glick for discussion. This research was supported by the Arts and Humanities Research Council [grant number AH/L015234/1].

References

Borg, E. (2004). *Minimal Semantics*. Oxford: Oxford University Press.

Braun, D. (1996). Demonstratives and their linguistic meanings. *Noûs*, 30, 145–173.

Braun, D. (2005). Empty names, fictional names, mythical names. *Noûs*, 39, 596–631.

Burgess, A. & Sherman, B., Eds. (2014). *Metasemantics*. New York: Oxford University Press.

Cappelen, H. (2008). The creative interpreter: Content relativism and assertion. *Philosophical Perspectives*, 22, 23–46.

Chomsky, N. (1986). *Knowledge of Language*. New York: Praeger.

Cresswell, M. (1973). *Logics and Languages*. London: Methuen.

DeRose, K. (2004). Single scoreboard semantics. *Philosophical Studies*, 119, 1–21.

Egan, A. (2009). Billboards, bombs and shotgun weddings. *Synthese*, 166, 251–279.

Glanzberg, M. (2014). Explanation and partiality in semantic theory. In Burgess & Sherman (2014) (pp. 259–292).

Heim, I. & Kratzer, A. (1998). *Semantics in Generative Grammar*. Oxford: Blackwell.

Jackendoff, R. (2002). *Foundations of Language*. New York: Oxford University Press.

Kaplan, D. (1977). Demonstratives: An essay on the semantics, logic, metaphysics, and epistemology of demonstratives and other indexicals. In J. Almog, J. Perry, & H. Wettstein (Eds.), *Themes from Kaplan* (pp. 481–564). New York: Oxford University Press.

Larson, R. & Segal, G. (1995). *Knowledge of Language*. Cambridge, MA: MIT Press.

Lewis, D. (1970). General semantics. *Synthese*, 22, 18–67.

Lewis, D. (1980). Index, context, and content. In *Papers in Philosophical Logic* (pp. 21–44). New York: Cambridge University Press.

Lewis, D. (1983). Languages and language. In *Philosophical Papers Volume I* (pp. 163–188). New York: Oxford University Press.

Liao, S. (2012). What are centered worlds? *Philosophical Quarterly*, 62, 294–316.

MacFarlane, J. (2014). *Assessment Sensitivity: Relative Truth and Its Applications*. Oxford: Oxford University Press.

Montague, R. (1974a). English as a formal language. In Montague (1974b), (pp. 188–221).

Montague, R. (1974b). *Formal Philosophy*. New Haven: Yale University Press.

Montague, R. (1974c). Pragmatics. In Montague (1974b), (pp. 95–118).

Neale, S. (2004). This, that, and the other. In A. Bezuidenhout & M. Reimer (Eds.), *Descriptions and Beyond* (pp. 68–182). Oxford: Oxford University Press.

Ninan, D. (2010). Semantics and the objects of assertion. *Linguistics and Philosophy*, 33, 355–380.

Nunberg, G. (1993). Indexicality and deixis. *Linguistics and Philosophy*, 16, 1–43.

Rabern, B. (2012). Against the identification of assertoric content with compositional value. *Synthese*, 189, 75–96.

Rabern, B. (2013). Monsters in Kaplan's logic of demonstratives. *Philosophical Studies*, 164, 393–404.

Recanati, F. (1993). *Direct Reference: From Language to Thought*. Oxford: Blackwell.

Santorio, P. (2012). Reference and monstrosity. *The Philosophical Review*, 121, 359–406.

Schiffer, S. (1996). Contextualist solutions to scepticism. *Proceedings of the Aristotelian Society*, 96, 317–333.

Schlenker, P. (2003). A plea for monsters. *Linguistics and Philosophy*, 26, 29–120.

Stalnaker, R. C. (1999). *Context and Content: Essays on Intentionality in Speech and Thought*. New York: Oxford University Press.

Stalnaker, R. C. (2014). *Contexts*. Oxford: Oxford University Press.

Thomason, R. (1974). Introduction. In Montague (1974b), (pp. 1–70).

Yalcin, S. (2014). Semantics and metasemantics in the context of generative grammar. In Burgess & Sherman (2014), (pp. 17–54).

PART III

Epistemological implications

9

EPISTEMIC CONTEXTUALISM AND THE SHIFTING THE QUESTION OBJECTION

Brian Montgomery

Epistemic contextualism is the thesis that the semantic value of a knowledge claim of the form "S knows that p" varies with the epistemic standards in play for the asserter at the time of assertion. Invariantists about "knowledge" – those who believe that the semantics of knowledge claims remain the same between contexts – have traditionally criticized contextualism in one of two ways. First, there is the common argument that the set of claims comprising contextualism is false. This may be done by arguing against the intuitions that motivate it, claiming that it gets the cases wrong, holding that it runs into semantic difficulties, or coming up with reasons for thinking that non-epistemic properties fail to effect knowledge claims. Objections of this type are discussed at length in other sections of this volume, and this will be the last that we discuss them here. Instead, we will focus on a separate objection that constitutes a metacritique of the entire contextualist's project. Consider the following:

> some of the most important epistemological views in recent years – e.g. contextualism, subject sensitive invariantism – have been grounded in large part in a close consideration of the semantics of knowledge ascriptions . . . the proper focus in epistemology should begin to shift back to traditional considerations involving justification, warrant, evidence, and so on – which is where it should have been all along.
>
> *(Lackey 2007, 619)*

Here Lackey expresses the belief that views like contextualism and subject sensitive invariantism aren't wrong so much as they are wrongheaded. In this way they serve as a red herring that distracts the epistemologist from the proper investigation. To put it another way, whatever the contextualist is doing when she talks about "knowledge", she isn't doing epistemology.

It is this second objection that we will examine in this chapter. As is usual with philosophy there are no easy answers to be had. It is clear that when an aestheticist discusses beauty that she is doing aesthetics, and that when a metaphysician writes about time he produces an essay that ought to be of interest to metaphysicians of time. But why then is the examination of "knows" so controversial within epistemology? In what follows I will attempt to answer the question of whether the epistemic contextualist is an epistemologist or not. But before we get there we will begin by examining arguments both pro and con. In the first section we will explore Ernest Sosa's influential critique of contextualism, before moving on to Hillary Kornblith's defense of

Sosa's position, as well as a related problem posed by Baron Reed. In the second section we will take a look at Keith DeRose's recent response to both Sosa and Kornblith. In the final section we will examine a possible solution that emphasizes the role that contextualism and theories of "knowledge" play in metaepistemology.

1 Contextualism is not epistemology

In this section we will explore some of the main criticisms of the second type. This will prove to be a deceptively difficult task, because at their heart many criticisms of the second type are really just special instances of the first and are so intimately comingled with them that they can appear inseparable. For instance, it is not at all unusual to find an invariantist argue that contextualism is irrelevant to epistemology *because* it gets the cases wrong in its inability to offer satisfactory answers to epistemological problems like skepticism, the lottery paradox, etc. Few, if any, arguments that we will examine in this section are without type-one criticisms.

This is really philosophy of language

One of the most common criticisms of epistemic contextualism is that it provides us with a fascinating thesis, but one that is properly construed as a thesis about linguistic entities, not epistemic ones. As we have seen in the preceding chapters, the epistemic contextualist holds that whether one can be truly said to know *p* varies based upon the relevant standards in play at the context of assessment. This is at its heart a *semantic* thesis. It is a thesis about the way in which the meaning of the word "knows" operates. This led Ernest Sosa (2000) to conclude that epistemic contextualism has "considerable plausibility as a thesis in linguistics or in philosophy of language," but suggests that it might "overreach" in its attempt to extend these semantic findings in epistemology (3).

To see why, he asks us to consider what he calls "the contextualist's fallacy", which he defines as "the fallacious inference of an answer to a question from information about the correct use of the words in its formulation" (Sosa 2000, 2). As he suggests, much can be learned by examining the semantics of a word, but rarely can we ever learn something about the nature of the thing itself. Consider the following:

(1)   People often utter truths when they say "Somebody loves me."
(2)   Does anybody love me?

The first (1) tells us something about the speaker – to wit, that sometimes the utterer of the sentence "Somebody loves me" speaks the truth. At best the semantic exploration in (1) tells us something trivial about the nature of the person's love life. What it doesn't give us is any sort of satisfying answer to the question expressed in (2). To conclude otherwise would be to commit the contextualist fallacy.

So much the worse for contextualist explorations of your love life. But what about knowledge? Consider the following:

(3)   People often utter truths when they say "I know that there are hands."
(4)   Do people ever know that there are hands?

There are ways of instantiating the value of "people" in (3) that are of little interest to epistemologists, but there are also ways of filling in the value for "people" where the speaker would not

The shifting the question objection

obviously commit the contextualist fallacy were she to say that (3) grants important insight into potential answers to (4). This is why Sosa is too cautious to dismiss the possibility out of hand.

Instead, he asks us to imagine the traditional "high" and "low" contexts that contextualism trades on. Imagine that the sentence

(5) Charlene knows that she has hands.

is uttered outside of philosophical discussion. Perhaps her friends Sal and Melinda are at a bar and engaged in a discussion about Charlene's lucrative career as a hand model and demure nature. In denying Charlene's faux modesty it would seem natural for one of her friends to assert (5). Now imagine that Sal and Melinda – both philosophy professors – discuss the problem of skepticism and use (5) in their discussion. Epistemic contextualists would predict that (4) is the case in the first example, but that the speaker of the negation of (4) in the second example cannot be said to utter a truth.

This is all standard contextualist fare so far, but Sosa soon enters more contentious material when he examines the relation between these high and low cases. Here he is willing to grant that anyone who utters (5) in a high context does not know it, but holds that the claim that the assertion of (5) in low justificatory contexts doesn't follow from this:

> From much discussion with undergraduates and ordinary folk, I am convinced that the term "know" and its cognates are sometimes so used as to make it true that the medievals just "knew" that the earth was flat (a view confirmed by the OED). In some ordinary contexts if someone is very sure that p, that makes it true to say that they "know" that p. Can that be relevant to our concern to understand the nature, conditions, and extent of this philosophical commodity that we constantly pursue, sometimes at great cost: namely, knowledge? Surely not. Nor should we conclude that at least in some ordinary contexts our medieval predecessors may be said to have enjoyed the knowledge that the earth is flat. That some sophomores call it "knowledge" hardly suffices to make it so, even if the attribution is correct in their context, by their definition.
>
> *(Sosa 2000, 8–9)*

Ultimately then, the epistemic contextualist, in Sosa's eyes, discusses two different conceptions of knowledge. There is the rigid high use of "knows" that is of interest to epistemologists, and the looser use of the phrase used by the rabble that is of little to no interest to epistemologists. This is fine and well as an examination of the semantics of "knows", but it reveals nothing about the nature of knowledge itself. To infer otherwise would be to commit the contextualist fallacy.

The skepticism objection

We want our epistemological theories to be put to work. Traditionally the main motivation behind epistemic contextualism has been its ability to offer novel and persuasive responses to the problem of external world skepticism (see Cohen 1999, 2000; DeRose 1995, 2011). Although some have argued that contextualism can help us resolve other epistemic problems, such as the lottery paradox (Cohen 1998; DeRose 1996), its ability to diagnose the difficulties with skepticism and offer a possible solution remain perhaps its single biggest selling point. That is why it would be disastrous for the epistemic contextualist to sever the link between the two. If it turned out that contextualism had nothing much of interest to say about the skeptical problem, then its epistemological importance is immediately in doubt. Here we'll take a look at two attempts to do just that.

Brian Montgomery

We begin with Hilary Kornblith who starts off his paper by stating that Sosa's critique is far too timid, arguing both that epistemic "contextualism is irrelevant to epistemology", and that the contextualist's "semantic thesis . . . does not explain the phenomenon [it] seeks to explain" (Kornblith 2000, 25). Kornblith begins by identifying two different kinds of skepticism: "Full Blooded Skepticism" (FBS) and "High Standards Skepticism" (HSS). FBS is, according to Kornblith, the kind of skepticism associated with Descartes's meditations and trades on the inability of a subject to ever be justified in her beliefs about the world:

> According to the skeptic, we are no more justified in believing that there is an external world than that there isn't. Indeed, take any two propositions about the external world: for example, the proposition that I am standing here now reading a paper about skepticism and the claim that I am now standing in the middle of a road with a very large truck heading straight toward me. If the skeptical argument works at all, it shows that I have no more reason to believe the first of these two claims than the second. The reason I don't know anything about the external world, according to the skeptic, is not that I have a small degree of justification for my beliefs when knowledge requires a larger degree of justification. Rather, the skeptic claims that I have no degree of justification whatever for my claims about the external world. None.
>
> *(Kornblith 2000, 25)*

On the other hand there is HSS, which holds that justification comes in degrees. According to this kind of external world skepticism, an epistemic subject may enjoy varying degrees of justification for her external world belief and its uneliminated skeptical counter-hypothesis. For instance, Mathilda may have a high degree of justification for her belief that her friend Charlene has hands, but similarly have a sufficiently high enough justification in the counter-possibility that Charlene is a handless brain in a vat to undercut her justification for the veridical belief from ever reaching the threshold where justified true belief becomes knowledge. According to Kornblith, this form of skepticism is "far less interesting" than FBS (Kornblith 2000, 26).

To make his case, Kornblith asks us to imagine a man from Vermont who stubbornly holds that the predicate "is cold" fails to apply to any temperature greater than −25°F. This eccentric holds that the temperatures approaching −25°F are gradable in a manner that reaches cold, and the temperatures below progressed onward in degrees of "colder". Kornblith reasons that the HSS skeptic is like the eccentric Vermonter, arbitrarily picking a point along a continuum and making the unsupported claim that *this* is the point where knowledge is no longer possible. Unsurprisingly, Kornblith holds that epistemic contextualism only responds to the "uninteresting" HSS. Moreover, he reasons, any attempt to respond to FBS in a contextualist manner merely supplements the theory with extraneous epistemic baggage that can be divorced from the semantic thesis without losing anything of merit.

Baron Reed provides us with a more recent attempt to show that the contextualist fails in her quest to respond to the skeptic (Reed 2010). Although he is willing to grant that contextualists provide an interesting response to the external world skeptic, he also holds that their enterprise is ultimately doomed to fail because the skeptic can simply reformulate her argument in a way that is immune to a contextualist response. To see how, Reed asks us to consider the "strength of one's epistemic position" (SEP). This rather unwieldy name belies a simple concept. As Reed uses the term, one's SEP is merely whatever it is (e.g. justification or warrant) that transforms true belief into knowledge. Using "H" and "BIV" to respectively stand for the propositions "I have hands" and "I am a handless brain in a vat":

124

The shifting the question objection

1 My SEP with respect to the proposition that H entails ~BIV is excellent.
2 If my SEP with respect to the proposition that H entails ~BIV is excellent, then my SEP for H cannot be much higher than my SEP for ~BIV.
3 My SEP with respect to ~BIV is poor.
4 ∴ My SEP with respect to H is poor.

(Reed 2010, 226)

Because the first and third premises are uncontroversial rephrasings of the traditional skeptical argument, and the second premise stems from an intuitively plausible version of the closure principle, the conclusion seems to follow:

> The conclusion says that my SEP for the proposition that I have hands is poor. The fundamental thesis of contextualism says only that the truth conditions of "know" assertions will be determined by the epistemic standards fixed by the conversational context. Though it is assumed that most of our beliefs meet the relatively lax standards operative in mundane conversations, it is compatible with contextualism that they do not. The skeptic has just produced an argument that shows they do not. What is worse, the contextualist is badly positioned to respond to the argument. Because SEP does not vary from one context to another, there is no chance that the contextualist response to skepticism will work here. And, because the contextualist has already conceded that the original skeptical argument (framed in terms of knowledge) cannot be directly refuted – hence the need to limit its forcefulness to certain conversational contexts – it doesn't look like the contextualist has any hope of there being a refutation of any kind for the new skeptical argument that parallels the old one. In the end, then, contextualism leaves us more, not less, vulnerable to skepticism.

(Reed 2010, 227)

If Reed is correct, then the contextualist is unable to respond to this newer form of skepticism, and the theory's epistemological importance has been severely undercut.

2 Contextualism is epistemology

Of course many epistemic contextualists believe that they are doing epistemology (mixed with the philosophy of language). Yet, few epistemic contextualists ever take the time to explicitly spell this out. Perhaps they see it as a given or don't consider it a strong enough objection to address in print. More likely than not, most simply don't think about it at all. There have, however, been almost no responses made directly to Sosa's and Kornblith's original criticisms. In this section we will take a look at responses offered by Keith DeRose (2011 and 2017), and Michael Blome-Tillman (2014).

Blome-Tillman on Sosa

In his *Knowledge and Presuppositions* Blome-Tillman (2014) diagnoses Sosa as erring in a significant way. He reasons that Sosa's criticism rests on the sloppiness of past contextual analyses. According to Blome-Tillman, in her haste to make her case, the epistemic contextualist has failed to properly separate off the use–mention distinction. A speaker uses a word or phrase when she utters it in a sentence and its semantic content refers to the thing that it picks out in the world. A speaker mentions a word or phrase when she utters it in a sentence and its semantic contentment refs to the word or phrase itself. Hence, in the examples below, (6) uses the phrase 'piece of cake', while (7) merely mentions it:

(6) That logic exam was a piece of cake.
(7) English speakers sometimes say "piece of cake" to convey that something was easy.

If Blome-Tillman is correct, then past contextualist analyses have failed to properly demarcate uses and mentions of "knows", thus resulting in the sort of confusion that made Sosa's critique possible. As the reader may have already noticed, in the section on Sosa, the numbered propositions that he analyses make knowledge claims themselves rather than report knowledge claims. This may seem like a subtle shift, but it is nevertheless an important one insofar as contextualist analyses in epistemology take the semantic functions of sentences about knowledge as their source of inquiry rather than sentences that the truth of individual knowledge claims. What Sosa's criticism lacks then is what the epistemic contextualist needs to make her case: disquotational schemas of the word "knows".[1]

DeRose on Sosa

In his 2011 work Keith DeRose left his readers with the promise to address Sosa's concerns in vol. 2 of his *Case for Contextualism*. DeRose (2017) confronts Sosa's worry in two ways: one polemical and the other substantive. In his initial assessment of the critique he begins by stating that it's "all wrong". Just as Sosa has (arguably) spent his career trying to answer the skeptic's challenge, DeRose sees himself as doing the same. Their methodology might be different, since DeRose uses "some (fairly low-tech) philosophy of language, and some talk about the truth-conditions of sentences containing 'know(s)'" (DeRose, 2017). None of this is done as a way to skirt the issue of skepticism, in DeRose's eyes, but rather as a way to answer the same issues that Sosa addresses. To use an analogy then, DeRose views Sosa as a carpenter who artificially limits the number of tools that he is willing to use to build a house. DeRose sees his toolbox as richer, and better off for it.

His second response, however, directly addresses Sosa's criticisms. Recall that Sosa asked us to consider the sentences:

(1) People often utter truths when they say "Somebody loves me."
(2) Does anybody love me?
(3) People often utter truths when they say "I know there are hands."
(4) Do people ever know that there are hands?

DeRose points to a dissimilarity between the two pairs that he believes creates a psychological confusion which undermines the case for contextualism. Notice how the first contains the indexical "me" in each of its sentences. Here the referent may be the same in each case, and virtually anyone who pays attention to them can recognize this. However, the story is different with the second pair. Few hearers are familiar with the contextualist view of "knows" semantics and, reckons DeRose, will fail to track the proper relationship between (3) and (4). Since the contextualist predicts that the raising of skeptical hypotheses "inclines us" to answer (4) in the negative, we may feel compelled to conclude that (3) is therefore false. But the average anti-skeptic who hears (3) without the standards raised is also inclined to agree with it and is therefore primed to reject skeptical hypotheses. "Not realizing that those usual affirmations are compatible with skeptical denials of knowledge", DeRose reasons, "we get confused." More specifically, this confusion results in a reader thinking that if (3) is true, then (4) must be answered in the positive, and considering (4) makes her think that (3) must be false. But, reasons DeRose, this is where contextualism forms an important new avenue to prior epistemological theorizing: it allows us to coherently respect both of these compelling intuitions in a way that Sosa's invariantism may not be able to.

DeRose on Kornblith

DeRose's response to Kornblith's criticisms takes three stages: (1) an examination of philosophical interest of the high standards skeptic, (2) a rereading of the role that the bold skeptic plays in his contextualism, and (3) a defense of epistemic contextualism's ability to respond to the skeptic. Since exegetical matters will lead us too far afield, let's focus on the first and third prongs of the author's response.

Recall that Kornblith compares the high stakes skeptic – the skeptic that he believes epistemic contextualists like DeRose respond to – to the eccentric Vermonter who holds that –25°F is the threshold for something to properly be called "cold". Kornblith sees this odd behavior as analogous to that of the high stakes skeptic who picks a threshold for knowledge and holds that few of our beliefs ever achieve that threshold. But, reckons DeRose, if it were the case that our "cold ascriptions" functioned in this way then it would be quite a surprise, one which would have ramifications on the metaphysics of "cold", as well as the philosophy of language. DeRose reasons that *mutatis mutandis* the same applies to knowledge claims. What's more, if the high stakes skeptic were to merely state her claim without giving a defense, then we might dismiss her as a harmless crank like our Vermonter. Yet, as DeRose points out, this isn't what the high stakes skeptic does. Instead she provides a valid argument composed of *prima facie* plausible premises. To reject it for being uninteresting is to overlook the fact that it takes independently plausible premises and uses them to construct an argument that strikes many as obviously unsound. Surely this makes it worth the study.

But even if we grant Kornblith the charge that the high stakes skeptic's activities are fundamentally jejune, DeRose reasons that the epistemic contextualist still has a response to the bold skeptic as well. Like the high stakes skeptic, the bold skeptic relies on premises which each have their own intuitive pull. Indeed, short of dismissing the skeptic out of hand, it's difficult to see what the best response could be. This leaves us with a dreadful predicament. We could (1) accept the bold skeptic's argument as correct and that we really do not know anything, (2) reject one or more of the bold skeptic's apparently innocent premises, or (3) argue that the bold skeptic's apparently valid argument is in fact invalid. DeRose argues that his brand of contextualism is the only game in town that allows us to choose a different option, one which respects the appeal of skeptical hypotheses, maintains that the argument is sound, and yet also allows for us to reject the claim that (under the right set of circumstances) we do not possess any knowledge.

3 Contextualism as metaepistemology

As we saw in the previous section, DeRose saw the chief virtue of his theory as its ability to both answer the skeptic's challenge while also allowing for the conflicting intuitions of the skeptic and the anti-skeptic to both come out correct. Such ecumenicalism is to be praised when it is possible. However, in offering his solution DeRose fails to develop any similarly robust and conciliatory position that would respect the intuition expressed by Sosa, Kornblith, and Reed that epistemic contextualism is not properly in the domain of epistemology, while also allowing for it to do epistemic work. Indeed, his response can be thought of as a kind of error theory where the invariantist about knowledge claims gets the proper role of contextualism wrong because of how counterintuitive the theory is. In this section we will see if we can do better. I shall sketch out a view of epistemic contextualism that admits its epistemic importance, while also doing justice to the positions examined in the first section.

However, in order to see how such a theory might go we must begin with a detour into ethics. Traditionally ethicists carve up their discipline into three distinct sub-disciplines. First there is normative ethics where philosophers work on developing theories of right and wrong or proper conduct. Second, there's metaethics where underlying concepts *about* ethics (e.g. moral motivation, the possibility of moral knowledge, etc.) are analyzed. Finally there is applied ethics, the branch of moral theorizing where the findings from normative ethics are applied to individual moral controversies (e.g. abortion, euthanasia, etc.). As Richard Fumerton noted in his groundbreaking book *Metaepistemology and Skepticism* (1995), there are parallels between ethics and epistemology. Although the division is rarely explicitly made, most traditional epistemological enquiries are what Fumerton refers to as "normative epistemology" (1), where we attempt to construct theories about how one ought to go about constructing her beliefs or respond to the skeptic. Analogously, there are metaepistemological questions about the metaphysical nature of knowledge, the extent to which belief is voluntary, and the structure that knowledge takes, to name but a few.[2]

Importantly, work in both meta-fields can inform, guide, and otherwise influence work done in the normative subdiscipline. To quote Fumerton:

> The importance of relating metaepistemological controversies to traditional issues in normative epistemology, particularly issues relating to the skeptical challenge, has never been more important. The internalism/externalism metaepistemological debate continues to rage, and its resolution has profound implications for the way in which philosophers should view issues in normative epistemology. Indeed, I believe that it is no exaggeration to suggest that if certain versions of externalism are correct, the history of epistemology is filled with philosophers who radically misconceive the nature of their enterprise. Moreover, if externalism is correct, the vast majority of contemporary philosophers are simply incompetent qua philosophers to address many of the questions that defined the history of western epistemology.
>
> *(1995, 2)*

In the same manner as those examples illustrated by Fumerton, we can see that metaepistemological considerations are no idle matter of interest to only the most esoteric investigations. Instead, they have a real importance that frequently impacts the nature and direction of philosophizing at the normative level.

Returning briefly to metaethics we find one of the most active and important discussions in the field in the last century is the debate about the meaning of moral language. Arguably this approach began with G. E. Moore's examination of the word "good" within his *Principia Ethica*, but has gone on to become perhaps the most discussed area of the field. Many of the explorations within the linguistics of moral language have fed into other projects within metaethical theory (e.g. the cognitivism/non-cognitivism debate), whereas others seem to have had a more direct impact on normative ethics. If, for instance, the relativist semantics developed by Jesse Prinz in his *The Emotional Construction of Morals* (2009) are correct, then the search for universal moral codes would almost certainly be misguided. Similarly, the work done in defense of metaethical contextualism in the writings of Mark Timmons (1998) and Peter Unger (1996) would, if proven sound, mean that all moral theorizing must take into account the context of evaluation.

It should not be too difficult to see where this excursion leads us. If the domains of normative epistemology and normative ethics run as strongly parallel as many philosophers think they do,

The shifting the question objection

then we would expect to find metaepistemological examinations about the way epistemic language works to have an impact on normative epistemic investigations. It is rather easy to find confirming instances of this prediction. For instance, Moorian paradoxical statements of the form "p, but I don't believe that p" have long been thought to reveal the intimate connection between belief and assertion. More recently, however, it has also been proposed that these infelicities can reveal constitutive elements of knowledge.[3] In a similar vein, epistemologists over the last two decades have been interested in the connection between assertion and knowledge or belief. As Timothy Williamson famously stated in his *Knowledge and Its Limits* (2000), "assertion is the exterior analogue of judgement, which stands to belief as act to state" (238). This has led numerous epistemologists to explore the connection between the act of assertion (and their content) with epistemic states.

It is in this area of metaepistemology that I believe we find the role of contextualist, relativist, and subject sensitive epistemic analyses. Studying the semantics and pragmatics of knowledge claims may not be "doing epistemology" in the same way that responding to Gettier cases or defending theories of justification are "doing epistemology", but as we have seen in this section epistemology is a wider field than just normative epistemology. It stands to normative epistemology as metaethical analyses of "good" or "ought" stand to normative ethics. In other words, semantic analyses of knowledge claims help to reveal the way that our understanding of knowledge operates in quotidian contexts as well as the unusual cases of hyperbolic doubt. Studying the way that knowledge claims operate may help us, as DeRose believes, uncover the multitude of assumptions (good or bad) that the external world skeptic makes in her argument that we know nothing. As such contextualist analyses of "knowledge" ought to be of interest to the epistemologist in so far as they are working on issues related to these.

So to return to the title of the piece, is epistemic contextualism epistemology? The answer is a qualified yes. Epistemology is a broad subject, but one that encompasses contextualism nonetheless. This answer respects the stance of both sides of the debate, and is compatible with their underlying intuitions. No, epistemic contextualists like DeRose and Cohen are not producing work in normative epistemology when they analyze the semantics of knowledge claims, but they are producing important metaepistemological work that ought to be of interest to anyone working in normative epistemology.

Notes

1 Blome-Tillman has a separate criticism of Sosa's reasoning that relies on his own brand of presuppositional epistemic contextualism. Those interested can find the relevant material in Blome-Tillman (2014, 51–52).

2 Although Fumerton never addresses the question of applied epistemology, there is undoubtedly such investigation as well with examinations questioning whether it is possible to have knowledge of God, certain scientific theories, etc.

3 See, for instance, Heumer (2008), where he considers the following problem sentences and concludes based on their infelicity that they reveal aspects of knowledge itself:

(1) It is raining, but I do not believe that it is.
(2) It is raining, but I believe that it is not.
(3) It is raining, but I do not know that it is.
(4) It is raining, but that isn't true.
(5) It is raining, but I have no justification for thinking so.
(6) It is raining, but my reason for thinking so is false.
(7) It is raining, but there are (non-misleading) facts that neutralize my reasons for believing that.
(8) It is raining, but my belief that it is was formed in an unreliable way.
(9) It is raining, but I would believe that even if it were false.
(10) It is raining, but I am not sure that it is.
(11) It is raining, but it is not certain that it is.

Brian Montgomery

References

Blome-Tillman, Michael. 2014. *Knowledge and Presuppositions.* Oxford: Oxford University Press.

Cohen, Stewart. 1998. "Contextualist Solutions to Epistemological Problems: Scepticism, Gettier, and Lotteries", *Australasian Journal of Philosophy* 76: 289–306.

———. 1999. "Contextualism, Skepticism, and the Structure of Reasons", *Noûs* 33: 57–89.

———. 2000. "Contextualism and Skepticism", *Philosophical Issues* 10: 94–107.

DeRose, Keith. 1995. "Solving the Skeptical Problem", *The Philosophical Review* 104: 1–52.

———. 1996. "Knowledge, Assertion, and Lotteries", *Australasian Journal of Philosophy* 74: 568–580.

———. 2011. *The Case for Contextualism, Vol 1.* Oxford: Oxford University Press.

———. 2017. *The Case for Contextualism, Vol 2.* Oxford: Oxford University Press.

Fumerton, Richard. 1995. *Metaepistemology and Skepticism.* Lanham, MD: Rowman and Littlefield.

Heumer, Michael. 2008. "Moore's Paradox and the Norm of Belief", in *Themes from G.E. Moore* (Nuccetelli, Susana and Gary Seay eds.). Oxford: Oxford University Press. 142–157.

Kornblith, Hilary. 2000. "The Contextualist Evasion of Epistemology", *Philosophical Issues* 10: 24–32.

Lackey, Jennifer. 2007. "Norms of Assertion", *Noûs* 41: 594–626.

Prinz, Jesse. 2009. *The Emotional Construction of Morals.* Oxford: Oxford University Press.

Reed, Baron. 2010. "A Defense of Stable Invariantism", *Noûs* 42: 224–244.

Sosa, Ernest. 2000. "Skepticism and Contextualism", *Philosophical Issues* 10: 1–18.

Timmons, Mark. 1998. *Morality without Foundations.* Oxford: Oxford University Press.

Unger, Peter. 1996. *Living High and Letting Die.* Oxford: Oxford University Press.

Williamson, Timothy. 2000. *Knowledge and Its Limits.* Oxford: Oxford University Press.

10

SKEPTICISM AND CONTEXTUALISM

Michael J. Hannon

Introduction

According to some powerful skeptical arguments, we know almost nothing. Contextualist theories of knowledge ascriptions have been developed with an eye toward resisting skepticism. Have the contextualists succeeded? After briefly outlining their view, I will consider whether contextualism about knowledge ascriptions provides a satisfactory response to one of the most popular and influential forms of skepticism. I conclude with some questions for the contextualist. As we'll see, the effectiveness of the contextualist solution to skepticism is far from settled.

1 What is epistemic contextualism?

"Contextualism" is an umbrella term for a variety of views, both inside epistemology and out. In epistemology, the most widely discussed version of contextualism is the view that knowledge-talk is context-sensitive. According to this view, the truth conditions of knowledge ascriptions (e.g. "S knows that p") and knowledge denials (e.g. "S doesn't know that p") vary depending on the context in which they are uttered (Cohen 1988; DeRose 1995; Lewis 1996). In what follows, I will be considering this type of contextualism.[1]

Let me start with a few clarifications. "Context" here means the conversational setting that is determined by speaker intentions, listener expectations, presuppositions in the conversation, and salience relations – what David Lewis calls the "conversational score" (Lewis 1979). What varies with context is the epistemic standard that a person S must meet in order to count as "knowing" some proposition p. Contextualists differ as to whether epistemic standards are a matter of the extent of relevant alternatives that need to be considered (e.g. Cohen 1988; Lewis 1996), the range of possible worlds in which the truth is tracked (e.g. DeRose 1995), or something else. They also disagree about the specific semantic character of "know" (e.g. indexical, vague, gradable, etc.). We can safely ignore these in-house disputes. What matters for our purpose is the following core feature of contextualism: there will be some contexts in which "S knows that p" requires for its truth that S has a true belief that p and meet a very high epistemic standard, while in other contexts an utterance of the very same sentence may require only that S meet some lower epistemic standard for its truth, in addition to S truly believing that p. Put differently,

131

what is expressed in certain contexts is that S knows that *p* relative to a low standard, and what is expressed in other contexts is that S knows that *p* relative to a high standard.[2]

The merits of this view are hotly debated in epistemology. My aim in this chapter is not to determine the plausibility of contextualist thesis that "knows" is context-sensitive – that is a large and complicated task to which this entire volume is a significant contribution. My goal, rather, is to evaluate the contextualist's solution to the problem of skepticism.[3] Perhaps the main virtue of contextualism is that it can allegedly solve the skeptical problem, and it is largely for this reason that contextualism has gained center stage in epistemology.

2 Skepticism

Skepticism takes many forms. Here I will focus on just one type of skepticism, albeit one that is both historically significant and widely discussed in recent epistemology: *Cartesian* skepticism.

Cartesian skeptical arguments are characterized by their use of "skeptical hypotheses," which describe undetectable cognitively debilitating states such as dreaming, hallucination, or victimization by an evil demon. Roughly, a hypothesis is "skeptical" if (a) its truth is inconsistent with some propositions we ordinarily take ourselves to know, and yet (b) the hypothesis is compatible with all our experience in favor of those ordinary propositions. To illustrate, consider the following brain-in-a-vat version of the skeptic's argument:

1   I don't know that I am not a handless brain in a vat.
2   If I don't know that I am not a handless brain in a vat, then I don't know that I have hands.
3   Therefore, I don't know that I have hands.

Although Descartes never mentions brains in vats, the origin of this argument can be traced to his *Meditations*, if not earlier. Many contemporary epistemologists, such as Keith DeRose (1995), Stephen Schiffer (1996), and Stewart Cohen (1999), provide essentially the same formulation of skepticism. Suitably articulated, the skeptic's argument will lead us to deny much of our putative knowledge of the world around us.

By extrapolating away from the details, we can provide a more general formulation of skepticism. For simplicity, let's say that O represents some ordinary proposition about the external world that we intuitively know (e.g. I have hands) and SH represents a suitably chosen skeptical hypothesis that is inconsistent with O (e.g. I am a handless brain in a vat). The general structure of the skeptic's argument is:

1   I don't know that not-SH.
2   If I don't know that not-SH, then I don't know that O.
3   Therefore, I don't know that O.

Let's call this simple version *the skeptic's argument*. DeRose thinks this argument is "clearly valid . . . and each of its premises, considered on its own, enjoys a good deal of intuitive support" (1999: 2–3). Cohen agrees that "both of these premises are intuitively quite appealing" (1999: 62).

The first premise is defended on the grounds that however unlikely or strange it might seem to suppose that I am in a skeptical scenario, it also seems true that I do *not* know that I am not in one – as DeRose says, "how *could* I know such a thing?" (1995: 2). Further, if I don't know whether or not I am in a skeptical scenario, then it seems that I do not know many things about the world around me. This claim derives its force from the notion that knowledge transfers across known entailments, and hence that some sort of closure principle holds for knowledge. Roughly:

if you know one proposition and also know that that proposition entails another, then you know the latter proposition. If we do not know the falsity of a skeptical scenario, however, then we can derive a skeptical result from the closure principle in the following way: if we know that O, then we know that not-SH; but we don't know that not-SH, so we don't know that O.

While there are some problems involved in finding a satisfactory articulation of the closure principle, the idea that knowledge is closed under known logical implication is widely accepted.[4] Denying this principle would license what DeRose calls "abominable conjunctions" (1995: 27–9). An example of an abominable conjunction is: "I know where my car is parked, but I don't know whether it has been stolen and moved." Another example is: "I know that I have hands, but I don't know that I'm not a handless brain in a vat." I will assume that some version of the closure principle holds.[5]

The skeptic's argument looks valid, and its premises are intuitively plausible. The problem is that the skeptic's conclusion seems false: it conflicts with our compelling belief that we *do* have all sorts of everyday knowledge. To doubt that we have such knowledge seems absurd – at least, to doubt it in any serious and lasting way. As Lewis puts it, "It is a Moorean fact that we know a lot. It is one of those things that we know better than we know the premises of any philosophical argument to the contrary" (1996: 549). The result is a paradox:

1   We have all sorts of everyday knowledge.
2   We don't know that we're not in a skeptical scenario.
3   If we don't know that we're not in a skeptical scenario, then we don't have all sorts of every-day knowledge.

This is a paradox because each of these jointly inconsistent propositions seems true. In order to escape the paradox, something has to give – but what and why?

At first blush it might look as if there are only three ways out of this paradox:

(a)   *Deny closure*: reject the idea that if S knows that p and S knows that p entails q, then S knows that q.
(b)   *Concession*: concede that we do not know most (or all) of what we thought we knew.
(c)   *Dogmatism*: maintain that we do know that we are not victims of a skeptical scenario.

None of these options is immediately appealing. I have already suggested that knowledge remains closed under known logical implication, so let's set (a) aside. Option (b) would allow the skeptic to rob us of our knowledge, whereas (c) seems groundless and even question begging.[6] A successful solution to the paradox must not just deny one of the three inconsistent propositions, it must also explain why we thought each proposition was true. In other words, a successful solution must explain why we thought there was a paradox in the first place.

This is just what contextualists allege they can do. The next section will explain how the context-sensitivity of knowledge ascriptions is supposed to resolve the skeptical paradox.

3 The contextualist solution to skepticism

While contextualist theories differ in their details (see Rysiew 2007: section 3.3), the contextualist solution to skepticism involves two basic elements: first, the contextualist claims that in ordinary contexts we often speak truly when we ascribe "knowledge" to others; second, in certain other contexts, such as those in which skepticism is seriously considered, the epistemic standards required to merit a knowledge ascription are much higher, and as a result speakers will deny "knowledge" with equal propriety and truth. The conditions for applying "knows" differ depending on the context we are in. This variation makes it possible for us to speak truly when we say "S knows that p" in contexts with low standards (e.g. "ordinary contexts"), even though we would speak falsely when uttering the same sentence in contexts with higher standards (e.g. "skeptical contexts").

But how does the skeptic create a context in which we can no longer truthfully say that we know many things? Contextualists disagree about how the standards get raised, including whether they *are* raised by merely considering skepticism.[7] I will return to this question in Section 4. For now, I'll simply adopt the common contextualist idea that the standards for "knowledge" are raised as moves in the conversation make salient various skeptical possibilities (Cohen 1988; DeRose 1995; Lewis 1996).[8] For example, if the skeptic makes salient the possibility that we are brains in vats, and we recognize that we cannot rule out this possibility, then we can no longer truthfully utter "I know that I have hands." This is because the operative standard now requires us to eliminate the possibility that we are handless brains in vats (which, presumably, we cannot do) in order to count as "knowing."

Contextualism allows us to escape the skeptical paradox in the following way. Although it initially seemed as though we were facing three mutually inconsistent propositions, the contextualist argues that these propositions aren't really inconsistent. When we ordinarily claim to "know" things what we mean is, roughly, that we know *relative to ordinary standards*. When faced with a skeptical challenge, however, what we mean is, roughly, that we don't know *relative to high standards*. We are first asserting one proposition and then denying another proposition, although both are expressed by the same words. The meaning of "know" shifts. But as long as the relevant contexts prescribe different standards, we do not logically contradict ourselves when uttering, in one context, "I know that I have hands," while uttering, in another context, "I don't know that I have hands." In ordinary contexts, the former claim is true and the latter claim is false; in skeptical contexts, the latter claim is true and the former is false.[9]

Why, then, did it *seem* as though there was a paradox? If the skeptic is not really denying what we have been asserting all along, why are we puzzled by skeptical arguments?

The answer is that we do not fully recognize the context-sensitivity of knowledge ascriptions. The contextualist is therefore committed to positing a degree of "semantic ignorance" (Schiffer 1996; Hawthorne 2004). We are ignorant of what we are really saying, and what the skeptic is saying, which misleads us into thinking the skeptic's conclusion is incompatible with our claims to "know" a variety of things. Contextualism thus combines a view about the semantics of knowledge ascriptions with an *error theory* according to which competent speakers are systematically misled by contextualist semantics (DeRose 1995: 40–1; Cohen 1999: 77).[10]

4 Objections and replies

The contextualist solution to skepticism has been touted as a major merit of the theory. However, this solution has been widely criticized. In this section, I will discuss several objections to the contextualist solution to skepticism.

Is contextualism too skeptic-friendly?

One of the most common objections to contextualism is that it is too concessive to the skeptic. This objection can be interpreted in several ways.[11] The most common interpretation is that contextualism is too skeptic-friendly, because as soon as skepticism is mentioned participants in the conversation can no longer truthfully claim to have "knowledge." In other words, merely

Skepticism and contextualism

mentioning the possibility that we are brains in vats would be enough to cause a dramatic upward shift in epistemic standards. Many, however, find it implausible that the skeptic wins every argument simply by mentioning a skeptical scenario (Schiffer 1996; Feldman 1999; Barke 2004; Brendel 2005; Willaschek 2007).

This objection is closely related to a second one; namely, that epistemological contexts are inevitably skeptical contexts (Feldman 2001; Pritchard 2002; Brueckner 2004). Lewis writes,

> Do some epistemology. Let your fantasies rip . . . In such an extraordinary context, with such a rich domain, it never can happen (well, hardly ever) that an ascription of knowledge is true.
>
> *(1996: 559)*

Why think epistemological contexts are inevitably skeptical? Because when we engage in epistemology, we routinely attend to skeptical possibilities. This allegedly creates a conversational context in which high epistemic standards prevail, so uttering "I know that I have hands" will, in this context, express the false proposition that one knows this *relative to high standards* (Schiffer 1996: 321).

Another consequence is that contextualists cannot claim to know the truth of their own thesis, for any discussion of contextualism must take place within a skeptical context. Fogelin (2000) says the contextualist cannot tell his story out loud (so to speak) without calling attention to the very things that undercut his story – i.e. skeptical possibilities. Thus, the contextualist cannot expound his view without succumbing to "the incoherence of attempting to eff the ineffable" (Fogelin 2000: 55).

Further, contextualism allegedly produces the curious result that we can never truthfully say, or even *think*, that we know that we are not brains in vats, since any consideration of this possibility automatically raises the epistemic standards (Schiffer 1996: 321; Davis 2004: 260; Engel 2004: 212).[12] Thus, while contextualists claim that in certain contexts we *do* know (relative to low standards) that we're not brains in vats, we can never truthfully utter this, or even think it. The *only* proposition expressible by an utterance of "I know that I'm not a brain in a vat" is the false proposition that one knows that one is not a brain in a vat relative to high standards. But many regard unspeakable and unthinkable knowledge to be a very peculiar form of knowledge. More drastically, Feldman (2001: 72) claims that the contextualist, in his context, cannot truthfully say (or think) that we know *anything* about the world around us.

A final way in which contextualism has been regarded as too concessive is this: the less we reflect on our knowledge, the more we seem to know (Engel 2004). The flip side is that the more we reflect on our knowledge, the less knowledge we have (Brendel and Jäger 2004: 150). Consider the following remark by Lewis:

> Maybe epistemology is the culprit. Maybe this extraordinary pastime robs us of our knowledge. Maybe we do know a lot in daily life; but maybe when we look hard at our knowledge, it goes away . . . Then epistemology would be an investigation that destroys its own subject matter.
>
> *(1996: 550)*

Lewis goes on to say that "knowledge is elusive"; it "vanishes" because epistemology plunges us into skeptical contexts (1996: 559, 560). This is an unsavory result.

A common response to these objections is that not every context in which skepticism is discussed is a skeptical context (DeRose 2000: 94–5; Montminy 2008: 4; Ichikawa 2011: 388;

Blome-Tillmann 2014: 36). Simply making S aware of a skeptical defeater is not sufficient to effect a change of an epistemic context with respect to S knowing that *p*. For example, imagine a jury that must decide whether Jones shot Smith. In their deliberations, the jury members may properly ignore the following possibility, even if it were mentioned by the defense lawyer in a desperate, last-ditch effort to save his client: "Ladies and gentlemen, I must point out that the prosecutor has failed to rule out the possibility that it was not Jones who fired the fatal shot but rather that there is an evil demon deceiving us!" Some possibilities may be properly ignored even when the stakes are high.

Although Lewis (1996: 559) suggests that mentioning a skeptical hypothesis will put in place very high epistemic standards, contextualists are not committed to this view. Contexts are not hostage to whatever "moves" are made by conversational participants. Thus, the skeptic would not win every argument by merely drawing attention to a previously unacknowledged skeptical defeater, nor would epistemology automatically place us in a skeptical context. Contextualists needn't accept the "skeptic-friendly" assumption that philosophical discussions of skepticism are governed by exceedingly high epistemic standards (DeRose 2009).

What, then, should the contextualist say about the mechanisms that cause a shift in the epistemic standards? A plausible idea is that to drive up the standards a skeptical possibility must not only be *mentioned*, but also *taken seriously* by participants in the context. DeRose shows some sympathy for this view. He says that one's conversational partner must "get away" with making a skeptical possibility relevant in order to raise the standard (DeRose 1995: 14, fn.21). Blome-Tillmann (2014) also claims that skeptical standards do not prevail in every context in which they are mentioned. On his view, whether a context of epistemological discussion is governed by high standards depends on what the speakers in the discussion pragmatically presuppose.[13] If epistemologists are pragmatically presupposing they are not brains in vats, then contexts of epistemological inquiry are not necessarily skeptical (Blome-Tillmann 2014: 53). Blome-Tillmann argues that speakers "can, to a certain extent, voluntarily decide what they take seriously and which propositions they presuppose; they have, to a certain extent, voluntary control over the content of 'know' in their contexts" (2014: 21). Thus, we can remain in a context in which we satisfy "know" even though the skeptic has drawn our attention to brains in vats.[14]

As we've seen, contextualists are not committed to the view that the epistemic standards skyrocket as soon as skepticism is mentioned. Consequently, they may reject the claim that epistemology is a context in which we rarely, if ever, meet the conditions to satisfy "knows *p*." From this it follows that contextualists can state their view without risking incoherence. As Montminy remarks, "contextualists need not embrace the skeptic's high standards; they simply need to point out that such standards are sometimes adopted by speakers" (2008: 6).

Now let's return to the question of whether epistemology robs us of our knowledge. This can be interpreted in two ways. On one interpretation, the amount of knowledge we have decreases when the epistemic standards go up (and increases when the standards go down). We literally lose and gain knowledge as the standards shift. Strictly speaking, however, contextualism does not entail that any knowledge is lost. Contextualism is a thesis about the truth conditions of knowledge sentences. On this view, it is true that a conscientious epistemologist, who strives to envisage all sorts of error possibilities, *cannot*, in her context, truthfully claim to "know" that she has hands. It is also true that a naïve person, in an ordinary context, *can* truthfully claim to "know" that he has hands. However, the naïve person is *not* in a better epistemic position than that of the epistemologist. Both people "know" they have hands relative to low standards and both do not "know" this relative to high standards. What contextualists investigate is how the knowledge claims made by these people are to be understood (Montminy 2008: 6). The conscientious investigator says something true when she utters "I don't know that *p*," since by that

Skepticism and contextualism

utterance she expresses the proposition that she does not know that p relative to high standards; and the naïve person says something true when he says "I know that p," since by that utterance he means that he "knows" that p relative to low standards.

On the second interpretation, epistemology "robs" us of our knowledge because we tend to speak *falsely* whenever we say that we "know" things in epistemological contexts. But I have argued that epistemology does not automatically plunge us into a skeptical context, so the sentence "No one knows anything" is not made true as easily as opponents to contextualism have suggested. This at least weakens the force of this objection, even if it does not remove it entirely.

Is contextualism irrelevant to epistemology?

Several philosophers who grant the truth of contextualism nevertheless doubt that contextualism is of any relevance to epistemology (Klein 2000; Sosa 2000; Feldman 2001). I will discuss two interpretations of this objection. The most common version of this objection is nicely expressed by DeRose:

> [Contextualism] has been known to give rise to the following type of outburst: "Your contextualism isn't a theory about *knowledge* at all; it's just a theory about *knowledge attributions*. As such, it's not a piece of epistemology at all, but of the philosophy of language."
>
> *(2009: 18)*

Contextualism, as mentioned earlier, is a thesis about the truth conditions of knowledge sentences – it is *not* a thesis about knowledge itself. Thus, it is misleading to say, as many contextualists have said, that *whether one knows* depends on the context (Feldman 2004: 25; Bach 2005: 54–5). It is more accurate to say that whether a sentence of the form "S knows that p" is true depends on the context. But if the focus of contextualism is on knowledge ascriptions and not knowledge itself, then how, even if contextualism is true, could it shed light on skepticism? Isn't skepticism about the extent of our *knowledge*?

Contextualists reject this characterization of their view (e.g. DeRose 2009: 18). Although they investigate the truth conditions of knowledge ascriptions, contextualists do not regard themselves as engaged in a very different inquiry from that of traditional epistemologists. Rather, they take themselves to be addressing the traditional philosophical problem of skepticism. Contextualists believe they are bringing the relevant philosophy of language to bear on the same *epistemological* issue that others have addressed in different ways. As DeRose writes, "To the extent that contextualism/invariantism is an issue in the philosophy of language, it's a piece of philosophy of language that is of profound importance to epistemology" (2009: 18). This is because how we proceed in studying knowledge will be greatly affected by how we come down on the issue of whether or not contextualism is true. To illustrate this point, DeRose draws an analogy with the free will debate:

> Those who work on the problem of free will and determinism should *of course* be very interested in the issue of what it means to call an action "free." If that could mean different things in different contexts, then all sorts of problems could arise from a failure to recognize this shift in meaning. If there is no such shift, then that too will be vital information. In either case, one will want to know what such claims mean.
>
> *(2009: 19)*[15]

137

Similarly, if "know" expresses different propositions in different contexts, then many epistemological problems may arise due to our ignorance of this fact (DeRose 2009). Thus, it is important to discern what it means to say that someone "knows" something in order to properly investigate knowledge.[16]

Feldman (1999, 2001) proposes another way in which contextualism might be irrelevant to epistemology. He claims that contextualism *per se* does not allow us to resolve the skeptical puzzle because one might be a contextualist and yet maintain that the standards for "knowledge" never get low enough for us to meet them (i.e. you might be a contextualist *and a skeptic*), or you might think the standards for "knowledge" are never high enough to entail skepticism (i.e. the standards vary but only at a low level). Neither of these types of contextualism would resolve the skeptical problem, and they would therefore be of limited significance to epistemology.

Although Feldman's point is true as far as it goes, the contextualist never claimed that *any* version of his view could resolve the skeptical challenge. Indeed, virtually every contextualist rejects the view that the standards for "knowledge" never get high enough to favor skepticism, since this view does not adequately explain our urge to deny "knowledge" when confronted with a skeptical challenge (and thus it would fail to explain part of the phenomena that motivated contextualism in the first place). Similarly, it would be implausible to defend a version of contextualism according to which the standards for "knowledge" never get low enough for us to meet them, for this view runs contrary to our everyday practice of ascribing knowledge. The most plausible version of contextualism is one where the standards for "knowledge" are often low enough to be met (thereby preserving the truth of our knowledge ascriptions in ordinary contexts), and yet sometimes they get so high that they are rarely, if ever, met (thus explaining the pull of skepticism).

Does contextualism mischaracterize skepticism?

According to some philosophers, contextualism does not shed much light on the problem of skepticism because the contextualist mischaracterizes the skeptic's position (Feldman 1999, 2001; Klein 2000; Kornblith 2000; Bach 2005; Ludlow 2005). More precisely, the contextualist improperly portrays the dispute between the non-skeptic and the skeptic as a difference between using laxer standards and stricter ones. In presenting her argument, however, the skeptic is not merely raising the standards for what it takes to "know." Rather, she is arguing that it is much tougher than we realized for a belief to qualify as knowledge *by ordinary standards* (Bach 2005: 68). The skeptic gets us to doubt whether we actually satisfy the same standards that we have always thought we satisfied, not merely some unattainably high standard (Feldman 1999, 2001; Klein 2000). In attempting to confine the plausibility of skeptical arguments to certain contexts, the contextualist ignores the fact that the skeptic purports to show that, contrary to common belief, ordinary knowledge attributions are generally false.

Kornblith (2000) makes a similar criticism. Central to his objection is a distinction between two types of skeptic: the Full-Blooded Skeptic and the High Standards Skeptic. The Full-Blooded Skeptic claims that "we are no more justified in believing that there is an external world than that there isn't," and that we "have no degree of justification whatever for [our] claims about the external world. None." (Kornblith 2000: 26). In contrast, the High Standards Skeptic is perfectly willing to grant there are differences in degree of justification that people have for their various beliefs about the external world; he simply denies that we ever reach some very high standard required for knowledge. Kornblith's main complaint is that the contextualist only answers the High Standards Skeptic, who is the far less interesting and worrying of the two.

Skepticism and contextualism

Why is the High Standards Skeptic less interesting and worrying than the Full-Blooded Skeptic? It is because the former, but not the latter, is willing to acknowledge "the importance and accuracy of substantive epistemological distinctions that we wish to make" (Kornblith 2000: 27). The High Standards Skeptic will admit that I am far more justified in believing that I am currently sitting down and writing this paper than I am in believing that I am a handless brain in a vat. Consequently, it is easy to decide what to believe because there are widely varying degrees of justification for propositions about the world around us. The High Standards Skeptic denies that we ever reach the level of justification needed to call such beliefs "knowledge," but this is "a wholly trivial and uninteresting position," says Kornblith (2000: 27). He writes, "This is not, of course, the skepticism of Descartes' First Meditation; it is, instead, a much more modest and less exciting form of skepticism" (2000: 26). The real threat is the Full-Blooded Skeptic who insists that all propositions about the external world are epistemically on par. It is this skeptic who is allegedly making "a historically important and philosophically interesting claim," according to Kornblith (2000: 27), and yet contextualism does nothing to address this argument.

How might the contextualist reply? In response to the skeptic's claim that we lack knowledge even by ordinary standards, the contextualist might accuse the skeptic of *mistakenly believing* this because she is confused by semantic ignorance. Although the skeptic purports to show that, contrary to common belief, our knowledge claims have always been false, perhaps she is just wrongly assuming that knowledge ascriptions have invariant truth conditions, and in making this assumption she commits the fallacy of equivocation. If knowledge ascriptions really are context-sensitive, then the skeptic is not actually denying what we thought we knew.[17] Instead, she makes the same type of semantic confusion that we make when we worry about skeptical arguments. Both parties are partially semantically ignorant of what's really going on, so neither of us realizes the context has shifted.

I think there's an element of talking past each other here. Contextualism is supposed to be a descriptive thesis about how we use language, whereas skepticism isn't usually a descriptive thesis. The skeptic isn't making a point about how we use language but rather a point about how we *should* use language, or something like that. So it is hard to see why this contextualist response is fully satisfying.[18]

As far as I know, no contextualist has in print dealt with Kornblith's Full-Blooded Skeptic.[19] Some anecdotal evidence suggests that many contextualists are not moved by this objection, but I'm not sure why. Perhaps it is because the skeptic is often portrayed as denying that we ever speak truly when, even in ordinary conversation, we claim to "know" things about the external world (see Hawthorne 2004: 53; Stanley 2005: 82; Davis 2007: 427; Rysiew 2007: 627). As DeRose (unpublished) points out, the skeptic of Descartes' First Meditation, whom Kornblith finds interesting, seems to be more like the High Standards Skeptic than the Full-Blooded Skeptic, contrary to Kornblith's own reading of Descartes. For example, Curley takes Descartes' conclusion to be: "None of my beliefs about ordinary-sized objects in my immediate vicinity are certain" (1978: 52). This certainly isn't Full-Blooded Skepticism. Further, DeRose (1992) argues that Descartes' own description of the "atheist geometer" makes his skepticism look milder than even the High Standards Skeptic. The geometer has not escaped from the skepticism established in the first meditation, and yet Descartes says he can "know clearly" that the geometrical theorem is true (Descartes 1967: vol. 2, 39). Thus, Kornblith's insinuation that Descartes is describing something more like the Full-Blooded Skeptic than the High Standards Skeptic seems false.

Perhaps another reason why contextualists have focused on the High Standards Skeptic is that he *is* more threatening than Kornblith suggests. If this skeptic were right, then we would speak falsely whenever we claim to "know" things about the external world. Kornblith says the truth of this claim would not be philosophically important news. However, the news that all our knowledge claims are false, including those made in ordinary conversation, certainly seems startling. "Know" is one of the ten most commonly used verbs in English (Davies and Gardner 2010), the most prominently used term in epistemic assessment (Gerken 2015), and is unlike almost every other word because it finds a precise meaning equivalent in every human language (Goddard 2010). These facts suggest that knowledge-talk plays an important and perhaps indispensable role in our communicative practices (see Hannon 2015). Why would such a common term in our language fail in such a radical way? If it did, that would be pretty interesting.

Do contextualists beg the question?

In presenting their argument, contextualists merely *assume* that we meet ordinary standards for knowledge. But are they entitled to this assumption? Isn't this *begging the question* against the skeptic? As Brueckner writes,

> Wait a minute. How do I know that any speaker is ever in an ordinary conversational context? Sure, in a normal, non-vat-world of the sort I take myself to inhabit, there are normal speakers who speak and write (and think) from within ordinary conversational contexts. But I don't know that there are any such contexts in my world, which may be a solipsistic vat-world.
>
> *(2004: 402)*

This worry has some merit. How could contextualists claim to be *defeating* the skeptic if one of the contextualist's key points merely presupposes that the skeptic is wrong?

The contextualist is not arguing that skepticism can be resolved in a way that would fully satisfy the skeptic. If that were the contextualist's goal, he would certainly beg the question. Rather, the contextualist is trying to provide a resolution to the skeptical paradox in a way that makes the most sense of all the intuitions involved. The contextualist will say his view is more plausible because he can explain three key facts: why the skeptic and the non-skeptic *think* they are contradicting each other; why skepticism seems threatening; and why we ordinarily *do* meet the standards for knowledge. In contrast, the skeptic is left with the burden of explaining why we are systematically mistaken about whether we have knowledge. By accounting for the plausibility of all the claims constitutive of the puzzle, the contextualist claims this solution is superior to rival positions, including the skeptic's.

5 Conclusion

Contextualism was recently judged to be the most popular view in the semantics of knowledge ascriptions.[20] One of the main virtues of this view is that it can allegedly resolve the problem of skepticism. However, this view is not without criticism. I've indicated how contextualists have, or might, reply to some objections, but the issue is far from settled. I'll conclude with three questions for the contextualist.

First, if the contextualist is right that merely considering a skeptical possibility is not sufficient to place me in a context with elevated standards, then why does it seem impossible to reasonably claim to know, say, that I am not a brain in a vat? *Whenever* I think about this possibility, it strikes me that I do not know it does not obtain. Second, on what grounds can we be said to know, even

Skepticism and contextualism

according to ordinary standards, that we are not brains in vats? We can't say that our evidence against this possibility is good enough because we have *no evidence whatsoever* that could count against it. Third, contextualists have not explained *why* there would be such diverse standards for "knowledge."[21] The contextualist merely points out that, given our linguistic behavior, we *do* seem to have them. But there are non-contextualist ways to explain our linguistic behavior (Stroud 1984; Rysiew 2001; Davis 2004; Stanley 2005; Brown 2006). For these and other reasons, the effectiveness of the contextualist solution to skepticism remains to be determined.[22]

Notes

1 This view differs from the sort of contextualism defended by Annis (1978) and Williams (1991). Pritchard (2002) discusses different types of contextualism. One might also be a contextualist about epistemic terms other than knowledge, such as certainty, justification, evidence, reliability, or understanding. My focus is strictly on knowledge.

2 This is a harmless simplification. Contextualists do not think there are just two standards governing the truth conditions of knowledge ascriptions (contra Malcolm 1952), but rather a wide variety (DeRose 1999). Elsewhere I have argued that "knows" is not a variable as contextualists typically claim (Hannon 2015).

3 The contextualist solution to skepticism would be implausible if contextualism were an incorrect account of the semantics of how we use the verb "know" in daily life. Thus, the primary grounds for contextualism must come from our knowledge-attributing (and knowledge-denying) behavior in ordinary, non-philosophical talk (DeRose 2009: 47). See ch. 2.

4 See Hawthorne (2004) for a discussion of the closure principle. The proposal that we should resolve skeptical worries by rejecting closure has been criticized by Cohen (1988: 105), Vogel (1990: 13), Feldman (1995: 487), Lewis (1996: 564), Schiffer (1996: 320), DeRose (2009: 29), and many others. In contrast, Dretske (1970), Nozick (1981), and Heller (1999) have denied closure.

5 Ch. 12 gives a related discussion of closure and contextualism.

6 Moore (1939) famously defended this strategy.

7 There is also a debate about whether the skeptic speaks *truthfully* when she attempts to impose higher standards. Suppose the skeptic is met with an "Aw, come on!" response from her listener, who continues to insist that he has knowledge. Who is speaking the truth? Contextualists often write as if the skeptic speaks truthfully in such a context (Lewis 1979: 355; DeRose 1995). Others have assumed that *both* the skeptic and her opponent are speaking the truth. DeRose (2004), however, rejects both of these views. In his view, neither the skeptic nor her opponent is speaking truthfully as they argue. Rather, both parties are making claims that are neither true nor false. For criticisms of this view, see Feldman (2004) and Gottschling (2004).

8 Although I will focus on salience (because it seems most relevant to skepticism), epistemic standards might also shift as a result of *practical interests* (Fantl and McGrath 2002; Stanley 2005). Consequently, what it takes to "know" that *p* might go up if it is very important for one to have a true belief that *p*.

9 The contextualist avoids rejecting the closure principle by contextualizing it: If X satisfies "knows *O*" in context C and satisfies "knows that *O* entails *P*" in C, then X satisfies "knows *P*" in C (Blome-Tillmann forthcoming). This metalinguistic version says that the non-contextualized closure principle expresses a truth as long as the conversational context is fixed.

10 One of the most important objections to contextualism is that semantic ignorance is implausible in the case of knowledge (see Schiffer 1996; Feldman 1999; Hofweber 1999; Rysiew 2001; Pritchard 2002; Davis 2004; Hawthorne 2004; Bach 2005; Conee 2005; Stanley 2005; Williamson 2005). A number of contextualists have replied to this objection (Neta 2003; Cohen 2005; DeRose 2009; Blome-Tillmann 2014). Unfortunately, I do not have space to discuss it here.

11 Here I draw on Montminy (2008).

12 This seems implied by DeRose's "Rule of Sensitivity" (1995: 36), although DeRose is careful to say that the standards for knowledge *tend* to raise when a person asserts that he does (or does not) know that he's not a brain in a vat.

13 S pragmatically presupposes *p* in context C iff S is disposed to behave, in her use of language, as if she believed *p* to be common ground in C (Blome-Tillmann 2014: 26). It is "common ground" that *p* in

a group G iff all members of G *accept* (for the purpose of the conversation) that *p*, and all *believe* that all accept that *p*, and all *believe* that all *believe* that all accept that *p*, etc. (Blome-Tillmann 2014: 23).

14 But what happens if, in a conversation, the skeptic refuses to pragmatically presuppose that we are not brains in vats? Blome-Tillmann says we are in a *defective context* (2014: 43–5). In such contexts, it is unclear whether we satisfy "knows" (or if epistemicism isn't your preferred theory of vagueness, there is a truth-value gap). This view is similar to DeRose (2004).

15 Robin McKenna suggests that the same analogy could actually illustrate the *irrelevance* of contextualism to epistemology. If the contextualist claim to solve the skeptical problem is like the claim that we can solve the debate between free will and determinism by pointing out that, in some contexts, "free" means something that is compatible with determinism (whereas in other contexts it doesn't), then those unsatisfied by this approach to free will would be similarly unsatisfied with epistemic contextualism.

16 Sosa (2000) also questions the relevance of contextualism to epistemology. See Blome-Tillmann (2007) for a reply. See also ch. 9.

17 Does this reply beg the question? I will discuss this objection in the next sub-section.

18 Thanks to Robin McKenna here.

19 After I wrote this chapter, Keith DeRose told me that he provides a thorough reply to Kornblith in ch. 4 of his unpublished monograph, "The Appearance of Ignorance: Knowledge, Skepticism, and Context, Vol. 2". This book is currently under review at Oxford University Press.

20 According to a recent survey, 40.1% of philosophers endorse contextualism, whereas 31.1% are invariantists, 2.9% are relativists, and 25.9% classify as "other" (Bourget and Chalmers 2014).

21 Although see Henderson (2009), Hannon (2013), and McKenna (2013) for an exception.

22 Thanks to Wesley Buckwalter, Elizabeth Edenberg, Stephen Grimm, Jonathan Ichikawa, Robin McKenna, and Mike Stuart for helpful comments and discussion.

Works cited

Annis, D. 1978. "A Contextualist Theory of Epistemic Justification." *American Philosophical Quarterly* 15 (3): 213–219.

Bach, K. 2005. "The Emperor's New 'Knows'." In G. Preyer & G. Peter (eds.), *Contextualism in Philosophy: Knowledge, Meaning, and Truth*. Oxford: Oxford University Press, 51–89.

Barke, A. 2004. "Epistemic Contextualism." *Erkenntnis* 61 (2–3): 353–373.

Blome-Tillmann, M. Forthcoming. "Skepticism and Contextualism." In B. Reed & D. Manchuca (eds.), *Skepticism: From Antiquity to the Present*. London: Continuum.

———. 2014. *Knowledge and Presuppositions*. Oxford: Oxford University Press.

———. 2007. "Contextualism and the Epistemological Enterprise." *Proceedings of the Aristotelian Society* 107 (1): 387–394.

Bourget, D. & Chalmers, D. 2014. "What Do Philosophers Believe?" *Philosophical Studies* 170 (3): 465–500.

Brendel, E. 2005. "Why Contextualists Cannot Know They Are Right: Self-Refuting Implications of Contextualism." *Acta Analytica* 20 (2): 38–55.

Brendel, E. & Jäger, C. 2004. "Contextualist Approaches to Epistemology: Problems and Prospects." *Erkenntnis* 61 (2–3): 143–172.

Brown, J. 2006. "Contextualism and Warranted Assertibility Manoeuvres." *Philosophical Studies* 130 (3): 407–435.

Brueckner, A. 2004. "The Elusive Virtues of Contextualism." *Philosophical Studies* 118 (3): 401–405.

Cohen, S. 2005. "'Contextualism Defended' and 'Contextualism Defended Some More'." In M. Steup & E. Sosa (eds.), *Contemporary Debates in Epistemology*. Malden, MA: Blackwell, 56–62, 67–71.

———. 1999. "Contextualism, Skepticism, and the Structure of Reasons." *Philosophical Perspectives* 13: 57–89.

———. 1988. "How to Be a Fallibilist." *Philosophical Perspectives* 2: 91–123.

Conee, E. 2005. "'Contextualism Contested' and 'Contextualism Contested Some More'." In M. Steup & E. Sosa (eds.), *Contemporary Debates in Epistemology*. Malden, MA: Blackwell, 56–62, 67–71.

Curley, E. 1978. *Descartes Against the Skeptics*. Cambridge: Harvard University Press.

Davies, M. & Gardner, D. 2010. *Frequency Dictionary of American English*. New York: Routledge.

Davis, W. 2007. "Knowledge Claims and Context: Loose Use." *Philosophical Studies* 132 (3): 395–438.

———. 2004. "Are Knowledge Claims Indexical?" *Erkenntnis* 61 (2–3): 257–281.

DeRose, K. 2009. *The Case for Contextualism*. Oxford: Oxford University Press.

Skepticism and contextualism

———. 2004. "Single Scoreboard Semantics." *Philosophical Studies*, 119 (1–2): 1–21.

———. 2000. "Now You Know It, Now You Don't." *Proceedings of the Twentieth World Congress of Philosophy* 5: 91–106.

———. 1999. "Contextualism: An Explanation and Defense." In J. Greco & E. Sosa (eds.), *The Blackwell Guide to Epistemology*. Malden, MA: Blackwell, 185–203.

———. 1995. "Solving the Skeptical Problem." *The Philosophical Review* 104 (1): 1–52.

———. 1992. "Contextualism and Knowledge Attributions." *Philosophy and Phenomenological Research* 52 (4): 913–929.

Descartes, R. 1967. The *Philosophical Works of Descartes*, Volume 2. Cambridge: Cambridge University Press.

Dretske, F. 1970. "Epistemic Operators." *The Journal of Philosophy* 67 (24): 1007–1023.

Engel, M. 2004. "What's Wrong with Contextualism, and a Noncontextualist Resolution of the Skeptical Paradox." *Erkenntnis* 61 (2–3): 203–231.

Fantl, J. & McGrath, M. 2002. "Evidence, Pragmatics, and Justification." *Philosophical Review* 111 (1): 67–94.

Feldman, R. 2004. "Comments on DeRose's 'Single Scoreboard Semantics'." *Philosophical Studies* 119 (1–2): 23–33.

———. 2001. "Skeptical Problems, Contextualist Solutions." *Philosophical Studies* 103: 61–85.

———. 1999. "Contextualism and Skepticism." *Philosophical Perspectives* 1: 91–114.

———. 1995. "In Defence of Closure." *Philosophical Quarterly* 45 (181): 487–494.

Fogelin, R. 2000. "Contextualism and Externalism: Trading in One Form of Skepticism for Another." *Philosophical Perspectives* 34 (1): 43–57.

Gerken, M. 2015. "The Roles of Knowledge Ascriptions in Epistemic Assessment." *European Journal of Philosophy* 23 (1): 141–161.

Goddard, C. 2010. "Universals and Variation in the Lexicon of Mental State Concepts." In B. Malt & P. Wolff (eds.), *Words and the Mind*. Oxford: Oxford University Press, 72–92.

Gottschling, V. 2004. "Keeping the Conversational Score: Constraints for an Optimal Contextualist Answer?" *Erkenntnis* 61 (2–3): 295–314.

Hannon, M. 2015. "Stabilizing Knowledge." *Pacific Philosophical Quarterly* 96 (1): 116–139.

———. 2013. "The Practical Origins of Epistemic Contextualism." *Erkenntnis* 78 (4): 889–919.

Hawthorne, J. 2004. *Knowledge and Lotteries*. Oxford: Oxford University Press.

Heller, M. 1999. "The Proper Role for Contextualism in an Anti-Luck Epistemology." *Philosophical Perspectives* 13: 115–129.

Henderson, D. 2009. "Motivated Contextualism." *Philosophical Studies* 142 (1): 119–131.

Hofweber, T. 1999. "Contextualism and the Meaning-Intention Problem." In K. Korta, E. Sosa, & X. Arrazola (eds.), *Cognition, Agency and Rationality*. Dordrecht: Kluwer, 93–104.

Ichikawa, J. 2011. "Quantifiers and Epistemic Contextualism." *Philosophical Studies* 155 (3): 383–398.

Klein, P. 2000. "Contextualism and the Real Nature of Academic Skepticism." *Philosophical Issues* 10: 108–116.

Kornblith, H. 2000. "The Contextualist Evasion of Epistemology." *Philosophical Issues* 10: 24–32.

Lewis, D. 1996. "Elusive Knowledge." *Australasian Journal of Philosophy* 74 (4): 549–567.

———. 1979. "Scorekeeping in a Language Game." *Journal of Philosophical Logic* 8 (1): 339–359.

Ludlow, P. 2005. "Contextualism and the New Linguistic Turn in Epistemology." In G. Preyer & G. Peter (eds.), *Contextualism in Philosophy: Knowledge, Meaning, and Truth*. Oxford: Oxford University Press, 11–50.

McKenna, R. 2013. "Epistemic Contextualism: A Normative Approach." *Pacific Philosophical Quarterly* 94 (1): 101–123.

Malcolm, N. 1952. "Knowledge and Belief." *Mind* 61 (242): 178–189.

Montminy, M. 2008. "Can Contextualists Maintain Neutrality?" *Philosophers' Imprint* 8 (7): 1–13.

Moore, G. E. 1939. "Proof of an External World." *Proceedings of the British Academy* 25 (5): 273–300.

Neta, R. 2003. "Contextualism and the Problem of the External World." *Philosophy and Phenomenological Research* 66 (1): 1–31.

Nozick, R. 1981. *Philosophical Explanations*. Cambridge, MA: Harvard University Press.

Pritchard, D. 2002. "Two Forms of Epistemological Contextualism." *Grazer Philosophische Studien* 64: 19–55.

Rysiew, P. 2007. "Epistemic Contextualism." In E. N. Zalta (ed.), *The Stanford Encyclopedia of Philosophy* (Winter 2011). URL = <http://plato.stanford.edu/archives/win2011/entries/contextualism-epistemology/>.

———. 2001. "The Context-Sensitivity of Knowledge Attributions." *Noûs* 35 (4): 477–514.

Schiffer, S. 1996. "Contextualist Solutions to Skepticism." *Proceedings of the Aristotelian Society* 96: 317–333.

Sosa, E. 2000. "Skepticism and Contextualism." *Philosophical Issues* 10: 1–18.

Stanley, J. 2005. *Knowledge and Practical Interests*. Oxford: Oxford University Press.
Stroud, B. 1984. *The Philosophical Significance of Skepticism*. Oxford: Oxford University Press.
Vogel, J. 1990. "Are There Counterexamples to the Closure Principle." In M. Ross & G. Ross (eds.), *Doubting: Contemporary Perspectives on Skepticism*. Dordrecht: Kluwer.
Willaschek, M. 2007. "Contextualism about Knowledge and Justification by Default." *Grazer Philosophische Studien* 74 (1): 251–272.
Williams, M. 1991. *Unnatural Doubts: Epistemological Realism and the Basis of Scepticism*. Malden, MA: Blackwell.
Williamson, T. 2005. "Knowledge, Context, and the Agent's Point of View." In G. Preyer & G. Peter (eds.), *Contextualism in Philosophy: Knowledge, Meaning, and Truth*. Oxford: Oxford University Press, 91–114.

11

CONTEXTUALISM AND FALLIBILISM

Keith DeRose

Contextualism in epistemology has been intimately related to fallibilism, though, due to some malleability in what's meant by "fallibilism," that relation has been presented in different ways. In one of contextualism's "founding documents," Stewart Cohen (1988), presented "fallibilism" as a form of sensibleness in epistemology, and contextualism as a way of achieving it; indeed, the paper was entitled "How to Be a Fallibilist."[1] David Lewis's (1996) contextualist manifesto, "Elusive Knowledge," by contrast, memorably construed "fallibilism" as a form of "madness," and presented contextualism as providing a way to "dodge the choice" between it and the even more intrusive madness of skepticism – to steer a course "between the rock of fallibilism and the whirlpool of skepticism" (550). The apparent difference here proves to be merely verbal, based on different uses of "fallibilism" (that we'll be in a position to quickly identify at the end of section 2).

In what follows, I will attempt to explain the relations among contextualism, skepticism, and different construals of "fallibilism," and I will distinguish between two contextualist ways of handling what we can call "infallibilist tensions," presenting them along with other, non-contextualist options for dealing with those tensions.

1 Contextualism, skepticism, and intuitive fallibilism

There seems to be an intuitive, but difficult-to-get-precise-about, sense in which we humans are fallible with respect to everything, or at least nearly everything, that we believe, and "fallibilism" is sometimes used to designate this fact about us.[2] But we will here be interested in uses of "fallibilism" in which it instead asserts that we can *know* things with respect to which we are fallible. "Intuitive fallibilism" can then be the position that knowing some fact is compatible with being fallible with respect to that fact in the murky-but-intuitive sense in question. Following Lewis's lead (1996: 449–450), then, we can set aside the issue of whether there are some narrow classes of beliefs with respect to which we are infallible – like perhaps a few concerning some simple necessary truths and some truths about our own present conscious experience.[3] For, whether or not we are infallible with respect to those special truths, common sense demands that our knowledge extends beyond those, to other truths, including many about the external world, with respect to which we seem to be fallible in the intuitive sense in question.

145

To see contextualism's relation to fallibilism, we look to contextualist treatments of skepticism. On typical contextualist analysis (on the "basic contextualist strategy" I outline at DeRose 1995: 4–7), the skeptic, in presenting her argument, manipulates the semantic standards for knowledge, thereby at least threatening to create a context in which she can truthfully say that we know nothing or very little. The hope is that by means of such an account, our ordinary claims to "know," and ordinary thoughts that we do "know" plenty, can be safeguarded from the apparently powerful attack of the skeptic, while, at the same time, the persuasiveness of skeptical arguments is explained.[4]

The standard contextualist treatment of skepticism then involves the claim/admission that there are standards for knowledge according to which the skeptic is right that we "know" nothing (or perhaps very little).[5] To employ a handy bit of semi-technical terminology,[6] the contextualist's account is not one on which we *simply know* what the skeptic denies we know; that is, it does not claim that any speaker using standard English, whatever their context, would be speaking truthfully if they said we "knew" these things. But it is an account on which almost all of our claims to "know" the items in question are true.[7]

This suggests a stance toward intuitive fallibilism. The contextualist (who takes the standard contextualist approach to skepticism) is not what we might call a "simple intuitive fallibilist": they will not hold that all of what gets called "knowledge" in standard English is compatible with being fallible with respect to the beliefs in question. But they will be a "relaxed intuitive fallibilist," holding that our ordinary claims to "knowledge" and ordinary thoughts to the effect that we "know" things (and indeed all such claims and thoughts that are not governed by the peculiar standards of philosophical skeptics) are compatible with our being fallible in the intuitive sense with what we say and think is "known." It also suggests the hope that the sense in which "knowledge" *is* incompatible with one's being fallible with respect to the item "known" can be used to explain (away) the phenomena that seem to support infallibilism.

2 Attempts at characterizing intuitive fallibilism, and the distinction between intuitive fallibilism and GC-fallibilism

But what is the intuitive way in which we are always, or almost always, fallible with respect to our beliefs? One prominent way of trying to spell this out construes our fallibility as a matter of our always, or almost always, failing to hold our beliefs on the basis of reasons or evidence that entails that those beliefs are true. "Intuitive fallibilism" (in its simple and relaxed varieties) would then be the position that we can know things to be true even when the evidence or reasons on which we base our beliefs in them don't entail the truth of those beliefs. This is the characterization that Cohen uses; "How to Be a Fallibilist" opens with these words:

> The acceptance of fallibilism in epistemology is virtually universal. Any theory of knowledge that endorses the principle that S knows q on the basis of reason r only if r entails q, is doomed to a skeptical conclusion. Fallibilist theories reject this entailment principle thereby avoiding this immediate skeptical result.
>
> *(1988: 91)*[8]

Cohen then offers contextualism (and, more particularly, a contextualist version of the relevant alternatives account of knowledge) as a way to handle the problems that confront such a fallibilist. However, I think that characterizations like Cohen's fail to really capture the intuitive distinction here.

Notice first that "infallibilism," as Cohen is construing it, does not actually by itself doom us to skepticism. A view that demands a tight connection between our reasons and any knowledge we might have – even one that demands that the tie be maximally tight – does not by itself ensure any strong skeptical results, since by itself it leaves it open that our reasons might abound. In an extreme case, if everything we normally took ourselves to know was among our reasons, then "infallibilism," construed as we are currently considering it, would not at all threaten *any* of our presumed knowledge. Similar remarks would apply to characterizations phrased in terms of "evidence," rather than "reasons" – and might be made a bit more urgent by the existence of Timothy Williamson's fairly prominent account of evidence on which E = K, as he puts it: our evidence is what we know to be the case (see Williamson 2000: 184–208). Skepticism would result from such forms of "infallibilism" *combined with* some suitably restrictive account of what our reasons or evidence might be.

And this points to one of the problems of this way of distinguishing between fallibilism and infallibilism. In addition to the problems such accounts face in their application to what seems to be our often shaky, fallibilist knowledge of necessary truths,[9] such accounts have trouble (that can overlap with the just mentioned problem) with *immediate knowledge*. Often, it seems, we know some proposition q on the basis of a reason, or piece of evidence, r, where r is some proposition distinct from q. And perhaps we know r to be the case on the basis of some yet other propositional reason, r2. But arguably, as we trace the lineage of reasons back, this basing of knowledge on deeper reasons comes to an end, and arguably, it can end in immediate knowledge, where some subject knows some proposition p to be the case, though her knowledge of p isn't based on any deeper propositional reasons (or any deeper propositional evidence). But it seems that, and nothing clearly rules it out that, immediate knowledge, so understood, can be the kind of shaky, uncertain "knowledge" that an intuitive fallibilist, but not an infallibilist, will accept as such. But how can a formulation of the type we are considering handle such cases? If we say that in cases of immediate knowledge of p, S has *no* propositional reason (or propositional evidence) for p (and so, presumably, doesn't need propositional reasons or evidence for p in order to know that p), then we of course can't differentiate fallibilist from infallibilist immediate knowledge in terms of whether S's propositional reasons (or evidence) for p entails p. And the other option would seem to be to say that in cases of immediate knowledge of p, p itself is S's reason (or evidence) for p. But then, of course, p *will* be entailed by S's reason for it in all cases of immediate knowledge, no matter how shaky they might be. The way of drawing the distinction exemplified here by Cohen would seem tenable only if we assume (rather boldly, I would think – indeed recklessly, relative to my sense of what could be said in defense of such an assumption) that our propositional reasons or evidence (or perhaps our "ultimate" propositional reasons or evidence, if you want to go that way) are themselves always things we know infallibly.

So it is natural to instead try to use a notion like that of epistemic *risk*, or *chances* or *possibilities* of error to draw the distinction: The infallibilist can be construed as holding that, while the fallibilist denies that, in order for S to know that p, there must be no risk (or perhaps "no risk whatsoever"), or perhaps no possibility or no chance ("whatsoever"), from S's point of view, that p is false.[10] These notions seem capable of applying to immediate as well as mediate knowledge, so as to differentiate in both places the infallibly certain from the at-least-somewhat-shaky.

The problem here is that (at least without the cryptic "whatsoever" qualification), such formulations misclassify some folks, including me, who seem to be intuitive fallibilists, as infallibilists. I take myself to be clearly an intuitive fallibilist, at least of the relaxed variety, but the way of drawing the distinction under consideration would style me an infallibilist. In the case of epistemic possibilities, I am on record as accepting an account on which S's not knowing that p is a truth condition for an assertion by S of "It's possible that not-p_{ind}," and, relatedly, as holding that conjunctions of the form "I know that p, but it is possible that not-p_{ind}," express "genuine inconsistencies" (DeRose 1991: 596–601).[11] My contextualism does muddy the waters a bit here.

I'm a contextualist about both epistemic modal statements and knowledge attributions, thinking that the meaning of these two types of statements "sway together," in Lewis's nice phrase,[12] so that, where the epistemic standards are held constant throughout the conjunction, as they are in normal contexts, "I know that p, but it's possible that not-P_{ind}" is inconsistent. So I think "I know that p" will often be true even though "It's possible that not-p_{ind}" is true as evaluated by *some* epistemic standard – but not the one at which "I know that p" is also true. Still, I seem a good (if muddy) example of someone who thinks that "I know that p" is inconsistent with "It's possible that not-p_{ind}," because I think their relation is much like that of "I am tall" and "I am not tall" – both of which could also be true if evaluated at different standards for tallness, but cannot be if the standards are kept constant.

We might want a way of marking the distinction between those who do and those who don't think that there is a real conflict between the likes of "I know that p" and "It's possible that not-p_{ind}," and one might well use "infallibilist"/"fallibilist" to mark that distinction, rightly putting me in the "infallibilist" camp. We can call this "GC-," for "genuine conflict," fallibilism and infalliblism. But then we should clearly distinguish this GC-fallibilism/GC-infallibilism from the "intuitive" use of the terms. Having made this distinction, we will try again to characterize the "intuitive" division in section 3, and will look a bit at the boundary between GC-fallibilism and GC-infallibilism in section 4.

First, however, we can now clear up the verbal disagreement between our contextualist authors (noted at the opening). The sensible fallibilism that Cohen seeks is intuitive fallibilism. Contextualists hope that their views can help make the world safe for such intuitive fallibilism – at least in its relaxed variety. The fallibilism that Lewis thinks sounds like "madness" is GC-fallibilism. We will consider how "mad" it is in section 4.

3 Characterizing intuitive fallibilism in micro-terms

Perhaps we can characterize intuitive fallibilism as the view that allows (simply, or in our more relaxed way) that we can have knowledge despite the existence of possibilities or "micro-possibilities" (or "micro-risks" and "micro-chances") of error, in the way I'm about to explain. This attempt certainly won't render our distinction maximally clear, but it can serve to forge a reasonable account of the relation between the intuitive notion of fallibility and some terms that employ an important part of our epistemic vocabulary ("possibility," "risk," "chance," in epistemic uses).

Consider Unger's old comparison of "knows" with "flat."[13] In the following section, we will consider some tensions between claiming to "know" something and admitting that there is some "possibility," "chance," or "risk" of error about the matter, from the speaker's point of view. Unger noted similar tensions between calling a surface "flat" and admitting that it had "bumps." Largely from such tensions, he concluded that if a surface is flat, then it has no bumps whatsoever. However, Unger claimed, just about all the physical surfaces we encounter, including those we typically describe as "flat," do in fact have some bumps, however small (and sometimes it might take a microscope to see them), and so, he argued, they are not actually flat (1975: 65). Unger concluded that we are just about always speaking falsely when we call an ordinary physical surface "flat."

Those who cling to the truth of our ordinary claims that surfaces are "flat" have several options as to what to say about Unger's argument and the microscopic "smallish bumps" he points out. Employing our semi-technical use of "simply," I suppose that one could bravely declare that the "irregularities" revealed by microscopes *simply* are not bumps, and anyone who calls them "bumps" in any context is speaking falsely. Those things simply aren't big enough to really constitute "bumps"! Alternatively, one could agree with Unger that it turns out that

Contextualism and fallibilism

almost all the physical surfaces we talk about, including those we typically call "flat," simply *do* have bumps, but hold that being flat, and being truthfully called "flat," is consistent with having (small enough) bumps. But many will be tempted by a contextualist approach to "bumps," saying that what counts as a "bump" varies with context. In most contexts, the microscopically small "irregularities" Unger points to don't rise to the level of counting as "bumps" – which is why we do (despite our standing knowledge of what the surfaces of physical objects are like) and can truthfully say of many ordinary physical surfaces in many contexts that they have "no bumps." (Or even, in some perfectly natural sense, "No bumps whatsoever": you worked for a long time sanding a tabletop to remove all the large bumps, but still left about ten "small bumps," as you were happy to call them. The next day, you sand those down. "Now there are no bumps whatsoever," you say, apparently [or at least this seems apparent to me] truthfully, despite the continued presence of Unger-bumps.) Relative to those contexts, the small "irregularities" that Unger writes of are what we might well call "micro-bumps": they are things that don't count as "bumps" relative to the context under discussion, but do count as "bumps" in other contexts, where they meet the lower thresholds in place for what is to count as a "bump." Such a contextualist line would seem to hold promise for accounting for the persuasiveness (such as it is, and this does seem to vary much from person to person) of Unger-like arguments for flatness skepticism. Perhaps pointing out such small irregularities and calling them "bumps" is a way of putting into place, or at least of pushing toward putting into place, standards by which they do count as "bumps" – of making what were just micro-bumps now count as "bumps." And here one can sense possibilities (that we won't here explore) for explaining the tensions that Unger exploits in ways that won't involve us in any jarringly incredible claims to the effect that almost all our positive ordinary claims to the effect that ordinary physical surfaces are "flat" are false.

It's easiest to make sense of a notion of "micro-bumps" when one accepts contextualism about "bump," so one can say, as I do above, that a micro-bump relative to context c is something that does not count as a "bump" in c, but does count as a "bump" in other contexts with more liberal standards. But suppose that for some reason (perhaps an irrational aversion to context-sensitivity) one is an invariantist about "bump," and so holds that, though the standards for what we are likely to *call* a "bump" may well vary a lot among contexts, what can be *truthfully* called a "bump" does not vary from context to context. Well, then, you won't think there are any micro-bumps relative to any contexts – at least given our current understanding of "micro-bump." But it seems you might still have good use for a related notion, which might well be given the same label. For, supposing you're not a *skeptical* invariantist like Unger, but instead think that the standards for what counts as a "bump" hold steady at some moderate level (at which microscopic "irregularities" certainly don't count), you will often face things much like those you would count as "bumps" but which you'll think don't – and that sometimes don't *quite* – rise to the level of counting as a "bump," and you might have use for a term like "micro-bump" to describe such things, where by this you will mean roughly: something much like a bump, but which doesn't rise to the level of being a bump; something that, if there were only more of it, would be a bump.[14] If we can make sense of such a notion (and I admit, it's not the clearest in the world), that should become our general notion, available to both contextualists and invariantists about "bump." We can use the explication just given, but relativize it to contexts: A micro-bump, relative to context c, is something which is much like the things that count as "bumps" in c, but which doesn't rise to the level of counting as a "bump" in c; it is something that, if there were only more of it, would count as a "bump" in c. For invariantists, the line between "bumps" and micro-bumps does not move from context to context. For contextualists, it does. This gives the contextualist an added aid in answering questions of the likes of "Wha'dya mean, 'something that, if there were only more of it, would count as a bump in c'?!": for the contextualist can often add that it is something that *does* count as a "bump" in contexts other than c, which are more liberal than c in counting things as "bumps."

Although it's not a physical notion of something we can visually imagine, we can utilize an analogous notion of "micro-risks" of error, understanding them to be micro-bumps in the epistemic road. A "micro-risk" of error, relative to context c, is something which is much like the things that count as "risks" of error in c, but which doesn't rise to the level of counting as a "risk" of error in c. It is something that, if there were only more of it, would count as a "risk" of error in c. This notion and/or closely related notions may be helpful in characterizing what "infallibilism" about knowledge is: perhaps we can say that the infallibilist, but not the fallibilist, holds that knowing that p is incompatible with there being risks *or even micro-risks* (and/or micro-possibilities, and/or micro-chances) of error with respect to p? And perhaps our fallibilist will be able to explain the tensions we looked at in the previous section in ways that won't involve us in any incredible claims to the effect that even the tiniest micro-risks of error are enough to make even ordinary claims to "know" something go false?

4 Contextualism and GC-fallibilism/GC-infallibilism: options for handling the infallibilist's tensions

We close by looking at the options by which intuitive fallibilists might seek to deal with the "infallibilist's tensions" (so-called because it is the infallibilist who is likely to point them out): tensions between claiming to know that p while, at the same time, making some admission about one's limited position with respect to a matter (like admitting that there is a risk that you might be wrong about p – or that there is a chance or a possibility that p is false, or that one may or might be mistaken). Two of the interesting intermediate options here are contextualist in nature (though the other options are also open to contextualists).

Let's start with a look at the kinds of tensions involved. Here is Rogers Albritton having some fun with how hard it is to combine "I know" with "I may be mistaken." He has just rejected the claim that "I may be mistaken" requires for its truth that the speaker have what J. L. Austin calls, not just a reason for thinking she may be mistaken, but a "*concrete* reason" for supposing so:

> But perhaps the point is that one gives people to understand by saying the sentence ["I may be mistaken"], and leaving it at that, that one does have some concrete reason to suppose that one may be mistaken or wrong, in the case at hand. If so, that "implicature," in Grice's term, should be easy to cancel. Like this: "I know he is honest. But I may be mistaken. I have no concrete reason, in this case, to suppose that I may be mistaken, much less that I am mistaken. But then, I didn't in that other case, either, though as you will recall I was disastrously mistaken, there. So if I were you, I wouldn't count on it that I'm not mistaken again. Obviously, I may be. I wouldn't say, "may well be." This chap is extremely convincing. But he may be dishonest, of course. Nevertheless, as I was saying, I know he's honest. That's the position."
>
> But this "position" doesn't exist. No implicature, if that's what it is, has been cancelled. On the contrary, the speaker has absurdly undermined what would have been a pretension to know, if he had said as much and shut up. Or does he know? Perhaps he does, and should have said so at the end, if not at the beginning, more emphatically, in which case he would have cancelled his rambling concession that he might be mistaken.
>
> The fact is, "I know" and "I may be mistaken" can't be gotten through a logical intersection by adroit steering and some sounding of horns. They inexorably collide.
>
> *(Albritton 2011: 5–6)*[15]

Contextualism and fallibilism

Similar observations would be plausible about the relation of "I know" to "There is some risk that I am wrong," or "There is some chance that I am wrong," or to any number of other ways of admitting some kind of possibility of error – or, again, of fallibility, in some good sense, with respect to the thing putatively known.

Of course, some may wonder just how inexorable, and how solid, is the collision of "I know" with "I may be mistaken" and with similar admissions of the chance or risk or possibility of error. My purpose here is to quickly survey the basic positions on such conflicts open to an intuitive fallibilist (of the simple or relaxed variety). Which strategy is most appealing to the intuitive fallibilist in a given case may depend on just how much of a tension you think there is, and how inexorable you find it to be. We will arrange the options according to how fallibilist, or how clearly fallibilist, they are in the GC-sense of that term. We are then arranging them by how genuine these positions take the conflict between the admission in question (e.g., "It's possible that not-p_{ind}") and the claim to know ("I know that p") to be. Alternatively, we can think of these strategies in terms of what they say about the skeptical inference from the admission in question to the denial of knowledge, e.g., "It's possible that not-p_{ind}; so, I don't know that p."

The reaction to the alleged tensions that would be the most zealously fallibilist in the GC-sense would be the way of flat denial (if I knew the Latin, I could get a zippy label for this way by filling in the blank of "*modus _____ tollens*"[16]): One who simply denied that there is any serious tension between the admission and the claim to know, nor even any appearance of validity to the skeptical inference, to be accounted for would certainly be a GC-fallibilist of the first order. I don't find that strategy credible in the cases before us (though I have witnessed the stance being [incredibly] adopted), but it should be included in our brief survey of options, not just for the sake of others who might react differently, but for the possibility of extending the scope of these strategy types to cover other admissions, where this strategy might make more sense.

A second stance that is a little less stringently GC-fallibilist, and that can be seen as roughly Moorean in methodological character, would be to admit that there is some slight intuitive pull toward finding the admission incompatible with the claim to know (and toward finding the inference valid), but to hold that it is so dominated an opposing intuitive push in the other direction that there is no call for trying to account for the slight pulls before reaching a secure verdict against them.

On the other extreme, a GC-*in*fallibilist of the first order holds that no standard use of "I know that p" can be true if "It's possible that not-p_{ind}" is true for the speaker at any epistemic standard by which that modal claim can be governed. Although it is in principle possible for a contextualist to hold this view, this kind of GC-infallibilist will likely be an invariantist, holding that for a given subject in a given situation there is just one epistemic standard that can govern both her knowledge claims and her epistemic modal statements,[17] and that the terms are connected in such a way that one cannot count as knowing that p if, according to the epistemic standard that must govern one's relevant modal claims, it is epistemically possible from one's point of view that p is false. Early Unger is a good example of an extreme GC-infallibilist, but one does not have to be a *skeptical* invariantist, nor an infallibilist in the intuitive sense, like him to be a fervent GC-infallibilist. In fact, I suspect this will be where many invariantists will land. A moderate invariantist, perhaps impressed by the apparent sharpness and inexorability of the collisions that occur in our "logical intersections," can adopt this view. Being moderate, she will think we often enough do simply know all manner of things, and will in those cases of knowledge conclude that "It is possible that not-p_{ind}" is simply false when said by one who possesses such knowledge of p. Early Unger combines infallibilism in the intuitive sense with extreme GC-infallibilism; our moderate invariatist, though, shows how such extreme GC-infallibilism can be combined with fallibilism in the intuitive sense.

That leaves the intermediate views, of which I will distinguish four. A view that acknowledges the existence of an at-least-apparent conflict that needs to be dealt with, and so isn't dismissive in the way that the GC-fallibilist views we've examined so far are, but which claims that the conflict is due to a Gricean conversational implicature generated by either the knowledge claim or by the relevant admission of fallibility, should clearly be classified as a GC-fallibilist view. This is the type of view that Albritton considers, but then rejects, in the quotation at the beginning of this section, and has been the focus of some of the wrangling over what we are here calling GC-fallibilism, since Patrick Rysiew presented such an account (2001: 492–8), setting off a battle over the tenability of such a mere "pragmatic" account of (some of) our clashes.[18] A related view would have it that the conflict is generated by a *conventional* implicature of one or both of the claims. This option would seem a bit more GC-infallibilist than the previous one, since on it the conflict is generated by the conventional meaning of the two sentences, even if not by their truth-conditional content. I am a bit leery of conventional implicatures myself (DeRose 2009: 88–9, n. 9), and should perhaps leave the classification of this position on our GC-scale to those who feel more at home with them, but I'm guessing that one who went for such an account of a tension should be construed as a GC-fallibilist.

The two intermediate positions that are left are both contextualist options. As I indicated in the previous section, my own position, at least with respect to the knowledge-epistemic possibility clash, is that the meaning of the two claims is such that what's expressed by "I know that p" is incompatible with what one would express by "It's possible that not-p_{ind}," *when both are evaluated at the same epistemic standard*. On this view, the inference "It's possible that not-p_{ind}; so, I don't know that p" is what we can call "Stine-valid": the conclusion does follow from the premise, so long as one evaluates both at the same epistemic standards, and thereby avoids committing, in Gail Stine's memorable words, "some logical sin akin to equivocation" (1976: 256). As I indicated in section 2, I think this view should be classified as a GC-infallibilist one, for, after all, on it, "I know that p" seems to be inconsistent with "It's possible that not-p_{ind}" in as strong a way as "I am tall" is inconsistent with "I am not tall."

Note, however, that the above option is only available where one is contextualist about both the knowledge claim and the admission of fallibility, so that the meanings of the two sentences can "sway together." There is an importantly different contextualist position available even for (but not only for) cases where the knowledge claim is subject to varying epistemic standards, but the admission of fallibility is not – or *vice versa*. On this position, the inference from the admission of fallibility to the admission that one does not know is not Stine-valid, but rather what we can call Stalnaker-reasonable. To illustrate, suppose you are an invariantist about, say, "There is at least some slight chance that not-p," thinking that such a claim is not governed by varying epistemic standards, and, say, you think it is almost always true. Being a good fallibilist in the intuitive sense, you'll think that people often speak truthfully when they claim to know things, even where, as is almost always the case (on your view), there is at least some slight chance from their point of view that the things they are claiming to know are false. You can then hold that "There is at least some slight chance that not-p; so, I don't know that p," while invalid, is a "reasonable inference" in something like the sense that Robert Stalnaker proposed in his (1975). To say that an inference is "Stalnaker-reasonable" is to say that the assertion of the premise affects the meaning of the conclusion so that the conclusion will, if need be, (tend to) come to express a proposition that must be true if the premise is true. In the case of our sample inference, you might think that bringing up the matter of a slight chance that not-p will be most germane to, and for that and/or other reasons may invoke, standards for knowledge at which slight chances of not-p are enough to block "knowledge" of p. On this view, then our sample skeptical inference is not valid: the conclusion can be false where the premise is true – so long as one keeps quiet about

Contextualism and fallibilism

that true premise. Rather, the assertion of the premise affects (or at least has a tendency to affect) the meaning of the conclusion in such a way that the latter comes to follow from the former.[19] Moving from the inference to the corresponding tension, on this type of view, putting "There is at least some slight chance that not-p" into play, tends to create (if need be) a context where "I know that p" is governed by standards that render it incompatible with (even) slight chances that not-p. In light of its ruling that knowledge can co-exist with the truth of the relevant claim of fallibility so long as that latter isn't actually made, I would classify this view as a GC-fallibilist one. That the knowledge-asserting sentence comes to (or has a tendency to come to) express a proposition incompatible with the admission of fallibility when the latter is put into play would be best thought of as an account of why knowledge of facts can misleadingly appear to be incompatible with, say, even slight chances to the contrary. This form of GC-fallibilism may be wrong (and I think it is), but it seems far from "madness."

The line between GC-fallibilism and GC-infallibilism, then, seems to me best placed so that it cuts right between our two intermediate, contextualist options. But we can all be good fallibilists in at least the relaxed version of the intuitive sense of that term.[20]

Notes

1 For a brief history of contextualism, focusing on its early years, and, of course, not at all covering any time after 2009, see (DeRose 2009: 26–9).

2 At (DeRose 1990: 289–2), I argue that this fallibility is not just a feature of the *human* condition, but would afflict any cognitive agent with beliefs that we can conceive of. Trent Dougherty (independently) expresses similar thoughts at (Dougherty 2011: 131–2).

3 For the record, I am among those who think that, in the intuitive sense in question, we are fallible with respect to all our beliefs, with no exceptions.

4 This anti-skeptical story is told much more fully, and defended, in (DeRose 2017).

5 Whether this is a claim or an admission will vary from anti-skeptic to anti-skeptic. Some may reluctantly admit it as the price they must pay for an at least somewhat undermining account of the skeptic's power. Others, of a less strident anti-skeptical orientation, may happily accept it. I tend to fall in the second category.

6 Here I use "simply know" as I do at (DeRose 2009: 228–9).

7 For discussion of whether contextualist accounts provide sufficient comfort, or whether they leave the most important skeptical worries unaddressed, see especially the "Irrelevant to Traditional Epistemological Reflection on Skepticism?" section of the "Contextualism and Skepticism" chapter of (DeRose 2017).

8 Such a formulation of fallibilism is not new to Cohen. Feldman, for instance, gives such a construal of fallibilism at (Feldman 1981: 266–7). See (Stanley 2005: 127) for an example of such a view which uses "evidence" where Cohen uses "reasons."

9 Baron Reed succinctly sums up this long-noted problem: "[W]here it is necessarily true that p, every justification will entail that p. But this will be so simply because everything entails a necessary truth" (2012: 586).

10 In a related move, Trent Dougherty explicates a notion of "epistemic probability," and construes fallibilism as the claim that we can know even where the epistemic probability for us of what is known is less than 1 (Dougherty 2011: 140–2).

11 The "ind" subscript indicates that P is to be kept in the indicative mood: "It's possible that she's the best"; not "It's possible that she should have been the best."

12 Lewis, writing about the link between similarity and counterfactual conditionals: "I am not one of those philosophers who seek to rest fixed distinctions upon a foundation quite incapable of supporting them. I rather seek to rest an unfixed distinction upon a swaying foundation, claiming that the two sway together rather than independently" (1973: 92). See (DeRose 2009: 19–20) for a little discussion of applications to epistemological language.

13 (Unger 1971); updated in Chapter 2 of (Unger 1975).

14 So micro-bumps will often "behave" in ways similar to bumps. So, to use an Unger-inspired illustration, just as you should be mindful of the potential effects of bumps in the field you're playing on when

planning a shot in croquet, or when you're predicting how likely your planned shot is to succeed, so, especially when it's an important shot and one that calls for much precision, you might do well to consider what some prominent micro-bumps might do to your shot.

15 These remarks are from a talk Albritton gave, I believe at the University of California, Irvine, I believe in 1987, a slightly fixed-up text of which was later published posthumously as (Albritton 2011). Albritton (who was my adviser) viewed the choice before us (in the terms we are here using) as being between the kind of implicature-based GC-fallibilism that he mentions and a quite thorough-going GC-infallibilism. A main push toward the birth of my contextualist views was the pressing sense that there were other – and better – important options here.

16 Trent Dougherty now informs me that he majored in Latin and he assures me that the term I'm looking for here is *"modus frickin tollens."*

17 For "Classical Invariantists," there will be only one set of epistemic standards that can ever govern knowledge ascriptions and epistemic modal statements. For "Subject-Sensitive Invariantists," we are instead speaking of the only epistemic standards that can be applied to particular subjects given certain features of those subjects' situations. For the distinction between the types of invariantists, see (DeRose 2009: 23–6).

18 See (Hawthorne 2004: 24–8) and (Stanley (2005) for criticisms of pragmatic accounts of the clash (aimed explicitly at Rysiew only in the case of Stanley), and (Dougherty and Rysiew 2009) for replies. This battle over the tenability of "pragmatic" accounts of our clashes is closely related to my wranglings with Rysiew over the tenability of his "pragmatic" account of the conversational data that is used in support of contextualism, which is the primary focus of (Rysiew 2001); see (DeRose 2009: 118–24).

19 In his (2015), Alex Worsnip provides a great example of a GC-fallibilist view of this type, but one on which it is the knowledge claim's effect on the meaning of the epistemic modal statement, rather than the other way around, that accounts for the clash in trying to make the claims together. I think Worsnip's should be classified as a GC-fallibilist view because, though he thinks that "I know that p, but it's possible that not-p" is inconsistent *wherever it is asserted*, on his view, the knowledge claim and the epistemic modal claim, and indeed their conjunction, can all be true together relative to many contexts (in which these claims are not uttered). That they cannot be truthfully asserted together accounts for why they misleadingly appear to be inconsistent. This grounds an important sense on which, for Worsnip, as opposed to a GC-infallibilist like me, there can be "Possibly False Knowledge." I don't accept Worsnip's account because I don't find his (4)–(7) (at 2015: 232) as felicitous as he does.

20 Thanks to Patrick Rysiew for helpful comments on a draft of this chapter, and especially to Trent Dougherty for comments and very helpful e-discussion of these matters.

References

Albritton, Rogers 2011. "On a Form of Skeptical Argument from Possibility," *Philosophical Issues* 21: 1–24.

Cohen, Stewart 1988. "How to Be a Fallibilist," *Philosophical Perspectives* 2: 91–123.

DeRose, Keith 1990. *Knowledge, Epistemic Possibility, and Scepticism*, Ph.D Diss., University of California, Los Angeles; University Microfilms International.

―――― 1991. "Epistemic Possibilities," *Philosophical Review* 100: 581–605.

―――― 1995. "Solving the Skeptical Problem," *Philosophical Review* 104: 1–-52.

―――― 2009. *The Case for Contextualism: Knowledge, Skepticism, and Context*, Vol. 1, Oxford: Oxford University Press.

―――― 2017. *The Appearance of Ignorance: Knowledge, Skepticism, and Context*, Vol. 2.

Dougherty, Trent 2011. "Fallibilism," in Sven Bernecker and Duncan Pritchard, eds., *The Routledge Companion to Epistemology*, New York and London: Routledge, 131–143..

Dougherty, Trent and Rysiew, Patrick 2009. "Fallibilism, Epistemic Possibility, and Concessive Knowledge Attributions," *Philosophy and Phenomenological Research* 78: 123–-132.

Feldman, Richard 1981. "Fallibilism and Knowing That One Knows," *Philosophical Review* 90: 266–282.

Hawthorne, John 2004. *Knowledge and Lotteries*, Oxford: Oxford University Press.

Lewis, David 1973. *Counterfactuals*. Cambridge, MA: Harvard University Press.

―――― 1996. "Elusive Knowledge," *Australasian Journal of Philosophy* 74: 549–567.

Reed, Baron 2012. "Fallibilism," *Philosophy Compass* 7/9: 585–596.

Rysiew, Patrick 2001. "The Context-Sensitivity of Knowledge Attributions," *Noûs* 35: 477–514.

Stalnaker, Robert 1975. "Indicative Conditionals," *Philosophia* 5: 269–286.

Stanley, Jason 2005. "Fallibilism and Concessive Knowledge Attributions," *Analysis* 65: 126–131.

Stine, Gail 1976. "Skepticism, Relevant Alternatives, and Deductive Closure," *Philosophical Studies* 29: 249–261.

Unger, Peter 1971. "A Defense of Skepticism," *Philosophical Review* 80: 198–219.

——— 1975. *Ignorance: A Case for Scepticism*, Oxford: Oxford University Press.

Williamson, Timothy 2000. *Knowledge and Its Limits*, Oxford: Oxford University Press.

Worsnip, Alex 2015. "Possibly False Knowledge," *Journal of Philosophy* 112: 225–246.

12

CONTEXTUALISM AND CLOSURE

Maria Lasonen-Aarnio

Epistemic contextualism in itself does not entail any stance on closure, but most contextualists have been friendly to both some form of closure of knowledge and closure of justification. Indeed, its claimed ability to solve a prevalent skeptical paradox while retaining an appealing closure principle for knowledge has been one of the main selling points of contextualism.[1] In what follows, I will briefly discuss various closure-based paradoxes and puzzles.[2] My goal will be to investigate whether contextualism provides resources for solving these paradoxes that are not available to non-contextualists. I will focus primarily on the closure of knowledge (as opposed to justification); unless otherwise indicated, by 'contextualism' I will mean contextualism about knowledge.[3]

I begin with the well-known skeptical paradox that contextualists have devoted most efforts to solving. I then discuss what I will call the problem of risk accrual, both as it applies to a multi- and single-premise form of closure, concluding with a discussion of a defeat-related problem. What will emerge is that it is far from clear whether contextualism in itself can help with closure-related problems and paradoxes other than, perhaps, the traditional skeptical paradox.

1 Formulating closure

According to contextualists, different uses of 'knows' can pick out different relations in different contexts. What is it that all of these relations have in common? Most agree, for instance, that only truths can be known, and that there is some sort of belief condition on knowledge. Further, a strong candidate for a structural feature common to all of the different knowledge-relations is closure.

Just how closure principles should be formulated in the first place is a topic of dispute. For many putative counterexamples, there is no consensus concerning whether they really are such, or whether they merely show the need to reformulate closure. It is clear that knowledge cannot be closed under *entailment* – for one thing, we don't believe everything entailed by our knowledge. A more promising idea is that knowledge is closed under *competent deduction*. Principles along the following lines are often taken to capture this idea:

Single-Premise Closure (SPC)

Necessarily, if S knows p and comes to believe q on the basis of competent deduction from p, while retaining knowledge of p throughout, then S knows q.

156

Multi-Premise Closure (MPC)

Necessarily, if S knows $p_1, \ldots, p_n$ and comes to believe q on the basis of competent deduction from $p_1, \ldots, p_n$, while retaining knowledge of $p_1, \ldots, p_n$ throughout, then S knows q.[4]

Many take the spirit of closure to be the idea that competent deduction from known premises is a way of extending knowledge, and state principles of the above sort to capture this idea.[5] But of course, coming to believe a proposition q on the basis of a competent deduction from a known proposition p may not extend one's knowledge in cases in which q is already known (perhaps on some other, non-inferential grounds). Further, even in cases in which one forms a belief in a proposition q for the first time on the basis of a competent deduction from known proposition(s), the above principles as such don't say anything about how it is that one knows q. For instance, the principles do not state that one knows q in virtue of knowing the propositions acting as the premises of one's deduction.[6]

Some think that the above principles need to be revised in light of counterexamples. What if, for instance, I competently deduce q from p, but acquire excellent reason to think that my deduction was incompetent? Many would argue that such evidence defeats my belief in q, thereby destroying my knowledge. One reaction is to build a clause into the above principles excluding the presence of such defeaters.[7] Note though that this would mean denying the idea that *competent deduction* is a way of extending knowledge; now competent deduction only extends knowledge in the absence of a certain kind of evidence.[8] My own view is that knowledge can be had even in the presence of such putative defeaters,[9] but nothing I say below rests on this. And more importantly, adding a defeat-clause to deal with the kind of case just mentioned does not solve the problems discussed below.

Now, standard formulations of closure won't do for the purposes of the contextualist: even if SPC and MPC (perhaps suitably tweaked) are true in the context in which I just asserted them, the contextualist wants them to be true in *all* contexts. Contextualists often express their endorsement of closure by saying that these principles hold *relative to any context*.[10] Perhaps the best way of making sense of this thought is to go metalinguistic:

Meta-Linguistic Single Premise Closure (MSPC)

For any context, any sentence of the form 'Necessarily, if S knows p and comes to believe q on the basis of competent deduction from p, while retaining knowledge of p throughout, then S knows q' is true.[11]

Similarly for MPC. On some contextualist views, it is impossible to utter the sentences stating such meta-linguistic versions of closure in any one context. But note that even if an instance of the meta-linguistic principles is not truly utterable, it can still be true. For instance, several contextualists have argued that merely mentioning a skeptical hypothesis changes the context.[12] If context shifts happen very easily, then knowledge of the deduced proposition will be difficult, if not impossible, to ascribe. For instance, I might start out knowing that I have hands, and being able to truly utter 'I know that I have hands.' Assume that I then come to believe that I am not a handless brain in a vat based on competent deduction from the proposition that I have hands. However, if forming this belief makes the possibility that I am a handless brain in a vat salient, thereby shifting the context, then despite my competent deduction, I cannot truly utter 'I know that I am not a handless brain in a vat.' It *looks* like closure fails, but instead, the context shifts in the middle of my deduction.

Maria Lasonen-Aarnio

2 Closure and skeptical paradoxes

Let 'S' denote a *skeptical hypothesis*, and 'O' denote some *ordinary claim* entailing ¬S. Here is a general form for a skeptical paradox to take:

(1) I don't know that ¬S.
(2) If I don't know that ¬S, then I don't know that O.
(3) I know that O.

We have a paradox because when we substitute 'S' and 'O' by suitable claims, each of (1)-(3) has a considerable degree of plausibility when considered on its own, even though they are jointly inconsistent.

I am considering this to be a closure-based paradox, but it is not wholly obvious what the role of closure is in creating the above paradox. First, (2) above doesn't entail anything as general as closure. Someone could deny closure – perhaps for some of the reasons to be discussed below, having to do with accrual of risks – while nevertheless conceding that for appropriate O and ¬S, it ought to be possible to come to know ¬S on the basis of one's knowledge of O. Nevertheless, closure is an appealing, general way of supporting the idea that knowledge of the suitable pairs of claims stands or falls together: if one knows some ordinary claim O, couldn't one simply deduce the relevant ¬S, thereby, by closure, knowing ¬S? Indeed, it is difficult to see how (2) could be supported without *some* closure-like generalization concerning pairs of propositions O and ¬S.

Philosophers who solve the paradox by denying (2) tend to deny closure.[13] However, closure does not entail (2). No plausible closure principle entails that anyone who knows O knows ¬S, even if the former entails the latter – for one thing, one might not even believe ¬S. Restricting the skeptical argument to subjects who have come to believe ¬S on the basis of competent deduction from O seems too modest for the purposes of the skeptic. A better strategy would be to build more into (1), the rough idea being that it's not just that I don't know ¬S, but that I couldn't come to know ¬S, not even if I were to believe it on the basis of a competent deduction from O. If the first premise is thus qualified, a proper closure principle can be plugged in place of (2).[14]

It is not my task here to provide a general characterization of what makes claims suited to play the roles of O and S in (1)-(3), but here is a pair that creates a well-known instance of the above skeptical paradox:

O: I have hands.
S: I am a handless brain in a vat stimulated into having exactly the kinds of experiences I would have if I were an ordinary human being with hands.[15]

Another class of similar paradoxes that I shall refer to as *Harman-style skeptical paradoxes* appeals not to seemingly distant skeptical possibilities, but to low-probability events like outcomes of lottery draws. Here is an example:

O: I will not be able to afford to donate 10 million dollars to Oxfam this year.
S: I will win the 10 million prize in the lottery I hold a ticket for.[16]

The reason why we have here a skeptical paradox is that for just about any ordinary claim it looks like we can think of a claim that will play the role of S. For instance, it seems that you know the result of a regional political election in a distant country based on reading a very brief report in the *New York Times*. But do you know that the *New York Times* did not contain a misprint (after all, misprints do sometimes occur)? Yet, if you do know that the *New York Times* reported *p* and that *p* is true, couldn't you just come to know by deduction that there was no misprint?

A prominent contextualist solution to at least the more traditional versions of the above kind of skeptical paradox will retain that we know both O and ¬S in any context, but that considering the skeptical hypothesis either changes the context in such a way that we no longer know either ¬S or O, or at least triggers cognitive mechanisms that are sensitive to context shifts in such a way as to make it appear as though we don't know ¬S.[17] On most views, the new context is one in which the standards for knowledge are higher than those in ordinary contexts, which explains why we know neither the relevant ¬S nor O.[18] The skeptic is wrong in thinking that pretty much any ordinary knowledge ascription is false. But at the same time, she may be right that in the context that considering the skeptical argument puts us into, my utterance of 'I don't know that I am not a handless brain in a vat' is true. What may appear like a failure of closure is really a shift, or at least a perceived shift, in the relation picked out by the word 'knows'.

This is not the place to discuss worries about the standard contextualist solution to the skeptical paradox. I do, however, want to note that a parallel resolution of the newer Harman-style skeptical paradox raises some worries of its own.[19] First, at least in print, epistemologists have been less willing to say that one could know that one's lottery ticket will lose just based on the odds than that one could know that one is not a brain in a vat.[20] It might be difficult to imagine contexts in which it would be relevant to assert 'I am not a handless brain in a vat,' but such sentences may not seem as categorically unassertable as 'My ticket will lose the lottery,' when one has merely the odds to go on. Still, the contextualist could dig in her heels here, insisting that since something has to give, it is simply wrong to think that one cannot know that one's ticket will lose the lottery merely based on the odds.[21] A second set of problems will be discussed in the next section: if I can know that my ticket will lose, surely I can know that yours will, too.

3 Lottery knowledge

According to the kind of contextualist solution discussed above to the newer Harman-style skeptical paradox, you can know, in an ordinary context, that your lottery ticket will lose just based on the odds. But presumably, you can then also know that your friend Li's ticket will lose. And that Al's will. (After all, they are just as likely to lose as you are!) In fact, assume that you know all of the ticket holders but one, Nina. You also know that the lottery has a winner. You then engage in some deduction, coming to believe that *none* of your friends will win. Upon hearing that the remaining ticket is Nina's, you deduce that Nina must hold the winning ticket. In fact, she does. But surely this is not something you can come to know in the way just described![22]

Apart from biting the bullet, contextualists have two main tactics to choose from. The first is to try to find resources in the contextualist position for resolving the puzzle without denying MPC, or its meta-linguistic version. One idea would be to look for a contextualist mechanism by which one cannot know, of *too* many people, that their tickets will lose. I first assert 'You know that your lottery ticket will lose.' And I continue: 'You know that Li's ticket will lose,' 'You know that Al's ticket will lose,' etc. But perhaps possibilities are popping in and out of salience as I make these assertions, thereby shifting the context. The idea is that in no context can *all* of the trouble-creating knowledge be truly ascribed to you.[23] Objective chance (or more generally, *risk* of error) sets a kind of cap on how much can be ignored in any one context. Note that unlike the different kinds of knowledge relations relevant to the contextualist's resolution of the skeptical paradoxes discussed above, none of these different knowledge relations need be more demanding than others. For instance, perhaps you start out knowing, of *n* friends, that their tickets will lose, and a context shift takes place as a result of which you know, of a *different* set of n friends, that their tickets will lose. In such cases, the raising of epistemic standards cannot be what explains the context shifts.

It won't do to merely stipulate the existence of a contextual mechanism ensuring the desired result. So what *does* explain these context shifts? For instance, what explains just which possibilities are salient? The possibility that Li's ticket wins, for instance, is supposed to be salient precisely when we are considering the lottery prospects of *other* people, not Li. Perhaps, for each friend whose ticket is *not* being considered, the possibility of that friend's ticket winning is salient. This in itself is a bit bizarre – contextualists normally think that it is the possibilities that are being attended to, considered, or taken seriously, that are salient.[24] Moreover, what happens if an ascriber simultaneously believes, of each of your friends – or of many of them – that you know that that friend lost the lottery? Recall that on the present proposal, objective chance (or, more generally, *risk* of error) sets a kind of cap on how much can be ignored in any one context; a set of possibilities cannot be ignored when there is a high chance that at least one of them is realized. If some, but not all, of these knowledge-ascriptios are true, then how are we to choose which? Any choice would seem *ad hoc*. But saying that none of them can be true also has some counterintuitive consequences. Whether the ascriber's mental tokening of the sentence 'You know that Li's ticket will lose' is true will depend on how many other similar beliefs, concerning other friends of yours, the ascriber holds.

The other option open to the contextualist (as to anyone else) is to deny MPC, claiming that while you know, of each friend, that they will lose the lottery, you cannot come to know by deduction that they *all* will lose or that Nina will win.[25] Denying MPC is denying the intuitive idea we started out with; namely, that competent deduction is a way of extending knowledge. Now it is only competent deduction from a *single premise*, or from premises that are *jointly not too risky*, that extends knowledge. Not surprisingly, those who deny MPC face many of the same sorts of counterintuitive consequences as those who deny SPC. Something very close to the kind of 'abominable conjunction'[26] worry DeRose raises for closure-deniers like Nozick arises for those who deny MPC: 'while you don't know that you will see *all* of your friends over the summer, you *do* know that you will see Li and that you will see Al and that . . . and those are all of your friends!'

Might contextualism provide resources for softening the blow of denying MPC? Wedgwood (2008) argues that though a multi-premise closure principle for justification fails on his contextualist view, counterexamples to it are *elusive*, which explains the appearance that the principle holds. One might attempt to make a similar move to explain the appearance that knowledge is closed under multi-premise deduction. Assume that a rational believer competently deduces a proposition q from premises $p_1, \ldots, p_n$ that she believes. She then considers whether she is justified in believing the premises and conclusion of the deduction. Wedgwood argues that in thus attending to her own situation, the believer focuses on a standard of justification that she can be guided by. Further, given the nature of outright belief, any standard for justified belief that a rational believer can be guided by is one on which her belief in q is justified so long as her beliefs in $p_1, \ldots, p_n$ are.[27] The result is that multi-premise closure is preserved in any token deduction a subject attends to. This is supposed to explain the appeal of the principle: a subject cannot attend to deductions in which the principle fails given the standards operative in her context.

Wedgwood's view of the appeal of multi-premise closure relies, of course, on contestable claims about the nature of belief, standards by which subjects can be guided, and context-shifting mechanisms. But even if we set aside any potential worries here, the view can only explain why it might seem to a subject that multi-premise closure holds for her *own* beliefs. However, the kind of 'abominable conjunction' worry raised above did not rely on a first-person perspective. Assume that we focus our attention on a rational believer, Rathika. It seems bizarre that Rathika could know, of each of her friends individually, that she will see them over the summer, know

Contextualism and closure

that these are all the friends she has, and be in no position whatsoever to know that she will see all of her friends over the summer. As such, Wedgwood's account does nothing to explain why multi-premise closure appears to hold even from a third-person perspective. Further, as a solution to the problem we started out with, the above proposal faces worries already discussed above. Consider the problem case discussed in which you deduce that Nina will win the lottery from your (assumed) knowledge, concerning each of the other ticket holders, that they will lose. Surely there is no standard by which you could thus come to know, prior to the draw, that Nina will win! The standard operative in your context had better not give you too much knowledge to create such trouble. But how, then, do we decide just which premises you know and which you don't? Again, isn't any choice bound to be *ad hoc*?

Further, some discomfort may remain even with the admission that you can know of each of your friends, just based on the odds, that they will lose the lottery. Consider the overall body of knowledge that you have. Perhaps the lottery has 1000 tickets. You know, of each of the losers, that they will lose. You also know that there is a winner. Although you may not be in a position to come to know that Nina is the winner, what you know entails this. Now assume that you *do* hold a belief about Nina: instead of deducing that Nina will win, you believe that she will lose based on the odds. Despite holding this false belief you can presumably still know, of all your friends, that they will lose. Knowledge seems to become just too easy to have: by believing of *every* person who holds a ticket in a lottery that they will lose, you get to know, of each loser, that they will in fact lose.

Let me now turn to a more general, though closely related, worry for MPC having to do with the accrual of risk. This worry arises even for those who deny that you could know that your lottery ticket will lose just based on the odds. The worry arises for contextualists and non-contextualists alike. But recall the main agenda of this piece: to discuss whether contextualism provides special resources for solving closure-based puzzles.

4 Accrual of risk and multi-premise closure

Even those who deny that one can know that one's ticket will lose the lottery in advance of hearing the result of the draw and just based on the odds will face a similar, though perhaps slightly less poignant, problem when it comes to MPC. Consider any ordinary claim you take yourself to know. I certainly think I know that my bike is where I locked it this morning, that Britain is going to leave the European Union, that I will be in the US in the fall like I planned I would, and that the marble the toddler just dropped in another room did not tunnel through the floor due to a bizarre quantum event. All of these claims have some non-zero *risk* of being false, a kind of risk that appears to have epistemic significance. When it comes to claims concerning the future, the risk in question might just be objective chance. But even if the toddler already dropped the marble, and the chance of its having tunneled through the floor is now zero, an accrual of risk worry still remains when a large enough body of such (putative) knowledge is conjoined.[28]

The problem is that when we conjoin enough claims, each of which has some, even if very slight, risk of being false, the result seems to be just too risky for knowledge.[29] That is, MPC seems to be at odds with the idea that knowledge is tolerant to *some*, but not too much, risk of error. As an instance of the puzzle, consider knowledge of the future in a non-deterministic world, as we can then focus on objective chance of falsehood as an instance of the relevant kind of risk. I know where I will be over the summer, where the next conference I am going to will be, where I will be in two minutes time, etc. Now assume that I conjoin all of this knowledge, believing a conjunction of very many claims about the future. Provided that my premises are suitably

161

independent, and that there are enough of them, the conjunction I believe will have a high chance of being false. Given plausible-seeming connections between chance and luck, the truth of the relevant conjunction now seems too lucky to constitute knowledge.[30]

What resources does contextualism provide to deal with this puzzle? Much of the dialectic already explored above can be replayed here. The option of rejecting MPC is not specific to contextualism. Neither is it clear whether the contextualist has resources to explain why we might erroneously be drawn to MPC. The other strategy was to appeal to some context-shifting mechanism ensuring that one cannot have *too* much knowledge of propositions that are individually risky in any one context. But much more would have to be said to show that a plausible context-shifting mechanism yields the desired result (for instance, why are possibilities being ignored salient?). Further, problems arise when we attempt to ascribe too much knowledge at once.[31]

That a risk-accrual related puzzle arises for multi-premise closure might seem obvious in light of the fact that multi-premise entailment does not preserve high probability. What is less obvious is that a risk-accrual worry also arises for single-premise closure.

5 Accrual of risk and single-premise closure

Consider the fact that a deduction of a proposition q from a proposition p can be competent, even though there was some risk that it would go wrong. For instance, perhaps there was a non-zero objective chance that one would infer from p some claim not logically entailed by it – even a false claim – without realizing that this had happened. Perhaps, for instance, there is always a chance of a bizarre quantum event taking place in one's brain that would cause one to perform a 'spoof' deduction, thereby forming a belief in a proposition merely seemingly deduced from something one knows. If we think such low-chance possibilities are incompatible with competence, then we are in danger of making competence such a demanding notion that ordinary human subjects never perform competent deductions.

Do the kinds of *deductive* risks described have epistemic significance? Consider a situation in which a subject has a very *high* risk of performing an incompetent deduction of the kind described above – perhaps, for instance, she has been given a drug that is almost certain to cause her to make a fundamental, unnoticed error in her reasoning. But assume that against the odds, she does not make such an error: she knows p, deduces q from p, and comes to believe q on this basis, retaining her knowledge of p. Now, at least a lot of epistemologists (the majority, I would guess) would judge that in this case the subject does not come to know q, for she could only too easily have come to believe a falsehood based on an erroneous piece of reasoning. It seems that competent deduction is only tolerant to deductive risk in small quantities.

Here, then, is a risk accrual worry for SPC. Consider a case in which you know p, but from the perspective of risk, only just. You then come to believe q based on a competent deduction from p. However, the deduction involves some risk. There are now two kinds of risks: a risk that p is false, and a risk that you inferred from p a false claim. When evaluating whether you know q, both risks must be taken into account. But these risks can pile up, taking you above the amount of risk that knowledge is tolerant to.[32] We have a puzzle, since according to SPC you know q. And yet, your belief in q appears too risky to constitute knowledge.

The puzzle can be resolved in ways that don't make special use of contextualist resources. For instance, one might dispute the claim that deductive risks have any relevance for knowledge: even if there is a high chance that one will commit a fundamental, unnoticed error in one's attempted deduction, as long as no such error occurs, the deduction can be competent, and extend knowledge.[33] Or, one might revert to a skepticism about competent deduction on which such risks are only too relevant, competent deduction being completely intolerant to them. And of course, one could reject SPC (or in the contextualist's case, MSPC). Alternatively, one might insist that rather than rejecting single-premise closure, such a solution merely requires reformulating the principle so as to rule out the kinds of cases discussed. But again, this would mean rejecting the idea that competent deduction from a single premise is a way of extending knowledge, opening the door to the kinds of abominable conjunctions discussed above.

What about distinctively contextualist solutions? Could the idea that when attributing knowledge to a subject, certain error possibilities are not salient, help here? The contextualist might try to couple this idea with the context-sensitivity of 'competent deduction', and a similar mechanism by which focusing on a given deduction can shift possibilities in which the subject makes a mistake out of salience. The hope would be that within any one context the standards for knowledge and competence are tied together in such a way as to ensure that an attributor can never attribute both knowledge of a premise and competence of a deduction in cases that are candidates for the kinds of closure failures discussed. Any such proposal faces problems analogous to those explored above. The contextualist must do much more than merely stipulate the existence of a contextual mechanism yielding the desired result: why does turning our gaze on a candidate piece of knowledge of a proposition p make the possibility that not-p disappear from salience? Further, what if knowledge of a proposition p and competence of a deduction of q from p are simultaneously ascribed? Moreover, having to appeal to both the context-dependence of 'knows' and that of 'competent deduction' raises worries of its own. The semantics of 'competent deduction' is supposed to be sensitive in a very specific way to just how the word 'knows' is used within a context (and vice versa): attributing knowledge of p to a subject can affect which possibilities are salient for the competence of her deduction of q from p. But what reason is there to think that the semantics of 'know' and 'competent deduction' are thus tied together?

Contextualism doesn't appear to provide special resources to solve the problem of risk-accrual for SPC. Before concluding, I want to discuss another, similar problem that doesn't arise from *actual* risk of error, but from a kind of *perceived* risk of error. It was observed above that a deduction can be competent, even if a subject has evidence for thinking that it is not. Many think that such evidence acts as a knowledge-destroying defeater of the deduced proposition. However, there is a trickier problem in the same ballpark.

Assume that Sara engages in a long chain of single-premise deductions. She starts out with a proposition p_0, and after 10,000 competent deductions, ends up believing $p_{10,000}$. Such chains raise the problem of risk accrual already discussed.[34] But now consider instead what Sara should think about her own epistemic standing with respect to $p_{10,000}$. When she reflects on her only human abilities and track record, it might be rational for her to be fairly confident that she has committed an error somewhere along the chain.[35] Note that it might be rational for Sara to think this even if the actual risk of committing an error was low. In so far as it is likely on Sara's evidence that some mistake occurred along the chain of deductions, and her only grounds for believing $p_{10,000}$ are deductive, it might appear that her belief in $p_{10,000}$ is now defeated. Closure seems to conflict with the idea that knowledge is tolerant to small, but only small, *perceived risks* of error.

What makes the problem tricky is that the seeming defeater has a global or holistic nature: it doesn't target any individual inference, but the inferential chain as a whole. Consider, for instance, Sara's deduction of p_1 from p_0. She shouldn't be at all confident that that deduction was incompetent; in fact, she should be confident that it was competent. And the same can be said of each individual deductive step: each step on its own looks very good. And yet, there appears to be a defeater for $p_{10,000}$. The verdict that Sara's belief in $p_{10,000}$ (and possibly also her beliefs in propositions preceding $p_{10,000}$ in the chain) is defeated is incompatible with closure. Moreover, it is difficult to see how SPC could be tweaked to deal with the problem in a way that doesn't trivialize the principle.[36]

163

Again, the contextualist might respond without making use of distinctly contextualist resources. Perhaps the right response is to reject closure of knowledge.[37] Or, perhaps the right response is to insist that Sara knows $p_{10,000}$ after all, and that we don't here have a real counter-example to closure.[38] I assumed above that closure generates the result that Sara knows $p_{10,000}$, since each step in her deduction was in fact competent. Might some form of contextualism be able to diagnose the puzzle by arguing that though closure *seems* to generate the result that Sara knows $p_{10,000}$, it doesn't in fact do so? Recall an idea mentioned above: 'competent deduction' is a context-sensitive term, and focusing on an individual deduction can have the effect of shifting error possibilities in and out of salience, thereby changing the context. Perhaps the context-shifting mechanisms works so that 'competent deduction' applies to each deduction in Sara's chain that an attributor individually shifts her gaze on. But in no one context do *all* of Sara's 10,000 deductions count as competent. This is because Sara has rational high confidence that not all of her deductions were competent. Hence, while it may appear that closure (MSPC) generates the result that Sara knows $p_{10,000}$, it in fact doesn't.

I leave it to the reader to consider objections to this proposal that are analogous to ones already discussed above. It is also worth asking whether it is plausible that perceived risk thus puts a cap on true ascriptions of competent deduction in any one context. Assume that you observe Li make a single, impeccable deduction, coming to believe a proposition q. The deduction also looks great to Li. However, a moment later she is told by a trustworthy source that she was given a reason-distorting drug with an overwhelmingly high chance of causing her to apply an invalid rule of inference. Again, many epistemologists would say that Li's belief in q is now defeated. But is it really true that her deduction was *incompetent*? Its appearing incompetent to Li doesn't entail that it is incompetent. Moreover, insisting that any seeming counterexample to closure that involves some sort of defeater also involves incompetent deduction is in danger of trivializing closure principles.[39]

6 Conclusions

I have explored several closure-based paradoxes and puzzles. In each case, a closure principle yields the verdict that a subject knows some proposition q, but other seemingly plausible assumptions yield the verdict that she doesn't. I discussed some distinctively contextualist treatments of these paradoxes, treatments that rely on some form of contextualism about knowledge or, in some cases, contextualism about competent deduction. I expressed skepticism especially about whether contextualists have special resources to deal with paradoxes created by combining closure with the idea that knowledge is tolerant to risk – whether actual or perceived – in small, but only small quantities.

Notes

1 See, for instance, Cohen (1988, 1999, 2000), DeRose (1995), Lewis (1996: 563–564), and Kvanvig (2007). Stine's (1976) criticism of Dretske (1970), who solved the skeptical paradox by denying closure, has been very influential.
2 As a very rough and ready characterization, what makes a paradox closure-based in this sense is not just reliance on an instance of closure, but a reliance on an instance that has been regarded as problematic. Closure-based paradoxes in the intended sense appear to put pressure on closure principles themselves.
3 Other closure-like principles also will be set aside. One example is a principle concerning evidence along the following lines: 'If S has evidence for p and p entails q, then S has evidence for q.' See, for instance, Neta (2003) for a defense of a similar principle.
4 These principles are very close to those discussed by Hawthorne (2004).
5 Cf. Williamson (2000: 117) and Hawthorne (2004: 36).

Contextualism and closure

6　This relates to the issue of *transmission* of justification and knowledge. Closure of knowledge (or justification) could hold even in cases in which one doesn't know (justifiably believe) the conclusion of a deductive inference in virtue of knowing (justifiably believing) the premise. It has been argued, for instance, that there is some sort of transmission failure in anti-sceptical arguments like 'I have a hand; Therefore, I am not a handless brain in a vat deceived into thinking that I have hands.' Wright (1985: 438, footnote 1) distinguishes between closure failure and transmission failure. See Silins (2005) for a discussion of closure and transmission.

7　For instance, Schechter (2013: 437) suggests a clause stating that 'S does not have a defeater for the claim that her deduction was competently performed.'

8　Hawthorne (2004: 35) leaves the notion of competent deduction very open. He seems to allow, for instance, that the presence of certain sorts of defeaters is incompatible with the competence of a deduction. In so far as I have a pre-theoretic grasp on the notion of *competent deduction*, it seems clear that a deduction leading to belief in a proposition *q* can be competent even if, for instance, one has evidence that it is not. (Similar remarks, I think, apply to other means for forming beliefs: I can perfectly *competently perceive* that *p* even upon being told by trustworthy authorities that my perceptual abilities are functioning unreliably.) In any case, if 'competent deduction' is understood so as to guarantee knowledge of the relevant deduced proposition *q*, then closure principles become trivial.

9　See Lasonen-Aarnio (2010).

10　See, for instance, Cohen (1988: 105).

11　Cf. Hawthorne (2004: 83). For alternative attempts to formulate contextualist closure in a metalinguistic way, see Schaffer (2007) and Blome-Tillman (2014).

12　Lewis's (1996: 559) 'Rule of Attention' has this consequence, given his view that mentioning a possibility entails attending to it.

13　See Dretske (1970) and Nozick (1981).

14　Such a strategy is pursued by Unger (1975: Chapter 1) and more recently by DeRose (2017, Appendix C).

15　In the end it may be that the best characterization of a skeptical hypothesis is a hypothesis that we feel at least some inclination to deny that we know. Nevertheless, see Cross (2010), and also DeRose (1995) for an approach largely based on Cross, and Neta (2003) for discussion.

16　See Harman (1968), Vogel (1987), and Hawthorne (2004) for this form of skeptical paradox. It might not be appropriate to call such hypotheses *skeptical*; Hawthorne, for instance, refers to them as *heavyweight*. Note that here O doesn't on its own entail ¬S, but at least it does so given salient background information, like the assumption that I would be able to donate the money were I to win the lottery. Alternatively, we can formulate S as follows: 'I will win the $10 million prize in the lottery I hold a ticket for, thereby being able to afford to donate 10 million dollars to Oxfam.'

17　The foundations for such a view were laid by Stine (1976), and the view was developed in more detail by Cohen (1988). Both Stine and Cohen work within the context of a relevant alternatives view of knowledge. See also DeRose (1995), Lewis (1996), and Neta (2003). As many contextualists note, people don't invariantly have the intuition that we don't know the relevant S. Several contextualists attempt to account for our varied reactions to skeptical arguments. See, for instance, Blome-Tillman (2014: 161) and DeRose (2017).

18　Neta (2003), for instance, has a different view on which the standards for knowledge don't change, but what counts as evidence differs depending on the context.

19　For a detailed discussion of extending the strategy to the newer Harman-style paradox, see DeRose (2017, Chapter 5). See also Hawthorne (2004, Chapter 2).

20　Hawthorne (2004: 87) has a brief critical discussion of a view on which one could know that one's ticket will lose just based on the odds.

21　Of course, the contextualist must do more than dig in her heels here: she needs to give a theory of knowledge that yields the desired verdicts. This is easier said than done. Take, for instance, a safety condition on knowledge. If knowing *p* requires avoiding false belief in *all* nearby worlds even in low-standards contexts, then one cannot know that one's lottery ticket will lose just based on the odds, for surely there are nearby worlds in which it wins. If in low-standards contexts error needs to be avoided merely in *most* nearby worlds, this problem is avoided, for one's ticket does lose in most worlds. By contrast, perhaps in high-standards contexts error must be avoided in all nearby worlds, and one thereby does not know that one's lottery ticket will lose. The problem then arises that we don't have an explanation of why it is that in high-standards contexts we don't know that we are not brains in vats, for presumably there are no nearby possibilities in which this is so.

22 See Hawthorne (2004: 6–7, 95).

23 Cf. Hawthorne (2004: 96–98).

24 See, for instance, Lewis's (1996) Rule of Attention.

25 This tactic is defended by DeRose (2017), though DeRose sees himself as re-formulating a multi-premise closure principle rather than denying it. Wedgwood (2008), who defends contextualism about justified belief, also denies a multi-premise closure principle for justification.

26 Here is DeRose (1995: 28) on Nozick: 'accepting his treatment involves embracing the abominable conjunction that while you don't know you're not a bodiless (and handless!) BIV, still, you know you have hands'.

27 Wedgwood (2008: 16) writes: 'It is part of the essential functional role of outright belief that if you have an outright belief in each member of a certain set of premises, and you deduce a certain conclusion from that set of premises, then you must either have an outright belief in that conclusion, or else retreat from having a full outright belief in every member of that set of premises.'

28 This is why I very much doubt that denying knowledge of future contingents solves the problem.

29 Hawthorne (2004: 46–50) discusses the problem.

30 See Hawthorne (2004, Chapter 1) and Hawthorne & Lasonen-Aarnio (2009).

31 In some ways these problems are more poignant in the present context. Given the high chance of each individual ticket losing any somewhat standard lottery, a lot of lottery knowledge can be ascribed to a subject before the threshold of risk that knowledge is tolerant to is crossed. But now consider a subject who *just* knows p, as the objective chance of p is just high enough to count as knowledge, and similarly *just* knows q. It looks like knowledge of even just these two propositions cannot then be simultaneously ascribed.

32 In Lasonen-Aarnio (2008) I spell out the worry in more detail. For instance, I demonstrate how taking into account deductive risk can create situations in which safe belief fails to be closed under competent deduction. DeRose (1999: 23, n. 14) raises a risk accrual worry for single-premise closure in a footnote, but given his formulation of the principle – he has both 's knows p' and 's knows that p entails q' in the antecedent of the principle – the problem raised is just a special case of the problem for MPC discussed above.

33 I feel some sympathy for such a view. Similarly, I am sympathetic to a view on which a subject in fake barn county can know that there is a barn before her, when she is in fact looking, and hence sees, a real barn, even if there was a high objective chance at a slightly earlier time that she would be looking at a barn facade.

34 Hawthorne and Lasonen-Aarnio (2009) also briefly discuss such long chains.

35 Schechter (2013) discusses the problem for closure of justification.

36 Cf. Schechter (2013).

37 See Schechter (2013).

38 The sense of epistemic failure on Sara's part if she sticks to her belief in $p_{10,000}$ even after becoming confident that she made an error somewhere along the chain must then be explained in some other way. Perhaps, for instance, she is displaying a kind of epistemic vice: she might know in this case, but her disposition would lead to retaining a false belief in other, similar cases (see Lasonen-Aarnio 2010).

39 See also note 8.

Works cited

Blome-Tillman, Michael 2014 *Knowledge and Presuppositions*, Oxford: Oxford University Press.

Cohen, Stewart 1988 'How to Be a Fallibilist', *Philosophical Perspectives* 2: 91–123.

——— 1999 'Contextualism, Skepticism, and the Structure of Reasons', *Philosophical Perspectives* 13: 57–88.

——— 2000 'Contextualism and Skepticism', *Philosophical Issues* 10: 94–107.

Cross, Troy 2010 "Skeptical 'Success', *Oxford Studies in Epistemology* 3: 35–62.

DeRose, Keith 1995 'Solving the Skeptical Problem', *Philosophical Review* 104.1: 1–52.

——— 1999 'Responding to Skepticism', in K. DeRose & T. A. Warfield (eds.), *Skepticism: A Contemporary Reader*, New York: Oxford University Press, 1–24.

——— 2017 *The Appearance of Ignorance: Knowledge, Skepticism and Context*, Volume 2, Oxford: Oxford University Press.

Dretske, Fred 1970 'Epistemic Operators', *Journal of Philosophy* 67.24: 1007–1023.

Harman, Gilbert 1968 'Knowledge, Inference, and Explanation', *American Philosophical Quarterly* 5: 164–173.

Contextualism and closure

Hawthorne, John 2004 *Knowledge and Lotteries*, Oxford: Oxford University Press.
Hawthorne, John & Lasonen-Aarnio, Maria 2009 'Knowledge and Objective Chance', in P. Greenough & D. Pritchard (eds.), *Williamson on Knowledge*, Oxford: Oxford University Press, 92–108.
Kvanvig, Jonathan L. 2007 'Contextualism, Contrastivism, Relevant Alternatives, and Closure', *Philosophical Studies* 134: 131–140.
Lasonen-Aarnio, Maria 2008 'Singe Premise Deduction and Risk', *Philosophical Studies* 141.2: 157–173.
———— 2010 'Unreasonable Knowledge', *Philosophical Perspectives* 24.1: 1–21.
Lewis, David 1996 'Elusive Knowledge', *Australasian Journal of Philosophy* 74.4: 549–567.
Neta, Ram 2003 'Contextualism and the Problem of the External World', *Philosophy and Phenomenological Research* 66.1: 1–31.
Nozick, Robert 1981 *Philosophical Explanations*, Oxford: Oxford University Press.
Schaffer, Jonathan 2007 'Closure, Contrast, and Answer', *Philosophical Studies* 133.2: 233–255.
Schechter, Josh 2013 'Rational Self-Doubt and Failure of Closure', *Philosophical Studies* 163.2: 429–452.
Silins, Nico 2005 'Transmission Failure', *Philosophical Studies* 126: 71–102.
Stine, Gail C. 1976 'Scepticism, Relevant Alternatives, and Deductive Closure', *Philosophical Studies* 29.4: 249–261.
Unger, Peter 1975 *Ignorance: A Case for Scepticism*, Oxford: Oxford University Press.
Vogel, Jonathan 1987 'Tracking, Closure, and Inductive Knowledge', in S. Luper-Foy (ed.), *The Possibility of Knowledge: Nozick and His Critics*, Totowa, NJ: Rowman & Littlefield, 197–215.
Wedgwood, Ralph 2008 'Contextualism about Justified Belief', *Philosophers Imprint* 8.9: 1–20.
Williamson, Timothy 2000 *Knowledge and Its Limits*, Oxford: Oxford University Press.
Wright, Crispin 1985 'Facts and Certainty', *Proceedings of the British Academy* 71, 429–472.

13

LOTTERIES AND PREFACES

Matthew A. Benton

1 Introduction

Consider a fair coin, which is now flipped. Should you believe that it won't land heads? Presumably not. Consider then a fair die, which is now rolled. Should you believe that it won't come up 6? Or consider two fair six-sided dice, which are now rolled. Should you believe, what is about 0.97 likely, that they won't both come up 1? Or consider four such dice, now rolled. Should you believe, what is about 0.999 likely, that they won't each come up 1?

Now consider a fair lottery of 1000 tickets, with one ticket guaranteed to win. Should you believe of any particular ticket (what is 0.999 likely) that it will not be drawn the winner? Many people will be tempted to answer this question similarly to how they answered the previous question, about four fair dice each coming up 1; namely, "yes" to both. This is because high probability is widely thought of as a good guide to what one may (and even should) believe. Implicit in this thought is the idea that the epistemically normative notions of what it is permissible (and obligatory) to believe encode some sort of threshold concerning how probable a proposition must be in order for one (acceptably) to believe it.

But if one may acceptably believe that any given ticket will lose, then presumably one may acceptably believe, on identical statistical grounds, that *each* of the lottery's 1000 tickets will lose. Suppose one does believe this of each ticket, that it will lose; yet in a typical lottery, one knows that some or other ticket will win, and so one would know that one of these lottery beliefs is false. This can seem paradoxical in that one seems to have epistemically acceptable grounds for believing each of a conjunction of propositions, even though one knows that the entire conjunction cannot be true.[1] Similar considerations plausibly arise in preface scenarios. Suppose you have painstakingly researched for writing a long non-fiction book, and have made many claims throughout the book manuscript. Upon finishing it, you write the preface, wherein it is customary to acknowledge, with due humility, that among the many hundreds of claims you have made, you are bound to have made a mistake: it is highly likely that some of your claims are false (see Makinson 1965). Nevertheless, given that you don't now know that any of your claims are false, or which ones they are if some are false, you stand by each of your claims. And if you stand by each of your claims, it seems that you also affirm their conjunction. This can seem paradoxical in that you, the author, seems to be claiming, on the one hand, a long conjunction, yet in the same text you claim that it's likely that the entire conjunction is not true.

This chapter provides a critical overview of how some contextualists in epistemology have approached lottery and preface scenarios. Although lotteries and prefaces raise several interesting issues concerning what one may or ought to believe, I shall focus my attention on what contextualists have said about knowledge and knowledge ascriptions with respect to the preface and lottery scenarios. For on the one hand, it is widely thought that an individual in a preface scenario can appropriately believe (and sometimes know) any particular claim made, but it is widely thought that in a lottery scenario one can perhaps appropriately believe that a ticket will lose even though the standard judgment is that one does not know it will. Yet on the other hand, when reflecting on the conjunction of such claims, it is also widely thought that one cannot know, and perhaps even should not believe, all of the conjoined claims at once.

Evaluating these paradoxes is of particular interest because what we commonly take ourselves to know can seem to depend on the truth of lottery outcomes, and our everyday knowledge can also seem to implicate us in being in a position to know, by deductive closure, the truth of lottery outcomes (Hawthorne 2004: ch. 1). The lottery paradox arguably relies on a *multi-premise closure* principle according to which knowledge may transmit from known premises to a known conclusion, for example:

> (MPC) If one believes a conclusion by competent deduction from some premises one knows, one knows the conclusion.[2]

MPC, or something similar, is initially quite plausible.[3] If I know that I won't be able to afford an African safari next year, it might seem that I can know what this logically entails; namely that I won't win a lottery or inherit a huge fortune; or if I know I will be in California in December, it might seem that I can know (what this entails) that I won't suffer an unexpected but fatal heart attack in the interim. But in a wide variety of mundane situations, we are willing to ascribe knowledge of the former claim, yet deny that one could (on similar grounds) know the entailed claim. Contextualists in epistemology offer an initially compelling explanation of this set of judgments, including those involving lotteries, while upholding a principle of closure.

2 Contextualism about knowledge and "know"

Contextualists concerned with knowledge ascriptions are broadly committed to a theory on which the truth-conditions of "know(s) that" are sensitive to the context in which it is used. The semantic contribution of "know(s) that" to a sentence is determined in part by the speaker (and interlocutors) at a conversational context. Just as indexical terms like "I" and "here" depend for their semantic contribution on the speaker or location of use, or gradable adjectives like "flat" or "tall" depend for their meaning on a standard being assumed by the speaker for what counts as flat or tall given the interests of the conversational context, so the semantic value of "know(s) that," according to contextualists, depends in part on the speaker's context of use. One attraction of contextualism is that it can explain the allure of skeptical arguments: they gain traction by subtly shifting the standard for the truth of knowledge ascriptions away from the manageable everyday standard to a much higher standard which is nearly impossible to meet. Thus in high standards skeptical situations, sentences of the form "S knows that p" are typically false.

Matthew A. Benton

David Lewis's contextualist (LC) approach purports to define knowledge in terms of both the subject's evidence and which possibilities the ascriber of knowledge is properly ignoring:

> (LC) S knows proposition P iff S's evidence eliminates every possibility in which not-P – Psst! – except for those possibilities that we are properly ignoring.
>
> *(1996: 554; repr. 1999: 425)*

Lewis's definition owes much to the "relevant alternatives" approach to theorizing about knowledge, which must provide an account of what and why certain alternatives count as "relevant."[4] As such, Lewis's definition is supplemented by several rules clarifying which possibilities may and may not be "properly" ignored (1996: 554ff.). I shall highlight only four. The *Rule of Actuality* says that "The possibility that actually obtains is never properly ignored; actuality is always a relevant alternative; nothing false may be properly presupposed" (1996: 554). The *Rule of Belief* states that a possibility believed by the subject to obtain is not properly ignored, whether or not she is right so to believe it. The *Rule of Resemblance* maintains that for two possibilities that saliently resemble each other, if one of them may not be ignored, neither may the other be properly ignored. And the *Rule of Attention* states that "a possibility not ignored at all is *ipso facto* not properly ignored" (1996: 559): those possibilities currently being attended to by the speaker and hearer are not properly ignored.

As written, LC provides a definition of knowledge itself, such that whether a subject S knows a proposition depends in part on the nature of S's evidence but also on features of the ascriber's conversational context: thus its final clause refers (with "we") to *us*, the ascribers, who might be speaking of whether S knows. If we take it straightforwardly as a definition of knowledge, it would seem to create (seemingly) absurd scenarios where a single subject can both know and not know a proposition at the same time. For if in S's own context, S is considering her evidence and whether she knows p, she might, given Lewis's rules, be properly ignoring all the possibilities not eliminated by her evidence, and so according to the definition, S indeed knows that p. But in another conversational context, some interlocutors are attending to a possibility $\neg p$, which is not eliminated by S's evidence, and thus according to the definition, S does *not* know that p. As such, taking LC as the definition of knowledge results in it defying the law of non-contradiction.[5]

Although though Lewis himself construes his task as defining knowledge, and although he conducts his discussion in the object-language of what it takes to know, he acknowledges (in his paper's final paragraph: 1996: 566–567) that LC should really be understood meta-linguistically rather than as a definition of knowledge itself. Stated more properly in meta-linguistic terms, Lewis's LC generates a straightforward semantics for "know(s) that" ascriptions ("AC" for *ascriber* contextualism), thus:

> (AC) X's ascription of the form "S knows that P" is true iff S's evidence eliminates every possibility in which not-P – Psst! – except for those possibilities that X and X's conversational participants are properly ignoring.

Where the ascriber is the subject, that is, where S = X, such that X is speaking of whether X herself knows, we get the result that whether X can truthfully claim that "I know that p" depends solely on X's evidence and whether X (and X's conversational partners) can properly ignore certain possibilities not eliminated by X's evidence. X can speak truly in self-ascribing such "knowledge" even while another ascriber (say, Joe) can simultaneously, and truthfully, claim that "X does not know that p," perhaps because Joe himself is attending to possibilities uneliminated by X's evidence. The semantics given by AC thus offers the truth-conditions for ascriptions and denials of "knowledge" relative to the alternatives being attended to or properly ignored in the ascriber's context; the AC contextualist need not be committed to there being a fact of the matter, independent of such conversational contexts, about whether a subject "knows."[6]

Two other prominent contextualists offer similar semantic accounts of ascriber contextualism. Cohen's (1988) proposal is that a subject S may be said, truly, to "know" a proposition p relative to a set of relevant alternatives, where the standards that govern which alternatives are *relevant* is a context-sensitive matter: "the truth-value of an attribution of knowledge is context-sensitive" in similar fashion to the way that indexical terms like "I" and "here" are sensitive to their context of utterance. "As such," Cohen says, "one speaker may attribute knowledge to a subject while another speaker denies knowledge to that same subject, without contradiction" (1988: 97). For Cohen, the shifting standards of what is relevant tracks the standard of epistemic justification required of the subject, by the speaker, in order for the speaker's knowledge ascription to be true. Similarly, DeRose defends a view on which

> the truth-conditions of knowledge-ascribing and knowledge-denying sentences (sentences of the form "S knows that p" and "S does not know that p" and related variants of such sentences) vary in certain ways according to the context in which they are uttered. What so varies is the epistemic standard that S must meet (or, in the case of a denial of knowledge, fail to meet) in order for such a statement to be true.
>
> *(2009: 2–3)*

For DeRose, the shifting standards govern the truth-tracking "strength of epistemic position" required of the subject, by the speaker, in order for the speaker's knowledge ascription to be true. For each of the above contextualist semantics, including AC, the underlying idea is the same: contextualists claim that "know(s)" expresses a different relation between a subject and a proposition depending on the ascriber's[7] context of use, where the conversational context sets the standard for what possibilities may be properly ignored, or what alternatives count as relevant, or how well the subject must be epistemically justified.[8]

3 Lotteries

When it comes to lotteries, the standard intuitive judgment is that a subject who believes that a given ticket will lose on the basis of the probabilities involved does not thereby know that the ticket will lose.[9] Given that setup, the standard semantic judgment, for at least a wide range of conversational situations, is that a denial along the lines of "S does not know that ticket 1 will lose," is true.[10]

Lewis claims that a contextualist who endorses a semantics given by AC along with Lewis's rules has an apt explanation of why. Such a denial would be true (when true) because the statistical evidence on which S might believe the ticket a loser makes likely a possibility (that ticket losing) which saliently resembles the possibility of every other ticket losing: the same statistical evidence is available for thinking of each and every ticket in a fair lottery that it will lose. But those possibilities, for each losing ticket, also saliently resemble the possibility that the eventual winning ticket (call it ticket w) loses; yet the Rule of Actuality says that possibility is not properly ignored. The Rule of Resemblance says that of two possibilities which saliently resemble each other, either both are properly ignored, or neither is properly ignored. Because the possibility that every other (losing) ticket wins saliently resembles the possibility that ticket w wins, one may not properly ignore the possibility that any particular ticket wins. As Lewis puts it, "These possibilities are saliently similar to one another: so either every one of them may be properly ignored, or else none may. But one of them may not be properly ignored: the one that actually obtains" (1996: 557).

171

One difficulty with this explanation, however, is that it seems to depend on the lottery having a winner: for it trades on the statistical resemblance between the winning ticket and the other (losing) tickets. But many lotteries do not have a guaranteed winner. In such lotteries, on a given day a ticket can be drawn but it may or may not correspond to a winning ticket holder.[11] For these lotteries, Lewis's view will predict that one fails to know that a given ticket is a loser only on those days when the drawn ticket has a winner. For all Lewis has said, lotteries whose drawings do not guarantee that the drawn ticket matches a sold winning ticket are lottery draws where, on the days where the drawn ticket produces no winner, we do know of each ticket that it loses. Yet the intuitive judgment of non-knowledge about losing tickets even extends to cases where there is no winning ticket (DeRose 1996: 571, fn. 6; Hawthorne 2004: 8, 15). To be worthwhile then, a viable contextualist approach must accommodate the commonsense judgments that (i) ordinary knowledge ascriptions are largely true in mundane situations; (ii) knowledge *denials* are true in high standard (especially skeptical) situations; and (iii) knowledge denials are typically (or at least can be) true when they concern statistical beliefs about lottery propositions, winner or no.

A contextualist strategy might exploit the fact that understanding what a standard lottery is involves grasping that each ticket (or number) is supposed to have an equally good chance of winning; and if every ticket is such that it is as likely to win as every other, then the possibility that any particular ticket wins should be salient to someone considering lotteries, including any ascriber (denier) considering whether a subject knows that a ticket wins. Given the standard statistical grounds for thinking a ticket will lose, the scenario of that ticket winning remains as likely as any other scenario, and thus it represents a salient possibility[12] where despite one's grounds, one's belief is mistaken. It is not the mere reliance on high probability that is the culprit, but reliance on probabilities structured of a standard lottery which are structured so as to make each ticket equally likely, or at least not appreciably differentially likely,[13] to win. As such, the lottery situation automatically installs an epistemic standard which is not met by relying on the lottery's statistical grounds, and thus knowledge denials of the form "S doesn't know that ticket x will lose," which implicitly regard S as relying only on a lottery's statistical belief-forming grounds, are rendered true.

However, Hawthorne (2002 and 2004: 94ff.) argues that any contextualist approach to this puzzle will have trouble given that a variety of our everyday knowledge claims, made without attending to lotteries or statistical considerations, can depend for their truth on statistical facts. For some of what I know about you (say, that you and I will meet for lunch tomorrow) may depend on you not winning the lottery (because if you win, tomorrow you will instead be busy collecting your prize and interviewing with the media).[14] But if my knowledge that we will meet for lunch depends on you not winning the lottery, and I cannot know you will not win, it may seem that I likewise cannot know that we will meet for lunch. (On the other hand, sticking to the claim that you do know we'll lunch may seem to license inferring from this knowledge that you *won't* win the lottery!)

The contextualist will insist that such mundane knowledge ascriptions can remain true even though they in some sense depend on lottery-like statistical facts; indeed, the contextualist is in principle committed to the idea that in some ascriber situations, a subject S can be said to "know" that he won't win the lottery, even if S happens to hold a lottery ticket in his pocket. For only when such statistical facts become salient to the *ascriber* will the conversational situation generate a new meaning for "know(s)" such that denying S "knowledge" is true. And the contextualist will maintain that a closure principle is upheld insofar as one may only infer from what one may, at a given context, be truthfully said to "know," so long as the meaning of "know" stays constant throughout the context of the deduction (inferring from "knowledge" had in a lower standards context to "knowledge" had in a higher standards context will be deemed illegitimate). Cases where it seems illegitimate to deduce the truth of ordinary knowledge ascriptions ("She knows

Lotteries and prefaces

that we will meet for lunch") to knowledge of an entailed truth ("Hence she knows that she won't win the lottery") are explained by appeal to a context shift rather than a failure of closure.

This approach can seem unsatisfying, however, for it can appear as though situations where lottery probabilities are salient end up revealing what was true all along: for if many such everyday knowledge ascriptions depend on lottery-like statistical facts, and we truthfully deny "knowledge" when reminded of this, the skeptic (speaking from a high standards skeptical context) can insist that you never spoke truthfully of having knowledge even when your conversational situation rightly didn't consider the relevance of statistical grounds.

The trouble becomes more pronounced when our mundane knowledge ascriptions undergo conjunction introduction. For even in situations where lottery-like odds seem to be far from relevant, the contextualist will allow that an ascriber can truthfully ascribe knowledge to a subject, and that ascriber can presumably conjoin this (given MPC) with other knowledge that the ascriber may claim for the subject.

Consider a case from Hawthorne (2004: 94–95). Suppose that Joe believes, knowing his friend Alfred's financial situation, that Alfred won't be able to afford an African safari this year. Joe also believes, on similar grounds, that his friend Bertha likewise won't have enough money for such a safari trip. Joe has 5000 such friends, of whom he believes this of them on similar grounds. On contextualism, in a situation[15] where we (the ascribers) are rightly not considering lotteries, a relation (call it "K") holds between Joe and each of these propositions about what his friends can afford, such that this relation makes true any claim we might make in that situation that Joe "knows" each of these truths.

But suppose further that Joe himself has deduced and come to believe that each of these 5000 friends, because they will not be able to afford a safari this year, will not win the lottery this year (assuming MPC). Suppose also that each of Joe's friends presently holds a ticket in a 5001-ticket lottery, and as it happens, the winning ticket is held by a non-friend. All of this is unbeknownst to us in our conversational situation. Contextualism allows that, nevertheless, the K relation can hold between Joe and these propositions about what his friends can afford, and that we, not needing to attend to the lottery applicable to Joe's friends, can still speak truly by ascribing, in our situation, "knowledge" to Joe of the entire conjunction.[16] "But," Hawthorne objects, "it seems crazy to suppose that in *any* context, 'know' expresses a relation that holds between an agent and the proposition that none of 5000 people will win the lottery when the agent has no special insider information and there are only 5001 lottery ticket-holders" (2004: 95, italics mine).[17] What is worse, if Joe himself has witnessed the distribution of tickets and sees that only one of the lottery tickets is held by a non-friend, and has deduced from what we say he "knows" and has come to believe that the non-friend will win, then K still holds (assuming MPC) between Joe and this proposition, for "the verb 'know' in the original context expresses a relation that holds between Joe and the proposition that his non-friend will win!"[18]

4 Prefaces

The lottery paradox gets traction by it seeming (probabilistically) reasonable to believe of each ticket that it will lose, which, when conjoined, would lead one to believe of each and every ticket that it will lose, even though one believes that some ticket will win. As such, it may be reasonable to have an inconsistent set of beliefs. But it also seems (intuitively) that one does not know (given just the probabilities) that a particular ticket will lose, and MPC vindicates this judgment by showing how absurd results would follow from knowing (on such grounds) which tickets are losers.

The preface paradox similarly relies on conjunction introduction, but it differs in that each individual belief from the manuscript, taken alone or in sequence, could each (by commonsense

173

standards) be knowledge. For the preface, the inclination to ascribe knowledge is threatened only once one contemplates conjunction introduction by considering all of the claims made in the manuscript and assessing the set as a whole for error. Thus the notion of risk of error in play in the preface is structurally different from that of the lottery, and the threat to MPC is all the more direct (see Williamson 2009: 4ff.).

Nevertheless, MPC retains some credibility here: for it would be bizarre for a speaker, in a given situation, to go through each claim in the book and ascribe knowledge to the author but then be unwilling to affirm the statement "The author knows all the claims made in the book." Situations in which one is indeed comfortable ascribing knowledge for each individual claim will likely be situations where one is similarly comfortable ascribing knowledge of the conjunction (as MPC would predict). But by the same token, being unwilling to ascribe knowledge of the manuscript's conjunction of claims plausibly correlates with thinking that at least one of its claims isn't known. Worth noting in this connection is the hesitancy of many actual authors to claim in a preface that they *have*, in fact, made a mistake somewhere; they thereby avoid actual inconsistency by noting that they "likely" or "surely" or "must" have made an error somewhere.[19]

However, we needn't consider actual prefaces to see the force of the paradox. One might know, because they tell you, that some of your friends will be attending the next philosophy conference; on similar grounds you might learn that 100 of your friends will be there (and indeed, all 100 show up). But though we might agree that you can know of each individual friend that they will attend, few will be inclined to agree that you can (by inferring from each such belief) come to know that all 100 will turn up (Hawthorne 2004: 48–49). This correlates with an uneasiness to claim that "All 100 will attend." But though we can be nervous about making such conjunction ascriptions (or ascriptions of knowing the conjunction), this uneasiness may be squared with MPC and the idea that the subject indeed can know the conjunction. For we might be susceptible to misleading evidence about the truth of a conjunction without thereby coming to drop any particular belief in the sequence. If it is possible for someone to know that p while believing that one does not know p,[20] then presumably one can continue to know a conjunction while believing (due to the misleading evidence) that one does not know the conjunction. And if knowledge is necessary but not sufficient for proper assertion, this would explain such uneasiness without impugning MPC.[21]

Such maneuvers aside, it looks as though the preface scenario generates a particularly tricky case for the contextualist about knowledge ascriptions. For an ascriber who goes through a long (or even short) sequence of knowledge ascriptions for some subject S need not feel any pressure of context-shift; but to capture the judgment that one cannot (normally) truthfully ascribe to S knowledge of its conjunction would require that merely introducing a conjunction ascription somehow shifts the context so drastically as to make the conjunction ascription false. Such a solution could be offered. But trading as it does on inductive grounds for thinking there must be some error in the sequence, the contextualist would need to provide a principled way of distinguishing between salient inductive grounds for thinking a subject has gone wrong specific to a preface-style case, and the salient inductive grounds we generally have for worrying about errors. Drawing that distinction without admitting skepticism looks to be a difficult task.[22]

Notes

1 See Kyburg (1961: 197 and 1970) for the original lottery paradox.
2 Williamson (2000: 117 and 2009). Hawthorne's version of MPC reads thus: "Necessarily, if S knows $p_1, \ldots, p_n$, competently deduces q, and thereby comes to believe that q, while retaining knowledge $p_1, \ldots, p_n$ throughout, then S knows that q" (2004: 33).

Lotteries and prefaces

3 Although I am sympathetic to closure, I don't intend to discuss the debate here. See Hawthorne (2004: 31–50 and 2014), Williamson (2009), and Dretske (2014). See also Maria Lasonen-Aarnio's "Contextualism and Closure," Chapter 12, this volume.

4 See especially Goldman (1976) and Stine (1976); for discussion of such a view with lotteries in view, see McKinnon (2013).

5 Another potentially absurd result: is LC committed to the possibility of S knowing some p precisely because there is no conversation at all in which speakers are considering whether p, or speaking of whether S "knows" that p? Suppose S has no evidence concerning p, but our conversation does not broach the matter of either p or $\neg p$ (and let us suppose that p is actual, and that S does not believe either p or $\neg p$, etc., so Lewis's other rules do not apply). Lewis says that "what is and what is not being ignored is a feature of the particular conversational context" (1996: 559). In the envisioned case then we are ignoring, and properly so, all the possibilities in which $\neg p$; but then S's evidence trivially eliminates every possibility in which $\neg p$ except for those we are properly ignoring, because, in our context, *every* $\neg p$ possibility is being properly ignored by us. Because the set of possibilities needed to be eliminated by S's evidence is null, then according to Lewis's definition (given its "iff" clause), S knows that p, despite S not believing p, and having no evidence for p whatsoever.

6 As such, the law of noncontradiction plausibly does not apply, for on AC there is no fact of the matter, independent of such ascribing (denying) contexts, about whether someone knows. DeRose (2009: 166ff.), another ascriber contextualist, thinks of "knows" on analogy with gradable adjectives such as "tall": there is plausibly no fact of the matter about who or what counts as tall, apart from ascribers' evaluations at a context.

7 Notice that Lewis's ascriber contextualism may be modified into a subject-centered contextualism (SC), by replacing the final clause's "we" with referent to S and those in S's context. But Lewis himself, though noting the possibility of a subject-centered approach like SC, prefers an ascriber contextualism (1996: 561). For approaches that center on the subject (but are thereby not semantically-contextualist), see Hawthorne (2004: ch. 4), and Stanley (2005: chs. 5–6).

8 Contextualists diverge on the mechanism for shifting the standards. For Lewis, certain possibilities previously properly ignored may become salient by the Rule of Attention; for Cohen, the mechanism is a similar rule of salience (1988: 109); for DeRose, a rule of sensitivity is the mechanism (1995: 37).

9 This judgment is widespread in (and outside of) philosophy. See DeRose, Cohen, and Lewis above, plus Harman (1973: 161 and 1986: 21), Nelkin (2000), Williamson (2000: 246–249), Hawthorne (2002 and 2004), and McKinnon (2013), among many others. See Turri and Friedman (2014) for empirical studies of non-philosophers' judgments, including the non-knowledge judgment, about lottery cases.

10 The contextualist, of course, is in a position to allow that some such knowledge-denials are false, for there might be contexts in which the ascriber *is* properly ignoring the possibility that a person wins.

11 Compare many actual lotteries where a computer generates a winning number by randomly selecting seven numbers (or by drawing balls with numbers on them); most days, the numbers correspond to no winning ticket having those numbers.

12 For discussion of what might make for such salience, and how it might rob one of knowledge, see Hawthorne (2004: 62ff and 168ff).

13 Even if some tickets are more likely to win than others, we are still apt to judge that one cannot know that a ticket in such a lottery will lose. Cf. Vogel (1990: 26 n. 8) and Hawthorne (2004: 8–9, 15ff).

14 See Harman (1973: 161) for this example.

15 Assume that Joe is not a part of our conversational situation.

16 Hawthorne (2004: 83) notes that the contextualist would have to ascribe to a metalinguistic closure principle; I ignore such complications here.

17 Someone might challenge the force of this objection by pointing out that the vignette loses sight of the context of ascription: we would be ascribing "knowledge" to Joe of the entire conjunction in a low standards context where we aren't attending to lottery considerations. Against this, note that Joe himself has deduced that none of his friends will win the lottery, when it was overwhelmingly likely that one of his friends would do so; the contextualist says that Joe "K"s that none of his friends will win the lottery even though that was overwhelmingly improbable.

18 Hawthorne (2004: 96–98) sketches a solution available to the contextualist who wants to respect MPC, which deploys a "New Rule of Belief" in the spirit of Lewis. But he notes that such a solution depends on "hyperactive context-shifting" to change the semantic value of "know" to make false the kind of knowledge ascriptions which arise in the above case.

19 Very few authors convey their humility by acknowledging (as Makinson 1965: 205 put it), that "not everything I assert in this book is true." Makinson's cited example (from R.L. Wilder) trades on a definite article: "the errors and shortcomings to be found herein are not [the] fault" of those who gave Wilder suggestions and criticisms.
20 Williamson (2011 and 2014) has argued that one can know *p* even though it is improbable on one's evidence that one knows *p*; in such cases, one might rationally believe that one doesn't know *p* yet continue to believe (and plausibly know) that *p*.
21 See especially Hawthorne (2004: 50) for this point. On whether knowledge is sufficient for assertion, see Lackey (2011 and 2016) and Benton (2016).
22 Many thanks to Max Baker-Hytch, Nathan Cockram, Jonathan Jenkins Ichikawa, and John Hawthorne for comments or discussion.

References

Benton, Matthew A. 2016. "Expert Opinion and Second-Hand Knowledge." *Philosophy and Phenomenological Research* 92: 492–508.
Cohen, Stewart. 1988. "How to Be a Fallibilist." *Philosophical Perspectives* 2: 91–123.
DeRose, Keith. 1995. "Solving the Skeptical Problem." *Philosophical Review* 104: 1–52.
———. 1996. "Knowledge, Assertion, and Lotteries." *Australasian Journal of Philosophy* 74: 568–580.
———. 2009. *The Case for Contextualism.* Oxford: Clarendon Press.
Dretske, Fred. 2014. "The Case against Closure." In Matthias Steup, John Turri, and Ernest Sosa (eds.), *Contemporary Debates in Epistemology*, 27–39. Malden: Wiley Blackwell, 2nd edition.
Goldman, Alvin I. 1976. "Discrimination and Perceptual Knowledge." *Journal of Philosophy* 73: 771–791.
Harman, Gilbert. 1973. *Thought.* Princeton: Princeton University Press.
———. 1986. *Change in View: Principles of Reasoning.* Cambridge: MIT Press.
Hawthorne, John. 2002. "Lewis, the Lottery, and the Preface." *Analysis* 62: 242–251.
———. 2004. *Knowledge and Lotteries.* Oxford: Clarendon Press.
———. 2014. "The Case for Closure." In Matthias Steup, John Turri, and Ernest Sosa (eds.), *Contemporary Debates in Epistemology*, 40–55. Malden: Wiley Blackwell, 2nd edition.
Kyburg, Henry. 1961. *Probability and the Logic of Rational Belief.* Middletown, CT: Wesleyan University Press.
———. 1970. "Conjunctivitis." In Marshall Swain (ed.), *Induction, Acceptance, and Rational Belief.* Dordrecht: Reidel.
Lackey, Jennifer. 2011. "Assertion and Isolated Second-Hand Knowledge." In Jessica Brown and Herman Cappelen (eds.), *Assertion: New Philosophical Essays*, 251–275. Oxford: Oxford University Press.
———. 2016. "Assertion and Expertise." *Philosophy and Phenomenological Research* 92: 509–517.
Lewis, David. 1996. "Elusive Knowledge." *Australasian Journal of Philosophy* 74: 549–567. Reprinted in Lewis (1999): 418–445.
———. 1999. *Papers in Metaphysics and Epistemology.* Cambridge: Cambridge University Press.
McKinnon, Rachel. 2013. "Lotteries, Knowledge, and Irrelevant Alternatives." *Dialogue* 52: 523–549.
Makinson, D. C. 1965. "The Paradox of the Preface." *Analysis* 25: 205–207.
Nelkin, Dana K. 2000. "The Lottery Paradox, Knowledge, and Rationality." *Philosophical Review* 109: 373–409.
Stanley, Jason. 2005. *Knowledge and Practical Interests.* Oxford: Clarendon Press.
Stine, Gail C. 1976. "Skepticism, Relevant Alternatives, and Deductive Closure." *Philosophical Studies* 29: 249–261.
Turri, John and Ori Friedman. 2014. "Winners and Losers in the Folk Epistemology of Lotteries." In James Beebe (ed.), *Advances in Experimental Epistemology.* New York: Bloomsbury Academic.
Vogel, Jonathan. 1990. "Are There Counterexamples to the Closure Principle?" In Michael D. Roth and Glenn Ross (eds.), *Doubting: Contemporary Perspectives on Skepticism.* Dordrecht: Kluwer Academic Publishing.
Williamson, Timothy. 2000. *Knowledge and Its Limits.* Oxford: Oxford University Press.
———. 2009. "Probability and Danger." *The Amherst Lecture in Philosophy* 4: 1–35.
———. 2011. "Improbable Knowing." In Trent Dougherty (ed.), *Evidentialism and Its Discontents*, 147–164. Oxford: Oxford University Press.
———. 2014. "Very Improbable Knowing." *Erkenntnis* 79: 971–999.

14

CONTEXTUALISM AND KNOWLEDGE NORMS

Alex Worsnip

Recent epistemology has seen a turn toward understanding the norms governing various practices in terms of knowledge.[1] Strikingly, such norms have been claimed as a data point both in favor of and against epistemic contextualism. In this chapter, I investigate the relationship of the two through a critical survey of the literature.

1 Knowledge norms introduced

"Knowledge norms", in the sense at work in this chapter, are norms that claim that knowledge is necessary and/or sufficient for something's being appropriate. Slightly more specifically, they tend to be claims that knowledge of a proposition p is necessary and/or sufficient for its being appropriate to do something related to p: for example, to assert p, to act on p, to employ p as a premise in one's reasoning, or even to believe p. Let us work with an example, the knowledge norm of assertion:

> **KNA.** S (epistemically) may assert p if and only if S knows p.

Some observations. First, because I have stated KNA as a biconditional, it commits one to both the sufficiency and the necessity of knowledge for permissible assertion. However, one might only want to endorse one of these two distinct claims. Such "one-direction" claims are still, in my sense, full-blooded knowledge norms. I am working with the biconditional simply to fix ideas.

Secondly, KNA uses the permissive modal 'may', rather than the requiring modal 'ought'. This, I take it, is orthodox. Most theorists would not want to endorse the (universally quantified) claim that if one knows p, one ought to assert p, even in some peculiarly epistemic sense of 'ought'. For surely it is at least sometimes permissible (in *every* sense) to remain silent about what you know. So as long as we hold on to the sufficiency direction of KNA, we will not want to use 'ought' to state it. However, assuming that 'ought Φ' entails 'may Φ', as it does on the orthodox semantics and logic for modals, KNA as stated already entails the claim that knowing p is *necessary* for it to be the case that one ought to assert p.[2]

177

Thirdly, note the qualifier 'epistemically' on 'may'. This is something of a term of art. The idea is that if S epistemically may assert p, there is nothing about S's epistemic position that makes it impermissible to assert p. Uncontroversially, there may be something non-epistemic that makes it impermissible for S to assert p, even when S knows p. For example, perhaps asserting p would be very hurtful to the listener, or betray a secret upon which someone's life depends.[3] Then asserting p is not morally permissible, but may still be epistemically permissible in our sense. These senses of 'may' are not obviously incommensurable: perhaps for asserting p to be permissible *simpliciter*, it must be permissible (at least) both epistemically and morally. But we can nevertheless use 'may' in a way that brackets non-epistemic factors and focuses only on epistemic permissibility. Note that this usage of 'may' is still a normative usage, rather than the purely expectational usage that is at work in sentences like "the train may be late" on their most natural readings – a usage that is, confusingly, also often called the "epistemic" sense of 'may'.

Fourthly, it is sometimes claimed that KNA is *constitutive* of assertion. The claim here is that part of what it is for something to be an assertion is that it be subject to KNA. This claim is ancillary to KNA itself. The point here is delicate. If KNA is a necessary truth, then nothing can be an assertion without being subject to KNA. However, plausibly there is more to constitutivity than this. Compare:

> **Reading-No Enslavement.** One may read a book only if reading the book does not lead to the enslavement and torture of the rest of humanity.

This claim seems true, and necessarily so, so nothing could be an act of reading a book unless it were subject to this norm. But it is not plausible that it is constitutive of the act of reading a book – part of what it is to read a book – that such an act is subject to Reading-No Enslavement. One thing that makes this clear is that one can specify what it is to read a book without any reference to Reading-No Enslavement. Moreover, there is no sense in which the act of reading a book involves "representing oneself" as staying away from enslavement and torture. Conversely, perhaps there is no way of telling whether something is an assertion (rather than some other speech act) that does not make reference to KNA – to the conditions under which the act is epistemically permissible. Perhaps all assertions "represent themselves" as satisfying KNA by being known.[4] If this were right, it might suggest that it is part of the very essence of assertion that it is governed by KNA, in a way that it is not part of the very essence of book-reading that it is subject to Reading-No Enslavement. But, as Reading-No Enslavement shows by analogy, this will not follow merely from KNA itself.

Briefly, without any claim to comprehensiveness, let's survey some of the data offered in favor of knowledge norms. The most fundamental kind of data that has been offered in favor of knowledge norms concerns the ways in which we naturally assess the relevant practices – assertion, action, reasoning – in terms of what a subject knows or knew. Consider, for example:

(1) You shouldn't have let my daughter play with your dog! For all you knew, it might have bitten her![5]

Note that here it isn't sufficient to excuse the act that the dog didn't *in fact* bite the daughter; the agent is still criticizable on the grounds that she didn't *know* that it wouldn't do so.[6] By contrast, the agent *can* defend herself like so:

(2) I knew that my dog wouldn't bite your daughter, since I know it has no teeth. So I didn't do anything wrong.

There are also certain "clashing" sentences where this clash may be well-explained by knowledge norms:

(3)   #I know that the ice will hold my weight, but I shouldn't cross in case it doesn't hold my weight.[7]

If knowing p is sufficient for relying on p in action, the oddness of (3) has an explanation.

In the case of assertion, some have claimed that knowledge norms explain the "clashes" of some utterances, in this case some famous "Moore-paradoxical" utterances:[8]

(4)   #It's raining, but I don't know it's raining.

This sentence's badness can be explained if knowledge is necessary for permissible assertion. For if one is only warranted in asserting the first conjunct if the second conjunct is false, no wonder the sentence sounds odd.

Interestingly, the badness of (3) and (4) support the *sufficiency* of knowledge for relying on p in action, and the *necessity* for knowledge for asserting p, respectively. One might expect there to be analogous sentences for the inverse cases (necessity for action and sufficiency for assertion), but those are harder to construct. It often at least not obviously incoherent to say that one is relying on something that one doesn't know. And the clash between saying one knows p and refusing to assert p can be explained without a knowledge norm: since 'knows' is factive, why would one be willing to assert that one knows p but not be willing to assert p? So the data in favor of knowledge-norms is complex. It may more strongly support sufficiency-norms for some practices (action) but more strongly support necessity-norms for other practices (assertion). And of course, it is open to theorists to accept knowledge norms about some practices but not others.[9]

2 The need for contextualists to "relativize" knowledge norms

As anyone reading this volume should know by now, contextualism is a semantic thesis about the word 'know(s)', according to which the semantic value of this term varies across conversational contexts. In some contexts, 'knows' expresses a concept that one must meet very demanding standards to satisfy; in other contexts, it expresses a concept that one must meet less demanding standards to satisfy. Moreover, on standard contextualist views, there can be true utterances both of 'S knows p' and of 'S doesn't know p', even holding fixed the same subject S, proposition p, and S's circumstances (evidence, practical situation, etc.) with respect to p. This will be so when S does meet the standards for knowing associated with the use of 'know' in lower-standards contexts, but fails to meet the standards for knowing associated with the use of 'know' in higher-standards contexts. As some contextualists have put the point, the subject knows$_{LO}$ but doesn't know$_{HI}$, or has "low-grade knowledge" but not "high-grade knowledge".

But it now becomes clear that, for a contextualist, it is radically indeterminate what KNA (understood as a sentence) says. What "grade" of knowledge is it that KNA says is required for permissible assertion? KNA itself is an implicitly universally quantified sentence stated in the course of abstract theorizing, so it's hard to say which semantic value of 'knows' the context in which KNA is uttered would determine.

Clearly, the contextualist cannot say that KNA is true on *every* value of 'knows', so that it holds in metasemantic generality, for this leads to contradictions. Since one can have low-grade knowledge while lacking high-grade knowledge, it cannot be that low-grade knowledge is sufficient for permissible assertion, but that high-grade knowledge is necessary for permissible assertion.[10]

A contextualist might next try specifying a single value of 'knows' that is the one picked out by 'knows' as it occurs in KNA. But which one? Given the diversity of potential semantic values for 'knows', it feels arbitrary to pick one privileged value of 'knows' that plays the crucial role of being necessary (and perhaps sufficient) for assertion; it is not even clear how one would go about specifying such a value. And once one says that one semantic value of 'knows' is privileged in this way, it seems that there will be pressure to say that this is the "core" or "real" sense of 'knows' in a way that undercuts contextualists' pluralism about the range of concepts that 'knows' can express.

So the most promising route is for the contextualist to instead modify KNA (and other knowledge norms), so that it is, as Keith DeRose calls it, "relativized" to a conversational context:[11]

> **KNA-Relativized.** S (epistemically) may assert p if and only if, in S's conversational context, the utterance 'I know p' would be true.

KNA-Relativized moves the right-hand side of KNA up one semantic "level". Although S is the subject here, that subject herself inhabits a particular conversational context, and is capable of self-attributing knowledge. The natural idea behind KNA-Relativized is that it is the subject's own conversational context, and the resulting value of 'know', that is relevant when it comes to assessing the normative appropriateness of the subject's utterances. However, it is important to see that KNA-Relativized does not collapse the normative appropriateness of asserting p with the normative appropriateness of asserting that one knows p.[12] The idea is that asserting p is appropriate only if a self-attribution of knowledge would be *true*, not that it is appropriate only if a self-attribution of knowledge would itself be *appropriate*. It is part of the original idea behind KNA that some utterances are true but inappropriate. So KNA-Relativized leaves open the possibility that sometimes one may assert p but may not assert that one knows p.

3 Knowledge norms and the contextualism-invariantism wars

Let's assume for the sake of argument that we want to accept some kind of knowledge norms, and ask whether this favors or hurts contextualism in the debate between contextualists and invariantists. Since we've already seen that contextualists should accept relativized versions of knowledge norms if they want to accept knowledge norms at all, it will be an important part of this task to consider whether there is any reason to prefer unrelativized norms over their relativized equivalents (or vice versa). We will consider, in turn, an argument against contextualism from knowledge norms (due to John Hawthorne) and an argument for contextualism from knowledge norms (due to Keith DeRose).

(a) Hawthorne's argument from knowledge norms against contextualism

Hawthorne (2004: 85–91) offers what is effectively an argument for preferring unrelativized knowledge norms to their relativized analogues. Hawthorne's case turns on exploiting potential differences between the context of someone ascribing knowledge and the context of the subject of their knowledge-attribution. Suppose that a subject S is in a low-standards conversational context but the ascriber is in a high-standards conversational context. And suppose that the subject's epistemic position with respect to some proposition p is such that, given these contexts, 'I know p' is true in the subject's mouth but 'S knows p' is false in the ascriber's mouth. By KNA-Relativized and the fact that 'I know p' is true in the subject's mouth, S (epistemically)

Contextualism and knowledge norms

may assert p. But then, since 'S knows p' is false in the ascriber's mouth, it should be true for the ascriber to say:

(5) S does not know p, but S may assert p.

Likewise, suppose that the subject is in a high-standards context but the ascriber is in a low-standards context. Then, 'I know p' is false in the subject's mouth and so, by KNA-Relativized, S (epistemically) may not assert p. But, since, 'S knows p' is true in the ascriber's mouth, it should also be true for the ascriber to say:

(6) S knows p, but S may not assert p.

According to Hawthorne, claims of the form of (5) and (6) sound odd; moreover, they clash with the fundamental idea that knowledge-attributions can be used to third-personally evaluate the propriety of assertions. But on the face of it, KNA-Relativized, together with contextualism about 'knows', commits us to the possibility that claims of the form of (5) and (6) can be true. By contrast, the unrelativized version of KNA seems to preclude the truth of (5) and (6). So, the unrelativized version of KNA does a better job of accounting for the intuitive role that knowledge-attributions play in the third-person evaluations of assertions.[13] Since the contextualist can only accept KNA-Relativized, and not KNA, this ultimately constitutes an objection to contextualism itself. Analogous arguments can be made for other knowledge norms.

How might a contextualist reply to this? There are two potential strategies: one that involves modifying KNA-Relativized, and one that involves arguing that KNA-Relativized does not really have the bad consequences that Hawthorne claims it has. Let's begin with the first strategy.

As we observed earlier, in relativizing KNA, the contextualist shifted the right-hand side of KNA up one semantic level, mentioning rather than using 'knows'. But the left-hand side of KNA-Relativized continues to use rather than mention the normative term ('may') that is used to evaluate assertions. But what if we also shifted the left hand side of KNA up one level, to mention rather than use 'may'? Then, we would get:

> **KNA-Doubly-Relativized.** An utterance of 'S (epistemically) may assert p' in a context C is true if and only if the utterance 'S knows p' in context C is true.[14]

By relativizing both sides of the biconditional, KNA-Doubly-Relativized brings third-person evaluations of the permissibility of assertions and third-person knowledge attributions back together. We are then back in a position where utterances like (5) and (6) could never be true, assuming that there is no context-shift in the course of their utterance.

Since the contextualist thinks that the semantic value of 'knows' can vary with the conversational context of the speaker, accepting KNA-Doubly-Relativized will commit her to also holding that the semantic value of 'may' can also vary with the conversational context of the speaker. Is this a problem? Hawthorne notes that "the relevant normative facts do *not* seem to be ascriber-dependent" (Hawthorne 2004: 86), but construed as an objection to the present view, this rests upon a simple use-mention conflation. The present view is not that the normative *facts* depend on the context of the ascriber (whatever that would mean), but rather that the semantic value of a normative term ('may') – and hence potentially the truth-value of utterances that use it – depends on the context of the ascriber. Ironically, this conflation parallels exactly the mistake in many critiques of contextualism about 'knows' far less sophisticated than Hawthorne's,[15] which falsely impute to contextualists the (borderline unintelligible) view that whether a subject

181

knows p depends on the context of "the ascriber" (whoever that is, given that this view makes no reference to any ascription). As Hawthorne himself points out, contextualism about 'knows' is instead the view that the semantic value, and hence potentially the truth-value, of the utterance "S knows p" varies with the context of ascription.[16]

In and of itself, the idea that the semantic value of 'may' (and other deontic modals) varies with conversational context is hardly odd; in fact, it is semantic orthodoxy.[17] Now, admittedly, the contextualist who accepts KNA-Doubly-Relativized is committed to something more specific than this. In particular, she is committed to allowing that the truth-value of utterances like "S may assert p" can depend in part on the standards for knowing p that are in play at the ascriber's, rather than the subject's, context. But I do not think this is obviously fatal. What unintuitiveness there may appear to be here can be further cushioned by a move that the contextualist makes in numerous other contexts: namely to insist that the standards that govern a conversational context are not mechanically determined by what is practically at stake for the speaker.[18] Rather, often, the interests and practical situation of the *subject* can be salient (perhaps *via* their being salient to the speaker, and part of what she intends to talk with reference to).[19] In contexts where she is talking about what the subject may assert or rely on, she will plausibly often be implicitly talking about what, *from the subject's perspective*, the subject may assert or rely on. In doing so, she may shift the contextually relevant value of 'knows'. KNA-Doubly-Relativized allows for this. It does not say that the contextually salient value of 'knows' must get fixed independently before determining the contextually salient value of 'may'; rather it allows for mutual influence between the two, as long as they always move along together.

For those who do not like KNA-Doubly-Relativized, let's explore the second strategy for resisting Hawthorne's argument. On this strategy, the contextualist hangs on to KNA-Relativized, but denies that it has the bad consequences that Hawthorne claims it does. This is the strategy pursued by DeRose (2009: ch. 7) in reply to Hawthorne. Again, we begin by recognizing that the practical situation of the speaker (construed narrowly as excluding indirect interest in or intention to discuss the practical situation of the subject) does not have a monopoly on determining the standards in play in the conversational context. Perhaps, when one talks about what the subject is warranted in relying on, one thereby tends to make salient standards for knowledge commensurate with what is practically at stake for the subject.

As DeRose notes, there is both a stronger and a weaker way of developing this view. On the stronger version, the claim is that in talking of what the subject is warranted in asserting or relying on, one automatically shifts the value of 'knows' to a value determined by the subject's practical interests. On this view, (5) and (6) will come out false, since in each sentence, the second conjunct affects the semantic value of 'knows' as it occurs in the first conjunct, in such a way as to make the first conjunct come out false. KNA-Relativized, then, turns out not to automatically entail that sentences (5) and (6) can be true when asserted. The weaker version of the view has it that by talking about what the subject is warranted in asserting or relying on, the speaker at least creates the *impression* that corresponding standards for 'knows' are in play in the conversation. On this view, utterances (5) and (6) can be true, strictly speaking, but they will be infelicitous, because in each sentence, the second conjunct generates an implicature that is at odds with the first conjunct. Like Moorean conjunctions such as 'it's raining but I don't believe it's raining', they will be (potentially) true, but unassertable.

In sum, it is far from obvious that contextualists cannot deal with the sense that there is something wrong with utterances of the form of (5) and (6).

(b) DeRose's argument from knowledge norms for contextualism

DeRose also offers a positive argument for contextualism from knowledge norms.[20] It begins with the observation that what one is epistemically permitted to assert often depends upon one's

Contextualism and knowledge norms

practical circumstances and what is at stake. When it doesn't matter much to you (and your audience) whether p, the epistemic standards for asserting p are lower than when it is extremely important whether p.[21]

Here the relativized version of KNA, conjoined with contextualism about 'knows', can seem to have the upper hand. For contextualists can say that, generally, these high-stakes situations raise the standards that must be met for 'I know p' to be true in the speaker's mouth. So KNA-Relativized predicts that the standards for permissibly asserting p will go up, correspondingly. By contrast, a view where 'know' is semantically invariant, conjoined with the unrelativized version of KNA, may seem to have difficulty making this prediction. If 'knows' always has the same semantic value, and whether one may assert p simply depends on whether one knows p in this single sense, it seems as though whether one epistemically may assert p cannot depend upon one's practical situation.

"Interest-relative" or "subject-sensitive" versions of invariantism avoid this problem by claiming that whether one knows p – even given a constant semantic value for 'knows' – can itself depend partly on one's practical situation and interests, such as how much it matters to one whether p.[22] On this view, whether it is permissible to assert p can depend on the practical stakes because whether one actually knows p can depend on the practical stakes.[23] However, DeRose also raises a related problem for interest-relative invariantism.[24] A subject can be in a situation where a single proposition p is relevant to one's assertion, reasoning, or actions in more than one way simultaneously. But maybe, with respect to one practical purpose, the stakes are low, but with respect to another practical purpose, the stakes are high. To give a slight variant on the concrete example that DeRose provides, suppose that Judith is simultaneously walking to the insurance office to purchase life insurance and talking on the phone to a friend about her teaching plans for next year. With respect to the first purpose, it seems that Judith may not rely on the proposition that she will be alive next year. For if Judith could rely on this, Judith could reason to the decision not to purchase life insurance. But with respect to the second purpose, it seems that Judith may rely on the proposition that she will be alive next year in outright asserting that she will be teaching philosophy of mind next year.

Now, DeRose points out that we are more likely to attribute knowledge that she will be alive next year to Judith if we are talking about her second purpose than if we are talking about the first. Contextualism accommodates this by saying that, depending on which purpose we are talking about, our standards will be different. Interest-relative invariantism, by contrast, doesn't seem able to mimic this explanation. Since she has both purposes simultaneously, interest-relative invariantists cannot vindicate both utterances attributing knowledge to Judith, and utterances attributing lack of knowledge to her.

I am not sure that this objection is decisive. Interest-relative invariantists, as the name suggests, posit that knowledge is (metaphysically) relative to interests. If it turns out that one can have different interests and purposes at a single time, it seems a relatively conservative extension of the view to explicitly relativize knowledge to different purposes, and say that Judith can know with respect to one purpose but not with respect to another. The interest-relative invariantist can then say that speakers are usually implicitly talking about whether Judith knows with respect to the purpose they are discussing. Admittedly, this concedes something to contextualism: sometimes 'Judith knows p' means 'Judith knows p relative to purpose X,' and sometimes it means 'Judith knows p relative to purpose Y.' But the contextualism conceded here is mild. Presumably all theorists already admit that knowledge-attributions are usually implicitly indexed to a time: 'Judith knows p,' uttered at time t, usually (but not quite always) means 'Judith knows p at time t.' Since different utterances occur at different times, there is a very mild kind of contextualism at work here. Relativizing to a purpose simply allows for an analogous maneuver given the possibility of simultaneously knowing with respect to one purpose, but not with respect to another, at a single time. It does not posit systematic variability in the standards for 'knows' of the sort that full-blooded contextualists are committed to.

I conclude that, so far as we have seen, commitment to knowledge norms does not win the day either for contextualism or for invariantism. Of course, this issue remains open to further debate. But in what remains, I want to focus on a different possibility: that contextualism itself might motivate *suspicion* of knowledge norms.

4 Reasons for contextualist suspicion of knowledge norms?

As I mentioned earlier, contextualism about deontic modals like 'ought' and 'may' is relatively orthodox in semantics. It is also increasingly popular in metaethics. Many of the theoretical issues surrounding contextualism about 'knows' find analogues in the literature on modals.[25] There is at least some pressure for contextualists about 'knows' to also be contextualists about modals.

This raises a question for proponents of knowledge norms. Knowledge norms say that assertion, action, and other practices are to be normatively assessed in terms of the acting agent's knowledge. But according to contextualism about modals – at least "flexible" versions of contextualism – there are many different bodies of information in terms of which actions can be assessed, and correspondingly different values of modals for each such body. Depending on our purposes in speaking, we can talk about what an agent ought to or may do relative to different bodies of information. To use the language that ethicists often use, there are values of 'ought' (and thus of 'may') that are more "objective" and those that are more "subjective". The knowledge-relative 'ought'/'may' seems to occupy an intermediate value. On the more "objective" side, we sometimes want to talk about what an agent ought to do relative to all the facts – even facts outside the agent's epistemic ken. This is particularly useful in advice-giving contexts where the advice-giver is better informed than the agent. On the more subjective side, we sometimes want to talk about what an agent ought to do relative to her beliefs – even those of her beliefs that do not amount to knowledge. This is particularly useful in cases where the facts are very contentious and so there is little conversational common ground about which of the agent's beliefs do amount to knowledge. Then we can say things like, "look, even given your own beliefs, you ought to do as I say."[26]

A flexible contextualist about modals does not deny that there are *some* values of 'ought' and 'may' that evaluate actions (and assertions, etc.) in terms of the subject's knowledge. However, the contextualist picture about modals does call into question the idea that knowledge norms occupy any special, privileged role with respect to this kind of evaluation, compared with evaluation in terms of beliefs, in terms of the totality of the facts, and so on. The challenge for proponents of knowledge norms is to identify some sense in which the knowledge-relative 'may' (and 'ought') does occupy such a special, privileged role in evaluation, or in deliberation, or some sense in which all other values of 'may' are fundamentally to be explained in sense of the knowledge-relative 'may'. These are important tasks for proponents of knowledge norms who do not wish to give a semantically naïve account of modals. I will close by mentioning a few challenges that attempts to execute them may face.

As our brief survey in section 1 suggested, knowledge often plays an important role in the evaluation of assertions and actions. But the contextualist about deontic modals may have debunking explanations of some of this data that does not appeal to knowledge norms. For example, consider the intuitive clash that we saw in sentences like

(3)   #I know that the ice will hold my weight, but I shouldn't cross in case it doesn't hold my weight.

Contextualism and knowledge norms

On one orthodox semantic proposal, by *saying* that one knows that the ice will hold one's weight, one proposes to add this piece of information to the contextually salient body of information.[27] But given that, 'shouldn't' will take a value on which the second conjunct is false. The crucial contention here is that it is the *mentioning* of the knowledge here, rather than one's actually having it, that guarantees that it features in the evaluation of action that follows. Indeed, we can argue that the data positively supports this explanation by contrasting (3) with:

(7)   I think I know the ice will hold my weight, but I shouldn't cross in case it doesn't hold my weight.[28]

(7) sounds much better than (3). However, on the explanation of (3)'s badness in terms of knowledge norms, (7) ought to be bad too. For given the knowledge norm, plus suitable claims about what actions (ought to) follow from relying on the proposition that the ice will hold one's weight, the second conjunct – 'I shouldn't cross in case [the ice] doesn't hold my weight' – will be true only if one doesn't know that the ice will hold one's weight. But in general it should be bad to say 'I think X, but Y', where Y obtains only if X does not obtain. Even though 'I think' hedges the assertion of X, even such a hedged assertion should be incompatible with the outright assertion of something incompatible with X. (Compare 'I think the hotel is on the left, but it's on the right.')

By contrast, our rival explanation of (3)'s badness in terms of the way that *claiming* knowledge updates the context for the use of 'shouldn't' gives a nice explanation of why (7) is better than (3). For (7) involves no outright claim to knowledge, but rather the hedged 'I think I know.' So we get no update to the information-base for 'should' that guarantees the falsity of the second conjunct.

(7) also provides an example of a deliberative context in which one seems to exclude something that one at least *may well* know from one's deliberations, thus providing a counterexample to the claim that it is the knowledge-relative 'should' (and 'may') that is always at work in deliberation. The speaker in (7) seems willing, in her practical situation, only to rely on things that she is *sure* she knows. She might well, by the lights of what she says, in fact know that the ice will hold her weight. But in this deliberative context she is nevertheless ruling out reliance on this proposition, whether she in fact knows it or not.[29]

Indeed, values of 'may' that are not knowledge-relative also appear to feature in criticism in many contexts. For example, suppose that, given everything you know, it is fine to let your dog play with children. But suppose that you also unjustifiably believe that your dog is very dangerous to children. And suppose also that you still casually let your dog play with my daughter. I might well criticize your action, even though it was perfectly responsible in light of what you knew. Your having done something that by the lights of your beliefs was dangerous to my daughter itself seems criticizable. And this is not even to get started on praise and criticism of actions in terms of one's *justified* beliefs that fall short of knowledge because they are unluckily false, or Gettiered.[30]

My own view, in light of all this, is that we can evaluate actions, assertions, and so forth either in terms of knowledge, or in terms of justified belief, or in other terms altogether, depending on our conversational purposes.[31] Now, proponents of knowledge-norms do allow that there can be different tenors of criticism that evaluate action not in terms of what the agent knew, but in terms of what (for example) the agent took herself to know. They propose somewhat breezily that these other tenors of criticism are all derivative on the central knowledge norm.[32] Now, it's easy to imagine how someone might try to use the knowledge-relative 'may' to analyze the other values of 'may'. One could claim, for example, that the fact-relative 'may' is used to talk about what would be permissible if one knew all the facts, and the belief-relative 'may' is used to talk about what would be permissible if all one's beliefs amounted to knowledge.

185

The problem here, though, is that any such strategy seems mimicable for the claim that one of the other senses of 'may' is fundamental. If we said that the fact-relative 'may' is fundamental, we could then say that the knowledge-relative 'may' is used to talk about what would be permissible if one's knowledge exhausted the facts, and the belief-relative 'may' to talk about what would be permissible if one's beliefs exhausted the facts. Similarly, if we said that the belief-relative 'may' is fundamental, we could say that the fact-relative 'may' is used to talk about what would be permissible if one believed all the facts, and the knowledge-relative 'may' to talk about what would be permissible if one believed only that which one knows.

So it isn't enough to simply produce a proposal for reducing all the senses of 'may' to one central sense. One has to actually show that proposal to be superior to its rivals, and that the proposal that no value of 'may' is any more fundamental than the others. It is not clear why the standard contextualist semantics for modals *needs* to be accompanied by any claim about fundamentality. In its more developed forms, it shows how we can get semantic predictions for 'ought' and 'may' given any potential body of information (and given other contextually variable parameters). Any claim about fundamentality can seem like a fifth wheel in such a theory; it is not required for the theory to make the right predictions.

Perhaps proponents of knowledge norms may yet be able to offer a full account that treats the knowledge-relative 'may' as fundamental and analyzes other semantic values of 'may' in terms of this central knowledge-relative notion. To do this convincingly, however, they must be more precise about what exactly the different normative notions in play are, how they fit together, and why we should take the knowledge-relative ones to be fundamental. And if potential counter-examples to knowledge norms are to be explained away in terms of "secondary" usages of normative terms, we need to be convinced that these usages really are secondary, and that it is not the knowledge-relative normative notion that turns out to be idiosyncratic or a term of art.[33]

If there is one crucial lesson for the literature on knowledge norms to take heed of, then, it is the need to think sophisticatedly not just about knowledge but also about norms and normativity. For example, Williamson writes at times[34] as if we need not necessarily have any genuine reason to comply with knowledge norms.[35] Knowledge norms are, on this view, "merely" constitutive, much like the rules of chess. The rules of chess help to tell us what the game of chess *is*, but it's easy to devise scenarios in which what one *really* ought to do is to break these rules, or even where there is really *no* genuine reason to comply with them. But such a view, applied to knowledge norms across the board, would clash strongly with the idea that action is genuinely *criticizable*, in some thick normative sense, whenever it violates the knowledge norm. These kinds of tensions, and the set of available normative and metanormative positions that arise from them, have received scant attention. The path to progress, here as in many other cases, lies in better integration of epistemology with the theory of normativity.[36]

Notes

1 See e.g. Williamson (2000: esp. ch. 11; 2005); DeRose (2002); Hawthorne (2004); Hawthorne & Stanley (2008); Fantl & McGrath (2009); Benton (2011); Turri (2011); Blaauw (2012).

2 Slightly more strongly, it also entails a wide-scoped version of the necessity-claim using 'ought': one ought to (assert p only if one knows p). This is Williamson's (2000: 243) formulation.

3 A complication: what one is permitted to assert or rely on, even in the sense we are interested in here, can sometimes depend on "pragmatic" or "non-epistemic" factors, such as what is at stake (see section 3b below). This may seem to collapse the distinction between epistemic and non-epistemic permissibility. However, going carefully, the distinction can remain intact. The claim is that when the stakes go up, the *epistemic* standards that one must meet in order to permissibly assert p become more stringent. So the idea

Contextualism and knowledge norms

is that practical factors can influence what is epistemically permissible. Asserting p might then become epistemically impermissible, because one's epistemic position is not strong enough to meet the new epistemic standards. This is still distinct from (im)permissibility that is non-epistemic in the sense that I am bracketing. In this latter sense, asserting p might be, for example, impermissible because asserting p will be rude or hurtful. This does not just make it the case that one has to be in a really strong epistemic position to assert p; rather, it makes it impermissible to assert p, no matter how strong one's epistemic position.

4 Indeed, the idea that to assert p is to "represent" oneself as knowing p predates the explicit idea that knowledge is the *norm* of assertion. See e.g. Unger (1975: ch. 6); Slote (1979).

5 The example is based on one given by Hawthorne & Stanley (2008: 572).

6 *Ibid.*

7 The example is based on one given by Fantl & McGrath (2009: 73–4, 82).

8 See e.g. Williamson (2000: 253); DeRose (2009: 96–7).

9 For discussion of some discontinuities between assertion and practical reasoning that may drive apart the norms for the two, see Brown (2012) and Worsnip (2015b: esp. 321). Some such discontinuities are especially pointed for contextualists. Suppose that the mentioning of error-possibilities with respect to p sometimes raises those error-possibilities to salience, such that one no longer 'knows' p by the conversational standards. It's plausible that the mentioning of such error-possibilities can also affect whether it is permissible to assert p. But is it really plausible that the mentioning of error-possibilities can make a difference to whether it is permissible to rely on p in one's reasoning? Such a verdict would be at radical odds with standard decision-theoretic pictures of rational action.

10 It does not help to retreat to a one-direction version of KNA, according to which knowledge is necessary or sufficient for epistemically permissible assertion, but not both. If one holds that knowledge is only necessary for epistemically permissible assertion, the idea that KNA holds in metasemantic generality would entail that assertion is warranted only when one meets the most demanding possible standards for 'knows', which seems too strong to be necessary. If one holds that knowledge is only sufficient for epistemically permissible assertion, the idea that KNA holds in metasemantic generality would entail that assertion is warranted whenever one meets the least demanding possible standards for 'knows', which seems too weak to be sufficient.

11 DeRose (2009: 99, 258–9). See also Hawthorne (2004: 88–9).

12 See DeRose (2009: 103–4) for an argument against such a collapse.

13 Both Hawthorne (2004: 89) and Fantl & McGrath (2009: 51) also make the simpler argument that unrelativized norms account for the intuitive ties between knowledge and assertion/action better than their relativized analogues, because they are simpler and because they link *knowledge* to assertion and action, rather than linking 'knowledge' to assertion and action. I think this is not decisive. The fundamental intuitive data we are trying to account for are those involving our tendency to *assess* assertions and actions in terms of knowledge – not an abstract theoretical claim about the relationship of knowledge to assertion and action. If the contextualist can show that a relativized principle accounts for that data equally well, I do not see why the unrelativized principle should be strongly preferred.

14 Cf. DeRose (2009: 260), though DeRose neither accepts this principle nor offers it as a way of dealing with Hawthorne's objections.

15 And which Hawthorne himself has been at pains to correct: see e.g. Hawthorne (2005: 39).

16 Hawthorne (2005). See also DeRose (2009: 212–25).

17 See, canonically, Kratzer (1981). For recent defenses and developments of this view see e.g. Björnsson & Finlay (2010); Kratzer (2012); Dowell (2013).

18 This point can be overlooked because of a slipperiness in usage of the word 'context', which can refer either to a context of *conversation* or to a *practical situation* (what the stakes are, etc.). The contextualist can and should deny that the standards in play in a conversational context are always mechanically determined by the practical situation of the speaker. The practical situations of others who are not the speaker may often be conversationally salient, even *to the speaker*. While in a broad sense it is the standards of the speaker that matter, the speaker's standards can be influenced by the practical interests of others.

19 See e.g. Greco (2008: esp. 424–5, 433–4); DeRose (2009: 246).

20 DeRose (2009: 98–102). See also Schaffer (2008).

21 The kind of permissibility here is still epistemic because, in this case, practical factors make it impermissible to assert p *via* raising the epistemic standards that one must meet to assert p. This is distinct from the case where practical factors make it impermissible to assert p quite independently of what epistemic position one is in. See note 3 above.

22 Even *classical* invariantists – invariantists who reject interest-relativism – have devised some interesting attempts to deal with the apparent stakes-sensitivity of warranted assertion and action. See e.g. Brown (2005); Williamson (2005); Nagel (2008).

23 See esp. Hawthorne (2004); Stanley (2005); Weatherson (2011). See also Fantl & McGrath (2009), though they leave open the possibility that both contextualism and interest-relativism are true. Chapter 19 of this volume takes up the contextualism/interest-relative invariantism debate.

24 DeRose (2009: 269–76).

25 See chapters 28–30 of this volume for explorations of analogies between contextualism about 'knows' and about modals and other normative terms.

26 These other values of 'may' are not accounted for by shifting to KNA-Doubly-Relativized. For KNA-Doubly-Relativized still always ties 'may' to what the agent counts as knowing in the conversational context. These usages of 'may', by contrast, allow for speakers to include information that the agent may not count as knowing even by the contextually salient standards, or to exclude information that the agent does count as knowing by these standards.

27 See e.g. Stalnaker (1999: ch. 4).

28 The example is analogous to those provided in Worsnip (2015a), where I pursue a similar line of argument against the view that all so-called "epistemic" usages of 'possible' must be understood in terms of the speaker's knowledge.

29 Williamson (2005: 230–5) notes, similarly, that subjects will, in high-stakes situations, only rely on propositions that they *know they know*. Williamson glosses a situation where the subject knows but isn't sure that she knows as one where relying on that proposition would be appropriate (in a semi-technical sense), but the subject isn't sure whether it would be appropriate. Though that maintains the letter of knowledge norms for the semi-technical notion of appropriateness, it also by the same token concedes that this notion of appropriateness is not always the one that is deliberatively relevant.

30 For criticisms of knowledge norms as compared with justified-belief (or similar) norms see e.g. Douven (2006); Lackey (2007); Stone (2007); Kvanvig (2009); Littlejohn (2009); McKinnon (2013).

31 This view should be distinguished from the superficially similar view that what is required to permissibly assert p (or rely on p in one's practical reasoning, etc.) is "context-sensitive" in the sense it changes according to the subject's practical situation (so that it might sometimes be knowledge, other times justified belief, etc.). (Compare Brown 2008; Gerken 2011; and Goldberg 2015.) This latter view as regards permissible assertion is analogous to interest-relative invariantism about knowledge-attributions, whereas mine is genuine *contextualism*, where this is a semantic thesis. The litmus test as to which account is preferable is whether (e.g.) "S may rely on p" can be true in some conversational contexts and false in others, without any change in S's own situation. If it can be, we should prefer the contextualist view that I favor.

32 See e.g. Williamson (2000: 243, 256–7; 2005: 227); Hawthorne & Stanley (2008: 586); DeRose (2009: 93–4).

33 Williamson (2000: 243) concedes that "false assertions are sometimes warranted in the everyday sense that they are sometimes reasonable." If knowledge-relative normative notions of warrant fails to be the "everyday sense" of such a term, we might doubt that they are really our central normative concepts.

34 E.g. Williamson (2000: 240; 2005: 232).

35 On this view, the knowledge norm of assertion is not really *normative* in the strong sense of the term employed by, e.g., Kolodny (2005).

36 Thanks to Nathan Cockram and Jonathan Ichikawa for helpful comments on a previous draft.

References

Benton, M. (2011). 'Two More for the Knowledge Account of Assertion,' *Analysis*, 71/4: 684–7.

Björnsson, G. & Finlay, S. (2010). 'Metaethical Contextualism Defended,' *Ethics*, 121/1: 7–36.

Blaauw, M. (2012). 'Reinforcing the Knowledge Account of Assertion,' *Analysis*, 72/1: 105–8.

Brown, J. (2005). 'Adapt or Die: The Death of Invariantism?,' *Philosophical Quarterly*, 55/219: 263–85.

——— (2008). 'Subject-Sensitive Invariantism and the Knowledge Norm for Practical Reasoning,' *Noûs*, 42/2: 167–89.

——— (2012). 'Assertion and Practical Reasoning: Common or Divergent Epistemic Standards?,' *Philosophy and Phenomenological Research*, 84/1: 124–57.

DeRose, K. (2002). 'Assertion, Knowledge, and Context,' *Philosophical Review*, 111/2: 167–203.

———— (2009). *The Case for Contextualism*. Oxford: Oxford University Press.

Douven, I. (2006). 'Assertion, Knowledge, and Rational Credibility,' *Philosophical Review*, 115/4: 449–85.

Dowell, J. (2013). 'Flexible Contextualism about Deontic Modals: A Puzzle about Information-Sensitivity,' *Inquiry*, 56/2–3: 149–78.

Fantl, J. & McGrath, M. (2009). *Knowledge in an Uncertain World*. Oxford: Oxford University Press.

Gerken, M. (2011). 'Warrant and Action,' *Synthese*, 178/3: 529–47.

Goldberg, S. C. (2015). *Assertion: The Philosophical Significance of a Speech Act*. Oxford: Oxford University Press.

Greco, J. (2008). 'What's Wrong with Contextualism?,' *Philosophical Quarterly*, 58/232: 416–36.

Hawthorne, J. (2004). *Knowledge and Lotteries*. Oxford: Oxford University Press.

———— (2005). 'The Case for Closure,' in M. Steup & E. Sosa (eds.), *Contemporary Debates in Epistemology*. Oxford: Blackwell.

Hawthorne, J. & Stanley, J. (2008). 'Knowledge and Action,' *Journal of Philosophy*, 105/10: 571–90.

Kolodny, N. (2005). 'Why Be Rational?,' *Mind*, 114/455: 509–63.

Kratzer, A. (1981). 'The Notional Category of Modality,' in H. J. Eikmeyer & H. Rieser (eds.), *Words, Worlds, and Contexts*. Berlin: de Gruyter.

———— (2012). *Modals and Conditionals*. Oxford: Oxford University Press.

Kvanvig, J. (2009). 'Assertion, Knowledge, and Lotteries,' in P. Greenough & D. Pritchard (eds.), *Williamson on Knowledge*. Oxford: Oxford University Press.

Lackey, J. (2007). 'Norms of Assertion,' *Noûs*, 41/4: 594–626.

Littlejohn, C. (2009). 'Must We Act Only on What We Know?,' *Journal of Philosophy*, 106/8: 463–73.

McKinnon, R. (2013). 'The Supportive Reasons Norm of Assertion,' *American Philosophical Quarterly*, 50/2: 121–35.

Nagel, J. (2008). 'Knowledge Ascriptions and the Psychological Consequences of Changing Stakes,' *Australasian Journal of Philosophy*, 86/2: 279–94.

Schaffer, J. (2008). 'Knowledge in the Image of Assertion,' *Philosophical Issues*, 18: 1–19.

Slote, M. (1979). 'Assertion and Belief,' in J. Dancy (ed.), *Papers on Language and Logic*. Keele: Keele University Library.

Stalnaker, R. (1999). *Context and Content*. Oxford: Oxford University Press.

Stanley, J. (2005). *Knowledge and Practical Interests*. Oxford: Oxford University Press.

Stone, J. (2007). 'Contextualism and Warranted Assertion,' *Pacific Philosophical Quarterly*, 88/1: 92–113.

Turri, J. (2011). 'The Express Knowledge Account of Assertion,' *Australasian Journal of Philosophy*, 89/1: 37–45.

Unger, P. (1975). *Ignorance: A Case for Skepticism*. Oxford: Oxford University Press.

Weatherson, B. (2011). 'Defending Interest-Relative Invariantism,' *Logos & Episteme*, 2/4: 591–609.

Williamson, T. (2000). *Knowledge and Its Limits*. Oxford: Oxford University Press.

———— (2005). 'Contextualism, Subject-Sensitive Invariantism, and Knowledge of Knowledge,' *Philosophical Quarterly*, 55/219: 213–35.

Worsnip, A. (2015a). 'Possibly False Knowledge,' *Journal of Philosophy*, 112/5: 224–46.

———— (2015b). 'Two Kinds of Stakes,' *Pacific Philosophical Quarterly*, 96/3: 307–24.

15

CONTEXTUALISM AND GETTIER CASES

John Greco

Epistemic contextualism is the thesis that the word "knows" and its cognates are context-sensitive. Put differently, sentences using the word "knows" and its cognates express different propositions in different conversational contexts. Roughly, Gettier cases are possible cases purporting to show that some analysis or definition of knowledge fails to state sufficient conditions for knowledge. The original Gettier cases were constructed by Edmund Gettier as counterexamples to the traditional analysis of knowledge as justified true belief (Gettier 1963). But as philosophers have tried to repair or replace that traditional analysis, subsequent Gettier cases have targeted those newer proposals (Shope 1983).

There have been few attempts in the literature to apply contextualist ideas to Gettier cases. The notable exception is David Lewis's "Elusive Knowledge," where he argues that his version of contextualism gives a unified treatment of Gettier cases, the lottery problem, and skepticism (Lewis 1996). Section 1 of this chapter looks more closely at the nature of Gettier cases. Section 2 considers Lewis's contextualist treatment of Gettier cases, and section 3 considers Stewart Cohen's influential critique of Lewis's approach. Section 4 offers a limited defense of my own contextualist treatment of Barn Facade cases. The chapter concludes that a contextualist approach is plausible for only some Gettier cases; specifically, those which elicit shifting intuitions about whether the subject in the case knows.

1 Gettier cases

Here are two now classic Gettier cases.

Someone Owns a Ford

On the basis of excellent reasons, S believes that her co-worker Mr. Nogot owns a Ford: Nogot testifies that he owns a Ford, and this is confirmed by S's own relevant observations. From this S infers that someone in her office owns a Ford. As it turns out, S's evidence is misleading and Nogot does not in fact own a Ford. However, another person in S's office, Mr. Havit, does own a Ford, although S has no reason for believing this.

(Adapted from Lehrer 1965)

Sheep on a Hill

A man takes there to be a sheep on the hill, basing his belief on convincing sensory experience. However, the man has mistaken a sheep-shaped rock for a sheep, and so what he sees is not a sheep at all. Nevertheless, unsuspected by the man, there *is* a sheep on another part of the hill.

(Adapted from Chisholm 1977)

Early reactions noted that, in these cases, the subject reasons through a falsehood en route to his or her true justified belief. For example, S reasons through the false belief that Nogot owns a Ford. This suggests the following fix for the traditional analysis:

S knows that p if and only if (1) p is true; (2) S believes that p; (3) S is justified in believing that p; and (4) S's reasons for believing that p do not essentially involve a falsehood.

However, subsequent cases showed that this fix does not work. For example,

Barn Facade

Henry is in the countryside and sees a barn ahead in clear view. On this basis he believes that the object ahead is a barn. Unknown to Henry, however, the area is dotted with barn facades that are indistinguishable from real barns from the road. However, Henry happens to be looking at a real barn.

(Adapted from Goldman 1976)

Zagzebski (1999) offers a helpful recipe for generating Gettier cases. First, take some proposed set of conditions for knowledge and construct a case where they are satisfied. Second, add a twist of bad luck, so that S's belief comes out false, despite satisfying all the conditions other than the truth condition. As Zagzebski notes, this will always be possible for accounts where the remaining conditions do not entail the truth condition. Finally, add a twist of good luck, so that S's belief comes out true after all. It is easy to see that this recipe could be used to generate all of the Gettier cases that we have seen so far.

We said that, roughly, Gettier cases are possible cases purporting to show that some analysis or definition of knowledge fails to state sufficient conditions for knowledge. This characterization of Gettier cases is only rough because not every example challenging sufficient conditions is considered to be a Gettier case. For example, consider the following definition of knowledge and the counterexample that follows it.

Lousy Definition: S knows that p if and only if (1) p is true, and (2) S has excellent reasons for believing that p.

Evidence without Belief

S has excellent reasons for believing that Jones will be at the party. Namely, she knows that Smith will be at the party, and she knows that Jones will go where Smith goes. But S fails to put two and two together, and so never forms the belief that Jones will be at the party. In fact, S does not form any beliefs at all about where Jones will be.

Plausibly, S does not know that Jones will be at the party because she does not even believe that he will be. **Evidence without Belief** shows that **Lousy Definition** does not state sufficient conditions for knowledge. But **Evidence without Belief** is plausibly not a Gettier case. Why not? Here is a suggestion: Gettier cases are directed specifically at the "plus" condition of accounts that state that knowledge is true belief *plus* something else. In other words, we assume that knowledge is true belief, and we consider what further conditions must be met to distinguish knowledge from "mere" true belief. Gettier cases target such proposals, purporting to show that the added condition or conditions still fail to be sufficient conditions.

That seems promising, but consider **Simple Lottery Case**, which is typically not considered to be a Gettier case: S believes that her lottery ticket will lose, basing her belief on excellent evidence that it is a fair lottery and that her chances of winning are very low. Intuitively, S's belief that she will lose the lottery is true and justified, but S does not know that she will lose the lottery. Thus **Simple Lottery Case** plausibly shows that true justified belief is not sufficient for knowledge. And yet **Simple Lottery Case** is typically not classified as a Gettier case. Why not? In truth, it is not easy to say. Perhaps the best we can do is to ignore this classification problem and proceed with an intuitive grasp of Gettier cases, guided by clear examples and by Zagzebski's recipe.

2 Lewis's contextualist treatment of Gettier cases

Lewis's contextualist account of knowledge ascriptions exploits the well-known context sensitivity of universal quantifiers.[1] In general, the scope of a quantifier is partly determined by conversational context. Here is Lewis:

> An idiom of quantification, like 'every', is normally restricted to some limited domain. If I say that every glass is empty, so it's time for another round, doubtless I and my audience are ignoring most of all the glasses there are in the whole wide world throughout all of time. They are outside the domain. They are irrelevant to the truth of what was said.
>
> *(1996: 553)*

Likewise, Lewis argues, knowledge ascriptions involve an implicit quantifier, and this makes them context-sensitive in a similar way.

> **Lewis's Definition:** Subject S *knows* proposition P iff P holds in every possibility left uneliminated by S's evidence; equivalently, iff S's evidence eliminates every possibility in which not-P.
>
> *(1996: 551)*

The "every" in Lewis's definition is context-sensitive. More specifically, the conversational context determines the domain of the quantifier by determining which possibilities can be properly ignored. Hence Lewis's infamous formulation:

> Our definition of knowledge requires a *sotto voce* proviso. S *knows* that P iff S's evidence eliminates every possibility in which not-P – Psst! – except for those possibilities that we are properly ignoring.
>
> *(1996: 554)*

Contextualism and Gettier cases

This gives us a general framework for understanding the implicit form of knowledge ascriptions. Lewis adds substance to his account by giving a list of rules for which possibilities can and cannot be properly ignored in a context. Three of those rules are especially important for present purposes.

First, the Rule of Actuality states that the possibility that actually obtains is never properly ignored. As Lewis points out, this rule acts as a truth condition on knowledge ascriptions. Second, the Rule of Belief states that a possibility that the subject believes to obtain is not properly ignored, and neither is one that he or she ought to believe to obtain.[2] Third, the Rule of Resemblance states that if one possibility saliently resembles another, then if one of these possibilities cannot properly be ignored, then the other cannot be properly ignored. The qualification that the resemblance must be *salient* is necessary, since every possibility resembles every other in some respect or another. As we shall see below, the Rule of Resemblance is among the rules that make Lewis's account a version of ascriber contextualism.

Finally, there is the Rule of Attention: if we are attending to a possibility, then it cannot be ignored. Here is what Lewis says about the rule, including a comment regarding its contextualist implications.

> Our final rule is the *Rule of Attention*. But it is more a triviality than a rule. When we say that a possibility is properly ignored, we mean exactly that; we do not mean that it *could have been* properly ignored. Accordingly, a possibility not ignored at all is *ipso facto* not properly ignored. What is and what is not being ignored is a feature of the particular conversational context. No matter how far-fetched a certain possibility may be, no matter how properly we might have ignored it in some other context, if in *this* context we are not in fact ignoring it but attending to it, then for us now it is a relevant alternative. It is in the contextually determined domain.
>
> *(1996: 559)*

Let us now consider how Lewis's account applies to skepticism and lottery cases. After that, we will be in a position to see how it applies to Gettier cases.

Lewis employs a now familiar contextualist strategy for addressing skepticism. The skeptic is right, Lewis argues, when she asserts that we "know" very little, because in the context of skeptical assertions the standards for "knowledge" are very high. But this concession to the skeptic has only limited implications regarding knowledge ascriptions in ordinary contexts, where the standards for "knowledge" are much lower. In effect, the contextualist is able to claim both (a) that the skeptic is correct in contexts where she utters sentences of the form "S does not know that P," and (b) that non-skeptical speakers are often correct when they utter sentences of the form "S does know that P" in ordinary contexts. On Lewis's view in particular, this is because different not-P possibilities are properly ignored in the different speaker contexts. More exactly, various skeptical possibilities are neither properly ignored nor eliminated by S's evidence relative to "extraordinary" contexts, i.e. contexts where epistemology is being done and skeptical possibilities are being considered. But those same skeptical possibilities are properly ignored, and thus need not be eliminated by S's evidence, relative to ordinary contexts. This is primarily due to the Rule of Attention, which says that possibilities that we are attending to are never properly ignored. And, of course, this is the essential difference between philosophical contexts and ordinary contexts on Lewis's view: in philosophical contexts, but not in ordinary contexts, various skeptical possibilities are brought to our attention, and so not properly ignored.

Why, according to Lewis, does S fail to know that she will lose the lottery, even when her reasons are excellent that she will lose? Here the Rule of Actuality and the Rule of Resemblance work together. The rule of Rule of Actuality makes it a relevant possibility that the actually winning ticket

193

will win. But that possibility saliently resembles the possibility that S's own ticket will win, and so the Rule of Resemblance requires that that possibility be eliminated by S's evidence. But of course S's evidence does not eliminate that possibility, and so S does not know that she will lose the lottery.

Or at least that is so relative to many contexts, and in particular those where the similarities among winning tickets are made salient. But relative to other contexts things are different. In other contexts, the Rule of Resemblance may not be similarly in play, and so one can "know" that S will lose. This is illustrated by the case of **Poor Bill**:

> Pity poor Bill! He squanders all his spare cash on the pokies, the races, and the lottery. He will be a wage slave all his days. We know he will never be rich. But if he wins the lottery (if he wins big), then he will be rich. Contrapositively: his never being rich, plus other things we know, imply that he will lose. So, by closure, if we know that he will never be rich, we know that he will lose.
>
> *(Lewis 1996: 565)*

Here is how Lewis explains the context shift.

> Salience, as well as ignoring, may vary between contexts. Before, when I was explaining how the Rule of Resemblance applied to lotteries, I saw to it that the resemblance between the many possibilities associated with the many tickets was sufficiently salient. But this time, when we were busy pitying poor Bill for his habits and not for his luck, the resemblance of the many possibilities was not so salient. At that point, the possibility of Bill's winning was properly ignored; so then it was true to say that we knew he would never be rich.
>
> *(1996: 565–6)*

Importantly, Lewis handles Gettier cases in a similar way. More exactly, the Rule of Actuality and the Rule of Resemblance work together to explain why S does not know in Gettier cases. In fact, Lewis thinks that Gettier cases and **Simple Lottery Case** can be assimilated. Thus he writes, "Though the lottery problem is another case of justified true belief without knowledge, it is not normally counted among the Gettier problems. It is interesting to find that it yields to the same remedy" (Lewis 1996: 557, n. 14).

Recall **Someone Owns a Ford**. The Rule of Actuality makes relevant the possibility that Nogot owns no Ford but Havit does. The Rule of Resemblance then kicks in to make relevant a possibility that saliently resembles this one: That Nogot owns no Ford, and neither does Havit. Since this possibility is left uneliminated by S's evidence, S does not know that someone in the office owns a Ford (Lewis 1996: 557).

Lewis handles **Barn Facade** in a similar fashion. The Rule of Actuality makes relevant the possibility that Henry is in the midst of numerous barn facades, indistinguishable from the real barn that he actually sees. The Rule of Resemblance make relevant a possibility that saliently resembles this one: that Henry is looking at a barn facade rather than a real barn. Since this possibility is left uneliminated by Henry's evidence, he does not know that he sees a barn (Lewis 1996: 557).

3 Cohen's critique of Lewis

Cohen (1998) takes issue with Lewis's claim that Gettier cases can be given a contextualist treatment. The central point behind Cohen's critique is that, unlike the problem of skepticism and lottery cases, Gettier cases do not evoke shifting intuitions regarding whether S knows. But then

Contextualism and Gettier cases

Gettier cases do not produce the sort of psychological and linguistic data that a contextualist framework is typically invoked to explain. Even worse, Lewis's contextualism seems to make the wrong prediction here. That is, it predicts that, relative to some contexts, knowledge ascriptions in Gettier cases will come out true. But that is implausible, Cohen argues. For example, here is what Cohen says regarding **Sheep on a Hill**:

> Surely it is very strange to suppose that there is any context of ascription in which one can truly say of S that he knows there is a sheep on the hill. The sentence, "S knows there is a sheep on the hill" looks false (at that world and time), regardless of who happens to be uttering it.
>
> *(1998: 298)*

To make the case against Lewis's account specifically, Cohen notes that some of Lewis's rules for proper ignoring are "subject-sensitive" while others are "speaker-sensitive." That is, some rules make proper ignoring depend on features of the subject, whereas others make proper ignoring depend on features of the speaker's conversational context. Importantly, the Rule of Resemblance, which is used in Lewis's treatment of Gettier cases, is speaker-sensitive, in that it makes proper ignoring a function of what is salient in the conversational context. But this creates a problem for Lewis, Cohen argues, precisely because it makes knowledge ascriptions in Gettier cases vary across conversational contexts in a way that they should not:

> Recall that according to Lewis's strategy for handling the Gettier cases, the subject fails to know P because there is an uneliminated not-P possibility that resembles actuality. . . . The problem for Lewis is that there is nothing to guarantee that the resemblance will be salient. In some contexts the resemblance will be salient, but in others it will not. And in those contexts where the resemblance is not salient, the not-P possibility will be properly ignored and the subject will know.
>
> *(1998: 296–7)*

For example, consider a case where, as in **Sheep on a Hill**, S mistakes a sheep-shaped rock for a sheep, but there is a sheep on another part of the hill, out of S's view. But in this case S's friend (call him A) is on the scene as well, and is unaware that S sees only a rock. Since the resemblance between actuality and the possibility that S sees only a rock on a sheepless hill is not salient for A, that possibility can be properly ignored in A's conversational context. Thus on Lewis's view, Cohen argues, "A truly ascribes knowledge to S. A can truly say 'S knows there is a sheep on the hill'" (1998: 297).

This makes the point by invoking the details of Lewis's view specifically. But as Cohen emphasizes, the result generalizes. In general, contextualist treatments of Gettier cases will have the result that the truth-values of knowledge ascriptions in those cases vary across speaker contexts, and this is a seemingly implausible result. The moral of the story, Cohen concludes, is that Gettier cases should be handled differently than the problem of skepticism and the lottery problem, where shifting intuitions better motivate a contextualist treatment. Put differently, knowledge ascriptions for Gettier cases should come out false across all ascriber contexts, and therefore should do so by virtue of a condition that is not ascriber sensitive.

Brogaard (2004) shows that, even with Cohen's point on board, the problem for contextualism here is tricky. For even if a contextualist theory does not explicitly diagnose Gettier cases by means of ascriber-sensitive conditions (as, for example, Lewis's does), such conditions might inadvertently make knowledge ascriptions in Gettier cases come out true. Brogaard argues that

195

this is indeed a problem for the version of contextualism defended in Cohen (1987). On Cohen's view, S knows that p just in case S's reasons for believing that p rule out all relevant alternatives, where the relevance of alternatives is relative to context. An alternative is relevant in a context, just in case, roughly, it is likely to be true or there is some reason for believing that it is likely to be true. Now consider a case that Brogaard argues makes trouble for Cohen:

Canary

S believes that Jones owns a canary in virtue of having seen him buy one the same morning. S is ignorant of the fact, however, that a divorce court deeded Jones's canary over to his wife, and that thousands of miles away Jones's aunt dies and leaves Jones her canary. Finally, suppose that it is rare that divorce courts award canaries to wives. Accordingly, that alternative is not relevant relative to normal standards.

(2004: 377)

Clearly, Brogaard argues, S does not know that Jones owns a canary. Moreover, this seems so independently of ascriber context. In particular, S cannot correctly ascribe to herself knowledge that Jones owns a canary. But on Cohen's view, at least as stated above, the alternative that Jones' canary has been lost in a divorce is not a relevant possibility in S's context, and so need not be ruled out for S to ascribe herself knowledge. One might argue on Cohen's behalf that the possibility is indeed relevant in S's context, perhaps because it is true in that context, and that suffices to make it relevant. But whether we should read Cohen's position this way is irrelevant to Brogaard's essential point, which is that contextualists must approach Gettier cases carefully. In the end, the moral that Cohen and Brogaard draw is the same: ascriber-sensitive conditions should not license knowledge ascriptions in Gettier cases. They should not do so by design, as Cohen argues, and they should not do so inadvertently, as Brogaard argues.

Ichikawa (2011) defends a neo-Lewisian version of contextualism against the objections raised by Cohen. In particular, Ichikawa seeks to preserve Lewis's idea that knowledge ascriptions are context-sensitive on the model of quantifiers and quantifier domains.

Ichikawa notes that Lewis's own contextualist account is in two parts: (a) a general thesis assimilating the context-sensitivity of knowledge ascriptions to that of quantifiers, and (b) a particular system of rules explaining the dynamics of context shifts. Ichikawa wants to preserve the insights of (a) while rejecting the specifics of (b). In fact, he argues, Lewis's efforts regarding (b) represent "an extremely ambitious meta-semantic project whose execution may be deeply flawed" (Ichikawa 2011: 387). Moreover, he argues, the contextualist need not replace Lewis's rules in (b) with a better system. On the contrary, the semantics for knowledge language are expected to be extremely complex, and unlikely to be captured adequately in any systematic way. This is relevant to Lewis's treatment of Gettier cases and Cohen's criticism of it. Specifically, there is nothing in Lewis's more general position that implies there will be context-sensitivity in Gettier cases. That is, nothing in the general position guarantees that features of Gettier cases will generate context sensitivity. Rather, it is Lewis's specific rules (in particular, the Rule of Resemblance and the Rule of Attention) that give this result. Accordingly, Ichikawa argues, "Cohen has offered an objection to the peripheral (b), not the central (a)" (2011: 393).

Having argued this much, Ichikawa nevertheless thinks that Lewis's own position does have resources for meeting Cohen's objections. The main idea is that Lewis's Rule of Resemblance does not require, as Cohen implies that it does, that possibilities generated by the rule must be salient in the ascriber context. On the contrary, Ichikawa argues, relevant *resemblances* must be salient. In his words, "The Rule of Resemblance requires salience of some property with respect to which a possibility is similar – not that the skeptical possibility itself be salient, or that the fact that actuality is similar to some skeptical possibility be salient" (Ichikawa 2011: 395).

Ichikawa illustrates the difference with a non-epistemic example.

Stucko

The crowd cheers as a clown pops out of the small car. 'Wow,' says Nephew, 'there was a clown in that car!' Aunt has seen this sort of thing before: 'Keep watching – not all the clowns are out yet.' Sure enough, out pops a second clown, and then a third, fourth, and fifth. 'I can't believe so many clowns fit inside! Are there any more clowns?' asks Nephew. 'No, all the clowns are out now,' says Aunt. But Aunt is wrong. Stucko is still in the car unseen, and can't get out.

(Adapted from Ichikawa 2011: 383–4, 394)

Stucko renders Aunt's last utterance false. He is in the relevant domain, and he is not out. But why is Stucko in the relevant domain? Ichikawa writes,

Plausibly because, in some relevant respect, he's similar to the clowns that Aunt intended to be talking about. This is consistent with Aunt's total ignorance of Stucko; it is not salient to Aunt that Stucko is similar to the other clowns. What is salient to Aunt is the relevant property: being a clown that is meant to jump out of this car tonight.

(2011: 395)

Let us agree that Ichikawa's defense of the neo-Lewisian view is correct as far as it goes. That is, let us agree that it is not an essential feature of the neo-Lewisian view that it licenses knowledge ascriptions in Gettier cases. Nevertheless, it would seem that the Cohen-Brogaard critique of contextualism still stands, for now no *contextualist* feature of the neo-Lewisian view is doing work in the treatment of Gettier cases.

A bit more carefully, it would seem that the neo-Lewisian view face a dilemma: Either it interacts with Gettier cases so as to make truth-values vary across ascriber contexts or it does not. If it does, then the Cohen-Brogaard critique stands, because intuitions do not shift in the way that the view predicts. If it does not, then contextualism is doing no work in the neo-Lewisian treatment of Gettier cases. That is, the ascriber-sensitive rules of the account are doing no work, and so the Cohen-Brogaard critique stands for that reason.[3]

Taking stock of the discussion so far, we can set out a dilemma for contextualist treatments of Gettier cases in general:

(1) For any given contextualist account C, either features of Gettier cases make the truth-value of knowledge ascriptions vary across contexts according to C, or they do not.
(2) If they do, then C is false, because truth-values of knowledge ascriptions in Gettier cases do not shift in the way that C predicts.
(3) If they do not, then contextualism is doing no work in C's treatment of Gettier cases. That is, the contextualist features of C are doing no work.

Therefore,

(4) No contextualist account gives an adequate treatment of Gettier cases. That is, no contextualist account, *qua* contextualist, gives an adequate treatment of Gettier cases.

One way to pursue a contextualist strategy is to reject premise (2), thereby denying the first horn of the dilemma. What is needed to make the strategy work is to find Gettier cases where relevant intuitions about knowledge do shift, and where contextualism can offer a plausible explanation of this. This strategy endorses Cohen's point that skeptical problems and lottery cases motivate contextualist treatments precisely because they elicit psychological and linguistic data that contextualism can explain. What it denies is that there are no Gettier cases that do the same.

4 Contextualism about Barn Facade cases

Greco (2012) argues that knowledge is a kind of success from ability, where abilities are understood as reliable dispositions and reliability is understood as relative to an environment.[4] More precisely,

> S has a cognitive ability A(R/C/D) relative to an environment E = S has a disposition to believe truths in a range R when in circumstances C and environment E, with degree of reliability D.

> S has knowledge only if S's believing the truth is attributable to S's cognitive abilities.
>
> *(Greco 2012: 18)*

For example, S has perceptual knowledge *that there is a barn in the yard* just in case S's true belief is attributable to S's perceptual abilities, formed in appropriate perceptual circumstances, and in an environment where S's perceptual abilities are sufficiently reliable.

We get a contextualist version of the position if we let relevant parameters be determined by (and vary across) ascriber contexts. On my own account, this is just what happens. More specifically, ascriber context picks out a relevant practical environment, defined by some set of information-dependent practical tasks and associated informational needs. It is this practical environment and associated informational needs that determines parameter values. Hence,

> An assertion "S knows that p" is true relative to a conversational context iff S's believing that p is produced by an exercise of intellectual ability (of the right sort★), and S's belief being so produced contributes (in the right way+) to S's having a true belief.
>
> > ★of a sort that would regularly serve relevant informational needs . . . as determined by the conversational context.
> > +in a way that would regularly serve relevant informational needs . . . as determined by the conversational context.
>
> *(Greco 2012: 20)*

Greco (2012) uses this framework to address **Barn Facade** and similar cases. The central idea is that in **Barn Facade** Henry does not know because Henry's true belief is not produced by a perceptual ability. More precisely, it is not produced by a perceptual disposition that is reliable relative to the environment that Henry is in. Of course, Henry's perceptual dispositions are *normally* reliable, i.e. reliable relative to normal perceptual environments. The problem is that Barn Facade County is not a normal perceptual environment. On the contrary, it is an environment where Henry *lacks* the ability to perceptually discriminate barns from non-barns.

As we have seen from previous sections, this approach will be plausible only if intuitions about such cases are unstable in ways that contextualism predicts and explains. Greco (2012) presents a range of cases to show that this is the case. First consider our original Barn Facade case:

Barn Facade

Henry is in the countryside and sees a barn ahead in clear view. On this basis he believes that the object ahead is a barn. Unknown to Henry, however, the area is dotted with barn facades that are indistinguishable from real barns from the road. However, Henry happens to be looking at a real barn.

Now consider two variations of the case (both adapted from Greco 2012):

Working Farm

Henry is visiting a working farm where there are several real barns and no barn facades. He is asked to retrieve a shovel from the barn located just ahead and begins walking in that direction. A farm in the next town is dotted with barn facades. However, Henry has never been in that town and never will be.

Tax Collector

Henry is a government employee, charged with counting barns in the area for the purposes of determining property taxes. Barn facades are not taxed in the same way that working barns are. Henry is a new employee who does not realize that the area is populated with barn facades, and he has not yet received the special training needed to distinguish barns from barn facades. Henry sees a real barn from the road and pulls out his log to record this.

Greco (2012) argues that there is pressure to ascribe knowledge in **Working Farm** and to deny knowledge in **Tax Collector**. The explanation is that knowledge ascriptions are sensitive to the informational needs of the relevant practical environment, and the relevant practical environments are significantly different in the two cases. Specifically, Henry's ability to distinguish barns from non-barns is perfectly reliable relative to the practical environment specified by **Working Farm**. However, Henry lacks an ability to distinguish barns from non-barns relative to the practical environment specified by **Tax Collector**. Put differently, Henry's perceptual abilities are adequate for the practical tasks in play in **Working Farm**, but not adequate for the practical tasks in play in **Tax Collector**.

Importantly, a contextualist treatment of **Barn Facade** cases does not require the details of the present framework. More generally, reliabilist theories of knowledge will invoke various parameters regarding the framing of reliable processes, the degree of their reliability, and their relevant environmental conditions. So long as the values of such parameters are allowed to vary across ascriber contexts, we get contextualist versions of reliabilism and similar resources for diagnosing Barn Facade cases.

We get a similar result for safety theories of knowledge. A safety condition requires that, in cases of knowledge, not easily would S's belief be false (Sosa 1999).[5] Such a condition can be interpreted as follows.

Safety. S's belief that p is *safe* just in case: in close possible worlds where S believes that p, p is true.

John Greco

Think of a space of possible worlds centered on the actual world and branching out according to some appropriate similarity ordering. S's belief that p is safe just in case: there are no close worlds where both S believes that p, and p is false. Put differently, we would have to go a long way off from the actual world to find a world where both S believes that p and p is false.

But how far off? Here we have another parameter that can be given a contextualist treatment. Specifically, one might hold that ascriber context determines the degree of safety required for "knows," with higher standards requiring true belief across a broader space of possible worlds. Applying this framework to our Barn Facade cases is straightforward: In the practical context specified by **Working Farm**, knowledge requires true belief out to worlds where Henry is involved in normal farm tasks under normal farm conditions. And, in fact, Henry's belief is safe by this standard. However, the practical context specified by **Tax Collector** requires more robust safety, out to worlds where Henry is engaged in tax collecting tasks and encountering barn facades. And, of course, Henry's belief is not safe by that higher standard.[6]

5 Conclusions

In conclusion, a contextualist treatment of Gettier cases is more or less plausible depending on whether intuitions about knowledge in such cases are unstable in ways that contextualism predicts and explains. In this respect, contextualism will be motivated (or not) in similar fashion as in skeptical problems and lottery cases. A number of standard Gettier cases evoke only the stable intuition that S does not know, and to that extent those cases resist a contextualist treatment. However, Barn Facade cases and other cases with a similar structure do seem to evoke shifting intuitions regarding whether S knows. To the extent that intuitions in these cases are predicted and explained by a contextualist treatment, these cases do serve to motivate a contextualist strategy.[7]

Notes

1 As Ichikawa (2011) points out, there are detractors, but the dominant view is that quantifiers are context-sensitive. If not, we can rephrase in terms of plausibility.
2 As Lewis says, "This is the only place where belief and justification enter my story." In this regard, notice that the Rule of Belief does not entail that, in cases of knowledge that *P*, S believes that *P* or that S is justified in believing that *P*. In fact, Lewis rejects belief and justification conditions for knowledge (1996: 556).
3 To be clear, the Cohen-Brogaard "critique" does not amount to an objection to contextualism (Cohen is himself a contextualist). Rather, it is an objection to contextualist treatments of Gettier cases. That is, it is an objection to the idea that contextualist resources can be fruitfully brought to bear on Gettier cases.
4 See also Greco (2007, 2010).
5 See also Pritchard (2005) and Greco (2012).
6 This general contextualist strategy for Barn Facade cases can be applied to other Gettier cases with similar structures. For example, see Epistemic Twin Earth (Kallestrup and Pritchard 2011) and Room Full of Liars (Goldberg 2007).
7 Thanks to Jonathan Ichikawa and Nathan Cockram for comments on an earlier version.

Bibliography

Brogaard, B. (2004), 'Contextualism, Skepticism, and the Gettier Problem', *Synthese* 139, 3: 367–386.
Chisholm, R. (1977), *Theory of Knowledge*, 2nd edition, Englewood Cliffs, NJ: Prentice-Hall.
Cohen, S. (1987), 'Knowledge, Context, and Social "Standards", *Synthese* 73: 3–26.
Cohen, S. (1998), 'Contextualist Solutions to Epistemological Problems: Scepticism, Gettier, and the "Lottery", *Australasian Journal of Philosophy* 76: 289–306.

Contextualism and Gettier cases

Gettier, E. (1963), 'Is Justified True Belief Knowledge?', *Analysis* 23, 6: 121–123.

Goldberg, S. (2007), *Anti-Individualism: Mind and Language, Knowledge and Justification*. Cambridge: Cambridge University Press.

Goldman, A. (1976), 'Discrimination and Perceptual Knowledge', *Journal of Philosophy* 73: 771–791.

Greco, J. (2007), 'The Nature of Ability and the Purpose of Knowledge', *Philosophical Issues* 17: 57–69.

Greco, J. (2010), *Achieving Knowledge*, Cambridge: Cambridge University Press.

Greco, J. (2012), 'A (Different) Virtue Epistemology', *Philosophy and Phenomenological Research* 85, 1: 1–26.

Ichikawa, J. (2011), 'Quantifiers and Epistemic Contextualism', *Philosophical Studies* 155, 3: 383–398.

Kallestrup, J. and Pritchard, D. (2011), 'Virtue Epistemology and Epistemic Twin Earth', *European Journal of Philosophy* 22, 3: 335–357.

Lehrer, K. (1965), 'Knowledge, Truth and Evidence', *Analysis* 25: 168–175.

Lewis, D. K. (1996), 'Elusive Knowledge', *Australasian Journal of Philosophy* 74, 4: 549–556.

Pritchard, D. H. (2005), *Epistemic Luck*, Oxford: Oxford University Press.

Shope, R. (1983), *The Analysis of Knowledge: A Decade of Research*, Princeton, NJ: Princeton University Press.

Sosa, E. (1999), 'How Must Knowledge Be Modally Related to What Is Known?', *Philosophical Topics* 26: 373–384.

Zagzebski, L. (1999), 'What Is Knowledge?' in J. Greco and E. Sosa, eds., *The Blackwell Guide to Epistemology*, Oxford: Blackwell.

PART IV

Doing without contextualism

16

'KNOWLEDGE' AND PRAGMATICS

Patrick Rysiew

1 Introduction

Linguistic phenomena have long served as an important source of data for epistemology. Considerations of 'what we would say', our ordinary knowledge-attributing habits and inclinations, etc., have helped to shape and constrain theories of knowledge, justification, and so on. But such considerations need to be handled with care, since our linguistic behavior and intuitions are shaped by a variety of factors. One of these is semantics, which has to do with linguistic items and the information they encode. Just as important, however, is pragmatics, which concerns the information arising from the tokening of such items – i.e., from *utterances*, or people's *saying things* – and the means by which such information is generated and recovered.[1]

It's often assumed that pragmatics has work to do only in special cases – for example, in understanding implicatures. Take Grice's well-known letter of recommendation example (1989: 33). Asked to write a testimonial for a student applying for a philosophy job, S writes (only)

(1) Mr. X's command of English is excellent, and his attendance at tutorials has been regular.

Here, S damns with faint praise, getting it across that his opinion of Mr. X as a philosopher is rather low. Similarly, in Grice's garage example (1989: 32), A is standing by an obviously immobilized car. B approaches, and the following exchange occurs:

    A: I'm out of petrol.
(2) B: There's a garage around the corner.

Here, Grice says, B implicates that the garage is, or at least may be, open.

The need for pragmatics is hardly restricted to such examples, however – and not just because pragmatic processes may also be essential to reference-fixing and resolving ambiguities. In standard examples of implicature, the speaker means what he says, but says it in order to communicate something further. Another sort of case that has gotten a lot of recent attention is a speaker's meaning and communicating something *other than* what s/he says. Such common departures from literal speech don't involve using words figuratively or ironically. Rather, they involve speakers' meaning and communicating something *more or less closely related to* what they say – something that 'resembles' it in some contextually salient way (Sperber & Wilson 1986b). (So the relevant form of non-literality is 'sentence nonliterality', as Bach (2001) calls it – none of the elements is being used figuratively, but the speaker doesn't mean quite what s/he says.) To take a well-worn example, an utterance of

(3) 'I've had [/haven't had] breakfast',

will typically communicate that the speaker has [/hasn't] had breakfast *that day*. And an utterance of

(4) 'You won't die',

said by a mother to her injured child, is liable to communicate that the child won't die *from the cut* – hence, that the injury isn't serious – not that the child is immortal (Bach 1994).

As such easily multiplied examples show, linguistic content often underdetermines communicated content. Though united in wishing to counter "the compulsion to treat all pragmatically derived meaning as implicature" (Carston 1988: 176), theorists differ as to the proper taxonomic handling of cases like those involving (3) and (4). Sperber and Wilson (1986a) and Carston (1988) call them 'explicatures'; Recanati (1993), 'strengthenings' of sentence meanings; and Bach (1994), 'implic*i*tures'. They also sometimes disagree about where specific examples fit within a given taxonomy,[2] how often sentences fail to express complete propositions, and whether 'what is said' is restricted to what's encoded in the words uttered or includes the qualifying material likely communicated by utterances of (2) and (3), for example.[3]

Such disagreements shouldn't obscure certain important points of agreement, however. First, all of the theorists just mentioned agree that what's communicated by a given utterance often departs from the information encoded in the uttered words. Second, they agree that the information communicated by an utterance can be more or less closely related to what's literally expressed. Thus, the content of sentence (1) differs markedly from what it's used to implicate, whereas (3) and (4) and what they're used to communicate are closely related.

What about (2)? Insofar as B communicates *that A can get service*, by the preceding reckoning, that would be counted as an implicature, since that information is hardly just an elaboration of the content of the uttered sentence. In this respect, the example resembles that involving (1). However, insofar as B's utterance of (2) communicates *that there's a garage around the corner that is (/might be) open* – a conceptual strengthening of the uttered sentence's content – it resembles the examples involving (3) and (4). Of course, there's no tension in seeing the example as involving both of these facts: as implicatures illustrate, one can perform one speech act and thereby (indirectly) perform another.

In any case, and to mark a final point of convergence among the relevant theorists, it's generally agreed that, in spite of the noted differences among examples such as those above, fundamentally the same type of pragmatic processes are involved in all. Indeed, both 'neo-Griceans' such as Bach and 'post-Gricean' relevance theorists such as Sperber and Wilson and Robyn Carston hold that the same very general principles are in play in understanding *literal* utterances. For, as Bach puts it, that the speaker means what she says is itself something that needs to be inferred, and inferred on the same grounds as her meaning something additional to or other than what she says (Bach 2006: 24–25; cf. Sperber & Wilson 1987: 708).

What grounds are those? According to one well-established view, what enables speakers to communicate what they intend, even when this departs from or goes beyond what they say, is the fact that our conversational exchanges are governed by Grice's (1989) Co-operative Principle (CP).[4] Or better, they are governed by the mutual presumption that others conform to CP (Bach & Harnish 1979: 62–65; Bach 2006: 24).

In discussing CP, Grice suggested various sub-maxims, under the headings of 'Quantity', 'Quality', 'Relation', and 'Manner'. Since it figures centrally in the discussion below, the role of relevance ('Relation') should be briefly illustrated. Thus, it's because B, in uttering (2), is presumed to be intending something that's relevant that his saying what he does communicates that the nearby garage is (/might be) open. Similarly, in the examples involving (3) and (4), it's not the obvious falsity of what's said – e.g., 'You're not going to die' – that triggers the inference to the information the speaker intends, any more than the obvious truth of the negated claim ('You're going to die') would be what the speaker relied upon in communicating that the injury was extremely serious. In either case, rather, it is a lack of relevant specificity in what is said that invites the appropriate inference (Bach 2001: 255–256).

A further crucial point illustrated by these examples is that conformity to CP doesn't require that the sentences uttered be maximally relevantly informative.[5] Indeed, as Saul puts it, "a key way of generating implicatures, according to Grice, is to violate maxims at the level of what is said" (2002: 364). Thus, for example, in their respective contexts, sentence (1) is under-informative, and (2) is not sufficiently relevant. In such cases, it's because the uttered sentences are not themselves maximally relevantly informative that speakers are able to communicate things over and above, or other than, what they say: they violate CP at the level of what is said but – and thereby – conform at the level of what's communicated (see, too, Grice 1989: 32–35; Neale 1990: 106, n. 19; van der Henst *et al.* 2002: 458).

One prominent alternative to the Gricean framework is relevance theory. According to Sperber and Wilson's *principle of relevance*, "every act of ostensive communication communicates the presumption of its own optimal relevance" (1986a: 158). Optimal relevance, in turn, is understood to be a matter (roughly) of minimizing processing costs while maximizing contextually relevant informational payoff (Sperber & Wilson 1986a). There are important questions about the extent to which Gricean and relevance-theoretic approaches are compatible (e.g., Saul 2002; Bach 2010). In what follows, however, we'll tend to employ the Gricean framework, though the key points could likely be rendered just as well in relevance-theoretic terms.[6]

2 Pragmatics and contextualism

It's uncontroversial among epistemologists that some data call for a pragmatic handling. For example, consider apparently non-factive uses of 'know(s)', as when it is said that ancient thinkers "knew" that the earth was flat. The majority view is that such utterances should not be taken literally – more specifically, that they involve 'protagonist projection' (Holton 1997), reflecting the point of view of the subject(s). Another example is Moore-paradoxical assertions – i.e., utterances of the form "*p*, but I don't believe that *p*" (Moore 1942: 543). These are odd-sounding, but not for semantic reasons. Neither must they be seen as involving implicature or impliciture (/explicature), either of which would require that the speaker *intend* to communicate (with the utterance of the first half of the sentence, '*p*') that s/he believes that *p*. Instead, the oddity can be explained by the familiar fact that belief is a condition on felicitous assertion (Grice 1989: 42; Bach 2006: 26) and thus that, whether or not one so intends, in asserting one represents oneself as believing (Rysiew 2007). Because that's so, and because pragmatically generated information can influence our intuitive response to an utterance, Moore-style assertions can persist in causing discomfort even in those who are aware that they involve no semantic inconsistency.

More controversial is whether pragmatics can help[7] explain the data that figure centrally in arguments for epistemic contextualism (EC), such as our intuitive responses to DeRose's Bank (1992) and Cohen's (1999) Airport Cases. In such examples, a scenario ('Low') in which a knowledge attribution seems correct is paired with one ('High') in which denying knowledge of the same subject seems correct, even though none of what would normally be regarded as epistemologically relevant factors have changed. The only clear difference between the cases is an increase in the practical importance of the subject's getting it right. EC is said to provide a natural resolution of this apparent tension: the content of sentences of the form '*S* does/doesn't know that *p*' vary, depending on the context, where 'context' is take to refer to features of the knowledge attributor(s)' psychology and/or conversational-practical situation. Acontextually, a knowledge sentence expresses (something like),

(5) *S* has a true belief and is in a strong$_C$ epistemic position with respect to *p*,

where strength of epistemic position is a function of the standards operative in the context, C; or, more simply,

(6) *S* has a true belief and that belief satisfies the contextually operative epistemic standards.[8]

With this view in place, the apparent tension between the relevant (Low) attribution and (High) denial dissolves. For what the relevant sentences actually express are,

> **(Low)** *S* has a true belief and is in a *moderately* strong epistemic position with respect to *p*, and
> **(High)** It's not the case that (*S* has a true belief and is in a *very* strong epistemic position with respect to *p*).

And these, of course, are perfectly compatible.

While EC has the result that each of the paired claims is true, a pragmatic response proposes that one member of the pair is false, even if the relevant assertion is pragmatically appropriate, and even if it seems true. (Following DeRose [1999], it has become common to refer to such views as involving a 'warranted assertability manoeuvre', or 'WAM'.) Some such accounts are sceptic-friendly, holding that the attribution of knowledge in Low is false, even if appropriately made (e.g., Unger 1975; Blaauw 2003; Schaffer 2004). Other, moderate invariantist views (e.g., Rysiew 2001, 2005, 2007; Black 2005; Brown 2006; Hazlett 2007; Pritchard 2010) explain, in pragmatic terms, why the knowledge-denial in High is apt, and even seems true, in spite of its literal falsity. There is disagreement among these theorists as to the proper form such an explanation should take. Below, we'll consider an account that appeals to Grice's maxim of Relation ('Be relevant!').

DeRose himself is sceptical about the prospects for a successful WAM here. In plausible WAMs,[9] DeRose says, we have some genuinely conflicting intuitions, such that we know in advance that something's going to have to be explained away. Further, a good WAM explains away one of the conflicting intuitions by appealing to the fact that the utterance of some truth generates a false implicature. (And it does so by appeal to some very general conversational principles.) But in the Bank and Airport Cases, these 'good-making' features are absent: First, our intra-contextual intuitions are in harmony (2009: 116). Second, and relatedly, the invariantist will have to explain an apparent truth in terms of an utterance of some *falsehood* generating a *true* implicature. And this, DeRose thinks, is implausible: "For, except where we engage in special practices of misdirection, like irony or hyperbole, don't we want to avoid falsehood both in what we implicate and (especially!) in what we actually say?" (2009: 114).

As Brown (2006: 411–419) – and, following her, Rysiew (2005: 59–62) – have argued, however, DeRose's scepticism about the prospects for a pragmatic handling of the relevant data is unwarranted. First, if the examples in question did not give rise to any apparent inconsistency – when we compare our intuitions across the Bank and Airport Cases, for example – there would be no reason to consider them interesting, much less to think that they might call for a contextualist handling. EC might imply that such an inconsistency is merely apparent, but that there is an inconsistency is an apparent truth all the same.

As to DeRose's second point, it may be true – special cases of indirection aside – that we want to avoid falsehood in what we say. But that's only insofar as we think that what we say is what we mean. However, as explained above, it's an established view that in many cases not involving any kind of irony, hyperbole, or figurative speech, the content of the uttered sentence fails to correspond to what the speaker intends to communicate. On that view, irony, figurative speech, etc., are limiting cases on a continuum of less than fully literal speech, rather than the best or only examples thereof. Further, as Brown says, "there is a wide range of non-figurative uses of language where one standard approach involves supposing that a literally false statement seems correct because it pragmatically conveys a truth" (2006: 415).[10] Indeed, that a speaker might make a literally false statement to communicate some truth is a corollary of the fact that violations of CP at the level of what is said are allowable when they enable conformity at the level of what's communicated. And that, in such a case, the statement itself can seem true is a consequence of the fact – which DeRose's own favored WAM exploits – that there is "a general tendency to confuse what a speaker merely represents as being the case in making an assertion with what the speaker actually asserts" (2009: 106; cf. 83).

With the previous points in place, the issue is simply whether there exists a plausible pragmatic explanation of the relevant data in terms of some general, and generally accepted, conversational principles. According to Rysiew and Brown, Gricean considerations operating through the maxim of Relation provide such an account. By way of background to her own presentation of such a view, Brown (2006: 425) illustrates how considerations of relevance function in Grice's garage example, introduced above. We'll do that here as well, in part because it will give us occasion to address a worry about the example that also arises, in general form, in cases of central interest to EC.

So, again: given A's evident need for gasoline, B's utterance of

(2) There's a garage around the corner,

implicates that the garage is or might be open; for otherwise the utterance would violate Relation. (Again, we may think this is an implic*i*ture; but either way, what's communicated is something that closely resembles what's said; and either way, that it's communicated is explained by the same general principles.) By the same token, if B thought that the nearby garage wasn't (at least possibly) open, his utterance would be misleading. "Rather," Brown continues, "in such a scenario, and assuming that she believes that there is no other nearby open garage, it would be correct for her to reply 'No, there's no garage nearby'. While this utterance is literally false, it pragmatically conveys the true claim that there is no open garage nearby" (2006: 425).

According to Blome-Tillmann, however, Brown's handling of the case fails. As Blome-Tillmann sees it, Brown is here assuming that, at least in the case of implicatures driven by Relation, the following principle holds:

> Converse Implicatures (CI):
> If an utterance of a sentence S conversationally implicates p in C, then an utterance of not-S conversationally implicates not-p in C.
>
> *(Blome-Tillmann 2013: 4306)*

However, CI is false of many implicatures, including many Relation implicatures.[11] Further, while agreeing that "B's utterance [here] conveys that there is no open garage nearby," Blome-Tillmann denies that this is an implicature. Rather, B's utterance communicates the latter because the proposition that there's no garage nearby *entails* that there's no open garage nearby (Blome-Tillmann 2013: 4307, n. 32). He continues:

> The fact that the phenomenon at issue is not a conversational implicature can be demonstrated further by the cancellability test: 'There's no garage nearby; but there's an open garage nearby' is contradictory in all contexts, because it semantically expresses a contradiction.
>
> *(Blome-Tillmann 2013: 4307, n. 32)*

In response, note first that Brown's handling of the example is hardly idiosyncratic: Garcia-Carpintero (2001: 113), e.g., cites the case as illustrating the inheritance of implicated contents in more complex constructions. Second, contrary to what Blome-Tillmann implies, one can implicate something that's entailed by what one says (Bach 2006: 24; Davis 2014: section 4). And of course, where what's implicated is entailed by what one says, cancellability will not be an appropriate test. Third (and again contrary to Blome-Tillmann), that the proposition that there's no garage nearby entails that there's no open garage nearby isn't sufficient for the latter's being communicated: not everything entailed by what one says is communicated; for something to be communicated, it must be plausibly regarded as intended (meant) by the speaker.[12] So we'd still need an account of why this particular entailment *is* communicated; and again, Relation provides the answer.[13]

Finally, consider the following natural elaboration of the case:

A: I'm out of petrol.
B: I'm sorry, there's no station nearby.
C (onlooker, to B): Isn't there a station just two blocks over?
B: Yes, but it's been closed for months.

Here, the two things B says can't both be true. Nonetheless, with his second utterance B is most naturally read, not as contradicting himself, but as making it clear just what he meant all along. For the same reason, if, after B has said, 'There's no station nearby,' A discovers that there is a nearby station but that it's shut down, there's no reason to think she would feel as though she'd been misled by B or that B had 'gotten it wrong'.

In sum, Blome-Tillmann has given us no reason to question Brown's handling of the garage example: her treatment of it faithfully illustrates the operation of considerations of relevance in everyday linguistic communication.

Let's proceed, then, to a specific proposed pragmatic handling of the data thought to lend support to EC. Briefly sketched, the account runs as follows: According to a widely held view, knowing requires (unGettiered) true belief plus the subject's being in a good epistemic position with respect to the proposition in question. What makes such a view invariantist is the idea that there is a fixed standard for the level of epistemic goodness knowledge requires. Even so, because a speaker is presumed to be conforming to Relation, in uttering a sentence of the form, '*S* knows that *p*', s/he is naturally taken to intend/mean that *S*'s epistemic position with respect to *p* is 'good enough' *given the epistemic standards that are operative in the context in question*. For, in naturally occurring situations,[14] it is only if speakers are so regarded that the presumption that their conversational contributions are maximally relevantly informative, and thus that they conform to CP, is preserved.

In the Airport Case, for example, it's mutually obvious that Mary and John want to ensure that their epistemic position with respect to the flight plan is *very* strong – strong enough to rule out the possibility of a misprint in their itinerary. Being in an epistemic position of such strength may or may not be required for knowing. Either way, due to considerations of relevance, it would be misleading of Mary and John to attribute knowledge to Smith, and so represent him as being in a good epistemic position, if they thought that his epistemic position wasn't so good as to put their shared and pressing concerns to rest – just as, in the garage example, it would be misleading to utter (2), 'There's a garage nearby', unless one thought it was (possibly) *open*. Parallel considerations apply to the knowledge denial: as *per* Brown above, the speaker who utters the negation of (2) is most naturally taken to mean that there is no *open* garage nearby; similarly, given that what's relevant to Mary and John is whether Smith is in a *very* strong epistemic position, their utterance of 'Smith doesn't know . . .' is most naturally taken to mean that it's not the case that Smith (has a true belief and) is in a *very* strong epistemic position – that his epistemic position isn't so good as to put their shared and pressing concerns to rest, that he can't rule out the possibility of a misprint, and so on.[15] Given what we're told, the latter thoughts seem not just highly relevant but true. And if they (we) read what's conveyed by the relevant utterance onto the sentence uttered, the knowledge denial will strike them (us) as true as well.

3 Some objections considered

One objection to the account just sketched, in certain of its forms, is that it is *ad hoc*. In the language of Rysiew (2001), knowledge requires an ability to rule out the relevant not-p alternatives; but, thanks to considerations of relevance, an attribution of knowledge pragmatically conveys that S can rule out the *salient* alternatives – i.e., the not-p alternatives that the conversants have in mind.[16] As DeRose at one time interpreted it (2002: 198, n. 17), Rysiew's view is that "an assertion of 'S knows that P' carries two separate but related meanings" – a 'semantic meaning' and 'a pragmatic meaning'; and the role of relevance is simply to get the hearer "to fasten on the second, pragmatic meaning" in cases where "the semantic content of 'S knows/doesn't know that P' is clearly irrelevant to the purposes at hand" (2002: 198, n. 17, cf. 2009: 118ff.). As Rysiew (2005: 63–64) explains, however, on his view nothing "has two meanings", and the role of relevance is (therefore) not simply to get the hearer to switch from one to the other. Rather, there is what the sentence means, and what the speaker means in uttering it; and Relation explains how an utterance of the former, given what it means, communicates the latter.

A second, more influential objection has it that the relevant pragmatic conveyances fail Grice's cancellability test (1989: 44). On the proposed account, an utterance of 'S knows that p' might pragmatically convey that S is in a very strong epistemic position – that S can rule out the not-p alternatives that are in play, that (consequently) there's no need for further investigation, and so on. However, the objection runs, "S knows, but S is not in an especially strong epistemic position," or "S knows, but S needs to check further," sound odd (Cohen 1999: 60). In response, we should first note, again, that "[s]peech act content is, in the jargon, a massive interaction effect" (Borg 2012: 15) – i.e., that what's communicated by a given utterance is the product of multiple factors (syntax, semantics, pragmatics, etc.). And, to the extent that our intuitions are attuned to the total message communicated, rather than just the semantic features of what is said, certain cancellations are apt to feel uncomfortable (Rysiew 2001: section 7; Brown 2006: 428; cf. Chomsky 1977: 4).

Our general tendency to read merely pragmatically generated information onto what we say aside, however, is there any reason to think that we might make such an error in the case at hand? After all, to return to the letter-writer case discussed above, no one is going to confuse what's said with what's communicated *there*, so why think it happens here? Several things are worth noting.

Patrick Rysiew

First, the pragmatic phenomena we're now considering are not "particularized" (Grice 1989: 37): that the speaker takes S to satisfy the contextually operative standards, to be able rule out the salient not-p alternatives, and so on, is inferable simply from her asserting the relevant sentence and the presumption that she's conforming to CP; unlike the example involving (1), very little in the way of specific knowledge of the context in which the relevant sentences are uttered is required (see Rysiew 2007). Second, while in the case at hand what the speaker means isn't what s/he says, unlike familiar tropes, say, none of the elements of the knowledge sentence is being used non-literally; the example thus involves a kind of non-literality that's harder to spot (Bach 2001: 249–250).[17] Third, and again unlike the letter-writer case, what's communicated in the present example closely resembles what's semantically expressed. Finally, while error about certain items in the lexicon might antecedently be rather unlikely, even those whose job it is to provide an account of the semantics of 'know(s)' disagree on the matter, sometimes significantly, and with some holding that the sort of thing said on the present account to be merely pragmatically conveyed is in fact required for knowing. For this reason too, it's not implausible that we might be prone to reading the latter type of information onto knowledge sentences.

Still, that we naturally make the mistake doesn't mean that we must do so. Thus, when the relevant information is spelled out explicitly, we can distinguish between (for example) a speaker's being in a strong, versus a *very* strong, epistemic position with regard to some p (the former being what knowledge requires, the latter being what an attribution of knowledge might convey). In fact, and returning to the issue of cancellability, that's essentially what's happening with certain instances of the allegedly problematic utterances, instances that *don't* sound odd at all. For instance, "S knows that p, but S can't rule out some *bizarre* not-p possibilities" or "S's epistemic position with respect to p isn't so strong that her belief that p would match the facts in *very* distant not-p worlds; but still, she knows that p" (Rysiew 2001: 495; Brown 2006: 428).[18] With these more natural utterances, the speaker's presenting information in a certain order, using stress selectively, and so on, makes it easier to understand what he's trying to get across; and when that's so, the appearance of inconsistency recedes.

DeRose's most recent objection to the pragmatic account we're considering, however, takes a different form. Here, the worry is not that it is *ad hoc*, that it leads to violations of cancellability, or that it posits an implausible form of error. Rather, it's that considerations of relevance simply wouldn't operate in the way the account requires. Here is the objection, as applied to the High variant of the Bank Case:

> how could relevance concerns drive the hearer from the semantic content posited by the theory to the theory's proposed pragmatic destination? The falsehood that, according to the account, the speaker has asserted would be very relevant to the concerns of the participants in this conversation. We will grant that the *issue* or the question of whether or not the subject knows$_H$[19] is the most relevant issue to the purposes at hand (and is therefore more relevant than is the question of whether he knows$_M$). . . . But that the speaker doesn't even know$_M$ that the bank is open on Saturdays – which according to Rysiew's account is what the speaker has asserted – would of course settle (in the negative) the salient question or issue of whether he knows$_H$. So, in saying that he doesn't 'know' that the bank is open on Saturdays, on Rysiew's account, the speaker asserts what would be an extremely relevant thought.
>
> *(DeRose 2009: 122)*

Thus, DeRose concludes, "it's hard to see how relevance concerns would drive the hearer to suppose that anything other than what was said is what the speaker intends to communicate" (2009: 124).

212

'Knowledge' and pragmatics

This objection of course recalls Blome-Tillmann's criticism of Brown's handling of the garage example. The core idea of each is that all of the work is being done by the fact that the sentence uttered entails information that's most relevant to the subjects. In Blome-Tillmann's criticism, this was taken to show that what's entailed is communicated but not implicated; here, it's being used to argue that what does the entailing is most plausibly thought to be what the speaker means.

In the present case, one response is that it's questionable whether the relevant entailment holds.[20] In the language of Rysiew (2001), DeRose's objection assumes that the set of relevant alternatives is a subset of the salient alternatives. In more general terms, it assumes that strength of epistemic position is a straightforward matter of variation along some one (or several) neatly ordered dimensions (cf. Bach 2005: 57, n. 11; DeRose 2009: 7, n. 3). In either form, the assumption is dubious.

However, even granting the assumption – i.e., even granting that 'S doesn't know$_M$ that p' entails that 'S doesn't know$_H$ that p' (and setting aside concerns about the shorthand: see n. 19) – the objection fails. For, first, both Grice and Sperber and Wilson make it clear that the fact that some information is somewhat relevant, even very relevant, won't suffice for its being communicated, and/or its being appropriately thought to be what the speaker intends.[21] What must be presumed is that what the speaker intends, given what he's said, affords maximal relevant informational payoff for least interpretative effort. Nor, for the same reason, does it matter that because 'S doesn't know$_M$ that p' is (we are for the sake of argument supposing) logically stronger, it "give[s] more information" than 'S doesn't know$_H$ that p' (see DeRose 2009: 123–124), for that extra information might tax attentional and inferential resources without itself contributing to a resolution of the issue of greatest immediate interest.

This leads to the second point: the reason the speaker communicates that S doesn't 'know$_H$ that p' is the same reason that B's utterance in the garage example communicates what *it* does – namely, because this further information speaks directly to "the most relevant issue to the purposes at hand" (DeRose 2009: 122), and because it is only on the supposition that he intends to communicate that information, and expects the hearer to recognize that intention, that the presumption that he is conforming to CP is preserved. As Sperber and Wilson put it, "when the speaker could not have expected his utterance to be relevant to the hearer without intending him to derive some specific contextual implication from it, then . . . that implication is also an implicature" (1981: 284; cf. Bach & Harnish 1979: 169).

Finally, consider the following natural elaboration of the case:

A: Banks do change their hours. Do you know the bank will be open tomorrow [Saturday]?
B: Well, no. I'd better go in and make sure.
C (onlooker, to B): But wait. You were there just two weeks ago on a Saturday. You have no reason to think that its hours have changed. In fact, you have, overall, very good reason to believe that the bank is open tomorrow.
B: Yes. But it's *very* important we get the check cashed before Monday. And I can't be sure that it hasn't changed its hours (etc.).

Here, if a moderate invariantist view is correct, the two things B says can't both be true (assuming his belief is true and unGettiered), since (given a true, unGettiered belief) being in an epistemic position as good as his apparently is suffices for knowing. Nonetheless, with his second utterance B is most naturally read, not as contradicting himself, but as making it clear just what he meant all along. For the same reason, if, after the fact, A and B learn that B did satisfy the (moderate) conditions that are, in fact, required for knowing, there's no reason to think A would feel as though, in saying 'No [I don't know]', B had misled her or had gotten it wrong.

213

In sum, then, even assuming that the relevant entailment holds, it is not "hard to see how relevance concerns would drive the hearer to suppose that anything other than what was said is what the speaker intends to communicate" (DeRose 2009: 124). Quite the contrary: the present reflections reinforce the idea that considerations of relevance favor the view that what the speaker intends to communicate is that his epistemic position isn't so strong as to satisfy the elevated standards that are in play.

The latter, of course, is just what DeRose (and others contextualists) think the speaker here would communicate. However, contextualists themselves owe us an account of how that happens. As we saw at the outset, pragmatics are required even in cases where the speaker means just what he says. That what he says, according to EC, itself encodes the relevant context-relative information – viz., (High) It's not the case that (S has a true belief and is in a *very* strong epistemic position with respect to p) – does not explain how the hearer grasps that that's what the speaker means (see Rysiew 2001: 506).[22] And now notice that, if DeRose's argument above is effective, it frustrates the contextualist at just this point. For if DeRose is correct, that S doesn't 'know$_M$' that p suffices to address "the most relevant issue to the purposes at hand" (by settling it in the negative), and so there's no reason for the hearer not to take *that* to be what the speaker means. The denial in High would then be correctly read as a simple negation of the Low attribution – which is precisely what contextualists want to deny. On the other hand, if there *is* a good account of how the hearer gets from an utterance of the relevant sentence to the speaker's meaning that S 'doesn't know$_H$ that p' (i.e., High), the pragmatic invariantist can avail herself of that as well. In short, both parties to the debate require a way of moving from the sentence uttered to what the speaker means thereby. Either there's a plausible story to be told here, or there is not. If not, that's equally problematic for both parties. But if so, it's not clear what benefit accrues from taking the speaker's meaning to be reflected in the content of the sentence itself (Rysiew 2001: section 10).

4 Conclusion

The aim of this chapter has been to provide an introduction to pragmatics and its relevance to debates surrounding EC. To give a good sense of how the relevant issues play out, we've focused on one particular pragmatic approach and some of the more prominent objections to it. The reader is reminded that there are other pragmatic accounts (and, no doubt, other objections). Also, while we have focused here on the handling of Low-High paired cases, there are other fronts on which EC and pragmatic considerations compete. These include concessive knowledge attributions (see n. 18) and considerations of the social function of 'know(s)'.[23] Like pragmatics itself, its bearing upon EC and the issues it brings to the fore is multi-faceted and under-appreciated.[24]

Notes

1 Theorists disagree as to how best to formulate the semantics-pragmatics distinction. The above characterization follows Bach (1999), who also argues against other formulations.
2 For example, Bach (2006: 28–29) suggests that most 'scalar implicatures' are really implicitures; and Bach & Harnish (1979: ch. 4) and Bach (1994: section 5) argue that metaphor and irony are best thought of as non-literal but direct speech acts, rather than implicatures.
3 Here, I use 'what is said' (as well as 'linguistic content' and 'the content of the sentence') to refer to the information encoded in expression-types, *modulo* disambiguation and reference-fixing.
4 "Make your conversational contribution such as is required, at the stage at which it occurs, by the accepted purpose or direction of the talk exchange in which you are engaged" (1989: 26).
5 The latter is Harnish's (1976) suggested compression of CP.
6 For a particular application of relevance theory to the case of EC, see Jary & Stainton, ch. 37, this volume.

'Knowledge' and pragmatics

7 There is no need to claim exclusivity here. Pragmatic explanations can complement psychological ones, for example. After all, pragmatics is already as much about psychology – the psychology of utterance-production and utterance-interpretation – as anything.

8 "When the content of knowledge-attributing sentences varies from context to context, what is varying are the epistemic standards, or how strong an epistemic position the subject must be in to count as knowing; the content of a given use of 'S knows that p' is that S (has a true belief that p and) meets the epistemic standards relevant to the context of utterance" (DeRose 2009: 34).

9 DeRose (2009: ch. 3) illustrates with the example of possibility statements, executing a 'WAM' on behalf of his preferred account of the semantics thereof.

10 The experiments of Gibbs & Moise (1997), Nicolle & Clark (1999), and Novacek (2001), for example, strongly suggest that intuitive assessments of 'what is said' are influenced by pragmatic factors. Indeed, Nicolle & Clark report that, in some cases, when asked to select the paraphrase that best reflects what a speaker has said subjects choose clear cases of implicatures.

11 Blome-Tillman cites (2003: 4307, n. 32), as a Relation-based counterexample to CI, Grice's letter-writer case – i.e., the example involving (1) above. 'Praising with faint damns' is a real phenomenon. But set that aside – the discussion here doesn't require that CI be true, even that it be true of all Relation implicatures. All that's required is (a) that 'pragmatic inheritance' does occur, and (b) that it is plausibly thought to occur in the present case (as well as in the cases of concern to EC). As to (a), implicitures [/explicatures] and definite descriptions provide examples (Brown 2006), as do (according to some) belief reports (Berg 2012 and others). As to (b), see the discussion below.

12 And intended to be communicated, in part, by means of the recognition of that intention. That communication involves such reflexive intentions is a key insight of Gricean theory.

13 Recall the discussion of utterances of (3) and (4) and their negations: the inference to what the speaker means is driven by Relation, not Quality ('Do not say what you believe to be false'); the presumed or likely truth-values of the sentences uttered – hence, what they do/don't entail – play no direct role.

14 As opposed to, say, in an epistemology class. There, if conditions are right, what attributions or denials of knowledge communicate might be just what the relevant sentences express.

15 There is no need to single out one such proposition as *the* thing the speakers mean. What's communicated can be vague or indeterminate.

16 There are important issues here about the role that salience considerations play, how they interact with practical interests, and so on. For criticism of Rysiew (2001) on this, see Brown (2006); Rysiew (2007) is meant to incorporate the relevant points.

17 Blome-Tillmann observes that even highly formulaic and idiomatic instances of hyperbole ('apologise a thousand times', 'cry a flood of tears') are easily detected as non-literal, as are metaphor and irony ('She's made of stone, this girl', A: 'John's an atheist' – B: 'Yes, and so is the pope') (2013: 4300–4302). Note that many such examples involve figurative speech, rather than the sort of non-literality being considered here. They also all typically exploit the obvious flouting of Quality (see n. 13) at the level of what is said – in Blome-Tillmann's terms, such "utterances . . . trigger an implicature *because* their semantic content cannot be readily added to the common ground" (2013: 4310). This is not true of the case under consideration here.

18 Such statements are examples of *concessive knowledge attributions* (CKAs) (Rysiew 2001) – that is, utterances of the form 'S knows that *p*, but it's possible that *q*' (where *q* entails not-*p*). The proper handling of CKAs is another front on which contextualists and pragmatic theorists (among others) compete. Lewis (1996) argues that CKAs state the basic fallibilist idea but are self-contradictory, the best fix being to adopt a certain version of EC. Stanley (2005) denies that the relevant claims express fallibilist thoughts. Dougherty & Rysiew (2009) argue that they do, but that their (sometimes) infelicity is pragmatic.

19 'Knows$_M$' and 'knows$_H$' are meant by DeRose to express S's satisfying moderate/high standards for knowing, the idea being that, according to the moderate invariantist a knowledge attribution/denial that semantically encodes that S does/doesn't know$_M$ that *p* might pragmatically communicate that S does/doesn't know$_H$ that *p*. While the expressions are intended merely as shorthand, they are misleading, as the invariantist need hardly grant that there are degrees or types of knowledge.

20 This is noted by Blome-Tillmann (2013: 4309–4310). Blome-Tillmann has his own concerns about the pragmatic account we're considering, only some of which are touched on here.

21 Sperber & Wilson (1986a) speak of *optimal* relevance. Bach (2010: 130; cf. Bach & Harnish 1979: 92) prefers *sufficient* relevance, which also permits the point just made. And Grice, in explicating Relation, writes: "I expect a [conversational] partner's contribution to be appropriate to the immediate needs at each stage of the transaction; if I am mixing ingredients for a cake, I do not expect to be handed a good

book, or even an oven cloth (though this might be an appropriate contribution at a later stage)" (1989: 28).

22 Neale (2007: 81–82) makes a similar point.

23 Henderson (2009) argues that such considerations provide a new rationale for EC. For a treatment of the topic in which pragmatics figure prominently, see Rysiew (2012).

24 For valuable feedback, and for help at various stages with the ideas expressed herein, I'm indebted to Jonathan Adler, Kent Bach, Jessica Brown, Nathan Cockram, Jonathan Ichikawa, Mike Raven, and Rob Stainton.

References

Bach, K. (1994) "Conversational Impliciture", *Mind & Language* 9: 124–162.

——— (1999) "The Semantics-Pragmatics Distinction: What It Is and Why It Matters", in K. Turner (ed.), *The Semantics-Pragmatics Interface from Different Points of View*. Oxford: Elsevier, pp. 65–84.

——— (2001) "Speaking Loosely: Sentence Nonliterality", in P. French and H. Wettstein (eds.), *Midwest Studies in Philosophy 25*. Malden, MA: Blackwell Publishers, pp. 249–263.

——— (2005) "The Emperor's New 'Knows'", in G. Preyer and G. Peter (eds.), *Contextualism in Philosophy: Knowledge, Meaning, and Truth*. Oxford: Clarendon Press, pp. 51–89.

——— (2006) "The Top 10 Misconceptions about Implicature", in B. J. Birner and G. Ward (eds.), *Drawing the Boundaries of Meaning*. Amsterdam and Philadelphia: John Benjamins, pp. 21–30.

——— (2010) "Implicature vs. Explicature: What's the Difference?", in B. Soria and E. Romero (eds.), *Explicit Communication*. New York: Palgrave MacMillan, pp. 126–137.

———, and M. Harnish (1979) *Linguistic Communication and Speech Acts*. Cambridge, MA: The MIT Press.

Berg, J. (2012) *Direct Belief*. Berlin: Walter de Gruyter.

Blaauw, M. (2003) "WAMing Away at Contextualism", *Nordic Journal of Philosophy* 4(1): 88–97.

Black, T. (2005) "Classic Invariantism, Relevance, and Warranted Assertability Manoeuvers", *The Philosophical Quarterly* 55(219): 328–336.

Blome-Tillmann, M. (2013) "Knowledge and Implicatures", *Synthese* 190(18): 4293–4319.

Borg, E. (2012) *Pursuing Meaning*. Oxford: Oxford University Press.

Brown, J. (2006) "Contextualism and Warranted Assertibility Manoeuvres", *Philosophical Studies* 130: 407–435.

Carston, R. (1988) "Implicature, Explicature, and Truth-theoretic Semantics", in R. M. Kempson (ed.), *Mental Representations*. Cambridge: Cambridge University Press, pp. 155–181.

Chomsky, N. (1977) *Essays on Forms and Interpretation*. Amsterdam: North Holland.

Cohen, S. (1999) "Contextualism, Skepticism, and the Structure of Reasons", in J. E. Tomberlin (ed.), *Philosophical Perspectives 13: Epistemology*. Atascadero, CA: Ridgeview, pp. 57–89.

Davis, W. A. (2014) "Implicature", in E. N. Zalta (ed.), *The Stanford Encyclopedia of Philosophy* (Fall 2014 Edition), URL = <http://plato.stanford.edu/archives/fall2014/entries/implicature/>.

DeRose, K. (1992) "Contextualism and Knowledge Attributions", *Philosophy and Phenomenological Research* 52(4): 913–929.

——— (1999) "Contextualism: An Explanation and Defense", in J. Greco and E. Sosa (eds.), *The Blackwell Guide to Epistemology*. Cambridge, MA: Blackwell, pp. 185–203.

——— (2002) "Assertion, Knowledge and Context", *The Philosophical Review* 111(2): 167–203.

——— (2009) *The Case for Contextualism*. Oxford: Oxford University Press.

Dougherty, T., and P. Rysiew (2009) "Fallibilism, Epistemic Possibility, and Concessive Knowledge Attributions", *Philosophy and Phenomenological Research* 78(1): 123–132.

Garcia-Carpintero, M. (2001) "Gricean Rational Reconstructions and the Semantics/Pragmatics Distinction", *Synthese* 128: 93–131.

Gibbs, R. W., and J. F. Moise (1997) "Pragmatics in Understanding What Is Said", *Cognition* 62: 51–74.

Grice, H. P. (1989) *Studies in the Way of Words*. Cambridge, MA: Harvard University Press.

Harnish, R. (1976) "Logical Form and Implicature", in T. Bever, J. Katz and T. Langendoen (eds.), *An Integrated Theory of Linguistic Abilities*. New York: Thomas Y. Crowell, pp. 464–479.

Hazlett, A. (2007) "Grice's Razor", *Metaphilosophy* 38(5): 669–690.

Henderson, D. (2009) "Motivated Contextualism", *Philosophical Studies* 142(1): 119–131.

Holton, R. (1997) "Some Telling Examples", *Journal of Pragmatics* 28: 625–628.

Lewis, D. (1996) "Elusive Knowledge", *Australasian Journal of Philosophy* 74(4): 549–567.

Moore, G. E. (1942) "A Reply to My Critics", in P. Schlipp (ed.), *The Philosophy of G. E. Moore*. Evanston: Tudor, pp. 535–677.

Neale, S. (1990) *Descriptions*. Cambridge, MA: The MIT Press.

—————— (2007) "Heavy Hands, Magic, and Scene-Reading Traps", *European Journal of Analytic Philosophy* 3(2): 77–132.

Nicolle, S., and B. Clark (1999) "Experimental Pragmatics and What Is Said", *Cognition* 69: 337–354.

Novacek, I. (2001) "When Children Are More Logical than Adults", *Cognition* 78: 165–188.

Pritchard, D. (2010) "Contextualism, Skepticism, and Warranted Assertibility Manoeuvres", in J. C. Campbell, M. O'Rourke and H. Silverstein (eds.), *Knowledge and Skepticism*. Cambridge, MA: The MIT Press, pp. 85–103.

Recanati, F. (1993) *Direct Reference*. Cambridge, MA: Blackwell.

Rysiew, P. (2001) "The Context-Sensitivity of Knowledge Attributions", *Noûs* 35(4): 477–514.

—————— (2005) "Contesting Contextualism", *Grazer Philosophische Studien* 69: 51–70.

—————— (2007) "Speaking of Knowing", *Noûs* 41(4): 627–662.

—————— (2012) "Epistemic Scorekeeping," in J. Brown and M. Gerken (eds.), *Knowledge Ascriptions*. Oxford: Oxford University Press, pp. 270–293.

Saul, J. (2002) "What Is Said and Psychological Reality", *Linguistics and Philosophy* 25: 347–372.

Schaffer, J. (2004) "Skepticism, Contextualism, and Discrimination", *Philosophy and Phenomenological Research* 69(1): 138–155.

Sperber, D., and D. Wilson (1981) "Pragmatics", *Cognition* 10: 281–286.

—————— (1986a) *Relevance*. Cambridge, MA: Blackwell.

—————— (1986b) "Loose Talk", *Proceedings of the Aristotelian Society* 6: 153–171.

—————— (1987) "Précis of *Relevance*", *Behavioral and Brain Sciences* 10: 697–754.

Stanley, J. (2005) "Fallibilism and Concessive Knowledge Attributions", *Analysis* 65(2): 126–131.

Unger, P. (1975) *Ignorance: A Case for Scepticism*. Oxford: Clarendon Press.

Van der Henst, J.-B., L. Carles, and D. Sperber (2002) "Truthfulness and Relevance in Telling the Time", *Mind & Language* 17(5): 457–466.

17
LOOSE USE AND BELIEF VARIATION

Wayne A. Davis

The use of 'S knows p' varies from context to context. Contextualist theories hypothesize that the truth conditions of 'S knows p' vary with things like salience, interests, and stakes. They promise to dissolve the problem of skepticism. I argue that the contextual variation results from pragmatic factors. The cases promising a philosophical payoff for contextualism involve variation in belief (Davis 2015): the speaker expresses different beliefs about whether S knows p. The everyday cases providing the best evidence for contextualism involve loose use (Davis 2007): the speaker means that S is close enough to knowing p for different purposes. Loose use is a common form of implicature related to hyperbole and irony. The loose-use account requires a strong invariant semantics, but not skepticism.

I Everyday variation and semantic theories

Attributions of knowledge often vary from context to context without any evident difference in the content, truth, or justification of what we believe. Representative cases each involve two contexts, A and B.

The bank case

A. Hannah and Bob are driving home on Friday. They had planned to stop at the bank, but notice long lines. Asked whether she knows if the bank will be open tomorrow, Hannah recalls going to the bank on Saturday, and says, "Yes, let's go then." **B.** Bob immediately reminds her that the funds must be in the bank by Monday morning, otherwise checks will bounce. Noting that banks sometimes change hours, he asks whether she really knows it will be open. Hannah pauses, and says, "No. We'd better go now."

The parking case

A. Dick and Jane are discussing how often they forget where they parked their cars. Jane asks, "Does Alan know his car is in section 5?" Dick answers, "Yes. He told me this morning." **B.** In nearly identical circumstances, Jack and Jill are talking about cars being stolen from even the safest neighborhoods. Jill asks the same question. Jack answers, "No. He hasn't checked."

Loose use and belief variation

Hannah believes the bank will be open on Saturday both before and after her husband's reminder, and her belief is true and justified throughout. Her reasons for believing the bank will be open do not change. Nor does the likelihood that the bank will be open given her evidence. These are stipulations of the case. Nevertheless, Hannah said she knows in A and does not in B. What she says seems natural and appropriate in both contexts.

The level of justification necessary for affirming knowledge is what differs in these examples. The subjects need more evidence in the B contexts for knowledge to be attributed. Contextualism, subject-sensitive invariantism, and relativism maintain that the standard of justification varies because the truth conditions of 'S knows p' depend on *truth-independent* factors – factors such as interests, stakes, and salience that are unrelated to whether 'p' is true, what reasons S has for believing p, the soundness of S's reasoning, and how likely 'p' is given S's evidence. *Contextualism* holds that the truth conditions depend on features of the *speaker's* context – the context in which 'S knows p' is *used* (Cohen 1986; DeRose 1992; Lewis 1996). On the most popular form, 'know' has a syntactically unmarked *indexical* element in addition to its tense. *Subject-sensitive invariantism* holds that the truth conditions depend on the *subject's* context (Annis 1978; Hawthorne 2004; Stanley 2005) and *relativism* on the *assessor's* context (MacFarlane 2005, 2014; Cappelen 2008). I advocate *classical* or *insensitive invariantism*, on which the truth conditions of 'S knows p' do not vary with truth-independent factors.

When speaker and subject differ, as in the parking case, the variation in knowledge claims tracks variation in the speaker's contexts. The subject Alan's context is the same. So subject sensitive invariantism does not account for the variation in this case. Subject-sensitive invariantism also implies, implausibly, that subjects can acquire knowledge by moving to contexts with lower stakes, and that it is correct to say of Hannah in B that she *used to know*, but *no longer knows*, that the bank will be open. Since the context of assessment might be neither the subject's nor the speaker's context, it is even more problematic. I will focus on contextualism.

Here is some of the evidence favoring an insensitive-invariant semantics. There is a wide variety of uncontroversially context-sensitive terms, but all behave differently from 'knows p' in several ways. For example, 'is flat' and 'is heavy' allow comparisons and relativizations, as do 'knows Paris,' 'knows how to dance,' and 'is justified in believing p.' But 'knows that p' cannot be qualified by *more* or *better*, and we never say things like: *He knows it's true by (or relative to) low standards, but not high standards; He knows it's true compared to Mary, but not Jane;* or *He knows it's true, but not perfectly.*

Contextualism would explain why Dick is not disagreeing with Jack, and why Hannah has not changed her mind about the bank. But it entails counterintuitively that Dick's knowledge claim does not contradict Jack's, and that Hannah's second knowledge claim is not a denial, retraction, or correction of her first. It also predicts that instances of (1) could be true and assertable when the speaker is in a high-standards context and S a low-standards context. For the speaker can recognize that S's epistemic position meets the low standard of S's context (making S's statement "I know p" true) while not meeting the high standard of the speaker's own context (making 'S does not know p' true there).

(1) S can truly say "I know p" even though S does not know p.

On the contrary, (1) seems contradictory in every context. Finally, knowing p seems to entail having enough evidence to assert p. Therefore, (2) seems absurd:

(2) Mary knows Tom was home last night, but she does not have enough evidence to assert that.

Contextualism allows (2) to be true, however, when the speaker is in a low-standards context and Mary is in a high-standards context.

These facts tell equally against 'know' being semantically ambiguous, with a weak and a strong sense: (1) has no true interpretation, unlike *S can truly say "I bought a plane" even though she did not buy a plane*, which could be true if the first occurrence of 'plane' means carpentry plane and the second airplane.

II Hyperbole and irony

A special problem for contextualism is that if S's only evidence is the extremely low probability of winning, then 'S knows that he will lose' never seems true – even in ordinary low-standards contexts. Consider:

The lottery case

A. Harry, the career dishwasher, says he is purchasing a Ferrari. Incredulous, Joe asks how he plans to pay for it. Harry responds, "I'm going to win the lottery." When he realizes Harry is serious, Joe blurts out, "That's ridiculous. You know you're not going to win." **B.** Wondering whether Joe has inside information about the lottery, Tom asks, "Does Harry really know that he is going to lose?" "Of course not," Joe replies, "but his chances of winning are infinitesimal."

Joe's use of 'know' in A is perfectly natural. Criticism would be inappropriate. Yet Joe's statement in A does not strike us as true no matter what context he is in. While we take what Joe said to be false, we accept his saying it because his point is that Harry's plan is irrational because he is too likely to lose.

The lottery case differs from the bank and parking cases because it involves *hyperbole*, a common figure of speech in which a speaker says that something is greater in a certain respect than he means or believes to emphasize how great it is in that respect. What the speaker *means* is not what the speaker *says*, and what the *speaker* means is not what the speaker's *sentence* means. In A, Joe meant that Harry has strong reason to believe he is not going to win. He meant that by saying something stronger, that Harry knows he is not going to win. Hyperbole involves what Grice (1989) called *implicature*: meaning or implying one thing by saying something else.[1] Specifically, hyperbole involves *conversational* implicatures: implicatures that are not part of the meaning of the sentence used, and depend on the speech context.

Hyperbole is typically signaled by intonation, and the obvious falsity of what is said. When a traveler remarks, "My suitcase weighs a ton," she will expect her audience to recognize that what she says is false (after all, she is carrying it), and infer that she meant something else. Joe also takes it to be obvious in A that what he said is false. We would expect Joe to have uttered 'know' with a special intonation. *Irony* resembles hyperbole in these respects, but the speaker's reason for implicating rather than saying what is meant differs. In irony, the purpose is to make light of, belittle, or mock what is said. In hyperbole, the speaker wants to emphasize how great something is in a certain respect. Joe is emphasizing how much justification Harry has to believe he will not win. For an example of irony, imagine that a Democrat is asked why some Republicans propose barring Muslims from entering the United States, and answers sarcastically, "They *know* all Muslims are terrorists." The Democrat means that they are far from knowing that, so this is another case of implicature. The Democrat's goal, though, is to emphasize how little justification the Republicans have for such a belief.

The variation in knowledge attributions in the bank and parking cases is not plausibly attributed to the difference between figurative and literal use (*pace* Schaffer 2004: 149). Hannah and Dick did not use any special intonation or expect it to be obvious that what they said is false. Their goal is not to either belittle the knowledge claim or emphasize how warranted it is:

> [O]rdinary speakers don't seem to regard their ordinary knowledge claims as exaggerations. Nor do they mark any distinction between what they literally know and what they only hyperbolically "know". When their knowledge claims are challenged, they don't say, "I was speaking hyperbolically", the way I would if you replied to my horse-eating boast by saying, "Not even a grizzly bear can consume an entire horse in one sitting."
>
> *(MacFarlane 2005: 206)*

MacFarlane's exaggeration that he could eat a horse differs from Joe's knowledge claim in the lottery case mainly in how big it is.

III Loose use

Pragmatic accounts of the bank and parking cases need not treat them as hyperbole (*pace* Hawthorne 2004: 116–8). Another common type of implicature is illustrated by the coffee case.

The coffee case

A. When the scoop comes up empty in the coffee jar, I yell to my wife, "The coffee is all gone." **B.** When my son comes down for breakfast a few minutes later, he announces that he needs a few coffee grounds for his science project, and then asks, "Is the coffee really all gone?" I say without hesitation, "No, there may be enough for you."

What I *say* in A contradicts what I say in B. But what I *mean* in A is that *the coffee is close enough to being all gone for current purposes* – making coffee. This is not what the sentence I use means. Yet by saying the coffee is all gone, I convey the less precise thought indicated. By ignoring irrelevant detail, I make my point more effectively. When my conversational purposes change in B, I speak more strictly. Since *what I mean* in the two cases is consistent, there is no sense that I am contradicting myself, nor that I have changed my mind about what is in the jar. Nevertheless, I would never claim that *what I said* was true in both cases. My use of 'all gone' displays the variability observed with 'know' even though 'all gone' does not have a sense sensitive to factors like salience, interests, or stakes.

When we use a sentence loosely, we conversationally implicate that it is a good enough *approximation* to the truth. This is an extremely common mode of speech, learned early in life. Most terms are used loosely some of the time, and some terms are almost always used with some looseness, such as those giving measurements on a continuous scale. If I say, "My son is 5 feet, 8 inches tall," I would be unlikely to mean that precisely. The absolute term *perfectly flat*, which strictly speaking means "having no bumps of any size or curvature of any degree," is another example, used more loosely by road builders than by woodworkers. In other cases, loose use is optional but often preferred, as 'all gone' illustrates.

In both loose use and hyperbole, there is a difference between what speakers mean and say. If speakers later deny what they said, they are not taken to have changed their minds. But the intent in hyperbole is to overstate the truth, whereas the intent in loose use is to approximate it. When astonished passengers describe their cruise ship as 5 miles long, they are not implying that the ship is close enough to being 5 miles long for current purposes. They are just exaggerating for effect. Harry is close enough to knowing given that the question in the lottery case is whether Harry's plan is rational. But Joe wants to emphasize how irrational Harry's plan is. In hyperbole, speakers expect hearers to notice the contrast between what was said and meant, and recognize what they said to be false. In loose use, the focus is on what is meant. The speakers may not know or care whether what they say is literally false. There is no special intonation.

Variation in strictness accounts for the bank and parking cases without the unacceptable linguistic consequences of contextualism. At first Hannah used "I know the bank will be open" loosely to mean that *she is close enough to knowing for their purposes*. She did not care whether strictly speaking she knows. Their purposes in A did not require precision. The difference between knowledge and well-justified true belief was immaterial. After her husband made the difference important, she used 'know' more strictly and meant that she is not close enough to knowing for the purposes of B. What Hannah *said* in B contradicts what she said in A, but what she *meant* in both contexts is consistent. Hannah did not imply that she changed her mind, and Jack was not disagreeing with Dick. The difference in usage is due to a difference in the desired level of approximation to truth and to a difference in the perceived truth value of implicatures referring to different purposes.

MacFarlane rejects loose use, too:

> If I say, "My tank holds 15 gallons," and someone calls me on it – "But the manual says it holds 14.5!" – I will say, "I was speaking loosely: what I meant was that it holds *about* 15 gallons." But if I say, "I know that my car is in my driveway" and someone calls me on it – "How can you rule out the possibility that it has been stolen?" – I will *not* say, "I was speaking loosely."
>
> *(2005: 207; see also 2014: 179)*

Speakers engaging in loose use do not always respond to challenges in the same way, however. If my wife challenged my claim that the coffee is all gone by saying, "Look, there are some grounds left," I would more likely respond either by rolling my eyes (if I thought she were being pedantic or cute) or by saying, "There's not enough to make a cup of coffee" (if I thought she were serious). Similarly, if Hannah's friend Alice challenged her knowledge claim by pointing out the possibility of a schedule change, Hannah might similarly have rolled her eyes. If she took Alice to be serious, she might say, "There's little chance of that," or "Strictly speaking you are right, but that doesn't matter."

As the last answer illustrates, MacFarlane's implication that the speaker would *never* acknowledge speaking loosely after claiming knowledge in such cases is unwarranted. Here is an example from DeRose intended to make a different point:

> [I]n HIGH (while talking to the police), Louise will say that she does "not know" that John was at work that day, even though she has claimed to "know" that very fact while she was in LOW (at the tavern). But now suppose the police officer questioning her has been in radio contact with another police officer who has arrived at the tavern since Louise left it, and challenges her as follows: "Hey, but didn't you say at the tavern that you *did* know that John was at work today?" It isn't obvious how Louise might best answer, but one thing that is fairly clear here is that it would be wrong for her to reply, "I didn't say that". . . . it seems much better (and, in fact, fine) for her to instead say, "I did say that, but I was speaking casually then."
>
> *(2009: 172)*

Loose use and belief variation

Note, too, that if I were asked in the A context of the coffee case, "Is the coffee strictly speaking *all* gone?" I would answer "No" if I knew a little was left. Similarly, If Hannah were asked in the A context, "Do you strictly speaking *know* the bank will be open," we would expect her to answer "No" as long as she remembered the possibility of a schedule change.

Unlike hyperbole and irony, one term is rarely used loosely without a network of terms being used loosely. 'There's no coffee' is as likely to be used loosely in A as 'The coffee is all gone.' And if someone asks, "Is that true?" in A, I would most likely reply, "Yes, it's true." What I would mean is that 'The coffee is all gone' is close enough to being true for my purposes. I would answer, "No, it is not true," in B because the same thing is not close enough to being true for the purposes of that context. A relativized Tarski formula applies: x is close enough to being F for purpose P iff 'x is F' is close enough to being true for P. Similarly, I would likely use 'I believe the coffee is all gone' to mean I am close enough to believing it is all gone. Applied to the bank case, we would expect Hannah to say "Yes" if asked in the A context whether it is true that she knows the bank will be open tomorrow, or whether she believes she knows, and "No" if asked in the B context.

Consider now whether I *asserted* that the coffee is all gone. I *said* that it is. But asserting requires more than saying. This is clear in irony. Someone who utters, "George Bush was a genius" to mean that he was an idiot said but did not assert that Bush was a genius. Asserting p requires meaning as well as saying p. Meaning p requires expressing the belief as well as the proposition p. Consequently assertion is unjustified unless belief is. Saying that Bush was a genius is not unjustified if it was not an assertion. Suppose my wife asks, "Did you assert that the coffee is all gone?" in A. Strictly speaking, that is not something I asserted because I did not (strictly speaking) mean that it is all gone. Still, I would surely answer "Yes" (unless I suspected she had taken an interest in speech acts). The difference between asserting and saying is not important when what I need is coffee. Irony and hyperbole differ from loose use in that the speakers' purposes make the difference between saying and asserting important. Was Hannah strictly speaking asserting as well as saying the bank will be open? It is hard to classify her act as an assertion given that she so readily said the opposite in the B context. She had little commitment to what she said. And even when we think she has insufficient justification, we cannot criticize her saying she knows the bank will be open in A.

IV Strong and weak invariant semantics

As with most philosophically interesting terms, I doubt we can find a definiens synonymous with 'know.' Nevertheless, I believe we can at least roughly characterize knowledge as *completely and nondefectively justified true belief.* Hence 'know' can be used loosely to implicate *close enough to completely and nondefectively justified true belief for contextually indicated purposes.* A belief is 'completely' justified provided it is either self-evident or based on evidence sufficient to establish its truth in any actual context. Such evidence justifies being psychologically certain. 'Defective' justification includes reasoning that has false steps (Gettier 1963) or is undermined by counterevidence the subject does not possess (Lehrer & Paxson 1969). Lottery cases involve justification that is nondefective but incomplete.

The requirement that justification be complete explains why sentence (2) seems absurd no matter what context Mary is in, and why no one knows the results of a lottery based solely on the odds. The requirement predicts, correctly in my view, that Hannah does not literally and strictly speaking know on Friday night that the bank will be open on Saturday. There are too many very real possibilities Hannah's evidence does not rule out: that the bank changed its hours since she last checked, that an unexpected thunderstorm would lead to a massive power outage, and so on. These things happen with some regularity. So what Hannah *says* in A is false, even though what she *means* (that she is close enough to knowing for current purposes) is true. In B, what she says and means are both true. The complete justification requirement does not entail general skepticism, however, without the supplementary thesis that we are never completely justified in believing anything, which I reject (see section V). While Hannah did not have enough evidence in either context to know the bank would be open on Saturday, she was completely justified in believing many things, such as that she was alive.

Pragmatic accounts of the contextual variation in knowledge claims could be combined with a weaker invariant semantics. 'Know' could be used loosely even if it required high rather than complete justification. The account would fail, however, for variants in which the A contexts require high justification while the B contexts require extremely high justification. And such a semantics would erroneously make 'S knows he will lose the lottery' true if all S knows is that there are a million other entrants.

Pragmatic accounts typically assume an invariant semantics so weak that the affirmations in the A contexts of the bank and parking cases are true while the denials in the B contexts are false.[2] This precludes attributing the difference between A and B to the difference between loose and strict usage. One problem for the weak invariantist is to provide a reason for believing that the threshold of justification required for knowledge is low enough to make the knowledge affirmations in the bank and parking cases true rather than high enough to make the knowledge denials false. Since the A and B uses are equally common and ordinary, the choice seems unmotivated. Another problem is to explain why the denials seem appropriate in the B contexts of the bank and parking cases, and why it seems imprudent for the subjects to act on knowledge they falsely (according to the theory) deny having. If Hannah really *knows* that the bank will be open on Saturday, why shouldn't they avoid the lines and come back Saturday? *They know, but should not take a chance* seems absurd.

Brown (2005b) and Williamson (2005: 234) propose that a *psychological bias* leads speakers in B and those evaluating them to overestimate the objective likelihood of error. The B contexts need not involve any overestimate, however. We may stipulate that Hannah knows that the bank schedule changes only once every three years, and has been closed Saturday only once in ten years. If the consequences of not depositing the check on time are sufficiently disastrous, she and we will correctly judge that they should not take a chance on the bank being closed. Our judgments about the lottery case are definitely not due to overestimating the likelihood of losing, given that the subject's evidence is stipulated to be the actual likelihood.

Rysiew (2001: 488–90) claims that 'I know the bank will be open' seems inappropriate in B because it would falsely implicate that Hannah can eliminate salient but epistemically irrelevant possibilities.[3] Unlike hyperbole, irony, and loose use, the implicature Rysiew postulates is not a general form of implicature. The weak invariantist semantics itself provides no reason to expect it. Furthermore, the inappropriateness of the positive knowledge claim would not explain the appropriateness of its allegedly false denial.

DeRose rejects pragmatic explanations of the variability of knowledge claims as unjustified "warranted assertability maneuvers":

> It's simply declared that it's the conditions of warranted assertability rather than of truth, that are varying with context, and the contextualist is then accused of mistaking warranted assertability for truth. To the extent that defenders of invariantism go beyond such bare maneuvers, their hints tend to point in the direct of *special* rules for the assertability of 'knows', such as 'If someone is close enough, for present intents and purposes, to being a knower, don't say that she doesn't know, but rather say that she knows.'
>
> *(2009: 89)*

*On my account (section III), Hannah did not, strictly speaking, *assert* that she knew the bank would be open, and such an assertion would not be *warranted* even in A. It was natural and appropriate for her to say she knows because she thereby meant that she is close enough to knowing, which is true and warranted in the A context. DeRose (2009: 87) requires an acceptable "WAM" to be derivable from general conversational rules by "Gricean reasoning." I have argued (Davis 1998, 2013) that such a requirement is unwarranted and unsatisfiable. DeRose (2009: 118–24) legitimately objects, though, that Rysiew's implicature is *ad hoc* and independent of the proposed semantics for 'know.' The same cannot be said, however, of the loose-use implicature. Loose use is even more general than hyperbole and irony. DeRose (2009: 125ff) criticizes Unger's (1975: 68–9, 83–7) loose-use account as applying only to "absolute" terms, like 'perfectly flat,' which have no application in the real world. But almost any term can be used loosely. When people ask where I was born, for example, I generally say "Detroit," though strictly speaking it was Highland Park, a small city surrounded by Detroit known to few elsewhere.

Invariantists generally fall in two groups: those like Unger who adopt the skeptic's standards of the B context of the epistemology case (section V), maintaining that strictly speaking nothing is known; and those like Rysiew who adopt the standard of the A context of the bank case, maintaining that people can know things despite having weak evidence for what they believe. The use of 'skeptical' and 'non-skeptical' for these forms of invariantism suggests incorrectly that they are jointly exhaustive. The invariantism I have sketched is an alternative to both.

V Belief variation

Loose use is distinct from *careless* use. We use a term carelessly if do not take proper care to verify that it applies (or is close enough to applying). This would occur if, when my son asked whether the coffee was really all gone, I answered "Yes" without looking closely enough to justify that claim. If I subsequently look carefully and say, "I was wrong: the coffee is not all gone," that change in what I say would result from a change in belief about the coffee.

Unenlightened usage reflects lack of education rather than care. A man saying that a particular table is precisely 3 feet long may mean exactly that because he never learned that all measurement has a range of error. If he measured carefully with the best instrument, his usage is unenlightened but not careless or loose. Once he learns about the limits of precision, he will, if candid, admit he was in all likelihood mistaken.

In loose usage, the speaker does not commit himself to what he strictly speaking said. Hence he cannot be criticized for being careless or ignorant just because what he said was not strictly speaking true. It is unfair to interpret Hannah as meaning that she strictly speaking knows the bank will be open. For then she would be subject to criticism that seems unwarranted. Either she failed to realize that schedules sometimes change or failed to check.

Variation in belief is thus another factor accounting for variation in usage. It is pragmatic because no matter what the truth conditions are, whether we use a sentence typically depends on whether we believe they are satisfied.

The change in the bank case does involve *a* change in belief. At first Hannah believes she is close enough to knowing for their purposes; later she does not believe it. There is no indication she ever believed what she strictly speaking said in A. So we cannot say she stopped believing that she knows the bank will be open. When I use 'belief variation' to refer to this additional factor accounting for whether or not we say 'p,' I mean specifically the difference between believing and not believing p.

I believe the epistemology case motivating much contextualist thinking is a paradigm case of belief variation.

Wayne A. Davis

The epistemology case

A. Like most people, David gives little thought to philosophical questions in every-day life. If asked, "Do you know whether you have a hand?" he would answer, "Yes, of course." He may hold up his hand as proof. **B.** In college, he takes epistemology. The professor patiently explains Putnam's skeptical hypothesis, and then asks whether David *knows* he is not a brain in a vat. As expected, David reflects that things would look and feel exactly the same to him if he were; and so, after some resistance, he answers "No." The professor then asks again whether David knows he has a hand, noting that if he knows that, then he must know he is not just a brain in a vat. David hesitates, and then concedes, "No, I guess not." Eventually, he says, "I was wrong in thinking I knew."

It is not plausible that David is using the term 'know' loosely in context A, assuming he is a typical student. In everyday contexts, David could not imagine being any closer to knowing he has a hand. He would regard himself as completely justified in believing such a thing. Nothing could be more certain, he might say. He would thus take his statement to be strictly speaking true. Ordinary careful reflection would not prompt a retraction or correction. In context B, moreover, David would say he *used to believe he knew* such things, but now he does not. David *disagreed* with his professor at first and *agreed* with her later. That is why David said, "I was wrong." The disagreement in the epistemology case makes it very different from the parking case. David similarly differs from Hannah in having *changed his mind*, and is likely to feel the sort of *embarrassment, regret*, and *dismay* that results from realizing we were wrong about something.

Further, unlike Hannah, David is also likely to regard himself in B as *enlightened* – superior intellectually to the way he was. One purpose of a liberal arts education is to get students to grow by making them question deep-seated beliefs and either replace them with better justified beliefs or get clear on why they should retain them. The process in epistemology differs little from what happens to students who have their belief in God shaken in philosophy of religion or their moral beliefs tested in ethics. Contextualism maintains, most implausibly, that when we are discussing skepticism in epistemology, we are not challenging students to either defend or abandon fundamental beliefs. All we are doing is exposing students to new contexts, to which their language responds sensitively.

Before David changed his mind, he probably experienced *mental conflict* and *uncertainty*. He may have felt he was confronting a paradox. If he is like most of us, he was pulled by the evidence of his senses to believe he knows he has a hand, while being pushed by the recognition that his sensory evidence is logically compatible with being a brain in a vat to believe he does not. He recognized that the propositions in (3) cannot all be true, but did not know which to give up. We may have the same difficulty right now.

(3) (a) I know that I have a hand.
    (b) If I know that I have a hand, then I know that I am not a handless brain in a vat.
    (c) I do not know that I am not a handless brain in a vat.

The contextualist attempts to resolve the paradox by claiming that (3)(a) is true in low-standards contexts while (3)(c) is true in high-standards contexts.[4] But when (3) presents David or us with a paradox, no context shifting is going on. We are in one context trying to decide whether (a) or (c) is true. The practical stakes are not changing. We are conflicted because we have to decide which of the contradictory propositions satisfy the standards we are applying.

Loose use and belief variation

Contextualism itself provides no more reason to expect a sense of paradox in the epistemology case than it does in (4).

(4) (a) Today is a weekday.
    (b) If today is a weekday, today is not Saturday or Sunday.
    (c) Today is Sunday.

These is no paradox in (4) because in no context are we pushed to believe both (a) and (c). (a) is true in most contexts and (c) in others.

Appeal to a shift between loose and strict usage is just as inadequate. There is no paradox in (5):

(5) (a) It is 3:00 pm.
    (b) If it is 3:00 pm, then it is not 3:01 pm.
    (c) It is not 3:01 pm.

Even when (5)(c) is strictly speaking true and (5)(a) false, (5)(a) may be close enough to being true and (5)(c) close enough to being false.

Weak invariantism has an equally hard time explaining why the choice between (3)(a) and (3)(c) is difficult. If the meaning of 'knows' is such that the truth of (3)(a) only requires David to have as much evidence as Hannah has in bank case A, then it should be obvious that (3)(a) is true and (3)(c) false, at least after David carefully distinguishes between what (3)(a) says and what it might implicate.

The contextualist account of the B context depends on a controversial philosophical assumption. Contextualism predicts that 'I know' is false in B only when it is assumed that David has to rule out the possibility of being a brain in a vat to know that he has a hand, but cannot. Cohen, Lewis, and DeRose side with the skeptic and assume that David's evidence does not suffice in B to establish and thereby know he has a hand. Non-skeptics like me take 'I know I have a hand' to be true in both A and B.

I submit that we have trouble deciding whether skepticism is correct because it requires answering a foundational question about the evidence required for knowledge. I believe firmly, for example, that the evidence of my senses is not only the best evidence that I have a hand, but all the evidence I need to know this. Yet the fact that I would have all the same evidence if I were a brain in a vat makes me wonder whether I need more to rule that possibility out. It makes me question, that is, whether the evidence of my senses is sufficient to establish that I have a hand. I convince myself that more evidence is unnecessary by recalling that the brain-in-the-vat hypothesis is completely ad hoc; that we have never observed a disembodied brain getting the same sensory stimulation as a real human, and cannot realistically see how anything like it could be arranged; that it is much more complex than the simple hypothesis that I have a hand; and so on. Still, the hypothesis is a logical possibility. I recognize others are unable to convince themselves that more evidence is unnecessary, and as a result have a skeptical moment. I remember having had one myself when first studying epistemology, and still wonder occasionally about the strength of my own reasons. I believe we vacillate over which proposition in the inconsistent epistemic triad to give up because we have no way of *settling* the question as to whether the evidence of our senses completely justifies believing we have a hand.

I thus believe that only a strong invariant semantics does justice to the epistemology case. On a weak invariantist semantics, it should be easy to accept (3)(a) over (3)(c). On a contextualist semantics, it should be easy to accept (3)(a) in some contexts and (3)(c) in others. In fact, the choice is never easy.

Wayne A. Davis

Notes

1 See Davis (2014) and (2016) for an introduction and references.
2 Cf. Rysiew (2001: 490); Bach (2005: 75); Brown (2005a: 280ff, 2005b, 2010); Williamson (2005: 225); Hazlett (2007).
3 See also Rysiew (2005); Brown (2005a, 2006); Hazlett (2007: 682).
4 Cf. DeRose (1992: 917, 1995: section 2, 1999: section 6, 2009: 41ff, 128); Lewis (1996: 434–5); Cohen (1999: 64–7).

References

Annis, D. B. (1978) A contextualist theory of epistemic justification. *American Philosophical Quarterly*, **15**, 213–219.
Bach, K. (2005) The emperor's new 'knows'. In *Contextualism in Philosophy: Knowledge, Meaning, and Truth*, eds. G. Preyer & G. Peter, pp. 51–90. Oxford: Clarendon Press.
Brown, J. (2005a) Adapt or die: The death of invariantism? *The Philosophical Quarterly*, **55**, 263–285.
Brown, J. (2005b) Williamson on luminosity and contextualism. *The Philosophical Quarterly*, **55**, 319–327.
Brown, J. (2006) Contextualism and warranted assertability manoeuvres. *Philosophical Studies*, **130**, 407–435.
Brown, J. (2010) Knowledge and assertion. *Philosophy and Phenomenological Research*, **81**, 549–566.
Cappelen, H. (2008) The creative interpreter: Content relativism and assertion. *Philosophical Perspectives*, **22**, 23–46.
Cohen, S. (1986) Knowledge and context. *Journal of Philosophy*, **83**, 574–583.
Cohen, S. (1999) Contextualism, skepticism, and the structure of reasons. *Philosophical Perspectives*, **13**(Epistemology), 57–89.
Davis, W. A. (1998) *Implicature: Intention, Convention, and Principle in the Failure of Gricean Theory*. Cambridge: Cambridge University Press.
Davis, W. A. (2007) Knowledge claims and context: Loose use. *Philosophical Studies*, **132**(3), 395–438.
Davis, W. A. (2013) Grice's razor and epistemic invariantism. *Journal of Philosophical Research*, **38**, 147–176.
Davis, W. A. (2014) "Implicature", *The Stanford Encyclopedia of Philosophy* (Fall Edition), ed. E. N. Zalta. Palo Alto, CA, URL= <http://plato.stanford.edu/entries/implicature>
Davis, W. A. (2015) Knowledge claims and context: Belief. *Philosophical Studies*, **172**, 399–432.
Davis, W. A. (2016) Implicature. *Oxford Handbooks Online*. ed. S. Goldberg. Oxford: Oxford University Press.
DeRose, K. (1992) Contextualism and knowledge attributions. *Philosophy and Phenomenological Research*, **52**, 913–929.
DeRose, K. (1995) Solving the skeptical problem. *Philosophical Review*, **104**, 1–52.
DeRose, K. (1999) Contextualism: An explanation and defense. In *The Blackwell Guide to Epistemology*, eds. J. Greco & E. Sosa, pp. 187–205. Oxford: Blackwell.
DeRose, K. (2009) *The Case for Contextualism: Knowledge, Skepticism, and Context, Vol. 1*. Oxford: Oxford University Press.
Gettier, E. L. (1963) Is justified true belief knowledge? *Analysis*, **23**, 121–123.
Grice, H. P. (1989) *Studies in the Way of Words*. Cambridge, MA: Harvard University Press.
Hawthorne, J. (2004) *Knowledge and Lotteries*. Oxford: Clarendon Press.
Hazlett, A. (2007) Grice's razor. *Metaphilosophy*, **38**, 669–690.
Lehrer, K., and T. D. Paxson (1969) Knowledge: Undefeated justified true belief. *Journal of Philosophy*, **66**, 225–237.
Lewis, D. (1996) Elusive knowledge. *Australasian Journal of Philosophy*, **74**, 549–567.
MacFarlane, J. (2005) The assessment sensitivity of knowledge attributions. In *Oxford Studies in Epistemology*, Vol. 1. eds. T. Gendler & J. Hawthorne, pp. 197–233. Oxford: Clarendon Press.
MacFarlane, J. (2014) *Assessment Sensitivity: Relative Truth and Its Applications*. Oxford: Oxford University Press.
Rysiew, P. (2001) The context-sensitivity of knowledge attributions. *Noûs*, **35**, 477–514.

Rysiew, P. (2005) Contesting contextualism. *Grazer-Philosophische Studien*, **69**, 51–69.

Schaffer, J. (2004). Skepticism, contextualism, and discrimination. *Philosophy and Phenomenological Research*, **69**, 138–155.

Stanley, J. (2005) *Knowledge and Practical Interests.* Oxford: Oxford University Press.

Unger, P. (1975) *Ignorance: A Case for Scepticism.* Oxford: Clarendon Press.

Williamson, T. (2005) Contextualism, subject-sensitive invariantism, and knowledge of knowledge. *Philosophical Quarterly*, **55**, 213–235.

18

SEMANTIC MINIMALISM AND SPEECH ACT PLURALISM APPLIED TO 'KNOWS'

Herman Cappelen

This chapter is an introduction to how the combination of two views – semantic minimalism and speech act pluralism ('SM+SAP', for short) – can be used to explain some aspects of our practice of making knowledge attributions. SM+SAP wasn't developed to account for issues in epistemology in particular. It was proposed as a solution to a very general linguistic phenomenon – a phenomenon that also happens to be exhibited by sentences containing 'knows'. The chapter is structured as follows:

- I first outline the general linguistic phenomenon/puzzle: how to resolve a tension between inter-contextual stability and variability, and I show how that puzzle arises with respect to sentences containing 'knows'.
- The next section outlines speech act pluralism and the arguments for it.
- I then outline semantic minimalism and the arguments for it.
- I show how SM+SAP explains the data/puzzle we started with.
- The final section outlines how SM+SAP has been used to defend skepticism.

First, a brief overview of where these topics are first discussed and the subsequent literature. There is now an extensive literature on semantic minimalism, speech act pluralism and their combination. Most of the discussion of those views is general, i.e., is not specifically about their application to epistemically relevant terminology. In what follows I focus on the version presented in Cappelen and Lepore (2004). Extensive discussion of the proposal in that book can be found in, e.g., Preyer (2007). A version of semantic minimalism is presented by Borg (2004, 2012). Relativism, e.g., the version advocated by John MacFarlane (2014), is also a version of minimalism, but that won't be discussed here.[1] A version of speech act pluralism is first advocated by Salmon (1991) and Cappelen and Lepore (1997), and later taken up by Soames (2002). While semantic minimalism is often discussed in connection with efforts to understand the semantic features of 'knows', speech act pluralism is less often appealed to, but one such effort is found in Cappelen (2005).

The general motivation: the tension between stability and variability

SM+SAP is a theory that was introduced in order to account for the following puzzling data pattern:

Minimalism and speech act pluralism

- **Variability:** *On the one hand*, contexts shape what we say to each other by uttering sentences. The context-sensitivity of what is said is wide-ranging along two dimensions: many words are context-sensitive and the range of potential meanings is wide. Moreover, what is said by an utterance is sensitive to features of context that are non-transparent to us: speakers and audiences have no easy cognitive access to the contextual mechanisms that shape what we say.

- **Stability:** *On the other hand*, what we say in uttering a sentence in a given context can easily be grasped and said again in a different context. We can tell others what someone told us, repeat a point we've made before, discuss the same question over and over again and remember what we have been told. In all these cases we say (or think) the same thing in different contexts. If someone says to me, 'There are many naked mole rats in Sweden and John knows that their behavior is very interesting', then I can easily tell this to other people. I can, for example, say to you, my reader:

> There are many naked mole rats in Sweden and John knows that their behavior is very interesting.

I'm confident that what I just told you, reader, is the same as what I was told, no matter what context you are in. This is so despite the fact that 'There are many naked mole rats in Sweden and John knows that their behavior is very interesting' is a paradigm of one of those sentences that variability applies to.

One of the central challenges for those trying to understand the nature of linguistic communication is to figure out how this tension is resolved. *If what we say is fixed in all kinds of ways by our speech contexts, how can what we say be so easily transferred across contexts?*

Below I say more about both stability and variability, but for ease of exposition, I will here sketch the solution provided by SM+SAP:

> **Preview of how SM+SAP resolves the tension between stability and variability:** According to *speech act pluralism*, many propositions are said by any one utterance. According to *semantic minimalism* there is one stable semantic content among the many propositions expressed: this minimal content is what is said in *all* contexts of utterance. The solution assumes a sharp distinction between semantic content, on the one hand, and what is said, on the other. With that distinction in hand, there is not even the appearance of a tension left: we can have variability in the plurality of propositions expressed/said (i.e. some of the propositions said can change between contexts) at the same time as we have stability (one content, the semantic content, is stable across contexts).

I now first say a bit more about the variability data and the stability data and then show how knowledge attributions instantiate the tension between stability and variability.

The variability data[2]

Start by considering some facts about sentences containing indexicals and demonstratives, i.e. expressions such as 'I', 'you', 'now', 'that', and 'here'. Sentences containing such words can exhibit three kinds of variability between contexts:

(i) *Variability in reference*: what is referred to by, e.g., 'you' varies between contexts of utterance.
(ii) *Variability in what is said*: as a result, what is said by such utterances varies. An utterance of 'I am happy' by John says something about John, but when Nora utters it she says something about

Nora. This is, in part, because of the change in reference. It is because John's utterance of 'I' refers to John and Nora's utterance of 'I' refers to Nora that they end up saying different things.

(iii) *Variability in truth value*: John's utterance of 'I am happy' can be true while Nora's utterance of the same sentence is false.

This kind of variability isn't restricted to obvious cases such as indexicals and demonstratives. The same data pattern can be found throughout language. For one illustration consider so-called *gradable adjectives*. In many settings, it would be true to say 'Josh is fast' because he runs marathons in under three and a half hours. However, when salient comparison is the speed of rockets, particles in accelerators, Olympic runners or leopards, it wouldn't be true to say 'Josh is fast' because, compared to any of those, he's not fast. It looks like, roughly, an occurrence of 'fast' is understood, in context, as 'fast for a . . .', where the dots are filled in by something like a comparison class (i.e., a class of objects we compare Josh to). Compared to the class of leopards Josh is not fast, but compared to the class of professional philosophers he's very fast. This comparison class is fixed in context.[3] What we find is variability along the three dimensions mentioned above: (i) variability in extension (the set of things that's in the extension of 'fast' varies between context utterance); (ii) a resulting variability in what is said (in one context the sentence is used to say that Josh is fast for a middle-aged philosophy professor and in another that he is fast compared to a leopard); and finally (iii) a variability in truth value (it's true that Josh is fast compared to middle-aged philosophy professors and false that he's fast compared to a leopard).

According to many epistemologists, 'knows' is one of the expressions that exhibits this pattern of variability. Here is a classic illustration from a paper by S. Cohen:

> Mary and John are at the L.A. airport contemplating taking a certain flight to New York. They want to know whether the flight has a layover in Chicago. They overhear someone ask a passenger Smith if he knows whether the flight stops in Chicago. Smith looks at the flight itinerary he got from the travel agent and responds, 'Yes I know – it does stop in Chicago.' It turns out that Mary and John have a very important business contact to make at the Chicago airport. Mary says, 'How reliable is that itinerary? It could contain a misprint. They could have changed the schedule at the last minute.' Mary and John agree that Smith doesn't really know that the plane will stop in Chicago. They decide to check with the airline agent. . . . [N]either standard is simply correct or simply incorrect. Rather, context determines which standard is correct. Since the standards for knowledge ascriptions can vary across context, each claim, Smith's as well as Mary and John's, can be correct in the context in which it was made. When Smith says 'I know . . . ,' what he says is true given the weaker standard operating in that context. When Mary and John say 'Smith does not know . . . ,' what they say is true given the stricter standard operating in their context. *And there is no context independent correct standard.*
>
> (1999: 58–9, emphasis in original)

The pattern is the same as in the previous cases. There is variability in the extension of 'knows' between contexts: the set of person/proposition pairs such that the person knows that proposition varies between contexts of utterance. As a result, what is said by an utterance of 'A knows that p' differs between contexts of utterance. Finally, truth values can vary: In one context of speech, it is true to say Smith knows (at t) that the flight stops in Chicago, while in another (John and Mary's context), that very same sentence is not true. There's disagreement about just what the source of the variability is. According to Cohen, the source is that what he calls 'standards of knowledge' vary between contexts – standards can go up and down, and evidence that suffices for knowing in one context will not suffice

Minimalism and speech act pluralism

in another. For more on the various kinds of variability involved in contextualist views, see, e.g., Cohen (1986, 1987), DeRose (1992, 1995), Lewis (1996), and Schaffer (2004, 2005).

The stability data

The previous section presented some evidence that what is said by sentences, and hence their truth values, can vary between contexts of utterance. The same sentence can be true when uttered in one context, and false when uttered in another. The goal of this section is to introduce a seemingly essential feature of language that, at least at first glance, appears to be in tension with the data in the previous section. It seems essential to language that we have inter-contextual stability in what we say. It is hard to see how language can perform the functions it in fact performs unless there is a fundamental form of inter-contextual stability in what is said by utterances of sentences (i.e. unless what is said does *not* vary between contexts). This section provides a brief introduction to the stability data. The goal of the next section is to show how SM+SAP can reconcile stability with variability.

There are two kinds of data that appear to show that what our sentences say does not vary between contexts:

(i)   Gathering, transmitting and using information requires contextual stability.
(ii) The way we say what other people have said requires stability across contexts.

Stability 1: information storage. Imagine a case where someone utters a sentence and thereby tells you something. Suppose this is done by uttering the sentence, 'Samantha, who is very smart, loves her friend Alex'. Call the context of this utterance *the Original Context.* Suppose what you've been told is somewhat important to you so you want to *remember* it. You want to store that information and be able to recall it later. This information can play a role in your reasoning about what to *do* later. For example, because she's very smart, you might ask Samantha for help with a project you're working on. Since you are a social creature, you might also want to *tell* others what you have been told. The central point in the argument is that widespread context-sensitivity makes these roles for what is said difficult, if not impossible to fulfill. Here is why: suppose what is said by uttering a sentence in a context is massively influenced by the specific features of that context. There are many contexts and so a large number of different things the sentence could say. It now seems challenging both to figure out how to store that information in memory and to figure out how to rearticulate it in new contexts. Suppose what you do is store *the sentence* in memory. Then remembering what it said would require keeping track of all the relevant contextual features that determined its content. We don't do that (even experts don't know what the relevant features are, and it would be a massive cognitive burden to keep it all in mind). Alternatively, we could try to remember a context *in*sensitive sentence that contains the same information. However, we don't know how to do that, and there might be no way to do that (or so the proponents of SM+SAP argue, see Carston 2002).

Stability 2: saying what others said. In slogan form, *the easiness of homophonic speech reports is direct evidence of inter-contextual content stability.* Here is what that means: imagine Jill uttering the sentence, 'In St Andrews, you can see the impressive ruins of a huge cathedral which took about 150 years to complete and was consecrated on July 5, 1318' while standing on Market Street at 1pm on July 1, 2015. Call that the Original Context. If you, the reader of this entry, ask yourself how you would report what Jill said, one answer you might come up with is the following:

> *The Report:* Jill said that in St Andrews you can see the impressive ruins of a huge cathedral which took about 150 years to complete and was consecrated on July 5, 1318.

You can use The Report to say what Jill said, *no matter what context you are in*. Even when you vary all aspects of the conversational setting (time, place, audience, topic, etc.) you can use The Report to say what Jill said. This is important because in The Report the words after 'Jill said that' are *exactly the same words as Jill used in the Original Context*. What this shows is that we can use the same words as she used to say the same thing that she said even as all the relevant aspects of the context vary. That makes it look as if those words say the same in every context (because in every context they can be used to say what she said). This is evidence that those words don't vary in meaning between contexts. If they did, they couldn't be used to say the same in each context – there would be contextual variability in what is said. In sum, what Cappelen and Hawthorne (2009) call 'the easiness of homophonic speech reports' can be used as evidence against claims of context-sensitivity. (For an introduction to this line of argument, see Cappelen and Dever 2016, Cappelen and Lepore 2005, Hawthorne 2006, and Williamson 2005).

Stability 1 and 2 applied to 'knows'. 'Knows' exhibits both kinds of stability. When we hear knowledge attributions, we need to store them in memory and to rearticulate them in new contexts. So inter-contextual storing and inter-contextual re-articulation is crucial. This seems to assume an important level of content stability. This is exhibited in the ease of homophonic inter-contextual speech reports: If I hear Nora say, 'Naomi knows flight KL407 stops in Chicago', I can use that very sentence as the complement of an indirect report and say something true about what was said by uttering, 'Nora said that Naomi knows that flight KL407 stops in Chicago'. I can do that in any (or at least a very broad range of) context(s). But if 'Naomi knows flight KL407 stops in Chicago' is context-sensitive, how then can it be used to say the same thing in every context, or at least a very broad range of contexts?

Strengthening of stability 2: indexicals and demonstratives don't exhibit that kind of stability. The case against widespread context-sensitivity can be strengthened as follows: for indexicals and demonstratives, homophonic saying-reports of the kind considered above are often not possible. Suppose Jill utters, 'I am happy', or 'I am here now', or 'I had fish for dinner yesterday'. Suppose you are tasked with saying what Jill said. How would you do it? Note that you cannot do it the simple way by just using her words to say what she said. If you tried any of the following homophonic reports, you would end up misreporting her:

- Jill said that I am happy.
- Jill said that I am here now.
- Jill said that I had fish for dinner yesterday.

Jill didn't talk about you, your time or your place. To report correctly, you have to make adjustments. You would have to take away the original indexical expressions ('I', 'here', 'now', 'yesterday') and replace them with ones that in your context denote what her words denoted in her context. You could try 'Jill said that Jill was happy' or 'Jill said that Jill was happy there and then' or 'Jill said that Jill had fish for dinner on Thursday' (assuming the original speech took place on Friday). The argument continues, and *this is exactly as expected if a word is context-sensitive. Context-sensitivity implies that you have to adjust and coordinate meanings between contexts.* Genuinely context-sensitive expressions (such as 'I', 'here', 'now' and 'yesterday') typically block homophonic disquotational reports. So, this argument concludes, expressions that make such reports easy, such as 'knows', are not genuinely context-sensitive. (For more on this argument, see Cappelen and Lepore 2004.)

How SM+SAP resolves the tension between stability and variability

So far we have seen an apparent tension (or at least an explanatory challenge) posed by stability and variability. Here is one way to structure responses to this tension:

Minimalism and speech act pluralism

(a) Deny variability (e.g., by questioning the judgments about contextual variability).
(b) Deny stability (e.g., by saying we typically recall and transmit *similar* information, not the same information).
(c) Preserve both stability and variability.

SM+SAP is a version of (c), and in what follows I don't outline the various version of (a) and (b). The goal of this entry is an exposition of SM+SAP, not of the whole field of possible solutions. For an overview of all solutions, see Cappelen and Dever (2016: ch. 3).

The basic idea behind SM+SAP is to deny a tacit but fundamental assumption that generates the appearance of a puzzle. The puzzle, as I articulated it, assumes *that there is just one thing which is said by the utterance of a sentence*. If we make that assumption, then it looks mysterious how we can have both variability and stability in what was said. Take a sentence like 'There are many naked mole rats in Sweden and their behavior is very interesting'. According to variability, that sentence can be used to say many different things in different contexts. According to stability, what it says is stable across contexts. Now, suppose instead *that each time one utters the sentence, it says many different things*. If so, then one of those can be stable across contexts while others may vary.

Let's call the view that an utterance of a sentence says only one thing (that there is only one what is said per utterance per context, so to speak) *what-is-said-monism* (*monism* for short). One salient option when faced with the problem outlined at the beginning of this chapter is to give up monism. The alternative is what I call *speech act pluralism* (*pluralism* for short). Pluralism is the view that in each context many things are said by an utterance of a sentence. If pluralism is true, we can easily reconcile the stability and variability data: one what is said is stable and then there is variability in the rest of what is said.

Structurally, the solution is clear enough, but it raises at least two tricky questions:

(i) Do we have any positive reason to think pluralism is true or is it simply an ad hoc move to solve the puzzle?
(ii) What is the stable element in all these cases?

First some brief remarks in reply to the first question. In the next section I turn to the second question.

Speech act pluralism

The primary evidence for pluralism is independent of the tension outlined above. Consider the following case: Jones is under suspicion of the murder of Smith, and is being interrogated by the police. Eventually Jones says, 'I'm the one who killed Smith'. The police can tell the press either of the following:

> 'Jones said that he is the murderer'.
> 'Jones said that he is guilty'.
> 'Jones said that he committed the heinous crime'.

These are all correct reports of what Jones said. Moreover, if you know that Smith is a Swede, and if that is important and relevant in your context, you can report Jones as having said that he killed a Swede. In short, the situation is this: Jones uttered the sentence, 'I'm the one who killed Smith', and we have a range of true speech reports. It follows that Smith said many things (he said that he is the murderer, that he is guilty, that he committed the heinous crime, that he killed the Swede, etc.).

There is nothing special about this particular case. In general, when someone utters a sentence there are many different true ways to say what he or she said. And so the point applies very generally: by uttering one sentence, a speaker says a plurality of things, not just one thing. (For more on speech act pluralism see Cappelen and Lepore 1997, 2004, 2005; Salmon 1991; and Soames 2002.)

The minimal what is said

I turn now to the second challenge for minimalistic pluralism: what is the stable component of what is said? When minimalists say that one thing said is 'minimal', they mean to indicate *that context plays a minimal role in shaping it*. This is as expected if we want a what-is-said that is shared across contexts (if it was influenced by context, it would vary between contexts and so not have cross-contextual stability).

Consider utterances of 'Naomi is smart' in different contexts. What is said by such utterances will depend on the contextually supplied comparison class. In some contexts, it can be used to say she is smart for a kid in kindergarten. In others, it can be used to say that she is smart compared to rocket scientists. This is just a way of repeating the variability data with respect to 'smart'. Speech act pluralism allows the proponent of SM+SAP to grant this. We are now looking for what these utterances have in common and why it is we can, for example, share that content across contexts in homophonic speech reports. There are many minimalistic answers to this question (for an overview, see Cappelen and Dever 2016, ch. 3). In what follows, I focus on the proposal in Cappelen and Lepore (2004). According to minimalists such as Cappelen and Lepore, the minimal what-is-said is this: *that Naomi is smart*. That is what is invariant between contexts. If we apply this line of thought to sentences containing 'knows', then the answer to the question would be analogous: the minimal content of 'a knows that p' is *that a knows that p*. There is nothing more to say. The obvious concern here is that this isn't very helpful. It is uninformative. Suppose you wonder: What exactly do these minimal what-is-said's tell us about the world? What is it to be known in the context-insensitive sense? A reply of the form "'a knows that p' is true just in case a knows that p" is unlikely to remove your puzzlement.

Cappelen and Lepore (2004, 2005) try to rebut this objection. Their central response goes as follows: if pressed on, for example, the question what it is to be know, *simpliciter*, the minimalist should explain why it is not her job to answer that question. In general, it is not the job of the theorist of meaning to tell us anything substantive about the conditions under which what we say is true. Consider Jill's utterance of 'Water is liquid'. Suppose a meaning theorist concludes that in uttering that sentence Jill says *that water is liquid*. Now consider the objection: that is insufficient as an account of what was expressed. To tell us what Jill said, you also have to tell us what it is to be liquid and what it is to be water. Surely, Cappelen and Lepore say, this is an unfair demand. It is unfair to demand from the meaning theorist that she provide answers to questions about what liquids are. That's a question for the physicist and the chemist. If we demanded such answers, then the meaning theorist would need a theory of the entire universe to present her theory of meaning and communication. That is clearly an unreasonable expectation. The same point applies to sentences containing 'knows': it's not that it's no more within the remit of a theory meaning to tell us what knowledge is than it is to tell us what it is to be a liquid.

That completes the brief overview of (a) the motivation for SM+SAP, (b) the motivation for speech act pluralism, (c) Cappelen and Lepore's version of semantic minimalism and (d) the relevance of these issues for efforts to understand how the English verb 'knows' functions.

SM+SAP in defense of skepticism

In the final part of this chapter I briefly outline how Cappelen (2005) uses SM+SAP to defend a version of skepticism. One way to think of this proposal: it takes SM+SAP and adds an assumption about the nature of knowledge. Recall that Cappelen and Lepore say that the semanticist has no more of an obligation to specify the nature of knowledge than an obligation to specify the nature of water or liquid. That said, it could still be that the semantics make it easier to defend a specific account of knowledge. In this case, the claim is that SM+SAP makes it easier to defend a version of skepticism.

Skepticism is the view that it's extremely hard to know something. Most or perhaps all of our positive knowledge ascriptions are false. Cappelen (2005) construes this as the claim that the propositions *semantically expressed* by all or almost all utterances of sentences of the form 'A knows that p' are false. The arguments for this are old and familiar; they typically involve evil demons, brains in vats, etc. The focus in what follows will not be on these familiar arguments. It will focus instead on how SM+SAP helps defend skeptics against a familiar objection and provide some additional support for the view.

SM+SAP as a reply to an influential objection to skepticism. Here is an influential objection to skepticism: skepticism is inconsistent with fundamental aspects of our linguistic behavior and our pre-theoretic judgments (what some people call 'intuitions'). Pre-theoretically, the skeptic seems to have a hard time explaining the context-sensitivity of what speakers say when they utter sentences of the form 'a knows that p'. According to DeRose:

> In some contexts, 'S knows that P' requires that S have a true belief that P and also be in a very strong epistemic position with respect to P, while in other contexts, the same sentence may require for its truth, in addition to S's having a true belief that P, only that S meet some lower epistemic standards.
>
> *(2002: 182)*

What makes for this difference? In the examples favored by the contextualist it is various practical factors (such as what is practically at stake) that vary between contexts of utterance. In other words, this sensitivity to contextual standards is not just brought out when thinking about skeptical possibilities – it is not just when speakers are in philosophical contexts that their standards shift. As DeRose points out:

> To make the relevant intuitions as strong as possible, the contextualist will choose a "high standards" case that is not as ethereal as a typical philosophical discussion of radical skepticism . . . it makes the relevant intuitions more stable if the introduction of the more moderate skeptical hypothesis and the resulting raise in epistemic standards are tied to a very practical concern, and thus seem reasonable given the situation.
>
> *(2002: 191)*

The problem for the skeptic is supposed to be this: if the semantic content of 'knows' invokes a super-high standard, and this content is invariant between contexts of utterance, the semantics will provide no explanation of the variability pointed about by DeRose and, it is assumed, these are the kinds of pre-theoretic judgments that a semantic theory for English should account for.

The Reply. According to Cappelen (2005), SM+SAP can explain this kind of data in a skeptic-friendly way. The assumption has been that the skeptic has to say that these pre-theoretic judgments are, somehow, mistaken, i.e. has to defend some kind of large-scale error theory about speakers' pre-theoretic judgments. A skeptic who endorses SM+SAP, can say the following:

(a) The semantic content of 'a knows that p' is hardly ever true, because the semantic value of 'knows' has few if any person/proposition pairs in its extension. This is revealed by familiar skeptical arguments. They show that knowledge is very difficult, if not impossible, to obtain.
(b) We assert many different propositions when we utter sentences of the form 'a knows that p'. We do not just assert the proposition semantically expressed.[4]
(c) Some of the propositions asserted (said, claimed, etc.) by an utterance of a positive knowledge attribution can be true even though the proposition semantically expressed is false.
(d) The totality of asserted propositions can vary from one context of utterance to another.

This is a brief sketch of how a skeptic who endorses SM+SAP can try to account for (at least some of) the variability appealed to by contextualists. For more details of this strategy, see Cappelen (2005) – where it is explained how this can be made compatible with e.g., the knowledge norm of assertion.

It is important to note that this argumentative strategy is available to *any* invariantist about 'knows' (i.e., to anyone who thinks 'knows' has a stable semantic content – no matter what she takes that content to be). It provides a recipe for how a stable semantic content for 'knows' can be made compatible with variability in what was said by utterances of 'a knows that p'. Why apply the strategy specifically as a defense of skepticism construed as the view that the semantic content of 'knows' is such that knowledge is very hard if not impossible to obtain? The reason that moves Cappelen (2005) is the ease with which skeptical considerations can get a grip in *any* context. Semantic content on this view is *always* among the expressed propositions. The ease with which skeptical arguments get a grip in *any* context is what makes it a good candidate being the semantic content, or so argues Cappelen (2005).

Notes

1 See chs. 20–23 of this volume.
2 The material that follows is a summary of material that can be found in the first three chapters of Cappelen and Dever (2016) and that again is a summary of material that can be found in Cappelen and Lepore (2005) and Cappelen and Hawthorne (2009).
3 Alternatively, think of it like this: there's a scale of speed and the cutoff for what counts as fast varies between contexts.
4 Here is one way to think about the connection between the semantic content, the proposition expressed and what is said on this kind of view: the semantic content is a proposition that is expressed by all utterances of 'Ka', and it is also always said by an utterance of 'Ka'. It is the stable part of the plurality of what is said. Utterances of 'Ka' will also express many other propositions, and all of these (or at least some of them) are also said. For more on how to think about the connection between semantic content, sayings and speech act pluralism, see Cappelen and Lepore (2005).

References

Borg, Emma (2004). *Minimal Semantics*. Oxford: Oxford University Press.
Borg, Emma (2012). *Pursuing Meaning*. Oxford: Oxford University Press.
Cappelen, Herman (2005). Pluralistic skepticism: Advertisement for speech act pluralism. *Philosophical Perspectives* 19 (1): 15–39.
Cappelen, Herman & Dever, Josh (2016). *Context and Communication*. Oxford: Oxford University Press.
Cappelen, Herman & Hawthorne, John (2009). *Relativism and Monadic Truth*. Oxford: Oxford University Press

Cappelen, Herman & Lepore, Ernie (1997). On an alleged connection between indirect speech and the theory of meaning. *Mind and Language* 12 (3&4): 278–296.

Cappelen, Herman & Lepore, Ernest (2004). *Insensitive Semantics: A Defense of Semantic Minimalism and Speech Act Pluralism*. Malden, MA: Blackwell.

Cappelen, Herman & Lepore, Ernie (2005). A tall tale: In defense of semantic minimalism and speech act pluralism. In Gerhard Preyer & Georg Peter (eds.), *Contextualism in Philosophy: Knowledge, Meaning, and Truth*. Oxford: Oxford University Press, 197–220.

Carston, Robyn (2002). *Thoughts and Utterances*. Malden, MA: Blackwell.

Cohen, Stewart (1986). Knowledge and context. *The Journal of Philosophy* 83: 574–583.

Cohen, Stewart (1987). Knowledge, context, and social standards. *Synthese* 73: 3–26.

Cohen, Stewart (1999). Contextualism, skepticism, and the structure of reasons. *Philosophical Perspectives* 13 (s13): 57–89.

DeRose, Keith (1992). Contextualism and knowledge attributions. *Philosophy and Phenomenological Research* 52 (4): 913–929.

DeRose, Keith (1995). Solving the skeptical problem. *Philosophical Review* 104 (1): 1–52.

DeRose, Keith (2002). Assertion, knowledge and context. *Philosophical Review* 111 (2): 167–203.

Hawthorne, John (2006). Testing for context-dependence. *Philosophy and Phenomenological Research* 73 (2): 443–450.

Lewis, David (1996). Elusive knowledge. *Australasian Journal of Philosophy* 74 (4): 549–567.

MacFarlane, John (2014). *Assessment Sensitivity: Relative Truth and Its Applications*. Oxford: Oxford University Press.

Preyer, Gerhard & Peter, Georg (eds.) (2007). *Context-Sensitivity and Semantic Minimalism: New Essays on Semantics and Pragmatics*. Oxford: Oxford University Press.

Salmon, Nathan (1991). The pragmatic fallacy. *Philosophical Studies* 63 (1): 83–97.

Schaffer, Jonathan (2004). From contextualism to contrastivism. *Philosophical Studies* 119 (1–2): 73–103.

Schaffer, Jonathan (2005). What shifts?: Thresholds, standards, or alternatives? In Gerhard Preyer & Georg Peter (eds.), *Contextualism in Philosophy: Knowledge, Meaning, and Truth*. Oxford: Oxford University Press, 115–130.

Soames, Scott (2002). *Beyond Rigidity: The Unfinished Semantic Agenda of Naming and Necessity*. Oxford: Oxford University Press.

Williamson, Timothy (2005). Knowledge, context, and the agent's point of view. In Gerhard Preyer & Georg Peter (eds.), *Contextualism in Philosophy: Knowledge, Meaning, and Truth*. Oxford: Oxford University Press, 91–114.

19

INTEREST-RELATIVE INVARIANTISM

Brian Weatherson

1 Introduction

One of the initial motivations for epistemological contextualism was that the appropriateness of self-ascriptions of knowledge seemed to depend, in some circumstances, on factors that were traditionally thought to be epistemologically irrelevant. So whether our hero S was prepared to say, "I know that p", would depend not just on how strong S's evidence for p was, or how strongly she believed it, but on factors such as how much it mattered whether p was true, or what alternatives to p were salient in her thought or talk.

It was immediately noted that this data point, even if accepted, is consistent with a number of theories of the truth of knowledge ascriptions. It might be that things like stakes and salient alternatives affect the assertability conditions of knowledge ascriptions, but not their truth conditions (Rysiew 2016 and this volume, Chapter 16). But let's assume that we've convinced ourselves that this isn't right, and that whether S can truly (and not just appropriately) say, "I know that p", depends on things like the stakes or salient alternatives.

It still doesn't follow that contextualism is true. It might be that in all contexts, whether an utterance of "S knows that p" is true depends on the stakes for S, or on the salient alternatives for S. That would be true, the idea is, whether S is talking about herself, or someone else is talking about her. The stakes, or salient alternatives, would affect the truth conditions of S's utterance not because she is the one doing the talking, but the one being talked about. The practical and theoretical situation of the ascribee of the knowledge ascription may be relevant, even if the practical and theoretical situation of the ascribor need not be.

This line of thought leads to the idea that knowledge itself is interest-relative. Whether an utterance here and now of "S knows that p" is true, i.e., whether S knows that p – depends on how much it matters to S that p is true or on which alternatives are salient to S. The thesis that knowledge is interest-relative is consistent with contextualism. It could be that whether a knowledge ascription is true depends on the interests of both the ascriber and the ascribee. In this chapter, however, I'm going to largely focus on the view that knowledge is interest-relative, but contextualism is false. On this view, the interests of the ascribee do matter to the truth of a knowledge ascription, but the interests of the ascribee do not.

This view is naturally called *interest-relative invariantism*, since it makes knowledge interest-relative, but it is a form of anti-contextualism, i.e., invariantism. The view is sometimes called *subject-sensitive*

240

Interest-relative invariantism

invariantism, since it makes knowledge relevant to the stakes and salient alternatives to the subject. But this is a bad name; of course whether a knowledge ascription is true is sensitive to whom the subject of the ascription is. I know what I had for breakfast and you (probably) don't. What is distinctive is which features of the subject's situation that interest-relative invariantism says are relevant, and the name interest-relative invariantism makes it clear that it is the subject's interests. There is one potential downside to this name; it suggests that the practical interests of the subject are relevant to what they know. I intend to use the predicate 'interest-relative' to pick out a class of theories, including the theory floated by John Hawthorne (2004), where the options that are salient to the subject make a difference to what the subject knows. If forced to defend the name, I'd argue that salience is relevant to the theoretical interests of the subject, if not necessarily to their practical interests. But the name is still potentially misleading; my main reason for using it is that 'subject-sensitive' is even more misleading. (I'll shorten 'interest-relative invariantism' to IRI in what follows. I'll return to the question of practical and theoretical interests in section 4.)

There are a number of ways to motivate and precisify IRI. I'll spend most of this chapter going over the choice points, starting with the points where I think there is a clearly preferably option, and ending with the choices where I think it's unclear which way to go. Then I'll discuss some general objections to IRI, and say how they might be answered.

2 Motivations

There are two primary motivations for IRI. One comes from intuitions about cases, the other from a pair of principles. It turns out the two are connected, but it helps to start seeing them separately.

Jason Stanley (2005) starts with some versions of the 'bank cases' due originally to Keith DeRose (1992). These turn on idiosyncratic, archaic details of the US payments system, and I find it hard to have clear intuitions about them. A cleaner pair of examples is provided by Ángel Pinillos (2012); here are slightly modified versions of his examples.

> Ankita and Bojan each have an essay due. They have, surprisingly, written word for word identical papers, and are now checking the paper for typos. The papers have no typos, and each student has checked their paper twice, with the same dictionary, and not found any typos. They are, in general, equally good at finding typos, and have true beliefs about their proficiency at typo-spotting.
>
> The only difference between them concerns the consequence of a typo remaining. If the paper is a borderline A/A- paper, a typo might mean Ankita gets an A- rather than an A. But the grade doesn't matter to her; she's already been accepted into a good graduate program next year so long as she gets above a C. But Bojan's instructor is a stickler for spelling. Any typo and he gets a C on the paper. And he has a very lucrative scholarship that he loses if he doesn't get at least a B on this paper. (Compare the Typo-Low and Typo-High examples in Pinillos.)
>
> *(199)*

The intuition that helps IRI is that Ankita knows she has no typos in her paper, and should turn it in, while Bojan does not know this, and should do a third (and perhaps fourth or fifth) check. Contextualists have a hard time explaining this; in this very context I can say, "Ankita knows her paper has no typos, but Bojan does not know his paper has no typos." If the intuition is right, it seems to support interest-relativity, since the difference in the practical situation between Ankita and Bojan seems best placed to explain their epistemic difference.

Alternatively, if there is a single context within which one can truly say, "Ankita knows her paper has no typos," and "Bojan does not know his paper has no typos," that's again something an interest-invariant contextualism can't explain. Either way, we have an argument from cases for a form of interest-relativity.

The argument from principles takes off from the idea that knowledge plays an important role in good deliberation, and that knowledge does not require maximal confidence. It is easiest to introduce with an example, though note that we aren't going to rely on epistemic intuitions about the example. Chika looked at the baseball scores last night before going to bed and saw that the Red Sox won. She remembers this when she wakes up, though she knows that she does sometimes misremember baseball scores. She is then faced with the following choice: take the red ticket, which she knows pays $1 if the Red Sox won last night, and nothing otherwise, or the blue ticket, which she knows pays $1 iff $2 + 2 = 4$, and nothing otherwise. Now consider the following principle, named K-Suff by Jessica Brown (2014).

K-Suff

If S knows that p, then S can rationally take p as given in practical deliberation.

The following trio seems to be inconsistent:

(1) Chika knows the Red Sox won last night.
(2) Chika is rationally required to take the blue ticket.
(3) K-Suff is true.

By (1) and (3), Chika can take for granted that the Red Sox won last night. So the value of the red ticket, for her, is equal to its value conditional on the Red Sox winning. And that is $1. So it is at least as valuable as the blue ticket. So she can't be rationally required to take the blue ticket. Hence the three propositions are inconsistent.

This is worrying for two reasons. For one thing, it is intuitive that Chika knows that the Red Sox won. For another thing, it seems this form of argument generalises. For almost any proposition at all, if Chika knows the red ticket pays out iff that proposition is true, she should prefer the blue ticket. So she knows very little.

How could this argument be resisted? One move, which we'll return to frequently, is to deny K-Suff. Maybe Chika's knowledge that the Red Sox won is insufficient; she needs to be certain or to have some higher-order knowledge. But denying K-Suff alone will not explain why Chika should take the blue ticket. After all, if K-Suff is false, the fact that Chika knows the payout terms of the tickets is not in itself a reason for her to choose the blue ticket.

So perhaps we could deny that she is rationally required to choose the blue ticket. This does seem extremely unintuitive to me. Intuitions around here do not seem maximally reliable, but this is a strong enough intuition to make it worthwhile to explore other options.

And IRI provides a clever way out of the dilemma. Chika does not know the Red Sox won last night. But she did know that, before the choice was offered. Once she has that choice, her knowledge changes, and now she does not know. The intuition that she knows is explained by the fact that relative to a more normal choice set, she can take the fact that the Red Sox won as a given. And scepticism is averted because Chika does normally know a lot; it's just in the context of strange choices that she loses knowledge.

The plotline here, that principles connecting knowledge and action run up against anti-sceptical principles in contrived choice situations, and that IRI provides a way out of the tangle, is familiar. It

Interest-relative invariantism

is, simplifying greatly, the argumentative structure put forward by Hawthorne (2004), by Fantl and McGrath (2002, 2009), and by Weatherson (2012). It does rely on intuitions, but they are intuitions about choices (such as that Chika should choose the blue ticket), not about knowledge directly.

Some discussions of IRI, especially that in Hawthorne and Stanley (2008) use a converse principle. Again following the naming convention suggested by Jessica Brown (2014), we'll call this K-Nec.

K-Nec

An agent can properly use p as a reason for action only if she knows that p.

I'll mostly set the discussion of K-Nec aside here, since my preferred argument for IRI, the argument from Chika's case, merely relies on K-Suff. But it is interesting to work through how K-Nec helps plug a gap in the argument by cases for IRI.

Buckwalter and Schaffer (2015) argue that the intuitions behind Pinillos's examples are not as solid as we might like. It's true that experimental subjects do say that Bojan has to check the paper more times than Ankita does before he knows that the paper contains no typos. But those subjects also say he has to check more times before he believes that the paper has no typos. And, surprisingly, they say that he has to check more times before he guesses the paper has no typos. They suggest that there might be interest-relativity in the modal 'has' as much as in the verb 'knows'. To say someone 'has' to X before they Y, typically means that it is improper, in some way, to Y without doing X first. That won't be a problem for the proponent of IRI as long as, at least in some of the cases Pinillos studies, the relevant senses of propriety are connected to knowledge. And that's plausible for belief; Bojan has to know the paper is typo-free before he (properly) believes it. At least, that's a plausible move given K-Nec.[1]

There is one other problem for argument from cases for IRI. Imagine that after two checks of the paper we tell Bojan that Ankita's paper is a duplicate of his, and she has checked her paper in just the same way he has checked his. And we tell him that Ankita does not overly care whether her paper is typo-free, but is confident that it is. We then ask him, does Ankita know her paper is typo-free? Many philosophers think Bojan should answer "No" here. And that isn't something IRI can explain. According to IRI, he should say, "I don't know." He can't say Ankita does know, since he doesn't know their common paper has no typos. But it's hard to see why he should deny knowledge. Keith DeRose (2009, 185) thinks this case is particularly hard for IRI to explain, while Brian Kim (2016) offers some possible explanations. This objection doesn't tell against the claim that knowledge is interest-relative, but it does threaten the invariantism. An interest-relative contextualist should say that everyone should deny Bojan knows his paper is typo-free, and Bojan should deny Ankita knows her paper is typo-free.

3 Odds and stakes

Interest-relative invariantism says that the interests of the subject make a difference to what she knows. This is a fairly vague statement though; there are a number of ways to make it precise. Right now I have interests in practical questions (such as whether I should keep writing or go to lunch) and in theoretical questions (such as whether IRI is true). Do both kinds of interests matter? We'll return to that question in the next section. For now we want to ask a prior question: when do practical interests matter for whether a subject knows that p? There are two main answers to this question in the literature.

Stakes

When the agent has a possible bet on p that involves large potential losses, it is harder to know that p.

Odds

When the agent has a possible bet on p that involves long odds, it is harder to know that p.

The difference between these two options becomes clear in a simple class of cases. Assume the agent is faced with a choice with the following structure:

* There is a safe option, with payout S.
* And there is a risky option, with good payout G if p is true, and bad payout B if p is false.

These choices need not involve anything like a 'bet', in the ordinary folk sense. But they are situations where the agent has to make a choice between a path where the payouts are p dependent, and one where they are independent of p. And those are quite common situations.

The **Stakes** option says that the relevant number here is the magnitude $S - B$. If that is large, then the agent is in a high-stakes situation, and knowledge is hard. If it is low, then the agent is in a low-stakes situation, and knowledge is relatively easy. (Perhaps the magnitude of $G - S$ is relevant as well, though the focus in the literature has been on examples where $S - B$ is high.)

The **Odds** option says that the relevant number is the ratio:

$$\frac{S - B}{G - S}$$

If that number is high, the agent faces a long-odds bet, and knowledge is hard. If that number is low, the agent faces a short odds bet, and knowledge is relatively easy.

If our motivation for IRI came from cases, then it is natural to believe **Stakes**. Both Bojan and Chika face bets on p at long odds, but intuition is more worried about whether Bojan knows that p than whether Chika does. (At least my intuition is worried about whether Bojan knows, and I've seen little evidence that Chika's case is intuitively a case of non-knowledge.)

But if our motivation for IRI came from principles, then it is natural to believe **Odds**. One way to think of the argument from principles for IRI is that it is a way to make all four of the following intuitive claims true:

1. Agents should maximise evidential expected utility; i.e., they should choose the option whose expected utility is highest if the utilities are the agent's own, and the probabilities are the evidential probabilities given the agent's evidence.
2. If an agent knows that p, she can ignore possibilities where p is false; i.e., she can make whatever choice is the rational choice given p.
3. Chika cannot ignore possibilities where the Red Sox lost; she should consider those possibilities because it is in virtue of them that the evidential expected utility of taking the red ticket is higher.
4. Agents with Chika's evidence, background, and dispositions typically know that the Red Sox won.

The first three principles imply that Chika does not know the Red Sox won. The only way to square that with the anti-sceptical fourth principle is to say that Chika is in some way atypical.

Interest-relative invariantism

And the only way she has been said to be atypical is in the practical choices she faces. But note that it is not because she faces a high-stakes choice: precisely one dollar is at stake. It is because she faces a long (indeed infinitely long) odds bet.

In the general case we discussed above, agents maximise expected utility by taking the risky choice iff:

$$\frac{S-B}{G-S} < \frac{Pr(p)}{1-Pr(p)}$$

where $Pr(p)$ is the probability of p given the agent's evidence. The actual magnitudes at play don't matter to what choice maximises expected utility, just the odds the agent faces. So if one's motivation to keep IRI is to square expected utility maximisation with natural principles about knowledge and action, it seems the relevant feature of practical situations should be the stakes agents face.

Why could it seem stakes matter then? I think it is because in high-stakes situations the odds an agent faces are typically long ones. It is much easier to lose large amounts of utility than to gain large amounts of utility. Bojan stands to lose a lot from a typo in his paper; he doesn't stand to lose much by taking the time to check it over. So a high-stakes situation will, at least typically, be a long-odds situation. So if we say the odds the agent faces are relevant to what they know, we can explain any intuition that the stakes at play are relevant.

Jessica Brown (2008, 176) also notes that cases where the agent faces long odds but low stakes raise problems for the stakes-based version of IRI.

4 What kind of interests?

Let's return to the question of whether theoretical interests or only practical interests are relevant to knowledge. There is some precedent for the more restrictive answer. Stanley's book on IRI is called *Knowledge and Practical Interests*. And he defends a theory on which what an agent knows depends on the practical questions they face. But there are strong reasons to think that theoretical reasons matter as well.

In the previous section, I suggested that agents know that p only if they would maximise expected utility by choosing the choice that would be rational given p. That is, agents know that p only if the answer to the question "What choice maximises expected utility?" is the same unconditionally as it is conditional on p. My preferred version of interest-relative invariantism generalises this approach. An agent knows that p only if the rational answer to a question she faces is the same unconditionally as it is conditional on p. What it is for an agent to face a question is dependent on the agent's interests. If that's how one thinks of IRI, the question of this section becomes, should we restrict questions the agent faces to just being questions about what choice to make? Or, should they include questions that turn on her theoretical interests, but which are irrelevant to the choices before her? There are two primary motivations for allowing theoretical interests as well as practical interests to matter.

The first comes from the arguments for what Jeremy Fantl and Matthew McGrath call the Unity Thesis (Fantl and McGrath 2009, 73–6). They are interested in the thesis that whether or not p is a reason for an agent is independent of whether the agent is engaged in practical or theoretical deliberation. But we don't have to be so invested in the ideology of reasons to appreciate their argument. Note that if only practical interests matter, then the agent should come up with different answers to the question "What to do in situation S" depending on whether the agent is actually in S, or they are merely musing about how one would deal with that situation. And it is unintuitive that this should matter.

245

Let's make that a little less abstract. Imagine Chika is not actually faced with the choice between the red and blue tickets. In fact, she has no practical decision to make that turns on whether the Red Sox won. But she is idly musing over what she would do if she were offered the red ticket and the blue ticket. If she knows the Red Sox won, then she should be indifferent between the tickets. After all, she knows they will both return \$1. But intuitively she should think the red ticket is preferable, even in the abstract setting. And this seems to be the totally general case.

The general lesson is that if whether one can take p for granted is relevant to the choice between A and B, it is similarly relevant to the theoretical question of whether one would choose A or B, given a choice. And since those questions should receive the same answer, if p can't be known while making the practical deliberation between A and B, it can't be known while musing on whether A or B is more choice-worthy.

In Weatherson (2012) I suggest another reason for including theoretical interests in what's relevant to knowledge. There is something odd about the following reasoning: the probability of p *is precisely* x, therefore p, in any case where $x < 1$. It is a little hard to say, though, why this is problematic, since we often take ourselves to know things on what we would admit, if pushed, are purely probabilistic grounds. The version of IRI that includes theoretical interests allows for this. If we are consciously thinking about whether the probability of p is x, then that's a relevant question to us. Conditional on p, the answer to that question is clearly no, since conditional on p, the probability of p is 1. So anyone who is thinking about the precise probability of p, and not thinking it is 1, is not in a position to know p. And that's why it is wrong, when thinking about p's probability, to infer p from its high probability.

Putting the ideas so far together, we get the following picture of how interests matter. An agent knows that p only if the evidential probability of p is close enough to certainty for all the purposes that are relevant, given the agent's theoretical and practical interests. Assuming that the background theory of knowledge is non-sceptical, this will entail that interests matter.

5 Global or partial?

So far I've described three ways to refine the defence of IRI.

1   The motivation could come from cases or principles.
2   The relevant feature that makes it hard to have knowledge could be that the agent faces a high-stakes choice, or a long-odds choice.
3   Only practical interests may be relevant to knowledge, or theoretical interests may matter as well.

For better or worse, the version of IRI I've defended has fairly clear commitments on all three; in each case, I prefer the latter option. From here on, I'm much less sure of the right way to refine IRI.

IRI, like contextualism, was introduced as a thesis about knowledge. But it need not be restricted that way. It could be generalised to a number of other epistemically interesting notions. At the extreme, we could argue that every epistemologically interesting notion is interest-relative. Doing so gives us a global version of IRI.

Jason Stanley (2005) comes close to defending a global version. He notes that if one has both IRI, and a 'knowledge-first' epistemology (Williamson 2000), then one is a long way towards globalism. Even if one doesn't accept the whole knowledge first package, but just accepts the thesis that evidence is all and only what one knows, then one is a long way towards globalism. After all, if evidence is interest-relative, then probability, justification, rationality, and evidential support are interest-relative, too.

Katherine Rubin (2015) objects to globalist versions of IRI. But the objections she gives turn, as she notes, on taking stakes, not odds, to be relevant.

If a non-global version of IRI could be made to work, it would have some theoretical advantages. It's nice to be able to say that Chika should take the blue ticket because the evidential probability of the Red Sox winning is lower than the evidential probability of two plus two being four. But that won't be a non-circular explanation if we also say that something is part of Chika's evidence in virtue of being known.

On the other hand, the motivations for interest-relativity of knowledge seem to generalise to all other non-gradable states. In ordinary cases, Chika could use the fact that the Red Sox won as a given in practical or theoretical reasoning. That is, she could properly treat it as evidence. But she can't treat it as evidence when deciding which ticket to take. So at least what she can properly treat as evidence seems to be interest-relative, and from there it isn't obvious how to deny that evidence itself is interest-relative, too.

There remains a question of whether gradable notions, like epistemic probabilities, are also interest-relative. One of the aims of my first paper on IRI (Weatherson 2005) was to argue that probabilistic notions are interest-invariant while binary notions are interest-relative. But if propositions that are part of one's evidence have maximal probability (in the relevant sense of probability), and evidence is interest-relative, that combination won't be sustainable.

In short, while the non-global version of IRI allows for some nice reductive explanations of why interests matter, the global version is supported by the very intuitions that motivated IRI. There is a danger here that whatever way the IRI theorist goes, they will run into insuperable difficulties. Ichikawa, Jarvis, and Rubin (2012) argue strongly that this danger is real; there is no plausible way to fill out IRI. I'm not convinced that the prospects are quite so grim, but I think this is one of the more pressing worries for IRI.

6 Belief, justification, and interest

If we decide that not everything in epistemology is interest-relative, then we face a series of questions about which things are, and are not, interest-relative. One of these concerns belief. Should we say that what an agent believes is sensitive to what her interests are?

Note that the question here concerns whether belief is constitutively related to interests. It is extremely plausible that belief is causally related to interests. As Jennifer Nagel (2008) has shown, many agents will react to being in a high-stakes situation by lowering their confidence in relevant propositions. In this way, being in a high-stakes situation may cause an agent to lose beliefs. This is not the kind of constitutive interest-relativity that's at issue here, though the fact this happens makes it harder to tell whether there is such a thing as constitutive interest-relativity of belief.

I find it useful to distinguish three classes of views about beliefs and interests:

1   Beliefs are not interest-relative. If knowledge is interest-relative, the interest-relativity is in the conditions a belief must satisfy in order to count as knowledge.
2   Beliefs are interest-relative, and the interest-relativity of belief fully explains why knowledge is interest-relative.
3   Beliefs are interest-relative, but the interest-relativity of belief does not fully explain why knowledge is interest-relative.

In Weatherson (2005), I suggested an argument for option 2. I now think that argument fails, for reasons given by Jason Stanley (2005). I originally thought option 2 provided the best explanation of cases like Chika's. Assume that Chika does the rational thing, and takes the blue ticket. She believes it is better to take the blue ticket. But that would be incoherent if she believed the Red Sox won. So she doesn't believe the Red Sox won. But she did believe the Red Sox won before she was offered the bet, and she hasn't received any new evidence that they did not. So, assuming we can understand an interest-invariant notion of confidence, she is no less confident that the Red Sox won, but she no longer believes it. That's because belief is interest-relative. And if all cases of interest-relativity are like Chika's, then they will all be cases where the interest-relativity of belief is what is ultimately explanatory.

The problem, as Stanley had in effect already pointed out, is that not all cases are like Chika's. If agents are mistaken about the choice they face, the explanation I offered for Chika's case won't go through. This is especially clear in cases where the mistake is due to irrationality. Let's look at an example of this. Assume Dian faces the same choice as Chika, and this is clear, but he irrationally believes that the red ticket pays out \$2. So he prefers the red ticket to the blue ticket, and there is no reason to deny he believes the Red Sox won. Yet taking the red ticket is irrational; he wouldn't do it were he rational. Yet it would be rational if he knew the Red Sox won. So Dian doesn't know the Red Sox won, in virtue of his interests, while believing they did.

Note that this isn't an argument for option 1. Everything I said about Dian is consistent with the Chika-based argument for thinking that belief is interest-relative. It's just that there are cases where the interest-relativity of knowledge can't be explained by the interest-relativity of belief. So I now think option 3 is correct.

We can ask similar questions about whether justified belief is interest-relative, and whether if so this explains the interest-relativity of knowledge. I won't go into as much detail here, save to note that on my preferred version of IRI, Dian's belief that the Red Sox won is both justified and rational. (Roughly, this is because I think his belief that the Red Sox won just is his high credence that the Red Sox won, and his high credence the Red Sox won is justified and rational. I defend this picture at more length in (Weatherson 2005). And while that paper makes some mistaken suggestions about knowledge, I still think what it says about belief and justification is broadly correct.) That is, Dian has a justified true belief that the Red Sox won, but does not know it. This is, to put it mildly, not the most intuitive of verdicts. I suspect the alternative verdicts lead to worse problems elsewhere. But rather than delving deeper into the details of IRI to confirm whether that's true, let's turn to some objections to the view.

7 Debunking objections

Many arguments against IRI are, in effect, debunking arguments. The objector's immediate conclusion is not that IRI is false, but that it is unsupported by the arguments given for it.

Arguments that people do not have the intuition that, for example, Bojan lacks knowledge that his paper is typo-free, do not immediately show that IRI is false. That's because the truth of IRI can be made compatible with that intuition in two ways. For one thing, it is possible that people think Bojan knows because they think Bojan betting that his paper is typo-free is, in the circumstances, a good bet.[2] For another thing, intuitions around here might be unreliable. Remember that one of the original motivations for IRI was that it was the lowest-cost solution to the preface paradox and lottery paradox. We shouldn't expect intuitions to be reliable in the presence of serious paradox. That consideration cuts both ways; it makes debunking objections to arguments for IRI from intuitions about cases look very promising. I think those objections are promising; but they don't show IRI is false.

Similarly, objections to the premises of the argument from principles don't strictly entail that IRI is false. After all, IRI is an existential thesis; it says that sometimes interests matter. The principles used to defend it are universal claims; they say (for example) that it is always permissible to act on knowledge. Weaker versions of these principles might still be consistent with, or even supporting of, IRI. But this feels a little desperate. If the premises of these arguments fail, then IRI looks implausible.

But there are still two methodological points worth remembering. Sometimes it seems that critics of principles like K-Suff reason that K-Suff entails IRI, and IRI is antecedently implausible, so we should start out suspicious of K-Suff. Now why might IRI be antecedently implausible?

I think to some extent it is because it is thought to be so revolutionary. The denial of interest-relativity is often taken to be a "traditional" view. This phrasing appears, for example, in Boyd (2016) and in Ichikawa, Jarvis, and Rubin (2012), and even in the title of Buckwalter (2014). And if this were correct, that would be a mark against interest-relativity. The "inherited experience and acumen of many generations of men" (Austin 1956–7, 11) should not be lightly forsaken. The problem is that it isn't true that IRI is revolutionary. Indeed, in historical terms there is nothing particularly novel about contemporary IRI. As Stephen R. Grimm (2015) points out, you can see a version of the view in Locke, as well as in Clifford. What's really radical, as Descartes acknowledged, is to think that the perspective of the Cartesian meditator is the right one for epistemology.

Perhaps what is unintuitive about IRI is that it makes knowledge depend on factors that are not 'truth-directed' nor 'truth-conducive'. There is a stronger and weaker version of the principle that might be being appealed to here. The stronger version is that IRI makes practical matters into one of the factors on which knowledge depends, and this is implausible. But IRI doesn't do this. It is consistent with IRI to say that only truth-conducive features of beliefs are relevant to whether they amount to knowledge, but how much of each feature one needs depends on practical matters. The weaker principle is that IRI makes knowledge counterfactually sensitive to features irrelevant to the truth, justification, or reliability of the belief. This is true, but it isn't an objection to IRI. Any theory that allows defeaters to knowledge, and defeaters to those defeaters, will make knowledge counterfactually sensitive to non-truth-conducive features in just the same way. And it is independently plausible that there are defeaters to knowledge, and they can be defeated.[3]

These are all reasons to think that IRI is not antecedently implausible. There is one reason to think it is antecedently plausible. On a functionalist theory of mind, belief is a practical notion. And it is plausible that knowledge is a kind of success condition for belief. Now it's possible to have non-practical success conditions for a state our concept of which is practical. But I don't find that a natural starting assumption. It's much more intuitive, to me at least, that the norms of belief and the metaphysics of belief would be tightly integrated. And that suggests that IRI is, if anything, a natural default.

That's not an argument for IRI, or of course for K-Suff. And there are important direct objections to K-Suff. Jessica Brown (2008) and Jennifer Lackey (2010) have examples of people in high-stakes situations who they say are intuitively described as knowing something, but not being in a position to act on it. I'm sympathetic to the two-part reply that Masashi Kasaki (2014) makes to these examples. The first thing to note is that these are hard cases, in areas where several paradoxes (e.g., lottery, preface, sceptical) are lurking. Intuitions are less reliable than usual around here. But another thing to notice is that it is very hard to say what actions are justified by taking p for granted in various settings. Brown and Lackey both describe cases where doctors have lots of evidence for p, and given p a certain action would maximise patient-welfare, but where intuitively it would be wrong for the doctor to act that way. As it stands, that's a problem for IRI only if doctors should maximise epistemic expected patient-welfare, and that principle isn't true. Kasaki argues that there isn't a way to fill out Lackey's example to get around this problem, and I suspect the same is true for Brown's example.

Finally, note that K-Suff is an extensional claim. Kenneth Boyd (2016) and Baron Reed (2014) object to a principle much stronger than K-Suff: the principle that what an agent knows should explain why some choices are rational for them. Both of them say that if IRI is inconsistent with the stronger principle, that is a serious problem for IRI. (In Boyd's case this is part of an argument that IRI is unmotivated; in Reed's case he takes it to be a direct objection to IRI.) Now I think IRI is inconsistent with this principle. Chika doesn't know the Red Sox won because she can't rationally choose the red ticket, not the other way around. But I don't see why the principle is so plausible. It seems plausible to me that something else (e.g., evidence) explains both rational choice and knowledge, and the way it explains both things makes IRI true.

8 Direct objections

Let's close with direct arguments against IRI. There are two kinds of arguments that I won't address here. One of these is the argument, developed in Ichikawa, Jarvis, and Rubin (2012), that there isn't a good way to say how far interest-relativity should extend. As I noted above, I agree this is a deep problem, and I don't think there is a good answer to it in the existing literature. The other kind are objections that only apply to the Stakes version of IRI, not the Odds version. One instance of this kind is the Dutch Book argument deployed by Baron Reed (2014). I think several instances of that kind of argument are successful. But the theory they succeed against is not IRI, but a sub-optimal version of IRI. So I'll stick to objections that apply to the Odds version.

IRI does allow knowledge to depend on some unexpected factors, but so do most contemporary theories of knowledge. Most contemporary theories allow for knowledge to be defeated in certain ways, such as by available but unaccessed evidence (Harman 1973, 75), or by nearby possibilities of error (Goldman 1976), or by mistakes in the background reasoning. The last category of cases aren't really contemporary; they trace back at least to Dharmottara (Nagel 2014, 58). And contemporary theories of knowledge also allow for defeaters to be defeated. Once we work through the details of what can defeat a defeater, it turns out many surprising things can affect knowledge.

Indeed, for just about any kind of defeater, it is possible to imagine something that in some ways makes the agent's epistemic position worse, while simultaneously defeating the defeater.[4] If interests matter to knowledge because they matter to defeaters, as is true on my version of IRI, we should expect strange events to correlate with gaining knowledge. For example, it isn't surprising that one can gain knowledge that p at exactly the moment one's evidential support for p falls. This consequence of IRI is taken to be obviously unacceptable by Eaton and Pickavance (2015), but it's just a consequence of how defeaters generally work.

IRI has been criticised for making knowledge depend on agents not allowing agents to get knowledge by not caring, as reflected in the following vivid quotes:

> Not giving a damn, however enviable in other respects, should not be knowledge-making.
> *(Russell and Doris 2009, 433)*

> If you don't know whether penguins eat fish, but want to know, you might think . . . you have to gather evidence. [But if IRI] were correct, though, you have another option: You could take a drink or shoot heroin.
> *(Cappelen and Lepore 2006, 1044–5)*

Let's walk through Cappelen and Lepore's case. IRI says that there are people who have high confidence that penguins eat fish, and they have this confidence for reasons that are appropriately connected to the fact that penguins eat fish. But one of them really worries about sceptical doubts, and so won't regard the question of what penguins eat as settled. The other brushes off excessive sceptical doubts, and rightly so; they are, after all, excessive. IRI says that the latter knows and the former does not. If the former were to care a little less, in particular if s/he cared a little less about evil demons and the like, s/he would know. Perhaps they could get themselves to care a little less by having a drink. That doesn't sound like a bad plan; if a sceptical doubt is destroying knowledge, and there is no gain from holding onto it, then just let it go. From this perspective, Cappelen and Lepore's conclusion does not seem like a reductio. Excessive doubt can destroy knowledge, so people with strong, non-misleading evidence can gain knowledge by setting aside doubts. And drink can set aside doubt. So drink can lead to knowledge.[5]

But note that the drink doesn't generate the knowledge. It blocks, or defeats, something that threatens to block knowledge. We should say the same thing to Russell and Doris's objection. Not giving a damn, about scepticism for example, is not knowledge-making, but it is knowledge-causing. In general, things that cause by double prevention do not make things happen, although later things are counterfactually dependent on them (Lewis 2004). And the same is true of not caring.

Finally, it has been argued that IRI makes knowledge unstable in a certain kind of way (Lutz 2014; Anderson 2015). Practical circumstances can change quickly; something can become a live choice and cease being one at a moment's notice. If knowledge is sensitive to what choices are live, then knowledge can change this quickly, too. But, say the objectors, it is counterintuitive that knowledge changes this quickly.

Now I'm not sure this is counterintuitive. I think that part of what it takes to know p is to treat the question of whether p as closed. It sounds incoherent to say, "I know a is the F, but the question of who is the F is still open." And whether a question is treated as open or closed does, I think, change quite rapidly. One can treat a question as closed, get some new reason to open it (perhaps new evidence, perhaps an interlocutor who treats it as open), and then quickly dismiss that reason. So I'm not sure this is even a problem.

But to the extent that it is, it is only a problem for a somewhat half-hearted version of IRI. The puzzles the objectors raise turn on cases where the relevant practical options change quickly. But even once a practical option has ceased to be available it can be hard in practice to dismiss it from one's mind. One may often still think about what to do if it becomes available again or about exactly how unfortunate it is that the option went away. As long as theoretical as well as practical interests matter to knowledge, it will be unlikely that knowledge will be unstable in just this way. Practical interests may change quickly; theoretical ones typically do not.

Notes

1 I'm suggesting here that, in some sense, knowledge is a norm of belief. For more on the normative role of knowledge, see Worsnip (2016).
2 Compare the response to Feltz and Zarpentine (2010) that I make in Weatherson (2011 §1), or the response to Lackey (2010) by Masashi Kasaki (2014 §5).
3 The argument of the last two sentences is expanded on greatly in Weatherson (2014 §3). The idea that knowledge allows for defeaters is criticised by Maria Lasonen-Aarnio (2014a). Eaton and Pickavance (2015) make an objection to IRI that does not take this point into account.
4 The argument of the last two sentences is expanded on greatly in Weatherson (2014 §3), where it is credited to Martin Smith. The idea that knowledge allows for defeaters is criticised by Maria Lasonen-Aarnio (2014b).
5 Wright (2004) notes that there often is not value in holding on to sceptical doubts, and the considerations of this paragraph are somewhat inspired by his views. That's not to endorse the idea that using alcohol or heroin is preferable to being gripped by sceptical doubts, especially heroin, but I do endorse the general idea that those doubts are not cost-free.

Bibliography

Anderson, Charity. 2015. "On the Intimate Relationship of Knowledge and Action." *Episteme* 12 (3): 343–53. doi:10.1017/epi.2015.16.

Austin, J.L. 1956–7. "A Plea for Excuses." *Proceedings of the Aristotelian Society* 57: 1–30.

Boyd, Kenneth. 2016. "Pragmatic Encroachment and Epistemically Responsible Action." *Synthese* 193 (9): 2721–2745.

Brown, Jessica. 2008. "Subject-Sensitive Invariantism and the Knowledge Norm for Practical Reasoning." *Noûs* 42 (2): 167–89. doi:10.1111/j.1468-0068.2008.00677.x.

———. 2014. "Impurism, Practical Reasoning and the Threshold Problem." *Noûs* 48 (1): 179–92. doi:10.1111/nous.12008.

Buckwalter, Wesley. 2014. "Non-Traditional Factors in Judgments about Knowledge." *Philosophy Compass* 7 (4): 278–89. doi:10.1111/j.1747-9991.2011.00466.x.

Buckwalter, Wesley, and Jonathan Schaffer. 2015. "Knowledge, Stakes and Mistakes." *Noûs* 49 (2): 201–34. doi:10.1111/nous.12017.

Cappelen, Herman, and Ernest Lepore. 2006. "Shared Content." In *The Oxford Handbook of Philosophy of Language*, edited by Ernest Lepore and Barry C. Smith, 1020–55. Oxford: Oxford University Press.

DeRose, Keith. 1992. "Contextualism and Knowledge Attributions." *Philosophy and Phenomenological Research* 52 (4): 513–29.

———. 2009. *The Case for Contextualism: Knowledge, Skepticism and Context.* Oxford: Oxford University Press.

Eaton, Daniel, and Timothy Pickavance. 2015. "Evidence Against Pragmatic Encroachment." *Philosophical Studies* 172: 3135–43. doi:10.1007/s11098-015-0461-x.

Fantl, Jeremy, and Matthew McGrath. 2002. "Evidence, Pragmatics, and Justification." *Philosophical Review* 111: 67–94.

———. 2009. *Knowledge in an Uncertain World.* Oxford: Oxford University Press.

Feltz, Adam, and Chris Zarpentine. 2010. "Do You Know More When It Matters Less?" *Philosophical Psychology* 23 (5): 683–706. doi:10.1080/09515089.2010.514572.

Goldman, Alvin I. 1976. "Discrimination and Perceptual Knowledge." *The Journal of Philosophy* 73 (20): 771–91.

Grimm, Stephen R. 2015. "Knowledge, Practical Interests and Rising Tides." In *Epistemic Evaluation: Purposeful Epistemology*, edited by David K. Henderson and John Greco, 117–37. Oxford: Oxford University Press.

Harman, Gilbert. 1973. *Thought.* Princeton: Princeton University Press.

Hawthorne, John. 2004. *Knowledge and Lotteries.* Oxford: Oxford University Press.

Hawthorne, John, and Jason Stanley. 2008. "Knowledge and Action." *Journal of Philosophy* 105 (10): 571–90.

Ichikawa, Jonathan Jenkins, Benjamin Jarvis, and Katherine Rubin. 2012. "Pragmatic Encroachment and Belief-Desire Psychology." *Analytic Philosophy* 53 (4): 327–43. doi:10.1111/j.2153-960X.2012.00564.x.

Kasaki, Masashi. 2014. "Subject-Sensitive Invariantism and Isolated Secondhand Knowledge." *Acta Analytica* 29: 83–98. doi:10.1007/s12136-013-0215-3.

Kim, Brian. 2016. "In Defense of Subject-Sensitive Invariantism." *Episteme* 13 (2): 233–51. doi:10.1017/epi.2015.40.

Lackey, Jennifer. 2010. "Acting on Knowledge." *Philosophical Perspectives* 24: 361–82.

Lasonen-Aarnio, Maria. 2014a. "The Dogmatism Puzzle." *Australasian Journal of Philosophy* 92 (3): 417–32. doi:10.1080/00048402.2013.834949.

———. 2014b. "Higher-Order Evidence and the Limits of Defeat." *Philosophy and Phenomenological Research* 88 (2): 314–45.

Lewis, David. 2004. "Causation as Influence." In *Causation and Counterfactuals*, edited by John Collins, Ned Hall, and L.A. Paul, 75–106. Cambridge: MIT Press.

Lutz, Matt. 2014. "The Pragmatics of Pragmatic Encroachment." *Synthese* 191 (8): 1717–40. doi:10.1007/s11229-013-0361-6.

Nagel, Jennifer. 2008. "Knowledge Ascriptions and the Psychological Consequences of Changing Stakes." *Australasian Journal of Philosophy* 86 (2): 279–94. doi:10.1080/00048400801886397.

———. 2014. *Knowledge: A Very Short Introduction.* Oxford: Oxford University Press.

Pinillos, Ángel. 2012. "Knowledge, Experiments and Practical Interests." In *Knowledge Ascriptions*, edited by Jessica Brown and Mikkel Gerken, 192–219. Oxford: Oxford University Press.

Reed, Baron. 2014. "Practical Matters Do Not Affect Whether You Know." In *Contemporary Debates in Epistemology*, edited by Matthias Steup, John Turri, and Ernest Sosa, 2nd ed., 95–106. Chichester: Wiley-Blackwell.

Rubin, Katherine. 2015. "Total Pragmatic Encroachment and Epistemic Permissiveness." *Pacific Philosophical Quarterly* 96: 12–38. doi:10.1111/papq.12060.

Russell, Gillian, and John M. Doris. 2009. "Knowledge by Indifference." *Australasian Journal of Philosophy* 86 (3): 429–37. doi:10.1080/00048400802001996.

Rysiew, Patrick. 2017. "Warranted Assertability Maneuvers." In *The Routledge Handbook of Epistemic Contextualism*, edited by Jonathan Jenkins Ichikawa, 205–17. London: Routledge.

Stanley, Jason. 2005. *Knowledge and Practical Interests*. Oxford: Oxford University Press.

Weatherson, Brian. 2005. "Can We Do Without Pragmatic Encroachment?" *Philosophical Perspectives* 19 (1): 417–43. doi:10.1111/j.1520-8583.2005.00068.x.

———. 2011. "Defending Interest-Relative Invariantism." *Logos & Episteme* 2 (4): 591–609.

———. 2012. "Knowledge, Bets and Interests." In *Knowledge Ascriptions*, edited by Jessica Brown and Mikkel Gerken, 75–103. Oxford: Oxford University Press.

———. 2014. "Probability and Scepticism." In *Scepticism and Perceptual Justification*, edited by Dylan Dodd and Elia Zardini, 71–86. Oxford: Oxford University Press.

Williamson, Timothy. 2000. *Knowledge and its Limits*. Oxford: Oxford University Press.

Worsnip, Alex. 2017. "Knowledge Norms." In *The Routledge Handbook of Epistemic Contextualism*, edited by Jonathan Jenkins Ichikawa, 177–89. London: Routledge.

Wright, Crispin. 2004. "Warrant for Nothing (and Foundations for Free)?" *Proceedings of the Aristotelian Society, Supplementary Volume* 78 (1): 167–212.

PART V

Relativism and disagreement

20

THE DISAGREEMENT CHALLENGE TO CONTEXTUALISM

Justin Khoo

Contextualism about "knows" is the view that knowledge ascriptions (sentences of the form "S knows p") may express different propositions in different contexts of utterance, even when the ascription contains no other context-sensitive vocabulary (throughout this chapter, I'll just refer to this view as "contextualism"). This view is contrasted with invariantism about "knows," which is the view that knowledge ascriptions containing no other context-sensitive vocabulary always express the same proposition in every context. Consider the following knowledge ascription:

(1)   Barack Obama knows that it is raining in Cambridge, MA.

The standard motivation for contextualism is that knowledge ascriptions like (1) intuitively have different truth values when uttered in different contexts, holding fixed the facts about the subject's (in this case, Obama's) epistemic situation (his evidence, beliefs about whether p, the truth of p, etc). Consider the following two contexts:

CONTEXT 1: Sue is talking with some friends at MIT (in Cambridge, MA); they are watching it rain outside. They have just learned that Obama, who is currently in the White House, has recently seen a weather report in which the reporter said that it is currently raining in Cambridge, MA. Sue then says, "Barack Obama knows that it is raining in Cambridge, MA."

CONTEXT 2: Jim is talking with some friends at Harvard (in Cambridge, MA); they are watching it rain outside. They have just learned that Obama, who is currently in the White House, has recently seen a weather report in which the reporter said that it is currently raining in Cambridge, MA. Jim then says, "Obama *thinks* that it's raining here in Cambridge. But he cannot rule out the possibility that the weather reporter is lying as part of an elaborate hoax. So, Barack Obama doesn't know that it is raining in Cambridge, MA."

Intuitively, when Sue utters (1), she says something true. However, it also intuitively plausible that when Jim utters the negation of (1), he says something true. Contextualism predicts that what Sue says is true and that what Jim says is true by predicting that (1) expresses a different proposition in CONTEXT 1 than it does in CONTEXT 2.[1] Call the proposition (1) expresses in CONTEXT 1 *knows-low* and the proposition (1) expresses in CONTEXT 2 *knows-high*. Because these

257

propositions are distinct, the negation of *knows-high* is compatible (in principle) with *knows-low* – in other words, both *knows-low* and ~*knows-high* may be true. That is how contextualism predicts that what Sue says and what Jim says are both true.

What I will call the *disagreement challenge to contextualism* is a way of turning this standard motivation for contextualism on its head. The problem is that some cases in which contextualism predicts that a knowledge ascription made in one context is compatible with the negation of that knowledge ascription made in another context are also cases in which the two speakers intuitively disagree. However, from the fact that the two speakers disagree it seems to follow that at least one of the propositions they assert must be false. Yet, the opposite is predicted by contextualism, since it predicts (*ex hypothesi*) that the propositions asserted by the two speakers are compatible (so that they may both be true together). So, contextualism predicts in such cases that the two speakers do not disagree, contrary to our intuition. Hence, contextualism is false.[2]

We can state a general disagreement argument against various contextualist theories as follows. First, let "X" denote some particular contextualist theory.[3] Say that X *compatibilizes* a knowledge ascription Φ and its negation ~Φ across contexts C1 and C2 iff X predicts that the proposition expressed by Φ at C1 is compatible with the proposition expressed by ~Φ at C2. We can now state a schematic disagreement argument against theory X as follows:

Disagreement

In some cases in which X compatibilizes Φ/~Φ across C1 and C2, the speaker uttering Φ in C1 disagrees with the speaker uttering ~Φ in C2.

Compatibility > No Disagreement

If the proposition asserted by the speaker uttering Φ in C1 is compatible with the proposition asserted by the speaker uttering ~Φ in C2, then the two speakers do not disagree.

Contextualism > No Disagreement

In all cases in which X compatibilizes Φ/~Φ across C1 and C2, X predicts that the speaker in C1 does not disagree with the speaker in C2.

> (This follows from **Disagreement**, **Compatibility > No Disagreement**, and the definition of "compatibilizes.")

So, X is false.

The strategy behind the argument is simple: pick your target contextualist theory, find a case in which that theory compatibilizes Φ/~Φ (for some knowledge ascription Φ and its negation ~Φ), and then instantiate the schematic argument above accordingly. This strategy of argument has been widely influential in the literature on contextualism.[4] In this chapter, I evaluate the prospects of stating a persuasive version of this challenge for contextualism and then consider and evaluate some responses to it on behalf of contextualism.

1 Motivating the argument

Why accept the premises of the disagreement argument sketched above? Let's start with the intuitive motivation behind the argument. Consider the following two dialogues:

The disagreement challenge

[Prime]
A: 231 is a prime number.
B: No, 231 is a not prime number.

[Doctor]
C: I'm a doctor.
D: #No, I'm not a doctor.

Two observations jump out about these dialogues. The first is that there is something defective about D's response to C in DOCTOR (that is why it is marked with a '#', to indicate some kind of oddity), while there is nothing odd about B's response to A in PRIME. The oddity in D's response seems to stem from the feeling that D is trying to reject C's assertion but does so for a reason that doesn't make sense (perhaps because what D says is compatible with what C says). By contrast, B has good grounds to reject A's assertion: B thinks what A says is false. In a slogan:

(i)   Rejection is *licensed* in PRIME but not in DOCTOR.

The second observation is that in PRIME it would be sensible for A to retract what she says were she to be convinced of what B says (perhaps by saying, "I was wrong; I take back what I said"). But in DOCTOR it wouldn't be sensible for C to retract what she says were she to be convinced of what D says. In a slogan:

(ii)   Retraction is *sensible* in PRIME but not in DOCTOR.

These two marks suggest that A and B disagree in PRIME, and that C and D do not disagree in DOCTOR. But what explains this contrast? A promising answer is that in PRIME what A says is *incompatible* with what B says (in the sense that at least one of their asserted propositions must be false), whereas in DOCTOR what C says is *compatible* with what D says (because it could be that C is a doctor and D is not, in which case both of their asserted propositions would be true). Underlying this explanation is the following hypothesis about disagreement.

<u>The Disagreement Hypothesis</u>

If S utters Φ and S' assertively utters $\sim\Phi$, then S and S' disagree only if the proposition expressed by Φ (as uttered by S) is incompatible with the proposition expressed by $\sim\Phi$ (as uttered by S').

This hypothesis explains both (i) and (ii). Take (i) first. On a standard account of assertion (due to Stalnaker 1978, 1999, 2002, 2014), to assert a proposition is to propose adding that proposition to the *common ground* of your conversation. The common ground of a conversation is the set of propositions that are all believed by everyone in the conversation and believed by everyone to be believed by everyone in the conversation (and so on iterated infinitely). To reject an assertion is to signal that you refuse to allow the asserted proposition into the common ground in your conversation. This theory of conversation explains why it makes sense for me to reject your assertion if I believe that the proposition you assert is false. I am a cooperative interlocutor, and thus I want the common ground to contain only true propositions. Since I think the proposition you assert is false, it makes sense for me to refuse to allow it into the common ground. By contrast, it does not make sense why I would reject your assertion if I (merely) believe and assert some other proposition that is compatible with the one you assert. In that case, both our asserted propositions may be true, so I have no reason to refuse to allow your asserted proposition into the common ground.

Regarding (ii), if I assert a proposition that is incompatible with what you assert, then if you come accept my assertion, you have reason to retract your earlier assertion. To not retract would be to leave in place your earlier proposal while accepting my later proposal; but, if both proposals were accepted, two incompatible propositions would become common ground, thus ensuring that at least one false proposition is common ground.[5] Thus, we can see how **The Disagreement Hypothesis** yields a promising explanation of our observations (i) and (ii).

Turning back to contextualism, notice that **The Disagreement Hypothesis** entails **Compatibility > No Disagreement**. Then, as we saw above, it follows from this that **Contextualism > No Disagreement**. Therefore, we only need to find evidence for (the relevant instance of) **Disagreement** to support the argument against contextualism.

2 Refining the challenge

We have just seen some reason to accept **Compatibility > No Disagreement**, which is the second major premise in our disagreement argument above. However, **The Disagreement Hypothesis** immediately faces a challenge. The problem is that it need not be the case that someone *says* something you think to be false for you to be licensed in rejecting their assertion. Conversational implicatures are aspects of what a speaker *means*, but not part of what they *say* (cf. Grice 1989). Thinking that something someone implicates is false is sufficient to make it linguistically appropriate to reject their claim (cf. Horn 1985):

> **[Cookies]**
> E: John ate some of the cookies.
> F: No, he ate all of them.

Notice in this case that E doesn't *say* that John didn't eat all of the cookies; all E has said is that John ate some of the cookies. In particular, E may follow up her claim with an explicit denial of that statement without contradicting herself: "John ate some of the cookies, and in fact he ate all of them." Nonetheless, what E says plausibly conversationally implicates that John didn't eat all of them. F thinks this is false, and that seems sufficient to license her denying E's claim, even though the propositions E and F assert are compatible.

Call cases like COOKIES, where one party rejects another's claim on the basis of thinking that something implicated by her utterance is false, cases of *implicature rejection*. Defenders of contextualism may point out that such cases challenge **The Disagreement Hypothesis**, for they are cases in which two speakers disagree (in a sense sufficient to license rejection) but in which they do not assert incompatible propositions.

However, notice that, although rejection is licensed in COOKIES, it wouldn't make sense for E to retract her claim were she to be convinced of what F says. That is, even supposing that E became convinced that John ate all of the cookies, it wouldn't make sense for her to reply, "I was wrong; I take back what I said."[6] And furthermore, although it seems intuitively correct that E and F disagree in COOKIES, it is clearly wrong that they disagree about whether John ate some of the cookies. Thus, there seems to be a sense in which E and F disagree in COOKIES, and a sense in which they do not disagree.

This observation suggests a strategy for insulating the disagreement challenge from the implicature rejection response. The new strategy is to stipulate a narrow sense of disagreement that both licenses rejection and makes sensible retraction and to formulate the challenge in

The disagreement challenge

those terms. As a helpful technical notion, say that A and B *strongly disagree* iff A and B make claims and:

(a) Were B to reject A's claim, that rejection would be linguistically appropriate,
(b) Were A to retract her claim in light of B's rejection, her doing so would be sensible.

(cf. MacFarlane 2014: 132–133)

Next, we reformulate our hypothesis about disagreement to be about strong disagreements:

The Strong Disagreement Hypothesis

If S utters Φ and S' assertively utters $\sim\Phi$, then S and S' *strongly disagree* only if the proposition expressed by Φ (as uttered by S) is incompatible with the proposition expressed by $\sim\Phi$ (as uttered by S').

We can see the appeal of this hypothesis about strong disagreement by thinking about COOKIES from the perspective of how assertions aim to update the common ground. In COOKIES, E and F assert compatible propositions, so both may become common ground without ensuring that the common ground contains a false proposition. Furthermore, in rejecting E's claim, F is not trying to block *what E asserts* from becoming common ground. Rather, in rejecting E's claim, F is trying to block something *E implicates* from becoming common ground. Thus, it would not be sensible for E to retract her claim after having accepted F's – since there were some cookies to be eaten, if John ate all of them, he ate some of them, and so what E and F said may both be true. Thus, it looks like retraction is sensible only if you accept the assertion of someone who asserts something incompatible with what you assert, and this is just what **The Strong Disagreement Hypothesis** predicts.[7]

With this strengthened disagreement hypothesis in hand, we may turn back to our disagreement argument from before. We now need to modify that argument to be about strong disagreements rather than just disagreements in general. We do so as follows:

Strong Disagreement

In some cases in which X compatibilizes $\Phi/\sim\Phi$ across C1 and C2, the speaker uttering Φ in C1 *strongly disagrees* with the speaker uttering $\sim\Phi$ in C2.

Compatibility > No Strong Disagreement

If the proposition asserted by the speaker uttering Φ in C1 is compatible with the proposition asserted by the speaker uttering $\sim\Phi$ in C2, then the two speakers do not *strongly disagree*.

(This follows from **The Strong Disagreement Hypothesis**.)

Contextualism > No Strong Disagreement

In all cases in which X compatibilizes $\Phi/\sim\Phi$ across C1 and C2, X predicts that the speaker in C1 does not *strongly disagree* with the speaker in C2.

(This follows from **Strong Disagreement**, **Compatibility > No Strong Disagreement**, and the definition of "compatibilizes.")

261

This argument is more compelling than the first, for it is not immediately undermined by cases of implicature rejection.

However, we still need evidence for **Strong Disagreement**, which will come from cases in which a contextualist theory X compatibilizes $\Phi/\sim\Phi$ across C1 and C2 in which both (a) and (b) hold. Given that the aim of contextualism is to predict a difference in our truth value intuitions about knowledge ascriptions in various contexts, what we want is a pair of contexts in which we intuit a difference in the truth value of "S knows that p" – if our target contextualist theory is thus to be plausible, it will compatibilize "S knows that p"/"S doesn't know that p" across those contexts. Then, we can ask whether (a) and (b) intuitively hold in those contexts.

A standard method for ensuring that the two contexts are distinct, while also allowing the speakers to be in contact with each other, is to consult intuitions in eavesdropper cases: these are cases in which one speaker is eavesdropping on another, and then jumps in to reject the latter speaker's assertion (cf. Egan et al. 2005, Egan 2007). Here is an example (modified slightly from an example in Schaffer & Knobe 2012):

[Eavesdroppers]

Hannah and Sarah arrive at the bank one Friday afternoon to deposit their paychecks. When they arrive, they find the lines to the bank are very long.

Hannah says, "Ugh, what a line! Let's come back tomorrow."

Sarah replies, "But some banks aren't open on Saturdays! Do you know if this one is?"

Hannah responds, "Yes, **I know this bank will be open tomorrow (Saturday)**. I was there two Saturdays ago, and it was open."

Sarah replies, "OK, let's come back then to deposit our paychecks."

Another customer in line, Henry, overhears Hannah and Sarah. Being the intrepid type, he politely inserts himself into their conversation, saying, "Sorry to interrupt, but no, **you don't know this bank will be open tomorrow**. Banks sometimes change their hours; so, maybe it won't be open this Saturday, even though it was open two Saturdays ago. My brother Leon once got into trouble when the bank changed hours on him and closed on Saturday. How frustrating! Just imagine driving here tomorrow and finding the door locked."

Intuitively, EAVESDROPPERS is a case in which a contextualist theory may be inclined to predict that both what Hannah says and what Henry says are true. Say that X is a contextualist theory that predicts this result – then, X compatibilizes "Hannah knows the bank will be open Saturday"/"Hannah does not know the bank will be open Saturday" across Hannah's and Henry's contexts.[8] However, in this case, it seems that Henry's rejection of Hannah's assertion is licensed; and furthermore, were Hannah to retract her claim in light of Henry's rejection, her doing so would be sensible. So, it seems that Hannah and Henry strongly disagree in this case. Thus, (the relevant instance of) **Strong Disagreement** is true. We have already established **Compatibility > No Strong Disagreement** (which follows from **The Strong Disagreement Hypothesis**), and thus **Contextualism > No Strong Disagreement**. Therefore, by this argument, we may conclude that theory X is false (it incorrectly predicts that Hannah and Henry are not strongly disagreeing).

Having articulated a reasonably plausible disagreement argument that is not undermined by considerations of implicature rejection, we turn next to some contextualist responses.

The disagreement challenge

3 Resisting Strong Disagreement

Given that there are two major premises in the disagreement argument sketched above, we will consider strategies for resisting each premise. In this section, we focus on arguments against (the relevant instance of) **Strong Disagreement**.

I can see at least two ways of resisting (the relevant instance of) **Strong Disagreement**. The first is to challenge the alleged intuitions marshaled in support of it; the second is to argue that such intuitions do not support (that instance of) **Strong Disagreement**. Now, generally, intuition-mongering is not a fruitful dialectical strategy. However, in the case at hand, since both contextualists and anti-contextualists generally agree that the intuitions at stake are semantic intuitions of fluent speakers of English (in this case), a promising methodological strategy may be to put these intuition-claims to the test and see if ordinary speakers really have such intuitions. Despite a recent surge in experimental philosophy testing the truth-conditional predictions of various versions of contextualism, I am not aware of any experimental work examining intuitions about disagreement in compatibility pairs.[9] I leave assessing this matter aside for future work. For now, we will move on to the second kind of strategy for resisting (the relevant instance of) **Strong Disagreement**.

Conceding that we have the relevant intuitions about rejection and retraction, one might continue to resist (the relevant instance of) **Strong Disagreement** by denying that the intuitions that the speakers in the two contexts strongly disagree support the claim that the two speakers in fact strongly disagree. In other words, the contextualist adopting this strategy holds that the strong disagreement intuitions in these cases are mistaken. We will say that one taking this line of defense is offering an **error theory** about these disagreement intuitions.[10]

In my view, the most plausible appeal to error theory about disagreement intuitions is due to Schaffer and Szabó (2014), who argue that "knows" is an adverbial quantifier (e.g., "usually," "always," etc.) on the grounds that its behavior is most analogous to that displayed by adverbial quantifiers.[11] Schaffer and Szabó also argue that we have independent reasons to think that adverbial quantifiers are context-dependent (i.e., their domains are restricted to relevant situations, which may be sensitive to the questions under discussion in that context). Yet we also find contextualist-unfriendly intuitions about rejection and retraction for knowledge ascriptions. Thus, Schaffer and Szabó reason as follows: since "knows" is an adverbial quantifier, which is a context-dependent expression, our intuitions about rejection and retraction regarding "knows" must be systematically mistaken.[12,13]

I am not yet convinced that Schaffer and Szabó's appeal to an error theory is fair at this point in the dialectic. After all, it may be that "knows" differs in some semantically significant way from ordinary adverbial quantifiers, which makes extending lessons from the former to the latter suspect. For instance, while it seems appropriate for Henry to reject Hannah's assertion in Eavesdropper, it is less plausible to do so when the targeted claim involves an ordinary adverbial quantifier instead:

[Chopsticks]
>   G (to a friend): On Mondays, John eats lunch at his favorite Chinese restaurant. He always eats with chopsticks.
>   H (listening in): #No, he sometimes eats with a fork; I had him over for dinner last Friday.

In this case, it seems clear that H has simply not understood what G has said, and thus her rejection of what G says here is misplaced (and hence odd). The dialogue in Chopsticks seems like that in Doctor in this respect. Yet, there is nothing odd about Henry's rejection of Hannah's claim in Eavesdropper – in other words, it patterns analogously to B's rejection of A's assertion in Prime. This gives us reason to think that "knows" behaves differently from ordinary adverbial quantifiers in the relevant respect; hence, we should not reason, as Schaffer and Szabó do, from the fact that knowledge ascriptions license cross-contextual disagreement intuitions, together with the claim that "knows" is semantically similar to an adverbial quantifier, to the conclusion that an error theory is called for to handle our intuitions of disagreement for knowledge ascriptions. Rather, the reasonable conclusion to draw, it seems, is that "knows" is semantically unlike an ordinary adverbial quantifier. Contra Schaffer and Szabó, it seems we should conclude that the data about rejection and retraction is evidence that "knows" is simply not context-sensitive, in contrast with ordinary adverbial quantifiers.

In the case of disagreement intuitions, the contrasts between PRIME and DOCTOR (and EAVESDROPPER and CHOPSTICKS) strongly suggest that it is something about the semantics of the expressions involved in these dialogues that is responsible for our diverging intuitions regarding them. Positing an error theory here is unsatisfying because merely making this move does not explain why we get such clear intuitive contrasts (and why we find "knows" falling on the context-insensitive side of the contrast). Supplemented with a plausible theory, answering this question would make the error theory defense significantly stronger. However, no such theory is on offer.[14]

4 Resisting the Strong Disagreement Hypothesis

We turn now to the other premise in the disagreement argument: **The Strong Disagreement Hypothesis**. Responding to disagreement arguments about other expressions (most notably, moral expressions, predicates of personal taste, and epistemic modals), some theorists have suggested resisting disagreement arguments at this juncture on the grounds that there are better (or at least equally good) explanations for why two speakers strongly disagree that do not demand that those speakers assert incompatible propositions. For instance, one might hold that the reason why two speakers strongly disagree is that they *disagree in attitude* rather than in what they say (cf. Björnsson & Finlay 2010, Huvenes 2012, 2014, 2015). Or one might hold that such speakers are engaged in a metalinguistic dispute over what the extensions of certain expressions should be (cf. Plunkett & Sundell 2013). Finally, one might hold that the two speakers disagree about how to update their contexts (cf. Khoo 2015, Khoo & Knobe forthcoming). The unifying theme of these responses is to resist the account of strong disagreements in terms of incompatibility at the level of what is asserted, and offer an alternative understanding of strong disagreements.

Consider the first strategy – that some strong disagreements are best understood as mere disagreements in attitude. One immediate worry with appealing to disagreement in attitude as an account of strong disagreement is that it is hard to see what sort of attitude would do the work in this case. In the case of moral claims, the attitude is plausibly that of moral approval or disapproval; in the case of disagreements of taste, the attitude is plausibly that of enjoying or finding pleasurable. However, when it comes to disagreements involving knowledge ascriptions, it is less clear what the relevant attitude should be. For instance, is it some kind of attitude of epistemic approval of the subject of the knowledge ascription, S? What would this involve? Perhaps it involves approving of or recommending various related actions of S, like acting on her belief, and so on. Suppose for now that this is the relevant attitude, and suppose that speakers in compatibility pairs disagree in attitude in this sense (cf. McKenna 2014, 2015).

With a suitable attitude in hand, we now consider whether one person having (and perhaps expressing, by making her claim) the attitude of approving of S acting on her belief that p and another having the contrary attitude towards S (and expressing it, by making her claim) would explain why the two individuals strongly disagree. One way to explore this hypothesis is to see whether rejection is licensed and retraction is sensible when the two speakers directly report having the relevant contrary attitudes. Thus, consider the following discourse:

The disagreement challenge

[Approval]
J: I approve of S acting on her belief that p.
K: I do not approve of S acting on her belief that p.

Here, it seems that whether rejection is licensed depends on what questions are under discussion in the context, as brought out in the following examples:

[Q1]
J and K have the same evidence as S regarding the proposition that p and are discussing
   whether they should act on their belief that p.
J: I approve of S acting on her belief that p.
K: No, I don't approve of S acting on her belief that p.

[Q2]
J and K are getting to know each other, and K has asked J what sorts of things he approves of.
J: I approve of S acting on her belief that p.
K: #No, I don't approve of S acting on her belief that p.

By contrast, rejection seems *always* licensed when contrary knowledge ascriptions are uttered. This is some reason to think that strong disagreements are not disagreements in attitude. A further reason comes from the fact that in APPROVAL, even if J were to be convinced that K does not approve of S acting on her belief that p, this alone would not be enough to make it reasonable for J to retract her claim.[15]

In response to challenges like these, a natural move would be to hold that *expressing* one's attitudes is not the same as *asserting that* one has them (a point familiar in the expressivism literature going back to Ayer 1936). However, notice that the person running the above challenge on the disagreement in attitude approach did not make the mistake of confusing expressing and asserting – rather, she was looking for a reason to think that some strong disagreements were merely disagreements in attitude. Making this move perhaps explains why we should not expect self-ascriptions of certain attitudes to pattern the same as expressions of those attitudes. However, it does not explain why expressions of conflicting attitudes give rise to strong disagreements. The proponent of the disagreement in attitude strategy owes us an account of why merely expressing contrary attitudes explains why rejection is licensed and retraction is sensible in these cases. Without such an account, we have no reason to think that its account of strong disagreements is better (or even on a par with) that given by **The Strong Disagreement Hypothesis**.

Plunkett and Sundell (2013) raise the possibility that many ordinary-looking disagreements are what they call "metalinguistic negotiations" (following Barker 2002, Ludlow 2008). When two people are metalinguistically negotiating the extension of some term *t*, they disagree about what should fall in the extension of *t* in their context. Crucially, in a metalinguistic negotiation, the two speakers may assert compatible propositions, since, in one speaker's context, the extension of *t* is different from what it is in the other speaker's context. Here is an example from Ludlow (2008):

[Athlete]
L and M are trying to write up a list of the greatest athletes of the 20th century.
L: Secretariat is an athlete.
M: No, Secretariat isn't an athlete.

As the case is to be understood, L "systematically applies the term 'athlete' in such a way as to include non-human animals" while M "systematically applies the term 'athlete' in such a way as to never include non-human animals. This holds true even when all of the relevant factual information is on hand, including, as noted, the facts about Secretariat's speed, strength, etc." (Plunkett & Sundell 2013: 16). This gives us strong prima facie reason to think that they mean different things by "athlete" and that what each says is true in her idiolect. Yet, even with this background in place, the two speakers seem to strongly disagree by making their claims. Intuitively,

(a) M's rejection of L's claim is linguistically appropriate.
(b) Were L to retract her claim in light of M's rejection, her doing so would be sensible.

I understand Plunkett and Sundell to be arguing as follows. First, they argue that there are some cases of strong disagreement that are best analyzed as metalinguistic negotiations (such as ATHLETE above). Because the speakers engaged in a metalinguistic negotiation may assert compatible propositions, this result immediately challenges **The Strong Disagreement Hypothesis**. But this principle was our main support in favor of **Compatibility > No Strong Disagreement**, so that premise of the disagreement argument is also undermined. Crucially, the disagreement argument fails because, for all that has been said so far, it may be that all of the relevant cases of cross-contextual disagreement are metalinguistic negotiations, and contextualism is compatible with cross-contextual metalinguistic negotiations. Granted, *if* one could establish that a particular cross-contextual strong disagreement involving knowledge ascriptions was not a metalinguistic negotiation, then Plunkett and Sundell's resistance strategy fails. However, Plunkett and Sundell suggest that it is not at all obvious how to establish (on independent grounds) that a given strong disagreement is *not* a metalinguistic negotiation. As such, they fashion the contextualist a "get out of jail free" card – whenever someone raises a case of cross-contextual strong disagreement, the contextualist may now propose that it is a metalinguistic negotiation about what the extension of "knows" ought to be rather than a first-order disagreement about whether the subject knows.

Plunkett and Sundell threaten to blunt the dialectical force of disagreement arguments. However, we might worry that their defensive strategy merely rescues contextualism on a technicality. After all, it is still an open possibility that some cross-contextual disputes between someone uttering "S knows p" and someone uttering "S doesn't know p" are first-order disagreements (in which the two speakers assert incompatible propositions) rather than metalinguistic negotiations, and in that case Plunkett and Sundell would seem to have to concede that contextualism would fail to predict that the two speakers disagree. Plunkett and Sundell's point is just that it may not be possible to independently establish that any given dispute is first order.

We may then wonder what our options are for independently establishing whether a dispute is first order or metalinguistic. Khoo and Knobe (forthcoming) offer a method for investigating whether two speakers who strongly disagree must assert incompatible propositions. Although they focus on moral claims (sentences like "What S did was morally wrong"), their strategy is straightforwardly applicable to the knowledge attributions. Khoo and Knobe's strategy is to explore whether ordinary speakers' intuitions about disagreement (focusing on rejection) pattern with their intuitions about incompatibility in what is said. In a series of empirical studies, they find that, in certain cases, intuitions about whether two speakers disagree come apart from intuitions about whether at least one of those speakers' claims must be incorrect (their measure of incompatibility in what the speakers assert). Specifically, in certain cases where A utters a sentence Φ and B utters $\sim\Phi$, ordinary speakers agreed that rejection is licensed and that it would be correct to say that A and B disagree, and yet in those same cases ordinary speakers also tended to disagree

The disagreement challenge

with the claim that at least one of their (A's or B's) claims must be incorrect.[16] In other words, ordinary speakers' intuitions provide evidence against **The Strong Disagreement Hypothesis**.[17] Hence, we have good reason to doubt the principle, and thus the disagreement argument against contextualism is undermined.[18] One table-turning upshot of this result is that semantic theories designed to make predictions in line with **The Strong Disagreement Hypothesis** are actually disconfirmed by ordinary speakers' intuitions.[19]

But then what are the speakers in cases like EAVESDROPPERS disagreeing about if not the propositions they assert? Khoo and Knobe propose understanding conversational disagreements (those in which one person rejects another's assertion and thereby puts pressure on the latter to retract) in terms of how the two speakers propose to update their conversational context. Recall from Section 2 that on Stalnaker's theory of communication when you assertively utter a sentence, you assert some proposition, and thereby propose to add that proposition to the common ground. Although Stalnaker's view is quite popular, it is possible to understand the update proposal made by assertive utterances in different ways. For instance, Lewis (1979) proposes thinking of a context as determining a "conversational score," which changes in response to various conversational moves. For instance, in addition to a common ground parameter of the score, it may contain parameters for questions under discussion, standards for what counts as "flat," and so on. Crucially, for our purposes, is the idea that the conversational score contains an epistemic standards parameter, which entails what epistemic properties one must have with respect to a proposition to count as "knowing" it.[20] Keith DeRose then proposes that assertive utterances of knowledge ascriptions are proposals (in part) to change this epistemic standards parameter (DeRose 2004). For instance, uttering "S knows p" is to propose (among other things) changing the epistemic standards of the context such that S counts as "knowing" p by those standards.

On this theory of communication, it may turn out that when A says "S knows p" in her context and B says "S doesn't know p" in her context, they both assert true propositions (owing to different epistemic standards being operative in their two contexts). Nonetheless, in making these assertions, A and B make incompatible proposals to update their contexts. This is because there is no context whose epistemic standards count S as "knowing" p and also count S as not "knowing" p. Thus, if A were to make her assertion in conversation with B and vice versa, they would be making incompatible proposals for that context. It seems plausible that this fact licenses A and B to reject each other's assertions, and make it sensible for one to retract in light of the other's rejection. It seems then that a scorekeeping model of conversation may provide some resources toward a contextualist-friendly explanation of the intuitions of disagreement in cases like EAVESDROPPERS.[21]

5 Concluding thoughts

Disagreements involving two parties, one of whom makes a knowledge ascription and the other of whom rejects that knowledge ascription, pose a serious challenge to contextualism. In this chapter, I sketched the challenge and discussed several strategies contextualists have pursued for resisting it. We have seen why some of these strategies may be more promising than others, and found a promising path for the contextualist to follow. However, extending this strategy about conversational disagreements to cases in which the disagreeing parties are not in conversation with one another is non-trivial (though, it is also not obvious one would need to do so to defend contextualism from the disagreement challenge). I leave it as an open question for future work whether we should give up contextualism (in favor of some form of invariantism, truth-relativist or otherwise) in light of considerations of disagreement.[22]

Notes

1 This kind of contextualism is sometimes called "indexical contextualism" to distinguish it from the view called "non-indexical contextualism" (cf. MacFarlane 2009). The key difference between the views is that non-indexical contextualism predicts that knowledge ascriptions always express the same proposition in every context of utterance, while "indexical contextualism" instead predicts that different contexts of utterance initialize different epistemic standards parameters – thus, allowing that the same knowledge ascription may be true when uttered in some contexts and false when uttered in other contexts. I will set aside this variation of contextualism in what follows.

2 This challenge is discussed in several chapters in this volume, including chs. 1, 5, 21, and 22.

3 Though united in their general commitments sketched above, different contextualist theories will differ over what propositions are expressed by "S knows that p" in certain contexts. I will be largely abstracting away from such details in this chapter.

4 See, in particular, Feldman (2001), Hawthorne (2004), Richard (2004), MacFarlane (2005, 2011, 2014), Stanley (2005), Brendel (2014), Kompa (2015). Theorists have employed analogous strategies for resisting contextualist theories of other expressions, for instance, gradable adjectives, moral expressions, epistemic modals, taste predicates, and future operators. See, for instance, Moore (1922), Stevenson (1937), Hare (1952), Kolbel (2002, 2004), Gibbard (2003), Egan et al. (2005), Huemer (2005), Lasersohn (2005, 2009, 2011), Egan (2007, 2010, 2012), Stephenson (2007), Brogaard (2008), Garcia-Carpintiero and Kolbel (2008), Thomson (2008), Baker (2012), and MacFarlane (2014).

5 It should be emphasized that often accepting an assertion and retracting an assertion will be tacit, in that one need not do anything overt to signal one does either. It is an interesting question how accepting and retracting are signaled – see Farkas and Bruce (2010) and Malamud and Stephenson (2015) for discussion.

6 It might be sensible for E to admit that she shouldn't have said what she did. Nonetheless, having said it, she need not take it back. Intuitively, it's not what she said that's problematic, it's what she didn't say (and hence implicated as false) that's at stake.

7 MacFarlane offers an alternative hypothesis of strong disagreement within his relativist semantic framework which he calls *preclusion of joint accuracy*. I won't go into these details here.

8 I changed the sentences to remove the indexicals "I," "you," and "tomorrow" to eliminate the extra complications introduced by these expressions. The issues raised by indexicals are distinct from the ones currently under discussion, which concern whether "S knows p" may express different propositions in different contexts, even when "S" and "p" contain no context-sensitive vocabulary.

9 I know of three relevant studies here. Knobe and Yalcin (2014) looked at intuitions about retraction involving epistemic modal claims, Khoo (2015) looked at intuitions about rejection regarding epistemic modal claims, and Khoo and Knobe (forthcoming) looked at intuitions about rejection regarding moral claims. All three studies found evidence that ordinary speakers intuit the relevant marks of strong disagreement even when the speakers are in different contexts.

10 Invoking an error theory to defend contextualism on this point goes back to Schiffer (1996); see also Hawthorne (2004), DeRose (2006), Schaffer and Szabó (2014). Contextualists have appealed to error theories in order to account for intuitions about homophonic inter-contextual speech reports, disagreement, and anaphora.

11 See ch. 26.

12 This is a more plausible appeal to an error theory than is usually on offer. Another strategy is simply to appeal to an error theory on the grounds that every theory in play must do so. For instance, DeRose (2006) voices this strategy regarding the intuition whether the two speakers' claims are compatible, which he reports some tendency among his undergraduate students to endorse. DeRose's point is that the intuition of incompatibility is itself incompatible with the intuitions appealed to by contextualists – namely, that what each speaker says is true. So, DeRose concludes, whatever way you go – invariantist or contextualist – you will need to appeal to some kind of error theory. The problem with this response as a defense of contextualism is that it threatens to give up the game. There is a view which aims to capture both the truth value intuitions and the incompatibility (or in our case, disagreement) intuitions: truth relativism (cf. MacFarlane 2005). On truth relativism, "S knows that p" expresses the same proposition in all contexts (in which "p" expresses the same proposition), but the truth of the proposition expressed by "S knows p" depends on the context in which it is assessed. According to truth relativism, in the compatibility pair, (i) what the first speaker says is true (as assessed at his context) and what the second speaker says is true (as assessed at her context), yet (ii) the two speakers disagree because (relative to any context of assessment) at least one of their asserted propositions must be false. Unless the

The disagreement challenge

proponent of this version of the error theory is willing to hold that theories invoking an error theory of some of the data are just as good (*ceteris paribus*) as theories which do not need to invoke an error theory for that data, she must concede that relativism about knowledge ascriptions is the superior view (on this point).

13 An alternative strategy is that the disagreement intuitions are the result of a (perhaps mistaken) presupposition that the relevant contextual parameter (in this case, maybe a parameter for epistemic standards) has the same value in both speakers' contexts. Cf. de Sa (2008, 2015) and Marques and Garcia-Carpintero (2014). See MacFarlane (2014) for critical discussion of this strategy.

14 A place to look for bolstering the contextualist's appeal to error theory here is the "pretense" theory of Lawlor (2005). However, because Lawlor's theory is a very non-standard version of contextualism (in which knowledge ascriptions are given an invariant semantics but combined with a pretense theory that generates contextualist-friendly truth conditions), I will set it aside for now.

15 Interestingly, as was pointed out to me by Tim Sundell (p.c.) in cases like these, J might say, "Well, we will have to agree to disagree," suggesting that J and K disagree in some sense in such cases.

16 The kind of case in which these intuitions come apart for moral claims are ones in which the two speakers' cultures value radically different things.

17 To appreciate why data from ordinary speakers' intuitions could undermine **The Strong Disagreement Hypothesis**, recall that its support derived from the explanation it gave of the contrasting intuitions of disagreement in dialogues like PRIME and DOCTOR. However, **The Strong Disagreement Hypothesis** explains this contrast only if it is tacitly accepted by ordinary speakers who have such contrasting intuitions in PRIME and DOCTOR (for instance, as part of their understanding of how words like "No" work in English). Thus, if intuitions about disagreement come apart from intuitions about incompatibility in what is said, this is evidence that **The Strong Disagreement Hypothesis** is not really what explains the relevant difference between PRIME and DOCTOR after all, and hence these intuitions are evidence against it.

18 Admittedly, more work needs to be done. For instance, Khoo and Knobe did not explore intuitions about retraction. Furthermore, as of the time of this chapter's publication, there is no empirical work exploring whether there is a similar contrast between intuitions about rejection and intuitions about incompatibility in what is asserted for knowledge ascriptions.

19 These include invariantist theories, as well as the truth-relativist theory of MacFarlane (2005, 2014).

20 What it is to "count as knowing p by standards e" is shorthand for the relevant notion in your theory of knowledge. It could be a degree of justification, or a set of alternative possibilities your evidence must rule out, some degree of reliability throughout nearby possible worlds, and so on.

21 A standard response to the DeRose "single scoreboard" theory of disagreement is that it does not extend to cases in which the two parties "merely *think* to themselves 'S knows that p' and 'S does not know that p,' respectively, or if one considers the other's written or taped comments months later" (MacFarlane 2014: 182). However, these are not cases in which our standard measures of disagreement (felicitous rejection and sensible retraction) are measurable (because there is no conversation between parties). As such, the disagreement challenge loses much of its force. It may still be that the two parties disagree in some technical sense (disagree★), but it is less clear that a semantic theory for "knows" needs to predict that two people disagree★ merely in virtue of having certain thoughts.

22 Thanks to Nathan Cockram, Jonathan Jenkins Ichikawa, Laura Khoo, Joshua Knobe, and Matt Mandelkern for comments and suggestions on previous drafts.

References

Ayer, Alfred J. 1936. *Language, Truth, and Logic*. London: Victor Gollancz.

Baker, Carl. 2012. Indexical Contextualism and the Challenges from Disagreement. *Philosophical Studies*, 157, 107–123.

Barker, Chris. 2002. The Dynamics of Vagueness. *Linguistics and Philosophy*, 25, 1–36.

Björnsson, Gunnar, & Finlay, Stephen. 2010. Metaethical Contextualism Defended. *Ethics*, 121, 7–36.

Brendel, Elke. 2014. Contextualism, Relativism, and the Semantics of Knowledge Ascriptions. *Philosophical Studies*, 168, 101–117.

Brogaard, Berit. 2008. Sea Battle Semantics. *Philosophical Quarterly*, 58(231), 326–335.

de Sa, Dan López. 2008. Presuppositions of Commonality. Pages 297–310 of: Garcia-Carpintero, Manuel, & Kölbel, Max (eds), *Relative Truth*. Oxford: Oxford University Press.

de Sa, Dan López. 2015. Expressing Disagreement: A Presuppositional Indexical Contextualist Relativist Account. *Erkenntnis*, 80, 153–165.

DeRose, Keith. 2004. Single Scoreboard Semantics. *Philosophical Studies*, 119, 1–21.

DeRose, Keith. 2006. "Bamboozled by Our Own Words": Semantic Blindness and Some Arguments Against Contextualism. *Philosophy and Phenomenological Research*, 73(2), 316–338.

Egan, Andy. 2007. Epistemic Modals, Relativism, and Assertion. *Philosophical Studies*, 133(1), 1–22.

Egan, Andy. 2010. Relativism about Epistemic Modals. Pages 219–241 of: Hales, Steven (ed), *Blackwell Companion to Relativism*. Oxford: Blackwell.

Egan, Andy. 2012. Relativist Dispositional Theories of Value. *The Southern Journal of Philosophy*, 50(4), 557–582.

Egan, Andy, Hawthorne, John, & Weatherson, Brian. 2005. Epistemic Modals in Context. Pages 131–170 of: Preyer, George, & Peter, George (eds), *Contextualism in Philosophy: Knowledge, Meaning, and Truth*. Oxford: Oxford University Press.

Farkas, Donka, & Bruce, Kim. 2010. On Reacting to Assertions and Polar Questions. *Journal of Semantics*, 27(1), 81–118.

Feldman, Richard. 2001. Skeptical Problems, Contextualist Solutions. *Philosophical Studies*, 103(1), 61–85.

Garcia-Carpintiero, Mauel, & Kölbel, Max (eds). 2008. *Relative Truth*. Oxford: Oxford University Press.

Gibbard, Allan. 2003. *Thinking How to Live*. Cambridge: Harvard University Press.

Grice, Paul. 1989. *Studies in the Way of Words*. Cambridge: Harvard University Press.

Hare, Richard Mervyn. 1952. *The Language of Morals*. Oxford: Oxford University Press.

Hawthorne, John. 2004. *Knowledge and Lotteries*. Oxford: Oxford University Press.

Horn, Laurence. 1985. Metalinguistic Negation and Pragmatic Ambiguity. *Language*, 61(1), 121–174.

Huemer, Michael. 2005. *Ethical Intuitionism*. New York: Palgrave Macmillan.

Huvenes, Torfinn Thomesen. 2012. Varieties of Disagreement and Predicates of Taste. *Australasian Journal of Philosophy*, 90, 167–181.

Huvenes, Torfinn Thomesen. 2014. Disagreement Without Error. *Erkenntnis*, 79, 143–154.

Huvenes, Torfinn Thomesen. 2015. Epistemic Modals and Credal Disagreement. *Philosophical Studies*, 172(4), 987–1011.

Khoo, Justin. 2015. Modal Disagreements. *Inquiry*, 58(5), 511–534.

Khoo, Justin, & Knobe, Joshua. Forthcoming. Moral Disagreement and Moral Semantics. *Nous*. doi: 10.1111/nous.12151.

Knobe, Joshua, & Yalcin, Seth. 2014. Context-sensitivity of epistemic possibility modals: experimental data. *Semantics & Pragmatics*, 7(4), 1–21.

Kölbel, Max. 2002. *Truth without Objectivity*. London: Routledge.

Kölbel, Max. 2004. Faultless Disagreement. *Proceedings of the Aristotelian Society*, 104, 53–73.

Kompa, Nikola. 2015. Contextualism and Disagreement. *Erkenntnis*, 80, 137–152.

Lasersohn, Peter. 2005. Context Dependence, Disagreement, and Predicates of Personal Taste. *Linguistics and Philosophy*, 28(6), 643–686.

Lasersohn, Peter. 2009. Relative Truth, Speaker Commitment, and Control of Implicit Arguments. *Synthese*, 166, 359–374.

Lasersohn, Peter. 2011. Context, Relevant Parts and (Lack of) Disagreement over Taste. *Philosophical Studies*, 156, 433–439.

Lawlor, Krista. 2005. Enough Is Enough: Pretense and Invariance in the Semantics of "knows that". *Philosophical Perspectives*, 19(1), 211–236.

Lewis, David. 1979. Scorekeeping in a Language Game. *Journal of Philosophical Logic*, 8, 339–359.

Ludlow, Peter. 2008. Cheap Contextualism. *Philosophical Issues*, 18, 104–129.

MacFarlane, John. 2005. The Assessment Sensitivity of Knowledge Attributions. Pages 197–233 of: Szabó Gendler, Tamar, & Hawthorne, John (eds), *Oxford Studies in Epistemology, Vol. 1*. Oxford: Oxford University Press.

MacFarlane, John. 2009. Nonindexical Contextualism. *Synthese*, 166(2), 231–250.

MacFarlane, John. 2011. What is Assertion? Pages 79–96 of: Brown, Jessica, & Cappelen, Herman (eds), *Assertion*. Oxford: Oxford University Press.

MacFarlane, John. 2014. *Assessment Sensitivity: Relative Truth and its Applications*. Oxford: Oxford University Press.

McKenna, Robin. 2014. Shifting Targets and Disagreements. *Australasian Journal of Philosophy*, 92(4), 725–742.

McKenna, Robin. 2015. Epistemic Contextualism Defended. *Synthese*, 192(2), 363–383.

Malamud, Sophia, & Stephenson, Tamina. 2015. Three Ways to Avoid Commitments: Declarative Force Modifiers in the Conversational Scoreboard. *Journal of Semantics*, 32(2), 275–311.

Marques, Teresa, & Garcia-Carpintero, Manuel. 2014. Disagreement about Taste: Commonality Presuppositions and Coordination. *Australasian Journal of Philosophy*.

Moore, George Edward. 1922. *Philosophical Studies*. New York: Harcourt, Brace and Co. Inc.

Plunkett, David, & Sundell, Tim. 2013. Disagreement and the Semantics of Normative and Evaluative Terms. *Philosophers' Imprint*, 13(23), 1–37.

Richard, Mark. 2004. Contextualism and Relativism. *Philosophical Studies*, 119, 215–242.

Schaffer, Jonathan & Knobe, Joshua. 2012. Contrastive Knowledge Surveyed. *Noûs*, 46(4), 675–708.

Schaffer, Jonathan, & Szabó, Zoltán Gendler. 2014. Epistemic Comparativism: A Contextualist Semantics for Knowledge Ascriptions. *Philosophical Studies*, 168, 491–543.

Schiffer, Stephen. 1996. Contextualist Solutions to Skepticism. *Proceedings of the Aristotelian Society*, 96, 317–333.

Stalnaker, Robert. 1978. Assertion. Pages 315–332 of: Cole, Peter (ed), *Syntax and Semantics 9: Pragmatics*. New York: Academic Press.

Stalnaker, Robert. 1999. *Context and Content*. Oxford: Oxford University Press.

Stalnaker, Robert. 2002. Common Ground. *Linguistics and Philosophy*, 25, 701–721.

Stalnaker, Robert. 2014. *Context*. Oxford: Oxford University Press.

Stanley, Jason. 2005. *Knowledge and Practical Interests*. Oxford: Oxford University Press.

Stephenson, Tamina. 2007. Judge Dependence, Epistemic Modals, and Predicates of Personal Taste. *Linguistics and Philosophy*, 30(4), 487–525.

Stevenson, Charles Leslie. 1937. The Emotive Meaning of Ethical Terms. *Mind*, 46(181), 14–31.

Thomson, Judith Jarvis. 2008. *Normativity*. Peru, IL: Open Court.

21
ON DISAGREEMENT

Torfinn Thomesen Huvenes

1 Introduction

The topic of this chapter is what it takes for two individuals to disagree. In the unlikely event that someone is expecting a simple and informative answer, they will be disappointed. The main goal of this discussion is to provide an overview of some of the main issues and challenges that come up when we try to answer that question.

The purpose of sections 2 and 3 is to set the stage for the main discussion. In section 2, I clarify the boundaries of the discussion. In section 3, I introduce and tentatively defend the assumption that disagreement is a psychological phenomenon. The main discussion takes place in sections 4–6. In section 4, I discuss what the attitudes of two individuals have to be like in order for them to disagree. A lot of the discussion focuses on the question of whether two individuals must have conflicting beliefs in order to disagree. In section 5, I propose that it makes sense to think of disagreement as a matter of having conflicting attitudes. I also consider two accounts of what it is for attitudes to be in conflict. In section 6, I discuss whether it is necessary to take into account the context in which the attitudes are held. This discussion is motivated by considerations involving propositions that have relative truth-values.

2 Preliminary distinctions

It will be useful to start out by drawing some distinctions that will help establish the boundaries of the discussion. First and foremost, the focus will be on disagreement. However, it would also have been possible to focus on agreement. Many issues involving disagreement also come up in the case of agreement, and vice versa.

Herman Cappelen and John Hawthorne (2009: 60) distinguish between agreement as a state and agreement as an activity. Agreement as an activity is a matter of doing something and requires some form of interaction between the individuals who are involved. For instance, if someone makes a statement, there is a sense in which someone else may agree by uttering the sentence "I agree" in response, regardless of what she thinks about the matter. Agreement as a state, on the other hand, does not require interaction. For instance, if someone in Bogota and someone in Kuala Lumpur both believe that the Earth revolves around the Sun, then they may agree even if they are completely unaware of each other. Cappelen and Hawthorne suggest that the progressive

use, as in "agreeing", is a sign that we are talking about the activity. That is also true of constructions like "agree to". As John MacFarlane (2014: 119) points out, this distinction also applies to
disagreement. In what follows, the focus will be exclusively on disagreement as a state.

Another distinction has to do with the relata of the disagreement-relation, the objects
which disagreement is a relation between. In what follows, the focus will be on disagreement
between two individuals. However, it seems that an individual may also disagree with, say, a
proposition, action or attitude. For instance, if John says that it is raining in New York and
Mary believes that it is not raining in New York, she may be taken to disagree with what
John said.

Furthermore, two individuals may disagree about something and fail to disagree about something else. For instance, Mary and John may disagree about whether Stockholm is the capital of
Sweden, but agree that Copenhagen is the capital of Denmark. This may suggest that we should
really focus on a three-place relation between two individuals and whatever it is that they disagree about. For similar reasons, MacFarlane (2014: 120) takes the target relation to be a relation
between an individual and a speech act or attitude in context. However, in what follows, this
complication will be downplayed as much as possible. That is a matter of convenience. In order
to simplify the discussion, it will often be convenient to simply focus on the conditions under
which there is something that two individuals disagree about.

3 Language and thought

The next step is to start to locate the factors that make it the case that two individuals disagree.
As a starting point, it is natural to think of disagreement between individuals as a psychological
phenomenon. I take that to mean that whether two individuals disagree always depends at least
partly on their attitudes, such as their beliefs. This is the line taken by Frank Jackson and Philip
Pettit in their discussion of moral disagreement:

> Moral disagreement, and indeed disagreement in general, is a psychological phenom-
> enon. The production of sentences make public our disagreements; it does not create
> them.
>
> *(1998: 251)*

For the purpose of the following discussion, I am going to follow Jackson and Pettit and take
disagreement to be a psychological phenomenon. That is a substantial assumption. It is also
common to talk about disagreement in connection with speech acts like assertion (MacFarlane
2007: 22, 2014: ch. 6; Egan 2014: 76). That makes it tempting to say that whether two individuals disagree does not always depend on their attitudes. It sometimes depends on what they say.
However, this is not as obvious as it may seem. When we talk about disagreement in connection
with speech acts like assertion, it is important to remember the distinction between disagreement
as a relation between individuals and disagreement as a relation between an individual and a
proposition or speech act.

It might be helpful to consider an example. Let us suppose that Mary asserts that Tolstoy wrote
War and Peace and John asserts that Tolstoy did not write *War and Peace*. This looks like a case
of disagreement, but the issue is by no means clear-cut. If Mary believes that Tolstoy wrote *War
and Peace* and John believes that Tolstoy did not write *War and Peace*, then it seems right to say
that they disagree. But if that is what is going on, the example does not give us a reason to think
that their disagreement does not depend on their attitudes. The disagreement can be explained
by their beliefs.

Alternatively, it could be that both Mary and John believe that Tolstoy wrote *War and Peace*. While Mary's assertion is sincere, John's assertion is insincere. This is a more interesting version of the example insofar as the facts about their beliefs are not indicative of any disagreement. However, it is no longer clear that Mary and John disagree. There could still be disagreement in the sense that Mary disagrees with what John said. But it does not obviously follow that Mary and John disagree.

The tentative conclusion is that this kind of example does not give us a reason to abandon the assumption that disagreement is a psychological phenomenon, but there is a lot of room for further discussion. It is also worth noting that even if disagreement is a psychological phenomenon, what we say can still provide evidence for disagreement because it can provide evidence about our attitudes, such as our beliefs.

4 Attitudes

At this point, a natural question is what the attitudes of two individuals have to be like in order for them to disagree. In particular, a question that will occupy a central role in the following discussion is whether two individuals disagree only if they have conflicting beliefs. It is uncontroversial that when two individuals disagree, this is sometimes a matter of them having conflicting beliefs. That is what is going on when Mary and John disagree about who wrote *War and Peace*. Mary believes that Tolstoy wrote *War and Peace* and John believes that Tolstoy did not write *War and Peace*. More needs to be said about what it is for beliefs to be in conflict, but for now it is sufficient to observe that the proposition that John believes is the negation of the proposition that Mary believes.

Many cases of disagreement fit this pattern. The more interesting question is whether they all do. In other words, the question is whether we ought to endorse the following view, in the form of a necessary condition for disagreement:

Conflicting Beliefs

Necessarily, two individuals disagree only if they have conflicting beliefs.

This view is not without supporters. Derek Parfit expresses the view very concisely: "For people to disagree, they must have conflicting beliefs" (2011: 385). MacFarlane even suggests that something along these lines may seem like an obvious view:

The obvious thing to say is that they disagree just in case

ACCEPT/REJECT. There is a proposition that one party accepts and the other party rejects.

Perhaps it is because Accept/Reject is such an obvious answer that philosophers have not wasted much ink on the question of what it is to disagree.

(2007: 22)

MacFarlane formulates the view in terms of acceptance and rejection instead of belief, but for present purposes that is not too important. While he goes on to emphasize how difficult it is to give necessary and sufficient conditions for disagreement, MacFarlane (2007: 24) still treats disagreement as a matter of accepting and rejecting propositions. However, in later work, he distances himself from Conflicting Beliefs as a necessary condition for disagreement (Mac-Farlane 2014: ch. 6).

While Conflicting Beliefs has its supporters, it also has its opponents. Following Charles L. Stevenson (1937, 1944, 1963), it is common to recognize a distinction between so-called "disagreement in belief" and so-called "disagreement in attitude" or "disagreement in interest". While the former involves conflicting beliefs, the latter involves a conflict of non-doxastic attitudes. Non-doxastic attitudes are attitudes other than beliefs, such as desires or preferences.

While Stevenson's distinction is influential, there is a sense in which his terminology of "disagreement in attitude" and "disagreement in belief" might be unhelpful. For the purpose of the present discussion, "attitude" is used in a broader sense that also applies to belief. Having that in mind, it makes less sense to talk about a distinction between disagreement in belief and disagreement in attitude. Having conflicting beliefs is just one way of having conflicting attitudes. If Stevenson is right, there are other ways of having conflicting attitudes. As far as I can see, this is merely a terminological point. For the purpose of the present discussion, the important idea is that it is possible for there to be disagreement that involves non-doxastic attitudes and not conflicting beliefs.

Stevenson is not alone in thinking that disagreement can involve non-doxastic attitudes. Normative expressivists, such as Simon Blackburn (1984: 168, 1998: 69) and Allan Gibbard (2003: 68–71), often appeal to disagreement involving non-doxastic attitudes in order to explain normative disagreement. Roughly speaking, normative expressivism is the view that normative sentences express non-doxastic attitudes. However, one does not have to be an expressivist in order to reject Conflicting Beliefs and think that disagreement can involve non-doxastic attitudes (Dreier 1999; Björnsson and Finlay 2010; Sundell 2010; Huvenes 2012, 2014; Egan 2014; MacFarlane 2014: ch. 6; Marques and García-Carpintero 2014; McKenna 2014; Marques 2015; Richard 2015).

A problem with Conflicting Beliefs is that there are cases of disagreement that it does not capture. Stevenson uses the following example to illustrate the distinction between disagreement in belief and disagreement in attitude or interest:

> Let me give an example of disagreement in interest. A. "Let's go to a cinema to-night." B. "I don't want to do that. Let's go to the symphony." A continues to insist on the cinema, B on the symphony. This is disagreement in a perfectly conventional sense.
>
> *(1937: 27)*

I take it that there is a way of understanding Stevenson's example such that the two individuals disagree, but do not have conflicting beliefs. They are talking about what they want to do and there is no indication that they have conflicting beliefs. Insofar as the example shows that it is possible to disagree without having conflicting beliefs, that means that Conflicting Beliefs is false.

In order to resist this conclusion, one could maintain that no matter how the example is fleshed out, it will either turn out that the two individuals do not disagree or that they have conflicting beliefs after all. For instance, there may be ways of fleshing out the example such that they disagree about what they ought to do or something along those lines. In that case, they could still be construed as having conflicting beliefs. One of them believes that they ought to go to a cinema and the other believes that they ought not to go to a cinema. However, as far as I can tell, the disagreement remains even if I assume that they do not have any relevant beliefs about what they ought to do.

If the two individuals in Stevenson's example do not have conflicting beliefs, then what explains their disagreement? A natural answer is that they have conflicting desires and that is sufficient for disagreement. One of them has the desire that they go to a cinema, while the other has the desire that they do not go to a cinema. This takes us back to the question of what the attitudes of two individuals have to like in order for them to disagree. If the proposed explanation of Stevenson's example is on the right track, disagreement is sometimes a matter of having conflicting desires.

The disagreement in Stevenson's example has a practical dimension. The two individuals are trying to settle on a course of action. But that is not necessary in order to have a disagreement involving conflicting desires. For instance, it could be that Mary and John disagree because Mary has the desire that the company hires Harry, while John has the desire that the same company does not hire Harry. That could be the case even if they are not involved in the decision in any way. As before, one could argue that the disagreement depends on them having a disagreement about whether Harry ought to be hired or whether he is the best candidate. But that is still not obvious. For instance, it could be that they both believe that Harry is one of several candidates that are equally qualified. That does not make it the case that they do not disagree, but it makes it more difficult to argue that they have to be understood as having a disagreement about whether Harry ought to be hired.

So far the focus has been on cases of disagreement involving conflicting beliefs or desires. But it also makes sense to talk about disagreement in connection with other attitudes. In addition to desires, Stevenson (1944: 3) mentions purposes, aspirations, wants and preferences. James Dreier (2009: 105–106) takes preferences, as opposed to desires, as his paradigm when he discusses attitudes that can be involved in disagreement. It is possible that the list can be extended even further. For instance, if someone likes something that someone else dislikes, that could also be a case of disagreement (Weatherson 2009: 347; Huvenes 2012). It is beyond the scope of this article to discuss all of these attitudes in detail. However, it would not be surprising if it turned out that disagreement could involve a wide range of attitudes.

Having said that, there are attitudes that probably do not belong on the list. For instance, it is more difficult to find cases of disagreement involving imagination. It is not sufficient for disagreement if someone imagines that so-and-so is the case and someone else imagines that so-and-so is not the case. In that case, there is no apparent conflict. This will be relevant when we consider what it takes for attitudes to be in conflict.

5 Conflict

In the previous section, it was proposed that disagreement could involve a range of attitudes. At this point, I propose to think of disagreement as always being a matter of having conflicting attitudes, with "attitudes" still being used in a broad sense that includes belief. That amounts to endorsing the following view, in the form of a necessary and sufficient condition for disagreement:

Conflicting Attitudes

Necessarily, two individuals disagree if only and if they have conflicting attitudes.

There is a sense in which this does not say much. For instance, someone who endorses CONFLICTING BELIEFS could endorse CONFLICTING ATTITUDES and insist that the only way of having conflicting attitudes is to have conflicting beliefs. The question is what the relevant attitudes are and what it takes for them to be in conflict. In the previous section, the focus was on the former question. In this section, the focus will be on the latter question.

There are several ways in which one might try to develop a substantive account of what it takes for attitudes to be in conflict. In what follows, the plan is to focus on two prominent proposals in the literature. It might be more accurate to talk about two families of proposals, but for present purposes we will gloss over some of the subtle differences. The first proposal appeals to rationality or coherence. The idea is that it is impossible for a single individual to rationally and coherently have both attitudes at the same time. Dreier (2009: 106) seems to have something like this in mind. It is also similar to what MacFarlane (2014: 121–123) calls "noncotenability" of attitudes. Let us state the proposal as follows:

Rationality

Necessarily, two attitudes are in conflict if and only if it is impossible for a single individual to rationally and coherently have both attitudes at the same time.

For instance, let us again suppose that Mary believes that Tolstoy wrote *War and Peace* and John believes that Tolstoy did not write *War and Peace*. It is arguably impossible for a single individual to rationally and coherently believe that Tolstoy wrote *War and Peace* and at the same time believe that Tolstoy did not write *War and Peace*. According to RATIONALITY, that is sufficient for Mary and John's beliefs to be in conflict.

The second proposal appeals to satisfaction. The idea is that it is impossible for both attitudes to be satisfied. There are several proposals along these lines in the literature (Jackson 2008; Marques and Garcia-Carpintero 2014: 718; Marques 2015: 6). Stevenson also makes some suggestions that point in this direction:

> The difference between the two senses of "disagreement" is essentially this: the first involves an opposition of beliefs, both of which cannot be true, and the second involves an opposition of attitudes, both of which cannot be satisfied.
>
> *(1963: 2)*

The proposal can be stated as follows:

Satisfaction

Necessarily, two attitudes are in conflict if and only if it is impossible for both attitudes to be satisfied.

It is worth noting that "satisfaction" is being used in a broad sense. Simplifying somewhat, for beliefs, satisfaction is a matter of the belief being true. In the case of desire, satisfaction is a matter of the desire being fulfilled. For instance, let us suppose that Mary has the desire that the company hires Harry, while John has the desire that the same company does not hire Harry. In that case, it is impossible for both Mary's desire and John's desire to be fulfilled. Similarly, if Mary believes that Tolstoy wrote *War and Peace* and John believes that Tolstoy did not write *War and Peace*, then it is impossible for both Mary's belief and John's belief to be true.

There are problems with both proposals, but let us start with RATIONALITY. One worry is that the plausibility of the proposal depends on what counts as rational and coherent. This is particularly worrisome once we take into accounts attitudes other than beliefs. For instance, Teresa Marques (2015: 6) raises the worry that the circumstances under which it is irrational to have a pair of attitudes like desires may be limited. Desires may not be subject to the right kind of coherence constraints. It may even be that it is never irrational to have a pair of desires. In that case, there would not be any cases of conflicting desires according to RATIONALITY.

The worry is not just that coherence constraints apply too narrowly. Let us suppose that desires are in fact subject to coherence constraints. If Mary has the desire to become a physicist and John has the desire not to become a physicist, one may be reluctant to say that this is sufficient for them to disagree. In this case, there is a sense in which Mary's desire only concerns what happens to her and John's desire only concerns what happens to him. However, one could argue that it is impossible to rationally and coherently have both attitudes. According to RATIONALITY, that means that they have conflicting attitudes. How pressing this worry is depends on what the contents of the desires are. For instance, the worry becomes more pressing if we think of the contents of the desires as properties, along the lines suggested by David Lewis (1979). In order to have both attitudes, one would have to have the desire to possess the property of becoming a physicist and the desire not to possess that property. On the other hand, if the content of Mary's desire is the proposition that she becomes a physicist and the content of John's desire is the proposition that he does not become a physicist, it is possible to rationally and coherently have both attitudes. In the next section, we will discuss further complications that have to do with the contents of propositional attitudes.

There are also problems with SATISFACTION. One worry is that we end up with less conflict and disagreement than we might have hoped. For instance, insofar as there is a conflict between liking something and disliking it, that conflict is not captured by SATISFACTION. If Mary likes the taste of haggis and John dislikes the taste of haggis, there is nothing that prevents their attitudes from being satisfied (Marques 2015: 6).

There is also the worry that we end up with too much conflict and too much disagreement. If it is impossible for an attitude to be satisfied, then that attitude is in conflict with any other attitude. For instance, it is impossible for the belief that $2 + 2 = 5$ to be true. That means that it is also impossible for the belief that $2 + 2 = 5$ and the belief that Nairobi is the capital of Kenya to be true. According to SATISFACTION, that means that these attitudes are in conflict. But that is not a great result. If Mary believes that Nairobi is the capital of Kenya and John believes that $2 + 2 = 5$, then that should not be sufficient for them to be disagree.

This is arguably a result of SATISFACTION being formulated in modal terms. MacFarlane (2014: 126) uses the term "preclusion" and talks about one attitude precluding the satisfaction of another. Using his terminology, we can say that two attitudes are in conflict if and only if the satisfaction of one attitude precludes the satisfaction of the other attitude. However, MacFarlane declines to give an analysis of "preclusion" in modal terms in order to avoid the problem with attitudes that it is impossible to satisfy. Perhaps no analysis of "preclusion" is required, but it is worth considering whether that could also be said about "conflict".

If the choice is between RATIONALITY and SATISFACTION, then it might be better not to choose. Even in the absence of a worked-out third alternative, it would be a mistake to assume that either RATIONALITY or SATISFACTION has to be correct. Perhaps some of the difficulties can be lessened by thinking of the proposals as identifying different varieties of conflict and disagreement, along the lines suggested by MacFarlane (2014: 119). But even that is not obvious.

6 Context

So far we have been ignoring an important complication. It is natural to think that whether two individuals have conflicting attitudes only depends on the attitudes that they have. For instance, it is sufficient for two individuals to disagree if one of them believes a proposition and the other believes its negation. But that turns out to be problematic if propositions have relative truth-values. In that case, one only also needs to take into account the contexts in which the propositions are believed (MacFarlane 2007: 23). In what follows, the focus will be on beliefs, but these issues are also relevant for other propositional attitudes. More generally, the idea is that whether there is a conflict of attitudes depends partly on the contexts in which the attitudes are held.

On disagreement

For instance, let us suppose that the contents of beliefs are so-called temporally neutral propositions, propositions that are true or false relative to times. If I believe the temporally neutral proposition that I am hungry, I believe something that is true relative some times, but false relative to other times. That is different from believing the temporally specific proposition that I am hungry at 2 p.m. on the 1st of January 2016. Using an example from MacFarlane (2007: 22) as a template, let us suppose that at 2 p.m. Mary believes the temporally neutral proposition that Harry is sitting and that at 3 p.m. John believes the temporally neutral proposition that Harry is not sitting. The proposition that John believes at 3 p.m. is the negation of the proposition that Mary believes at 2 p.m., but Mary and John do not disagree. Their beliefs concern different times and it is possible that John was sitting at 2 p.m., but at 3 p.m. John was not sitting. Similar cases can be constructed if propositions are true or false relative to other parameters, such individuals or locations.

One might take this to be a problem for the view that the contents of beliefs are temporally neutral propositions (Cappelen and Hawthorne 2009: 98). If Mary believes the temporally specific proposition that Harry is sitting at 2 p.m. and John believes the temporally specific proposition that Harry is not sitting at 3 p.m., the propositions they believe are consistent and it is not surprising that they do not disagree. However, MacFarlane (2007: 22–23) argues that the point can also be made if propositions are true or false relative to possible worlds. That is significant insofar as the view that propositions are true or false relative to possible worlds is more widely accepted than the view that propositions are true or false relative to times. Let us suppose that Mary, who inhabits the actual world, believes that Mars has two moons and that John, who inhabits another possible world, believes that Mars does not have two moons. The proposition that John believes is the negation of the proposition that Mary believes, but Mary and John do not disagree.

It should be noted that these examples, involving individuals in different worlds, are contentious. Cappelen and Hawthorne (2009: 64) argue that MacFarlane's example does not work. It does not show that there are two individuals, one who believes that Mars has two moons and one who believes that Mars does not have two moons, who despite this fail to disagree. To say that there is a possible world in which someone believes that Mars does not have two moons, does not entail there is someone who believes that Mars does not have two moons. It only entails that it is possible that there is someone who believes that Mars does not have two moons. MacFarlane (2007: 23, 2014: 128) argues that the point can be made without talking about individuals in different possible worlds. Instead, we can ask whether Mary disagrees with the belief state that John would have had in the counterfactual situation. However, questions remain about how these counterfactuals ought to be understood and how they should be evaluated (Cappelen and Hawthorne 2009: 64–66; MacFarlane 2014: 128).

The lesson that MacFarlane (2007: 23) wants to draw is that we need to take into account the contexts in which the attitudes are held. For present purposes, it is not necessary to go into too much detail about how one might do that. One strategy is to adopt SATISFACTION and to be more careful about what this amounts to in the case of belief. This is more or less what MacFarlane (2007: 23, 2014: ch. 6) does by introducing the term "accuracy". Let us suppose that propositions are true or false relative to possible worlds and times. In that case, a belief is accurate if and only if the proposition that is believed is true relative to the possible world and time that is relevant in the context of the belief. In that case, we can say that a belief is satisfied if and only if it is accurate. This seems to work as intended in the case of temporally neutral propositions. While the time that is relevant in Mary's context is 2 p.m., it is 3 p.m. that is relevant in John's context. In that case, all it takes for both beliefs to be accurate is that at 2 p.m. Harry is sitting, but at 3 p.m. he is not sitting. According to SATISFACTION, that means that there is no conflict of attitudes.

279

Torfinn Thomesen Huvenes

However, there may be problems that this does not solve. Let us suppose that the proposition that John believes is the negation of the proposition that Mary believes, but that their beliefs are accurate. In that case, one might want to deny that they have conflicting attitudes. However, if Mary were to believe that John believes something false, that belief would also be accurate (MacFarlane 2007: 25). As Cappelen and Hawthorne (2011: 452) point out, then it should make sense for John to utter the sentence "She believes that what I believe is false, but she doesn't disagree with me." But that sounds strange, to say the least. This problem may be less pressing if we are only considering propositions that are true or false relative to times. In that case, the belief report would typically be in the past tense and that arguably makes it easier to make sense of what John is saying. However, if one takes propositions to be true or false relative to other parameters, such as individuals or locations, this response is not available.

It should be noted that the preceding discussion also ignores complications having to do with a so-called "relativist" position. For instance, it has been proposed that sentences that contain predicates of taste like "fun" and "tasty" express propositions that are true or false relative to different individuals or standards or taste (Kölbel 2002; Lasersohn 2005; Stephenson 2007; Richard 2008; Egan 2010; MacFarlane 2014: ch. 7). Similar ideas have been discussed in connection with other expressions, including knowledge ascriptions (Richard 2008: 166–176; MacFarlane 2014: ch. 8). Relativists have claimed to be in a strong position when it comes to making sense of disagreement. Let us suppose that Mary believes that haggis is tasty and John believes that haggis is not tasty. Roughly speaking, the idea is that this is sufficient for Mary and John to disagree even if the proposition that haggis is tasty is true relative to Mary's standards and false relative to John's standards. But that requires a standard of taste parameter to be treated differently from, say, a time parameter. If the relevant times are different, as in the cases above, there is no disagreement. But if their standards of taste are different, there can still be disagreement. Much has been written about this (Dreier 2009; Francén 2010; Lasersohn 2013; Egan 2014: 94–98; MacFarlane 2014: ch. 8; Richard 2015), but a proper treatment of these issues is beyond the scope of the present discussion.

7 Concluding remarks

While many issues remain unresolved, it is worth taking note of some of the points that have been made. In particular, there are reasons to think that it is possible to disagree without having conflicting beliefs. While disagreement sometimes involves conflicting beliefs, it may also involve conflicting non-doxastic attitudes, such as desires or preferences.

It is natural to think of disagreement as a matter of having conflicting attitudes, with "attitude" being used in a broad sense that includes belief. However, it is unclear whether there is a worked-out and satisfactory account of conflicting attitudes. There are problems with the two proposals that we considered. Perhaps these problems can be overcome, or perhaps it is possible to develop another alternative, but that remains to be seen. As an additional complication, it may be that whether there is a conflict of attitudes also depends on the contexts in which the attitudes are held. However, this depends on some contentious issues having to do with propositions that have relative truth-values.

References

Björnsson, G. and Finlay, S. (2010). Metaethical Contextualism Defended. *Ethics*, 121, 7–36.
Blackburn, S. (1984). *Spreading the Word*. Oxford: Oxford University Press.
Blackburn, S. (1998). *Ruling Passions*. Oxford: Oxford University Press.

Cappelen, H. and Hawthorne, J. (2009). *Relativism and Monadic Truth*. Oxford: Oxford University Press.

Cappelen, H. and Hawthorne, J. (2011). Reply to Lasersohn, MacFarlane, and Richard. *Philosophical Studies*, 156, 449–466.

Dreier, J. (1999). Transforming Expressivism. *Noûs*, 33, 558–572.

Dreier, J. (2009). Relativism (and Expressivism) and the Problem of Disagreement. *Philosophical Perspectives*, 23, 79–110.

Egan, A. (2010). Disputing about Taste. In R. Feldman and T. Warfield (Eds.), *Disagreement* (p. 247–286). Oxford: Oxford University Press.

Egan, A. (2014). There's Something Funny about Comedy: A Case Study in Faultless Disagreement. Erkenntnis (special issue on disagreement edited by Daniel Cohnitz and Teresa Marques), 79, 73–100.

Francén, R. (2010). No Deep Disagreement for New Relativists. *Philosophical Studies*, 151, 19–37.

Gibbard, A. (2003). *Thinking How to Live*. Cambridge, MA: Harvard University Press.

Huvenes, T. (2012). Varieties of Disagreement and Predicates of Taste. *Australasian Journal of Philosophy*, 90, 167–181.

Huvenes, T. (2014). Disagreement without Error. *Erkenntnis* (special issue on disagreement edited by Daniel Cohnitz and Teresa Marques), 79, 143–154.

Jackson, F. (2008). The Argument from the Persistence of Moral Disagreement. In R. Shafer-Landau (Ed.), *Oxford Studies in Metaethics: Volume 3* (p. 75–86). Oxford: Oxford University Press.

Jackson, F. and Pettit, P. (1998). A Problem for Expressivism. *Analysis*, 58, 239–251.

Kölbel, M. (2002). *Truth without Objectivity*. London: Routledge.

Lasersohn, P. (2005). Context Dependence, Disagreement, and Predicates of Personal Taste. *Linguistics and Philosophy*, 28, 643–686.

Lasersohn, P. (2013). Now-World Indices and Assessment-Sensitivity. *Inquiry*, 56, 122–148.

Lewis, D. (1979). Attitudes De Dicto and De Se. *The Philosophical Review*, 88, 513–543.

MacFarlane, J. (2007). Relativism and Disagreement. *Philosophical Studies*, 132, 17–31.

MacFarlane, J. (2014). *Assessment Sensitivity*. Oxford: Oxford University Press.

McKenna, R. (2014). Shifting Targets and Disagreement. *Australasian Journal of Philosophy*, 92, 725–742.

Marques, T. (2015). Disagreeing in Context. *Frontiers in Psychology*, 6, 1–12.

Marques, T. and García-Carpintero, M. (2014). Disagreement about Taste: Commonality Presuppositions and Coordination. *Australasian Journal of Philosophy*, 92, 701–723.

Parfit, D. (2011). *On What Matters*. Oxford: Oxford University Press.

Richard, M. (2008). *When Truth Gives Out*. Oxford: Oxford University Press.

Richard, M. (2015). What is Disagreement? In *Truth and Truth Bearers* (p. 82–114). Oxford: Oxford University Press.

Stephenson, T. (2007). Judge Dependence, Epistemic Modals, and Predicates of Personal Taste. *Linguistics and Philosophy*, 30, 487–525.

Stevenson, C. L. (1937). The Emotive Meaning of Ethical Terms. *Mind*, 46, 14–31.

Stevenson, C. L. (1944). *Ethics and Language*. New Haven: Yale University Press.

Stevenson, C. L. (1963). The Nature of Ethical Disagreement. In *Facts and Values* (p. 1–9). New Haven: Yale University Press.

Sundell, T. (2010). Disagreements about Taste. *Philosophical Studies*, 155, 267–288.

Weatherson, B. (2009). Conditionals and Indexical Relativism. *Synthese*, 166, 333–357.

22

CONTEXTUALISM, RELATIVISM, AND THE PROBLEM OF LOST DISAGREEMENT

Elke Brendel

Introduction

Disagreement has been receiving attention in the recent debate between contextualists and relativists. A central challenge for contextualism and relativism is to account for the phenomenon of disagreement while still capturing the idea of context-sensitivity. In what follows, I focus on the prospects for epistemic contextualism and relativism to account for our intuitions concerning disagreement about *knowledge ascriptions*. The discussion is also briefly extended to *epistemic modal claims*. I will examine whether contextualist and relativist semantics allow us to model situations of disagreement and certain related phenomena of rejection and retraction. In particular, I analyze the "problem of lost disagreement," which can be considered the largest threat to indexical contextualism. It is argued that this problem can be avoided within nonindexical contextualism and truth-value relativism. However, both relativist and contextualist semantics seem unable to address *substantial* forms of disagreement about knowledge ascription.

First, a brief explication of the key notions *disagreement*, *contextualism*, and *relativism* is in order. Roughly speaking, a *disagreement* consists in a situation where two parties have contradictory opinions about a particular subject matter. Two parties are in disagreement only if there is a certain state of conflict that can only be resolved by at least one of the parties changing or retracting his/her opinion about the contentious issue (see MacFarlane 2014: 123).[1] A disagreement does not necessarily presuppose an actual conversational situation of dispute. People can be in disagreement without knowing it (see, for example, Cappelen/Hawthorne 2009: 60f. and MacFarlane 2014: 119). The opposing parties do not even need to be different subjects. It is possible, for example, to disagree with "one's past self."

In order to distinguish *contextualism* from *relativism*, it is helpful to characterize these notions in terms of *use-sensitivity*, *use-indexicality*, *assessment-sensitivity*, and *assessment-indexicality* (see, for example, MacFarlane 2005b: 326 and 2014: 79f.). Generally speaking, a sentence is *use-sensitive* if and only if the truth-value of the proposition it expresses depends on features of the context of use, as, for example, on features of the world, the speaker, or the location or time of the sentence utterance. A sentence is *use-indexical* if and only if it expresses different propositions at different contexts of use. So, for example, the sentence "I am tired" is *use-indexical*. It expresses different propositions when uttered by different speakers. When uttered by speaker A, it expresses the proposition that A is tired (at the time of utterance); when uttered by speaker B, it expresses the proposition that B is tired (at

282

the time of utterance). "I am tired" is also *use-sensitive*. It expresses a true proposition just in case the speaker is tired (at the time of utterance), and it expresses a false proposition if the speaker is not tired (at the time of utterance). For a sentence which is *use-indexical but not use-sensitive* consider, for example, the sentence "If I am tired, I am tired." This sentence expresses different propositions when uttered by different speakers, but its truth-value does not depend on features of the context of use: it is true at all contexts of use. According to certain temporalists, such as Arthur Prior or David Kaplan, a sentence like "Jonathan is talking" is *use-sensitive without being use-indexical*. It expresses (at all contexts of use) the proposition that Jonathan is talking. Nevertheless, the truth-value of this proposition depends on whether Jonathan is talking at the time of utterance.

According to John MacFarlane, we need *contexts of assessment* in addition to contexts of use to model proper relativist semantics. For MacFarlane, a sentence is *assessment-sensitive* if and only if the truth-value of the proposition it expresses depends on features of the context of assessment, i.e., the context from which the use of a sentence is assessed. A sentence is *assessment-indexical* if and only if it expresses different propositions relative to different contexts of assessment.[2] As we will see in the following, *contextualists* regard *knowledge ascriptions*, in a certain sense, as *use-sensitive*. *Knowledge ascriptions* are *sentences* of the form "S knows that p" (where S is the epistemic subject, and p is a proposition). In an *indexical contextualist* semantics, knowledge ascriptions are not only use-sensitive but also *use-indexical*, whereas *nonindexical contextualists* treat knowledge ascriptions as *use-sensitive without being use-indexical*. *Relativism* about knowledge ascriptions, in contrast, is the view that knowledge ascriptions are *assessment-sensitive*. In particular, according to MacFarlane's *truth-value relativism*, knowledge ascriptions are assessment-sensitive but *not assessment-indexical*.[3]

Indexical contextualist semantics of knowledge ascriptions and the problem of lost disagreement

According to contextualism, the truth-value of the proposition expressed by a knowledge ascription depends, inter alia, on whether the epistemic subject S can meet the standards for knowledge that are in play at the context of use c_U, i.e., at the context of the speaker or the knowledge ascriber.[4] Contextualists normally refer to two major components at c_U that determine the standards for knowledge: stakes and error-possibilities. The more that is at stake for the knowledge ascriber – i.e., the more important it is for the knowledge ascriber that p is right – the higher the standards for knowledge are at c_U, and, as a consequence, the more difficult it gets for S to meet those standards (see, for example, DeRose 1992: 914). Furthermore, the knowledge ascriber's mentioning or considering of an error-possibility regarding p can raise the standards for knowledge at c_U (see, for example, DeRose 1992: 915, or David Lewis's "rule of attention" in Lewis 1996: 559), and if S is not able to rule out those error-possibilities, the proposition expressed by "S knows that p" turns out to be false at c_U.

Almost all contextualists about knowledge ascriptions are *indexical* contextualists (see, for example, Cohen 1988, 2000; DeRose 1992, 2005, 2009; Lewis 1996). For them, knowledge ascriptions are not only use-sensitive but also *use-indexical*, i.e., they express different propositions at different contexts of use. For an indexical contextualist, in ascribing knowledge that p to S by uttering "S knows that p," a speaker A thereby says that S knows that p *according to A's standards for knowledge*. And if another speaker B with higher or more stringent standards for knowledge utters "S does not know that p," B thereby says that S does not know that p *according to B's standards for knowledge*. In claiming "S does not know that p," B does not say something that contradicts what A says when claiming "S knows that p." If S can meet A's but not B's standards for knowledge (and if the other conditions for S's knowing that p are fulfilled), both speakers A and B say something true. So there does not seem to be any disagreement between A and B about the question of whether S knows that p or not. There is no conflict that needs to be settled, and neither A nor

B should rationally be motivated to reject what the other has said – or to retract what they have said in order to reach agreement.

Let us illustrate this so-called "problem of lost disagreement" with an example (see also Brendel 2014: 103f.): Anna parks her bicycle in front of the university library and goes into the library to read. An hour later her friend Bertha shows up and (with the intent to borrow Anna's bike) asks Anna whether she knows where her bicycle is. Anna remembers having parked the bicycle in front of the library, and she has no reason to doubt that her bicycle is parked there. Thus, she believes that her bicycle is parked in front of the library and responds to Bertha: "Of course, I know where my bicycle is. It is parked in front of the library." Let us assume that Anna's bicycle is indeed parked in front of the library. According to contextualism, not only does Anna's knowledge self-ascription express a true proposition in Anna's context, but also Bertha, who is not considering any error-possibilities to Anna's belief, would say something true when she uttered "Anna knows that her bicycle is parked in front of the library" at her context $c_U B$ (context of use governed by the standards for knowledge of the speaker Bertha).

Remembering that there have been many bicycle thefts in front of the university library recently, Carla, another of Anna's friends, considers the possibility that thieves might have stolen Anna's bicycle – a possibility that Anna, given her current epistemic situation where she is sitting inside the library with no sight of the bike racks, cannot rule out. Fortunately, no thieves are around at the time when Anna's bicycle is parked in front of the library. However, for a contextualist, Carla says something *true* when claiming "Anna does not know that her bicycle is parked in front of the library" at her context $c_U C$ – a context in which the possibility that Anna's bicycle might have been stolen is salient.

Indexical contextualism has it that Bertha's knowledge ascription expresses the proposition that Anna knows that her bicycle is parked in front of the library according to Bertha's standards for knowledge operative at $c_U B$, and Carla's utterance expresses the proposition that Anna does not know that her bicycle is parked in front of the library according to Carla's higher standards for knowledge at $c_U C$. Thus, Bertha and Carla have not asserted incompatible propositions. The opinions they have expressed with their utterances do not contradict each other. According to an indexical contextualist approach, Bertha and Carla only appear to disagree, and are actually talking past each other. Neither Bertha nor Carla is therefore rationally warranted in rejecting what the other has said. Even if Carla confronts Bertha with her worry that Anna's bicycle might have been stolen, there is no need for Bertha to retract what she said. What she said when uttering "Anna knows that her bicycle is parked in front of the library" at $c_U B$ remains true even after learning about an error-possibility she hitherto ignored. Even if Bertha, after becoming aware of such an error-possibility, now claims "Anna does not know that her bicycle is parked in front of the library," her claim is made in a context with higher standards and does not contradict what she said earlier. There is, so to speak, no disagreement between Bertha in higher-standards context and her "past self" in lower-standards context.[5]

This consequence of lost disagreement seems to be a severe problem for contextualism. Intuitively, there is a disagreement between Bertha and Carla. Carla seems to be warranted in rejecting what Bertha said. Furthermore, after seriously considering the possibility that Anna's bicycle might have been stolen, it appears to be rational for Bertha to retract what she said before.[6]

Epistemic relativism, nonindexical contextualism, and the problem of lost disagreement

MacFarlane has sharply criticized contextualism for its alleged incapability to address intuitions about disagreement. For him, the "problem of lost disagreement" is the "Achilles' heel of contextualism" (MacFarlane 2014: 118). According to MacFarlane, *truth-value relativism*[7] can

The problem of lost disagreement

avoid the problem of lost disagreement while still capturing the idea of the context-dependency of knowledge ascriptions. MacFarlane's relativist account has it that knowledge ascriptions are *assessment-sensitive*, i.e., the truth-values of the propositions they express (at a context of use and assessed from a context of assessment) depend, inter alia, on the standards for knowledge of the *assessor* (see, for example MacFarlane 2005a and 2014, ch. 8).[8] It is important to note that in Mac-Farlane's relativist semantics, knowledge ascriptions are *not assessment-indexical*. They express the *same* proposition uttered at all contexts c_U and assessed from all contexts c_A. But since knowledge ascriptions are assessment-sensitive, this proposition can nevertheless vary its truth-value relative to the standards of knowledge at c_A. So, "S knows that p" uttered at c_U and assessed from c_A expresses the proposition that S knows that p, and the truth-value of this proposition depends on whether S can meet the standards for knowledge at c_A. Thus, if one speaker utters "S knows that p" at c_U1 and another speaker utters "S does not know that p" at c_U2, these sentences, according to relativism, express *contradictory* propositions, and assessed from a context c_A only one of these propositions can be true: if S meets the standards for knowledge at c_A (and all other conditions for knowledge are fulfilled), "S knows that p" uttered at c_U1 and assessed from c_A expresses a *true* proposition, and "S does not know that p" uttered at c_U2 and assessed from c_A expresses a *false* proposition – and vice versa for the case in which S does not meet the standards for knowledge at c_A. Thus, it seems that a relativist semantics makes room for modeling intuitions of disagreement and certain rejection and retraction phenomena. Assessed from Carla's higher-standards context c_AC, the proposition Bertha's knowledge ascription expresses is false, and, as a consequence, Carla can rationally reject what Bertha has said. And if Bertha considers the possibility that Anna's bicycle might have been stolen, she can now assess (from c_AB) her former knowledge claim uttered at c_UB as expressing a false proposition. So, she can retract what she said before.

But it should be noticed that the capacity of relativist semantics to address the problem of "lost disagreement" is primarily due to the assumed *nonindexicality* of knowledge ascriptions. In order to explain and model certain phenomena of rejection and retraction it does not seem necessary to regard knowledge ascriptions as *assessment-sensitive*. A *nonindexical* contextualist account (see, for example, Kompa 2002, 2015; MacFarlane 2009, 2014: 88–90), according to which knowledge ascriptions are *use-sensitive without being use-indexical*, seems to be able to capture intuitions of disagreement as well. In contrast to indexical accounts, nonindexical contextualism has it that the propositions expressing knowledge ascriptions do not contain the speaker's standards for knowledge as an indexical element. Bertha's utterance simply expresses the proposition that Anna knows that her bicycle is parked in front of the library, and Carla's utterance expresses the proposition that Anna does not know it. So, as in relativism, Bertha's and Carla's knowledge ascriptions do express *contradictory* propositions. Thus, Bertha and Carla are in disagreement and it seems appropriate for Carla to reject what Bertha has said. And if Bertha seriously considers the possibility that Anna's bicycle might have been stolen, it is rational for her to disagree with her "past self" and retract the proposition expressed by her earlier knowledge ascription. However, in treating knowledge ascriptions as *use-sensitive*, nonindexical contextualism is still contextualist in character. The truth-value of the proposition that Anna knows that her bicycle is parked in front of the library depends on the standards for knowledge at the *context of use* – *not* the context assessment.

Although nonindexical contextualism can account for the problem of lost disagreement, Mac-Farlane nevertheless objects that nonindexical contextualism still fails to address some important intuitions about rejection and retraction. For MacFarlane, rejection and retraction target speech acts, such as assertions – and not their contents (see, MacFarlane 2014: 108–110). Although relativism and nonindexical contextualism both predict that from Carla's perspective, the content of Bertha's utterance at c_UB is false, it is only in a relativist framework that there is ground for Carla to reject Bertha's *utterance* of the knowledge claim (and for Bertha to retract the utterance

285

she made earlier). In a contextualist framework, the relevant context of evaluating a knowledge ascription is the *context of utterance* c_U. That Bertha's knowledge ascription uttered at c_UB expresses a true proposition is, so to speak, an "eternal truth," according to a contextualist semantics – no matter if the knowledge ascription would have expressed a false proposition uttered at c_UC. If an utterance of a knowledge ascription was made in accordance with the epistemic standards at c_U (and if the other truth-conditions for the knowledge ascription are met), there is no rationale for a contextualist to reject such an *utterance*. In a relativist semantics, however, the relevant context of evaluating a knowledge ascription is the *context of assessment* c_A. Thus, an utterance of a knowledge ascription made at c_U can be rejected by an assessor whose standards for knowledge at c_A differ from the utterer's standards for knowledge at c_U.

But is this capacity to explain rejection and retraction of *utterances* of knowledge ascriptions really an important advantage of truth-value relativism over nonindexical contextualism, as MacFarlane claims? A nonindexical contextualist could argue against MacFarlane that rejection and retraction is not necessarily confined to assertions. Contrary to MacFarlane, a nonindexical contextualist could contend that there are situations where it makes sense to reject (or retract) *what* was said but not *that* it was said. In particular, these could be situations in which the speaker when uttering a knowledge ascription "S knows that p" at c_U is *not at fault*, i.e., in which the speaker makes her utterance in accordance to the standards for knowledge that are in play at c_U (and in which p is true, S believes that p, and S meets the standards for knowledge at c_U). While MacFarlane emphasizes that "withdrawing an assertion [. . .] is not tantamount to conceding that one was at fault in making it" (2014: 110), a nonindexical contextualist could instead argue that if an utterance of a knowledge ascriptions doesn't involve any kind of mistake, although one can change one's mind vis-à-vis the content of the utterance when the standards for knowledge change, one should nevertheless adhere to the utterance itself. So, it is not obvious that the semantic treatment of rejection and retraction of *utterances* of knowledge ascriptions really constitutes a conclusive selling point for relativism or motivates embracing a much more complicated semantics than nonindexical contextualism.

Epistemic relativism and the problem of lost substantial disagreement

So far we have seen that disagreement "gets lost" within an indexical contextualist semantics, whereas nonindexical contextualism as well as relativism can account for our intuitions about disagreement. Nonindexical contextualism, however, does not allow for rejecting or retracting *utterances* of knowledge ascriptions – a consequence a nonindexical contextualist might happily accept. But regardless of whether we embrace a contextualist or a relativist semantics of knowledge ascriptions, we face another difficulty that I propose to call the *problem of lost substantial disagreement*.

In what follows, the problem of lost substantial disagreement will be discussed with a focus on relativism, though a similar argument can be put forward with regard to contextualism as well. In a relativist framework, a disagreement between two assessors A1 and A2 about a knowledge ascription of the form "S knows that p" (used at a context c_U) can arise when the truth-value of the proposition this knowledge ascription expresses varies from A1's context of assessment c_A1 to A2's context of assessment c_A2. In such a case of disagreement, A1 and A2 have conflicting opinions about whether S knows that p. From their respective contexts of assessment, they cannot consistently adopt the view of the other. But according to relativism, there are *no assessment-independent standards of correctness*. So, even if two assessors A1 and A2 have a disagreement about whether S knows that p, the disagreement can be *nonsubstantial*.[9] A disagreement about whether S knows that p is nonsubstantial, according to a relativist semantics of knowledge ascriptions, if

The problem of lost disagreement

the opposing parties are both right about all the context-insensitive components of a knowledge ascription, and the disagreement only results from the different contextual standards for knowledge. So let us assume that, as used at c_U1 and assessed from c_A1, "S knows that p" expresses a true proposition, and as used at c_U2 and assessed from c_A2, "S knows that p" expresses a false proposition. Let us further assume that both assessors A1 and A2 *correctly* assume that p is true, that S believes that p, and that S can meet A1's but not A2's standards for knowledge. In such a case the opposing assessments only result from the different standards for knowledge in play at the contexts of assessment. Since those standards are only governed by the assessor's stakes or by the error-possibilities the assessor happens to consider, neither A1 nor A2 is wrong in assessing the knowledge claim in accordance to their respective standards for knowledge. As long as the assessors stick to their contexts, the disagreement cannot be settled. In a case of nonsubstantial disagreement, a dispute about who is right and who is wrong and an attempt to reach agreement seems to be inappropriate, and maybe even disrespectful to the subjective opinions of the disputants. In such a situation one should, as Gottlob Frege remarks, "espouse the principle: *non disputandum est*" (Frege 1979: 233, quoted in MacFarlane 2014: 118).[10]

According to relativism, if S can meet Bertha's standards for knowledge but not Carla's (and if the other conditions for knowledge are fulfilled), neither Bertha nor Carla were wrong when they came to different conclusions when assessing an utterance of "Anna knows that her bicycle is parked in front of the library." They have both correctly assessed an utterance of a knowledge ascription, relative to separate perspectives where different standards for knowledge are in play.

However, the above disagreement between Bertha and Carla does not appear to be merely nonsubstantial. Carla, who knows about the recent bicycle thefts and considers the possibility that Anna's bicycle might have been stolen, appears to be in a *superior* epistemic position compared to Bertha. It therefore seems to be correct for Carla to assess from c_AC the knowledge ascription as expressing a false proposition, and it seems to be correct for her to reject what Bertha said when Bertha uttered at c_UB "Anna knows that her bicycle is parked in front of the library."

But, according to relativism, assessed from Bertha's context in which the possibility of bicycle thefts is not considered, Carla's knowledge-denying claim expresses a *false* proposition. As long as Bertha is ignorant of the possibility of bicycle thefts, she stays in her lower-standards context and, as a result, her knowledge-affirming utterance remains true, relative to her ignorant perspective. That is why according to relativism, even if Bertha and Carla have a disagreement about whether Anna knows that her bicycle is parked in front of the library, neither Bertha nor Carla are rationally required to revise their opinions, as long as they don't change their standards for knowledge. But intuitively there is a *substantial* disagreement between Bertha and Carla: given Carla's epistemically superior position, Carla is right in rejecting what Bertha has said – but not vice versa.[11]

This problem of lost substantial disagreement is similar to a difficulty Richard Dietz has pointed out with regard to relativist accounts of *epistemic modal* claims (see Dietz 2008). Roughly, epistemic modal claims are sentences expressing the epistemic possibility or impossibility of a proposition, such as "It might be that p" or "It cannot be that p."[12] In contextualist accounts, epistemic modal claims are *use-sensitive*: An epistemic modal claim of the form "It might be that p" expresses a true proposition at c_U just in case p is not ruled out by the epistemic state of the speaker (or a contextually relevant group) at c_U.[13] In MacFarlane's truth-value relativist account, epistemic modal claims are *assessment-sensitive*: used at c_U and assessed from c_A an epistemic modal claim of the form "It might be that p" expresses a true proposition just in case p is not ruled out by the epistemic state of the assessor (see MacFarlane 2014: ch. 10). So, for example, the epistemic modal claim "There might be a counterexample to Fermat's Last Theorem" expresses a true proposition when uttered at and assessed from the epistemic perspective of an ignorant assessor

287

A1 who does not know that Fermat's Last Theorem was proved by Andrew Wiles in 1994. A1 is therefore warranted in rejecting what an informed person A2, who knows about Wiles's proof, says when uttering "There cannot be a counterexample to Fermat's Last Theorem." But this appears to be counterintuitive. In particular, if the above epistemic modal claims are made after 1994, A1 in ignoring common mathematical knowledge should not be warranted in rejecting an epistemic modal claim made by a mathematically informed person.

MacFarlane tries to address Dietz's problem of *ignorant assessors* by allowing his relativist account to be more flexible with regard to the truth-determining contexts. In his so-called flexible relativism, it is still the context of assessment that determines which epistemic perspective is relevant for the evaluation of epistemic modal claims, but, depending on the intentions and goals of the assessor, in some situations – for example, when "the primary point of assessment is critical evaluation of the speaker's assertion" (MacFarlane 2014: 17) – the relevant context could be the *speaker's* information.[14]

Flexible relativism can explain why we sometimes *resist* rejecting or retracting epistemic modal claims when the focus of interest is on what the speaker's informational state was when she made her claim. With knowledge ascriptions, however, we are much less inclined to resist rejection or retraction. Our informed mathematician A2 could, in a somewhat generous mood, claim: "A1, given her deficient information state, said something true when saying that there *might* be a counterexample to Fermat's Last Theorem." And the uninformed and ignorant person A1, after getting the information that Fermat's Last Theorem had been proved, could entrench by claiming: "I wasn't wrong. When I said that there might be a counterexample to Fermat's Last Theorem, I didn't know that the theorem had been proved. So, I don't take back what I said." But it seems to be unacceptable if Carla claimed: "Bertha didn't say something false. She just didn't think about the bicycle thefts in front of the library recently and didn't consider the possibility that Anna's bicycle might have been stolen." And it would also be unacceptable if Bertha, after becoming aware of the possibility of bicycle thefts, claimed: "I do not take back what I said. I said something true. I just didn't consider the possibility of bicycle thefts when I made my earlier knowledge claim."[15]

But even with regard to epistemic modal claims, flexible relativism doesn't seem to provide a *general* solution to the problem of ignorant assessors. MacFarlane stresses the point that his relativist account of epistemic modal claims is "solipsistic" i.e., it is the epistemic perspective of the single assessor that counts – and not the epistemic perspective of a "contextually relevant group" which might include informed assessors (see MacFarlane's critique of attempts to widen the relevant epistemic perspective to a contextually relevant community in MacFarlane 2014: 243–245). So, if an ignorant assessor is simply not interested in the perspective of others while trying "to guide her own inquiry" (MacFarlane 2014: 260), she need not take the epistemic state of others into account.

Conclusion

Let us briefly take stock. It has been argued that *indexical contextualism* about knowledge ascriptions faces the problem of *lost disagreement* and cannot account for certain phenomena of rejection and retraction. Yet it was shown that *nonindexical contextualism* is capable of addressing the problem of lost disagreement. Although in contrast to relativism, nonindexical contextualism does not allow for rejection and retraction of certain *utterances* of knowledge ascriptions; the *contents* of those utterances can nevertheless be rejected or retracted within a nonindexical contextualist semantics. A main objection against relativism was put forward in terms of the problem of *lost substantial disagreement* or the problem of *ignorant or uninformed assessors*. Because standards for

The problem of lost disagreement

knowledge are only governed by the single assessor's stakes or the error-possibilities the assessor happens to consider, relativism has difficulties in accounting for substantial disagreements due to superior or deficient standards among the assessors. It was shown that the problem of uninformed or ignorant assessors also appears for truth-value relativist accounts of *epistemic modal claims* and that MacFarlane's "flexible relativism" does not provide a general remedy for such a problem. So at the end of the day, the phenomenon of disagreement remains one of the main challenges for both epistemic contextualism and epistemic relativism.

Notes

1 This notion of disagreement as a certain state of intersubjective conflict is spelled out in various different ways in the literature – see, for example, John MacFarlane's distinction between *noncotenability* and *preclusion of joint accuracy* (MacFarlane 2014, ch. 6) or Teresa Marques's concept of (doxastic) disagreement as a certain kind of incompatibility of doxastic attitudes (Marques 2014). Nikola Kompa, in contrast, embraces a "rather thin" notion of disagreement characterized by two necessary conditions: the intuition of conflict and the existence of something to disagree on (see Kompa 2015: 128), and Timothy Sundell defines "disagreement" as the "relation between speakers that licenses denial" (Sundell 2011: 274). See also ch. 21.
2 Throughout this chapter, I will take *propositions*, i.e. the content of uttered sentences, as truth-bearers. Sentences when uttered (used) *express* propositions. The proposition expressed by an uttered (and in a relativist semantics also assessed) sentence is *said* by the speaker (or assessor) of the sentence.
3 The reader should be aware that the terms "contextualism" and "relativism" are used quite differently in the literature. In particular, Max Kölbel favors a view he calls "genuine relativism" (see, for example, Kölbel 2004) – a view that in this chapter is named "nonindexical contextualism." In contrast to Kölbel, I will assume (with MacFarlane) that the key to the distinction between contextualism and relativism lies in the distinction between *use*-sensitivity and *assessment*-sensitivity.
4 Of course, a proposition expressed by a knowledge ascription of the form "S knows that p" at c_U can only be true if p itself is true at the world and time of c_U, and if S believes that p at the world and time of c_U.
5 The same applies, of course, to Anna's self-knowledge ascription in an indexical contextualist account: when Anna after considering the possibility that her bicycle might have been stolen and, as a consequence, no longer claims to know that her bicycle is parked in front of the library (though she still believes that her bicycle is parked there), she thereby says something that doesn't contradict what she said before.
6 DeRose has tried to solve the contextualists problem of lost disagreement in terms of his "single-scoreboard" semantics (see DeRose 2004). According to this account, there is a single scoreboard in a given conversation that "registers" the truth-conditions of the propositions expressed by the knowledge ascriptions made by the parties to a conversation. The score can change as the conversation progresses, but at any time there is a single score that governs the truth-conditions of the propositions expressed by all knowledge ascriptions made by the speakers in the conversation (see DeRose 2004: 6). However, a problem of DeRose's single scoreboard semantics is its limitation to "intra-conversational disagreement" (see MacFarlane 2007: 21). As MacFarlane objects, single-scoreboard semantics "doesn't give us enough disagreement. It gives us disagreement only within the bounds of a single 'conversation'" (MacFarlane 2007: 20). As said at the outset, people can have a disagreement even if they do not actually disagree with each other in a conversational dispute.
7 The chapter will not discuss other forms of relativism, such as, for example, *content* relativism (see, for example, Egan/Hawthorne/Weatherson 2005: 154 or MacFarlane 2014: 72f.). In what follows, the terms "relativism" or "relativist semantics" always refer to MacFarlane's *truth-value* relativism.
8 Even in a relativist semantics, the truth-value of a knowledge ascription still depends, of course, on whether p is true at the world and time of c_U and on whether S believes that p at the world and time of c_U.
9 A nonsubstantial disagreement is similar to what has been called "faultless disagreement" in the debate about relativism. Max Kölbel defines "faultless disagreement" as a situation where neither of the two thinkers A and B in believing and judging contradictory propositions "has made a mistake (is at fault)" (Kölbel 2004: 54). Many relativists, including Kölbel, contend that the existence of faultless disagreement is one of the main motivations to embrace relativism. However, MacFarlane has recently dissociated himself from the use of "faultless disagreement" (see MacFarlane 2014: 136). In contrast to the somewhat

ambiguous term "faultless disagreement," the notion "nonsubstantial disagreement" used in this chapter is confined to disagreement about knowledge ascriptions in which there are no assessor-independent correctness criteria for knowledge standards and in which the disagreement only rests on the different standards operative at the contexts of assessment.

10 A similar argument of lost substantial disagreement applies to contextualism as well, since in a contextualist account the knowledge standards are solely determined by the speaker's stakes or error-possibilities.

11 In a similar vein, Adam Carter observes that in a relativist semantics, "cognitive superiority (vis-à-vis *p*) and evidential superiority (vis-à-vis p) don't entail *standards* superiority (or even standards equality) vis-à-vis *p* [. . .]" (Carter 2014: 170). According to Carter, relativism fails to address the epistemic role of doxastic revision in disagreements with recognized epistemic superiors.

12 For a discussion of what epistemic possibilities are and what counts as an epistemic modal, see, for example, Chalmers (2011) and Swanson (2011).

13 In an indexical contextualist account, epistemic modal claims are also *use-indexical*, i.e., they express different propositions at different contexts of use c_U. Thus, "It might be that p" expresses the proposition that p is epistemically possible for the speaker (or a contextually relevant group) at c_U.

14 DeRose makes a similar move in attempting to address the problem of ignorant assessors for contextualism (see DeRose 2005: 189).

15 Of course, we sometimes do resist retraction even in cases of knowledge ascriptions, especially when far-fetched or highly unlikely error-possibilities are mentioned or when the mentioning of error-possibilities is completely unmotivated. But in most other cases higher knowledge standards are regarded as epistemically superior to lower standards. We therefore tend to retract knowledge ascriptions when confronted with hitherto ignored error-possibilities that we cannot rule out. We have, as John Hawthorne claims, a strong "inclination to reckon ourselves more enlightened with regard to our former self (on the topic of knowledge) when possibilities of error become salient" (Hawthorne 2004: 106, 122f.).

References

Brendel, Elke (2014): "Contextualism, Relativism, and the Semantics of Knowledge Ascriptions", *Philosophical Studies* 168, 101–117.

Cappelen, Hermann/Hawthorne, John (2009): *Relativism and Monadic Truth*, Oxford: Oxford University Press.

Carter, J. Adam (2014): "Disagreement, Relativism and Doxastic Revision", *Erkenntnis* 79, 155–172.

Chalmers, David J. (2011): "The Nature of Epistemic Space", in: A. Egan/B. Weatherson (eds.): *Epistemic Modality*, Oxford: Oxford University Press, 60–107.

Cohen, Stewart (1988): "How to be a Fallibilist", *Philosophical Perspectives* 2, 91–123.

Cohen, Stewart (2000): "Contextualism and Skepticism", *Philosophical Issues* 10, 94–107.

DeRose, Keith (1992): "Contextualism and Knowledge Attribution", *Philosophy and Phenomenological Research* 52, 913–929.

DeRose, Keith (2004): "Single Scoreboard Semantic", *Philosophical Studies* 119, 1–21.

DeRose, Keith (2005): "The Ordinary Language Basis for Contextualism, and the New Invariantism", *Philosophical Quarterly* 55, 172–198.

DeRose, Keith (2009): *The Case for Contextualism*, Oxford: Oxford University Press.

Dietz, Richard (2008): "Epistemic Modals and Correct Disagreement", in: M. García-Carpintero/M. Kölbel (eds.): *Relative Truth*, Oxford: Oxford University Press, 239–262.

Egan, Andy/Hawthorne, John/Weatherson, Brian (2005): "Epistemic Modals in Context", in: G. Preyer/G. Peter (eds.): *Contextualism in Philosophy*, Oxford: Clarendon Press, 131–168.

Frege, Gottlob (1979): *Posthumous Writings*, Chicago: University of Chicago Press.

Hawthorne, John (2004): *Knowledge and Lotteries*, Oxford: Clarendon Press.

Kölbel, Max (2004): "Faultless Disagreement", *Proceedings of the Aristotelian Society* 104, 53–73.

Kompa, Nikola (2002): "The Context Sensitivity of Knowledge Ascriptions", *Grazer Philosophische Studien* 64, 1–18.

Kompa, Nikola (2015): "Contextualism and Disagreement", *Erkenntnis* 80, 137–152.

Lewis, David (1996): "Elusive Knowledge", *Australasian Journal of Philosophy* 74: 549–567.

MacFarlane, John (2005a): "The Assessment Sensitivity of Knowledge Attributions", in: T. Gendler/J. Hawthorne (eds.): *The Oxford Studies in Epistemology, Vol. 1*, Oxford: Oxford University Press, 197–233.

MacFarlane, John (2005b): "Making Sense of Relative Truth", *Proceedings of the Aristotelian Society* 105, 321–340.

The problem of lost disagreement

MacFarlane, John (2007): "Relativism and Disagreement", *Philosophical Studies* 132, 17–31.
MacFarlane, John (2009): "Nonindexical Contextualism", *Synthese* 166, 231–250.
MacFarlane, John (2014): *Assessment Sensitivity. Relative Truth and Its Applications,* Oxford: Oxford University Press.
Marques, Teresa (2014): "Doxastic Disagreement", *Erkenntnis* 79, 121–142.
Sundell, Timothy (2011): "Disagreement about Taste", *Philosophical Studies* 155, 267–288.
Swanson, Eric (2011): "How Not to Theorize about the Language of Subjective Uncertainty", in: A. Egan/B. Weatherson (eds.): *Epistemic Modality*, Oxford: Oxford University Press, 249–269.

23

EPISTEMOLOGICAL IMPLICATIONS OF RELATIVISM

J. Adam Carter

Relativists about knowledge ascriptions think that whether a particular use of a knowledge-ascribing sentence, e.g., "Keith knows that the bank is open," is true depends on the epistemic standards at play in the *assessor's* context – viz., the context in which the knowledge ascription is being assessed for truth or falsity. Given that the very same knowledge ascription can be assessed for truth or falsity from indefinitely many perspectives, relativism has a striking consequence. When I ascribe knowledge to someone (e.g., when I say that, at a particular time, "Keith knows that the bank is open"), what I've said does not get a truth-value absolutely, but only relatively. If this semantic thesis about the word "knows" and its cognates is true, what implications would this have for epistemology, the philosophical theory of knowledge? The present aim will be to engage with this mostly unexplored question, and then to consider how the epistemological conclusions drawn might bear on the plausibility of a relativist semantics for "knows".

Epistemic relativism and relativism about "knows"

Traditionally, the term "epistemic relativism" has been used to pick out a wide class of philo-sophical positions. Wittgenstein (1969), Rorty (1979), Hacking (1982), and Feyerabend (1987), to name a few, have often been branded "relativists" for maintaining that (broadly speaking) knowledge, justification, rationality, epistemic norms and the like are the products of a plurality of conventions and frameworks of assessment and that their authority does not extend beyond the contexts giving rise to them.[1] One very natural way of glossing what it is an epistemic relativist wants to say is that – in short – knowledge, just like other epistemic standings, depends always on context. There is no way, as Rorty (1989) put it, to "escape" the various contingencies of the knowledge-ascribing situations in which we find ourselves, no "neutral standpoint" of epistemic evaluation.

However, this quick gloss should be initially perplexing: epistemological *contextualists* also fly under the banner that knowledge depends always on context (albeit, contexts of a specific sort). Contextualists after all think that whether any given knowledge-ascribing sentence (e.g., "Keith knows that the bank is open") is true depends on the speaker's context[2] by depending on the epistemic standards at play when the speaker is using a knowledge-ascribing sentence. Contex-tualism is more or less mainstream in contemporary epistemology. But isn't epistemic *relativism* supposed to be radical?

Implications of relativism

Given that contextualists, like traditional epistemic relativists, embrace the dictum (generally construed) that knowledge depends always on context, is contextualism best understood as a particular *version* of relativism? Or, alternatively, are traditional construals of "epistemic relativism" perhaps not as radical or iconoclastic as we've been inclined to think?

According to John MacFarlane (2014), it's the latter that is the case.[3] Philosophically interesting relativism must go a crucial step further than many of the disparate views that have been branded "epistemic relativism" have gone.[4] To appreciate why he thinks so, consider the following two example sentences: (1) is a reference point in the contextualist literature; (2) is a reference point in the (traditional) relativist literature.

(1) "Keith knows that the bank is open."
(2) "Galileo knows that the Earth revolves around the Sun."

Contextualists (e.g., DeRose 1992, 2009) insist that the extension of "knows" in (1) varies with the context in which (1) is *used*, and accordingly (1) can express different propositions and have different truth-conditions in different contexts (of use).[5] For instance, if I utter, "Keith knows that the bank is open," in a context where it is of dire importance whether Keith can make a withdrawal, (1) comes out true only if Keith meets very demanding epistemic requirements. And this is because, for the contextualist, what I've *said* when I utter (1) in a high-stakes context is something like

(1*) *Keith knows$_{high}$ that the bank is open.*

And this is a different proposition than what I've uttered (using the same sentence) in relaxed practical circumstances, viz.,

(1**) *Keith knows$_{low}$ that the bank is open.*

Likewise, for the contextualist, what goes for (1) goes for (2). I've expressed a different proposition, with different truth-conditions,[6] when I utter (2) in an academic context (i.e., *Galileo knows$_{low}$ that the Earth revolves around the Sun*) than I do when the fate of the world rides on Galileo's cognitive life (i.e., *Galileo knows$_{high}$ that the Earth revolves around the Sun*).

What does the traditional epistemic *relativist* say about (1) and (2)? By "traditional" epistemic relativist, I mean the kind of "Rorty-style" epistemic relativist which has recently drawn the sustained criticism of Paul Boghossian (2006). As Boghossian sees it, the traditional epistemic relativist regards (2) as depending on context in the following way: firstly, the epistemic relativist says there are "no absolute facts" of the form (2), (i.e., *S knows that p.*) And so, if a person S's knowledge ascriptions are to have any prospect of being true, we must not construe his utterances of the form

"Galileo knows that the Earth revolves around the Sun."

as expressing the claim

Galileo knows that the Earth revolves around the Sun.

but rather as expressing the claim.

(2*) *According to the epistemic system C, that I, S, accept, Galileo knows that the Earth revolves around the Sun.*

293

And, what goes for (2) goes for more mundane knowledge ascriptions, such as (1), which Bog-hossian's epistemic relativist tells us expresses the explicitly relational proposition:

(1***)   *According to the epistemic system C, that I, S, accept, Keith knows that the bank is open.*

Putting this all together, DeRose and Rorty can thus agree that statements like (1) and (2) do not get a truth-value, *simpliciter,* but only relative to a standards parameter whose value is supplied by the context in which (1) and (2) are used. In this respect, the views are equally radical, or equally unradical.

Moreover – and this is a point MacFarlane stresses – both the contextualist and the traditional epistemic relativist embrace the following thesis with respect to utterance tokens of (1) and (2):

> *Knowledge Ascription Absolutism*: Utterance tokens of knowledge-ascribing sentences have their truth-values absolutely.[7]

As MacFarlane sees it, an epistemic relativist of a philosophically interesting[8] sort is going to do more than merely insist that knowledge depends always on context, but also, to go a step further: to *reject* Knowledge Ascription Absolutism.

MacFarlane's semantics for "knows", which gives what he calls a *context of assessment* a semantically significant role, takes this further step and denies Knowledge Ascription Absolutism.

New epistemic relativism

This section briefly outlines the key features of "new" epistemic relativism (along the lines sketched by MacFarlane[9]), after which the implications for this view in epistemological theory will be canvassed.

First some terminology. Following MacFarlane (2014, 60) we can distinguish a *context of assessment* from the more familiar notion of a *context of use* in the following way:

> *Context of use*: a possible situation in which a sentence might be used and where the agent of the context is the user of the sentence.
> *Context of assessment*: a possible situation in which a use of a sentence might be assessed, where the agent of the context is the *assessor* of the use of a sentence.
> *(MacFarlane 2014, 60)*

Whereas relativising knowledge-ascribing sentence truth to merely a context of use is compatible with Knowledge Ascription Absolutism, relativising knowledge-ascription sentence truth to a context of assessment is not.[10]

On MacFarlane's view, truth-relativism of the philosophically interesting sort with respect to "knows" maintains that when I say that "Keith knows the bank is open," the truth of what I just said depends (in part) on a context of assessment – viz., this utterance token gets a truth-value only once the standard of the *assessor* is specified. Accordingly, my claim that "Keith knows the bank is open" can be at the same time true relative to a context of assessment (e.g., in which "Bob" is evaluating my claim) where ordinary "low" standards are in place, yet false relative to a context of assessment in which "Rene" is evaluating my claim, and where Cartesian standards are in place.[11]

Since the same knowledge ascription can be assessed from an indefinite number of perspectives, there are only perspective-relative answers to the question whether what I say when I ascribe knowledge to someone is true.[12] Indeed, even holding fixed the standards operative in my context, what I say can be true relative to some assessment contexts and false relative to others. My knowledge ascription does not get its truth-value absolutely.[13]

In three different places, MacFarlane (2005, 2011, 2014) has defended a "master argument" for an assessment-sensitive semantics for knowledge attributions. Here is the core strand of argument he's defended on each occasion:

Master Argument for Assessment-Sensitive Semantics for Knowledge Attributions

(3) Standard invariantism, contextualism and subject-sensitive invariantism all have advantages and weaknesses.
(4) Relativism preserves the advantages while avoiding the disadvantages.
(5) Therefore, prima facie, we should be relativists about knowledge attributions.

Premise (3) is more or less uncontroversial. One interesting line of question is whether, premise (4) of MacFarlane's master argument is true.[14] For the present purposes, though, we can set this aside.

The question that will be of interest now is: if we *do* have good reason to embrace a truth-relativist semantics for "knows", then how should this affect our epistemological theorising? What is the *upshot* for this view in epistemology – viz., that is, of giving "knows" a semantic treatment such that knowledge ascriptions do not have their truth-values absolutely? This is the question to which the remainder of this discussion will be concerned.

Implications of relativism

Equivalence and reduction

Knowledge is the central subject matter around which epistemological theorising is organized.[15] If "knows" gets a relativist treatment, we should expect that other epistemic notions, which are connected in various ways with knowledge, will as well. Here I'll consider epistemic notions which stand (modulo certain substantive commitments) in *equivalence, reductive* and *normative* relations (respectively) to "knows" and its cognates.

Other epistemic items	Relation to knowledge
Evidence	Equivalence (E = K)
Knowledge-how	Reductive (Intellectualism)
Knowledge norms	Normative

Take, as a starting point, a very tight conceptual connection: Williamson's (2000) knowledge-evidence equivalence thesis, $E = K$, according to which "knowledge, and only knowledge, constitutes evidence . . . S's evidence [is] S's knowledge, for every individual or community S in any possible situation" (183).[16]

$E = K$ is controversial, though the proposal has become increasingly attractive for those sympathetic with the knowledge-first approach in epistemology. Suppose one combines $E = K$ with MacFarlane-style relativism about "knows". In short, the relativist about "knows" had better be prepared to embrace the view that evidence ascriptions are assessment-sensitive, or give up $E = K$. Consider, after all, that the proponent of $E = K$ is submitting that the claim that

S's evidence includes E if, and only if, S knows E is extensionally correct in all metaphysically possible worlds.[17] If knowledge ascriptions are assessment-sensitive, but evidence ascriptions *weren't*, then, possibly, a claim of the form "S knows E" could be true as uttered at c_1 and assessed from c_2, even when "S's evidence includes E" is false as uttered at c_2 and assessed at c_2, a result that stands in tension with the $E = K$ proponent's commitment to regarding the claim that S's evidence includes E if, and only if, S knows E as extensionally correct in all metaphysically possible worlds.

The epistemological "bleed over" from an assessment-sensitive semantics for "knows" to other epistemic notions connected to knowledge isn't limited to equivalence relations. Let's consider now a reductive relation, one embraced by intellectualists about knowledge-how.[18]

Gilbert Ryle's (1945) distinction between knowing-how and knowing-that had for decades been taken for granted. But this is no longer so. Intellectualists about knowing-how, following Stanley and Williamson (2001), insist that knowing how to do something is a species of propositional knowledge – viz., that knowing-how is a kind of knowing-that.[19] As Stanley (2011a) puts the core intellectualist insight:

> you know how to ride a bicycle if and only if you know in what way you could ride a bicycle. But you know in what way you could ride a bicycle if and only if you possess some propositional knowledge, viz. knowing, of a certain way w which is a way in which you could ride a bicycle, that w is a way in which you could ride a bicycle.
>
> *(209)*

Intellectualism isn't for everyone.[20] But let's consider: what is the state of play for philosophers who embrace intellectualism about knowledge-how as well as an assessment-sensitive semantics for propositional knowledge ascriptions? Again, in short: it is hard to see knowledge-how ascriptions would *not* be assessment-sensitive, too. Suppose, for reductio, that knowing how to do something is just a kind of propositional knowledge and that the truth-conditions for knowing how to do something (e.g., as in the case of attributions of the form "Irina knows how to perform a salchow") are *not* assessment sensitive, but the truth-conditions for proposition knowledge are. So we can suppose that "Irina knows that p" has assessment-sensitive truth-conditions, where p is a proposition specifying a way, w, which is a way in which Irina could perform a salchow. This would be perplexing to say the least. One way to make this point is in terms of absolute truth-values. If I antecedently embrace intellectualism and assert, "Irina knows how to perform a salchow," I regard myself as having said something that is true if and only if Irina knows some proposition. If my ascription to Irina of knowledge of that proposition does not get an absolute truth-value, then it's puzzling to see how my knowledge-*how* ascription to Irina would. Thus, for intellectualists about knowledge-how, no less than proponents of $E = K$, it looks like a MacFarlane-style semantics for "knows" generates further epistemological commitments.

Normativity and value

I've suggested elsewhere that similar arguments can be made in the case of reductive accounts of understanding-why, and even (though perhaps more controversially) for certain accounts of epistemic justification.[21] I want to now consider the implications for an assessment-sensitive semantics for "knows" within the context of epistemological debates about epistemic norms and epistemic value. Let's begin with norms.

Here are two that are popular nowadays: the knowledge norms of assertion and action.

296

Implications of relativism

One must: assert that p only if one knows p.

(Williamson 2000, 243)

Treat the proposition that p as a reason for acting only if you know that p.

(Hawthorne and Stanley 2008, 578)

If we assume *ex ante* MacFarlane's semantics for "knows", then proponents of the knowledge norms for action and assertion face an interesting position: they will be forced to embrace a view we can call *normative non-absolutism* with respect to assertion and action.

Call normative absolutism the view that a particular speech act, at a particular time, has its normative properties absolutely. For example, if I violate the norm governing permissible assertion by asserting a at t_1, then (on normative absolutism) it's not the case that, at t_2, my utterance token a can "no longer have violated" the norm of assertion at t_1, and vice versa.

Denying normative absolutism has its costs. As Gareth Evans (1985) puts the point:

> Just as we use the terms 'good' and 'bad', 'obligatory' and 'permitted' to make an assessment, once and for all, of non-linguistic actions, so we use the term 'correct' to make a once-and-for-all assessment of speech acts. . . . if a theory of reference permits a subject to deduce merely that a particular utterance is now correct but later will be incorrect, it cannot assist the subject in deciding what to say, nor in interpreting the remarks of others.
>
> *(349)*

If "knows" gets a relativist treatment, then – at least in so far as we are inclined to embrace the knowledge norm of assertion – there can be no assessment, once and for all, of assertions.[22] And what goes for the knowledge norm of assertion goes for knowledge norms of action as well as belief, practical reasoning and the like. In each case, one can embrace such a knowledge norm, alongside a relativist treatment for "knows" only by giving up normative absolutism.

While knowledge norms are often embraced by those sympathetic to the knowledge-first approach, a more general axiological insight about knowledge is embraced even more widely.[23] The idea is, put crudely, that knowledge is more epistemically valuable than mere true opinion. Call this the *value insight*. As Duncan Pritchard (2009) puts it, if we didn't take something like the value insight for granted in epistemology, "then it would be simply mysterious why knowledge has been the focus of so much of epistemological theorising, rather than some other epistemic standing like justified true belief" (19).

One interesting implication a relativist treatment of "knows" would have, for epistemological theorising, is that it's not clear how the value insight can continue to be maintained. The insight, unpacked more carefully, is that for any given proposition, it's better (from a purely epistemic or intellectual point of view) to know that proposition than to merely truly believe the proposition but fail to know it.[24]

Suppose A says, "Keith knows that the bank is open." The value insight implies that if this claim is true, then the state of affairs in virtue of which it is true is more epistemically valuable than is the state of affairs of Keith's *merely* truly believing that the bank is open, but not knowing this. A relativist semantics for "knows" implies that, since the truth of what A just said about Keith's mental life can be assessed from indefinitely many perspectives, there are only perspective-relative answers to the question whether the state of affairs characterising Keith's mental life is more valuable than were Keith to merely truly belief that the bank was open.

297

New relativism: wider epistemological implications

The previous section outlined several specific ways in which a relativist semantics for "knows" would have some consequences, more broadly, in epistemological theory. I want to close by gesturing to a bigger-picture issue.

Compare epistemology with paleontology, which studies life prior to the Holocene epoch, primarily by scientifically studying the fossil record. Paleontology is organized around certain rules about how inferences are best drawn to conclusions about ancient life. If paleontologists began playing by very different rules – suppose they began relying on tea leaves more so than the fossil record – paleontology would no longer be valuable in telling us with accuracy about ancient life. The value of the practice, in light of these new rules, wouldn't sustain the practice.

In recent work, John Turri (Forthcoming) argues that a rule normatively sustains a practice when the value achieved by following the rule explains why agents continue following that rule, thus establishing and sustaining a pattern of activity.

The practice of epistemology, or epistemological inquiry is, like paleontology, also organized around certain rules – the rules which epistemologists take for granted when engaging in typical first-order debates. Imagine the nearest world where epistemologists (replete with their dispositions to do epistemology as usual) wake up to find themselves convinced by arguments for a relativist semantics for "knows". Epistemologists, having woken up with this revelation, accordingly reject Knowledge Ascription Absolutism. Suddenly, the rules change dramatically.

There would be no point, for example, in continuing to follow one of the most basic rules which sustains the practice of epistemology: that universal generalizations about knowledge stand to be legitimately challenged by pointing to imagined knowledge cases. There is, as Williamson (2007) puts it, a kind of "cognitive weight analytic philosophers rest on thought experiments" (180). And analytic epistemology is a paradigmatic example of an area in analytic philosophy where thought experiments are relied upon.[25]

But epistemologists, having woken with commitments to rejecting Knowledge Ascription Absolutism, would have little reason to continue playing by such rules anymore. For example, even if most individuals agree that, within a given thought experiment *T*, a subject *S*'s claim that Keith knows that the bank is open is true, this could not in itself constitute evidence one way or another for whether Keith *really knows* that the bank is open. After all, given that the relativist semantics for "knows" rejects Knowledge Ascription Absolutism, this isn't the sort of thing for which individuals' willingness to attribute knowledge would be evidence. At any rate, there would be no reason to rest much (as Williamson says) "cognitive weight" on what individuals say about such cases like *T*, to the end of theorising about the *nature* of knowledge.

Putting this all together: if we were to suppose that epistemologists embraced MacFarlane's semantics for "knows," we should expect them to find little point in carrying on by following the same rules. The "new rules" would not normatively sustain, in Turri's sense, the practice of theorising about knowledge in the way epistemologists *traditionally* have.

Trivially, the current rules do normatively sustain the practice. The theoretical value achieved by following the rules characteristic of epistemology plausibly explains why epistemologists continue to pursue traditional projects. Some practices are more valuable than others. To the extent that the practice of epistemology (along traditional lines) *is a valuable* one – replete with the kind of rules epistemologists take for granted in practice – we have either (i) prima facie reason to be skeptical that a relativist semantics for "knows" is tractable or, alternatively, (ii) prima facie reason to be skeptical that our theory of knowledge attributions should inform the epistemologist's theory of knowledge.[26,27]

Notes

1 See Baghramian and Carter (2015 §1). For some recent overviews of various forms of epistemic relativism, see Baghramian (2004), Boghossian (2006 Ch. 5–6), Kusch (2010), Siegel (2013), Seidel (2014), and Carter (2016 Ch. 3–5).

2 And this is because, according to the (attrib/uter) contextualist (e.g., DeRose 1992), sentences like "Keith knows that the bank is open" can express different propositions in different conversational contexts. Cf., however, Williams (2007) for a very different kind of view under the description of "contextualism".

3 See also MacFarlane (2005).

4 As I note later, MacFarlane regards various views which have been traditionally regarded as "epistemic relativism" as better classified as forms of contextualism.

5 Jonathan Schaffer (2004) defends a related view, *contrastivism*, which treats "knows" as invariably expressing a ternary relation with a slot for a contrast proposition provided by the context. Schaffer himself regards this position as a "sibling" to contextualism, though it is sometimes regarded as form of contextualism. Cf., Brogaard (2008) for another non-standard version of contextualism about "knows" which Brogaard describes as *perspectivalism*.

6 For an introduction to truth-conditional semantics, see Heim and Kratzer (1998 §1).

7 Knowledge Ascription Absolutism could just as easily be framed in terms of sentence truth. On MacFarlane's view, the kind of relativism that parts ways interestingly from absolutism can be expressed either in terms of sentence truth (following the semantic framework of Lewis 1980) or in terms of propositional truth (following the semantic framework of Kaplan 1989). As Wright (2007) notes, a familiar way to capture the kind of relativism MacFarlane advances is in terms of utterance tokens, understood as "an actual historic voicing or inscription of a sentence of a certain type" (262).

8 Indeed, as MacFarlane (2014, 33, fn. 5) sees it, the view which Paul Boghossian (2006) recently (and influentially) challenged, at length, under the description of "epistemic relativism" isn't really that interesting. It was really a form of contextualism, modeled on Gilbert Harman's (1975) moral relativism which was itself, according to MacFarlane, a kind of contextualism.

9 For some similar relativist treatments of "knows", see Richard (2004). Cf. Kompa (2002) for an earlier example of a similar view, though one which might be aligned more closely with non-indexical contextualism. I am focusing on MacFarlane's presentation of the view here as it has been developed in the most detail (e.g., 2005, 2011 and 2014) and has generated the most discussion.

10 See, for instance, MacFarlane (2014, 49, 67, 73, fn. 3, 89, *passim*).

11 For MacFarlane, then, the answer to the question of why contextualism, as well as Rorty-style epistemic relativism, is not on the interesting side of the relativist's line is that while the contextualist can, no less than the relativist, recognize a "standards" parameter, for the contextualist, its value will be supplied by the context of use, whereas the relativist (proper) takes it to be supplied completely independently of the context of use, by the context of assessment. See Baghramian and Carter (2015 §5) for an overview. See also MacFarlane (2007, 2011, 2012b).

12 See, for example, MacFarlane (2011). Independent of the specification of an assessor's standard, my claim that Keith knows that the bank is open simply lacks a truth-value much as, by comparison, an indexical expression such as "I have been to Tahiti" simply lacks a truth-value independent of contextual facts about the context of use (i.e., which pick out to whom "I" refers).

13 For two accessible overview discussions of MacFarlane's view, see Baghramian and Carter (2015 §5) and Carter (2016 Ch. 7).

14 For some recent criticism on this point, see Stanley (2005 Ch. 7, 2015), Cappelen and Hawthorne (2010) and Carter (2016 Ch. 7–8). Cf., Partee (2004).

15 The longstanding concern with the project of analysing propositional knowledge is a testament to this. For an overview, see Ichikawa and Steup (2014).

16 See also Williamson (1997).

17 Compare: Ichikawa and Steup (2014), who make a similar point regarding the commitments of proponents of K = JTB.

18 Stanley and Williamson (2001); Stanley (2011a).

19 Stanley (2011b, 207, 2011a, 122), *passim*.

20 For a sample of some recent criticisms of intellectualism, see Noë (2005), Toribio (2008), Poston (2009), Cath (2011) and Carter and Pritchard (2015a, 2015b, Forthcoming). For an idiosyncratic version of intellectualism which embraces that knowing how to do something is in virtue of propositional

attitudes, but which does not embrace *propositionalism*, the thesis that knowledge-how is a propositional knowledge relation, see Bengson and Moffet (2011).

21 See Carter (2014) for the argument that a MacFarlane-style semantics for "knows" must be paired (for the reductivist about understanding-why) with an assessment-sensitive semantics for understanding-why ascriptions. I also, in Carter (2016 Ch. 8), make a more detailed argument for why a relativist treatment of "knows" has a range of other implications in epistemology, beyond some of the highlights I'm able to cover here.

22 While a stock objection to truth-relativist semantics, more generally, is that an implication is that assertions are not once-and-for all assessable, the typical sort of relativist response doesn't have purchase against the tension just described between a relativist treatment for "knows" and the knowledge norm of assertion, specifically. For instance, in response to Evans' challenge, MacFarlane embraces a kind of "meet the challenge" norm for assertion which he thinks preserves the integrity of assertion. See Mac-Farlane (2003). Cf., Kölbel (2004, 308). However, redeploying this kind of move is an option only if one isn't *already* committed to a particular norm of assertion. So, for one who antecedently embraces the knowledge norm of assertion, a truth-relativist semantics for "knows" is going to have, as a consequence, normative non-absolutism in the case of assertion.

23 Cf., Kvanvig (2003) for criticism.

24 For discussion on this point, see Carter, Jarvis, and Rubin (2013).

25 This point is perhaps on clearest display in the post-Gettier literature. See here Shope (1983) for a review.

26 For an argument in favour of this kind of conclusion, see Hazlett (2010). Cf. Carter (2016 Ch. 8–9).

27 Thanks to Jonathan Jenkins Ichikawa and Brian Rabern for helpful comments.

References

Baghramian, Maria. 2004. *Relativism*. London and New York: Routledge.

Baghramian, Maria, and J. Adam Carter. 2015. "Relativism." In *Stanford Encyclopaedia of Philosophy*, edited by Edward N. Zalta, Fall 2015, 1–46. http://plato.stanford.edu/entries/relativism/.

Bengson, John, and Marc Moffet. 2011. "Nonpropositional Intellectualism." In *Knowing How: Essays on Knowledge, Mind, and Action*, edited by John Bengson and Marc Moffet, 161–95. Oxford: Oxford University Press.

Boghossian, Paul. 2006. *Fear of Knowledge: Against Relativism and Constructivism*. Oxford: Oxford University Press.

Brogaard, Berit. 2008. "In Defence of a Perspectival Semantics for 'Know'." *Australasian Journal of Philosophy* 86 (3): 439–59.

Cappelen, Herman, and John Hawthorne. 2010. *Relativism and Monadic Truth*. Oxford: Oxford University Press.

Carter, J. Adam. 2014. "Relativism, Knowledge and Understanding." *Episteme* 11 (1): 35–52.

———. 2016. *Metaepistemology and Relativism*. London: Palgrave Macmillan.

Carter, J. Adam, and Duncan Pritchard. 2015a. "Knowledge-How and Epistemic Luck." *Noûs* 49 (3): 440–53.

———. 2015. "Knowledge-How and Cognitive Achievement." *Philosophy and Phenomenological Research* 91 (1): 181–99.

———. Forthcoming. "Knowledge-How and Epistemic Value." *Australasian Journal of Philosophy*.

Carter, J. Adam, Benjamin Jarvis, and Katherine Rubin. 2013. "Knowledge and the Value of Cognitive Ability." *Synthese* 190 (17): 3715–29.

Cath, Yuri. 2011. "Knowing-How Without Knowing-That." In *Knowing How: Essays on Knowledge, Mind and Knowing How: Essays on Knowledge, Mind, and Action*, edited by John Bengson and Marc Moffett, 113–35. Oxford: Oxford University Press.

DeRose, Keith. 1992. "Contextualism and Knowledge Attributions." *Philosophy and Phenomenological Research*. JSTOR, 52: 913–29.

———. 2009. *The Case for Contextualism: Knowledge, Skepticism, and Context, Vol. 1* Oxford: Oxford University Press.

Evans, Gareth. 1985. "Does Tense Logic Rest on a Mistake?" In *Collected Papers: Gareth Evans*, edited by Gareth Evans, 346–63. Oxford: Clarendon Press.

Feyerabend, Paul. 1987. *Farewell to Reason*. London: Verso.

Hacking, Ian. 1982. "Language, Truth and Reason." In Martin Hollis & Steven Lukes (eds.), *Rationality and Relativism*, 48–66. Cambridge, MA: MIT Press

Harman, Gilbert. 1975. "Moral relativism defended." *The Philosophical Review* 84 (1): 3–22.

Hawthorne, John, and Jason Stanley. 2008. "Knowledge and Action." *Journal of Philosophy* 105 (10): 571–90.

Hazlett, Allan. 2010. "The Myth of Factive Verbs." *Philosophy and Phenomenological Research* 80 (3): 497–522.

Implications of relativism

Heim, Irene, and Angelika Kratzer. 1998. *Semantics in Generative Grammar*. London: Blackwell.

Ichikawa, Jonathan Jenkins, and Matthias Steup. 2014. "The Analysis of Knowledge." In *The Stanford Encyclopedia of Philosophy*, edited by Edward N. Zalta, Spring 2014. http://plato.stanford.edu/archives/spr2014/entries/knowledge-analysis/.

Kaplan, David. 1989. "Demonstratives." In *Themes from Kaplan*, edited by J. Almog, J. Perry and H. Wettstein, 481–563. Oxford: Oxford University Press.

Kölbel, Max. 2004. "Faultless Disagreement." *Proceedings of the Aristotelian Society (Hardback)*, 104: 53–73. 1. Wiley Online Library.

Kompa, Nikola. 2002. "The Context Sensitivity of Knowledge Ascriptions." *Grazer Philosophische Studien* 64 (1): 1–18.

Kusch, Martin. 2010. "Epistemic Replacement Relativism Defended." In *EPSA Epistemology and Methodology of Science: Launch of the European Philosophy of Science Association*, edited by Mauricio Suarez, 165–75. Dordrecht: Springer.

Kvanvig, Jonathan L. 2003. *The Value of Knowledge and the Pursuit of Understanding*. Cambridge: Cambridge University Press.

Lewis, David. 1980. "Index, context and content." In: *Philosophy and Grammar*, edited by S. Kanger and S. Ohman, 79–100. Amsterdam: Reidel.

MacFarlane, John. 2003. "Future Contingents and Relative Truth." *Philosophical Quarterly* 53 (212): 321–36.

———. 2005. "Making Sense of Relative Truth." *Proceedings of the Aristotelian Society* 105: 305–23. 1. Wiley Online Library.

———. 2007. "Relativism and Disagreement." *Philosophical Studies* 132 (1): 17–31.

———. 2011. "Relativism and Knowledge Attributions." In *The Routledge Companion to Epistemology*, edited by Duncan Pritchard and Sven Bernecker, 536–544. London: Routledge.

———. 2012. "Relativism." In *The Routledge Companion to Philosophy of Language*, edited by Delia Graff Fara and Gillian Russell. London: Routledge.

———. 2014. *Assessment Sensitivity: Relative Truth and Its Applications*. Oxford: Oxford University Press.

Noë, Alva. 2005. "Against Intellectualism." *Analysis* 65: 278–90.

Partee, Barbara. 2004. "Comments on Jason Stanley's 'on the Linguistic Basis for Contextualism'." *Philosophical Studies* 119: 147–59.

Poston, Ted. 2009. "Know-How to Be Gettiered?" *Philosophy and Phenomenological Research* 79 (3): 743–47.

Pritchard, Duncan. 2009. "Knowledge, Understanding and Epistemic Value." *Royal Institute of Philosophy Supplement* 64: 19–43.

Richard, Mark. 2004. "Contextualism and Relativism." *Philosophical Studies* 119 (1): 215–42.

Rorty, Richard. 1979. *Philosophy and the Mirror of Nature*. Princeton, NJ: Princeton University Press.

———. 1989. *Contingency, Irony and Solidarity*. Cambridge: Cambridge University Press.

Ryle, Gilbert. 1945. "Knowing How and Knowing That: The Presidential Address." *Proceedings of the Aristotelian Society* 46: 1–16. JSTOR.

Schaffer, Jonathan. 2004. "From Contextualism to Contrastivism." *Philosophical Studies* 119 (1): 73–103.

Seidel, Markus. 2014. *Epistemic Relativism: A Constructive Critique*. London: Palgrave Macmillan.

Shope, Robert K. 1983. *An Analysis of Knowing: A Decade of Research*. Princeton: Princeton University Press.

Siegel, Harvey. 2013. *Relativism Refuted*. Dordrecht: Springer.

Stanley, Jason. 2005. *Knowledge and Practical Interests*. Oxford: Oxford University Press.

———. 2011a. *Know How*. Oxford: Oxford University Press.

———. 2011b. "Knowing (How)." *Noûs* 45 (2): 207–38.

———. 2016. "On the Case for Truth-Relativism." *Philosophy and Phenomenological Research* 92 (1): 179–188.

Stanley, Jason, and Timothy Williamson. 2001. "Knowing How." *Journal of Philosophy* 98: 411–44.

Toribio, Josefa. 2008. "How Do We Know How?" *Philosophical Explorations* 11 (1): 39–52.

Turri, John. Forthcoming. "Sustaining Rules: A Model and Application." In *Knowledge First: Approaches in Epistemology and Mind*, edited by J. Adam Carter, Emma C. Gordon, and Benjamin Jarvis. Oxford: Oxford University Press.

Williams, Michael. 2007. "Why (Wittgensteinian) Contextualism Is Not Relativism." *Episteme* 4 (1): 93–114.

Williamson, Timothy. 1997. "Knowledge as Evidence." *Mind* 106 (424): 717–41.

———. 2000. *Knowledge and Its Limits*. Oxford: Oxford University Press.

———. 2007. *The Philosophy of Philosophy*. Oxford: Oxford University Press.

Wittgenstein, Ludwig. 1969. *On Certainty*. Oxford: Blackwell.

Wright, Crispin. 2007. "New Age Relativism and Epistemic Possibility: The Question of Evidence." *Philosophical Issues* 17 (1): 262–83.

PART VI

Semantic implementations

24

THE SEMANTIC ERROR PROBLEM FOR EPISTEMIC CONTEXTUALISM

Patrick Greenough and Dirk Kindermann

1 Introduction

Epistemic Contextualism is the view that "knows that" is semantically context-sensitive and that properly accommodating this fact into our philosophical theory promises to solve various puzzles concerning knowledge.[1] Yet Epistemic Contextualism faces a big – some would say fatal – problem: *The Semantic Error Problem*.[2] In its prominent form, this runs thus: speakers just don't seem to recognise that "knows that" is context-sensitive; so, if "knows that" really is context-sensitive, then such speakers are systematically in error about what is said by, or how to evaluate, ordinary uses of "S knows that p"; but since it's wildly implausible that ordinary speakers should exhibit such systematic error, the expression "knows that" isn't context-sensitive.[3]

We are interested in whether, and in what ways, there is such semantic error; if there is such error, how it arises and is made manifest, and, again, if there is such error, to what extent it is a problem for Epistemic Contextualism. The upshot is that some forms of The Semantic Error Problem turn out to be largely unproblematic. Those that remain troublesome have analogue error problems for various competitor conceptions of knowledge. So, if error is any sort of problem, then it is a problem for every extant competitor view.

2 Epistemic Contextualism

Broadly conceived, Epistemic Contextualism (hereafter: Contextualism) is the view that the truth-value of "S knows that p" is sensitive to the epistemic standards which obtain in the context of use.[4] These standards fix how strong the epistemic position of the subject S needs to be in order for this sentence to be true. So, in some context, a speaker may truly utter "S knows that p", while in a different context, a speaker may truly utter "S does not know that p", even though these contexts merely differ in respect of the epistemic standards – and so remain the same in respect of epistemic position.

Specific forms of Contextualism differ as to what this sameness of epistemic position amounts to. For convenience, we assume it amounts to the sameness of the evidence of the subject S.[5] Furthermore, there are various accounts as to what raises or lowers the epistemic standards. For simplicity, we assume the standards are fixed by which error possibilities are salient (ignoring,

305

e.g., practical stakes). We shall also assume that there are just two contexts: *high-standards contexts* (hereafter: HIGH), where far-fetched error possibilities are salient, and *low-standards contexts* (hereafter: LOW), where such error possibilities are not salient. Any differences between this simplified version and specific contemporary forms of Contextualism shouldn't matter to our discussion.

3 Modest versus Ambitious Contextualism

Modest Contextualism merely gives a theory of the meaning and use of "S knows that p" and thus involves: accounting for the intuitive judgments concerning the truth, or assertibility, of this sentence; making sense of (dis)agreement involving such sentences; and specifying the norms of assertion and retraction for such sentences. *Ambitious Contextualism*, meanwhile, deploys the insights gained from Modest Contextualism to resolve a range of puzzles concerning knowledge, such as Cartesian Scepticism, lottery scepticism, the dogmatism paradox, the puzzle of easy knowledge, and so on. As we shall see, semantic error problems have been leveled against both kinds of Contextualist projects.[6]

4 Kinds of semantic error: preliminary distinctions

Broadly, semantic error is some kind of mistake, made by a speaker, with respect to some semantic property of a word or string of words. A prototypical case is where a speaker is mistaken about what a word means. Such a mistake, we assume, typically comes with some false, usually implicit, belief, and typically manifests itself by some mistaken (potential) use of the word. Semantic error can be a mistake about a semantic feature that is in principle accessible to ordinary speakers or about an elusive semantic feature which only a theorist of language may be privy to. To isolate the relevant kinds of error we are interested in, it will help to sketch some preliminary distinctions:

(1) *Semantic error versus semantic ignorance*: Semantic error involves more than mere ignorance; it typically involves some false (implicit) belief about some semantic property of an expression.[7] Such a false (implicit) belief will typically be made manifest by some misuse of the expression in question.

(2) *Global versus local semantic error*: A speaker makes a *local* semantic error if she uses the word in ways incompatible with the semantic theory only in specific kinds of use situations (such as the sceptical argument); a speaker makes a *global* semantic error if she uses the word in ways incompatible with the semantic theory in all kinds of use situations.

(3) *Universal versus individual semantic error*: Semantic error is *universal* (with respect to a language community) if all (or nearly all) competent speakers of that language community are in error. It is *individual* (with respect to a language community) if it occurs only in a single competent speaker of the language.

(4) *Systematic vs non-systematic semantic error*: Given a particular kind of use situation (e.g., the sceptical argument), a speaker who always uses the expression in a particular, erroneous way is *systematically* semantically in error. One who does so only in some instantiations of a given kind of use situation is *non-systematically* in error.[8]

As we shall see, Contextualism is allegedly committed to positing a kind of semantic error which is systematic, universal, and multiply local.

The Semantic Error Problem

5 Ambitious Contextualism and Cartesian Scepticism

Ambitious Contextualism, as mentioned above, seeks to resolve various epistemological puzzles. With respect to Cartesian Scepticism, it typically proceeds as follows:

(i) The basic form of the (Cartesian) Sceptical Argument (SA) is this:

Premise A: I don't know that not-SH.
Premise B: If I don't know that not-SH then I don't know that O.
Conclusion C: I don't know that O.[9]

Here O stands for some ordinary claim (e.g., *I am in London*), and SH for some sceptical hypothesis (e.g., *I am a brain in a vat being "fed" non-veridical experiences of the external world*).

(ii) SA represents a paradox: the premises A and B are (initially) highly plausible; the conclusion C is (initially) highly implausible; yet, the reasoning from A and B to C is (taken to be) valid.

Standardly, to resolve a paradox one must discharge two explanatory tasks. The first is to establish some fault with the reasoning, premises, or presuppositions of the argument, or establish that the conclusion is not so toxic after all. The second is to explain just why we, epistemologists and the folk alike, mistakenly thought that some premise, rule of inference, or presupposition was true/valid, or explain why, contra initial appearances, the conclusion is not so toxic after all.

To discharge the first explanatory task, Ambitious Contextualism proceeds thus:

(iii) Premise A introduces a sceptical hypothesis thus raising the standards to HIGH. Premise A is true in HIGH because my epistemic position is too weak to meet the standards for "I know that not-SH" to be true.[10]

(iv) Premise B is true as used in both LOW and HIGH.[11]

(v) So, for Ambitious Contextualism, SA turns out to be a sound argument *at least in HIGH*: the premises A and B, used in HIGH, are both true, the reasoning is deductively valid, and so the conclusion C, as derived in HIGH, is true, too.

(vi) In contrast, the conclusion C is false when used in LOW. That's because when sceptical error possibilities are not salient, my epistemic position *is* strong enough to meet the epistemic standards.

(vii) For Ambitious Contextualism, the upshot of (v) and (vi) is that although the sceptical argument does indeed show that knowledge ascriptions turn out to be false when used in HIGH, it falls short of establishing that ordinary knowledge ascriptions are false when used in LOW. Thus, the sting of SA has, allegedly, been drawn because it fails to establish *tout court* that I lack knowledge of ordinary propositions.[12]

6 Local and Global Semantic Error

What of the second task? This amounts to explaining why we (initially) take C to be false, despite the fact that, as used in SA, it is true. Contextualism's explanation is as follows:

(viii) Despite its use in SA, we mistakenly treat the conclusion C as if it was used in LOW, and thus we treat it as expressing the false proposition it would express in LOW. Furthermore, we are unaware of our assessing, when considering SA, this false proposition rather than the true proposition C expresses in the HIGH context of SA. This explains why we (initially) find C so implausible despite the fact that it straightforwardly follows from plausible premises.[13]

307

So, if SA is a paradox, with initially plausible premises and a (simultaneously) implausible conclusion, then, according to Ambitious Contextualism, the speaker of SA makes a certain *Local Semantic Error:*

> *Local Semantic Error:* The speaker of SA mistakenly takes C, when derived in SA, as saying something false.

In a much discussed paper, in which the Semantic Error Problem first rose to prominence, Schiffer (1996) offers an explanation of the source of this Local Semantic Error:

> [SA] strikes us as presenting a profound paradox merely because we're ignorant of what it's really saying, and this because we don't appreciate the indexical nature of knowledge sentences.
>
> *(p. 325)*

Here, Schiffer has a specific version of Contextualism in mind, namely, *Indexical Contextualism,* according to which utterances of "S knows that p" can express different propositions in contexts where the epistemic standards differ (see below).

With the help of our distinctions from section 4, we reconstruct Schiffer's reasoning as follows: Firstly, we have:

> *Global Indexical Ignorance:* The speaker of "S knows that p" is ignorant of the fact that this sentence can say different things in different contexts of use (which merely differ with respect to the epistemic standards).

Since such ignorance of indexicality will, plausibly, lead the speaker to treat "S knows that p" as having an invariant content (across contexts which merely differ with respect to the epistemic standards), we then have:

> *Global Indexical Error:* The speaker mistakenly takes "S knows that p" to say the same thing across these contexts.

Furthermore, if we assume, for the time being, that the relevant context-sensitivity is exhausted by indexicality, then we can derive the more generic error claim:

> *Global Context-Sensitivity Error:* The speaker mistakenly takes "S knows that p" to have the same truth-value across contexts (which merely differ with respect to the epistemic standards).

Given this, and the fact that the speaker takes "I don't know that O", as used in ordinary contexts, to be false, the Local Semantic Error immediately follows: the speaker mistakenly takes C, when used/derived in SA, to be false.

7 The Semantic Error Problem for Ambitious Contextualism

Does this pose a serious problem for Ambitious Contextualism? Schiffer thinks so: "while this error theory is an inevitable corollary of the semantics the Contextualist needs to sustain her

The Semantic Error Problem

solution to Cartesian Scepticism, it's a pretty lame account of how, according to her, we came to be bamboozled by our own words" (p. 329). Why exactly? Schiffer (1996) says:

> Since a knowledge sentence is supposed to express different propositions in different contexts even if it contains no apparently indexical terms, one naturally thinks of a "hidden-indexical" theory of knowledge sentences [. . .] What's hard to see is how the hidden-indexical proposal can sustain the idea that fluent speakers systematically confound their contexts, so that even when they're in a context in which [HIGH] is the induced standard occurring in the false proposition they have just asserted, they mistakenly think they've just asserted a true proposition, a proposition that evidently contains the standard [LOW] that would be induced by an utterance of the problematic sentence in a quite different context. It's as though a fluent, sane, and alert speaker, who knows where she is, were actually to assert the proposition that it's raining in London when she mistakenly thinks she's asserting the proposition that it's raining in Oxford. Actually, the situation is even much more problematic. For the speaker would not only have to be confounding the proposition she's saying; she'd also have to be totally ignorant of the sort of thing she's saying.
>
> *(p. 326)*

Moreover, Schiffer thinks that attribution of Global Indexical Ignorance and, in turn, Error is independently needed by the Contextualist because

> no ordinary person who utters 'I know that p', however articulate, would dream of telling you that what he meant and was implicitly stating was that he knew that p relative to such-and-such standard.
>
> *(p. 326)*

And so, if "knows that" is an indexical, this person is not only wrong about what particular proposition is being expressed, *but also ignorant of the very kind of proposition being expressed*. That's why they mistakenly take "S knows that *p*" to express the same proposition across all contexts.[14]

Schiffer concludes that the kind of error attribution needed by Indexical Contextualism is "extreme" and "has no plausibility: speakers would know what they were saying if knowledge sentences were indexical in the way the Contextualist requires" (p. 328). In effect, Schiffer is making the claim that the required error attribution is highly implausible because the kind of Global Indexical Ignorance/Error he thinks is needed to explain the Local Semantic Error would represent a hitherto unprecedented form of semantic error that no other indexical words exhibit – the error attribution would be just too ad hoc to be taken seriously.

8 Schiffer's Local Semantic Error Objection regimented

A regimentation of Schiffer's *Local Semantic Error Objection* against Ambitious Contextualism thus runs:

(1) The Sceptical Argument SA is a paradox with plausible premises, A and B, and an implausible conclusion C.

(2) Ambitious Contextualism entails that SA is in fact sound – at least when run in HIGH.

(3) So according to Ambitious Contextualism, the conclusion of SA is non-toxic because it falls short of establishing that ordinary standards for knowledge are not met.

309

(4) However, Ambitious Contextualism also needs to explain why we were drawn into the paradox in the first place and, in particular, explain why we took the conclusion to be so implausible.

(5) Contextualism can do this only if it posits that the speaker of SA is making a Local Semantic Error whereby they mistakenly take C, when derived in SA, as saying something false.

(6) Such a Local Semantic Error is only to be explained via positing a kind of Global Indexical Error whereby the speaker does not appreciate the indexical nature of "knows that" and so mistakenly treats C, when derived in SA, as expressing the same proposition it expresses when used outside of the sceptical argument.

(7) But Global Indexical Error represents a hitherto unprecedented form of error that no other indexical words exhibit.

(8) Hence, attribution of such error is implausible.

(9) There is no other theory of context-sensitivity which can be appealed to which can explain the Local Semantic Error.

(10) Thus, there is no plausible Contextualist response to SA.

How should Contextualism respond?

9 Two initial responses

9.1 Response one: get used to it!

One immediate response is to concede that the requisite global error is indeed unprecedented but deny this makes the required error attribution implausible. So, reject the move from (7) to (8) in the Local Semantic Error Objection above. One way to do this is to reason as follows.[15] There is substantial and reasonably stable disagreement amongst competent users of "knows that" as to whether premise A of SA is true. If moderate invariantism is true then premise A, as used in SA, is false.[16] If (scepticism-friendly) Contextualism is true then premise A, as used in SA, is true. Either way, a large number of competent speakers are in error as to the truth-value of premise A – at least as used in SA. So, either way, an error theory is needed. However, as DeRose (2006) puts it,

> there may be some reason for thinking it's more problematic to suppose that many speakers are blind to the context-sensitivity of their own words than to suppose that many are blind to the context-*in*sensitivity of their own words. But it's not easy to see how to give any credible argument for such an asymmetry and it's perhaps best not to stretch to anticipate how such an argument might go.
>
> *(p. 335, emphasis in original)*

The upshot is that while Contextualism does indeed require an unprecedented error attribution this does not make this error attribution implausible *all things considered*, because it will be no more implausible than the unprecedented error theory needed by competing invariantist theories of knowledge.

This response is plausible to the degree to which its pessimism is warranted. Is there no good way to "stretch" and argue for the superiority of an error attribution for invariantism, or for Contextualism? Work published around the time and after DeRose's pessimistic response gives reason to believe that a more sophisticated weighing of pros and cons is possible, once the views' profile of error attributions and, hence, need for an error *theory*, comes into sharper relief.[17]

9.2 Response two: favor Modest over Ambitious Contextualism

A second initial response concedes that Schiffer's Local Semantic Error Objection is effective against a Contextualist treatment of SA but maintains this just shows that Modest Contextualism should be preferred over Ambitious Contextualism.

Firstly, such a response robs Contextualism of much of its philosophical interest since it is not equipped to address Cartesian Scepticism (and related puzzles). Secondly, and more tellingly, Modest Contextualism is still subject to a Global Semantic Error Objection which is effectively embedded in the Local Semantic Error Objection given above. Let's now see why this is so.

10 Schiffer's Global Semantic Error Objection

It's worth distinguishing a crude from a more sophisticated form of the Global Semantic Error Objection. The crude form runs as follows: indexicality should be obvious; since "knows that" is not obviously indexical, it's not indexical. The underlying idea is semantic transparency: if speakers, in their linguistic behavior, are unaware of some putative feature of meaning, then the feature does not exist. On this view, there is just no room for Indexical Semantic Error. But semantic transparency is implausible. As Schaffer and Szabo (2014) put it: "Virtually every sophisticated semantic theory posits all sorts of non-transparent features. Non-obvious context sensitivity is just more of the same" (p. 534).[18]

The more sophisticated form of the objection, encountered briefly above, proceeds as follows:

(1) "Knows that" is a standard kind of indexical (either an indexical verb or a hidden indexical or some other familiar kind of indexical).
(2) If "knows that" is a standard indexical then competent users should be able to recognise this.
(3) Such users are in a position to recognise this only if they are able to articulate or clarify the proposition that gets expressed by "S knows that p" (in some context of use).
(4) But competent users are not typically able to articulate or clarify the proposition that gets expressed.
(5) So, "knows that" is not a standard kind of indexical.
(6) So, if "knows that" is an indexical, its indexicality is unprecedented.
(7) But such unprecedented indexicality is just ad hoc and thus "has no plausibility".[19]

In effect, Schiffer presumes that a speaker who is semantically competent with regard to the class of indexical expressions in question satisfies something like the following thesis:

> *Content Articulation Thesis*: Semantic competence with regard to an indexical sentence S requires that speakers be able to specify what is said by S (in some context c) by articulating a natural language sentence that literally expresses the proposition originally asserted (in c).

11 An initial response to the Global Semantic Error Objection

An initial response is that the Content Articulation Thesis is too demanding. Competent speakers do not generally have to be able to articulate semantic content when using context-sensitive expressions. For instance, articulating the contextually determined modal base of a modal auxiliary like "might" – as is done, e.g., by expressions like "in view of my/x's current information" or "in view of orthodox Christian moral principles" – is not always something competent speakers can do. Similarly, articulating a token quantifier's restricted domain (as in "in this apartment", "among the students in this class") can be difficult. Moreover, even a speaker who says "It's raining" (Schiffer's example) and responds to repeated requests regarding what she meant by pointing out that what she meant is just that *it is raining* can count as a competent speaker. She may not be particularly attuned to differences between what she said (the words she used) and what meaning she expressed, and she may not be sensitive to the interpretive needs of her hearer, but this by itself does not show she is not competent. Examples like these are legion.

12 The Global Semantic Error Objection strengthened

Even if the Content Articulation Thesis is too strong, Schiffer's objection can be modified thus: if "knows that" is context-sensitive in the way gradable adjectives or "hidden indexicals" are (substitute a given Contextualist's favorite model of context-sensitivity), then how come speakers are *much better* at clarifying what they meant using gradable adjectives etc. than they are with knowledge ascriptions? How come they have prepositional phrases such as "in London" for the articulation of location or "for a basketball player" for the articulation of a comparison class to a use of "tall" more readily at hand than they have any phrases articulating epistemic standards? Note this challenge does not rely on the Content Articulation Thesis, merely on the difference between the ease of articulation with "knows" and paradigmatic examples of the Contextualist's favorite model of context-sensitive expressions (cf. Hawthorne 2004, pp. 104–5).

13 Responding to the strengthened Global Semantic Error Objection

Contextualists can meet this challenge in two ways. First, they can point to semantic or non-semantic features that plausibly distinguish "knows that" and knowledge from the relevant context-sensitive model expressions and their subject matters. Thus, Blome-Tillmann (2014, section 4.4) explains our lesser propensity to clarify knowledge ascriptions by the dependence of knowledge claims' felicity on the pragmatic presuppositions of the original context of utterance and the fact that a speaker's clarification would involve conceding that the presuppositions that are needed to render her original knowledge ascription true were absent, thereby making clarification "pragmatically incoherent". A parallel dependence on pragmatic presuppositions is not systematically present with uses of gradable adjectives.

Cohen, relatedly, observes that, more generally, semantic ignorance with context-sensitive expressions comes in degrees. (His response is not targeting content articulation in particular.) He explains our high degree of ignorance with respect to "knows" by pointing out that *knowledge* is a normative concept; possession of knowledge is valuable. Hence, Contextualism's "good news" is that we can ascribe a lot of that valuable good (in everyday contexts). The "bad news" is that we nevertheless don't always meet the highest epistemic standards. A similar "good news, bad news" Contextualist account holds for gradable adjectives like "flat". The difference in semantic ignorance between "flat" and "knows" is due to the fact that "we find [the bad news] much easier to accept in the case of flatness than knowledge because ascriptions of flatness do not have the normative force that ascriptions of knowledge/justification do" (Cohen 2004, p. 193; see also Cohen 2005, p. 61f and Neta 2003, pp. 407–9).

Second, Contextualists can also meet the articulation challenge by denying any relevant differences in articulatory ability. Thus, Schaffer and Szabo (2014), for instance, could respond – in line with their response to another strand of the semantic error objection – that speakers are *not* worse in articulating the content of knowledge ascriptions than they are with other relevant context-sensitive expressions: A-quantifiers such as the adverb "always" or modal auxiliaries such as "might", "can", and "must". The asymmetries only show that "knows" is not like gradable adjectives or "hidden indexicals" in its context-sensitivity.

This latter response is a special instance of a popular Contextualist strategy to argue that the attributed error is not ad hoc – *pace* step (7) in the Schiffer's Global Semantic Error Objection (section 10) – because similar error patterns can be found with the (particular Contextualist's chosen) analogous class of context-sensitive terms (whether or not the error is just as grave as with "knows"). For instance, Cohen (1999, pp. 77–9) argues that while speakers are prone to ascribing flatness to paradigmatic tables, they may be led to deny that some paradigmatic table is flat in the context of setting up a sensitive scientific experiment, when microscopic bumps in the table's surface are salient. Moreover, they take their denial to be in conflict with their previous lenient ascription of flatness to the same table. But since there is, just like for "knows", strong evidence in favor of the context-sensitivity of gradable adjectives like "tall", it is plausible to assume that speakers are simply unaware of the context-sensitivity of "tall", and thus mistakenly withdraw their flatness ascription in light of raised standards. Indexical Error is thus argued to be well-attested with other kinds of expression that are context-sensitive in ways similar to "knows" (cf. also Blome-Tillmann 2008, 2014, section 4.1; Cohen 2004, 2005, p. 60f.; DeRose 2006, pp. 327–31, 2009, pp. 168–74).

The force of this response depends on the independent evidence there is in favor of a Contextualist semantics of the model context-sensitive expression (gradable adjectives, quantified noun phrases, adverbial quantifiers, modal auxiliaries, etc.) and also largely on intuitive judgments: do the Contextualist's particular model context-sensitive expressions in fact have use patterns relevantly similar to knowledge claims, or do their use patterns not require a Contextualist error attribution? To our knowledge, this question still awaits empirical testing.

14 The self-undermining objection

Our discussion so far has revolved around Schiffer's original error case(s) against Contextualism, as it already prefigures most of the strands of error objections levelled against Contextualism. But there is a yet another dimension along which Indexical Error may be thought to be worrisome. MacFarlane (2005) gives expression to this worry when he claims that there is a general problem with attributing (semantic) error to competent speakers:

> [A] *general* problem with positing speaker error to explain away facts about use is that such explanations tend to undermine the evidential basis for the semantic theories [Contextualism, moderate and strict invariantism, subject-sensitive invariantism] they are intended to support. All of these semantic theories are justified indirectly on the basis of facts about speakers' use of sentences, and the more error we attribute to speakers, the less we can conclude from these facts.[20]
>
> *(p. 215)*

MacFarlane makes this dialectical point after having argued that all the mentioned theories face commitment to some error attribution or other. For instance, according to MacFarlane, Contextualists make the wrong predictions about speakers' cross-contextual truth ascriptions to knowledge ascriptions and their willingness to retract. Thus, suppose Cem asserts "I know that my car is parked in the driveway" and is subsequently presented with error possibilities to the effect that car thieves are often nearby. This is likely to raise the epistemic standards, and Cem is now inclined to say that his assertion in the previous context was false. Moreover, MacFarlane claims, Cem will treat it as false: if challenged, he will retract his earlier knowledge claim, e.g., by saying "I was wrong. I take that back. I didn't know my car is parked in the driveway" (cf. also Hawthorne 2004, p. 163; Williamson 2005, p. 220).

313

There are two ways in which error attributions may be considered generally troublesome:

(1) The "double-edged sword" (MacFarlane 2005, pp. 213–16). A particular error that explains the use facts that are troubling one view may equally explain other use facts that are troubling another view. For instance, Contextualists' attribution of error to explain cross-contextual truth ascriptions and retraction data runs the risk of equally explaining the data that Contextualists may use in their case against other views. If the involved error is one of projecting the relevant features of one's own context of use onto other contexts of use, subject-sensitive, or interest-relative, invariantists (Fantl & McGrath 2009; Hawthorne 2004; Stanley 2005) may use this sort of projection error to explain why speakers do not treat temporal and modal operators as shifting epistemic standards, e.g., in "Before you mentioned car thieves roaming the neighbourhood, I *did* know that my car is parked in the driveway" – use facts that are not predicted by subject-sensitive invariantist semantics. Attributions of semantic error may end up levelling the dialectical playing field.

(2) Overgeneration. Explaining a given set of data by attributing error risks overgeneration: other data that proponents of a view claim *support* their view may also be explained by the attributed error, thus undermining the evidential basis for the view.[21]

15 Responding to the self-undermining objection

Self-undermining objections can be understood as challenges to the semantic view rather than knock-down objections. As it stands, many error attributions are mere diagnoses of the ways in which speakers diverge from the alleged 'correct' use of "knows". There are some attempts to meet this challenge by providing more specific *psychological error theories* – theories that explain the error by appeal to some general psychological phenomena rather than merely call some use facts erroneous. Both the dialectical double-edged sword and the overgeneration problems can be defused for a particular semantics if a specific error theory can be shown to explain all and only those use facts which it is needed to explain. That is, it may be shown that the error theory doesn't explain further use facts that allegedly support the semantics (defusing overgeneration worries), and that it cannot be co-opted by rival semantic theories to explain their own troubling use facts (defusing the double-edged sword worry). See section 18.

Our discussion so far has focused on the varieties of error objections levelled against Contextualism and the responses available to Contextualists. We have not specifically addressed versions of these objections based on further kinds of data: cross-contextual judgments about the truth/acceptability of knowledge ascriptions and retraction (e.g., Hawthorne 2004; MacFarlane 2005; Stanley 2005; Williamson 2005); agreement and disagreement (e.g., see also chapter 20, "The Disagreement Challenge to Contextualism"). Contextualism, however, isn't the only view suffering from error objections. A full appreciation of the force of Contextualism's error objections requires taking into account the proliferation of error objections in the debate on knowledge ascriptions. In what follows, we illustrate two of the ways in which error objections multiply in the debate on knowledge ascriptions: as objections against relativism (section 16) and against moderate invariantists who supplement their invariant semantics with a variable pragmatics (section 17).

16 Generalizing the challenge: relativism's Index Error

A basic point in favor of Contextualism is the variability in speakers' acceptance, or rejection, of knowledge ascriptions depending on the context they are in. Classical invariantists have trouble accounting for this contextual variability. They, too, appear to be in need of error attributions to

The Semantic Error Problem

ordinary speakers (cf. section 9.1) – or of some other way to account for contextual variability (cf. section 17). MacFarlane (2005) extends this point to further views. The upshot in his paper is that while all major non-relativist views are stuck with some problematic error attributions (or worse options), his assessment-sensitive, relativist semantics of knowledge ascriptions is error attribution–free and should be preferred on these grounds.

In response, Montminy (2009) and Kindermann (2013) have argued that relativism about knowledge ascriptions faces its own semantic error objections.[22] Assessment-sensitive relativism about knowledge ascription is, very roughly, the view that while a given instance of "S knows [doesn't know] that p" expresses the same content across different contexts of use, this content may vary in truth-value with the epistemic standards operative in different contexts of assessment.[23] Kindermann (2013) objects that relativism faces a version of Schiffer's objection: a satisfactory relativist solution to the sceptical paradox must explain the appearance of paradox by appeal to an attribution of semantic error to assessors. However, the kind of error relativists need to ascribe differs from Indexical Error, which Contextualists must ascribe (see section 6).[24] For relativists, however, "knows" does not induce the expression of different contents at different contexts of utterance. In contrast, a content expressed by a given knowledge sentence may be true at one assessor's circumstances of evaluation – or "index" and false at another assessor's index. As a result, the kind of ignorance relativists must attribute to assessors is "Index Ignorance":

> *Index Ignorance*: Speakers are ignorant of the fact that the truth value of contents expressed by sentences of the form "S knows [doesn't know] that p" can vary with the epistemic standards in the index.[25]

But Index Ignorance, the objection concludes, is implausible. Speakers and assessors do not fall for the appearance of paradox with regard to other, standard, features of the index, or circumstances of evaluation, such as world and time.

17 Generalizing the challenge: error in pragmatic invariantist accounts

A popular strategy for classical invariantists is to explain the variability of acceptance and rejection of knowledge ascriptions that makes for the basic evidence in favor of Contextualism by appeal to general pragmatic mechanisms (see chapters 16–18). Brown (2006) and Rysiew (2001, 2007), among others, pursue this strategy for moderate invariantists who need to explain, among other things, why speakers in HIGH are prone to reject knowledge ascriptions and to accept knowledge denials. Put simply, these invariantists argue that an utterance of "S knows that p" in a context of utterance pragmatically implicates, rather than semantically expresses, that S is in a good enough position to meet the epistemic standards operative in the context. Hence, an utterance of "S knows that p" in HIGH may semantically express something true but pragmatically implicate a falsehood when S is in a good enough position to meet the invariant moderate epistemic standard but not the contextually determined high standard.[26]

What is important to note is that this pragmatic strategy is designed to mimic the predictions of a Contextualist semantics. In consequence, the strategy is faced with (some of) the Contextualist's recalcitrant data. As Kindermann (2016) argues, pragmatic invariantists cannot account for the sceptical paradox or retraction data without attributing an implausible form of speaker error.[27] Therefore, appeals to pragmatic mechanisms are no alternative to error attributions; they incur their very own versions of error objections.

Sections 16 and 17 served to illustrate by way of two examples that every extant view of the meaning and use of knowledge ascriptions is faced with the attribution of some error to speakers.

If this is right, then the dialectical playing field is somewhat levelled. What is needed is, first, a more careful comparison of the kinds of attributed error and a thorough investigation of the criteria that render one error attribution plausible and another implausible; and second, a view's error attributions need to be substantiated by plausible psychological accounts that *explain* why the error occurs systematically in just those use situations for which the view must attribute it. Some such accounts have been sketched on behalf of invariantist accounts. We will take a look at these before closing.

18 Psychological error theories

Another popular invariantist strategy is to explain (away) the intuitive, 'erroneous' judgments not supported by their semantics appeals to some general cognitive mechanism, which interferes with semantic processing and for which we have independent empirical evidence. Hawthorne (2004), for instance, sketches a psychological error theory on behalf of subject-sensitive invariantism. He appeals to a general-purpose heuristic underlying many judgments under uncertainty: psychological research on heuristics and biases shows that in our probability and frequency judgments we use a small number of heuristics that are cognitively effective and often lead to correct judgments, but equally result in biases that may skew our judgments. One such heuristic is the psychological 'availability' of relevant events: In assessing the probability or frequency of an event, we sometimes rely on the ease with which instances of the type can be brought to mind (cf. e.g., Tversky & Kahneman 1973). Similarly, speakers ascribing knowledge in HIGH, to whom certain error possibilities become salient, or 'available', tend to pessimistically overestimate the knowledge-destroying danger of these error possibilities and as a result come to deny knowledge. Moreover, Hawthorne claims, they tend to project their overestimations of these error possibilities onto the subject's position and come to also deny knowledge of the subject. Thus, reliance on the availability heuristic in assessing the epistemic danger of non-knowledge-destroying error possibilities may lead to erroneous judgments; attributors in HIGH are pessimistically biased.

Others have developed similar psychological explanations to help moderate insensitive invariantism explain the data. Williamson (2005) also appeals to the availability heuristic. Nagel's (2008, 2010a, 2010b) accounts draw on the bias called "epistemic egocentrism"; and Gerken (2012, 2013) develops his epistemic focal bias account within the framework of dual process theories.[28]

Whatever the merits of these accounts, invariantists' attempts to integrate epistemological work on knowledge that with empirical results from cognitive science are clearly moving the debate in the right direction. Existing attributions of *linguistic* ignorance and error – such as Contextualists' error attributions – do not involve a psychological account of how and why speakers deviate from correct use. Invariantists' psychological error theories can claim to deliver just this kind of explanation.

It is worth noting that it is open to Contextualists to co-opt the psychological strategy and explain error in terms of more general cognitive mechanisms. These mechanisms may interfere with the proper execution of semantic competence under certain conditions, leading to systematic errors. On this strategy, then, Contextualists may argue that speakers' semantic competence with "knows" itself is flawless, but that it is skewed under certain conditions by general psychological processes that are not inherently semantic.

19 Conclusion

The Semantic Error Problem for epistemic Contextualism comes in the form of different kinds of error objections, from observations about different facts about ordinary speakers' and philosophers' use of knowledge ascriptions. Contextualism's need to attribute semantic error to speakers

The Semantic Error Problem

to account for some use data is seen by some opponents as constituting a decisive objection (e.g., Schiffer 1996); to some proponents, it's further evidence in favor of Contextualism (Schaffer & Szabo 2014). Here, we haven't taken a definite stance on the force of the Semantic Error Problem for Contextualism. Our main goal has been to chart the different versions of error objections and available responses for Contextualists and to introduce a number of useful distinctions between error attributions as well as different kinds of semantic ignorance and error. Our discussion should serve to highlight two under-appreciated points. First, error objections are ubiquitous in the debate about knowledge ascriptions. None of the major extant views accounts for all the use facts without any special pleading. Second, error objections are best understood as challenges to Contextualism, and other views, to provide an error *theory* – a substantial psychological explanation of why speakers systematically, in particular kinds of situations, use knowledge ascriptions in ways that diverge from the semantics' predictions. So the force of error objections against Contextualism ultimately depends on whether Contextualism has a better explanation of the use data that is erroneous given a Contextualist semantics than other views' explanations of the use data that is erroneous given their semantics.

Given the ubiquity of error objections, the debate does and will benefit greatly from two developments. First, a more systematic comparison and evaluation of different views' needed error attributions (as attempted, e.g., in Kindermann 2012). Second, the development of psychologically substantial error theories that explain some given error rather than merely describe it (cf. section 18).

Notes

1 Blome-Tillmann (2008, 2009, 2014), Cohen (1987, 1999, 2004, 2004a, 2005), DeRose (1995, 2006, 2009), Goldman (1976), Ichikawa (2011), Lewis (1996), Neta (2003), McKenna (2013), Schaffer (2004a, 2004b), Schaffer and Szabo (2014), Stine (1976) and others.

2 Semantic error has hitherto been called "semantic blindness". However, a blind person's visual apparatus works in ways that produce (some degree of) lack of visual information (relative to a norm), rather than in the delivery of misinformation. This, we'll argue, is in contrast to the semantic case. Moreover, since semantic error is apt to be seen as a bad thing, the use of "semantic blindness" runs the risk of being an ableist metaphor.

3 Various (related) problems are found in: Bach (2005), Conee (2005), Davis (2004), Feldman (1999), Hawthorne (2004), MacFarlane (2005), Schiffer (1996), Stanley (2004, 2005) and Williamson (2005).

4 Contextualism is here neutral between Indexical Contextualism and Non-Indexical Contextualism. The former entails that there can be a difference in propositions expressed across contexts of use, while the latter holds that the content of "S knows that p" is invariant but can be true relative to one set of epistemic standards and false relative to another. See MacFarlane (2009).

5 That's controversial if evidence is constituted by, e.g., what one knows (see Williamson 2000), but nothing turns on this issue below.

6 See Schaffer and Szábo (2014) for a form of Modest Contextualism.

7 Here, we do not intend to commit to a view of semantic competence in terms of (implicit) beliefs about the semantic properties of expressions in the language. Talk of (implicit) belief is simply picked as one way to conceptualize, e.g., the difference between semantic ignorance and error.

8 Cf. MacFarlane (2005, p. 215).

9 See Cohen (1987), DeRose (1995), Lewis (1996) and Stine (1976).

10 Here we outline what DeRose (1995) calls the "scepticism-friendly" version of Contextualism.

11 One forceful reason: it would be an "abominable conjunction", in both LOW and HIGH, to assert: I know that O but I don't know that not-SH (DeRose 1995, section 7).

12 We take such a semantic story to subsume the meta-semantic story as to why the salience of error produces a high-standards context, and the non-salience of error produces a low-standards context.

13 Cf. Schiffer (1996).

14 Schiffer also considers two further implementations of Indexical Contextualism. The first treats "knows" as an indexical verb which picks out different knowledge relations (e.g., knows$_{HIGH}$, knows$_{LOW}$) in

different contexts. He thinks this does no better than hidden-indexical Contextualism (p. 327). The second appeals to the idea that "knows that" is vague, plus the idea that such vagueness entails that the penumbra/extension of "knows that", like that of "flat", can vary with the standards operative in the context of use (pp. 327–8). While Schiffer finds such variability plausible, he alleges that it will not help because we are "perfectly aware when it is going on". So, again, Contextualism cannot accommodate the kind of error theory needed.

15 Here we adapt DeRose (2006, pp. 333–6) who instead uses judgments as to whether those who assert and those who deny premise A (or indeed C) are genuinely disagreeing.

16 Moderate invariantism is the view that "S knows that p" is not relevantly context-sensitive and that subjects are able to meet the epistemic conditions for knowing.

17 See, for instance, the work on psychological error theories in Nagel (2008, 2010a, 2010b), and Gerken (2013), and a systematic comparison of the main contenders' error ascriptions in Kindermann (2012).

18 Schaffer and Szabo (2014) continue: "Indeed we suspect that those who endorse the transparency premise must ultimately be the sort of radical invariantists who only allow for context sensitivity with core indexicals and demonstratives." See also Blome-Tillmann (2014, 107–10) against transparency.

19 Similarly, Hawthorne (2004,104–7) argues that if "knows that" was context-sensitive in a way similar to that of gradable adjectives ("empty", "flat"), then speakers should be able to avail themselves of "clarification" techniques to state more precisely what they meant. A speaker who asserts "That is flat" and is then challenged with "Well, it's got a few small holes in it" would be able to clarify what she meant by saying, e.g., "All I meant is that it is flat *for a football field.*" But no such natural linguistic devices of clarification seem available in the case of knowledge ascriptions. According to Hawthorne, the theorist's locution "relative to high standards" is not a natural clarification device speakers have in their repertoire. (Though see Ludlow (2005) for a list of natural language expressions which are in use with knowledge ascriptions and may count as clarification devices.) MacFarlane (2005, section 2.3) puts the articulation/clarification point in the context of retraction: I will retract rather than reformulate/articulate my previous knowledge ascription in a way to show it consistent with my current claims. See also Feldman (2001, p. 74, pp. 78–9).

20 MacFarlane (2014, 180–1) makes this point specifically against Contextualism. Cf. Conee 2005.

21 A more specific self-undermining objection concerns a tension in Schiffer's (1996, 326–7) Local Semantic Error Objection: With respect to the sceptical paradox, he claims that (i) a speaker interprets the proposition in the conclusion C as false and the proposition expressed by premise A as true; and (ii) yet she is "totally ignorant of the sort of thing she's saying" because she can't articulate it. But note that in order to have strong intuitive judgments of truth and falsity, the speaker must have determinate if implicit views of what is said. If she was "totally ignorant" of which proposition the conclusion expresses, she would be at a loss in evaluating it for truth and falsity.

22 The broad worry also besets Non-Indexical Contextualism.

23 Kölbel (2009) and Richard (2008) also endorse relativism about knowledge ascriptions. See also chapters 22 ("Contextualism, Relativism, and the Problem of Lost Disagreement") and 23 ("Epistemological Implications of Relativism").

24 Cf. the notion of "Content-Blindness" in Kindermann (2013).

25 Cf. Åkerman and Greenough (2010) on the distinction between (Strong and Weak) Content Blindness and (Strong and Weak) Truth Blindness.

26 Cf. Greenough (2011) who advocates Norm-Relativism – a form of Invariantism under which there is a demanding norm of assertion in HIGH (assessment contexts), and a less demanding norm of assertion in LOW (assessment contexts). Unlike the various competitor forms of Invariantism such a view can handle retraction data (without succumbing to relativism about truth).

27 See also Dimmock and Huvenes (2014).

28 See also chapter 7, "The Psychological Context of Contextualism", by Nagel and Smith.

Bibliography

Åkerman, J. and Greenough, P. (2010). "Vagueness and Non-indexical Contextualism." In: Sawyer, S. (ed.). *New Waves in Philosophy of Language.* New York: Palgrave, 8–23.

Bach, K. (2005). "The Emperor's New 'Knows'." In: Preyer, G. and Peter, G. (eds.). *Contextualism in Philosophy: Knowledge, Meaning, and Truth.* Oxford: Oxford University Press, 51–89.

Blome-Tillmann, M. (2008). "The Indexicality of 'Knowledge'." *Philosophical Studies* 138(1), 29–53.

Blome-Tillmann, M. (2009). "Contextualism, Subject-Sensitive Invariantism, and the Interaction of 'Knowledge'-Ascriptions with Modal and Temporal Operators." *Philosophy and Phenomenological Research* 79(2), 315–31.

Blome-Tillmann, M. (2014). *Knowledge and Presuppositions*. Oxford: Oxford University Press.

Brown, J. (2006). "Contextualism and Warranted Assertibility Manoeuvres." *Philosophical Studies* 130(3), 407–35.

Cohen, S. (1987). "Knowledge, Context, and Social Standards." *Synthese* 73(1), 3–26.

Cohen, S. (1999). "Contextualism, Skepticism, and the Structure of Reasons." *Noûs* 33, 57–89.

Cohen, S. (2004a). "Contextualism and Unhappy-Face Solutions: Reply to Schiffer." *Philosophical Studies* 119(1), 185–97.

Cohen, S. (2004b). "Knowledge, Assertion, and Practical Reasoning." *Philosophical Issues* 14, 482–91.

Cohen, S. (2005). "Contextualism Defended." In: Steup, M. and Sosa, E. (eds.). *Contemporary Debates in Epistemology*. Malden, MA: Blackwell, 56–62.

Conee, E. (2005). "Contextualism Contested." In: Steup, M. and Sosa, E. (eds.). *Contemporary Debates in Epistemology*. Malden, MA: Blackwell, 47–56.

Davis, W. (2004). "Are Knowledge Claims Indexical?" *Erkenntnis* 61(2), 257–81.

DeRose, K. (1995). "Solving the Skeptical Problem." *The Philosophical Review* 104(1), 1–52.

DeRose, K. (2006). "'Bamboozled by Our Own Words': Semantic Blindness and Some Arguments against Contextualism." *Philosophy and Phenomenological Research* 73(2), 316–38.

DeRose, K. (2009). *The Case for Contextualism*. Oxford: Oxford University Press.

Dimmock, P. and Huvenes, T.T. (2014). "Knowledge, Conservatism, and Pragmatics." *Synthese* 191(14), 3239–69.

Fantl, J. and McGrath, M. (2009). *Knowledge in an Uncertain World*. Oxford: Oxford University Press.

Feldman, R. (1999). "Contextualism and Skepticism." *Noûs* 33, 91–114.

Feldman, R. (2001). "Skeptical Problems, Contextualist Solutions." *Philosophical Studies* 103(1), 61–85.

Gerken, M. (2012). "On the Cognitive Bases of Knowledge Ascriptions." In: Brown, J. and Gerken, M. (eds.). *Knowledge Ascriptions*. Oxford: Oxford University Press, 140–70.

Gerken, M. (2013). "Epistemic Focal Bias." *Australasian Journal of Philosophy* 91(1), 41–61.

Goldman, A. (1976). "Discrimination and Perceptual Knowledge." *The Journal of Philosophy* 73, 771–91. Reprinted in Goldman, A. 1992, *Liaisons: Philosophy Meets the Cognitive and Social Sciences*, Cambridge, MA: The MIT Press, 85–103.

Greenough, P. (2011). "Truth-Relativism, Norm-Relativism, and Assertion." In: Brown, J. and Cappelen, H. (eds.). *Assertion: New Philosophical Essays*, Oxford: Oxford University Press, 197–231.

Hawthorne, J. (2004). *Knowledge and Lotteries*. Oxford: Oxford University Press.

Ichikawa, J. (2011). "Quantifiers, Knowledge, and Counterfactuals." *Philosophy and Phenomenological Research* 82(2), 287–313.

Kindermann, D. (2012). "Perspective in Context. Relative, Truth, Knowledge, and the First Person." PhD Dissertation, University of St Andrews.

Kindermann, D. (2013). "Relativism, Sceptical Paradox, and Semantic Blindness." *Philosophical Studies* 162(3), 585–603.

Kindermann, D. (2016). "Knowledge, Pragmatics, and Error". *Grazer Philosophische Studien* 93, 429–57.

Kölbel, M. (2009). "The Evidence for Relativism." *Synthese* 166(2), 375–95.

Lewis, D. (1996). "Elusive Knowledge." *Australasian Journal of Philosophy* 74(4), 549–67.

Ludlow, P. (2005). "Contextualism and the New Linguistic Turn in Epistemology." In: Preyer, G. & Peter, G. (eds.). *Contextualism in Philosophy: Knowledge, Meaning, and Truth*. Oxford: Oxford University Press, 11–50.

MacFarlane, J. (2005). "The Assessment-Sensitivity of Knowledge Attributions." In: Gendler, T.S. and Hawthorne, J. (eds.). *Oxford Studies in Epistemology I*. Oxford: Oxford University Press, 197–233.

MacFarlane, J. (2009). "Nonindexical Contextualism." *Synthese*, 166(2), 231–50.

MacFarlane, J. (2014). *Assessment-Sensitivity: Relative Truth and Its Applications*. Oxford: Oxford University Press.

McKenna, R. (2013). "Epistemic Contextualism: A Normative Approach." *Pacific Philosophical Quarterly* 94(1), 101–23.

Montminy, M. (2009). "Contextualism, Relativism, and Ordinary Speakers' Judgments." *Philosophical Studies* 143(3), 341–56.

Nagel, J. (2008). "Knowledge Ascriptions and the Psychological Consequences of Changing Stakes." *Australasian Journal of Philosophy* 86(2), 279–94.

Nagel, J. (2010a). "Epistemic Anxiety and Adaptive Invariantism." *Philosophical Perspectives* 24, 407–35.

Nagel, J. (2010b). "Knowledge Ascriptions and the Psychological Consequences of Thinking about Error." *The Philosophical Quarterly* 60(239), 286–306.

Neta, R. (2003). "Skepticism, Contextualism, and Semantic Self-Knowledge." *Philosophy and Phenomenological Research* 67, 396–411.

Richard, M. (2008). *When Truth Gives Out*. Oxford: Oxford University Press.

Rysiew, P. (2001). "The Context-Sensitivity of Knowledge Attributions." *Noûs* 35(4), 477–514.

Rysiew, P. (2007). "Speaking of Knowing." *Noûs* 41(4), 627–62.

Schaffer, J. (2004a). "From Contextualism to Contrastivism." *Philosophical Studies* 119(1), 73–103.

Schaffer, J. (2004b). "Skepticism, Contextualism, and Discrimination." *Philosophy and Phenomenological Research* 69(1), 138–55.

Schaffer, J. and Szabó, Z.G. (2014). "Epistemic Comparativism: A Contextualist Semantics for Knowledge Ascriptions." *Philosophical Studies* 168(2), 491–543.

Schiffer, S. (1996). "Contextualist Solutions to Scepticism." *Proceedings of the Aristotelian Society* 96, 317–33.

Stanley, J. (2004). "On the Linguistic Basis for Contextualism." *Philosophical Studies* 119, 119–46.

Stanley, J. (2005). *Knowledge and Practical Interests*. Oxford: Oxford University Press.

Stine, G.C. (1976). "Skepticism, Relevant Alternatives, and Deductive Closure." *Philosophical Studies* 29, 249–61.

Tversky, A. and Kahneman, D. (1973). "Availability: A Heuristic for Judging Frequency and Probability." *Cognitive Psychology* 5, 207–32.

Williamson, T. (2000). *Knowledge and Its Limits*. Oxford: Oxford University Press.

Williamson, T. (2005). "Contextualism, Subject-Sensitive Invariantism, and Knowledge of Knowledge." *The Philosophical Quarterly* 55(219), 213–35.

25

CONVERSATIONAL KINEMATICS

Robin McKenna

Introduction

Contextualism is the view that knowledge ascriptions – utterances of sentences containing the word "knows" – express different propositions in different contexts of utterance. Consider these examples:

LOW: Hannah and Sarah are discussing whether the bank is open on Saturdays. Hannah recalls it was open on a previous Saturday. She says, "I know that the bank is open on Saturdays." Sarah agrees.

HIGH: Laura and Sarah are discussing whether the same bank is open on Saturdays. Sarah says, "Hannah has been in there on Saturday before." But Laura replies, "Banks can change their opening hours. Hannah doesn't know that the bank is open." Sarah agrees.[1]

Assume the bank is open. The thought is that Hannah's knowledge ascription and Laura's knowledge denial are both true, even though we can specify that Hannah's epistemic position is the same in both cases (for dissent, see Brown 2006; Nagel 2008; Rysiew 2001). The contextualist explanation is that their respective uses of "knows" have different semantic values.[2] Let's say that an utterance of "S knows that p" is true in a context c iff S's evidence rules out all of the alternatives in which not-p that are relevant in c, where different sets of alternatives are relevant in different contexts (see Blome-Tillmann 2014; Ichikawa 2011; Lewis 1996).[3] The alternative in which the bank has changed its opening hours is relevant in HIGH (Laura and Sarah take it seriously), but isn't relevant in LOW (Hannah and Sarah don't consider it). So Hannah's use of "knows" refers to a property the possession of which would allow Hannah to rule out one set of alternatives, whereas Laura's use of "knows" refers to a property the possession of which would allow Hannah to rule out another set. Because (let's assume) Hannah has the former property but not the latter, Hannah's knowledge ascription is true, whereas Laura's is false.[4]

Contextualism says that the semantic values of uses of "knows" depend on features of the context of utterance. But what features? In other words, what makes an alternative relevant (or, an epistemic standard appropriate)? Jason Stanley (no friend of contextualism) suggests this answer:

On a standard account of context-sensitive expressions, their semantic contents, relative to a context, are determined by facts about the intentions of the speaker using that expression. On this account, the reason that a use of (for example) 'that cat' refers to a particular cat is because of the linguistic meaning of 'that cat', together with the referential intentions of the user of that expression on that occasion. Call the view that all context-sensitive expressions behave in this manner the *intention-based* view of context-sensitive expressions.

(2005: 25)

The intention-based view says that the set of relevant alternatives in a context is the set of alternatives those in the context intend to be talking about. But the contextualist need not accept this view. First, it may well be false. David Kaplan (1989a) has argued that the semantic values of uses of pure indexicals (e.g. "I") and demonstratives (e.g. "that") don't depend on referential intentions. If Catriona says, "I am tired", she refers to Catriona, not whoever she intended to refer to (maybe Catriona thinks she is Laurie). If I say, "that café", while pointing at Café Landtmann, I refer to Café Landtmann, not whichever café I intended to refer to (maybe I thought I was pointing at Café Central). If Kaplan is right, then the semantic values of uses of some context-sensitive expressions don't depend on referential intentions.[5]

Second, here's Stewart Cohen (a prominent contextualist) on the question of what determines the standards:

This is a very difficult question to answer. But we can say this much. The standards are determined by some complicated function of speaker intentions, listener expectations, presuppositions of the conversation, salience relations, etc., by what David Lewis calls the conversational score.

(1999: 61)

Cohen only says that speaker intentions are part of the story. Consequently, it is at best unclear whether he accepts the intention-based view.[6]

Cohen's picture (based on Lewis 1979) is roughly as follows. The speakers in a conversational context make various conversational moves. These moves are informed by their intentions, expectations, presuppositions and purposes. Catriona says she "knows" that the train leaves at 3 p.m. Morven points out that they need to catch this train and asks if Catriona has seen the latest timetable. Catriona says she has, and the next train is at 3 p.m. Laurie suggests there might be a problem on the track, and the train won't leave until later. Catriona admits she can't rule this out. As this conversation develops, the set of relevant alternatives expands. At first, the alternative in which there is a problem on the track was irrelevant (it hadn't occurred to anyone). At the end, the alternative is relevant (everyone accepts it is worth considering). Their conversational moves determine the set of relevant alternatives. The set of relevant alternatives depends on the 'dynamics' or 'kinematics' of conversation. For want of a better label, I'll call this 'conversational contextualism'. Conversational contextualism is broader than the intention-based view. Conversational contextualism says that the set of relevant alternatives depends on conversational kinematics. The intention-based view says that the set depends on a particular aspect of conversational kinematics, viz. the speaker's referential intentions.

The chapter has three parts. In section 1, I outline the most sophisticated version of conversational contextualism, which is the view defended by Michael Blome-Tillmann (2009, 2014). In section 2, I argue that conversational contextualism faces serious problems. Put briefly, conversational contextualism makes it too hard to count as "knowing" in contexts where the speakers have relevant false beliefs about the epistemic situation of the subject they are evaluating. In section 3, I consider three responses to this objection. I argue that none of them are successful, so we have reason to abandon conversational contextualism. But my conclusion is not that we have reason to abandon contextualism. While the literature has focused on views that tie the set of relevant alternatives to conversational kinematics, one can be a contextualist without tying the set of relevant alternatives to conversational kinematics. I finish by briefly sketching what this kind of view might look like.

1 Conversational contextualism

Our question is: what makes an alternative relevant? Lewis (1996) provides a list of rules specifying exactly when an alternative is relevant. In this section I outline Lewis's rules, and explain why Blome-Tillmann's (2009, 2014) modified list of rules rectifies the failings of Lewis's.

Lewis gives us four rules (see Lewis 1996: 554–9):[7]

> RULE OF ACTUALITY (RA): If an alternative in which not-p is actual, then that alternative is relevant in c.[8]
>
> RULE OF BELIEF (RB): If the subject believes (or should believe) an alternative in which not-p is actual, then that alternative is relevant in c.
>
> RULE OF RESEMBLANCE (RRE): If an alternative in which not-p saliently resembles another relevant alternative (made relevant in some other way), then that alternative is relevant in c.
>
> RULE OF ATTENTION (RTT): If an alternative in which not-p is not ignored in c, then that alternative is relevant in c.

Some comments are in order. RA ensures that a knowledge ascription is true only if the relevant proposition is true: "S knows that p" is true only if p is true. RB ensures that a knowledge ascription is true only if the subject doesn't (or shouldn't) believe that an alternative in which p is false is actual: "S knows that p" is true only if S doesn't (or shouldn't) believe that p is false.

RRE is a little less clear. The basic thought is that there may be a number of respects in which an alternative resembles an alternative that is already relevant, and whether any of those respects are salient depends on the context (see Lewis 1996: 557–66). Perhaps the most serious problem with RRE is that it allows that there are contexts in which one can truly say that the subject in a Gettier case "knows" (these are contexts where the alternatives in which the Gettierized subject's belief is false don't saliently resemble actuality).[9]

Lewis's defence of RTT is brief:

> [RTT] is more a triviality than a rule. When we say that a possibility is properly ignored, we mean exactly that; we do not mean that it *could have been* properly ignored. Accordingly, a possibility not ignored at all is *ipso facto* not properly ignored.
>
> *(1996: 559)*

However, as Blome-Tillmann (2009, 2014: ch. 1) has argued, RTT should be rejected. I will outline his argument before turning to his proposed replacement for RTT. Consider this case:

> TEENAGER: Laurie is lying in bed. She hears her teenage son's bedroom window open, so she gets up and looks out. She sees someone who looks a lot like her son jumping out onto the ground below. She goes into the bedroom and finds it empty. She concludes that her son has slipped out, and spends the night fuming. In fact, this is exactly what happened. In the morning she challenges him: "I know you went out late last night.

I heard you." The son responds: "How do you know? It's possible that you dreamt the whole thing."

If the son continues to insist it's possible that Laurie dreamt the whole thing (the 'dreaming alternative'), then the dreaming alternative isn't ignored. But, if it isn't ignored, then, according to RTT, it's relevant. Assuming Laurie can't rule the dreaming alternative out, the son speaks truly when he denies that Laurie "knows" he went out. Because this is counter-intuitive, RTT should be rejected.

TEENAGER gives us good reason to reject RTT because it shows that RTT makes it too hard for Laurie to count as "knowing". In order to count as "knowing" in her present context, Laurie has to somehow convince her son to ignore the dreaming alternative. But this isn't a condition Laurie should have to meet in order to count as "knowing" her son slipped out. Given the strength of her evidence, it is obvious that Laurie counts as "knowing". As I will put it in what follows, RTT is at odds with epistemological orthodoxy. While epistemologists dispute whether subjects in various real and imaginary cases can truly be said to "know" (e.g. fake barn cases), they agree that there are a number of paradigm cases in which "knowledge" can truly be ascribed.[10] Our case is such a paradigm: Laurie has excellent grounds for thinking her son has slipped out, nothing funny is going on, and Laurie has no reason to think anything funny is going on. Sense perception doesn't get much (epistemically) better than this.[11] So epistemological orthodoxy says that the right thing to say is that Laurie "knows" her son slipped out.[12] Of course, this is not to say that this is the verdict everyone would give, much less the verdict everyone would give if they were rational. If someone had the false belief that something funny was going on – that Laurie was being tricked, say – they might deny that Laurie "knows". But epistemological orthodoxy tells us that they would be speaking falsely in doing so, albeit for understandable reasons (this point will be important in section 2).[13]

Turning to Blome-Tillmann's (2009) account, he replaces RTT with what he calls the 'rule of pragmatic presupposition' (RPP) (see pp. 249–56). To understand RPP, we need the notions of 'common ground' and 'pragmatic presupposition', which Blome-Tillmann takes from Robert Stalnaker. The basic thought is that in making their conversational moves speakers often presuppose that their audience has relevant information. If I say, "My wife is ill", I presuppose that my audience is aware that I have a wife. In doing so I take it to be common ground that I have a wife (I don't expect the response to be "You have a wife?").[14] Here is Stalnaker summarizing the basic idea:

> [T]he common ground is just common or mutual belief, and what a speaker presupposes is what she believes to be common or mutual belief. The common beliefs of the parties to a conversation are the beliefs they share, and that they recognize that they share: a proposition [p] is common belief of a group of believers if and only if all in the group believe that ϕ, all believe that all believe it, all believe that all believe that all believe it, etc.
>
> *(2002: 704)*

So Stalnaker offers these characterizations of common ground and pragmatic presupposition:

> COMMON GROUND: The common ground in a conversational context c is the body of propositions that all the conversational participants accept, all believe that all accept, all believe that all believe that all accept, and so on.
> PRAGMATIC PRESUPPOSITION: A conversational participant S pragmatically presupposes p in c iff S believes p to be common ground in c.

While Blome-Tillmann accepts this basic picture, he proposes an amendment to PRAGMATIC PRESUPPOSITION:

PRAGMATIC PRESUPPOSITION★: A conversational participant S pragmatically presupposes *p* in c iff S *is disposed to behave as if* she believes *p* to be common ground in c.

(2009: 253)

His reasons for doing so need not detain us here. The important point is that he uses these notions to formulate a replacement for RTT:

RULE OF PRAGMATIC PRESUPPOSITION (RPP): If an alternative in which not-*p* is compatible with the conversational participants' pragmatic presuppositions in c, then that alternative is relevant in c.

(Blome-Tillmann 2009: 256)

While RPP has a lot to recommend it, two considerations are particularly important. First, it appeals to two notions – Stalnaker's notions of common ground and pragmatic presupposition – that are independently motivated. Second, it seems to deal with TEENAGER. The case can end in one of two ways. Either the son realizes Laurie won't consider the dreaming alternative, in which case he ceases to insist on it, and so is no longer disposed to behave as if he believes it to be common ground that the alternative needs to be ruled out. Or the son continues to insist Laurie dreamt it all, in which case we end up in what Stalnaker calls a 'defective context'. In such contexts, it is at best unclear what alternatives are relevant, and at worst indeterminate. While this may not sound like an improvement on RTT, Blome-Tillmann argues (convincingly) that it is (see Blome-Tillmann 2009: 268–72).[15]

There are other aspects of Blome-Tillmann's view. While he accepts RA and RB, he proposes an alternative to RRE, and he thinks we need to add some additional rules (see Blome-Tillmann 2014: chs. 3, 5). But RPP is the core of his view. Accordingly, my criticism in section 2 will focus on RPP. While RPP provides a compelling account of the way in which the set of relevant alternatives depends on the conversational context, I will argue that it faces serious problems.

2 Problems for conversational contextualism

In this section I will argue that RPP is as much at odds with epistemological orthodoxy as RTT. I will start by presenting the argument. I will then explain why this problem is an instance of a more general problem for a certain kind of view of semantic context-sensitivity.

Consider this case:

REAL BARNS: Catriona and Sorcha are driving through a rural area. Their friend Morven has told them that there is a particularly fetching red barn in the area, so they have been looking out for it. But Catriona has just remembered that someone told them this is the dreaded fake barn county, where almost all of the barn-shaped objects are actually fake barns. However, unbeknownst to Catriona and Sorcha, this information is entirely false. Not only are there no fake barns here, there are no fake barns for hundreds of miles. Catriona and Sorcha are discussing whether Morven actually saw a red barn in light of their (mis)information. Catriona says, "Morven doesn't have the skill to distinguish between real barns and all these fakes that are around here. So she doesn't know that there was a red barn."

Catriona and Sorcha aren't just disposed to behave as if Morven saw a fake barn, they believe that she saw a fake barn. Indeed, given their misleading evidence, their belief that she saw a fake barn is reasonable. So, according to RPP, the alternative in which Morven saw a fake barn is relevant. Because Morven can't rule it out (we can assume she lacks the required discriminatory capacities) it follows that Catriona's utterance is true.

I would submit that this is as counter-intuitive as the verdict RTT gives about TEENAGER (I briefly discuss whether it is in section 3). My diagnosis of the problem parallels my diagnosis of the problem with RTT and TEENAGER. This is a clear case in which epistemological orthodoxy says it would be right to say that Morven "knows". Her belief was formed by a perceptual process that is reliable in normal conditions, conditions are normal, and she has no reason to think anything funny is going on. Sense perception doesn't get much better.[16] Again, this is not to say that this is the verdict that everyone would give, much less the verdict that everyone would give if they were rational. Given their false beliefs, the reasonable thing for Catriona to say in REAL BARNS might be that Morven doesn't "know". But there's a difference between it being reasonable to say something and that thing being true. Epistemological orthodoxy says that Catriona speaks falsely in denying that Morven "knows". But RPP tells us she speaks truly. So RPP is also incompatible with epistemological orthodoxy.

This problem is an instance of a general problem for a certain kind of view of semantic context-sensitivity. In a recent paper Torfinn Huvenes and Andreas Stokke (2015) argue against a view they call 'information centrism'. According to information centrism, contexts can be identified with bodies of shared information that are characterized in terms of the propositional attitudes of the conversational participants (Huvenes & Stokke 2016: 302). As Michael Glanzberg puts it, according to this view:

> The context of an utterance is the collection of propositions presupposed by participants in the conversation at the point of utterance . . . The expression *I* winds up referring to the speaker because it will be common ground among participants in a conversation who is speaking at a given time, and that *I* picks out that person.
>
> *(2015: 304)*

To see the problem with information centrism, consider this case:

> CASTOR AND POLLUX: Castor and Pollux are identical twins, and are virtually indistinguishable. In school Castor was a model student, while Pollux got into trouble and was ultimately expelled. Their parents managed to keep this event secret, and the twins changed school. After a few years, they and their parents were the only ones to know about Pollux's tainted academic history. Later in life, a series of physical accidents and psychological complications arose, and as a result people got the identities of the twins mixed up so that *everyone*, including themselves, came to believe that Castor is Pollux, and that Pollux is Castor. One day, sitting in a café with some friends, Castor feels the urge to come clean, and after taking a deep breath, says, "I was expelled from school."
>
> *(Huvenes & Stokke 2016: 4)*

Huvenes and Stokke think that it is intuitive that Castor's use of "I" refers to Castor, not Pollux. So his utterance is false. But, because it is common ground that the speaker is Pollux, information centrism says that Castor's use of "I" refers to Pollux. The problem with information centrism is that it ties the semantic values of uses of context-sensitive expressions to the common ground, but the common ground can contain relevant false propositions (here,

Conversational kinematics

that the speaker is Pollux).[17] As we have seen, the problem with RPP is that it ties the relevance of alternatives to pragmatic presuppositions and the common ground, but the conversational participants can pragmatically presuppose relevant false propositions (here, that Morven saw a fake barn, because she's in fake barn county). So the problem is caused by the same structural feature. The problem with RPP is an instance of a more general problem for views of semantic context-sensitivity that tie the semantic values of uses of context-sensitive expressions to features of the conversational context (common ground, pragmatic presuppositions) that can contain relevant false propositions.[18]

3 Possible responses

In this section I will canvass three responses to my argument against RPP and conversational contextualism. My tentative conclusion will be that the responses can be dealt with, and so the argument stands. I finish by briefly adverting to a different sort of contextualism.

First, I have been arguing against RPP, not conversational contextualism. Why can't the conversational contextualist propose a replacement for RPP that deals with REAL BARNS? The onus is on the conversational contextualist to provide the replacement, and I am not optimistic about her prospects. Here's why. Conversational contextualists hold that an alternative being relevant is a matter of it being appropriately related to things like the common ground, speaker intentions, expectations and pragmatic presuppositions. The problem with tying the relevance of alternatives to the common ground is that the common ground reflects the speakers' possibly false beliefs about what the world is like. Because it reflects their possibly false beliefs, the common ground can contain false propositions. Catriona and Sorcha deny that Morven "knows" because they falsely believe that she is in a fake barn case. But speaker intentions, expectations and pragmatic presuppositions also reflect the speakers' possibly false beliefs about the world. So it is unlikely that conversational contextualism can be salvaged by replacing RPP.

Second, one might deny that RPP's verdict in REAL BARNS is counter-intuitive. Whether the verdict is generally regarded as counter-intuitive is an empirical matter, which I won't speculate about here. Instead, I want to emphasize that RPP and RTT suffer from a common problem: both are incompatible with epistemological orthodoxy. My argument was not (just) that it is counter-intuitive to say that Catriona speaks truly when she denies that Morven "knows". The deeper diagnosis was that epistemological orthodoxy rules that it is *wrong* to deny that Morven "knows". But this was also the deeper diagnosis of what goes wrong with RTT in TEENAGER. What we need is an argument that the way in which RTT goes against orthodoxy is problematic, whereas the way in which RPP goes against orthodoxy isn't.

One might be tempted to point out the obvious difference between REAL BARNS and TEENAGER. REAL BARNS exploits the fact that RPP allows false but reasonable beliefs to affect which alternatives are relevant. TEENAGER exploits the fact that RTT allows uncooperative conversational partners to affect which alternatives are relevant. Perhaps the latter is problematic, whereas the former isn't.[19] However, it isn't hard to construct variants on REAL BARNS where the conversational participants are uncooperative:

CONSPIRACY: As before, except that Catriona and Sorcha have managed to convince themselves that the government has secretly been replacing real barns in the area with fake barns. But, not only is there no such conspiracy, they have no actual evidence that this is going on. They are both just inclined to believe any conspiracy theory they come across. Catriona says, "Morven *thinks* she saw a red barn, but we know better. There's this massive conspiracy going on. She doesn't know that there was a red barn."

327

Here, both Catriona and Sorcha are behaving in an epistemically uncooperative way. Because of this, RPP rules that the alternative in which Morven saw a fake barn is relevant.

Ultimately, I suspect that arbitrating this dispute requires getting clear on the extent to which a semantic view of a natural language expression like "knows" is beholden to the philosophical theorist's view of the extension of that expression (and vice versa). If the epistemologist says that it is right to say that a subject "knows", is it a problem for the contextualist if she has to hold that there are contexts in which it would be true to say that the subject doesn't "know"? It doesn't necessarily have to be. Just think of the contextualist solution to scepticism, according to which there are contexts in which it would be true to deny that we "know" much, if anything (see DeRose 1995). But the contextualist offers this as a solution to a deep epistemological problem. What deep epistemological problem is solved by holding that there are contexts in which it is true to deny that Morven "knows"?

Third, one might deny that the contextualist has to give rules stating when an alternative is relevant. Jonathan Jenkins Ichikawa (2011) gives a nice statement of this view:

> [M]any metasemantic questions about the role of context in picking out a modal base for knowledge attributions remain here unanswered. Some philosophers will be dissatisfied for this reason. In my view, such philosophers are demanding too much at once. To understand knowledge attributions as context-sensitive on the model of quantifiers, and to show that they shift in the same sorts of ways, is a substantive and interesting philosophical conclusion. Of course questions remain unanswered; these questions have unanswered analogues for quantifiers, as I've repeatedly emphasized in this paper. Such considerations, therefore, do not undermine the contextualist approach to knowledge, any more than they undermine the widely accepted contextualist approach to quantifier domains.
>
> *(398)*

There is much that I agree with here. It would be a mistake to argue that contextualism is false on the basis of cases like REAL BARNS. After all, nobody would argue that "I" isn't context-sensitive on the basis of cases like CASTOR AND POLLUX. But my aim is not to argue that contextualism is false. My aim is to argue that the best contextualist view should not advert to features of conversational kinematics. So the burden is on me to suggest what an alternative account might look like.

The contextualist says that the semantic values of uses of "knows" depend on the context. The problem is to specify the features of context on which they depend. In trying to answer this question we might profit from looking at some of the broader literature. While discussions of contextualism in epistemology have focused on a particular view defended by the likes of Blome-Tillmann, Cohen, DeRose, Ichikawa and Lewis, there are other views on which epistemic properties and/or epistemic vocabulary depend on contexts. Take, for instance, Helen Longino's 'critical contextual empiricism', on which some content A which is accepted by a community C is knowledge for C just in case A accurately represents its intended object, is supported by the data available to C and has survived critical scrutiny from as many perspectives as are available in C (see Longino 2002: 135–6). One could give this view a semantic spin: uses of "knows" refer to a property the possession of which requires one to be in a position to satisfy certain norms. One counts as "knowing" something (e.g. a scientific theory) only if one can show that it is supported by the available data and survives critical scrutiny from as wide a variety of perspectives as are available. Because different data and perspectives will be available in different communities, what these norms require of one depends on and varies with the context. While there are issues with her story (see Longino 2002: 145–65; Rolin 2011), Longino offers a clear and compelling

Conversational kinematics

answer to our basic question: we can characterize contexts in terms of various norms. We must meet these norms in order to count as "knowing". Because what we need to do to meet the norms depends on the context, whether we count as "knowing" depends on the context, too.

4 Conclusion

Conversational contextualism is the view that the semantic values of uses of the expression "knows" depend on conversational kinematics. In this chapter I have argued against a particular version of conversational contextualism, on which an alternative is relevant in a context if it is compatible with the common ground in that context. Much like Lewis's RTT, this view conflicts with epistemological orthodoxy. While I haven't made a conclusive case against conversational contextualism, I hope this chapter provides ample motivation for considering alternative ways of thinking about contextualism.[20]

Notes

1 These are modified versions of DeRose's (1992) 'bank cases'.
2 Strictly speaking, this is just a contextualist explanation. Some contextualists hold that uses of "knows" refer to the same relation in all contexts, but that relation has an argument place that varies with the context of utterance. For discussion see Schaffer (2004) and Schaffer and Gendler Szabó (2013).
3 I use "S", "p" and "c" as schematic letters for subjects, propositions and contexts, respectively.
4 I sometimes talk about epistemic standards, the idea being that different standards are appropriate in different contexts. For instance, a strict standard is appropriate in HIGH, whereas a laxer standard is appropriate in LOW. For discussion of the differences between 'relevant alternatives contextualism' and 'shifting standards contextualism', see Ichikawa (2017) and Schaffer (2005).
5 While most agree that "I" is a pure indexical in Kaplan's sense, it is unclear whether there are any other pure indexicals. Kaplan's account of demonstratives is controversial (see Bach 1992; King 2014; Reimer 1991), and he abandoned it (see Kaplan 1989b).
6 DeRose (2009: 135–6) makes similar remarks. I discuss Blome-Tillmann (2009; 2014) and Lewis (1996) below.
7 I ignore Lewis's (1996: 558–9) three 'permissive' rules of reliability, method and conservatism. They make no difference in what follows.
8 Lewis means actual in the world of the subject to whom "knowledge" is ascribed, not actual in the world of the ascriber (the two come apart when "knowledge" is ascribed to counterfactual subjects).
9 Lewis (1996: 557–8) took this to be a virtue of RRE. But Brogaard (2004) and Cohen (1998) show that it is a vice.
10 These cumbersome locutions are necessary because contextualists hold that uses of the expression "knows" refer to different properties in different contexts. Epistemologists don't have any views about the property referred to by uses of "knows" in the context of writing this chapter. But they do have views about when it is right (and wrong) to ascribe "knowledge". For instance, it is wrong to ascribe "knowledge" to a subject in a Gettier case.
11 If you think it does, add whatever is required.
12 If the contextualist were out of the room, the defender of epistemological orthodoxy would add that the reason why it is right to say that Laurie "knows" her son slipped out is that Laurie knows her son slipped out.
13 Does this apply in conversational contexts where skeptical scenarios are taken seriously? This is tricky because the contextualist solution to skepticism requires that there are contexts where it can be true to say that subjects lack "knowledge" even though epistemological orthodoxy tells us that they can truly be said to "know" (see DeRose 1995). Because none of the cases I discuss involve sceptical scenarios I set this complication aside.
14 Sometimes my act of saying "My wife is ill" makes it common ground that I have a wife. This phenomenon is known as presupposition accommodation. For discussion see Karttunen (1974), Lewis (1979) and Stalnaker (1974).
15 Blome-Tillmann's response here has a lot in common with DeRose's (2009: Ch. 4) 'single scoreboard semantics'. For criticism of single scoreboard semantics see Montminy (2013).

329

16 If you think that it does, add whatever you think is needed. In particular, if you think the argument relies on reliabilism, add that Morven has whatever non-reliabilist extras are required (e.g. reflective access to grounds in virtue of which she is justified in believing there was a red barn).

17 Can other views avoid the problem? Bach (1992) argues that views, on which the semantic values of uses of context-sensitive expressions depend, on referential intentions can. I lack the space to consider this more general issue here.

18 I have been talking as if the context of utterance entirely determines the set of relevant alternatives. But, as Ichikawa (2017: Ch. 1) emphasizes, the set of relevant alternatives depends on facts about the subject's circumstances as well as the context of utterance. While this complicates the objection developed in this section, I doubt it makes a difference. The objection just requires that satisfying RPP is sufficient for an alternative to be relevant.

19 Perhaps the former is problematic, too. Maybe the set of relevant alternatives depends on what epistemic standards the conversational participants would use if they were better informed, or something like that. I defend a view like this in McKenna (2014), but the view I defend is not a variety of conversational contextualism.

20 Thanks to Michael Blome-Tillmann, J. Adam Carter, Michael Hannon, Torfinn Huvenes and Jonathan Jenkins Ichikawa. Research on this chapter was assisted by funding from the ERC Advanced Grant Project "The Emergence of Relativism" (Grant No. 339382).

Bibliography

Bach, Kent (1992). Paving the Road to Reference. *Philosophical Studies* 67 (3): 295–300.

Blome-Tillmann, Michael (2009). Knowledge and Presuppositions. *Mind* 118 (470): 241–94.

——— (2014). *Knowledge and Presuppositions.* Oxford: Oxford University Press.

Brogaard, Berit (2004). Contextualism, Skepticism, and the Gettier Problem. *Synthese* 139 (3): 367–86.

Brown, Jessica (2006). Contextualism and Warranted Assertibility Manoeuvres. *Philosophical Studies* 130 (3): 407–35.

Cohen, Stewart (1998). Contextualist Solutions to Epistemological Problems: Scepticism, Gettier, and the Lottery. *Australasian Journal of Philosophy* 76 (2): 289–306.

——— (1999). Contextualism, Skepticism, and the Structure of Reasons. *Philosophical Perspectives* 13: 57–89.

DeRose, Keith (1992). Contextualism and Knowledge Attributions. *Philosophy and Phenomenological Research* 52 (4): 913–29.

——— (1995). Solving the Skeptical Problem. *Philosophical Review* 104 (1): 1–52.

——— (2009). *The Case for Contextualism: Knowledge, Skepticism, and Context.* Oxford: Oxford University Press.

Glanzberg, Michael (2002). Context and Discourse. *Mind and Language* 17 (4): 333–75.

Huvenes, Torfinn & Andreas Stokke (2015). Information Centrism and the Nature of Contexts. *Australasian Journal of Philosophy* 94 (2): 301–314.

Ichikawa, Jonathan Jenkins (2011). Quantifiers and Epistemic Contextualism. *Philosophical Studies* 155 (3): 383–98.

——— (2017). *Knowledge in Theory and Context.* Oxford: Oxford University Press.

Kaplan, David (1989a). Demonstratives. In Joseph Almog, John Perry & Howard Wettstein (eds.), *Themes from Kaplan.* New York: Oxford University Press: 481–563.

——— (1989b). Afterthoughts. In Joseph Almog, John Perry and Howard Wettstein (eds.), *Themes from Kaplan.* New York: Oxford University Press: 565–614.

Karttunen, Lauri (1974). Presuppositions and Linguistic Context. *Theoretical Linguistics* 1: 181–94.

King, Jeffrey (2014). Speaker Intentions in Context. *Noûs* 48 (2): 219–37.

Lewis, David (1979). Scorekeeping in a Language Game. *Journal of Philosophical Logic* 8 (1): 339–59.

——— (1996). Elusive Knowledge. *Australasian Journal of Philosophy* 74 (4): 549–67.

Longino, Helen (2002). *The Fate of Knowledge.* Princeton, NJ: Princeton University Press.

McKenna, Robin (2014). Normative Scorekeeping. *Synthese* 191 (3): 607–25.

Montminy, Martin (2013). The Role of Context in Contextualism. *Synthese* 190 (12): 2341–66.

Nagel, Jennifer (2008). Knowledge Ascriptions and the Psychological Consequences of Changing Stakes. *Australasian Journal of Philosophy* 86 (2): 279–94.

Reimer, Marga (1991). Demonstratives, Demonstrations, and Demonstrata. *Philosophical Studies* 63 (2): 187–202.

Rolin, Kristina (2011). Contextualism in Feminist Epistemology and Philosophy of Science. In Heidi Grasswick (ed.), *Feminist Epistemology and Philosophy of Science*. Dordrecht: Springer: 25–44.

Rysiew, Patrick (2001). The Context-Sensitivity of Knowledge Attributions. *Noûs* 35 (4): 477–514.

Schaffer, Jonathan (2004). From Contextualism to Contrastivism. *Philosophical Studies* 119 (1–2): 73–104.

——— (2005). What Shifts? Thresholds, Standards, or Alternatives?. In Gerhard Preyer & Georg Peter (eds.), *Contextualism in Philosophy: Knowledge, Meaning, and Truth*. Oxford: Oxford University Press: 115–30.

Schaffer, Jonathan & Zoltán Gendler Szabó (2013). Epistemic Comparativism: A Contextualist Semantics for Knowledge Ascriptions. *Philosophical Studies* (2): 1–53.

Stalnaker, Robert (1974). Pragmatic Presuppositions. In Milton Munitz & Peter Unger (eds.), *Semantics and Philosophy*. New York: New York University Press: 197–214.

——— (2002). Common Ground. *Linguistics and Philosophy* 25 (5–6): 701–21.

Stanley, Jason (2005). *Knowledge and Practical Interests*. Oxford: Oxford University Press.

26

'KNOWLEDGE' AND QUANTIFIERS

Nathan R. Cockram

1 Background: contextualism about 'knows'

Contextualism is a linguistic thesis about the word 'knows'. Roughly, it is the thesis that the truth-conditions of knowledge ascriptions are sensitive to features embedded in the conversational context of the ascription. Whether a subject can truly be said to 'know' a proposition, on this view, thus shifts along with shifts in the relevant features of the conversational context. Now exactly what features ascriptions are sensitive to has been cashed out in different ways by different proponents of contextualism;[1] however, what they all share is a common commitment to this pattern of 'shifty' truth-conditions for knowledge ascriptions.[2] As such, contextualism has two distinct components, one semantic, the other epistemic. The epistemic component has to do with the relationship between 'knowing' and shifts in evidential standards. The semantic component, by contrast, concerns the vindication of the claim that 'knows' is a context-sensitive term. Often, this vindication proceeds through the presentation of arguments suggesting that the pattern of use exhibited by knowledge ascriptions is consistent with their fitting within a broader family of context-sensitive terms. Different contextualists have taken knowledge ascriptions to be subsumable under different families of context-sensitive terms. DeRose, among others, has argued that 'knows' is best understood as an indexical such as 'I'.[3] Cohen, by contrast, has argued that 'knows' is best understood as functioning in a similar manner to gradable adjectives like 'tall' or 'flat'.[4] And Lewis, Ichikawa, and Blome-Tillmann have argued that 'knows' is best understood as having a semantic role analogous to a universal quantifier.[5]

The primary focus of this chapter is on the semantic component of contextualism, and more specifically with the proposal that 'knows' has a semantic function similar to a universal quantifier. In what follows, I will provide a summary of the view and describe some of the motivation for taking this route in the defence of 'knows' as context-sensitive. I will then look at some of the major criticisms of the view as given by Stanley (2004, 2005) and Schaffer and Szabo (2013). The final section of the chapter will be devoted to replies to these criticisms.

2 'Knows' as a universal quantifier

What exactly is it to say that 'knows' has a semantic function similar to a universal quantifier? To answer this, we need to first take a brief look at the semantics of quantifiers more generally. It is relatively uncontroversial that the domain which a universal quantifier like 'all' ranges over is

'Knowledge' and quantifiers

context-sensitive. For instance, suppose that you and Sally are at the beer store. If Sally, looking at the bottles of beer, utters:

(1) 'All of the beer looks tasty.'

It is intuitively clear that the proposition expressed by the utterance ranges over all of the beer *in the store*, rather than all of the beer *in the universe*, where the context of the utterance – in this case, the beer store – determines the particular domain required to assess its semantic value. As a result, which proposition is expressed by Sally's utterance of a token of (1) will depend on her context. For instance, in context c1, where what is conversationally salient is the beer in the store, her utterance will express the following proposition:

(2) 'All of the beer$_{store}$ looks tasty.'[6]

But in context c2, her kitchen, Sally's utterance will express a different proposition, e.g.

(3) 'All of the beer$_{kitchen}$ looks tasty.'[7]

One natural way to see that (1) expresses different propositions in different contexts is to see that what Sally says with (1) seems to suggest different equivalent propositions in different contexts. For example, in c1 it looks like what she uttered is equivalent to:

(4) 'All of the beer in the store looks tasty.'

But this clearly isn't equivalent to what she uttered in c2. Rather in this context, it looks like (1) is equivalent to:

(5) 'All of the beer in the fridge looks tasty.'

Different theorists have tried to account for the context sensitivity of universal quantifiers in different ways. At least three separate strategies are to be found in the literature. One strategy, the 'syntactic ellipsis approach', accounts for domain restriction at the syntactic level, by taking the sentences in which quantifiers are embedded to covertly include a contextually determined subsentential constituent which, together with the contextually insensitive portion of the sentence, determines the domain of the proposition.[8] So, using the above example, if Sally is looking in her fridge, and utters:

(6) 'All of the beer looks tasty.'

What she is expressing, at the propositional level, is just:

(7) 'All of the beer *in the fridge* looks tasty.'

A second strategy accounts for domain restriction at the pragmatic level, by taking embedded quantifiers to communicate a domain via familiar Gricean mechanisms.[9] More specifically, according to the pragmatic view:

(8) 'All of the beer looks tasty.'

expresses the false proposition that every beer in the universe is tasty (to Sally). However, the intended audience can, through general pragmatic mechanisms and the context (Sally looking at the fridge), infer that she is intending to communicate the true proposition that 'all of the beer *in the fridge* look tasty.' Third, there is the semantic strategy, of which this chapter is exclusively concerned. This view, roughly, takes sentences bound by a universal quantifier to include, at the propositional level, a variable which (together with an index) acts as a function from context to domain. Thus, Sally's quantifying over 'all' of the beer has the following general structure:

(9) 'All of the beer$_c$ looks tasty.'

Where $_c$ contributes to the semantic value of the proposition expressed by determining the set or domain of bottles, each of which must look tasty in order for it to be true. So when Sally is looking at her fridge, the proposition expressed will be:

(10) 'All of the beer$_{\text{fridge}}$ looks tasty.'

Which will be true iff, at the relevant world of assessment, all of the beer in Sally's fridge has the property of being tasty to Sally.

Following suit, some contextualists like Lewis (1996), Blome-Tillmann (2009), and Ichikawa (2011a, 2017) have argued that 'knows' displays a similar type of context-sensitivity to 'all' or 'every'. On this account, knowledge ascriptions function like universal generalizations: the semantic value of a knowledge ascription is determined by the domain of possibilities it ranges over, where the domain is a function from a context to a set of possibilities. One natural starting point for this view, a starting point taken up by Lewis, is the thought that if 'knowing' that P requires that a Subject S's evidence eliminate all not-P possibilities, and if what constitutes the domain of 'every' possibility is itself a context-sensitive matter, then 'knowing' P will, roughly, be a matter of P holding on the basis of evidence e within that contextually determined domain C. That is to say, if this is the way that knowledge ascriptions proceed, then 'knows' functions semantically in a manner analogous to 'every'. As Lewis puts it:

> What does it mean to say that every possibility in which not-P is eliminated? An idiom of quantification, like 'every' is normally restricted to some limited domain. If I say that every glass is empty, so it's time for another round, doubtless I and my audience are ignoring most of the glasses that there are in the whole wide world through all of time. They are irrelevant to the truth of what was said. They are outside the domain.
>
> Likewise, if I say that every uneliminated possibility is one in which P, or words to that effect, I am doubtless ignoring some of all the uneliminated alternative possibilities that there are. They are outside of the domain, they are irrelevant to the truth of what was said.[10]

Lewis can be understood in the above passage as taking 'every' and 'all' to be a *model* for understanding the putative context-sensitivity of 'knows'. When I ascribe 'knowledge' to a subject, I am saying that her evidence is sufficient to rule out all not-P cases, where crucially, what domain constitutes 'all' depends on what error possibilities are contextually salient, and expands or contracts accordingly. The following is his definition of what it is for a subject to 'know':

> 'S knows proposition P' is true in context C iff 'P holds in every possibility left uneliminated by S's evidence' is true in C; equivalently, if 'S's evidence eliminates every possibility in which not-P' is true in C.[11]

On this account, when one utters a sentence of the form 'S knows that P', the proposition expressed by the utterance will depend on how the domain of possibilities is restricted by the property of being properly ignored. Furthermore, what particular domain the proposition expressed by the utterance ranges over, and thus which not-P possibilities must be eliminated by S's evidence, depends upon a syntactically unrepresented context variable, which acts as function returning a concrete domain of possibilities. This function will take the conversational context as input, because this context determines which possibilities are properly ignored and which are not. For example, if Sally says, on the basis of her perceptual evidence e ('I see hands'):

(11) 'I know that I have hands.'

In an everyday, non-sceptical context with a domain encompassing only nearby possibilities, her utterance will express something approximating the following proposition:

(12) 'I know$_{everyday}$ that I have hands.'

Which will be true if and only if every possibility context *everyday* provides as the relevant domain is one in which her believing that she has hands on the basis of e rules out her being handless. It seems, furthermore, that in this context Sally does know that she has hands: we properly ignore sceptical scenarios in such contexts. By contrast, if she utters (12) in sceptical context, say a context with a drastically expanded domain where the brain-in-a-vat (BIV) hypothesis is salient, her utterance will express something approximating the following proposition:

(13) 'I know$_{sceptical}$ that I have hands.'

Which will be true if and only if every possibility in context *sceptical* is one in which e rules out her being handless. In this context, it seems that she doesn't know that she has hands, as there are unignored – i.e. conversationally relevant – possibilities left uneliminated by her evidence in which her having hands fails to obtain.[12] The BIV world, for one, is uneliminated by her evidence inasmuch as her perceptual evidence of her hands is compatible with her being envatted; had she been envatted, she would still think she had hands.[13]

3 Criticisms of 'knows' as a universal quantifier

In this section I will focus on two of the most comprehensive and extended critiques of the universal quantification model found in the literature: Stanley (2005) and Schaffer and Szabo (2013). The latter present four arguments against the model, the first three of which are adopted from more general linguistic considerations which they take to undermine each proposed semantic model for 'knows' (i.e. indexicals, gradable adjectives, and universal quantification). Each of the four arguments in question will be summarized in 3.1–3.4 below. Stanley[14] deploys an argument designed to show that because quantifiers can shift domain mid-sentence, the contextualist can't cash out her solution to the sceptical paradox. This argument will be outlined in 3.5. First, however, a note on methodology.

The authors in question attempt to undermine the universal quantification model in a broadly inductive manner by highlighting disanalogies between 'knows' and quantificational determiners such as 'all'. More specifically, the broad pattern of argumentation exemplified by each criticism is as follows. First, examples or scenarios are used to demonstrate that 'knows' functions quite differently from quantificational determiners in natural language.[15] Second, it is argued that this difference in function in natural language is strong evidence that 'knows' isn't properly modelled as a quantifier in the manner advocated by Lewis, Ichikawa, and Blome-Tillmann.

3.1 Homophonic reporting (disquotation)

Competent English speakers can and will naturally track and update the use of context-sensitive terms across contexts, because these terms often do not allow homophonic reporting (e.g. disquotation) across context.[16] For instance, if Sally says, while at home:

(14) 'All of the boots are in the closet.'

Billy, at the boot store, won't be able to felicitously disquote Sally as follows:

(15) 'Sally said that all the boots are in the closet.'

Because if he is speaking at the boot store, (15) would be infelicitous (and false) due to the difference in context between Sally's utterance and Billy's report. This resistance to disquotation is, according to Shaffer and Szabo, a feature of most context-sensitive terms.[17] They argue, however, that 'knows' doesn't display this resistance. For example, if Sally says:

(16) 'I know where I put my glasses.'

Billy, speaking the next day, can felicitously disquote Sally as follows:

(17) 'Sally said that she knows where she put her glasses.'

There is no tendency to see (16)-(17) as infelicitous or otherwise inappropriate; as unlike (9)-(10) there is no need to update the supposedly context-sensitive token in this utterance. Schaffer and Szabo take this as a serious disanalogy.

3.2 Disagreement

Another point of disanalogy raised by Schaffer and Szabo concerns disagreement. The basic thrust of the argument is as follows. In general, there is no tendency for competent speakers to disagree, or at least seem to disagree, when they make divergent claims regarding a paradigmatic context-sensitive term like 'I' or 'all'. On the other hand, such speakers do tend to see themselves as disagreeing when they make divergent knowledge claims. For instance, if Sally and Billy are having a telephone conversation, and Sally, who has just put her beer in the fridge, says:

(18) 'All of the beer is put away.'

'Knowledge' and quantifiers

It would be exceedingly odd for Billy, who is messy and has left his beer on the table, to subsequently answer by saying:

(19) 'That's wrong! Not all of the beer is put away!'

In other words, Billy will feel no inclination to disagree with Sally's utterance because he understands that she is making a quantificational claim about the beer in her house, not his. This is in stark opposition, they argue, to how people use 'knows'. Suppose once again Sally and Billy are sitting together in a car. Sally, who is not at all disposed to scepticism, and is thus in a low-standards context, utters:

(20) 'I know that I have hands.'

Billy, however, has read some Descartes, and is thus disposed to be much more sceptical. Considering Sally's utterance in a higher-standards context, where demon-style worlds are relevant, he replies:

(21) 'You are wrong, you don't know that you have hands.'

Here we naturally take Billy to be disagreeing with or negating Sally's self-ascription of knowledge. However, if contextualism is correct, then it appears as if Sally and Billy aren't actually disagreeing, because they are expressing different propositions relative to different contexts. This is a problem, the objection continues, because unlike disagreements which occur over other context-sensitive terms, we take disagreements over knowledge ascriptions to be substantive and genuine.[18] This is a significant point of disanalogy according to Schaffer and Szabo;[19] a disanalogy also, it should be noted, emphasized by MacFarlane (2007, 2009), in the context of arguing for his assessment-relativism, and Hawthorne (2004), in the context of his argument for interest-relative invariantism.[20]

3.3 *Semantic ignorance*

A third point of disanalogy suggested by Schaffer and Szabo is, following Schiffer (1996) and Hawthorne (2004),[21] what can be called 'semantic ignorance'. This argument takes off from the same linguistic data which motivates the disagreement objection: competent speakers of English display no tendency to be confused regarding the referent of paradigmatic context-sensitive terms.

For instance, if Judy, speaking on the phone to Billy, says:

(22) 'All of the dishes are put away.'

Billy will understand that the 'All' in Judy's utterance here picks out the domain *all of the dishes at Judy's house*. That is, he won't have any tendency to reply by saying:

(23) 'No, all of the dishes are not put away!!'

Because he won't confuse the truth-conditions of Judy's use of 'All'; he will pick out what domain her utterance ranges over. But, the objection goes, it is a standard part of the contextualist treatment of sceptical scenarios to attribute a widespread tendency to confuse the

337

truth-conditions of 'knows' in the face of certain error possibilities. More specifically, consider the following argument adopted from Schiffer:

(a)   I don't know that I'm not a BIV.
(b)   If I don't know that I'm not a BIV, then I don't know that I have hands.
(c)   Therefore, I don't know that I have hands.[22]

The argument looks like a paradox inasmuch as the two premises look true yet the conclusion false. According to the contextualist, however, the appearance of paradox is misleading, as each premise and the conclusion is in fact true. This is for the following reason. Because the first premise conversationally introduces a sceptical scenario, each premise is actually expressing the following propositions:

(d)   I don't know$_{high}$ that I'm not a BIV.
(e)   If I don't know$_{high}$ that I'm not a BIV, then I don't know that I have hands.
(f)   Therefore, I don't know$_{high}$ that I have hands.

And as a result, the argument is sound: we don't know that we have hands once the BIV possibility has been made conversationally salient. What made the third premise look false, on this account, is that speakers are systematically confusing which proposition the third premise is expressing; they are confusing its truth-conditions with the proposition that the premise *would have* expressed in a low standards context, i.e. 'Therefore, I don't know$_{low}$ that I have hands.' Thus, as Schaffer and Szabo make clear, the contextualist solution to the paradox is to posit an *error theory*: competent English speakers are often quite ignorant about the context in which a knowledge ascription is made – and as a result misjudge its truth-value. But, the objection continues, this is quite unlike the behavior of other context-sensitive terms like 'all' or 'I': competent speakers *don't* display a widespread tendency to confuse the context or the truth-value of such terms. So we allegedly arrive at another significant disanalogy between 'knows' and other context-sensitive terms.[23]

3.4 Lack of a nominal expression

Schaffer and Szabo also provide an argument against the quantification model for 'knows' based upon syntactic considerations. As they explain, standard quantificational determiners like 'all' combine with a nominal expression ('the eggs'); where the nominal expression plays the role of fixing the domain (i.e. the extension of 'all'). Knowledge ascriptions, however, lack this structure; they don't (at least typically) combine with a nominal expression. This is, in their view, another significant point of disanalogy.[24]

3.5 Free shifting within a discourse

Jason Stanley (2005) presents a further argument against the universal quantification model for the semantics of 'knows'. The argument exploits a general feature of context-sensitive terms – their ability to shift mid-discourse – as a means of undermining a key contextualist thesis. The root of the objection proceeds from the observation that context-sensitivity can be traced to individual terms, rather than the discourse or conversational context itself. As Stanley puts it:

> Since semantic context-sensitivity is traceable to an individual element, multiple occurrences of that element in a discourse should be able to take on differing values. In the case of an utterance such as 'This is larger than this', where two different objects are

'Knowledge' and quantifiers

pointed to by the person uttering the sentence, this feature is obviously confirmed. But it is present in a broader range of constructions.[25]

For instance, the following utterance is felicitous:

(24) 'Every sailor waved to every sailor.'

Here, domains are, within a single context, freely shifting mid-sentence: the natural way to read (24) is that some group of sailors, say every sailor on HMS *Pinafore*, are waving to some other group of sailors, say every sailor left on the pier. This natural reading would, however, be impossible if the discourse set the domain, as (24) would instead have to be read as suggesting that every sailor waved to him/herself, which is clearly infelicitous (at least without special reason to think otherwise). Stanley takes such examples as evidence that free shifting is a general feature displayed by all context-sensitive terminology, including quantifiers.[26]

With the free shifting data on the table, Stanley then suggests that it generates a problem for contextualism. Consider the following so-called 'abominable conjunction':

(25) 'Sally knows that she has hands, but she doesn't know that she's not a brain-in-a-vat.'

Contextualists such as Lewis have argued that it is a significant virtue of the theory that it can explain why sentences like (25) are infelicitous: they are so because the mention of the BIV possibility shifts the conversational context such that epistemic standards required to know that one has hands are raised significantly; a shift which renders the first conjunct both false and unassertable.[27] This strategy only works, as Stanley notes, if we assume that a single domain governs both uses of 'knows'; a domain which is determined by the discourse rather than freely shifting individual terms. But if 'knows' functions like other context-sensitive terms, a point which contextualists seem to accept, then given free shifting we must, according to Stanley, read each instance of 'knows' in (25) as behaving like each instance of 'every' in (24). That is, if they wish to model 'knows' upon quantifiers, the contextualist is thus committed to reading each instance of 'knows' in (25) as ranging over distinct domains. However, such a reading, as Stanley emphasizes, renders (25) both felicitous and possibly true:

> Distinct occurrences of the same context sensitive term can have different interpretations within a discourse. We should therefore expect distinct occurrences of the instances of 'knows that p' to allow for the possibility of distinct interpretation within a discourse. But this opens the contextualist up to a number of objections that she does not otherwise face. Furthermore, if this is so, some of what contextualists say about the virtues of their theories over other theories falls by the wayside.[28]

Because context-sensitive terms admit of free shifting, 'knows' should also admit of it. But this means that the contextualist is committed to holding intuitively repugnant abominable conjunctions to be felicitous. Or, if the contextualist rejects free shifting to save her strategy of dealing with abominable conjunctions, she does so at the cost of rendering 'knows' completely disanalagous to all other context-sensitive language, making the theory semantically *ad hoc*. That is, according to Stanley the contextualist is faced with the following dilemma:

(i) Either she can accept the free-shifting data, meaning that she is thus committed to the felicity of intuitively repugnant abominable conjunctions. This undercuts a central theoretical virtue of contextualism.[29]

339

(ii) Or she can reject the free-shifting data, meaning that she is thus committed to taking 'knows' to be context-sensitive despite lacking a general feature displayed by all other context-sensitive language (free shifting); a disanalogy which threatens to render contextualism semantically *ad hoc*.

This is a dilemma because neither option looks promising to the contextualist: either way she is left (for different reasons) with an implausible metasemantic theory. Stanley takes this implausibility as providing good grounds for rejecting a context-sensitive semantics for 'knows' outright (and thus by extension for rejecting the universal quantification model).

4 Replies

This section will provide an overview of the most prominent replies to the criticisms summarized above. Ichikawa (2011a, 2017) and Mion (2013) both provide replies on behalf of the quantifier model to Stanley's argument from free shifting described in 3.5. These replies will be reconstructed in 4.1 and 4.2, respectively. Schaffer and Szabo argue that a new semantics for quantifiers can avoid the criticism they leveled at the model in their (2013) and summarized in 3.1–3.4; this reply will be discussed in 4.3.

4.1 Free shifting I: Ichikawa

Ichikawa (2011a, 2017) takes on board the data which suggests that context-sensitive terms display free shifting mid-sentence, but *contra* Stanley, he argues that this data is ambiguous, and certainly doesn't conclusively show that the universal quantification model licences the felicity of abominable conjunctions.

Ichikawa affirms that the domain of 'every' can shift within a short period in a particular conversation; and as such he agrees with Stanley's reading of the following, which involves putatively context-sensitive universal and existential noun phrases:

(26) 'Every van Gogh painting is in the Dutch National Museum.'
(27) 'That's a change: when I visited last year, I saw every van Gogh painting, and some of them were definitely missing.'[30]

Stanley takes the natural reading of this dialogue to be as follows. The 'every' in (26) and 'some' in (27) range over all of the van Gogh paintings in existence; whereas the 'every' in (27) ranges over the van Gogh paintings in the Dutch National Museum (at the time of the visit). Despite this agreement, however, Ichikawa argues that the free shifting data identified by Stanley and exemplified by (26)-(27) *does not* have the anti-contextualist upshot the latter suggests it does; as it doesn't in fact imply that a Lewisian-style contextualism is committed to the felicity of abominable conjunctions, nor does it suggest a strong disanalogy between 'knows' and other quantifiers. As he puts it:

> But this [free shifting] does not imply, as Stanley suggests it does, that Lewisian contextualism predicts abominable conjunctions to be acceptable. It does not even imply that there is any significant disanalogy between knowledge ascriptions and quantifiers.[31]

As indicated above, Ichikawa's strategy for undermining Stanley's argument is to demonstrate that the linguistic data which supposedly supports the former in fact does no such thing. More specifically, he argues that Stanley's interpretation of the free-shifting data is implausibly strong and thus unfair to the contextualist. Why? Because it relies upon the assumption that because domains are related to individual terms, sentences with multiple quantifiers can *always* be rendered felicitous by being read as involving a mid-sentence domain shift. For if they are always felicitous, then obviously if 'knows' is a quantified expression one must thereby be committed to taking abominable conjunctions as (implausibly) felicitous. But, according to Ichikawa, this simply isn't the case: while we sometimes accommodate the felicity of such assertions by shifting domains, we certainly don't always or automatically do this. For one thing, he argues, domain shifting doesn't render the natural reading of abominable conjunctions involving quantified expressions in any way felicitous. Thus Stanley is wrong to think that a proponent of the quantificational model who accepts domain shifting is committed to abominable conjunctions. So the dilemma is false. Consider the following sentence:

(28) 'Bill's evidence eliminates all possibilities in which he lacks hands, but Bill's evidence does not eliminate all possibilities in which he is a handless brain-in-a-vat.'[32]

(28) Ichikawa argues, is very similar to an abominable conjunction like (25). Despite this, he contends that it is very hard to find a felicitous and true reading of (28); intuitively, it seems more like a straightforward contradiction like the following:

(29) 'Every sailor is on deck, but some sailors are below deck.'[33]

However – and this is the key point – if Stanley's interpretation of the free-shifting data was correct, (28) *should* be straightforwardly felicitous; as the two tokens of 'all', as instances of quantification, have independent domains. The fact that (28) is infelicitous, however, suggests that it is more like (25) than (26)-(27). This is a point of analogy between quantifiers like 'all' and 'knows', not a disanalogy; and it suggests, importantly, that domain shifting *doesn't* straightforwardly licence abominable conjunctions as Stanley believes it does. For if it did, (28) should sound fine. So, if Ichikawa is correct, the data motivating domain-shifting is much less straightforward than Stanley assumes, and his argument is unfair to the contextualist. For while it is certainly correct that free domain shifting is a feature of universal quantification, examples like (28) show that free shifting doesn't automatically render any sentence involving quantified noun phrases which displays this behavior felicitous. Thus, Ichikawa maintains, there is no sense in which affirming the existence of domain shifting commits the proponent of the quantificational model to the felicity of abominable conjunctions.

4.2 Free shifting II: Mion

Giovanni Mion (2015) also presents an argument in reply to Stanley's free-shifting argument outlined in 3.5. As we have seen, Stanley's criticism of the quantificational model turns on free shifting: because domains are related to individual terms; sentences with multiple quantifiers can always be rendered felicitous by reading the terms as having separate domains. Thus if 'knows' is like a quantifier it licences the felicity of repugnant abominable conjunctions. According to Mion, however, it is not clear that such a semantics is correct, as:

> it is not obvious that different occurrences of the same quantified expression (at the same syntactic level) within a discourse could be associated with different domains. Therefore it is not obvious that in order to function like a quantifier, different occurrences

341

of 'knowledge' (at the same syntactic level) within a discourse could be associated with different domains.[34]

If free shifting is actually impossible, then we have a way of rejecting the second horn of Stanley's dilemma, for the fact that abominable conjunctions are infelicitous on the universal quantificational model would not imply that it is semantically *ad hoc*.

But why think that it is impossible after all? The problem, according to Mion, here drawing upon Christopher Gauker (2010), is that Stanley's preferred semantics, which includes free-shifting, licences the felicity of intuitively contradictory sentences such as the following:

(30) 'Every student is happy and some student is not happy.'
(31) 'Dumbo is small, and Mickey is large, and Dumbo is larger than Mickey.'
(32) 'France is hexagonal, but Italy is not boot shaped.'[35]

The fact that these sentences sound quite odd, according to Gauker and Mion, suggests that in general[36] it is not the case that context-sensitivity is a feature of linguistic items; rather, it is a feature of the discourse. For if we take context sensitivity in the latter way, we have an explanation of the oddity of (30)-(32) not available on the semantic model like the one endorsed by Stanley (which permits free shifting within a single context): in each case, two contradictory semantic values are being read off the same context parameter.[37] Both Gauker and Mion take this explanatory deficiency of the Stanley model as grounds for rejecting it in favour of an alternative, discourse-level model for context sensitivity.[38]

Thus, if Mion is correct, and we have reason to think that the Stanley model of domain-shifting is incorrect, we thus have no reason to think that there is any serious disanalogy between 'knows' and other quantifiers on this score: the appearance of universal smooth domain shifting argued by Stanley is misleading, as many conjunctive sentences containing context-sensitive terms resist such a reading. So, the argument goes, the dilemma he poses is false, and of no real danger to the proponent of contextualism.

4.3 A-quantifiers as fitting troublesome data

Despite producing a series of objections (see 3.1–3.4 above) to the quantificational model, Schaffer and Szabo (2013) take these objections to only show that a certain approach to the quantificational model is flawed, rather than showing the approach per se to be flawed. More specifically, they take these objections to show the inadequacies of the so-called 'D-quantifier' model; however, they argue that a slightly different approach to quantification, the so-called 'A-quantifier' model, can avoid the criticisms in question.

Using the work of linguist Barbara Partee (1995)[39] as a starting point, Schaffer and Szabo distinguish A- and D-quantifiers in the following way. D-quantifiers are so named because they are modelled on *determiners*, and thus typically have a tripartite [quantifier] [restrictor] [scope] structure which features an overt restrictor in the syntax.[40] For instance, the noun phrase:

(33) 'All dogs bite.'

is a D-quantificational sentence following this structure: here 'dogs' restricts the scope of the quantifier. A-quantifiers, on the other hand, are modelled on *adverbs*, and thus do not typically involve noun phrases. A good example of an adverbial quantifier is 'always', as we see in Quine's (1980) famous example:[41]

'Knowledge' and quantifiers

(34) 'Tai always eats with chopsticks.'

Importantly, D-quantifiers don't select domains in the same manner as A-quantifiers; as (34) shows, they don't feature an overt restrictor in the syntax; the restrictor, typically, is instead provided by the context of use. For instance, (34) could equally mean:

(35) 'Whenever he eats with anything, Tai eats with chopsticks.'

Or

(36) 'Whenever he does anything with chopsticks, Tai eats with them.'

Depending on the presuppositions operating within the context.[42] Schaffer and Szabo argue that there is reason to think that 'knows' functions like an A-quantifier, and that adopting this alternate model can save the view from what they consider to be the four major linguistic objections to it (which I summarize in 3.1–3.4).[43] More specifically, they take the four arguments to suggest a set of constraints upon a plausible context-sensitive semantics for 'knows', and contend that the A-quantificational model, unlike the D-quantificational model, can meet them. The relevant constraints are as follows:[44]

(i) A plausible contextualist semantics, given the arguments from homophonic reporting, disagreement, and semantic ignorance, should not predict smooth tracking across contexts.
(ii) A plausible contextualist semantics should not, given the argument from the lack of a nominal expression, require an overt expression to constrain the context-sensitivity.

Regarding the first constraint, Shaffer and Szabo argue that linguistic evidence suggests that speakers display a consistent inability to track A-quantifiers across contexts in the manner highlighted by the arguments from homophonic reporting, disagreement, and semantic ignorance. To this end, they ask us to consider the adverbial quantifier 'always'. Suppose Sally utters:

(37) 'Claire always steals the Diamonds.'

This sentence can be, according to Schaffer and Szabo, quite comfortably and felicitously disquoted by Billy as:

(38) 'Sally said that Claire always steals the diamonds.'

even if the context has shifted.[45] Additionally, they argue that adverbial quantifiers can accommodate the disagreement data where the D-model fails. For instance, if James and Sally are speaking on the telephone, and James is aware of a circumstance in which David rather than Claire stole the diamonds, if Sally utters (38), James can felicitously answer by saying:

(39) 'That's false! Claire doesn't always steal the diamonds.'

In other words, there is a tendency for competent speakers to disagree when they make divergent claims which involve an adverbial quantifier in the same way that there is when they make divergent claims involving 'knows'. This is a point of analogy rather than disanalogy. A similar point can be made, according to Schaffer and Szabo, about semantic ignorance arguments of the type advanced by Schiffer: if 'knows' is an A-quantifier, then there is no reason to think that the contextualist solution to the sceptical puzzle is *ad hoc*, for the lack of smooth tracking is a general phenomenon.[46] Regarding the second constraint, Schaffer and Szabo argue that this model of quantification is also immune to the argument from the lack of a nominal expression. For as we have seen, A-quantifiers don't display the tripartite syntactical form typical of D-quantifiers, and thus there is no reason to expect them to combine with a domain-fixing nominal expression. The domain of an A-quantifier is determined by the context of utterance and various background presuppositions rather than a syntactically displayed determiner. So the objection, in their view, has no force against a model which takes 'knows' to function like an A-quantifier.[47]

Schaffer and Szabo conclude that adverbial quantification is a viable option for modelling the context-sensitivity of 'knows'. For the four objections they outline only look plausible if we assume that the correct semantics must be modelled on D-quantificational noun phrases. But such an assumption is erroneous, they argue, given the availability of the alternate A model, which doesn't fall prey to the aforementioned objections.

5 Conclusion

This chapter has been concerned with providing a general overview of the major arguments for and against the proposal that the semantics for 'knows' should be modelled upon the semantics of universal quantifiers. As we have seen, several contextualists, such as Lewis, Ichikawa, and Blome-Tillmann, argue that, like quantifiers such as 'all', knowledge ascriptions are 'shifty' and range over a contextually determined domain which determines the semantic value of the proposition uttered. To the contrary, however, critics such as Stanley and Hawthorne have argued that the linguistic evidence suggests that there are significant disanalogies between paradigmatic quantifiers such as 'all' and 'knows'; they take these disanalogies to be a good reason to reject the quantificational model outright. It is ultimately controversial, however, as to whether these criticisms pose a serious threat to the model as proponents of the view, such as Ichikawa, Mion, and (in a qualified form) Schaffer and Szabo, have argued that 'knows' is much less disanalagous to paradigmatic quantifiers than critics have supposed. Ultimately, providing a viable semantic model for contextualism is an ongoing research project in epistemology, and it is clear that the quantificational model merits further exploration.[48]

Notes

1 Some contextualists like Cohen (1988) take the shifty data as suggesting that the amount of evidence needed in order to for a subject to 'know' depends on conversational contexts. Others, such as DeRose (1992, 2009), take the data as suggesting that the modal space in which a subject's belief tracks the truth expands or contracts relative to conversational standards. Relatedly, Lewis (1996) and Ichikawa (2011a) take the data as suggesting that the relevant alternatives, which a subject's belief must be sensitive to in order to 'know', shift with conversational standards. Interestingly, then, what features one takes knowledge ascriptions to be sensitive to is related to the internalist/externalist distinction.

2 The data motivating contextualism is often presented via hypothetical cases such as the well-known 'bank case'. Here we are given two vignettes involving a husband and wife who need to deposit a cheque. In one case, where not much is at stake, it seems as if the husband 'knows' the bank will be open in the morning when asked by his wife. In the other, however, it seems as if he doesn't 'know'. It is a puzzle for traditional theories of knowledge because in each case the belief is true, and he has the same amount of evidence. Contextualists can account for the data via shifting standards. For more, see DeRose (2009), chapter 1.

3 Keith DeRose (1992).

4 Stewart Cohen (1988).

'Knowledge' and quantifiers

5 David Lewis (1996). Jonathan Ichikawa (2011a, 2011b).
6 More formally, the semantics of (2) are something like '[$\forall$x(Bx is Ty($f(d)$)], where $f(d)$ represents a function from a context to a domain of evaluation. Thus, the truth conditions of (3) require every beer in the domain produced as the value of d be tasty; e.g.:

(2) 'All the B looks tasty' is true relative to d if and only if every beer in the domain d provides as the value of B looks tasty.'

We represent the function to d and its contribution to the semantic value of the proposition as beer$_{store}$ in (2); it makes clear the fact that what the proposition actually gets expressed by (2) partly depends upon this function. This is why the proposition expressed differs from (3); its contribution to the semantic value of the proposition isn't the same as (3); in the latter, d contextually returns a different domain (the fridge). Thus, what is required for all the beer to look tasty has changed. This semantic model is adopted from Jason Stanley and Zoltan Gendler Szabo (2000).
7 One natural way to see that (1) expresses different propositions in different contexts is to see that what Sally says with (1) seems to suggest different equivalent propositions in different contexts. For example, in c1 it looks like what she uttered is equivalent to:

(1) 'All of the beer in the store is looks tasty.'

But this clearly isn't equivalent to what she uttered in c2. Rather in this context, it looks like (1) is equivalent to:

(2) 'All of the beer in the fridge looks tasty.'

For more, see Stanley and Szabo (2000), pp. 231–232.
8 Cf. Stanley and Szabo (2000), pp. 236–239.
9 Grice (1989). See Stanley and Szabo (2000), pp. 239–245.
10 Lewis (1996), pg. 553.
11 Lewis's own formulation makes a statement about knowledge, rather than 'knowledge'. Accordingly, I have adopted Ichikawa's (2017) version, which casts Lewis's claim in full metasemantic generality about what it takes for a subject to 'know'.
12 Again, same test as in the case of 'all'; we can see that the paraphrases of (12) would be different in different contexts.
13 At least assuming that we don't hold a disjunctive theory of perception. In that case, our evidence (as factive) might thereby rule out the BIV possibility. See Ichikawa (2017).
14 Stanley also, it should be noted, puts forth his own variants of the three general arguments deployed by Schaffer and Szabo. See Stanley (2005).
15 Or the quantificational model as it has been generally presented in the literature; Jonathan Schaffer and Zoltan Gendler Szabó (2013) argue that a new form of the quantificational model, which models 'knows' along the lines of an A-quantifier, can actually vindicate the semantic side of the contextualist thesis. This argument will be surveyed below.
16 Herman Cappelen and Ernest Lepore (2005).
17 Schaffer and Szabo (2013), pg. 500.
18 For instance, if Billy and Sally disagreed over a context-sensitive predicate of taste such as 'delicious', we would naturally take Billy's objection to be borne out of his confusion over the truth-conditions of the predicate, rather than suggesting that they actually do disagree. For more, see Torfinn Huvenes (2012).
19 Schaffer and Szabo (2013), pp. 500–501.
20 John MacFarlane (2007, 2009) takes the disagreement challenge to contextualism as a point in favour of his assessment-relativism, which he argues can accommodate disagreement in a perfectly natural manner. John Hawthorne (2004) argues that his version of interest-relative invariantism has a better time accommodating disagreement than contextualism based upon considerations outlined in 3.2.
21 John Hawthorne (2004), chapters 2 and 4, and Stephen Schiffer (1996).
22 Schiffer (1996), pg. 317.
23 Schaffer and Szabo (2013), pp. 504–505.
24 Schaffer and Szabo (2013), pp. 506–507.
25 Stanley (2005), pg. 57.

26 As Stanley puts the point on pg. 61 of his (2005): "It is no surprise that different occurrences of one and the same context-sensitive expression can have different values within the same discourse. For context-sensitivity is linked not to the *discourse*, but to a particular context-sensitive *term*."

27 Cf. Lewis (1996), pp. 564–565.

28 Stanley (2005), pg. 62.

29 Stanley (2005), pp. 66–68.

30 Stanley (2005), pg. 65.

31 Jonathan Ichikawa (2017). (Unpublished manuscript version, pg. 30.)

32 Ichikawa (2017), manuscript, pg. 30.

33 Ichikawa (2017), manuscript, pg. 30.

34 Giovanni Mion (2015).

35 Christopher Gauker (2010).

36 All context-sensitive terms other than pure indexicals. See Gauker (2010), pp. 267–269.

37 As Gauker puts it: "For each of the sentences [(30)-(32)], the oddness can be explained as follows: For each of these sentences, there is a parameter p of interpretation, the value of which is set by the context of utterance c, such that there is a conjunct S_1 in the sentence and a kind K of values that p can take such that S_1 is true relative to c only if the value of p in c is of kind K, and there is another conjunct S_2 that can be true in c only if the value of p in C is *not* of kind K. Consequently, the sentence of a whole is true in no context" (2010, pg. 268).

38 Neither Mion nor Gauker is particularly explicit about the details of why sentences such as 'Every student is happy, and some student is not happy' are in fact odd and prima facie contradictory. Consequently, I have had to reconstruct the argument from a few different places. Gauker (2010) makes the argument I am concerned with here in the context of advocating an alternative semantics for context-sensitive language which he calls 'Global Domains'. The key upshot of the global domains approach is that, in general, context-sensitive language doesn't function like a Kaplanian (1989) indexical (functions from characters to content), but rather specifies a relation between a property and a set of things, where the set is determined by the context, rather than the individual lexical item. The view is motivated via examples like (30)-(32).

39 Barbara Partee (1995).

40 Schaffer and Szabo (2013), pg. 507

41 Cf. Willard Van Orman Quine (1980).

42 As may be apparent, A-quantification is the phenomenon at work in so-called 'Donkey Sentences'.

43 Schaffer and Szabo (2013) provide the reader with a number of linguistic examples designed to provide independent motivation for the thesis that 'knows' functions like an A-quantifier rather than a D-quantifier. For reasons of space, I am forced to omit discussing them here. See pp. 522–536.

44 There are actually five constraints according to Schaffer and Szabo. However, because only two are directly relevant to the objections summarized in section 3, I shall omit the others. See pp. 532–533.

45 Schaffer and Szabo (2013), pg. 533.

46 Schaffer and Szabo (2013), pg. 508.

47 Schaffer and Szabo (2013), pp. 523–524.

48 Thanks to Jonathan Ichikawa for helpful comments on numerous draft versions of this chapter.

References

Blome-Tillmann, Michael. (2008). The Indexicality of 'Knowledge'. *Philosophical Studies* 138 (1):29–53.

Blome-Tillmann, Michael. (2009). Knowledge and Presuppositions. *Mind* 118 (470):241–294.

Cappelen, Herman and Lepore, Ernest. (2005). *Insensitive Semantics: A Defense of Semantic Minimalism and Speech Act Pluralism*. Cambridge, MA: Blackwell Publishing.

Cohen, Stewart. (1988). How to be a Fallibilist. *Philosophical Perspectives* 2:91–123.

DeRose, Keith. (1992). Contextualism and Knowledge Attributions. *Philosophy and Phenomenological Research* 52 (4):913–929.

DeRose, Keith. (2009). *The Case for Contextualism*. Oxford: Oxford University Press.

Gauker, Christopher. (2010). Global Domains Versus Hidden Indexicals. *Journal of Semantics* 27 (2):243–270.

Grice, Paul. (1989). *Studies in the Way of Words*. Harvard: Harvard University Press.

Hawthorne, John. (2004). *Knowledge and Lotteries*. Oxford: Oxford University Press.

Huvenes, Torfinn. (2012). Varieties of Disagreement and Predicates of Taste. *Australasian Journal of Philosophy* 90:167–181.

'Knowledge' and quantifiers

Ichikawa, Jonathan. (2011a). Quantifiers and Epistemic Contextualism. *Philosophical Studies* 155 (3):383–398.

Ichikawa, Jonathan. (2011b). Quantifiers, Knowledge, and Counterfactuals. *Philosophy and Phenomenological Research* 82 (2):287–313.

Ichikawa, Jonathan. (2017). *Contextualising Knowledge*. Oxford: Oxford University Press.

Kaplan, David. (1989). Demonstratives. In J. Almog, J. Perry & H. Wettstein (eds.), *Themes from Kaplan*. Oxford: Oxford University Press, pp. 481–563.

Lewis, David. (1996). Elusive Knowledge. *Australasian Journal of Philosophy* 74 (4):549–567.

MacFarlane, John. (2007). Relativism and Disagreement. *Philosophical Studies* 132 (1):17–31.

MacFarlane, John. (2009). Nonindexical Contextualism. *Synthese* 166 (2):231–250.

Mion, Giovanni. (2013). Epistemic Disagreements: A Solution for Contextualists. *Studia Philosophica Estonica* 6 (1):15–23.

Mion, Giovanni. (2015). Does *Knowledge* Function Like a Quantifier? A Critique of Stanley. *Philosophical Inquiries* 3 (2):9–16.

Partee, Barbara. (1995). Quantificational structures and Compositionality. In E. Bach, E. Jelinek, A. Kratzer & B. Partee (Eds.), *Quantification in Natural Languages*. Dordrecht: Kluwer Press, pp. 541–601.

Quine, W. V. O. (1980). *Elementary Logic*. 3rd Edition. Harvard: Harvard University Press.

Schaffer, Jonathan and Szabo, Zoltan Gendler. (2013). Epistemic Comparativism: A Contextualist Semantics for Knowledge Ascriptions. *Philosophical Studies* (2):1–53.

Schiffer, Stephen. (1996). Contextualist Solutions to Scepticism. *Proceedings of the Aristotelian Society* 96:317–333.

Stanley, Jason. (2004). On the Linguistic Basis of Contextualism. *Philosophical Studies* 119 (1–2):119–146.

Stanley, Jason. (2005). *Knowledge and Practical Interests*. Oxford: Oxford University Press.

Stanley, Jason and Szabo, Zoltan Gendler. (2000). On Quantifier Domain Restriction. *Mind and Language* 15 (2–3):219–261.

Stine, Gail. (1974). Skepticism, Relevant Alternatives and Deductive Closure. *Philosophical Studies* 29 (4):249–261.

27
GRADABILITY AND KNOWLEDGE

Michael Blome-Tillmann

Epistemic contextualism ('EC'), the view that the truth-values of knowledge attributions may vary with the context of ascription, has a variety of different linguistic implementations. On one of the implementations most popular in the early days of EC, the predicate 'knows p' functions semantically similarly to gradable adjectives such as 'flat', 'tall', or 'empty'. In recent work Jason Stanley and John Hawthorne have presented powerful arguments against such implementations of EC. In this chapter I briefly systematize the contextualist analogy to gradable adjectives, present Stanley's argument against the analogy, and offer a contextualist response that abandons the analogy in favor of modeling the semantics of 'knows p' along the lines of quantifier expressions. I then present Hawthorne's objection to the views presented, and finally conclude by outlining an argument to the effect that 'knows p' is an automatic indexical and as such to be expected to function differently from many other indexicals that the term has been compared to in the literature. I finally point out that no analogy should be expected to be perfect, and that no harm is done by postulating some unique behavior of 'knows p'.

1 The analogy to gradable adjectives

Jason Stanley has argued recently that the analogy between 'knows p' and gradable adjectives hypothesized by early contextualists breaks down on the syntactic side; 'knows p' doesn't behave like a gradable expression.[1] To get a better understanding of this objection let us take a brief look at the syntax and semantics of gradable adjectives.

It is often held among semanticists that the contents of gradable adjectives have semantic links to scales measuring the gradable property associated with the adjective at issue. For instance, the content of 'tall' is taken to have a link to a scale of height, the content of 'flat' a link to a scale of flatness, and the content of 'empty' a link to a scale of emptiness.[2] According to such *scalar analyses* of gradable adjectives, (1) is to be analyzed as in (2), where 'δ_F' denotes a function mapping objects onto values of a scale of flatness and the variable 'v_{minFC}' denotes a value on that scale separating the domain of 'flat' into its positive and negative extensions in context C:[3]

(1) A is flat.

(2) $\geq (\delta_F (A); v_{minFC})$.

Gradability and knowledge

More intuitively, (2) is to be read as follows:

(3) The value A takes on a scale of flatness is at least as great as the minimal value required for counting as satisfying 'flat' in context *C*.

According to the scalar analysis, positive 'flat'-ascriptions have a logical form similar to the logical form of comparative 'flat'-ascriptions. To see this, note that the scalar analysis assigns the logical form as depicted in (5) to the comparative statement (4):

(4) A is flatter than B.
(5) $> (\delta_F (A); \delta_F (B))$.

Again, more intuitively, (5) is to be read as in (6):

(6) The value A takes on a scale of flatness is greater than the value B takes on a scale of flatness.

According to the scalar analysis, at the level of logical form, positive 'flat'-ascriptions comprise a contextually determined comparison value that is unarticulated at the level of surface structure.

Let us return to epistemic contextualism. Owing to their emphasis on the analogy to gradable adjectives, some early defenders of EC were tempted to take over the scalar analysis for their purposes and claim that 'knows p' is to be modeled semantically analogously to 'flat': just as the content of 'flat' is semantically linked to a scale of flatness, the content of 'knows p' is semantically linked to a scale of *epistemic strength*, the degree of epistemic strength required for a belief to satisfy 'knows p' varying with context.[4] According to this view, (7), which is to be read as in (8), gives the logical form of 'knowledge'-ascriptions:

(7) $\geq (\delta_{ES} (b_x); v_{minKC})$.
(8) The value x's true belief b takes on a scale of epistemic strength is at least as great as the minimal value required for counting as satisfying 'know' in context C.[5]

Thus, according to the analogy between 'knows p' and gradable adjectives, 'knows p' is context-sensitive in virtue of having a semantic link to a scale of epistemic strength, which is modeled in a contextually variant way by postulating a hidden variable whose value is provided by the respective context of ascription. The analogy seems straightforward and is intuitively plausible, and it isn't further surprising that it has figured prominently in the early literature on EC.

2 Stanley's objection

Even though the above view appears fairly natural at first glance, Jason Stanley objects to it on the basis of syntactic evidence. Here is Stanley:

> If [. . .] the semantic content of 'know' were sensitive to contextually salient standards, and hence linked to a scale of epistemic strength (as 'tall' is linked to a scale of height), then we should expect this link to be exploited in a host of different constructions [. . .]. The fact that we do not see such behavior should make us at the very least suspicious of the claim of such a semantic link.[6]

Exactly what kind of syntactic constructions does Stanley have in mind? As previously indicated, Stanley claims that, as a matter of empirical fact, expressions whose contents are semantically linked to scales are usually gradable. As he shows in great detail, however, 'knows p' is not gradable: it neither accepts standard degree modifiers such as 'very', 'quite', or 'extremely' nor comparative and superlative constructions with 'more' and 'most' or the degree morphemes '-er' and '-est'. Here are some exemplary constructions demonstrating this syntactic difference:

(9) FLAT/EMPTY
   x is very/quite/extremely flat/empty
   x is flatter/emptier than y
   x is the flattest/emptiest F

(10) KNOW:
   $\star x$ very much/quite/extremely knows that p
   $\star x$ knows that p more than y
   $\star x$ knows that p most[7]

Let us recap Stanley's argument. In addition to the syntactic data in (10), Stanley's argument rests on what I shall call the *Gradability Constraint*:

Gradability Constraint (GC): If a natural language expression e has an unarticulated semantic link to a scale s, then e is gradable along s.

From (GC) and the rather uncontroversial assumption that 'knows p' is not gradable, Stanley infers that the content of 'knows p' doesn't have a semantic link to a scale of epistemic strength. If the content of 'knows p' doesn't have such a link, however, then 'knows p' cannot be context-sensitive along the lines of gradable adjectives, for — according to the scalar analysis — such adjectives are context-sensitive precisely because their contents are linked to scales. Epistemic contextualism is implausible, the argument goes, because its analogy between 'knows p' and gradable adjectives breaks down on the syntactic side.[8]

I assume here that the contextualist has to grant Stanley that her analogy to gradable adjectives breaks down on the syntactic side: 'knows p' isn't gradable. But should the contextualist accept (GC)? As a first attempt towards a rejection of (GC), it might be argued that 'knows p' behaves distributionally in a very different way from gradable adjectives because it is a verb. However, as Stanley points out, there are straightforwardly gradable verbs. Here is 'like':

(11) Like
   x likes y very much/a lot
   x likes y more than z
   x likes y most

As Stanley admits, 'knows p' differs from 'like' in being factive and taking a sentential complement. The contextualist might thus be tempted to argue that we shouldn't expect 'knows p' to exploit its semantic link to a scale syntactically in the same way in which 'like' does. 'Knows p' might, after all, be non-gradable for purely syntactic reasons.

Even though this response seems attractive initially, Stanley counters it convincingly by showing that a fairly straightforward distinction can be drawn between gradable and non-gradable verbs, which suggests that (GC) doesn't hold for adjectives only.[9] In fact, Stanley even offers an example of a gradable factive verb taking sentential complements. Here is 'regrets p':[10]

Gradability and knowledge

(12) REGRET

> x very much regrets that p
> x regrets that p more than y/more than that q
> x regrets that p most

Since 'regrets p' is gradable, we may assume that its content has a semantic link to a scale measuring degrees of regret – that is, (13), which is to be read as in (14), gives the truth-conditions of 'regrets p'-ascriptions:

(13) $\geq(\delta_R (x, p); v_{minRC})$.

(14) The value x takes with regard to p on a scale of regret is at least as great as the minimal value required for counting as satisfying 'regret' in context C.[11]

If 'knows p' were semantically linked to a scale of epistemic strength in the way in which 'regrets p' is linked to a scale of regret, then we should expect 'knows p' to be gradable, too. But since 'knows p' is clearly not gradable, it also doesn't have a semantic link to a scale of epistemic strength, and therefore isn't context-sensitive in the way gradable adjectives are.

Stanley's objection seems very strong indeed. If an expression has a semantic link to scale, it exploits that link syntactically in the form of gradability. The fact that 'knows p' isn't gradable is evidence in support of the view that 'knows p' doesn't have a semantic link to a scale and thus isn't context-sensitive along the lines outlined in (8).

3 Abandoning the analogy: the quantifier view

In light of Stanley's objection it is tempting to abandon the contextualist analogy to gradable adjectives in favor of an alternative model. To see what I have in mind, note that, as Stanley is well aware, the gradability objection puts at risk only some versions of epistemic contextualism – namely, precisely those that model the semantics of 'knows p' along the lines of scalar analyses such as the one proposed above in (8): the gradability objection is only an objection to those versions of contextualism that postulate a semantic link between 'knows p' and a scale of epistemic strength. Of course, Stanley is correct that, on the face of it, the syntactic data speak rather strongly against such scalar approaches to 'knows p' – as have been defended, for instance, by DeRose and Cohen. However, it is important to note that David Lewis's versions of contextualism, for instance, doesn't rely on the scalar approach.

To illustrate this point further, note that according to David Lewis's approach to EC the semantics of 'knows p' is modeled along the lines of (L):

> (L) A subject S satisfies 'knows p' in context $C \leftrightarrow S$'s evidence e eliminates every $\neg p$-world, except for those that are properly ignored in C.

According to (L), 'knows p' is a modal quantifier whose domain of counter possibilities is restricted by a context-dependent property – the property of being properly ignored in C. As Ichikawa puts it aptly, on Lewis's approach '"knows" is a context-sensitive modal whose base is fixed by a series of rules.'[12] Thus, the context-sensitivity of 'knows p' is, according to Lewis, modeled rather differently than on scalar approaches: according to (L), 'knowledge'-attributions do not comprise, at the level of logical form, reference to scales of any type.

Lewis's account accordingly sidesteps the gradability objection, for the defender of (L) can simply grant Stanley that 'knows p' doesn't behave like a gradable expression, and explain this fact by noting that 'knows p' doesn't have a semantic link to a scale of epistemic strength. Moreover,

351

note that the fact that the Lewisian contextualist can dispense entirely with other contextualists' talk of 'epistemic standards' as merely metaphorical. This presents a crucial advantage for the Lewisian contextualist, for it is talk about 'epistemic standards' that – when taken literally – gives rise to the impression that 'knows p' should be linked to a scale of epistemic strength, justification, or evidential support, as explicated in (8).[13]

Predictably, the Lewisian idea that 'knows p' works more like a quantificational expression has become popular recently. The main defenders of the view are Blome-Tillmann (2009, 2014), Ichikawa (2011a, 2011b), and Schaffer and Szabo (2014), who argue that 'knows p' works similarly to the A-quantifier expression 'always'.[14]

4 Further problems: clarification techniques

While Stanley's objection can be countered by the quantificational approach, this isn't so obvious for another powerful linguistic objection to the analogy to gradable adjectives that is due to John Hawthorne (2004). As Hawthorne points out, DeRose and Cohen's analogy between 'knows p' and gradable adjectives is implausible for reasons that go beyond the problem of syntactic gradability. For, in addition to being syntactically gradable, adjectives such as 'flat' and 'empty' come, as Hawthorne observes, with a fine-grained system of modifiers that can be used to indicate or clarify the particular standards of flatness or emptiness that are prevalent at one's context. 'Knows p', however, doesn't seem to accept similar constructions.

To illustrate this issue further, suppose I say, 'That meadow is flat,' and you challenge my assertion by pointing out that there are some molehills in it. In such a situation, there are – as Hawthorne observes – three different strategies available to me:

(i) Concession
I concede that my earlier belief was wrong and try to find new common ground: 'I guess you are right and I was wrong. It's not really flat. But let's agree that . . .'

(ii) Stick to one's guns
I claim that the challenge does not undermine what I said. I say ['That meadow is flat']. You point out some small bumps. I say: 'Well, that doesn't mean it isn't flat'.

(iii) Clarification
I clarify my earlier claim and then protest that your challenge betrays a misunderstanding of what I believe and what I was claiming. There are various sorts of 'hedge' words that can be invoked in aid of this kind of response.[15]

Hawthorne then focuses on the third type of strategy – the clarification strategy – and gives three examples of how it can be implemented:

Example 1
Assertion: The glass is empty.
Challenge: Well, it's got some air in it.
Reply: All I was claiming is that it is empty of *vodka*.

Example 2
Assertion: The field is flat.
Challenge: Well, it's got a few small holes in it.

352

Gradability and knowledge

Reply: All I was claiming is that it is flat *for a football field*.
(Or: 'All I was claiming is that it is *roughly* flat.')

Example 3
Assertion: He'll come at 3 p.m.
Challenge: He's more likely to come a few seconds earlier or later.
Reply: All I meant is that he'll come at *approximately* 3 p.m.[16]

As these examples demonstrate, we have a rich repertoire of natural language devices for implementing the clarification technique when it comes to 'flat' and 'empty'. We can use prepositional phrases ('PPs') such as 'for a football field' and 'of vodka' or adverbial phrases ('AdvPs') such as 'enough to play golf' and 'enough to refill' to clarify sensitivity to particular standards of flatness and emptiness, respectively.

Interestingly, however, there are no natural language expressions that we can use to clarify sensitivity to so-called epistemic standards: gradable adjectives come with a rather rich system of modifiers that is unavailable with regard to 'knows p'.[17] As Hawthorne emphasizes, it is due to the unavailability of such constructions that we usually react to epistemic challenges by either conceding that we were mistaken, as in strategy (i), or by sticking to our guns, as in strategy (ii).[18] But why is it that 'knows p' doesn't accept 'for'-PPs, 'of'-PPs, 'enough to'-AdvPs, or similar constructions clarifying sensitivity to particular 'epistemic standards'?

One might be tempted to think that, given our considerations from the previous section, the answer is fairly obvious: since 'knows p' isn't context-sensitive in virtue of having a semantic link to a scale of epistemic strength, it's not further surprising that it doesn't accept the same types of modifier phrases as gradable adjectives. As we have already seen in the previous sections, the syntax of 'knows p' is rather different from the syntax of gradable adjectives, and we already admitted there that this is so because the semantics of 'knows p' is plausibly rather different from the semantics of gradable adjectives – namely, quantificational.

Such a response to the worry at hand, however, can quickly be shown to be unsatisfactory. For even though Hawthorne addresses the standard contextualists' analogy between 'knows p' and gradable adjectives only, an analogous objection can be made with respect to the Lewisian quantificational account. Consider the example of quantified noun phrases ('QNPs'): we can usually clarify the intended domains of QNPs quite straightforwardly – namely, by appending prepositional phrases or often by simply adding predicates:

(15) A: Tom drank all the beer.
       B: No, he didn't. There's still some in the basement.
       A: I didn't mean all the beer *in the house*; I meant all the beer *in the fridge*.
(16) A: All the leaves are brown.
       B: No, they aren't. Look, the ones of your indoor bonsai are still green.
       A: I didn't mean the leaves *of my indoor plants*; I meant the leaves *of the trees outside*.

The italicized phrases in (15) and (16) serve to clarify the intended domain of the quantified noun phrases. Moreover, note that the context-sensitivity of yet further context-sensitive expressions that we might compare 'knows p' to can be indicated or clarified straightforwardly by means of natural language clarifying devices: the intended content of 'left' and 'right', for instance, can be made obvious by adding the phrases 'from my perspective' or 'from Hannah's perspective', while the hemisphere-sensitivity of season expressions can be made explicit by appending 'in the northern hemisphere' or 'in the southern hemisphere'. Finally, note that the sensitivity of 'local'

353

and 'nearby' to a subject's perspective can be made explicit by adding phrases such as 'to me', 'to you', or 'to Tom'. Here are a few examples illustrating this point:

(17) I meant local/near to you.
(18) I meant right/left from my point of view/from my perspective.
(19) I meant spring/autumn in the northern/southern hemisphere.

Given that all of the mentioned context-sensitive expressions come with clarificatory devices, the question arises as to why 'knows p' doesn't seem to allow for similar constructions. If 'knows p' were in fact context-sensitive, shouldn't we expect it to be modifiable in a similar way?

5 'Knowledge' as an automatic indexical

Note in response to the above challenge that absence of clarifactory devices for 'knows p' is by no means surprising. In fact, there is a large number of indexicals the context-sensitivity of which cannot be clarified or made explicit by appending additional linguistic material. In particular, note that clarification strategies never work for so-called *automatic indexicals* — that is, for indexicals whose contents are fixed independently of the speaker's intentions. To see in more detail what I have in mind, let us take a brief look at the distinction between *automatic* and *intentional* indexicals.

As David Kaplan (1989) has pointed out, these two types of indexicals — Kaplan prefers the terminology of 'pure indexicals' and 'true demonstratives' — differ in how their contents are fixed on a given occasion of use. While the content of a tokening of a true demonstrative such as 'he', 'she', 'this', and 'that' is always to some extent determined by the speaker's intentions or accompanying actions, this is not the case for pure indexicals such as 'I', 'today', and 'tomorrow'. For instance, the content of a tokening of 'that' is always partly determined by a more or less explicit manifestation of the speaker's intention to refer to a given object, such as accompanying pointing gestures or the provision of other contextual clues. Pure indexicals, however, are — as Perry (2001) puts it — *automatic* in the sense that their contents are fixed *independently* of the speaker's intentions or manifestations thereof.

A tokening of 'I', for instance, always has as its content the speaker of the context, regardless of whether the speaker actually intends to refer to herself or points at somebody else while speaking. Assuming that indexicals usually have a descriptive character, the crucial point with regard to Kaplan's and Perry's distinction is that the descriptive character of pure indexicals doesn't contain intentional concepts, whereas the descriptive character of impure indexicals does. The conditions fixing the content of pure or automatic indexicals at a context C do not place restrictions on the speaker's intentions, whereas the conditions fixing the content of true demonstratives or intentional indexicals at a context C do.[19]

Next, note that automatic indexicals do not accept modifier phrases clarifying the factors that they are sensitive to. Consider the examples of 'I', 'here', and 'today'. Expressions that aim at shifting the reference of these expressions should — given their automaticity — be expected to be rather awkward or even nonsensical, for they are attempting to do something that is linguistically impossible. The following examples confirm exactly this prediction:

(20) Given that you are the speaker, I'm hungry.
(21) Relative to you as speaker, I'm hungry.
(22) Relative to tomorrow, it is raining today.
(23) Given that it is tomorrow, it is raining today.
(24) Relative to Moscow as place of utterance, it's cold here.

As these examples demonstrate, there seem to be no modifiers or operators that can shift the content of automatic indexicals in ways in which this is possible for expressions such as gradable adjectives or season expressions.

Is 'knows p' an automatic or an intentional indexical? According to some contextualists, it is an automatic indexical. Blome-Tillmann (2014), for instance, defends *Presuppositional Epistemic Contextualism* (PEC), according to which the semantic content of 'knows p' at a context is partly fixed by what is pragmatically presupposed at the context. Thus, on Blome-Tillmann's account, speaker intentions do not play a direct role in fixing the content of 'knows p'. However, let us leave aside PEC for the moment, and consider the question of whether what speakers intend to express by their use of the word 'knows p' at a context C can intuitively make a difference as to what 'know p' expresses at C. The answer to this question is that this seems impossible; if we want to change the content of 'knows p' we have to change the context (which amounts, according to PEC, to changing what we pragmatically presuppose). In other words, 'knows p' receives its content at a context C independently of what content the speaker intends to express by tokening 'knows p' in C; the content of 'knows p' is, at a given context, fixed independently of the speaker's intentions.[20] 'Knows p' is accordingly a pure indexical, and as such – in Perry's words – automatic.

Next, note that 'knows p' is in this respect crucially different from 'spring', 'autumn', 'left', 'right' and even from gradable adjectives such as 'tall' and 'empty' and QNPs. Clearly, speaker intentions can determine the hemisphere, the perspective, or the relevant comparison class or standard of tallness or emptiness, respectively. That is why we have at our disposal phrases to implement the clarification technique for those expressions – sometimes our intentions aren't readily accessible or obvious to our hearers, and in those cases we need linguistic devices such as those in (15)-(19) to make explicit our intentions. With respect to automatic indexicals, however, such expressions have no linguistic purpose: since automatic indexicals receive their Kaplan content automatically and invariably from the context of utterance, there can never be any uncertainty about what content the speaker could have meant to express (unless one is ignorant about the context).

The characterization of 'knows p' as an automatic indexical helps resolve another linguistic objection to standard contextualism that is also due to Jason Stanley. As Stanley points out, the standards governing the semantics of gradable adjectives and quantified noun phrases can sometimes shift mid-sentence. Here are three of Stanley's examples illustrating the phenomenon:[21]

(25) That butterfly is large, but that elephant is not large.
(26) If you have a car, Detroit is nearby, but if you are on foot, it is not nearby.
(27) Every sailor waved to every sailor.[22]

As is obvious from Stanley's examples, gradable adjectives as well as quantified noun phrases can shift their content mid-sentence. But, as Stanley observes, this is not possible with respect to 'knowledge'-ascriptions.

While this is surely worrying news for contextualists who model the semantics of 'knows p' on the basis of the scalar approach presented in the previous section, it should be clear by now that this is not a problem for views according to which 'knows p' is an automatic indexical (such as PEC). As can be demonstrated easily, the automatic indexicals 'I', 'today', and 'tomorrow', for instance, do not shift their contents mid-sentence:

(28) #I am hungry, but I am not hungry.
(29) #Tomorrow will be the 18th of October 2011, but tomorrow will not be the 18th of October 2011.
(30) #Today is my birthday, but today is not my birthday.

355

Michael Blome-Tillmann

Since automatic indexicals such as those above do not change their content mid-sentence, we shouldn't (on the assumption that 'knows *p*' is an automatic indexical) – *pace* Stanley – expect 'knows *p*' to do so.[23]

6 Concluding remarks

With respect to the syntax of 'knowledge'-ascriptions, we can admit that 'knows *p*' differs significantly from gradable adjectives without risking the credibility of EC. Contextualists are not committed to the view that 'knows *p*' is semantically linked to a scale of epistemic strength. 'Knows *p*', therefore, shouldn't be expected to display the same syntactic features as gradable adjectives. In this chapter we also countered the clarification technique objection by drawing attention to the fact that 'knows *p*' is most likely – and in any case according to Presuppositional Epistemic Contextualism – an automatic indexical and that no automatic indexicals can be modified in ways that are exploited by the clarification technique objection. The contextualist may thus happily retreat to the view that 'knows *p*' is linguistically exceptional in a fairly harmless sense: 'knows *p*' is – as far as I can see – the only expression that has a quantificational structure, is sensitive to what is pragmatically presupposed at the context of ascription, and is thus an automatic indexical. This combination of properties is unique, and we should therefore not expect 'knows *p*' to function in each and every linguistic respect exactly like other non-obviously context-sensitive expressions or like recognized indexicals – whether gradable adjectives, QNPs, or core indexicals. In summary, the uniqueness of 'knows *p*' shouldn't worry us too much, as long as a coherent, illuminating, and systematic account of this uniqueness can be given.

Notes

1 See Stanley (2004, 2005, Ch. 2).
2 See Kennedy (1999) for such an account of gradable adjectives.
3 There will probably be no definite cut-off point for any gradable adjective here, but rather an area where it is unclear whether the adjective applies or not – that is, a penumbra. Gradable adjectives are vague. However, I take it that vagueness and context-sensitivity are two distinct semantic phenomena.
4 The versions of EC to be found in Cohen (1988, 1999) and DeRose (1995) can be read along these lines. DeRose gives the notion of epistemic strength an externalist reading, while Cohen interprets it along internalist lines.
5 I ignore the fact that 'knows *p*' might not be linked to a linear scale of epistemic strength but rather to a partial ordering of belief-states. Note that many gradable adjectives are linked to partial orderings rather than to linear scales: 'interesting', 'justified', and 'easy' are obvious examples.
6 Stanley (2004, p. 130 and 2005, p. 45).
7 As Stanley (2005, pp. 39–40) points out, constructions such as 'knows better than anyone', etc. are idiomatic and therefore do not indicate the gradability of 'knows *p*'.
8 Cohen (1999, p. 60) argues that 'know' needn't be gradable, because it is context-sensitive in virtue of entailing 'justified', which is gradable and, according to Cohen, context-sensitive. Stanley (2005, Ch. 4) objects to this maneuver on a variety of grounds, and I shall therefore refrain from addressing the issue. Let me mention, however, a further possible doubt one might have about Cohen's maneuver. Even though 'justified' is gradable, it might be disputed that it is indexical: 'justified', it might be argued, is more likely to be sensitive to the subject's rather than to the ascriber's context.
9 See Stanley (2004, pp. 127–129, 2005, pp. 40–41).
10 Further examples of gradable verbs are 'like', 'suspect', 'believe', 'hope', 'flatten', 'level', and 'empty'.
11 Note that the phrase 'in context *C*' does not necessarily signal indexicality here. The contextual variability with regard to what counts as satisfying 'regret' is minimal, possibly even null.
12 Ichikawa (2011b, p. 392).
13 It should be noted, however, that Stanley's objection is a valid objection against accounts such as DeRose's, which takes talk of epistemic strength literally and at face value. DeRose (1995) defines epistemic strength in terms of how far throughout modal space one's beliefs are true. With respect to Stanley's

gradability objection, Lewis's account has a clear advantage over DeRose's and over other versions of EC that measure epistemic strength in terms of degrees of justification (see Cohen 2001 for such a view).

14 See ch. 26.

15 Hawthorne (2004, p. 104).

16 Hawthorne (2004, p. 104).

17 However, see Ludlow (2005) for examples of expressions that might be used to indicate epistemic standards.

18 Hawthorne (2004, p. 105).

19 What is the descriptive character of the demonstratives 'this' or 'that'? Even though their character might initially seem to be unanalyzable, it can be explicated as 'the object the speaker intends to perceptually or cognitively focus on in context C' or as 'the object the speaker intends to refer to in context C'. These explications of the character of 'this' or 'that' provide us with a reasonably systematic and informative account of the interaction between context on the one hand and the content of 'this' or 'that' on the other.

20 Of course, the speaker's intentions can influence the content of 'knows p' at the speaker's context, but only insofar as the speaker's intentions influence her pragmatic presuppositions: if speaker intentions partly determine what a speaker pragmatically presupposes, then they may also partly (and indirectly) determine the content of 'know'. However, they do not directly determine the content of 'know', as they do in cases of intentional indexicals such as 'this' and 'that'.

21 See Stanley (2004, pp. 135–136, 2005, p. 60).

22 Ichikawa (2011a) points out that quantifier shifts are not always obvious, as in 'All of the bottles are on the table, but some of the bottles are in the fridge.' But note that there is still a disanalogy here, for the alleged quantifier shifts in the case of 'knowledge'-ascriptions are never obvious, not only sometimes. Moreover, note that the intended domains in a sentence such as the one just mentioned can be made obvious by adding additional linguistic material ('beer bottles' vs. 'soda bottles'), which is not possible with respect to 'knowledge'-attributions.

23 I have argued elsewhere that the unavailability of the clarification strategy and, accordingly, of constructions such as 'for'-PPs and 'enough to'-AdvPs offers an explanation of Cohen's observation that the context-sensitivity of 'knows' is a little less obvious than that of gradable adjectives. See Blome-Tillmann (2014).

References

Blome-Tillmann, M. (2008). "The Indexicality of 'Knowledge'." *Philosophical Studies* **138**(1): 29–53.

Blome-Tillmann, M. (2009). "Knowledge and Presuppositions," *Mind* 118/470: pp. 241–294.

Blome-Tillmann, M. (2014). *Knowledge and Presuppositions.* Oxford, Oxford University Press.

Cohen, S. (1988). "How to Be a Fallibilist." *Philosophical Perspectives* **2**: 91–123.

Cohen, S. (1999). "Contextualism, Skepticism, and the Structure of Reasons." *Philosophical Perspectives* **13**: 57–89.

Cohen, S. (2001). "Contextualism Defended: Comments on Richard Feldman's Skeptical Problems, Contextualist Solutions." *Philosophical Studies* **103**: 87–98.

DeRose, K. (1995). "Solving the Skeptical Problem." *The Philosophical Review* **104**: 1–52.

Hawthorne, J. (2004). *Knowledge and Lotteries.* Oxford, OUP.

Ichikawa, J. (2011a). "Quantifiers and Epistemic Contextualism." *Philosophical Studies* **155**(3): 383–398.

Ichikawa, J. (2011b). "Quantifiers, Knowledge, and Counterfactuals." *Philosophy and Phenomenological Research* **82**(2): 287–313.

Kaplan, D. (1989). Demonstratives. *Themes from Kaplan.* J. Almog, J. Perry and H. Wettstein. Oxford/New York, OUP: 481–563.

Kennedy, C. (1999). *Projecting the Adjective: The Syntax and Semantics of Gradability and Comparison.* New York, Garland.

Ludlow, P. (2005). Contextualism and the New Linguistic Turn in Epistemology. *Contextualism in Philosophy – Knowledge, Meaning and Truth.* G. Preyer and G. Peter (eds.). Oxford, OUP: 11–50.

Perry, J. (2001). *Reference and Reflexivity.* Stanford, CSLI Publications.

Schaffer, J. and Z. G. Szabó. (2014). "Epistemic Comparativism: A Contextualist Semantics for Knowledge Ascriptions." *Philosophical Studies* **168**(2): 491–543.

Stanley, J. (2004). "On the Linguistic Basis for Contextualism." *Philosophical Studies* **119**: 119–146.

Stanley, J. (2005). *Knowledge and Practical Interests.* Oxford, OUP.

PART VII

Contextualism outside 'knows'

28

MORAL CONTEXTUALISM AND EPISTEMIC CONTEXTUALISM

Similarities and differences

Berit Brogaard

1 Introduction

Suppose you are a devoted and motivated vegetarian on moral grounds. When you are out with your meat-eating friends, you often lecture them about the harms their meat-eating habits are inflicting on innocent animals. Some of your friends proclaim that they agree that the common industrialized treatment of farm animals is abhorable, and that they therefore stay away from meat from large-scale industries and only eat meat from small farmers committed to the proper treatment of their farm animals. They claim that because of this commitment they are doing nothing wrong when they sink their teeth into the prepared flesh of animals. In a desperate attempt to encourage your friends to see the wrongness of their culinary habits, you cite their reluctance to eat meat from dogs, cats, horses and humans. But your meat-eating friends remain unconvinced.

Exchanges about moral matters of this kind often take center stage in our day-to-day conversations with friends, relatives, partners and colleagues. But what are we saying when we engage in this type of discourse? Are we saying something that has a truth-value? Or are we merely expressing a reaction to particular actions or types of actions?

Old-school expressivists about moral discourse hold that although an expression like 'Eating meat is wrong' has a surface structure that makes it look like a statement with a truth-value, it is in fact a performative sentence without a truth-value (Blackburn, 1993, 2006; Gibbard, 1990; Hare, 1952). They typically further hold that these expressions are what John Austin called 'inhabitives' (1962) or what John Searle called 'expressives' (1969) – speech acts that express attitudes and social behavior, such as, congratulations, apologies and toastings. In other words, our moral exclamations serve to express the speaker's attitudes and emotions in response to the action in question. An expression of the sentence 'it's wrong to eat meat' is equivalent in content to an expression of a sentence such as 'Booh to eating meat!', and an expression of the sentence 'it's good never to eat meat' is equivalent in content to an expression of a sentence such as 'Hooray for never eating meat!'

The best-known challenge to this sort of view is the Frege-Geach problem (Geach, 1965; Searle, 1962). Consider the following argument.

If it is wrong to eat meat, then I will not order the beef tartare.
It is wrong to eat meat.
Therefore, I will not order the beef tartare.

This argument seems like a perfectly valid instance of Modus ponens. Yet if the antecedents of the first premise and the second premise are performatives, then it is not in fact a valid argument. An argument is valid just in case the premises could not be true while the conclusion is false. But if the second premise and the antecedent of the first premise do not have truth-values, then this condition can only be trivially satisfied.

Owing in part to the Frege-Geach problem, most thinkers with expressivist inclinations now adopt a view that takes moral expressions to have truth-values in spite of serving a non-descriptivist function. For example, one might hold that an expression of the sentence 'it's wrong to eat meat' has a truth-value but that its function is not to describe what is objectively right or wrong but rather to applaud vegetarianism or encourage meat-eaters to change their culinary habits.

Considerations of this kind can serve to motivate a form of moral contextualism. If a moral expression like 'it is wrong to eat meat' has a truth-value but does not serve to describe an objective fact in the world, then there are good reasons to think that we cannot apply standard semantics to the discourse. On standard semantics, the sentence 'it is wrong to eat meat' has the same truth-value regardless of who utters the sentence. Given non-descriptivism, however, moral expressions are not simply true or false, regardless of who utters the sentence. Their truth-value depends on our attitudes, emotions or individual moral standards. This can be accommodated within a contextualist semantics.

Contextualist semantics has been more frequently discussed in the literature on 'know' than in the literature on moral discourse. It has been suggested that the way 'know' functions in ordinary language requires a modification of standard semantics. To what extent our ordinary-language use of the word 'know' reflects the nature of knowledge is a further, substantial question. It could be that our ordinary use of 'know' is idiomatic in the same way that 'the sun is rising' is idiomatic. No one of a sane mind would conclude on the basis of the fact that we treat 'the sun is rising' as being accurate when the sun appears in the horizon in the morning that the sun is moving around the earth. 'Know', however, depicts a mental state, not a physical state in the universe. This may provide us with the requisite grounds for thinking that our use of 'know' reflects the nature of knowledge. Whether or not this is the case, however, will not be the topic of this chapter, although I shall return to it briefly at the end. The main aim of this chapter is to compare moral and epistemic contextualism. As we will see, the main difference lies in the nature of the standards that enter into the evaluation of the discourse.

The structure of the chapter is as follows. In the next section, I will look closer at the function of moral discourse as a motivation for moral contextualism and briefly consider whether epistemic contextualism might be similarly motivated. In section 3, I will compare moral and epistemic contextualism. In sections 4 through 6, I will look at the main arguments that have been advanced in favor of moral and epistemic contextualism, specifically retraction arguments and arguments from disagreement. These arguments will also serve to reveal some of the main differences between moral and epistemic contextualism. Finally, in the concluding remarks I will briefly consider whether the semantics of epistemic and moral expressions might have any implications for the nature of knowledge and morality.

2 The functions of moral and epistemic discourse

Even on the assumption that there are objective facts about morality, it is tempting to think that moral discourse often serves purposes other than (or maybe in addition to) simply describing what is objectively right or wrong. Upon seeing chicks stamp each other to death in a cruel chicken farm, I might exclaim 'That is just so wrong' as an expression of my moral disgust in

Moral and epistemic contextualism

response to the events I witness. 'That restaurant is bad; they use eggs from caged chickens' might serve both the function of expressing my disapproval of the restaurant's eggs and that of urging you to change your mind about going to the restaurant. Although it is an option to argue that I am either objectively right or wrong when I make these kinds of statements, one might also hold that the accuracy of these statements reflect their function. On this view, standard semantics will be unable to account for the accuracy conditions of the statements, and, as noted in the previous section, one natural option here is to turn to a contextualist semantics. We will look closer at the different types of contextualist semantics below. First, however, let us look at how non-descriptivism about 'know' might likewise serve to motivate a contextualist semantics for 'know'.

A contextualist semantics for 'know' is typically motivated by how 'know' is used in ordinary language. We will return to that in the following sections. Non-descriptivism about mental state expressions (e.g., 'believe' and 'know'), however, can also be used to motivate a contextualist semantics for these expressions. Mental state expressions can be used in a number of non-descriptivist ways in ordinary language (Lesson, 2016; Ryle, 1949; Sellars, 1956; Thomasson, 2008). Belief talk might serve a commitment-withholding function. For example, I might say, 'I believe Eli is in his office', to avoid fully committing myself to the proposition that he is in his office (Sellars, 1956). By contrast, knowledge talk may serve to emphasize my commitment to the truth of a proposition. For example, I might say, 'I know Eli is in his office', in reply to someone who expresses doubt in the proposition. Belief talk might also serve to make sense of puzzling behavior. For example, if a woman runs out of a building screaming, we can offer a causal explanation of this behavior by noting that the building was on fire, if indeed it was on fire, but if we know the building wasn't on fire, we cannot explain her behavior by stating that the building was on fire. However, we might *make sense* of the woman's behavior by attributing the belief that the building was on fire to her, thereby intending to provide an interpretive/hermeneutic rather than a causal explanation of her actions (Lesson, 2016: 85; Tanney, 2013: 8). This function carries over to claims about the lack of knowledge. If the question of whether the building was on fire has been addressed, and everyone except the screaming woman has been told that there is no fire, we can still make sense of the woman's behavior by noting that she didn't know the building wasn't on fire. This also applies to first-person reports. If I say, 'Sorry, I didn't know you were in line', after cutting in in front of you, the function of this talk may serve to excuse my rude behavior.

When we use mentalistic talk to *make sense* of our behavior or the behavior of others, we are not describing underlying mental states. Rather, the attributions of the mental states are accurate if they succeed in making sense of the otherwise puzzling behavior. On a standard analysis of knowledge, lack of knowledge is compatible with belief. Yet, if I firmly believe that you are in line despite not having strong evidence for believing it, saying, 'sorry, I didn't know you were in line', would not succeed in making sense of my rude behavior. One might argue that my pathetic excuse to the effect that I didn't know you were in line was inaccurate (rather than simply misleading).

In circumstances like these, knowledge claims appear to function in much the same way as claims to believe. Here is another case illustrating the same point. Suppose you and I are having a disagreement about whether the majority of the students in our undergraduate class know the capital of The Netherlands (Hawthorne, 2002: 253–4).[1] I argue that the majority know it, you argue that the majority don't know it. After our disagreement turns into a bet, we ask each student to write down the answer to the question on a piece of paper. We then count the correct and incorrect answers. As it turns out, most students correctly replied 'Amsterdam,' and only a few mistakenly replied 'The Hague', which is not the capital but the seat of government. We both agree that I won the bet. Neither of us cares about how the students hit upon the right answer. If they simply had a sufficient degree of belief that Amsterdam is the capital of The Netherlands, that suffices to count them as knowing the capital of The Netherlands.

There may be other circumstances, however, where knowledge talk requires more traditional requirements to be satisfied in order for a knowledge claim to be deemed accurate. Consider Keith DeRose's (1992) bank cases:

> *Bank Case A.* My wife and I are driving home on a Friday afternoon. We plan to stop at the bank on the way home to deposit our paychecks. But as we drive past the bank, we notice that the lines inside are very long, as they often are on Friday afternoons. Although we generally like to deposit our paychecks as soon as possible, it is not especially important in this case that they be deposited right away, so I suggest that we drive straight home and deposit our paychecks on Saturday morning. My wife says, "Maybe the bank won't be open tomorrow. Lots of banks are closed on Saturdays." I reply, "No, I know it'll be open. I was just there two weeks ago on Saturday. It's open until noon."
>
> Bank Case B. My wife and I drive past the bank on a Friday afternoon, as in Case A, and notice the long lines. I again suggest that we deposit our paychecks on Saturday morning, explaining that I was at the bank on Saturday morning only two weeks ago and discovered that it was open until noon. But in this case, we have just written a very large and very important check. If our paychecks are not deposited into our checking account before Monday morning, the important check we wrote will bounce, leaving us in a very bad situation. And, of course, the bank is not open on Sunday. My wife reminds me of these facts. She then says, "Banks do change their hours. Do you know the bank will be open tomorrow?" Remaining as confident as I was before that the bank will be open then, still, I reply, "Well, no. I'd better go in and make sure."
>
> *(DeRose, 1992: 913)*

In Bank Case B, where a lot is at stake for the speakers and the question of whether the bank will be open comes up, Keith's initial claim 'I know the bank will be open tomorrow' is inaccurate. His belief that the bank will be open the next day together with his circumstantial evidence does not suffice to make it the case that his knowledge claim is true. Here the function of the knowledge talk is to prevent a disaster from happening and evidence and anti-luck requirements need to be in place in order for the knowledge claim to be deemed accurate.

If the different functions of knowledge talk impose different requirements on the conditions under which the discourse is deemed accurate, then this type of discourse cannot be treated as having the same truth-value regardless of when the claim is made. One way to accommodate the variations in accuracy conditions for knowledge claims is to take the truth-value of knowledge claims to vary with the epistemic standards of the speaker.[2]

In both the moral and the epistemic cases, then, we might accommodate non-descriptivism by making modifications to standard semantics. Let us look at how this works first for the case 'know' and then for the moral case.

3 Contextualist semantics

One way to modify standard semantics to accommodate a kind of truth-evaluable discourse that may, but need not, describe objective facts in the world is to turn to a contextualist semantics.[3] Contextualism about knowledge is the view that the truth-conditions of knowledge claims may vary from speaker to speaker (Cohen, 1987; DeRose, 1995; Lewis, 1996). For example, the sentence 'Keith knows that the bank will be open tomorrow' may be true in the mouth of one speaker but false in the mouth of another.

Moral and epistemic contextualism

We can distinguish between two types of contextualism: indexical and non-indexical contextualism (MacFarlane, 2009). According to indexical contextualism, the content of 'know' may vary with the context of the speaker. On this view, 'know' is on a par with pure indexicals such as 'I', 'now' and 'here'. The sentence 'I am hungry' picks out different propositions when you and I utter it. When I utter the sentence 'I am hungry', it expresses the proposition that I am hungry, and when you utter it, it expresses the proposition that you are hungry. The context-sensitivity of 'I' is grounded in the variability of the linguistic meaning, or Kaplanian character, of the word. According to David Kaplan (1989), the linguistic meaning, or character, of 'I' is a function from a context of use (also known as the 'context of utterance') to the speaker in that context. Within a given context of use, the function provides an outcome, viz., whoever is the speaker in that context. Within that context the speaker thus becomes the content of 'I'. Indexical contextualists make a similar claim about 'know'. On their view, the linguistic meaning, or character, of 'know' is a function from a context of use to a particular knowledge property. In a particular context of use, the function will provide a knowledge property as an output, and this property thereby becomes the content of 'know' in that context. In high-stakes contexts or contexts where the possibility of error is made salient, the knowledge property becomes much harder for anyone to possess.

Non-indexical contextualists agree with the indexical contextualist that the truth-value of knowledge claims varies across contexts of use but they disagree with the indexical contextualist that this is due to a variation in the content of the knowledge claim (MacFarlane, 2009). They hold that the content of knowledge claims is the same across all contexts of use but that the truth-value nonetheless varies across those contexts. This type of stability of content but instability of truth-value is possible because the propositional contents of utterances are true or false only relative to a circumstance of evaluation (also sometimes known as an 'index of evaluation').

According to the framework suggested by Kaplan (1989), the circumstance of evaluation is a pair consisting of a world and a time determined by the context of use. Given this framework, consider the content of an utterance of the sentence 'John is hungry', which does not contain any indexicals. If John is actually hungry, then the context of this utterance is true relative to the actual world but false relative to a world in which John just ate. Likewise, if John is now hungry, and the sentence 'John is hungry' is uttered now, then the content of the utterance is true. But if the sentence had been uttered yesterday right after John's Super Bowl mega-feast, then relative to that time the content of the utterance would have been false.

The non-indexical contextualist relies on the circumstance of evaluation to account for how knowledge claims can have the same content across different contexts and yet have different truth-values. But they modify the parameters that enter into the circumstance of evaluation. The circumstance of evaluation is not simply a pair consisting of a world and a time. Rather, they argue, the circumstance of evaluation also contains a speaker parameter that reflects the speaker's epistemic state (which is a function of what is at stake for the speaker and how salient the possibility of error is). So, on this view, the content of an utterance like 'Keith knows that the bank will be open tomorrow' is true or false only relative to the speaker's epistemic state, despite the fact that the content is invariant across different contexts of use.

The semantics for moral contextualism is analogous to that for epistemic contextualism. Whereas contextualists about 'know' include individual *epistemic* standards among the parameters constituting the context of use (Brogaard, 2008c; Cohen, 1987; DeRose, 1995; Lewis, 1996), moral contextualists include individual *moral* standards among the parameters constituting the context of use (Brogaard, 2008a; Dreier, 1990; Harman, 1975; Norcross, 2005a, 2005b; Unger, 1995). When moral expressions are treated as indexicals, the view is referred to as 'indexical contextualism'. When moral expressions retain their content across contexts but have different truth-values in different circumstances of evaluation, the view is referred to as 'non-indexical contextualism'.

365

Berit Brogaard

According to moral indexical contextualism, a sentence like 'eating meat is wrong' has the content *eating meat is wrong relative to Brit's moral standards or attitudes*, when expressed by Brit and has the content *eating meat is wrong relative to Eli's moral standards or attitudes* when expressed by Eli. Assuming Brit thinks it is wrong to eat meat and Eli thinks it is okay to eat meat, the utterance is true when uttered by Brit but false when uttered by Eli.

Moral non-indexical contextualism does not build the individual moral standard into the content of moral expressions but takes the individual moral standard to affect which circumstance of evaluation the content is evaluated relative to. 'It is wrong to eat meat' has the content *it is wrong to eat meat* regardless of who is uttering the sentence. But the content *It is wrong to eat meat* may have different truth-values relative to different circumstances of evaluation. Assuming again that Brit thinks it is wrong to eat meat and Eli thinks it is okay to eat meat, the content is true relative to a circumstance of evaluation that contains Brit's moral standards but false relative to a circumstance of evaluation that contains Eli's moral standards.

Like epistemic contextualism, moral contextualism is thus first and foremost a view about the content of moral discourse or alternatively about ways of determining the truth-values of moral discourse. As noted above, nondescriptivism about moral or epistemic discourse can serve to motivate moral and epistemic contextualism. But the more common way to motivate these views is to argue that they are dictated by our ordinary-language use of the relevant expressions. In what follows I will look closer at some ordinary-language arguments for epistemic and moral contextualism. In these sections I will also discuss some differences between the nature of epistemic and moral standards. As we will see, although moral standards can change over time, they do not appear to be sensitive to what is at stake in the same way as epistemic standards are.

4 The retraction argument for a non-standard semantics for 'know'

Moral and epistemic contextualism are not typically motivated by non-descriptivist considerations but more often by how the expressions 'wrong' and 'know' function in ordinary language. One oft-discussed ordinary-language argument in favor of epistemic contextualism is the argument from retraction. As a brief review of a retraction case, consider the following (adapted from MacFarlane, 2005a):

> *The Retraction Case for 'Know'*
>   *Normally I am perfectly happy to say, 'I know that my car is in the driveway'. But on one occasion I am particularly obsessed with the possibility that a car thief might have stolen my car. The following exchange transpires between you and me:*
>
> Me: . . . So, you see, I don't know that my car is in the driveway.
> You: But a few hours ago you said that you knew it was there.
> Me: I was wrong. I didn't know that it was in the driveway back then either.
>
> (200)

This type of case has been presented as part of an argument in favor a non-indexical contextualist semantics (see, e.g., Brogaard, 2008c) as well as a variant on contextualism, also known as relativism (see, e.g., MacFarlane, 2005a). Epistemic relativism differs from epistemic contextualism in taking either the content or the truth-value of knowledge claims to vary across judges (also sometimes known as 'assessors') (Kölbel, 2002; Kölbel, 2003; MacFarlane, 2005a, 2005b; Richard,

2004). A judge (or assessor) can, but need not, be the person making the knowledge claim. If a speaker S_1 makes a knowledge claim at t_1 and a different person S_2 evaluates the knowledge claim at t_2, then it is the context of S_2 that matters to either the nature of the content or the truth-value of the knowledge claim. So, knowledge claims have their truth-values only relative to a context of utterance *and* a context of assessment (i.e., the context of the judge). For example, if John says, 'I know my car is in the driveway', and the possibility of error is not salient to him, then according to his context of assessment, the knowledge claim may be true but if someone else to whom the possibility of error is salient assesses the claim at a later time, then relative to this person's context of assessment, the knowledge claim may be false.

The retraction argument in favor of a relativistic semantics for 'know' runs as follows:

Although it initially may seem as if the retraction data motivate indexical contextualism about 'know', relativists have argued that this is not so (e.g., MacFarlane, 2005a). We often act as if the standards for 'know' are context-invariant: if reminded of a discrepancy in our knowledge ascriptions owing to a context-shift, we will hesitate to say things like 'what I said was merely that I met the standards for "know" that were in place when I was making the earlier claim'. Instead we will say: 'I was wrong. I thought I knew back then, but I didn't' (MacFarlane, 2005a). This sort of evidence, the relativists argue, provides a compelling case against indexical contextualism. To see this, consider a condensed version of what John said in the aforementioned discourse fragment.

> John at t_1: I know my car is in the driveway
> John at t_2: I was wrong. I didn't know that my car was in the driveway back then.

If indexical contextualism is true, then the contents of knowledge claims vary across the contexts of speakers. So, when John denies that he knew that the car was in driveway earlier, he is really saying something false, because at the earlier time John was in an epistemic state where the content of his utterance contained a knowledge property that was easy to come to possess. So, the content of his utterance back then was true, even if the content of any new knowledge claim he may later make is false. The fact that John fails to see this makes him *semantically blind*. This sort of blindness can be seen as a strike against indexical contextualism.

The most common form of relativism is one that takes only the truth-value of knowledge claims to vary with the judge but maintains that the content is invariant across contexts of assessment (Kölbel, 2004; see Weatherson, 2009 for the alternative view). Since the truth-value of John's earlier knowledge claim has its truth-value only relative to John-qua-judge (i.e., John at time t_2), it is true at t_2 that John didn't know that the car was in the driveway at t_1. So, it seems that the retraction data support relativism rather than indexical contextualism about knowledge.

In previous work, I have argued that non-indexical contextualism is a viable alternative to relativism (Brogaard, 2008c). When John at t_2 says, 'I didn't know the car was the driveway,' what we are evaluating is the following claim:

(1) The sentence 'I know my car is in the driveway,' as uttered by me earlier today, was false.

Taken at face value, the felicity of this sentence should be puzzling from any standard contextualist point of view. For the sentence that is evaluated occurs in a direct speech report, and it is normally thought that words that occur inside a direct speech report do not change their original content or extension.

However, as François Recanati has argued (2004: paragraph 3.2), there is good reason to think that a quoted sentence in a direct report is sometimes used, not simply mentioned. One reason is that the quoted material in a direct speech report may be available for copying, as in:

(2) 'I'm going to see the dean,' she said; and she did.

'And she did' is elliptical for 'and she did see the dean'. So, the elided material 'see the dean' is available for copying. But this suggests that the quoted material is used. For if the sentence were merely mentioned, the quoted material would not be available for copying, witness '"I'm going to see the dean" is a sentence; and she did.'

Another reason to think a quoted sentence in a direct report is used, not simply mentioned, is that expressions in the matrix clause can depend anaphorically on expressions in the quoted sentence. Consider, for instance:

(3) 'Give me your money$_i$, or I'll shoot,' he said, but I didn't give it$_i$ to him.

The pronoun 'it' in the matrix clause is anaphoric on 'your money'. But this requires that 'your money' picks out an individual for 'it' to refer to.

Recanati suggests that contextual cues associated with direct speech reports (e.g., quotation marks, lead-up, etc.) create a shifted context that determines the contents of the indexicals in the report. So, in the case of my assertion of 'And then John said, "I am leaving now"' the content of 'I' is John, not me, and the content of 'now' is a time in the past, not the current time. Direct speech reports can thus be considered context-shifters, or 'monsters', as Kaplan called them (1989: 510). Kaplan thought there weren't any context-shifting operators in English, but didn't rule out direct-speech-report shifts.

Given Recanati's account of direct speech reports, the case against the indexical contextualist may be formulated as follows: Pure indexicals like 'I' and 'now' *do* seem to change their content in direct speech reports. 'Know', on the other hand, does *not* seem to change its content when it occurs in a direct speech report. So, 'know' is not an indexical. Hence, indexical contextualism is false.

Non-indexical contextualism, by contrast, is not ruled out by these data. Following Kaplan (1989), the context of use plays two distinct roles: it fixes the value of indexicals, and it determines a default circumstance of evaluation. Context-shifters (or monsters) shift the content of indexicals (they operate on character). Non-indexical contextualism holds that the content of 'know' is constant across context. But if the content of 'know' is constant across context, it is unsurprising that 'know' is insensitive to the operations of context-shifters.

It might, of course, be thought that context-shifters shift not only the parameters of the context of use, but also the circumstance with respect to which a proposition is evaluated. There would indeed be nothing incoherent about an operator that operated on both context and circumstance. But direct speech report markers do not function in this way. To shift the parameters of the circumstance of evaluation we need a circumstance-shifter (e.g., a tense marker). For example, the proposition expressed by 'I am hungry' is evaluated with respect to the circumstance of evaluation determined by the context of use in an assertion of 'John says, "I am hungry,"' but it is evaluated with respect to a shifted circumstance in an assertion of 'John said, "I am hungry."'

Our problematic sentence, viz. 'The sentence "I know that my car is in the driveway," as uttered by me (John) earlier, was false' contains a circumstance-shifter, namely the past-tense operator. But the past-tense operator is selective: it operates on the time parameter, not the judge parameter. So, the circumstance of evaluation with respect to which the quoted sentence

Moral and epistemic contextualism

is interpreted is a triple of this world, a time in the past, and John, as he is currently constituted. In short: direct speech reports do not shift the judge parameter of the circumstance of evaluation because they do not operate on circumstances.

So, non-indexical contextualism is no worse off than relativism in terms of explaining the retraction data. In the next section I turn to retraction arguments for 'wrong' and look at how retraction cases involving moral expressions differ from those involving 'know'.

5 Retractions of moral claims

As for the case of 'know', retraction arguments also provide fairly good evidence in favor of a relativistic semantics or a non-indexical contextualist semantics for moral expressions. Consider a moral retraction case analogous to the epistemic case.

Moral Retraction Case for 'Wrong'
  Two years ago Brit was a vegetarian. She would often make claims to her meat-eating friends about their morally wrong culinary habits. Brit has now changed her mind about the wrongness of meat-eating. She is no longer a vegetarian. The following exchange transpires between Brit and her friend Eli:

Brit: . . . so, you see, it's okay to eat meat.
Eli: But two years ago you said that it was wrong to eat meat.
Brit: I was wrong. It wasn't and isn't wrong to eat meat.

In a case like this where a person changes his or her mind about a moral issue, retractions of earlier claims seem to be exceedingly common. It would, indeed, have been rather odd for Brit to have claimed that she was right back then but wrong now that she has changed her moral attitudes towards meat-eating. As the case illustrates, we tend to treat our own moral standards as objective, thereby condemning our own past attitudes.

Indexical contextualism applied to moral expressions treat 'morally wrong' as an indexical. So, if indexical contextualism were correct for moral claims, we should expect the retraction dialogue above to sound just as odd as the following exchange.

  Brit has just told Eli that she is hungry. Unbeknownst to Eli, Brit grabs a large sandwich from the fridge and eats it. The following exchange transpires between Brit and Eli:

Eli: You are hungry. So, let's get some food.
Brit: I am not hungry.
Eli: But five minutes ago you said you were hungry.
Brit: I was wrong back then. I wasn't hungry.

If Brit is sincere, we would have expected her to reply that she was hungry five minutes ago but that her state of hunger has changed because she ate a sandwich. In the moral case it is unusual for speakers to refer to their change of moral attitudes as a way of justifying why they could be right about saying one thing in the past and also be right about saying the opposite later on. Together with considerations motivating non-objective truth-values for moral claims, the retraction case thus supports relativism or non-indexical contextualism.

Although the epistemic and moral retraction cases look alike, there is an important difference between the two types of cases, however. In the epistemic case, it is the obsession with a possibility

369

that would make the speaker's earlier claim wrong that drives the retraction. In the moral case, the retraction is prompted by a change of moral attitudes. Knowledge claims are thus more elusive than moral claims. If you start obsessing about car thieves, you might retract your claim to know that your car is in the driveway. The retraction does not amount to a change in your core beliefs. In fact, the next day when you are no longer obsessing about car thieves, you may be perfectly content with stating that you know your car is in the driveway. Sincere retractions of moral claims, on the other hand, *do* appear to amount to a change in the speaker's core beliefs. If Brit were to retract her claim to the effect that it is okay to eat meat the next day, we would question the sincerely of her remark on the previous day or assume that she had undergone another radical change of attitude overnight.

Thus, whereas retractions of epistemic claims reflect a change in what is at stake for the speaker/judge or what is salient to him or her, retractions of moral claims reflect a change in the speaker's/judge's core beliefs. Retraction arguments thus nicely illustrate the differences between moral and epistemic contextualism. Disagreements about moral or epistemic issues serve as another way to illuminate the differences between the two positions. I turn to those cases next.

6 Arguments from disagreement

Disagreements about moral issues have sometimes been used to advocate non-indexical moral contextualism as well as moral relativism (e.g., Brogaard, 2008a, 2012; Kölbel, 2003). I will return to the success of these arguments below. It should be pointed out, however, that this type of argument is not usually advanced in favor of epistemic contextualism or epistemic relativism, as speakers who happen to disagree about a particular knowledge claim very quickly seem to come to an agreement, at least if they discuss their reasons for their claims. In DeRose's (1995) bank case, Keith may initially say, 'I know the bank will be open tomorrow,' not considering what will happen if the bank is not open. His wife, however, may be all too aware of the disastrous consequences that may ensue if the bank is closed. Accordingly, she may disagree with Keith that he *knows* that the bank is open on Saturday. But once she reminds Keith what is at stake if the bank is not open on Saturday and brings up the possibility that the bank may have changed its hours, Keith is likely to agree with her that he does not actually know.

Moral disagreements are much more likely to persist than disagreements about claims to know. If you disagree with another person about a moral issue, you are very likely to stick to your guns, almost regardless of how many reasons the other person fires in your direction. This is a reflection of the fact that moral standards are tied to the speaker's core beliefs, whereas epistemic standards are more closely tied to what is at stake for the speaker or what is salient to him or her.

Because moral disagreement are closely tied to the speaker's core beliefs, they have been used as arguments favoring a contextualist or relativist approach to moral discourse. However, initial appearances to the contrary, the arguments do not support just any old form of contextualism. They seem to favor non-indexical contextualism or relativism. Since this chapter is not concerned with adjudicating between non-indexical contextualism and relativism, let us focus on how the argument from faultless disagreement favors non-indexical contextualism.

In disagreements about facts, one of the discussants is wrong, even if we don't know who. For example, if I maintain that it is Monday and you deny it, one of us is at fault. If one is a non-descriptivist about moral discourse, then the function of moral discourse is not to describe objective facts but, for instance, to express one's moral attitudes. In that case, then, we should not expect disagreement to be due to one of the speakers being wrong about objective facts

Moral and epistemic contextualism

of the matter. And this is indeed what we find. To see this, consider the following moral disagreement:

Brit: . . . so, it's wrong to eat meat.
Eli: No, it's okay to eat meat if the animals don't suffer.
Brit: You are wrong. It's wrong to eat meat, even if the animals don't suffer.

If Brit's and Eli's claims serve to express their moral attitudes, their respective claims should be accurate even if their statements appear to contradict each other. Indexical contextualism cannot easily explain faultless disagreement. This is because indexical contextualism treats moral expressions such as 'wrong' as indexicals. So, given indexical contextualism, the above exchange is semantically equivalent to the following discourse fragment:

Brit: . . . so, according to my moral attitudes, it's wrong to eat meat.
Eli: No, according to my moral attitudes, it's okay to eat meat if the animals don't suffer.
Brit: You are wrong, according to my moral attitudes. According to my moral attitudes, it's wrong to eat meat even if the animals don't suffer.

This exchange makes no more sense than the following pseudo disagreement:

Brit: . . . so, I am hungry.
Eli: No, I am not hungry.
Brit: No, I am hungry.

If indexical contextualism is right, and moral expressions function semantically in the same way as indexicals, then what appears to be disagreements are not disagreements at all.

Given non-indexical contextualism, there is a proposition that Brit and Eli disagree about, viz., the proposition that it is wrong to eat meat. So, the disagreement is meaningful but it is not faulty. Brit and Eli can both be right insofar as the proposition that Brit and Eli disagree about is true relative to Brit's standards but not relative to Eli's standards.

The argument from faultless disagreement in favor of non-indexical contextualism can also be made on a different level of moral disagreement. This is because contextual theories turn on the fact that they include the speaker's moral standards as a factor relevant for determining the truth-value of sentences containing moral expressions. The truth-value of the sentence 'Murder is wrong' depends not only on the nature of murder, but also on the nature of the speaker's moral standards. But if this is so, then the question arises how we are to understand the semantics of a sentence concerning the moral standards themselves. Presumably we want our semantics to handle not only sentences such as 'It is right to pay your taxes,' but also sentences such as 'My moral standards are correct.' But it is difficult to see how we can do that, given indexical contextualism. Given indexical contextualism, the proposition expressed by an utterance of 'My moral standards are correct' is equivalent to 'according to my moral standards, my moral standards are correct.' So, it turns out to be true in the way in which the proposition expressed by an utterance of 'If it is right to maximize utility, then it is right to maximize utility' is true: it is true at all circumstances of evaluation.

Non-indexical contextualism does not run into this problem. This is because it takes the variability in the truth-values of moral claims to be due to the moral standards that figure in the circumstances of evaluation. An expression of the sentence 'My moral standards are correct' expresses the proposition *Brit's moral standards are correct* when I utter it. But this proposition is not

371

true in all circumstances of evaluation. It is not true in circumstances of evaluation that include standards that are different from mine.

The argument from faultless disagreement in favor of non-indexical contextualism (or relativism) has had its fair share of criticism. In their monograph *Relativism and Monadic Truth* Herman Cappelen and John Hawthorne argue that disagreement data by themselves do not establish whether an expression is context-sensitive. In order to show whether an expression is context-sensitive, they argue, we will need a test that gives 'center stage to the verbs "agree" and "disagree"' (2009: 54). The test they propose can be illustrated by means of an example. If A says, 'Mary has had enough. She has had three slices of cakes', and B says, 'Mary has had enough. She is going to leave her husband,' then we cannot correctly infer 'A and B agree that Mary has had enough.' The infelicity of the agreement report is supposed to illustrate that 'had enough' is context-sensitive. It has different contents in different contexts.

Consider another one of their examples. John says, 'Bill has died', in response to the question 'Why did Bill not show up at the pub last week? And Janet says, 'Bill hasn't died', in answer to the question 'Why did Bill's children not get their inheritance last year?' Cappelen and Hawthorne conclude that 'The claim "Janet and John disagreed about whether Bill had died" is clearly infelicitous' (2009: 98).

The test they propose, however, is not really a test of context-sensitivity but rather a test of whether an agreement or a disagreement is genuine. As Cappelen and Hawthorne point out, the test works as a true test of shared content because 'agree' in agreement reports fails to be distributive. Two individuals cannot independently agree about anything. Agreement is a joint effort involving a shared content. Here is another way to put the same point: For disagreement to take place between two speakers, it is not sufficient that one speaker denies something that another speaker asserts. Genuine disagreement requires that two speakers are debating a shared content and would be prepared to assign different truth-values to that content.

Despite what they claim, Cappelen and Hawthorne's test in fact lends credence to disagreement data. If Brit and Eli are discussing whether it is wrong to eat meat, it is perfectly felicitous to say 'Brit and Eli disagree about whether it is wrong to eat meat.' The discussants are prepared to assign different truth-values to a shared content, viz. the content *it is wrong to eat meat*. Indexical contextualism, however, fails the test. If Brit expresses the content *it is wrong to eat meat by Brit's standards*, and Eli expresses the content *it is not wrong to eat meat by Eli's standards*, then there is no shared content being subject to debate. Both speakers should be prepared to assign the same truth-value to each of the contents. Given non-indexical contextualism, by contrast, there is a shared content to which Brit and Eli are prepared to assign different truth-values, viz. the content *it is wrong to eat meat*.

7 Concluding remarks

As we have seen, moral contextualism and epistemic contextualism are analogous as far as the semantics is concerned. Our ordinary use of the expressions 'wrong' and 'know' support a non-standard semantics: either relativism or non-indexical contextualism. But the analogy ends here. The standards that determine the truth-value of moral claims and knowledge claim behave quite differently. Epistemic standards are easily influenced by what is at stake for the speakers or how salient possibilities of errors are to them. Moral standards, on the other hand, reflect the speakers' core beliefs. While these beliefs can change, they are not likely to change, dependent on what is at stake or how salient the possibility of error is to them. One reason they do not seem to exert this behavior may be that moral expressions are not factive operators. 'Know', by contrast, is factive. If I say, 'I know that the bank will be open tomorrow,' then this entails that the bank will be open tomorrow. If a lot hinges on whether the bank is open tomorrow, I might retract or withhold my claim until I can gather more evidence. In the moral case, however, there is often not further mind-altering evidence to gather for or against the accuracy of a claim. I may succeed in convincing someone that it is wrong to eat meat by showing them pictures of how industrial animals are treated but if I am unsuccessful, there is no easy route forward. I cannot simply go to a farm to double-check whether the treatment of farm animals makes it wrong to eat meat the way that I can go to the bank to check their opening hours. This is not to say that there are no cases in which we would want to withhold a moral claim until we can gather further evidence. If someone is accused of murder, we would want to collect as much evidence as possible before making the claim that the accused actually did anything wrong. But in this case it is not the wrongness of the act of murder that is in question but whether the accused committed the act.

As noted in the introduction, whether the semantics for 'know' and 'wrong' can tell us anything about knowledge and morality is a substantial question. It does not follow from the fact that we use a particular expression in a particular way that the state depicted by the expression is in fact the state we are really interested in when investigating the issue. Such is the case with idioms like 'the sun is rising.' The idiom may depict a seeming but it has no implications for physical facts about heavenly matters.

In the case of mental states, such as knowledge, however it may be argued that there is nothing to the mental state beyond what can be gathered from our discourse about it. This is the idea underlying nondescriptivism. Unless we are willing to identify mental states with their underlying neural states, mental states cannot easily be observed from a language-independent point of view. We cannot go take a peek at a person's mental states. If we want to know something about a person's mental states, one of the best things we can do is analyze the language we ordinarily use to attribute mental states to them on the basis of their behavior. Or we can use methods for gathering first-person reports about their mental states. But as these methods depend on the language we use to talk about mental states, it is hard to see a role for mental states that is completely independent of our discourse about them. For the case of morality, it is much more difficult to determine whether moral states are best considered objective properties of actions or mental attitudes toward actions. It is quite plausible that many other factors matter to the nature of morality besides the ways in which we happen to converse about it.[4]

Notes

1 's knows the capital of The Netherlands' is semantically equivalent to 's knows what the capital of The Netherlands is,' which, in turn, is true just in case s knows that Amsterdam is the capital of The Netherlands (see Brogaard, 2008b, 2009).
2 This is one way but not the only way; see Hawthorne (2004), Stanley (2005), and ch. 19, and the discussion of relativistic semantics in Part V of this volume, as well as below.
3 A contextualist semantics, of course, *can* describe objective facts in the world just as indexicals like 'I' and here' can, but if one is motivated by the idea that mental-state discourse (e.g., discourse involving 'know' and 'believe') can function in non-descriptive ways, a modification of standard semantics is needed. As noted above, one semantics that can account for non-descriptive discourse is a contextualist semantics.
4 For helpful comments on an earlier version of this essay I am grateful to Jonathan Ichikawa.

References

Austin, J.L. (1962). *How to Do Things with Words*, 2nd Edition, eds. J.O. Urmson and M. Sbisá. Cambridge, MA: Harvard University Press.
Blackburn, S. (1993). "Morals and modals", in *Essays in Quasi-Realism*. Oxford: Oxford University Press.
Blackburn, S. (2006). "Antirealist expressivism and quasi-realism", in D. Copp (ed.), *The Oxford Handbook of Ethical Theory*. Oxford: Oxford University Press, 146–162.

Brogaard, B. (2008a). "Moral Contextualism and Moral Relativism", *Philosophical Quarterly* 58: 385–409.

Brogaard, B. (2008b). "Knowledge-the and Propositional Attitude Ascriptions", *Grazer Philosophische Studien* 77 (1):147–190.

Brogaard, B. (2008c). "In Defense of a Perspectival Semantics for "Know", *Australasian Journal of Philosophy* 86: 439–459.

Brogaard, B. (2009). "What Mary Did Yesterday: Reflections on Knowledge-wh", *Philosophy and Phenomenological Research* 78 (2): 439–467.

Brogaard, B. (2012). "Moral Relativism and Moral Expressivism", *Southern Journal of Philosophy* 50 (4): 538–556.

Cappelen, H. and Hawthorne, J. 2009. *Relativism and Monadic Truth*. Oxford: Oxford University Press.

Cohen, S. (1987). "Knowledge, Context, and Social Standards", *Synthese* 73: 3–26.

DeRose, K. (1992). "Contextualism and Knowledge Attributions", *Philosophy and Phenomenological Research* 52(4): 913–929.

DeRose, K. (1995). "Solving the Skeptical Problem", *The Philosophical Review* 104: 1–52.

Dreier, J. (1990). "Internalism and Speaker Relativism", *Ethics* 101: 6–26.

Geach, P.T. (1965). "Assertion", *The Philosophical Review* 74(4): 449–465.

Gibbard, A. (1990). *Wise Choices, Apt Feelings: A Theory of Normative Judgement.* Oxford: Clarendon Press.

Hare, R.M. (1952). *The Language of Morals.* Oxford: Clarendon Press.

Harman, G. (1975). "Moral Relativism Defended", *Philosophical Review* 84: 3–23.

Hawthorne, J. (2002). "Deeply Contingent a Priori Knowledge", *Philosophy and Phenomenological Research* 65 (2): 247–269.

Hawthorne, J. (2004). *Knowledge and Lotteries.* Oxford: Oxford University Press.

Kaplan, D. (1989). "Demonstratives," in J. Almog, H. Wettstein, and J. Perry (eds.), *Themes from Kaplan.* New York: Oxford University Press, 233–249.

Kölbel, M. (2002). *Truth without Objectivity.* London: Routledge.

Kölbel, M. (2003). "Faultless Disagreement", *Proceedings of the Aristotelian Society* 104: 53–73.

Kölbel, M. (2004). "Indexical Relative versus Genuine Relativism", *International Journal of Philosophical Studies* 12: 297–313.

Lesson, S.B. (2016). *Making Ourselves Intelligible – Nondescriptive and Propositional Attitudes,* A Dissertation submitted to the faculty of the University of Miami in partial fulfillment of the requirements for the degree of Doctor of Philosophy.

Lewis, D. (1996). "Elusive Knowledge", *Australasian Journal of Philosophy* 74: 549–567.

MacFarlane, J. (2005a). "The Assessment Sensitivity of Knowledge Attributions," in T. Szabo-Gendler and J. Hawthorne (eds.), *Oxford Studies in Epistemology 1.* Oxford: Oxford University Press, 197–233.

MacFarlane, J. (2005b). "Making Sense of Relative Truth", *Proceedings of the Aristotelian Society* 105: 321–339.

MacFarlane, J. (2009). "Nonindexical Contextualism," in *Relative Truth,* ed. B. Brogaard, *Synthese* 166 (2): 231–250.

Norcross, A. (2005a). "Contextualism for Consequentialists", *Acta Analytica* 20: 80–90.

Norcross, A. (2005b). "Harming in Context", *Philosophical Studies* 123: 149–173.

Recanati, F. (2004). *"Indexicality and Context-shift,"* Conference Paper, Workshop on Indexicals, Speech Acts, and Logophors, Harvard University: 11–20.

Richard, M. (2004). "Contextualism and Relativism", *Philosophical Studies* 199: 215–242.

Ryle, G. (1949). *The Concept of Mind.* London: Hutchinson and Co.

Searle, J.R. (1962). "Meaning and Speech Acts," *Philosophical Review* 71 423–432.

Searle, J. (1969). *Speech Acts: An Essay in the Philosophy of Language.* Cambridge: Cambridge University Press.

Sellars, W. (1956). "Empiricism and the Philosophy of Mind", *Minnesota Studies in the Philosophy of Science* 1 (19): 253–329.

Stanley, J. (2005). *Knowledge and Practical Interests.* Oxford: Oxford University Press.

Tanney, J. (2013). *Rules, Reason, and Self-knowledge.* Cambridge, MA: Harvard University Press.

Thomasson, A.L. (2008). "Phenomenal Consciousness and the Phenomenal World," *Monist* 91 (2):191–214.

Unger, P. (1995). "Contextual Analysis in Ethics", *Philosophy and Phenomenological Research* 58: 1–26.

Weatherson, B. (2009). "Conditionals and Indexical Relativism", in *Relative Truth,* ed. B. Brogaard, *Synthese* 166 (2): 333–357.

29

CONTEXTUALISM ABOUT EPISTEMIC REASONS

Daniel Fogal and Kurt Sylvan

1 Introduction

Ordinary talk is rife with claims about epistemic reasons. Consider, for example:

'There's no reason to think Yetis exist.'
'We have a reason to believe your account was accessed by a third party.'
'The dark clouds approaching are a reason to think it will rain.'

We will call sentences like these 'normative epistemic reasons ascriptions' ('ERAs' for short), since they are used to ascribe or deny reasons that normatively support beliefs. For simplicity, we will focus on unmodified ERAs like those above; talk of 'good'/'bad' reasons, 'strong'/'weak' reasons, etc., introduces further complexities. Normative reasons are standardly contrasted with *explanatory* and *operative* reasons. Perhaps the *reason why* Smith thinks he will never get a job is that he is depressed – this is an explanatory reason. But the fact that he is depressed needn't be *his* reason for so believing – i.e., it needn't be an *operative* reason for him. We aren't directly concerned with these kinds of reasons.

The line between different kinds of reasons isn't perfectly sharp, however, and it's common to take all of them – including normative reasons – to be essentially explanatory in nature. To be a reason of any kind is, in part, to help explain something. What distinguishes normative reasons from the rest is partly a matter of the kind of explanation involved – mere explanatory reasons are typically causal, while normative reasons are not – and partly a matter of their *explanandum* – what normative reasons help explain are normative facts. Which normative facts? Three main answers have been defended. According to the first, for r to be a normative reason for an agent S to A (where A is some action or attitude) is for r to play a certain role in explaining why S *ought* to A (Broome 2004, 2013). According to the second, for r to be a normative reason for S to A is for r to play a certain role in explaining why it would be *good* for S to A (Finlay 2014). And according to the third, for r to be a normative reason for S to A is for r to play a certain role in explaining why there is *reason* (mass noun) for S to A (Fogal 2016). Evidence for the third option will be provided below.

The main goal in what follows is to survey some ways in which ERAs appear to be context-sensitive and to outline a framework for thinking about the nature of this context-sensitivity that is intimately related to their explanatory function. These are the main tasks of sections 2 and 3.

375

We won't pretend to have covered all forms of apparent context-sensitivity, nor to have settled the question of their nature and source. Surprisingly little work has been done on ERAs, despite the fact that ERAs strike us as more promising candidates for contextualist treatment than knowledge ascriptions. Our primary aim is thus to bring increased attention to an underexplored issue.

2 Data

In this section, we highlight several ways in which ERAs appear to be context-sensitive. To maintain neutrality between pragmatic and semantic explanations of such appearances, the initial judgments (or 'data') we consider are not presented as directly concerning the *truth conditions* of ERAs. Instead, they concern their *acceptability conditions* – roughly, the circumstances in which it is acceptable for a competent speaker who knows all the relevant non-semantic facts to use the ERAs.

2.1 Sensitivity to relevant alternatives

Some apparent contextual variability in the acceptability of ERAs is triggered by changes in which alternative hypotheses are relevant in the conversational context (cf. Dretske 1970; Stine 1976). Consider a relatively ordinary context in which we are asked whether some animal in a picture is a zebra. In such a context, it would be acceptable to say:

(1) The fact that it is striped is a reason to believe it is a zebra.

But now consider a context in which the possibility that the animal is a cleverly disguised mule – one with painted stripes, etc. – is being seriously entertained. In that context, (1) would be significantly less acceptable – so much so that its negation (2) seems OK:

(2) The fact that it is striped is not a reason to believe it is a zebra.

The acceptability of ERAs hence appears to be sensitive to which alternative hypotheses are contextually relevant. In particular, such patterns suggest that a claim of the form 'p is a reason to believe q' will be acceptable in a context c only when it is true that

(Alt) p is a reason to believe q rather than r_i,

where r_i are the relevant alternative hypotheses to q in c.

Epistemic contextualism in its earliest form was closely related to such a view. While the debate between Stine and Dretske focused on 'knows', both made analogous claims about 'reason(s)'.[1] More recent elaborations of this idea in the literature on ERAs tend to fall under the heading of 'contrastivism', with contrastivists arguing that the reason(s)-relation has an extra argument place for relevant alternatives, or 'contrasts', an argument place filled by context but phonologically null (Sinnott-Armstrong 2008; Snedegar 2013a, 2015, 2017).

The status of this view depends in part on what relevance amounts to, and how it is determined. If the relevance of an alternative is determined solely by facts about the *subject* of the ERA – say, by facts about their mental states, evidence, or situation more generally – then no support accrues for contextualism, since the relevant alternatives won't vary across conversational contexts. If, on the other hand, the relevance of an alternative is determined partly by facts about the *speaker*, then (some form of) contextualism would follow, since the relevant alternatives could vary with the speaker across contexts.

Contextualism about epistemic reasons

There are other possible explanations of the data involving (1). In particular, one might think that the relevant version of (Alt), along with various other natural strengthenings of (1) – e.g., the claim that the stripes are a *strong* or *weighty* reason to believe that the animal is a zebra – are merely pragmatically conveyed (cf. Schroeder 2007). On this view, even if an utterance of (1) might pragmatically convey something false in a context in which the possibility of the animal being a cleverly disguised mule is entertained, the proposition semantically expressed by (1) is true: the fact that the animal is striped *is* a reason to believe that it is a zebra, even though it may not be a *decisive* or even a particularly *good* reason, and even though it may not be a reason to believe that it is a zebra *rather than* a cleverly disguised mule. As evidence of their pragmatic status, one might point out that many such strengthenings appear to be cancellable. For example, in the original context one might utter (1) and then continue: 'Of course, it's hardly decisive – perhaps it's just a cleverly disguised mule.' Similarly, in the second context one might utter (1) and then continue: 'I realize, though, that the stripes are just as much a reason to believe it is a cleverly disguised mule – I don't mean to rule that possibility out.'

Even if we can explain why, despite being true, (1) is unacceptable in a context where the cleverly disguised mule possibility is entertained, it remains to be explained why (2) is acceptable despite being *false* (cf. Snedegar 2013b). The unacceptability of (1) despite its truth was traced to the unacceptability of what was pragmatically conveyed. Analogously, we might try to explain the acceptability of (2) in such a context by appealing to the acceptability of what it would pragmatically convey – e.g., the fact that it is striped is not a *sufficiently good* reason to believe that it is a zebra, or is not a reason to believe that it is a zebra *rather than a cleverly disguised mule*. Alternatively, one might think (2) is acceptable when seemingly false only if 'not' is interpreted metalinguistically, in which case (2) wouldn't actually be false (cf. Horn 1989). In particular, a metalinguistic use of 'not' might have the effect of saying that the fact that it is striped shouldn't *count* or *be considered* as a reason to believe that it is a zebra in the relevant context – perhaps, again, because it's not sufficiently good, or doesn't bear on the question of whether it's a zebra or instead a cleverly disguised mule.

Assuming utterances of (1) and/or (2) would normally pragmatically convey something of the form of (Alt), there remains the question of *how* that happens – i.e., what pragmatic 'mechanism' is underwriting the process. Here a variety of stories might be told. For example, one might think that the relevant instance of (Alt) has the status of a conversational implicature. For in normal contexts it will be fairly clear which alternatives are relevant, with one of the conversational goals being to decide between them. If so, then it would be pointless to utter (1) unless one also wanted to communicate something (Alt)-like (cf. Grice 1989's Maxim of Quantity), and although one *could* make an explicitly contrastive claim instead of uttering (1), doing so would be needlessly verbose (cf. Grice's Maxim of Manner). Another possibility would be to claim that (1) can be used to directly but *implicitly* communicate what utterances taking the form of (Alt) *explicitly* communicate, as the result of some process of so-called pragmatic enrichment (cf. Sperber and Wilson 1986; Bach 1994; Recanati 2004). For more on the similarities and differences between conversational implicature and various forms of pragmatic enrichment, see chapters 16 and 37.

Alternative semantics provides another way to explain how (1) can be used to communicate something (Alt)-like. According to alternative semantics, the general function of focus is to evoke alternatives, and an additional semantic value for each sentence posited to accommodate this fact (Rooth 1992). Sentences therefore come with both ordinary semantic values and focus semantic values, with the latter consisting of a set of alternatives. As Rooth (1996) notes,

> The basic idea [can] be illustrated with the question-answer paradigm. The question [does Ede want tea or coffee?] determines the basic answers "Ede wants tea" and "Ede wants

coffee". Similarly, focus in the answer [Ede wants [coffee]$_F$] indicates that propositions obtained by making substitutions in the position of the focused phrase – propositions of the form "Ede wants y" – are alternatives to the actual answer. Congruence is simply a matter of the question and answer characterizing the answer set consistently.

(276)

On this view, a sentence like (1) will thus have a focus semantic value in addition to its ordinary semantic value, with the former depending on which phrase is focused. The sentence [The fact that it is striped is a reason to believe it is a [zebra]$_F$], for example, will have as its focus semantic value the set of propositions of the form "The fact that it is striped is a reason to believe it is an X," with possible values of X being contextually constrained.

2.2 Sensitivity to questions

A related kind of apparent context-sensitivity is connected to the explanatory nature of reasons ascriptions. As many have observed, it seems a truism that reasons ascriptions – and explanations more generally – are answers to 'why'-questions (cf. Hempel 1965; Bromberger 1966; van Fraassen 1980; Jenkins 2008).[2] The questions ERAs answer concern why certain normative facts obtain. On this picture, one would expect the acceptability of ERAs to be sensitive to the question(s) under discussion, which may vary contextually.

To illustrate, consider a general theory (e.g., nominalism about properties) with its specific variants (e.g., trope theory and predicate nominalism), and to which there is a general alternative (e.g., realism about universals). Suppose the following questions interest us:

(Q1) Why believe trope theory rather than realism about universals?
(Q2) Why believe trope theory rather than predicate nominalism?

If we focus on (Q1), the following claim seems acceptable:

(3) The fact that trope theory provides a parsimonious ontology is a reason to believe it.

But if we instead focus on (Q2), (3) seems significantly less acceptable – after all, trope theory and predicate nominalism are similarly parsimonious. It's a further question whether (3) is *false* in such a context. We thus face a similar range of choices as above in offering a semantic and/or pragmatic explanation of the context-sensitivity.

It's worth noting that (Q1) and (Q2) are normative or deliberative questions. They concern why we should believe something, and the facts appropriately cited as reasons in response to them help settle the relevant question. Often, however, the questions that interest us aren't normative. How then should we interpret ERAs in contexts in which normative questions aren't under discussion, even implicitly?[3] Although space precludes detailed discussion, we doubt there are such contexts. Suppose, for example, that I ask you whether our neighbor Jim is home. You look across the street and see his car in the driveway. You then say, 'Well, I'm not sure, but the fact that his car is in the driveway is a reason to think he's home.' This response fails to answer the original question concerning Jim's location, but it's not completely irrelevant. Instead, you opt out of answering the original question by expressing uncertainty concerning the correct answer and seek to provide the next best thing – namely, information relevant to answering the question.[4] Here the question is theoretical, rather than practical, and information relevant to it will typically take the form of *evidence* concerning the truth or

Contextualism about epistemic reasons

falsity of possible answers. In other words, it will take the form of *reasons to believe* one answer rather than another. Given your inability to answer the original, non-normative question – namely, whether Jim is home – the natural thing to do is to pivot and provide an answer to a related, normative one – namely, whether there is any reason to think Jim is home (and if so, why). We think something like this is true in general when we use ERAs in answering seemingly non-normative questions.

Assuming the acceptability of ERAs is indeed sensitive to the question(s) under discussion, there's a further issue concerning whether it's distinct from sensitivity to relevant alternatives. It's standard in semantics, for example, to treat questions as presenting sets of alternatives, or possible answers. If so, then the question-sensitivity of ERAs would amount to sensitivity to relevant alternatives. This form of relevant alternatives contextualism would have the advantage of being able to draw from, and build on, the active and ongoing research program in formal semantics and pragmatics concerning the question under discussion, along with many other ways in which information in a discourse can be structured (see, e.g., Roberts 2012a, 2012b).

2.3 Sensitivity to information

Changes in which body of information is relevant provide another example of how the acceptability of ERAs appears to vary depending on the context of utterance (cf. Cohen 1986). Indeed, there is growing recognition that the familiar (and not necessarily binary) distinction between more 'objective' and more 'subjective' readings of claims concerning normative reasons for action extends to ERAs (cf. Schroeder 2008, 2011, 2015).[5]

Suppose Jones is a detective at the scene of a crime who stumbles across evidence that implicates Smith, a notorious criminal, though Jones lacks information needed to connect the dots. And imagine Jane, another detective, has the same information as Jones. Jones wonders aloud whether Smith is the culprit. Turning to Jones, Jane says:

(4) Perhaps – but as of now we don't have a single reason to believe that he did it.

Smith, meanwhile, overhears Jane's claim – he has a habit of lurking around crime scenes in disguise – and mutters to himself:

(5) Ha! They do have a reason to believe I did it right under their noses, though they'll never appreciate it.

Assuming both (4) and (5) are acceptable, one might take this as evidence that ERAs are always relativized – if only implicitly – to bodies of information, and that which body of information is relevant may vary between contexts, and perhaps even within a context. On this view, (4) might express the proposition that *relative to the information actually possessed by the detectives*, the detectives lack a reason to believe Smith committed the crime. (5), by contrast, might express the proposition that *relative to some enhanced body of information*, the detectives have a reason to believe that Smith committed the crime. This yields a view on which ERAs are *information-sensitive* in much the way deontic modals like 'ought' are thought to be.[6]

Henning (2014) pursues the apparent analogy between 'reason(s)' and 'ought', arguing that claims of the form 'r is a reason for S to believe that p' can be used to communicate an indefinite number of propositions of the form

($\star$) Relative to body of information i, r is a reason for S to believe that p.

379

According to Henning, any body of information can, in principle, determine the value of the parameter i. Candidates include the following:

(i) The information possessed by some relevant individual.
(ii) The information possessed by some relevant group or community.
(iii) The information easily-accessible-in-principle by some relevant individual or group.
(iv) All the information in the world.

Those wishing to defend invariantism about ERAs in the face of data concerning information-sensitivity face a challenge like those wishing to defend invariantism about deontic modals.[7] We cannot discuss those challenges in depth, but we take it to be an uphill battle.

2.4 Sensitivity to standards and thresholds

A consideration r can be a reason to believe p even if r doesn't entail p. Indeed, it often seems sufficient that r raises p's probability to some degree. To *what* degree, however, must r raise the probability of p in order to count as a reason for believing p? One might think there's no fixed answer to this question, and that ERAs can be true or false in different contexts depending on the stringency of the relevant threshold or standard. Consider, for example, a claim like the following:

(6) Lena has a reason to think John was at work today – she saw his coat and hat hanging outside his office door.

In a causal discussion at a tavern, (6) might be perfectly acceptable. But when being interviewed by a detective trying to determine whether John was at the scene of the crime, it might not be.[8] Such a contrast, insofar as it exists, could be taken as a reflection of different standards being operative in the two contexts. In the first context, for example, in order for r to count as a reason to believe p, perhaps r just needs to increase the probability of p to some degree or other, whereas in the second context perhaps r needs to *substantially* increase the probability of p. Alternatively, such a contrast may be susceptible to a pragmatic explanation. It's plausible, for example, that (6) would normally be used to communicate something more than the mere fact that Lena has a reason to believe John was at work, and what that reason is. In particular, it would be used to communicate something (via either conversational implicature or pragmatic enrichment) about the *strength* of Lena's reason – namely, that it was a relatively strong reason (cf. Schroeder 2007). And it is unsurprising that what counts as a 'strong' reason can vary between contexts depending on the operative standards (and, at least indirectly, stakes), since gradable adjectives like 'strong' are plausibly context-sensitive in this way (cf. Stanley 2005; Kennedy 2007). So even if talk of reason(s) *per se* isn't sensitive to standards or thresholds, talk of strong/weak/good/bad/ reasons will be.

Standards-sensitivity figured prominently in early discussions of contextualism. Stine (1976)'s view, for example, was doubly contextualist. She was a relevant alternatives contextualist about knowledge ascriptions, but her preferred account of relevance was understood in terms of epistemic reason(s) – according to her 'an alternative is relevant only if there is some reason to think that it is true' (252). But Stine also embraced a standards-relative contextualism about ERAs, arguing that the context-sensitivity of knowledge ascriptions is

> directly mirrored by the fact that we have different standards for judging that there is some reason to think an alternative is true, i.e., relevant. We can point out that some

Contextualism about epistemic reasons

philosophers are very perverse in their standards (by *some* extreme standard, there is some reason to think there is an evil genius, after all) . . . [and] in fact they have played on an essential feature of the concept.

(254)

What might such an 'extreme' standard – one relative to which there is some reason to think there is an evil genius – look like? There are various possibilities. For example, one might operate with a standard according to which *r* is a reason to believe *p* if (but not necessarily only if) *r*'s being true would explain *p*. Assuming the existence of the relevant evil genius would explain the fact that I have the perceptual experiences that I do (among other things), it might then be acceptable to utter the following:

(7) There is a reason to think there is an evil genius.[9]

One might then think that although the proposition expressed by (7) is true in contexts like the one just envisaged, in normal contexts – i.e., when a different standard is operative – it is false. Alternatively, one might think the proposition expressed by (7) is true in normal contexts as well, with its unacceptability being explained by familiar pragmatic means.

2.5 *Reasons and background conditions*

Two further kinds of apparent context-sensitivity in ERAs parallel kinds of context-sensitivity in causal talk. Firstly, as with causal talk, what is most naturally cited as a reason and what is treated as a mere 'background' condition seems contextually variable. Consider a match being struck and lighting. Although some might claim that only the striking of the match is a (or 'the') cause of the fire – with the presence of oxygen merely being a background condition – there are contexts in which the underlying metaphysics remains much the same and yet what we're inclined to count as a (or the) cause changes. Imagine that the match is being repeatedly struck in a vacuum when oxygen suddenly rushes in, or that we are aliens from an oxygen-deficient planet observing the striking from afar (cf. Putnam 1982). Here it would be natural for the presence of oxygen to be cited as a cause, and not merely a background condition.

It's plausible to view this contextual variability as a form of information-sensitivity, where what varies between contexts is not which body of information is relevant *per se* but instead which parts of that information are taken for granted or held fixed for the purposes of communication, and which parts are highlighted or viewed as especially noteworthy. This isn't to deny that there are meaningful distinctions to be drawn between different metaphysical roles that certain facts or events may play in explaining other facts or events. But it *is* to deny that ordinary language reliably tracks such distinctions. Differences in communicative relevance needn't reflect differences in metaphysical significance.

The same dialectical situation arises with respect to ERAs. Imagine a world, for example, in which only smokers with gene X get cancer, with an incident rate of 40%. Imagine further that the world is divided into two isolated populations, P1 and P2. In P1, it is common knowledge that most people have gene X but few people smoke. In P2, it is common knowledge that few people have gene X but most people smoke. Now, imagine the following possible answers to the question of what reasons there are to think that a given person will get cancer:

(8) The fact that a person smokes is a reason to think she will get cancer.
(9) The fact that a person has gene X is a reason to think she will get cancer.

The acceptability of these claims will likely vary depending on the population. In particular, (8) will be significantly more acceptable than (9) in P1 while in P2 the reverse pattern will hold. As before, it's plausible to view this as a form of information-sensitivity, since the only relevant differences between the populations concern the information at their disposal. But just because it's more natural to cite one fact rather than the other in a particular context needn't reflect a difference in epistemological significance. Differences in communicative relevance needn't reflect differences in epistemological significance any more than they reflect differences in metaphysical significance.[10]

2.6 Reasons as representatives

There is a second parallel between causal claims and ERAs that one of us has explored elsewhere (Fogal 2016). In response to the fact that what we're inclined to cite as 'the cause' of an event varies greatly from context to context, Lewis (1973) famously remarked:

> I have nothing to say about these principles of invidious discrimination. I am concerned with the prior question of what it is to be one of the causes (unselectively speaking). My analysis is meant to capture a broad and nondiscriminatory concept of causation.
>
> *(559)*

However, as Swanson (2010, 2012) argues, a similarly 'invidious' contextual variability infects our judgments involving 'a cause' or 'one of the causes', and failure to appreciate it has led subsequent theorizing astray. According to Swanson, the events we cite as causes function as 'representatives' of the causal chains leading them to the effect; as a result, whether a given causal claim is acceptable partly depends on what else has been cited as a cause (and hence used as a representative) in the context.

The acceptability of ERAs appears to exhibit the very same sort of variability. To illustrate, suppose Candice looks through a window and sees a room filled with smoke. In explaining what grounds she has to believe there's a fire you might say either of the following:

(10) That fact that she sees smoke is a reason for Candice to believe there's a fire.
(11) The fact that smoke is a sign of fire is a reason for Candice to believe there's a fire.

But it would be unacceptable to say any of the following:

(12) #The fact that she sees smoke is a reason for Candice to believe there's a fire, and so is the fact that smoke is a sign of fire.
(13) #The fact that she sees smoke and the fact that smoke is a sign of fire are both reasons for Candice to believe there's a fire.
(14) #Candice sees smoke and knows that smoke is a sign of fire, so she has two reasons to believe there's a fire.

ERAs like (12)-(14) seem guilty of 'double-counting'. What this shows − assuming the above pattern of judgments generalizes − is that the facts we usually cite as reasons are not *themselves* sources of epistemic support. Instead, they function communicatively as *representatives* of a larger cluster of facts that together (and only together) provide such support. What can be appropriately cited as a reason in a given context will thus partly depend on what else we've cited as a reason, since citing one fact as a reason − and hence as a representative of a given cluster − robs other facts belonging to that cluster of the representative role they might have otherwise played.

Contextualism about epistemic reasons

This reinforces the point that we should be wary of assigning undue significance to the facts we cite as reasons in using ERAs. It's doubtful that the sight of smoke is epistemically relevant in a way that the known connection between smoke and fire is not, and arguably it's only in virtue of both taken together that Sally has reason to believe there's a fire. The facts we usually cite as reasons don't *themselves* play a privileged epistemic role.

It is debatable whether the representative-like role facts cited as reasons is merely pragmatic or instead partly semantic. One might think (12)-(14) are defective solely in virtue of being pointless, irrelevant, misleading in virtue of generating a false implicature, etc., despite being true. Note, however, that there don't appear to be continuations of (12)-(14) in the relevant context that cancel or eliminate their infelicity, contrary to what one might expect if their defectiveness was purely pragmatic. Their defectiveness seems more akin to that involved in certain cases of presupposition failure, which is often treated as a partly semantic phenomenon.[11]

3 Reasons and explanation

The analogies between reasons talk and causal talk run deep. The similarities become less surprising once it is realized that claims about reasons and about causes are both *explanatory claims*, and essentially so. That is, they are claims the point of which is to explain *why* things (facts, states, events, whatever) are the way they are, rather than merely report *how* things are. This point of commonality is controversial, but not without precedent. Here is Strevens (2007), for example, on the explanatory nature of causal claims:

> the role of causal claims in science and everyday life is not to express basic metaphysical facts about causal connections, but rather to extract from the basic causal facts an understanding of how causal connections work together to bring about certain states of affairs. The question of the meaning of causal claims turns out to be less a question about metaphysics, then, and more a question about understanding or explanation . . . [it has] been an error – a major and pervasive error – for causal metaphysicians to have focused so great a part of their energies on causal claims.
>
> *(107)*

We think an analogous point holds with respect to ERAs, since reasons help to explain normative facts. Which normative facts do reasons help explain? In the introduction we noted that there have been three main proposals, and that our sympathies are with the third – that for r to be a reason (count noun) for S to A is for r to help explain why there is *reason* (mass noun) for S to A. To bring out the essentially explanatory nature of ERAs, it will help to say more.

Intuitively, count nouns denote (classes of) 'things' that are countable and hence can occur with cardinal numerals ('one', 'two', 'three'. . .) and take plural form (-s), while mass nouns denote 'stuff' that's not countable and hence do not occur with cardinal numerals and are generally singular or unmarked. There's a lot to be said about the mass/count distinction, but what matters most is that 'reason' in its normative sense is regularly used both ways. Superlative and comparative claims concerning what one has *most* or *more* reason to do, for example, are commonplace and obviously not equivalent to the corresponding superlative and comparative claims concerning what one has most or more *reasons* to do. The same goes for quantitative judgments concerning how *much* reason there is, whether there is *enough* reason, and so on. 'Reason' is hardly unique in being used as both a mass noun and a count noun; indeed, it is common for nouns in languages with mass-count syntax to be used both ways, and there are well-established patterns underlying such alternations.

This raises a question about the relationship between mass and count uses of 'reason'. Although space precludes detailed discussion, the relationship is plausibly the same as that which holds between mass and count uses of 'pleasure', 'sorrow', and 'light' (see Fogal 2016). Just as pleasures are sources of pleasure, sorrows are sources of sorrow, and lights are sources of light, so normative reasons are 'sources' (or grounds) of normative reason – i.e., they are sources of normative support. Importantly, however, there's an explanatory asymmetry involved: in each case the 'things' denoted by the count noun (pleasures, lights, reasons) are functionally defined in terms of the role they play in explaining the 'stuff' denoted by the mass noun (pleasure, light, reason), rather than vice versa. So just as it would be a mistake to analyze pleasure in terms of pleasures, or light in terms of lights, so it would be a mistake to analyze reason in terms of reasons. Instead, we should analyze normative reasons in terms of reason (i.e., normative support): reasons to φ are things which play a certain role in explaining why there is reason to φ. This view readily explains why (†) is intuitively equivalent to (††)-(†††):

(†)   The dark clouds approaching *are a reason* to think it will rain.
(††) The dark clouds approaching *give us reason* to think it will rain.
(†††) There are dark clouds approaching, and *that's why there is reason* to believe it'll rain.

Notice that the fact cited as *a reason* in (†) is cited as *that which explains why there is (mass-y) reason* in (††)-(†††). It's hence plausible to view claims about normative reasons as inherently explanatory. Given that ordinary explanatory claims are widely agreed to be context-sensitive, it's only to be expected that ERAs – and reasons ascriptions in general – are context-sensitive, and in much the same way.[12] We can profitably understand the question-sensitivity and information-sensitivity of ERAs as symptoms of this fact, since explanatory claims are sensitive to both.

None of this directly settles the matter concerning the precise nature of the context sensitivity at issue with ERAs, or how best to model it as part of a serious semantic theory. This remains an open question. Schaffer (2012) makes a similar point concerning the context-sensitivity of causal claims, concluding his survey by arguing not only that 'we do not yet have a clear understanding of context sensitivity as it arises for causal claims,' but also that this is 'everyone's problem' (55). We think the same is true of the context-sensitivity of ERAs and reasons claims more generally.

The good news is that there is a clear direction for research, at least on the assumption that the context-sensitivity of ERAs is an instance of the context-sensitivity of explanatory claims more generally: to better understand the semantics and pragmatics of the former, we need to better understand the semantics and pragmatics of the latter. Despite the controversies that have plagued debates about explanation and our explanatory practice over the past few decades, genuine progress has been made, and we should expect many of the lessons learned in the debates over causal and scientific explanation to carry over to normative explanation and locutions used to provide such explanations.[13] However, philosophers interested in explanation rarely try to provide semantically sophisticated analyses of explanatory terms themselves, or integrate their accounts into a larger semantic framework.[14] This is perhaps unsurprising – the information-sensitivity of explanatory claims is deep and pervasive, and so it is only to be expected that natural language evolved in such a way that sentences containing explanatory locutions are always evaluated relative to a question and/or an informational background, without there being any simple rules governing such relationships. This is in sharp contrast to the rules governing indexicals like 'I'. There nonetheless remains much interesting and important work to do by philosophers and linguists alike in better understanding our explanatory practice as well as the variety of different locutions we use in the service of providing explanations, such as ERAs.

4 Conclusion

While hard work remains, there is much to be said in favor of contextualism about ERAs. This matters. Given the variety of challenges confronting contextualism about knowledge ascriptions (cf. Stanley 2005; see also chapters 25, 27, and 25), one might be forgiven for thinking that contextualism in epistemology more generally is implausible. But there is a lot more to epistemic language than 'knows', and careful examination of the linguistic evidence in other cases – such as ERAs – encourages revival of the contextualist project. There are many important disanalogies between 'reason(s)' and 'know(s)'. This includes the fact that unlike 'knows', 'reason' is gradable when used as a mass noun (there can be more or less reason to φ) and is conceptually linked with a scale of normative weight or strength even when used as a count noun (some reasons are better/worse/stronger/weaker than others). There are also several avenues of possible support for contextualism about ERAs that lack obvious analogues in the case of 'knows', as the data in sections 2.3, 2.5, and 2.6 illustrate. So pessimism about contextualism about knowledge ascriptions does not warrant pessimism about contextualism about other epistemic terms.

Notes

1 Dretske (1970: 1017–1020) discusses pro tanto reasons talk; Dretske (1971) discusses overall reasons talk. Dretske (1972) contains a seminal discussion of contrastive statements in general, including ones concerning explanatory reasons.

2 These answers may only be partial, rather than full, and merely possible, rather than actual.

3 Thanks to Justin Snedegar for raising this issue.

4 Indeed, as Jonathan Shaheen (p.c.) notes, the hesitation marker 'well' is often used to signal that you are doing something other than providing a complete answer to a question.

5 One common way of drawing the distinction is in terms of the reasons there are for some agent S to A (objective reasons) and the reasons S has to A (subjective reasons). Although we grant that there is an important distinction in the vicinity, there are many complications concerning how such a distinction is to be understood, and how (if at all) it manifests itself in ordinary thought and talk. It seems doubtful the distinction is encoded in natural language – talk of reasons 'there are' and reasons 'had' is (for the most part) interchangeable. See Sæbø's (2009) for a semantic analysis of 'have'-sentences that predicts and explains their interchangeability with 'there is'-sentences. For a possible complication concerning this equivalence, see Broome (2013: 65).

6 Cf., e.g., Kolodny and MacFarlane (2010) and Dowell (2011). Another parallel with deontic modals arises if we consider the much-discussed mineshafts case, where a miner lacking full information seemingly acceptably utters 'I ought to block neither shaft,' and someone with more information says 'No, you ought to block shaft A.' Many philosophers assume the two disagree. A parallel claim might be made about Jane and Smith when they utter (4) and (5) – a parallel that would be strengthened if Smith's remark were prefaced by 'That's false . . .' This might suggest that ERAs are sensitive to the context of assessment (cf. MacFarlane 2014). The data surrounding cases of apparent disagreement is more complicated than commonly thought, however – see chapter 20.

7 For a recent overview, see Bronfman and Dowell (forthcoming).

8 Cf. DeRose (2009: 4–5).

9 It may help to imagine a continuation of (7) that explicitly cancels any implication of strength – e.g., 'though it's not a very good reason'. Cf. Schroeder (2007).

10 Jonathan Shaheen (p.c.) noted that this can be reinforced by finding a context involving members of P1 in which something like (9) is acceptable. Consider, for example, the following:

A: I know Jane smokes, unlike everybody else around here, but I really didn't think she'd get cancer.

B: Me neither. But as you know, Jane has gene X, and that is a reason to have thought she would get cancer.

11 For an introduction to presupposition (and presupposition failure), see Beaver and Geurts (2014).

12 This is after possible ambiguity is controlled for – see, e.g., Shaheen (forthcoming).

13 This is especially true if Skow (2016) is right that theories of explanation are best understood as theories of reasons why, given that normative reasons are just a special kind of reason why.
14 There are some exceptions – see, e.g., Nickel (2010).

References

Bach, K. 1994. "Conversational Impliciture." *Mind & Language* 9(2): 124–162.
Beaver, D. and Geurts, B. 2014. "Presupposition" in Zalta, Edward N. (ed.) *The Stanford Encyclopedia of Philosophy* (Winter 2014 Edition), URL = <http://plato.stanford.edu/archives/win2014/entries/presupposition/>.
Bromberger, S. 1966. "Why-Questions" in Colodny, R. (ed.) *Essays in Contemporary Science and Philosophy.* Pittsburgh: University of Pittsburgh Press.
Bronfman, A. and Dowell, J. Forthcoming. "The Language of Reasons and Ought" in Star, D. (ed.) *The Oxford Handbook of Reasons and Normativity.* Oxford: Oxford University Press.
Broome, J. 2004. "'Reasons'" in Wallace, R. J., Smith, M., Scheffler, S. and Pettit, P. (eds.) *Reason and Value: Themes from the Moral Philosophy of Joseph Raz.* Oxford: Oxford University Press.
Broome, J. 2013. *Rationality through Reasoning.* Oxford: Wiley Blackwell.
Cohen, S. 1986. "Knowledge and Context." *Journal of Philosophy* 83: 574–583.
DeRose, K. 2009. *The Case for Contextualism.* Oxford: Oxford University Press.
Dowell, J. L. 2011. "A Flexible Contextualist Account of Epistemic Modals." *Philosophers' Imprint* 11(14): 1–25.
Dretske, F. 1970. "Epistemic Operators." *Journal of Philosophy* 67: 1007–1023.
Dretske, F. 1971. "Conclusive Reasons." *Australasian Journal of Philosophy* 49: 1–22.
Dretske, F. 1972. "Contrastive Statements." *The Philosophical Review* 81: 411–437.
Finlay, S. 2014. *A Confusion of Tongues: A Theory of Normative Language.* Oxford: Oxford University Press.
Fogal, D. 2016. "Reasons, Reason, and Context" in Lord, E. and Maguire, B. (eds.) *Weighing Reasons.* Oxford: Oxford University Press.
Grice, H. P. 1989. *Studies in the Way of Words.* Cambridge, MA: Harvard University Press.
Hempel, C. 1965. "Aspects of Scientific Explanation" in *His Aspects of Scientific Explanation and Other Essays in the Philosophy of Science.* London: Collier-Macmillan.
Henning, T. 2014. "Normative Reasons Contextualism." *Philosophy and Phenomenological Research* 88: 593–624.
Horn, L. 1989. *A Natural History of Negation.* Chicago: University of Chicago Press.
Jenkins, C. S. 2008. "Romeo, René, and the Reasons Why: What Explanation Is." *Proceedings of the Aristotelian Society* 108: 61–84.
Kennedy, C. 2007. "Vagueness and Grammar: The Semantics of Relative and Absolute Gradable Adjectives." *Linguistics and Philosophy* 30: 1–45.
Kolodny, N. and MacFarlane, J. 2010. "Ifs and Oughts." *Journal of Philosophy* 107(3): 115–143.
Lewis, D. K. 1973. "Causation." *Journal of Philosophy* 70: 556–567.
MacFarlane, J. 2014. *Assessment Sensitivity Relative Truth and Its Applications.* Oxford: Oxford University Press.
Nickel, B. 2010. "How General Do Theories of Explanation Need to Be?" *Nous* 44(2): 305–328.
Putnam, H. 1982. "Why There Isn't a Ready-Made World." *Synthese* 51: 141–167.
Recanati, F. 2004. *Literal Meaning.* Cambridge: Cambridge University Press.
Roberts, C. 2012a. "Information Structure in Discourse: Towards an Integrated Formal Theory of Pragmatics." *Semantics & Pragmatics* 5(6): 1–69.
Roberts, C. 2012b. "Information Structure: Afterword." *Semantics and Pragmatics* 5(7): 1–19.
Rooth, M. 1992. "A Theory of Focus Interpretation." *Natural Language Semantics* 1: 75–116.
Rooth, M. 1996. "Focus" in Lappin, S. (ed.) *The Handbook of Contemporary Semantic Theory.* Oxford: Blackwell.
Sæbø, K. J. 2009. "Possession and Pertinence: The Meaning of 'Have'." *Natural Language Semantics* 17(4): 360–397.
Schaffer, J. 2012. "Causal Contextualism" in Blaauw, M. (ed.) *Contrastivism in Philosophy: New Perspectives.* London: Routledge.
Schroeder, M. 2007. *Slaves of the Passions.* Oxford: Oxford University Press.
Schroeder, M. 2008. "Having Reasons." *Philosophical Studies* 139: 57–71.
Schroeder, M. 2011. "What Does It Take to 'Have' a Reason?" in Reisner, A. and Steglich-Petersen, A. (eds.) *Reasons for Belief.* Cambridge: Cambridge University Press.

Contextualism about epistemic reasons

Schroeder, M. 2015. "Knowledge Is Belief for Sufficient (Subjective and Objective) Reason." *Oxford Studies in Epistemology* 5: 226–252.

Shaheen, J. Forthcoming. "Ambiguity and Explanation." *Inquiry*. DOI:10.1080/0020174X.2016.1175379.

Sinnott-Armstrong, W. 2008. "A Contrastivist Manifesto." *Social Epistemology* 22(3): 257–270.

Skow, B. 2016. *Reasons Why*. Oxford: Oxford University Press.

Snedegar, J. 2013a. "Negative Reason Existentials." *Thought* 2: 108–116.

Snedegar, J. 2013b. "Reason Claims and Contrastivism about Reasons." *Philosophical Studies* 166: 231–242.

Snedegar, J. 2015. "Contrastivism about Reasons and Oughts." *Philosophy Compass* 10(6): 379–388.

Snedegar, J. 2017. *Contrastive Reasons*. Oxford: Oxford University Press.

Sperber, D. and Wilson, D. 1986. *Relevance: Communication and Cognition*. Oxford: Blackwell.

Stanley, J. 2005. *Knowledge and Practical Interests*. Oxford: Oxford University Press.

Stine, G. 1976. "Skepticism, Relevant Alternatives, and Deductive Closure." *Philosophical Studies* 29: 249–261.

Strevens, M. 2007. "Mackie Remixed" in Campbell, J., O'Rourke, M. and Silverstein, H. (eds.) *Causation and Explanation*. Cambridge MA: The MIT Press.

Swanson, E. 2010. "Lessons from the Context-Sensitivity of Causal Talk." *Journal of Philosophy* 107(5): 221–242.

Swanson, E. 2012. "The Language of Causation" in Fara, D. and Russell, G. (eds.) *The Routledge Companion to the Philosophy of Language*. London and New York: Routledge.

van Fraassen, B. 1980. *The Scientific Image*. Oxford: Oxford University Press.

30

CONTEXTUALISM ABOUT EPISTEMIC MODALS

J. L. Dowell

Suppose I tell you, "Sobel must be in his office."[1] There are (at least) two distinct propositions I could be aiming to communicate. First, I could be remarking on his commitments, communicating, roughly, that every action open to him compatible with meeting those commitments locates him in his office. But, second, I could be remarking on what follows from the information available to me, roughly, that my information entails that he's in his office. A contextualist about modals holds that which proposition is expressed by a sentence containing a modal expression like "must" is a function of the context of utterance. A contextualist about modals in their epistemic use – illustrated by the second reading of my utterance – holds that the proposition expressed by such a use is likewise a function of the context of utterance. The canonical view of modal expressions in English, due primarily to Angelika Kratzer, is contextualist in this sense (Kratzer 1977, 1981, 1991a, 1991b, 2012; Lewis 1975). The core idea is that necessity modals function like universal quantifiers over possibilities, possibility modals like existential ones. In the case of epistemic modals, quantificational domains are restricted to worlds compatible with some body of information. Which body that is is determined by context.

The central focus here is consideration of some of the most powerful recent objections to contextualism about epistemic modals, as well as replies to those objections. The main conclusion is that none of these objections have the force proponents suggest. In the final section, I'll consider briefly what constraints, if any, acceptance of contextualism about epistemic modals places on one's theoretical options for understanding the nature of knowledge and the semantics of knowledge ascriptions, as well as how a contextualist about such ascriptions might borrow a strategy for defending contextualism about epistemic modals, pursued below.

Methodology and making sense of the data

The most frequently cited data for deciding between rival semantic hypotheses for modal expressions are competent speakers' truth-assessments of modal sentences in stipulated scenarios. (Sometimes I will refer to the combination of the sentence in a scenario as a "case".) A second sort of data sometimes appealed to, though with less frequency, are judgments about warrant. When an assessment is widely shared, it is standardly presumed to place a constraint on any semantics for such vocabulary: any semantic hypothesis must be such as to vindicate that assessment – that is, an utterance judged true must come out true and one judged warranted must come out reasonable.[2] For ease of exposition, call any assessment that rightly plays this evidential role "strong data".

One question about this practice is: how must scenarios be characterized in order for speakers' reactions to play this evidential role? Two constraints on these characterizations should be uncontroversial. First, they should be stated in such a way that it is reasonable to expect speakers' judgments to be reliable. (Call this "the reasonable reliability constraint".) If we assume that a semantic hypothesis must render a "true" judgment true, we should have good reason to think that that judgment is in fact correct. Second, a judgment's standing as strong data should be theoretically neutral in the sense that the grounds for according it that standing should not presuppose the falsity of any semantic hypothesis at issue. If a characterization is defective by the lights of a contending hypothesis, we should not require that hypothesis to vindicate speakers' assessments. (Of course, if such assessments are widespread, each contending hypothesis should fit with a plausible *explanation* of this fact, even if not a vindicating explanation.) Call this "the neutrality constraint". As we'll see, the failure of each of the challenges to contextualism we'll consider here stems from a failure to meet these constraints on characterizations.

Flexible contextualism and relativism about epistemic modals

In a moment, we'll consider an example of the kind of case thought by many to require revisions to the canonical contextualist view (Lennertz 2014; MacFarlane 2015; Moss 2015; von Fintel and Gillies 2011). But first a similar, warm-up case to help clarify the first of these constraints on characterizations.

Coffee Shop-That

Imagine you're in a coffee shop and overhear the following conversation taking place behind you.

George: Hey! Look! It's Joe! What's he doing here? I thought he was in China!
Sally: That's not Joe. He looks like Joe in profile, but wait until he fully turns around. See?
George: You're right; that's not Joe.

Coffee Shop-That is a perfectly ordinary sort of conversation to overhear; there is nothing odd or marked about any of the utterances that make it up. Here are two questions about it. First, what propositions are in its Common Ground, the set of propositions presumed to be true for the purposes of conversation? If this is all that one knows about the conversation, it is not at all clear. Second, what are the most salient discourse referents, objects made salient in the context that are available to be referred to by a demonstrative, like "that"? This, too, is unclear from the characterization of the case.

A few observations about this case are relevant for our purposes. First, in our position as eavesdroppers, we have sufficient information about the conversation to tell that it sounds like perfectly ordinary, intelligible English. But, second, given how little we know of the discourse context, especially which is the most salient discourse referent, we're unable to assess what either Sally or George has said for its reasonableness or truth. This means that, if we find ourselves with such judgments, they are not strong data. The problem here is precisely that the reasonable reliability constraint is not met. Given how underdescribed the case is, we're unable to tell whether George's original assertion, that that is Joe, is warranted, or whether Sally's challenge is, or whether George is right to retract. Interestingly, though, despite this, we'd be surprised to learn that both George and Sally are quite mistaken by the end of the conversation – we expect, at the very least, the presence of someone who looks at least a bit like, but isn't, their friend Joe.

What explains this pattern of reactions? Here are a few hypotheses:

(i) We expect interlocutors to be rational and cooperative. So, we incline towards charity, i.e. towards available interpretations that are at least reasonable and, ideally, both reasonable and true.

(ii) In defective contexts, when it is not clear what a speaker has said, we decide between available interpretations, when we can, by maximizing reasonableness, assuming cooperation.

(iii) For similar reasons, we assume, where we can, circumstances of evaluation that maximize truth.

For familiar, Gricean reasons, these hypotheses are independently plausible. Moreover, together, they explain our pattern. What's going on is this: first, because we assume interlocutors are rational and cooperative, we'd be surprised to learn that there is no person salient to Sally and George who resembles their acquaintance, Joe. So, we decide between possible discourse contexts for their conversation by assuming a context that has a discourse referent required to maximize reasonableness. We may even go farther – we may find ourselves assuming circumstances of evaluation that maximize truth. BUT, since we can be wrong about which possible discourse context and circumstances of evaluation are the actual ones, the strength of our opinion does *not* make our assessments reasonably reliable and so not strong data for hypotheses about the semantics of demonstratives. (If that isn't already clear, imagine turning around only to find nothing saliently animate to serve as an even prima facie eligible discourse reference for "that". Since we can't rule out that this is so of George's and Sally's actual context and circumstances, we're not in a position to judge the reasonableness or truth of what they each say.)

Compare this case with the case MacFarlane offers as his most powerful motivation for relativism about epistemic modals (MacFarlane 2014, chapter 10). (Call this case *Coffee Shop-Might*.)

> Suppose you are standing in a coffee line, and you overhear Sally and George discussing a mutual acquaintance, Joe:

> *Sally:* Joe might be in China. I didn't see him today.
> *George:* No, he can't be in China. He doesn't have his visa yet.
> *Sally:* Oh, really? Then I guess I was wrong.
> (MacFarlane 2014: 240)

Below, I'll sketch MacFarlane's grounds for thinking this case poses an insurmountable challenge to contextualism. But first I'll offer a few observations about the case that are neutral with respect to the contending hypotheses he aims for it to test. Like *Coffee Shop-That*, *Coffee Shop-Might* is a perfectly ordinary conversation, with nothing odd or marked about any of its utterances. Here, too, though, it's not clear which propositions make up the conversation's Common Ground. Do Sally and George know Joe equally well – and does each presuppose that each does? Or is it presupposed that one of them knows Joe better, is in more frequent contact with him, than the other? Or perhaps Sally and George each know Joe, but barely knows the other, and nothing is commonly presupposed about how much each knows about Joe's whereabouts. These are amongst the possible Common Grounds compatible with MacFarlane's characterization of his case. Given that the Common Ground is an important interpretive resource for determining the content of context-sensitive expressions, we can already see why MacFarlane's case does not yet meet the neutrality constraint: one contending hypothesis is contextualism about modals, and here (as will become clear shortly) MacFarlane's case does not include sufficient information to decide between possible contextualist readings. It is question-begging at best to presuppose that a theory must vindicate judgments about a case that are defective by the lights of that theory.

Soon we'll see what difference this failure to supply a Common Ground makes to what it's reasonable to conclude from his example. But first we need a bit more about contextualism on the table so we can see what lesson MacFarlane himself draws from it. On my view, as on Kratzer's, epistemic modals such as "might" and "must" function as quantifiers over a restricted domain of possibilities:[3] a claim of the form 'Might φ' is true just in case at least one possibility in the domain is a φ-possibility, whereas 'must φ' is true just in case every one is. That domain gets restricted by the modal base, f, a function supplied by the context, that takes a world of evaluation w and delivers a set of worlds compatible with a body of information, where which body of information is selected is a function of the value for $f(w)$. A bit more formally,

$$[\text{might } \varphi]^{f,w} = 1 \text{ iff } \exists w': w' \in \cap f(w): [\varphi]^{f,w'} = 1$$
$$[\text{must } \varphi]^{f,w} = 1 \text{ iff } \forall w': w' \in \cap f(w): [\varphi]^{f,w'} = 1$$

According to MacFarlane, Coffee Shop-Might poses a serious challenge to contextualism because there is no single value for f the context could select that would fit with all of our judgments about the case. As he writes,

> It seems that George is contradicting Sally and rejecting her claim. It also seems that, having learned something from George, Sally concedes that she was wrong. Finally, it seems appropriate for her to retract her original claim, rather than continuing to stand by it.
>
> If all of this is right, then any view about epistemic modals must have answers to the following questions:
>
> *Warrant Question:* On what basis did Sally take herself to be warranted in making her first claim?
>
> *Rejection Question:* On what basis did George take himself to be warranted in rejecting Sally's claim as incorrect?
>
> *Retraction Question:* On what basis did Sally concede that she was wrong, after George's intervention? What did she learn from George's remark that made her retract her original claim?
>
> <div align="right">(<i>MacFarlane 2014: 240–241</i>)</div>

MacFarlane argues that there is no single body of information that context could select in this case to provide answers to these questions that fit with the judgments he attributes to speakers. A view that held that the relevant value for f is *the information the speaker has at the time of her utterance in w*, could provide a plausible answer to the Warrant Question, but not to the Rejection and Retraction Questions. (George, for example, shouldn't reject what Sally has said, if that is the value for f that context selects.) To answer those questions, suppose instead the contextualist holds that context selects for f the information had by some larger group in w, for example, that of the conversational participants or of those participants and anyone listening in on that conversation (such as yourself eavesdropping in the coffee shop). Though such a reading would provide answers to the Rejection and Retraction Questions that fit with the judgments MacFarlane attributes to speakers, it could not provide such an answer to the Warrant Question. (Sally would not be warranted in asserting that Joe's being in China is compatible with what's known together by herself and anyone eavesdropping on her conversation. After all, she's not in a position to know what they know.) Only a relativist view, MacFarlane reasons, that allows multiple bodies of information to be relevant to the assessment of a single utterance, could provide plausible answers to these questions.[4] Since our concern is the standing of the case as he describes it to pose a real challenge to contextualism, the details of his positive view need not concern us. Suffice it to say that there have been a number of revisions to the canonical view motivated by the assumption that cases like this one put real pressure on it.[5]

To see that the case generates no such pressure, return again to the observation that the case provides no real information about what's in the conversation's Common Ground. The case as described is compatible with a number of different possible Common Grounds, and which one is thought to be in play in Coffee Shop-Might makes a difference to our judgments. To see this, consider more carefully three different ways of filling out that case:

> *Characterization 1*: Sally and George know Joe equally well (communicate with him equally often, etc.) and know that they do. Both know and know that the other knows that Joe is planning on traveling to China soon. Propositions representing these facts, then, are in the Common Ground. Further features of the case not in the Common Ground: George knows something Sally doesn't; namely, that Joe has had unusual trouble obtaining his visa and hasn't received it yet.
>
> *Judgments*: Common speaker judgments about Coffee Shop-Might under this characterization include: (i) Everyone speaks reasonably. (ii) What George has said is true. (iii) It's at least fine, perhaps good, for Sally to retract.
>
> *Characterization 2*: George knows Joe better than Sally and both Sally and George know this (George communicates much more frequently with Joe than Sally). Propositions representing these facts, then, are in the Common Ground. Further features of the case not in the Common Ground: as before, George knows something Sally doesn't; namely, that Joe has had unusual trouble obtaining his visa and hasn't received it yet.
>
> *Judgments*: (i) Sally speaks less reasonably than in CG1. (ii) As before, George speaks reasonably. (iii) It's good for Sally to retract.
>
> *Characterization 3*: Sally knows Joe better than George and both Sally and George know this (Sally communicates much more frequently with Joe than George). Propositions representing these facts, then, are in the Common Ground. Further features of the case not in the Common Ground: Sally knows something George doesn't—that Joe has gotten his visa.
>
> *Judgments*: (i) Sally speaks reasonably. (ii) George speaks less reasonably than he does in either of the first two characterizations of the case. (iii) What George said is false (or certainly not clearly true). (iv) Sally's retraction is odd.

What is going on here? According to the flexible contextualist view I have defended, epistemic modals are context-sensitive in the way that Kaplan suggests demonstratives are (Dowell 2011). What is referred to by the use of a demonstrative, he suggests, is partly a function of speaker's intentions, partly a function of how the world is. Thus, in saying "that is the greatest philosopher of the twentieth century", I may mistakenly say that Spiro Agnew is, by indicating a spot in which it is known that a portrait of Rudolph Carnap habitually resides, unbeknownst to me recently replaced by one of Agnew (Kaplan 1989a, 1989b).

Similarly, which proposition a speaker expresses in using a sentence containing an epistemic modal depends upon which body of information is selected as a function of $f(w)$. My view,

Contextualism about epistemic modals

flexible contextualism, holds that the value for *f*, roughly, a property of a body of information, is determined by the speaker's publicly manifestable intentions. These are intentions which, in the non-defective case, context is able to manifest to a reasonable audience.[6] (For example, if context manifests the speaker's intention to make a claim about what's possible, given just her own information at a certain time, the value for *f* will, taking *w* as an argument, deliver the set of worlds compatible with the body of information that has that property in *w*.)

The Common Ground is an important interpretive resource. The point is a familiar one. Stalnaker's Common Ground is now part of the linguist's standard toolkit for explaining how linguistic communication and coordination are possible.[7] Flexible contextualism borrows this tool for the purposes of explaining how speakers are able to manifest their domain-determining intentions to a reasonable audience. As we saw above, which possible Common Ground is the one in play for the conversation in Coffee Shop-Might makes a difference to our judgments about the reasonability of the utterances that make it up. And which additional facts, perhaps as unknown circumstances in which the conversation takes place, are assumed to be part of the characterization of the scenario, makes a difference to our judgments about which utterances express truths.

This ignorance means that, as in the case of Coffee Shop-That, we're unable to correctly assess what either Sally or George has said for its reasonableness or truth. And that means that, here, too, if we find ourselves with such judgments, for example, the judgments MacFarlane assumes, they are not strong data. The problem here is precisely that the reasonable reliability constraint is not met. Given how underdescribed the case is, given, for example, that we are not in a position to rule out that their conversation's Common Ground is CG3, we're not in a position to assess what each of them has said for reasonability or truth. This means that vindicating the judgments MacFarlane attributes to respondents in cases such as the original, underdescribed Coffee Shop-Might, is not a constraint on the plausibility of a semantic theory, contrary to what many have assumed.[8]

Many though, have felt the force of MacFarlane's arguments and so presumably share his judgments in the underdescribed case. What explains this? Drawing on consideration of Coffee Shop-That, the following hypotheses suggest themselves:

(i) In our position as eavesdroppers, we're able to track the conversation between George and Sally well enough to tell that it sounds like perfectly ordinary, intelligible English.

(ii) But, given how little we know of the discourse context, especially what's in the Common Ground, we're not in a position to reasonably assess what either Sally or George has said for its warrant or truth.

(iii) However, as Grice has taught us, we expect interlocutors to be rational and cooperative. So we incline towards charity, i.e. towards available interpretations that are at least reasonable and, ideally, both reasonable and true.

(iv) In defective contexts, when it is not clear what a speaker has said, we decide between available interpretations, between possible contexts, compatible with what we know, when we can, by assuming a context that maximizes reasonableness, assuming cooperation.

(v) Similarly, we assume, where we can, circumstances of evaluation that maximize truth.

(vi) Some ways of filling in the Common Ground for MacFarlane's underdescribed case generates the judgments he presumes. For example, in Characterization 1, above, Sally is reasonable to assume that Joe's being in China is compatible with what they together know, given what's in the Common Ground. But she's wrong about this. So, she's reasonable to retract, and what George has said is true. Given that there is a way of filling out MacFarlane's underdescribed case so as to maximize reasonableness and truth, it is no surprise that some respondents charitably presuppose such a conversational context.

393

This fully explains the data within the confines of the canonical view, while drawing only on independently well-motivated, Gricean resources.[9]

Non-factualist theories

In a series of recent papers, Seth Yalcin argues for a view he calls "Non-factualism" about epistemic modals. There are a number of different ways of spelling out the details of a Non-factualist proposal which don't concern us. The central idea is that the function of unembedded epistemic modal statements is not to describe how things are. If this is correct, then the canonical contextualist view is not. Our focus is on so-called "epistemic contradictions", the existence of which Yalcin regards as establishing this. On this, he writes:

Notice that the following sound[s] awful.

(1)   #It's raining and it might not be raining.

Let us call sentences like [this one] – sentences of the . . . form $[\varphi \wedge \Diamond \sim \varphi]$ . . . epistemic contradictions. Why do epistemic contradictions like (1) . . . sound awful?

   At first glance, a descriptivist-friendly explanation seems easy enough. A descriptivist might try saying that [(1)] sound[s] terrible because, thanks to the semantics of epistemic modals, [it] truth-conditionally entail[s]

(3)   #It's raining and I don't know it's raining

relative to context. Obviously, (3) is Moorean-paradoxical. Therefore, says the descriptivist, (1) . . . should be pragmatically defective in whatever way (3) is defective . . .

   The situation is not so simple, however. (1) . . . [is] more than merely pragmatically defective. The conjuncts [in (1)] are incompatible in a more robust sense. We can see this when we attempt to embed these conjunctions into larger constructions. Consider, for instance, the [imperative]:

(4)   #Suppose it's raining and it might not be raining.

[(4)] sounds incoherent and self-defeating. [In contrast to] . . .

(6)   Suppose it's raining and I don't know it's raining.

. . . Or, again, epistemic contradictions never sound acceptable in the antecedent position of an indicative conditional:

(7)   #If it's raining and it might not be raining, then . . .

Conditionals that begin in this way seem beyond repair. But Moorean paradoxical sentences are acceptable in this environment . . .[10]

For ease of exposition, I'll sometimes call the judgments Yalcin reports about these sentences as characterized above "Yalcin judgments". If Yalcin is right about the data, then it's hard to see how a Kratzer-style contextualist theory could account for them. Recall that such a view holds

Contextualism about epistemic modals

that might-claims are true or false depending upon whether their prejacents are compatible with a salient body of information. So, such a contextualist should allow that there should be some points of evaluation at which sentences such as (1) are true, namely, whenever it's not raining is compatible with the contextually determined body of information and "it's raining" is true, given the circumstances of evaluation.

Fortunately, it's easy to see that the data are not as Yalcin suggests. Suppose we grant Yalcin that initial, ordinary speaker reactions to these sentences are as described. Still, we have no grounds for thinking those judgments meet the reasonable reliability requirement. In addition, as I'll show, we have positive reason to think they do not meet the neutrality requirement. To see that they don't meet the first, recall that the reasonable reliability requirement holds that, in order to constitute strong data, speaker judgments must be reasonably expected to be reliable. That is because, to be strong data, those judgments must be such that a theory need vindicate them. But a theory needn't vindicate unreliable judgments: if a case is characterized in such a way that there is no reason to think speakers are in a position to properly assess the sentences at issue along the relevant dimension (truth, warrant, or felicity, for example), then we have no reason to treat those assessments as ones a theory need vindicate. In Yalcin's discussion of these sentences here and elsewhere, we have no characterization of a case at all: We have no context to help provide clues as to which proposition might be expressed, and we have no circumstances of evaluation against which to assess possible truth. The sole basis for our reactions is the sentences themselves or, in the case of (7), a partial sentence. So, it would be useful for assessing what sort of evidential weight it is reasonable to assign the reactions Yalcin reports to consider examples of such 'contradictions' in a filled out case and see whether we still have those reactions. Here's one:

Raincoat

Imagine a parent who asks his young daughter to bring her raincoat to school.

Dad: "Melina, would you please bring your raincoat today?"
Melina: "But it's not raining! I don't want to bring my raincoat!"
Dad: "Yes, but look at the sky. It might rain, so you should bring your raincoat."
Melina: "Ugh! But suppose it *doesn't* rain! Then I'll have carried my raincoat for nothing! What a pain!"
Dad: **"Well, suppose it doesn't, but might rain**. In that case, you should still bring your raincoat as a precaution."

The father's supposition here is not only not contradictory; it is perfectly clear. Anyone who has engaged in cost-benefit reasoning under conditions of uncertainty is familiar with considering scenarios of just this kind: scenarios in which one's information is compatible with a possibility that turns out not to be actual.

To avoid any appearance that the above phenomena is limited to cases concerning uncertainty about the future and that corresponding suppositions about the present are contradictory, we can consider a similar case about the present:

Windowless office

Drone 1: "I'm off to lunch! Hmmm . . . I've got my good shoes on – I wonder whether it's raining."

Drone 2: "Well, look. Either it's raining or it isn't. If it isn't, but it might be raining, you should bring your umbrella just in case. And if it is raining, you definitely want your umbrella."

Drone 1: "Yes, good point."

What Drone 2 says here sounds fine. This is explained by "it isn't, but might be raining . . ." denoting just the sort of proposition a flexible, Kratzer-style contextualist predicts: a proposition that is true at a point of evaluation just in case it is not raining at the world, time, and place of evaluation, but it's raining is compatible with the information had by Drones 1 and 2 together.

That the provision of a context of utterance causes our judgments to switch is evidence that the judgments Yalcin reports in his underdescribed case are not reasonably treated as reliable. But, the lack of any characterization of a point of evaluation in Yalcin's original cases suffice by itself to settle the point: it is agreed on all sides that sentences are only true or false relative to points of evaluation. Without the specification of a point of evaluation against which to assess truth, no speaker, regardless of how competent or confident of their judgment, is in a position to work out the truth of a sentence. So, Yalcin judgments are not strong data.

This complete lack of any contextual set up also suffices to show that the cases as described do not meet the neutrality constraint: in order for those cases to be non-defective by the lights of the contending, contextualist theory, they must be characterized in sufficient detail that speakers are in a position to identify and accurately assess the proposition expressed by the lights of that theory. This is an additional reason to think that the Yalcin judgments are not strong data.

Finally, though here is not the place to press the point, it is hard to see how to explain the felicity of the sentences in *Raincoat* and *Windowless Office* within the framework of a semantic theory, such as Yalcin's, designed to predict that they are contradictory.[11]

Knowledge-attributions and the nature of knowledge

The MacFarlane and Yalcin challenge cases to contextualism are arguably the most widely discussed and influential in recent literature on epistemic modals. Suppose we conclude from their failure to pose genuine challenges that a Kratzer-style contextualist account of modal expressions, at least in their epistemic uses, still deserves its canonical status. Here I consider two questions that arise if we accept this conclusion. First, what, if any, constraints does its acceptance place on an account of the nature of knowledge or the semantics of knowledge-attributions? Second, might the above strategy for responding to MacFarlane's case against contextualism about epistemic modals be borrowed to develop a reply to his case against contextualism about knowledge-attributions?

Taking these questions in order, the answer to the first seems to be "no obvious, direct constraints". If there are any, they would require independently motivated auxiliary assumptions to generate. To see this, consider first the relationship between theories about the nature of knowledge and semantic theories for knowledge-attributions. It may well be that sentences of the form <S knows that p> have truth-conditions that vary in some way with the context of utterance – or, for that matter, they may be invariant in the propositions they express, but receive different truth-values relative to indices that are more finely individuated than worlds, for example, worlds and information, or worlds and practical interests. Any such shifty semantics for knowledge-attributions is in principle compatible with the idea that "knowledge" as used by traditional epistemologists has a special sense, perhaps one tied to the use of that word in seminar rooms. On such a view, that use would invariably track a single cognitive state (or cognitive state–world relation), one whose nature the epistemologist aims to understand.

Something analogous is true of the relation between contextualism about epistemic modals (or other alleged sources of truth-shiftiness, such as relativism) and the semantics of knowledge-attributions. In principle, contextualism about epistemic modals is compatible with an invariant-ist semantics for such attributions, one which does not hold that indices that determine truth are more fine-grained than worlds (or perhaps situations). That said, though, one might think that the two semantic theories constrain each other; what one thinks about the semantics of attri-butions will place constraints on what one can say about the semantics of modals, or vice versa. Here I explore one such possible constraint.

One place some philosophers see the two as intersecting is in giving a full semantics for sen-tences of the form <I know that P and it might be that not-P>. As John Hawthorne (2012) writes,

> Claims of the form 'I know P and it might be that not-P' tend to sound odd. One natural explanation of this oddity is that the conjuncts are semantically incompatible: in its core epistemic use, 'Might P' is true in a speaker's mouth only if the speaker does not know that not-P.
>
> *(493)*

If Hawthorne is right, then a semantics for knowledge-attributions constrain a semantics for epistemic modals by requiring that the body of information to which their truth is sensitive include the speaker's knowledge.

Unfortunately, it's not clear what Hawthorne means by 'core epistemic use',[12] though it is clear what role he takes that phrase to play. He appears to concede that there are some clear, epistemic uses of "it might be that P" where the relevant body of information does not include the speaker's.[13] In any case, as there clearly are such cases, the concession is needed.[14] von Fintel and Gillies (2008) discuss one such case.

Mastermind

Pascal and Mordecai are playing Mastermind. Pascal is to guess the number and type of pieces Mordecai has hidden, and Mordecai has begun giving him hints.

Pascal: "There might be two reds."
Mordecai: "Yes. There might be."[15]

What Mordecai says here is fine, even if he knows that he has hidden only one red piece. Flex-ible contextualism can easily explain this speaker-exclusion: in the context of a guessing game, communicating information about what's possible given one's own information would defeat the purpose. This makes it clear that Mordecai is adopting Pascal's epistemic perspective in giving him hints. Here he is affirming that it is compatible with the information Pascal has that two reds are hidden.[16]

In calling such cases "non-core epistemic uses", Hawthorne treats them as providing no evi-dence against his central thesis. The trouble is that, if the incompatibility is genuinely semantic, there should be no such cases or, at any rate, it should be explained how speaker-exclusion is communicated pragmatically, though the semantics are speaker-inclusive. In any case, cases such as *Mastermind* suggest that there is no direct route from the prima facie oddness of <I know that p, but it might be that not-P> to speaker-inclusion as a constraint on a semantics for epistemic modals. As we've seen from the above methodological observations and consideration of *Coffee*

Shop-Might, establishing such a constraint requires an examination speakers' reactions to a full range of fleshed out, non-defective cases.

Returning very briefly now to our second question: Might the above strategy for explaining MacFarlane's eavesdropper cases suggest a contextualist-friendly strategy for responding to his retraction challenge cases to contextualism about knowledge-attributions?[17] Though it's not clear to me that such a strategy would ultimately be successful, it's clear enough what a sketch of such a strategy would look like. To be successful, such a contextualist would need to develop an independently motivated account of how contexts supply the needed value or values to generate propositions expressed at contexts of utterance.[18] They would then need to show that, in non-defective versions of those retraction cases, the propositions shown to be expressed on those independent grounds fit with widespread speaker truth- and warrant-assessments of the relevant utterances. This would be no quick task, in part because such a contextualist should insist at least on the provision of a minimal Common Ground in order for a case to meet the reasonable reliability constraint, while it is not clear how to do this from MacFarlane's discussion of the retraction cases in his (2014) or the (2005) discussion the (2014) discussion directs his reader to. Multiple versions of those cases, with different Common Grounds supplied, would need to be considered.

Notes

1 Thanks to Nathan Cockram, Jonathan Ichikawa, Bryan Pickel, and Brian Rabern for discussion.
2 For this assumption see Egan (2007), Egan, Hawthorne, and Weatherson (2005), Egan and Weatherson in their introduction to their (2011) volume, Lennertz (2014), MacFarlane (2011, 2015), Moss (2015), von Fintel and Gillies (2008, 2011), and Yalcin (2007, 2011). For brief discussions of the method itself, see Mathewson (2004) and Portner (2005).
3 To keep the discussion simple, I focus on just these two epistemic modal expressions, though there are others, such as probability operators, that any full treatment needs to account for.
4 See MacFarlane (2014: chapter 10) for details.
5 See, for example, Egan (2007), von Fintel and Gillies (2011), and Moss (2015). For discussion of a similar case without a positive proposal, see Lennertz (2014).
6 For more on this publicity constraint on contexts, see Dowell (2011, 2013).
7 See, for example, Stalnaker (1999).
8 For discussion in addition to MacFarlane (2011, 2015), see Egan (2007), von Fintel and Gillies (2011), Egan, Hawthorne, and Weatherson (2005), and Lennertz (2014). See also Moss (2015), who alludes to some of these discussions as grounds for rejecting truth-conditional theories of epistemic modals.
9 Though there is not space here to fully press the point, a nice feature of this account is that these resources suffice also to explain the Knobe and Yalcin's (2014) data, which empirically confirm an earlier observation from Dowell (2011) that speaker reactions in eavesdropper cases are not as MacFarlane (2011, 2014) and others (Egan 2007) have assumed, but are instead split and indecisive. For a detailed account of how this pattern is easily explained by flexible contextualism with the Gricean resources already on the table, see Dowell (2011).
10 (2011) pp. 300–301. See also his (2007) pp. 464–5.
11 Although the Yalcin judgments are not strong data, if the judgments he reports to the contextless sentences are widespread and firm, there is still a pattern to be explained. For an such an explanation in the framework of a dynamic semantics, see Stojnic, manuscript. For a contextualist explanation, see Roberts, manuscript. Finally, for a contextualist explanation that draws on Stojnic's work, see Dowell, manuscript.
12 He appears to concede this at (2012) p. 495.
13 Though it's not entirely clear, he appears to concede this on (2012) pp. 494–5.
14 See, for example, the Mordecai example from von Fintel and Gillies (2008) p. 90 and the treasure hunt example from Dowell (2011) pp. 21–2.
15 (2008) p. 90.
16 For further discussion of such cases, see Dowell (2011) p. 21.
17 MacFarlane (2005, 2014).

Contextualism about epistemic modals

18 To do this they might, for example, draw on my account of how modal propositions get determined, sketched in Dowell (2011, 2013).

References

Dowell, J. L. (2011), 'A Flexible Contextualist Account of Epistemic Modals', in *Philosophers' Imprint* 11(14): 1–25.

Dowell, J. L. (2013), 'Flexible Contextualism about Deontic Modals: A Puzzle about Information-sensitivity', in *Inquiry* 56: 2–3, 149–178.

Dowell, J. L. Manuscript. 'The Linguistic Case for Expressivism Reconsidered'.

Egan, A. (2007), 'Epistemic Modals, Relativism, and Assertion', in *Philosophical Studies* 113(1): 1–22.

Egan, A. (2011), 'Relativism about Epistemic Modals', in *A Companion to Relativism*, ed. S. D. Hales, 219–241. Malden, MA: Wiley-Blackwell.

Egan, A., J. Hawthorne and B. Weatherson. (2005), 'Epistemic Modals in Context', in *Contextualism in Philosophy*, eds. G. Preyer and G. Peter, 131–169. New York: Oxford University Press.

Egan, A. and B. Weatherson (eds.) (2011). *Epistemic Modality*. Oxford: Oxford University Press.

von Fintel, K. and A. Gillies. (2008), 'CIA Leaks', in *Philosophical Review* 117: 77–98.

von Fintel, K. and A. Gillies. (2011), '"Might" Made Right', in *Epistemic Modality*, eds. B. Weatherson and A. Egan, 108–130. Oxford: Oxford University Press.

Hawthorne, J. (2012), 'Knowledge and Epistemic Necessity', in *Philosophical Studies* 158: 493–501.

Kaplan, D. (1989a), 'Demonstratives: An Essay on the Semantics, Logic, Metaphysics, and Epistemology of Demonstratives and Other Indexicals', in *Themes from Kaplan*, eds. J. Almog, J. Perry, and H. Wettstein, 481–563. Oxford: Oxford University Press.

Kaplan, D. (1989b), 'Afterthoughts', in *Themes from Kaplan*, eds. J. Almog, J. Perry, and H. Wettstein, 481–563. Oxford: Oxford University Press.

Knobe, J. and S. Yalcin. (2014), 'Epistemic Modals and Context', in *Semantics and Pragmatics* 7(10): 1–21.

Kratzer, A. (1977), 'What "Must" and "Can" Must and Can Mean', in *Linguistics and Philosophy* 1(3): 337–355.

Kratzer, A. (1981), 'The Notional Category of Modality', in *Words, Worlds, and Contexts*, eds. H. Eikmeyer and H. Rieser, 38–74. Berlin/Boston: de Gruyter.

Kratzer, A. (1991a), 'Modality', in *Semantics: An International Handbook of Contemporary Research*, eds. A. von Stechow and D. Wunderlich, 639–650. Berlin/Boston: de Gruyter.

Kratzer, A. (1991b), 'Conditionals', in *Semantics: An International Handbook of Contemporary Research*, eds. A. von Stechow and D. Wunderlich, 651–656. Berlin/Boston: de Gruyter.

Kratzer, A. (2012), *Modals and Conditionals: New and Revised Perspectives*. Oxford: Oxford University Press.

Lennertz, B. (2014), 'Simple Contextualism about Epistemic Modals is Incorrect', in *Thought: A Journal of Philosophy* 3(4): 252–262.

Lewis, D. (1975), 'Adverbs of Quantification', in *Formal Semantics of Natural Language*, ed. E. L. Keenan, 3–15. Cambridge: Cambridge University Press.

MacFarlane, J. (2005), 'The Assessment-sensitivity of Knowledge-attributions', in *Oxford Studies in Epistemology*, eds. T. Gender Szabo and J. Hawthorne, 1: 197–234. Oxford: Oxford University Press.

MacFarlane, J. (2011), 'Epistemic Modals Are Assessment-sensitive', in *Epistemic Modality*, eds. B. Weatherson and A. Egan, 108–130. Oxford: Oxford University Press.

MacFarlane, J. (2014), *Assessment Sensitivity*. Oxford: Oxford University Press.

Matthewson, L. (2004), "On the Methodology of Semantic Fieldwork", in *International Journal of American Linguistics*, 70(4): 369–415.

Moss, S. (2015), 'On the Semantics and Pragmatics of Epistemic Vocabulary', in *Semantics and Pragmatics* 8: 1–81.

Portner, P. (2005), *What Is Meaning? Fundamentals of Formal Semantics*. Malden, MA: Blackwell.

Roberts, C. Manuscript. 'The Character of Epistemic Modality'.

Stalnaker, R. (1999), 'Assertion', in *Context and Content*, 78–95. Oxford: Oxford University Press.

Stojnic, U. Manuscript. 'Content in a Dynamic Context'.

Yalcin, S. (2007), 'Epistemic Modals', in *Mind* 116(464): 983–1026.

Yalcin, S. (2011), 'Nonfactualism about Epistemic Modality', in *Epistemic Modality*, eds. B. Weatherson and A. Egan, 295–332. Oxford: Oxford University Press.

31
CONTEXTUALISM ABOUT BELIEF ASCRIPTIONS

Roger Clarke

This chapter does two main things by way of discussing contextualism about belief ascriptions: on one hand, I will survey a range of different accounts of belief recently defended in print; on the other, I will sketch some ways of arguing for contextualism about belief ascriptions. Most of the accounts of belief I'll survey do not entail b-contextualism,[1] but instead take belief to be situation-sensitive in one or another way. One of the lines of argument I'll sketch, then, aims to motivate b-contextualism by appeal to belief's situation sensitivity.

The first part of the chapter, then, is given over to a survey of situation-sensitive accounts of belief. Section 1 sets up a problem all of these views aim to solve, and sections 2–5 discuss four different types of situation-sensitivity. Few of the philosophers whose views are covered here explicitly consider the question of b-contextualism – that is, sensitivity of belief ascriptions to the ascriber's context, rather than sensitivity of belief to the believer's situation – and none of them explicitly defend b-contextualism.[2] In section 6, I supply a sketch of an argument that any of these views of belief as situation-sensitive gives motivation for adopting b-contextualism as well.

The final two sections get at b-contextualism more directly. First, section 7 outlines Eric Schwitzgebel's phenomenal, dispositional account of belief. Unlike the views surveyed in in sections 2–5, this is an explicitly b-contextualist account.

Finally, I offer a belief-analogue of a familiar sort of argument for k-contextualism: case pairs. Section 8 describes a single agent whom one speaker correctly describes as believing and another speaker correctly describes as not believing a proposition p.

1 Full and partial belief: a lottery problem

All of the situation-sensitive accounts of belief we are about to encounter are motivated at least in part[3] by the problem of reconciling full belief (outright belief or belief *simpliciter*) with partial belief (degree of belief or credence). It's natural to think the two notions of belief relate in a straightforward way: to fully believe something is to have a high enough degree of belief. That is, the following is a natural thought:

> *Simple Threshold*: There is a threshold value $r < 1$ such that, for any agent S, time t, and proposition p, S believes p at t iff, at t, S has credence in p above r.[4]

(Note that *Simple Threshold* is situation-insensitive: the threshold value r applies to all agents and propositions, at all times.)

The difficulty for *Simple Threshold* stems from the conflicting norms of rationality on full and partial belief. Full belief is standardly thought to be governed by a norm of *logical* coherence: one ought not to believe contradictions, and one ought to believe the logical consequences of one's beliefs. Partial belief, on the other hand, is standardly thought to be governed by a norm of *probabilistic* coherence: one's credences should obey the axioms of probability.

Logic and probability give us different norms, but why think they conflict? The lottery problem of Kyburg (1961) gives a nice illustration. Suppose we have a fair lottery with n tickets – that is, exactly one ticket will win, and each ticket has an equal chance of winning. Where p_i is the proposition that ticket i wins, we have $\Pr(p_i) = 1/n$, for any $1 \leq i \leq n$. Rationality should, then, permit one to assign credence $1/n$ to each proposition p_i. Now consider the proposition that ticket i will *lose*, equivalent to $\overline{p_i}$. If our credences obey the probability axioms, we will assign this proposition a credence of $(n - 1)/n$. By making the lottery large enough – that is, by increasing the number of tickets n – we can then bring our credence in ticket i's losing as close to 1 as we like. In particular, whatever the threshold r for full belief, we can set our credence in ticket i's losing above r; thus, we have a full belief that ticket i will lose, for each i. But it is a logical consequence of these n beliefs that *no* ticket will win. Thus we have contradictory requirements: logical coherence requires us to believe no ticket will win, but we assign credence 1 to the proposition that exactly one ticket will win. Something has to give.

Each of the views we will consider in this section avoids the lottery problem by postulating one or another kind of situation sensitivity. Since *Simple Threshold* postulates a single threshold value necessary and sufficient for belief *for all agents, times, and propositions*, all of these views, by virtue of their situation sensitivity, violate *Simple Threshold*. In section 2, we find views on which the **threshold** for full belief varies across situations. In section 3, we find views on which different situations induce different **partitions** on the space of possible worlds. Effectively, then, different situations make different sets of propositions relevant; the views of belief we'll encounter in that section involve quantifying over a set of relevant propositions in bridging full and partial belief. Section 4 considers views on which the bridge between full and partial belief quantifies over the live **options** available to the believer, much as the previous section quantified over relevant propositions. All three of these sections deal with views on which partial belief is situation-invariant, but the bridge principle between full and partial belief is situation-sensitive. In section 5, on the other hand, we encounter views on which full belief is situation-sensitive because **credences** themselves are situation-sensitive. In each section, I will describe how the relevant sort of situation-sensitivity solves the lottery problem and discuss how such an account of belief might be independently motivated. After all, we hope for more than an *ad hoc* response to a very specific sort of puzzle.

Finally, in section 6, I consider generally how a view of belief as situation-sensitive in one of these ways may ground a case for contextualism about belief ascriptions.

Much as I mean in the following sections to give the impression of widespread support for situation-sensitive views of belief, there is hardly a consensus that something like this is correct. See Stalnaker (1984: 80–1), Maher (1986: 383), Foley (1993: 199), and Kaplan (1996: 101) for denials of belief's situation-sensitivity; and see Buchak (2014) and Ross and Schroeder (2014) for recent arguments that belief cannot be reduced to credence at all, let alone in one of the situation-sensitive ways to be outlined in the following.

2 Shifting thresholds

Notice the order of quantifiers in *Simple Threshold*:

> *Simple Threshold*: There is a threshold value $r < 1$ such that, for any agent S, time t, and proposition p, S believes p at t iff, at t, S has credence in p above r.

In setting up the problem, we first suppose a threshold value r to have been given, then construct a lottery large enough to get S's credence in losing over r: then we conclude that S must believe, inconsistently, that ticket 1 is a loser, that ticket 2 is a loser, . . ., that ticket n is a loser, and also that one of these tickets is not a loser.

Let's try modifying the threshold principle by shuffling our quantifiers:

> *Shifty Threshold*: For any agent S and time t, there is a threshold value $r < 1$ such that, for any proposition p, S believes p at t iff, at t, S has credence in p above r.

Here's the difference. *Simple Threshold* has it that there is some threshold value dividing belief from non-belief across the board, regardless of situation, believer, or proposition believed; *Shifty Threshold*, on the other hand, says that the difference between belief and non-belief in any given proposition does come down to whether one's credence is above or below some threshold, but agents in different situations can have different threshold values.

Now, when we try to set up the lottery problem, we can't run the usual construction. That is, given *Shifty Threshold*, we can't count on the threshold value r being determined in advance of our specifying a situation – in advance of our specifying the size of the lottery. Perhaps a rational agent faced with a lottery of size n will always have a threshold for belief set so that $r > (n-1)/n$, so that the agent does not believe that ticket i will lose, for any i. If we can avoid attributing the latter beliefs, we avoid attributing inconsistency. Problem solved.

How can we motivate such a view of belief? Ganson (2008) gives one line of argument. If one believes that p, we can expect one to act as if p. That is, if one believes that p, and one thinks that the best thing to do given p is A, we expect one to do A. She suggests the following condition as necessary for belief that p: "believing that p to a degree which is high enough to ensure that one is willing to act as if p is true, where one's being willing to act as if p means that what one is in fact willing to do is the same as what one would be willing to do, given p" (Ganson 2008: 451).

Similar remarks, albeit less clearly endorsed, can be found in Fantl and McGrath (2009: ch. 5).

Shifting-threshold views of belief can be found in Kyburg (1983), Bach (2005), Ganson (2008), Sturgeon (2008), Fantl and McGrath (2009: ch. 5), and Leitgeb (2013, 2014, forthcoming).

3 Shifting partitions

Leitgeb (2013, 2014, forthcoming) invokes shifting thresholds for full belief, as described in the previous section, but also posits another way belief might be situation-sensitive: the way we *partition* logical space may change across situations.

Here's a way of understanding the idea: suppose we have a quantificational account of full belief in the following sense: we say that an agent believes p if, or only if, *for all (relevant) propositions q*, p bears some relation to q. Examples: the agent's credence in p conditional on q is high enough, i.e., above some threshold s (Leitgeb); the agent's preferences conditional on q are the same as the agent's preferences conditional on the conjunction p and q (Weatherson). We can understand a partition of logical space as generating a set of propositions over which such a clause quantifies. The partition, so to speak, gives us a collection of atomic propositions.

In general, on this sort of view, more coarse-grained partitions (allowing fewer atomic propositions) make full belief easier to come by; more fine-grained partitions (allowing more atomic propositions) make it harder.

Leitgeb appeals to shifting partitions to explain the lottery case. He says that when the question at hand is *which ticket will win*, the appropriate partition has n cells, one for each ticket, containing those worlds where ticket i wins (for $1 \leq i \leq n$). On the other hand, when the question at hand is *will my ticket win*, the appropriate partition has only two cells: a cell where one's ticket wins and a cell where one's ticket loses. In the latter case, but not the former, Leitgeb's framework allows an ideally rational agent to believe that her ticket will lose. But in the case where our ideally rational agent believes her ticket will lose, the partition of logical space does not allow her to frame the question whether someone else's ticket will also lose; thus we avoid the contradictory requirement that she believe of each ticket that it will lose.

Lotteries aside, why accept partition-sensitivity? In a nutshell, the main benefit of Leitgeb's view is that it lets us keep three apparently conflicting desiderata on a unified view of full and partial belief: logical norms for full belief, probabilistic norms for partial belief, and a threshold principle linking the two. The lottery problem is simply an illustration of the apparent conflict between these three desiderata – one application among many Leitgeb provides.

Shifting-partition views of belief can be found in Weatherson (2005, 2012, 2016) and Leitgeb (2013, 2014, forthcoming).

4 Shifting options

In a series of papers, Brian Weatherson (2005, 2012, 2016) defends a view of belief that

> start[s] with the functionalist idea that to believe that p is to treat p as true for the purposes of practical reasoning. To believe p is to have preferences that make sense, by your own lights, in a world where p is true."
> *(Weatherson 2005: 421)*

Here's a concise statement of the basic idea:

> Very roughly, to believe that p is simply to have the same attitudes, *towards all salient questions*, unconditionally as you have conditional on p.
> *(Weatherson 2016: 218, emphasis added)*

In particular, if one believes that p, then one prefers A to B conditional on p iff one prefers A to B unconditionally. The emphasized clause above gives us Weatherson's situation-sensitivity:[5] the question (for example) whether it would be better to accept or reject some bet on whether p is only salient in situations where the bet might be offered; in other situations, one's attitudes towards this question make no difference to one's beliefs.

Apply this to the lottery. Plausibly, in a lottery situation, one has some options that one disprefers unconditionally, but would prefer conditionally on ticket i's losing: for example, *throw away ticket i* or *sell ticket i for a minimal sum*. It is difficult to construct a lottery scenario where one's preferences are unchanged by conditionalizing on ticket i's losing – so it is difficult to construct a lottery scenario where one believes ticket i will lose, by Weatherson's lights.

Note that Weatherson's view as articulated here does *not* commit him to *Shifty Threshold* (section 2). Recall, with added emphasis:

Shifty Threshold: For any agent S and time t, there is a threshold value r such that, *for any proposition p*, S believes p at t iff, at t, S has credence in p above r.

Weatherson's view does not entail that, even having fixed an agent and a time, there will be any threshold value appropriate for all propositions. Consider an agent faced with two options, A and B. Suppose the agent's credences and utilities are as in the following table:

Table 31.1 Some credences and utilities.

	$p\&q$	$p\&\neg q$	$\neg p\&q$	$\neg p\&\neg q$
Credence	90%	5%	3%	2%
$u(A)$	0	0	100	0
$u(B)$	0	40	0	0

For this agent, A's unconditional expected value (EV) is 3 units, and B's is 2 units, so the agent unconditionally prefers A to B. Likewise, the agent prefers A to B conditional on q (positive EV versus zero EV, conditional on q). But conditional on p, the agent prefers B to A. So on (a simplified version of) Weatherson's view, the agent cannot believe p because of her conditional and unconditional preferences with respect to A and B. On the other hand, her preferences with respect to A and B are consistent with her believing q. Therefore, for all that we've said about the agent's preferences, she might believe q, but she cannot believe p. According to *Shifty Threshold*, though, she must believe p if she believes q, since she has a higher credence in p (95% versus 93%).

The shifting-threshold views cited at the end of section 2 can all be read as shifting-options views as well; see also Weatherson (2005, 2012, 2016) and Fantl and McGrath (2009).

5 Shifting presuppositions

Clarke (2013) takes a slightly different tack. All the above accounts take credence to be situation-invariant, but give a situation-sensitive bridge principle linking credence to full belief; Clarke instead takes credence itself to be situation-sensitive, and identifies full belief with credence 1.

In fact, Clarke (2013) argues for two theses we might want to separate. These are, first, that belief is credence 1, and, second, that credence is situation-sensitive, with the believer's situation determining a space of alternative possibilities. Clarke's argument for the package of both theses is as follows: (a) belief-as-credence-1 is usually thought to be too demanding – belief is common, credence 1 is rare – but the reasons for thinking so are undermined by the situation-sensitivity of credence; (b) belief-as-credence-1 avoids notable drawbacks of the simple threshold view; and (c) accepting the situation-sensitivity of credences does not undermine the usual benefits of credence-centric approaches to epistemology and philosophy of science. Now suppose we're unconvinced by the case for (a) and/or (c). Then we might want to reject the identification of belief with credence 1, but we might nevertheless think that full belief is situation-sensitive in roughly the way he claims credence is.

We can think of the present sort of situation-sensitivity as analogous to a relevant alternatives account of knowledge: to believe that p is to rule out (doxastically), or reject, all relevant

Contextualism about belief ascriptions

alternatives to *p*. One might lose a belief that *p* not because one has changed one's mind about whether any possibility is actual, but because more possibilities have become relevant or salient. This sort of shift gives us a response to the lottery: in a lottery situation, one is likely to take seriously – to count as relevant – the possibility where one's ticket wins; and unless one has nefarious friends with inside information about the lottery draw, one will have no reason to rule out this possibility. Thus, contrary to *Simple Threshold*, one will not believe that one's ticket will lose, since there is a relevant counter-possibility one does not rule out.

Note that the response to the lottery problem given here does not necessarily require any particular thesis connecting belief and credence. One can certainly tell the same story in terms of credences given certain such theses – Clarke identifies doxastic "ruling out" with assigning zero credence, so that one lacks belief in the lottery case because one gives positive credence to one's ticket winning – but the story stands on its own terms. One might, for example, think belief cannot be reduced to credence at all, as Buchak (2014) and Ross and Schroeder (2014) have recently argued.

What advantages, then, are there to postulating this sort of situation-sensitivity for full belief, setting credence aside? Greco (forthcoming) develops an anti-idealizing motivation for this sort of picture: we finite agents cannot, in general, deal with the full range of possible worlds, and so simplify our cognitive lives by selectively ignoring irrelevant possibilities. Greco also argues for a parallel between this situation-sensitive picture of belief and conversational dynamics: the way the set of doxastically relevant possibilities can change mirrors the way conversationally relevant possibilities change in response to information entering the conversational common ground; Clarke (manuscript) pursues a similar line of argument.

Shifting-presupposition views of belief can be found in Clarke (2013, forthcoming), Greco (forthcoming), and, arguably, Levi (1980). See also Nozick (1981: 96ff) for a sketch of a similar proposal.

6 From situation-sensitivity to context-sensitivity

We've now seen four kinds of situation-sensitive accounts. One's situation might determine a *threshold* such that one believes only those propositions in which one has credence over the threshold; it might determine a *partition*, contributing a set of propositions over which some quantifier in a condition on belief ranges; it might determine a set of *options*, again governing a quantifier in a condition on belief; or it might determine a set of *presuppositions*, bounding a space of salient possibilities. None of the authors cited above argue explicitly for b-contextualism,[6] but neither do they explicitly reject it. In this section, I sketch how one might motivate b-contextualism based on accepting a situation-sensitive account of belief.

So suppose at least one of these accounts is correct. Then belief is situation-sensitive, which I take to mean (for present purposes) that belief is not a binary relation between agent and proposition, but a ternary (at least) relation between agent, proposition, and some feature(s) of the agent's situation.[7]

Here are two hypotheses about how the situation-sensitive belief relation might figure in the semantics of belief ascriptions. First hypothesis: when we ascribe to *S* the belief that *p*, we diagonalize. That is, the implicit third argument place is filled by *S*'s situation. Second hypothesis: the implicit third argument place is filled in some other way, determined by the context of ascription. Sometimes *S*'s situation provides the missing parameter, but sometimes it comes from elsewhere.

I think the second hypothesis is more plausible, no matter which sort of situation-sensitivity we posit. We ascribe belief for lots of reasons: sometimes I make claims about another's beliefs because I want to predict how they will behave; sometimes because I care how they would answer a question my interlocutors are thinking about; sometimes because I want to ascribe group membership. These aims (and others unmentioned) can come apart: it's not hard to imagine someone who says one thing – sincerely! – and does another. (In the next section, such cases will play a crucial role for Schwitzgebel's contextualist view of belief; see the articles cited there for a plethora of examples.)

In short, a situation-sensitive view of belief lends itself naturally to a contextualist view of belief ascriptions. This contrasts with the analogous view about knowledge: pragmatic encroachment on knowledge is usually set up as an alternative to k-contextualism. Why the difference? It might be that the "know"-analogue of the previous paragraph's claims about belief ascriptions is less attractive: we might be happy to admit variation or flexibility in our reasons for ascribing belief, but think there is less variation in our reasons for ascribing knowledge. I won't pursue that thought further here; but the parallel with pragmatic encroachment is worth exploring.

7 Schwitzgebel's phenomenal, dispositional account

Schwitzgebel (2002) defends a "phenomenal, dispositional account of belief". The central notion for Schwitzgebel's account is of a *dispositional stereotype*: for each proposition p, there is a cluster of dispositions we are apt to associate with belief that p. For example, the belief that there is beer in the fridge is associated with dispositions to open the fridge if someone asks for beer, to say "Yes" if asked whether there is beer in the fridge, to experience surprise if one sees no beer on looking in the fridge, and so on. None of these dispositions is a necessary condition for belief that there is beer in the fridge: if I am stingy, I won't open the fridge when you ask for beer; if I am uncooperative, I won't answer your questions; if I believe the beer is invisible, I won't be surprised at seeing no beer in the fridge; but despite all this I might believe there is beer in the fridge. Nevertheless, *typically*, when one believes that there is beer in the fridge, one has these dispositions and others like them.

According to Schwitzgebel, then, to believe that p "is nothing more than to match *to an appropriate degree and in appropriate respects* the dispositional stereotype for believing that p" (2002: 253, emphasis added). When we are happy to count a stingy and uncooperative agent as unequivocally believing there is (invisible) beer in the fridge, it is because they possess enough of the other stereotypical dispositions: e.g., dispositions to use the proposition that there is beer in the fridge as a premise in practical reasoning, to open the fridge when thirsty, and so on.

The emphasized words in the quote above lead to Schwitzgebel's contextualism. Different conversational purposes and assumptions can mean differences in both how closely an agent must match the stereotype to count as believing, and what sort of deviations from the stereotype are excusable. One and the same agent might match the stereotype closely enough and in the ways that count for one conversation, but not for another.

> Suppose, for example, that a child studying for a test reads, "The Pilgrims landed at Plymouth Rock in 1620," and remembers this fact. She is a bit confused about what Pilgrims are, though: She is unsure whether they were religious refugees or warriors or American natives. Now does she believe that the Pilgrims landed at Plymouth Rock in 1620? She deviates from the stereotype in some respects: She will not conclude that Europeans landed at Plymouth Rock in 1620; and when she imagines the event, she may bring some inappropriate images to mind. In some contexts – e.g., if we are talking about her likely performance on a history dates quiz – we might be inclined to describe her as believing this fact about the Pilgrims; in other contexts we would not.
>
> (*Schwitzgebel 2002: 257*)

Contextualism about belief ascriptions

Let us add: not only are we inclined to say different things about the child in different conversations, but our inclinations track the truth conditions of the things we might say. Thus, an utterance of "[the child] believes the Pilgrims landed at Plymouth Rock in 1620" would be true in a conversation where her beliefs matter primarily as a matter of predicting her performance on a test; yet the same utterance would be false in a conversation where it is important whether she can make appropriate inferences from the Pilgrims' landing.

This example of the confused child is one of many Schwitzgebel offers in a series of papers (2001, 2002, 2010) under the heading "in-between believing". On Schwitzgebel's view, belief that *p* is a vague property: some agents definitely believe that *p* and some definitely lack belief that *p*, but others are *in between* believing and not believing. This is to be understood in terms of dispositional stereotypes: the clear cases are agents who robustly match (or robustly fail to match) the dispositional stereotype for belief that *p*; the in-between cases are agents who match the stereotype partially or incompletely. The in-between cases will generally leave us uncomfortable simply saying that the agent does or does not believe that *p* (as indeed it seems misleading simply to say without elaboration that the child described above believes the Pilgrims landed at Plymouth Rock in 1620). However, conversational context can specify a subset of the stereotype, or a degree of matching, as relevant. In such conversations, we may be happy to attribute belief or lack thereof without further elaboration; and we may utter apparently conflicting things about the same agent in different conversations. Schwitzgebel writes:

> This vagueness and context-dependency does not undermine the value of belief ascription, but rather makes it flexible and responsive to our needs as belief ascribers. Similar vagueness and context-dependency can be found in the ascription of character traits, providing them with a similar flexible utility. The numerous examples in this paper will, I hope, help to support the view that talk about belief can be vague and flexible in this way and still quite useful – more useful in fact than an approach that rigidly insists on determinate yes-or-no answers to all questions about what people believe.
>
> *(2002: 253)*

8 Truman

I conclude by offering a story analogous with k-contextualists' case pairs. For reasons of space, I won't give an extensive discussion of it – if the Bank Cases teach us anything, it's that millions of interpretations of such stories are possible. Nevertheless, I think it worth showing that something along the lines of the best-known argument for k-contextualism may also be available for b-contextualism:

> There's a bird in the garden. Truman, an avid birder, is watching the bird from inside the house. He's writing a list of the bird species he sees in the garden this morning. After a moment's careful observation, he adds Western Wood-Pewee to his list. He then stands up and leaves for another part of the house, out of sight and out of earshot of the yard. All this is being recorded and broadcast live: Truman is on a reality TV show. Shortly after Truman leaves his view of the yard, the broadcast shows an exterior shot of the bird, who briefly sings; Truman does not hear it, as is clear to the show's audience.
>
> Alima and Arthur are watching Truman on TV. They are fans of the show, and aspiring birders. They enjoy the show partly because they can learn about birds by watching Truman identify them. They see Truman as an authority on birds. Arthur is looking away when the cameras show Truman adding Western Wood-Pewee to his list, but he

sees the bird. He asks Alima what kind of bird it is. Alima replies, "Truman thinks it's a Western Wood-Pewee."

Elsewhere, Bart, Betty, and Begbie are also watching Truman's show. They, too, are birders, and they are watching Truman's show with their entire birding club. Unlike Alima and Arthur, Bart and Betty know that a Rare Bird Alert has recently been issued in the Los Angeles area, where Truman's show is filmed, and where Bart and Betty live: an Eastern Wood-Pewee has recently been sighted in the area. Los Angeles is well outside the Eastern Wood-Pewee's range. Here's what Sibley (2003: 280) says about the Eastern Wood-Pewee, *Contopus virens*: "Essentially identical in habits and appearance to Western Wood-Pewee [*Contopus sordidulus*], but range barely overlaps; reliably distinguished only by voice, most easily the song."[8]

When they see the bird sing on TV (after Truman has absconded), a dispute breaks out among the birding club about whether the bird in Truman's yard was a Western or an Eastern Wood-Pewee. As a measure to ease tensions and resolve the dispute, Bart suggests polling the opinions of the assembled experts; Betty offers to record the votes. Since everyone present regards Truman as an authority on birds, Betty asks which camp Truman belongs to: should he be recorded as voting Eastern or Western? Begbie says, pointing at the TV screen, which now shows Truman's list, "He thinks it's a Western."

Bart responds, "No, he doesn't think it's a Western. He wrote that it's a Western Wood-Pewee, but he didn't hear it sing. He hasn't even thought about whether it's a Western or an Eastern – he knows you can only tell the difference by listening. Don't put him on either side."

Both Alima and Bart speak naturally and truthfully. It seems Alima is correct to attribute to Truman the belief that the bird is a Western Wood-Pewee, and it seems Bart is correct to deny the same belief of Truman. This needs to be explained.

Contextualism about belief ascriptions allows a straightforward explanation: Alima and Bart seem to speak truly because they do. Despite the surface appearance of a contradiction, they do not, in fact, contradict one another. It is possible for Truman to "believe" the bird is a Western, in Alima's sense, and also not "believe" the bird is a Western, in Bart's sense.

Note that the following type of response does not help the anti-contextualist. One might respond: "*I* wouldn't say what Bart says. Rather than deny that Truman thinks it's a Western, I would say something else – maybe that he thinks it's a Western, but you shouldn't include his vote because his belief isn't reliable, or something like that." But the contextualist needn't argue that what Bart says is better than this alternative. What, I claim, needs to be explained is that what Alima and Bart each say is natural and acceptable; I do not claim that there are no other things, even in some sense better things, Bart might have said instead.

An effective anti-contextualist response needs to address what Bart says, not what he could have said instead. As I said above, space prevents a full discussion of possible responses to the case. My aim in this brief section is just to sketch the beginning of a case-based argument for b-contextualism, analogous to the traditional case pair–based argument for k-contextualism.[9]

Notes

1 For convenience, I'll use "b-contextualism" as shorthand for "contextualism about belief ascriptions." I'll also use "k-contextualism" in a similar way when it helps to avoid ambiguity.

2 Well, almost none. Sturgeon (2008: 142) very briefly argues that "believes p" is a gradable expression and therefore context-sensitive.

Contextualism about belief ascriptions

3 The accounts of Weatherson (2005) and Ganson (2008) are also centrally motivated by debates over subject-sensitive invariantism. Both hope to, as Weatherson puts it, "do without" pragmatic encroachment about the normative dimension of knowledge: that is, both views have it that there is pragmatic encroachment on justified belief, but only because there is pragmatic encroachment on belief *simpliciter*. (Weatherson's later writing on this topic no longer claims to do without non-doxastic pragmatic encroachment on knowledge completely, having been persuaded by Stanley's Ignorant High Stakes bank case; see Weatherson 2012: 77). Bach (2005), similarly, adopts a situation-sensitive view of belief in objecting to k-contextualism.

4 This threshold principle is sometimes called the "Lockean Thesis", following Foley (1993: ch. 4). And, indeed, Foley does endorse the principle I call *Simple Threshold* in that chapter. However, Foley's "Lockean Thesis" is a principle about *rational* belief and *rational* degrees of belief, and I prefer to follow Foley on this point: the Lockean Thesis, then, says that there is a threshold value s such that one is *rational* to believe p iff one is *rational* to have credence in p above s. Above-threshold credence in something one does not believe is, then, impossible according to *Simple Threshold*, but merely irrational according to the Lockean Thesis.

5 See also section 3: the less-simplified version of Weatherson's view also involves shifting partitions. Simplifying less: if one believes that p, then *for all active propositions* q, one has the same attitudes conditional on q alone as one has conditional on the conjunction $p\&q$. The clause emphasized here yields shifting partitions; see Weatherson (2005: 423) for discussion of what it is for a proposition to be "active".

6 Leitgeb is carefully neutral on this question: he gives a formal framework for representing ideally rational belief featuring something like situation- or context-sensitivity, but he leaves it open how the framework is to be interpreted. It could be that what an ideal agent believes is situation-sensitive, or that what an agent is correctly described as (rationally) believing is context-sensitive. See Leitgeb (2014: 149ff) for discussion. See also footnote 2..

7 This is not the only way of understanding situation-sensitivity. Situation-sensitivity might mean instead that belief is a binary relation between an agent and a proposition, but one whose holding or otherwise depends on some third situational factor. The "present purpose" I appeal to in the main text is: building a plausible case for b-contextualism based on situation-sensitivity. For the argument sketched in the main text to succeed, it is true, this understanding of situation-sensitivity as ternarity would need to be defended; but for the present, I'll settle for its being one plausible interpretation of the situation-sensitive views surveyed above. Thanks to Jonathan Jenkins Ichikawa for pressing me on this point.

8 Thanks to Rebecca Gindin-Clarke for suggesting the example of Eastern and Western Wood-Pewees.

9 Thanks to Jonathan Jenkins Ichikawa for comments on a draft of this chapter.

References

Bach, K. (2005) "The Emperor's New 'Knows'", in G. Preyer and G. Peter (eds.), *Contextualism in Philosophy: On Epistemology, Language and Truth*, pp. 51–89. Oxford: Oxford University Press.

Buchak, L. (2014) "Belief, Credence, and Norms", *Philosophical Studies* **169**, 285–311.

Clarke, R. (manuscript) "Assertion, Belief, and Context." Available at http://www.rogerclarke.org/research.

Clarke, R. (2013) "Belief Is Credence One (In Context)", *Philosophers' Imprint* **13**(11), 1–18.

Clarke, R. (forthcoming) "Preface Writers Are Consistent", *Pacific Philosophical Quarterly*. doi:10.1111/papq.12130.

Fantl, J. and M. McGrath (2009) *Knowledge in an Uncertain World*. Oxford: Oxford University Press.

Foley, R. (1993) *Working without a Net: A Study of Egocentric Epistemology*. Oxford: Oxford University Press.

Ganson, D. (2008) "Evidentialism and Pragmatic Constraints on Outright Belief", *Philosophical Studies* **139**(3), 441–58.

Greco, D. (forthcoming) "How I Learned to Stop Worrying and Love Probability 1", *Philosophical Perspectives*.

Kaplan, M. (1996) *Decision Theory as Philosophy*. Cambridge: Cambridge University Press.

Kyburg, H. (1961) *Probability and the Logic of Rational Belief*. Middletown, CT: Wesleyan University Press.

Kyburg, H. (1983) "Rational Belief", *The Behavioral and Brain Sciences* **6**, 231–45.

Leitgeb, H. (2013) "Reducing Belief Simpliciter to Degrees of Belief", *Annals of Pure and Applied Logic* **164**(12), 1338–1389.

Leitgeb, H. (2014) "The Stability Theory of Belief", *Philosophical Review* **123**(2), 131–71.

Leitgeb, H. (forthcoming) *The Stability of Belief: How Rational Belief Coheres with Probability*. Oxford: Oxford University Press.

Levi, I. (1980) *The Enterprise of Knowledge: An Essay on Knowledge, Credal Probability, and Chance*. Cambridge, MA: MIT Press.

Maher, P. (1986) "The Irrelevance of Belief to Rational Action", *Erkenntnis* **24**(3), 363–84.

Nozick, R. (1981) *Philosophical Explanations*. Cambridge, MA: Belknap.

Ross, J. and M. Schroeder (2014) "Belief, Credence, and Pragmatic Encroachment", *Philosophy and Phenomenological Research* **88**(2), 259–88.

Schwitzgebel, E. (2001) "In-Between Believing", *Philosophical Quarterly* **51**(202), 76–82.

Schwitzgebel, E. (2002) "A Phenomenal, Dispositional Account of Belief", *Noûs* **36**(2), 249–75.

Schwitzgebel, E. (2010) "Acting Contrary to Our Professed Beliefs, or the Gulf between Occurrent Judgment and Dispositional Belief", *Pacific Philosophical Quarterly* **91**, 531–53.

Sibley, D. A. (2003) *The Sibley Field Guide to Birds of Western North America*. New York: Alfred A. Knopf.

Stalnaker, R. (1984) *Inquiry*. Cambridge, MA: MIT Press.

Sturgeon, S. (2008) "Reason and the Grain of Belief", *Noûs* **42**(1), 139–65.

Weatherson, B. (2005) "Can We Do without Pragmatic Encroachment?", *Philosophical Perspectives* **19**(1) 417–43.

Weatherson, B. (2012) "Knowledge, Bets and Interests", in J. Brown and M. Gerken (eds.), *Knowledge Ascriptions*, pp. 75–103. Oxford: Oxford University Press.

Weatherson, B. (2016) "Games, Beliefs and Credences", *Philosophy and Phenomenological Research* **92**(2): 209-236.

32

COUNTERFACTUALS AND KNOWLEDGE

Karen S. Lewis

1 Introduction

The standard semantics for counterfactuals comes from Stalnaker (1968, 1981), Lewis (1973, 1986) and Kratzer (1977, 1981). Abstracting away from differences between the accounts, the basic semantics is as follows:

A would-counterfactual $P \: \square \rightarrow Q$ is true (at w) iff all the closest
P-worlds (to w) are Q-worlds.

Traditionally, the semantics for counterfactuals is thought to have a limited kind of context-sensitivity. That is, most of the time, there is a consistent way in which the closest P-world(s) are selected (relative to the world of evaluation); what counts as the closest P-world does not vary based on the conversational context. There are some exceptions to this. Lewis discusses Quine's famous case of Caesar in Korea, arguing that in some conversational contexts (1) is true, while in other contexts (2) is true, and this depends on what facts are being held fixed in the context:

(1) If Caesar had been in command in Korea, he would have used the atom bomb.
(2) If Caesar had been in command in Korea, he would have used catapults.

Stalnaker (1981) endorses the idea that in some contexts, different worlds count as equally similar due to negligible differences (whereas those differences might not be negligible in other contexts). For example, in a case in which we have a line in the margin of a book that is actually just less than an inch, and are considering counterfactuals about how long it would be if it was more than an inch long, worlds in which the line is a little more than an inch up to worlds where it is 2 or 3 inches might count as equally similar (suppose the margin is 3 inches wide).

Aside from these sorts of considerations, counterfactuals on these views are not deeply contextualist; people generally speak of their truth values absolutely, not relative to conversational context. But there are several puzzles that plague this basically invariantist semantics for counterfactuals; ones that bear striking similarity to the sort of puzzles used to motivate contextualism for 'know' and other terms. These have motivated Ichikawa (2011) and Lewis (2016, Forthcoming) to argue for a thoroughly contextualist semantics for counterfactuals. In section 2, I explore the

411

various motivations for counterfactual contextualism. In section 3, I discuss and compare both my and Ichikawa's versions of counterfactual contextualism. Finally, in section 4, I examine the relationship between contextualism for counterfactuals and for knowledge, arguing that though a close relationship between a contextualist semantics for counterfactuals and one knowledge is elegant, it faces problems.

2 Motivations for counterfactual contextualism

Counterfactuals enter into several puzzles that, if accepted at face value, appear to have the power to undermine the truth of nearly all contingent counterfactuals. Call this the problem of *counterfactual skepticism*. Most people generally believe that there are true contingent counterfactuals (in fact, lots of them), in that they are accepted as true by native speakers in ordinary conversation, and used theoretically in philosophy, psychology, history, artificial intelligence and other disciplines. One of the most straightforward ways to resolve this tension is to adopt some version of a contextualist semantics for counterfactuals.[1]

2.1 Puzzle 1: mights and woulds

Consider an ordinary contingent counterfactual, one we are normally certain is true. For example, suppose I was holding my favorite mug just now as I stood in the middle of the kitchen. I did not drop it, but we think it true that:

(3)   If I had dropped my mug, it would have fallen to the kitchen floor.

A skeptic might come along and warn us: *Not so fast. Isn't it possible*, she asks, *that I might have very swiftly caught the mug before it reached the floor?* Though I'm not known for my coordination, this is not beyond the realm of what I am physically capable of doing, and it seems to support the truth of the might-counterfactual (4):

(4)   If I had dropped my mug, I might have deftly caught it before it fell to the floor.

This directly supports the truth of (5):

(5)   If I had dropped my mug, it might not have fallen to the kitchen floor.

To borrow a term from DeRose (1999), (5) inescapably clashes with (3). In fact, it sounds very much like a contradiction.

(6)   #If I had dropped my mug, it might not have fallen to the kitchen floor; if I had dropped my mug, it would have fallen to the kitchen floor.

The problem generalizes when we take into consideration the fact that our best physics seems to support indeterministic laws. If indeterministic interpretations of quantum mechanics are correct, then there is some chance (albeit very, very small) of almost anything happening, such as my mug quantum tunneling to China, which supports the truth of (7):

(7)   If I had dropped my mug, it might have quantum tunneled to China (and so not fallen to the floor).

Counterfactuals and knowledge

This counterfactual also supports the truth of (5), and so we are again faced with the inescapable clash of (6).

Even if it turns out that deterministic statistical mechanics is the right physics, the problem remains. For the vast majority of counterfactual conditionals, and for virtually all ordinary counterfactual conditionals, the antecedent is underdescribed in terms of the microphysical detail by which it occurs. There are very many precise ways in which I could have dropped my mug (the exact position of my hand, the exact position of the mug in my hand, the strength with which I dropped it, etc.). Statistical mechanics tells us that while the vast majority of these initial conditions lead to the expected outcome, i.e., the mug falling to the floor, at least some initial condition is such that it macroscopically looks just like the ones in which things go normally; but things don't go normally, for example, my mug flies sideways and lands safely on the counter. If statistical mechanics is right, then it is true that:

(8) If I had dropped my mug, it might have flown sideways and landed safely on the counter.

And again, we have the same clash of woulds and mights. It should be pretty clear that the above sorts of considerations generalize to all or almost all contingent counterfactuals without explicit mention of probability in the consequent.

These sorts of undermining might-counterfactuals don't just come about from extremely low probability events like quantum tunneling or rare feats of amazing coordination. They can often come about when dealing with much more ordinary, merely somewhat low probability events. For example, suppose I had a party to which you were invited, but did not come. Much to your dismay, you missed an extraordinary party. Shockingly, Lady Gaga showed up for about 20 minutes! I tell you that you really should have accepted my invitation, as:

(9) If you had come to the party, you would have seen Lady Gaga.

This is the sort of counterfactual that is commonly accepted as true in conversation. But the skeptic need not look very far to find undermining might-counterfactuals, for it also seems true that:

(10) If you had come to the party, you might have been sick to your stomach and so in the bathroom the whole time Lady Gaga was there.

Or, given your disposition for getting lost in philosophical conversation:

(11) If you had come the party, you might have been out on the deck lost in philosophical conversation and not noticed the commotion inside when Lady Gaga was there.

Such examples are also easy to multiply.

As Hájek (ms) points out, we need not invoke might-counterfactuals to present this sort of problem. Invoking chance (in the case of indeterminism) or indeterminacy (in the case of determinism) directly is enough – as Hájek puts it, *chanciness undermines wouldiness* (or *indeterminacy undermines wouldiness*). Merely pointing out that the dropping of a mug is a chancy event, in that it could turn out that the mug lands on the floor, but it could also turn out that it quantum tunnels to China or is caught in a swift act of coordination is enough, it seems, to undermine our confidence in the truth of counterfactuals like (3). (The same goes for the party case.)

2.2 Puzzle 2: the similarity ordering

The clash between woulds and mights is not the only way to get counterfactual skepticism off the ground. On a Lewisian-style similarity ordering, many of the undermining worlds are among the closest worlds. Lewis's system of weights is as follows:

1   It is of the first importance to avoid big, widespread, diverse violations of law.
2   It is of the second importance to maximize the spatio-temporal region throughout which perfect match of particular fact prevails.
3   It is of the third importance to avoid even small, localized, simple violations of law.
4   It is of little or no importance to secure approximate similarity of particular fact, even in matters that concern us greatly.

(Lewis, 1986, pp. 47–8)

Provided the antecedent is not true at the actual world, the closest worlds are generally an exact match to the actual world until some time not long before the antecedent occurs, at which point there is a small violation of law (e.g., a particle in a different place, a neuron fires that didn't actually fire) that brings the antecedent about. Then the laws of the actual world do what they will, and if they bring about the consequent in all the closest worlds, the would-counterfactual is true. If the laws are the indeterministic ones of quantum mechanics, the problem is the clearest. By hypothesis, the very same history, up to and including the same small miracle that brings about the antecedent, will lead to, say, a mug falling to the floor in one world and tunneling to China in another. This is just what it means for the actual laws to be the indeterministic laws of quantum mechanics. But even if the laws are actually the deterministic laws of statistical mechanics, the problem persists. This is because the antecedent is underdescribed, and so there are many equally good small miracles, in the sense that they are equally small violations of the law that will bring about the antecedent. In other words, there is indeterminacy in how the antecedent is brought about. Provided that one of these equally good small miracles brings about the initial conditions that lead to weird things happening – and I don't see why it wouldn't – worlds in which the mug flies sideways and lands safely on the counter are also equally close. Even if one does not ascribe to Lewis's particular system of weights, any natural interpretation of a similarity ordering in the spirit of Lewis, i.e., ones in which the closest worlds are those in which minor changes are made to incorporate the antecedent without contradiction and nothing more, will predict that these are among the closest worlds.[2] This is not to say that it is impossible to introduce a different similarity ordering; this is just the strategy of Lewis (1986) in introducing the notion of a quasi-miracle and Williams (2008) in invoking typicality. Changing the similarity relation in some way like this is one possible response to the puzzle.[3]

What about the more ordinary cases, like my deftly catching the mug before it falls or your being out on the deck and missing Lady Gaga at my party? Arguably, a natural similarity ordering is going to count some of these among more distant worlds, but some among the closest worlds, depending on the case and the facts about the actual world. By hypothesis, I am not a terribly coordinated person. So worlds in which I catch the mug before it falls to the floor are probably not among the closest worlds.[4] Here is a case where the pressure from might-counterfactuals and chanciness comes apart from the pressure from similarity. But other cases are not so clear. Suppose, as I did in the above case, that like most philosophers, you are prone to getting embroiled in philosophical debate and losing track of your surroundings. Given that you weren't at the party, there is no fact of the matter regarding exactly where you would have been standing had you been there at the time Lady Gaga arrived (let's also assume you don't have any peculiarities like always standing in the same spot at parties or always next to the same person). There are many

Counterfactuals and knowledge

ways in which you could have been present at the party, given that there were many people in the kitchen, many in the living room, and many out on the deck. Different small miracles lead you to be at the party in slightly different ways, and so standing at slightly different spots. (Or, if this example doesn't convince you, there are different times at which you arrive at and leave from the party. Some of these times do not have you overlap with Lady Gaga's surprise appearance.) So even some of the ordinary cases seem to be among the closest worlds on a natural similarity ordering. If this is the case, again we are threatened with counterfactual skepticism.

2.3 Puzzle 3: clashing would-counterfactuals

Counterfactual skepticism can also be motivated by a third kind of puzzle, one involving only would-counterfactuals, as Ichikawa (2011) presents it. Consider the case of the party again. You didn't come to my party, and so you missed Lady Gaga's surprise appearance. You regret not coming because:

(12) If you had come to the party, you would have seen Lady Gaga. But of course, it is also true that:
(13) If you had come to the party and been distracted by philosophical conversation out on the deck, you would not have seen Lady Gaga.

And this also seems to undermine our confidence in (12):

(14) #If you had come to the party and been distracted by philosophical conversation out on the deck, you would not have seen Lady Gaga. But of course, if you had come to the party, you would have seen Lady Gaga.

This data was first noted in publication by von Fintel (2001), who attributes the observation to Irene Heim in a seminar at MIT. Essentially, the observation is that conditionals like (12) and (13) form a consistent sequence, often called a *Sobel sequence*. But it seems they are only consistent when they are in that order. Reverse the order, and it sounds inconsistent. Both von Fintel and later Gillies (2007) take this data to support the need for a dynamic semantics for counterfactual conditionals.[5] But we can also take this data, as Ichikawa does, as a skeptical puzzle and a motivation for a contextualist account of counterfactuals.[6]

There have been various solutions to these three puzzles proposed in the literature. Hájek (ms) embraces counterfactual skepticism and proposes an error theory to account for our ordinary judgments. DeRose (1999) proffers a solution to the inescapable clash between woulds and mights by adopting a Stalnakerian semantics in which all might-counterfactuals are would-counterfactuals with a wide scope epistemic possibility operator ranging over them, and the clash is explained as pragmatic. Lewis (1986) and Williams (2008) aim to solve the problem from similarity, altering the similarity ordering to relegate the pesky worlds to more distant realms. von Fintel (2001) and Gillies (2007) give dynamic semantic accounts and Moss (2012) gives a pragmatic account of the reverse Sobel sequence data (Gillies also offers an account for the clash between mights and woulds). Putting aside other issues with each of these views, one major problem is that they each address only the puzzle they are designed to account for; the solutions cannot be extended to the other puzzles (with the exception of Hájek's error theory, which is an embrace of counterfactual skepticism rather than a solution to it, and Gillies' view, which applies to two out of three). It is possible that each puzzle represents a distinct phenomenon that warrants a distinct explanation. But at least on the surface, taken together, these seem to be related phenomena. A contextualist semantics for counterfactuals can explain them all, and this is certainly a theoretical virtue.

415

3 Counterfactual contextualism

Contextualism for counterfactuals, like contextualism for knowledge, can take many forms. I'll describe my preferred view, which is one version of the view I defend in Lewis (2016). In essence, it is a Lewisian-style variably strict conditional semantics that takes both similarity and relevance to contribute to the closeness ordering. I will then briefly compare it to Ichikawa's 'all cases' version of contextualism.

There are two central components to my preferred version of counterfactual contextualism. First, counterfactuals are sensitive not just to the most similar worlds, but to the worlds that are relevant given the conversational context. Second, the pragmatic effect of both might- and would-counterfactuals can be to expand what possibilities are relevant in the context. Beginning with the semantic component, the truth-conditions of a would-counterfactual are as follows:

> For all contexts c, $P\square\!\!\rightarrow Q$ is true in c (at w) iff all the closest P-worlds (to w) are Q-worlds, where closeness is a function of both similarity and relevance.

Mights are the duals of woulds ($P\diamondsuit\!\!\rightarrow Q =_{def} \neg(P \square\!\!\rightarrow\neg Q)$) so:

> For all contexts c, $P\diamondsuit\!\!\rightarrow Q$ is true in c (at w) iff some closest P-worlds (to w) are Q-worlds, where closeness is a function of both similarity and relevance.

Both similarity and relevance contribute to what counts as a closest world: worlds that are most similar might not be among the closest because they are simply not relevant to the conversation, and worlds that are not among the most similar might be among the closest because they are relevant in the context. Picturesquely speaking, relevance can take worlds that are among the most similar and move them farther away, and take worlds that are less similar, though not *too* dissimilar, and move them to the closest sphere.

What notion of conversational relevance is at play here? It is relevance both to the purpose of asserting a counterfactual and to conversational purposes more generally. Counterfactuals are often used for making predictions, expressing regret or making dispositional claims. This means that the actual world is always relevant if it is an antecedent world. (This corresponds to Ichikawa's invocation of Lewis's *rule of actuality*.) High probability outcomes (conditional on the antecedent) are also always relevant. It doesn't matter whether the conversational participants are aware of the probabilities or the facts that make them so; high probability outcomes cannot legitimately be ignored. Conversely, low probability outcomes can be ignored when they are not otherwise relevant to conversational purposes. *How* high counts as high (or how low counts as low) depends on the standards of precision operant in the conversation. Conversations about scientific experiments will have different standards from casual conversation, and conversations about quantum physics experiments will have different standards from conversations about biology experiments. Conversational participants have limited control over these measures of relevance. Once the conversational purposes and standards of precision are in play, they cannot legitimately ignore the actual world or high probability outcomes, even if they are completely ignorant of the actual world or the relevant probabilities.

The conversational participants can shift the conversational purposes or standards of precision by explicitly or indirectly introducing previously unconsidered possibilities. Two (of many) ways of so doing are to utter a might-counterfactual or would-counterfactual that includes a previously unconsidered possibility. For example, suppose we are engaged in casual conversation and

416

have not yet considered quantum physics. In this case, (3), repeated here as (15), is true when initially uttered in the conversation:

(15) If I had dropped my mug, it would have fallen to the kitchen floor.

But if you say (16) or (17), you introduce possibilities previously legitimately ignored in the conversation:

(16) If you had dropped your mug, it might have quantum tunneled to China (and so not fallen to the floor).
(17) If you had dropped your mug and it had quantum tunneled to China, it would not have fallen to the floor.

In the context in which (16) is asserted, it is technically false, since we have been legitimately ignoring worlds in which quantum events occur (and so none of the closest worlds are quantum worlds). But we tend to interpret speakers charitably, and it is clear that you are trying to shift conversational standards. So the context is (at least temporarily) shifted to include quantum worlds, making (16) true in the newly accommodated context. (17) is straightforwardly true, since even in the casual context the closest (i.e. most similar and relevant) mug-dropping worlds in which quantum tunneling occurs are presumably worlds in which the cup does not fall to my kitchen floor. Whether such assertions *permanently* change the conversational context depends on the conversational participants. I can stand my ground and refuse to accommodate, maintaining that quantum outcomes are simply irrelevant to what we are talking about. Or I can acquiesce, accepting the shift in conversational standards, in which case (15) is not true in the new context. (If the conversational participants disagree about whether accommodation should take place, disagreement or negotiation can ensue.) This is similar in spirit to Ichikawa's version of Lewis's *rule of attention*. Something being salient is not enough for it to become relevant; it must be taken seriously. To this I'd also like to add another point. Another way in which the conversational context cannot be permanently changed by making something salient is if the possibility made salient is very dissimilar; perhaps one way to understand this rule is that when considering counterfactuals one should never take seriously very dissimilar possibilities unless the antecedent requires it. So, for example, suppose, in a casual context, I am holding a reliable dry match that I never strike and truly say:

(18) If I had struck this match just now, it would have lit.

(19) is also true, since the most relevant similar worlds in which the match is soaking wet and struck, it does not light:

(19) If I had struck this match just now and it had been soaked overnight, it wouldn't have lit.

But it doesn't induce any change to the context. If (18) is uttered subsequently, it is still true, since given that the match in question is actually dry (and perhaps assuming some other plausible facts about the lack of proximity of water or the unlikelihood of people soaking matches around these parts), worlds in which it was soaked overnight are just too dissimilar to be relevant (even though we just mentioned them). In other words, accommodation cannot legitimately occur. Similarly, (20) cannot be made true by accommodation in the same context:

(20) If I had struck this match just now, it might have been soaked overnight.

We are now in a position to see how contextualism addresses all of the skeptical puzzles presented in section 2. First, it can explain the inescapable clash between woulds and mights, while vindicating our intuition that many would-counterfactuals are true. Would-counterfactuals like (15) are true *in many contexts*, particularly the casual contexts of ordinary conversation (but also potentially in historical, psychological, philosophical or scientific contexts). In many contexts, it is legitimate to ignore relatively low probability outcomes like my swift catching of the mug, quantum tunneling or statistically unlikely flying to the counter. But when an undermining might-counterfactual is raised, as long as the conversational shift it brings about is accommodated, what counts as relevant changes, and (15) is not true in this newer, more precise context. The same goes when we are face to face with the chanciness of things. Contrary to what Hájek argues, on this view, it is not that chanciness undermines wouldiness; rather it is that chanciness, when raised to salience and accommodated in the conversational context, undermines wouldiness (a much less catchy slogan, admittedly). *Mutatis Mutandis* for indeterminacy.

The second puzzle challenged the truth of most contingent counterfactuals based on the fact that at least many of the undermining worlds are among the closest on a natural similarity ordering. The contextualist view addresses this problem in that the closeness ordering is no longer merely a matter of similarity, but a combination of similarity and relevance. Quantum worlds, for example, may be among the most similar, but they are often not among the most relevant, and thus will often not be among the closest.

Finally, the third puzzle concerned sequences of clashing would-counterfactuals, or reverse Sobel sequences. On the present view, (12), repeated here as (21), is true in the context in which it is asserted, because it is a context that legitimately ignores the relatively low probability possibilities in which you come to my party and don't see Lady Gaga anyway.

(21) If you had come to the party, you would have seen Lady Gaga.

(13), repeated below as (22), is true in the same context, since, given the facts about the situation, all the most similar-relevant worlds in which you are at the party and distracted by philosophical conversation out on the deck are worlds in which you miss Lady Gaga.

(22) If you had come to the party and been distracted by philosophical conversation out on the deck, you would not have seen Lady Gaga.

But (22) also makes this previously unconsidered possibility salient in the conversation. And given that it is not too distant – you are a philosopher, after all, and there were many other philosophers at the actual party – it becomes relevant, and can no longer be legitimately ignored. So (21) is not true in the new context.

In this way contextualism explains why many would-counterfactuals are often true in the first place, but also why they seem to clash with other counterfactuals that apparently undermine their truth. They do clash with these other counterfactuals, but not in a way that undermines their truth once and for all. Counterfactual skepticism is avoided; many counterfactuals that we think are true are in fact true. The caveat is that they are not true in every context, though they are true in many contexts.

The other version of contextualism defended in print is the 'all cases' version defended by Ichikawa (2011). On his view, would-counterfactuals are contextually restricted strict conditionals:

> *If A were the case, C would be the case* is true just in case all of the A possibilities are C possibilities (Psst! – except those possibilities we're properly ignoring).
>
> (p. 296)

While Ichikawa only addresses the third of the three skeptical puzzles discussed above, his version of contextualism also has the potential to solve all three in a similar way. The problem with the similarity relation doesn't arise because a similarity ordering isn't invoked at all; as long as the right possibilities are properly ignored, many counterfactuals will come out as true in many contexts. He could also define might-counterfactuals as the duals of woulds, so that they are simply contextually restricted existential quantifiers over possibilities. Might-counterfactuals, like woulds, introduce new possibilities, thereby changing the context, in much the same way I've described above, explaining the clash between woulds and mights.

The central difference between my version of contextualism and Ichikawa's is the logic of counterfactuals; since his is a strict conditional account and mine a variably strict conditional account, they differ in which rules of inference they validate. Let's begin with what the two views have in common. Substitution of equivalents is valid in both frameworks. That is, if the context does not shift when logical equivalents are substituted for each other, then the substitution will be valid. Clearly, if all A possibilities are C possibilities and the B possibilities are just the A possibilities, then all B possibilities are C possibilities (and the same for D possibilities instead of C possibilities, where C and D are logically equivalent). Similarly, if the closest A-worlds are all C-worlds, and the A-worlds just are the B-worlds, then the closest B-worlds are all C-worlds (and similarly for substituting the logically equivalent D for C). But the validity is also limited in its applicability, since very often substituting a logical equivalent will place us in a different context, and so it won't be true that the A possibilities range over the same domain as the B possibilities. This is because logical equivalents can raise different possibilities to salience. For example, consider (23) vs. (24), where ϕ_1 through ϕ_n are all the possible ways in which a mug can fall described on a microphysical level:

(23) If I had dropped my mug, it would have fallen to the kitchen floor.
(24) If I had dropped my mug, it would have fallen to the kitchen floor in manner ϕ_1 or manner $\phi_2 \ldots$ or ϕ_n.

In this case, (24) makes salient microphysical detail, and thus puts us in a much more precise context than (23). Quantum events and other low probability outcomes are going to be relevant in the context of (24) while they are not in that of (23).

Both theories can endorse agglomeration as a reasonable inference, in the sense that whenever the premises are truly asserted, the conclusion is true in the same context:

Agglomeration: $A \mathbin{\square}\!\!\rightarrow B, A \mathbin{\square}\!\!\rightarrow C \vdash A \mathbin{\square}\!\!\rightarrow (B \And C)$

This is good, since it is an overwhelmingly intuitive principle. However, neither account validates the principle, since counterexamples come in the following form. Consider a fair lottery with a million tickets that is in fact never played. The premises are each of the form *If the lottery had been played, ticket 1 would not have won, If the lottery had been played, ticket 2 would not have won*, and so on for each of the million tickets. Now consider these relative to a context in which low probability outcomes, such as those that have a one in a million chance of occurring, are legitimately ignored. Each premise then comes out true. But apply the principle of agglomeration, and the conclusion is certainly false at any context: *If the lottery had been played, ticket 1 would not have won and ticket 2 would not have won . . . and ticket 1,000,000 would not have won.* Hence, agglomeration is not a valid principle for a contextualist account of counterfactuals. But it is important to note that these counterexamples can only be constructed for contexts in which the premises are *not asserted*. On both accounts under consideration, if these million premises (or even a small subset of them) were asserted, they would land us in such a context in which low probability outcomes *do* matter and the premises wouldn't be true. So a version of agglomeration *qua* reasonable inference is still applicable.

The two frameworks differ on antecedent strengthening, contraposition and transitivity.

Antecedent strengthening: A □→ C ⊢ (A & B) □→ C
Contraposition: A □→ C ⊢ ¬C □→ ¬A
Transitivity: A □→ B, B □→ C ⊢ A □→ C

Ichikawa's strict conditional semantics validates all of these; apparent counterexamples are due to shifts in context. By contrast, my semantics invalidates these rules of inference, as it is a variably strict conditional semantics. Apparent counterexamples to antecedent strengthening and contraposition would generally not be able to be explained away anyway, because for the single premise rules there is no context shift between premise and conclusion. Unlike Ichikawa's account, on my view would-counterfactuals generally induce a context-shift, if they induce one at all, after, and not before, their semantics is calculated.[7] Therefore the standard counterexamples in the literature to these rules are also genuine counterexamples on my account.[8]

Are there benefits to one account or the other? On the one hand, Ichikawa's semantics is simpler. One might think that the ideal account is a strict conditional one; historically we only moved away from such an account to a variably strict one because of the counterexamples. If the alleged counterexamples can be explained away by appealing to context-sensitivity, this is a very appealing picture. On the other hand, there may be good reasons for wanting a semantic account of the invalidity of antecedent strengthening rather than a pragmatic one. For example, against background assumptions that the match in question is extremely reliable and there is no water for miles around, it seems (25a) and (25b) are genuinely true together at the same context and are not simply consistent because of a context shift like in the case of *Everything in the fridge is edible* and *Not everything in the fridge is edible*.

(25a) If I had struck this match, it would have lit.
(25b) If I had struck this match and it was wet, it would not have lit.

For Ichikawa to account for this, the conversational participants have to (at least temporarily) take seriously worlds in which the match is wet, even if it has already been explicitly established in the conversation that the match wouldn't have been wet, e.g. the following is perfectly coherent: *There is no water anywhere, so if I had struck this match, there is no way it would have been wet. So (25a). Still, (25b) is true.* Now, it could be that there are very subtle shifts in context like this when it comes to sequences of counterfactuals, but one might think that the story of the two match examples is a lot more straightforward than that, especially when at the same time conversational participants would likely *not* agree to *If the match had been struck, it might have been wet*, even if this possibility only has to be considered temporarily.

On the other hand, validating transitivity seems like an advantage over my account, because as far as I can tell all the traditional counterexamples do involve an intuitive context shift between the premises and conclusion. Ichikawa's semantics nicely explains that data. So the logical considerations, though pertinent, do not without further consideration seem to point decisively in either direction.[9]

4 Counterfactuals and knowledge

What is the relationship, if any, between contextualism for counterfactuals and for knowledge? They have very similar motivating skeptical puzzles. Both the first and third puzzles presented in

Counterfactuals and knowledge

section 2 closely parallel standard arguments when it comes to skepticism about knowledge. As Ichikawa emphasizes, clashing would-counterfactuals like (14) closely resemble the "abominable conjunctions" of DeRose (1995), such as:

(26) I don't know that I am not a brain in a vat, but I do know that I have hands.

This is similarly true for the clashes between woulds and mights. The possibility that I am a brain in a vat seems to undermine my knowledge that I have hands in the same way the pesky possibilities raised by the skeptics in sections 2.1 and 2.3 undermine the relevant counterfactuals. And Hawthorne (2004: p. 5, fn. 10) points out that the lottery puzzle for knowledge parallels the second puzzle for counterfactuals, the pressure from similarity.

Because at least the puzzles that motivate the contextualist views are so similar, are there any other connections between contextualism for knowledge and counterfactuals?[10] In my work on the subject, I have made no claims either way about a connection between contextualism for counterfactuals and for knowledge. But Ichikawa argues that the domain over which counterfactuals range is the very same domain over which knowledge claims range. Call this *identity contextualism* for short.

Ichikawa endorses a Lewis-style contextualism for knowledge, essentially:

S knows that p if and only if S's evidence eliminates all the p-cases, where 'all' is a context-sensitive restricted quantifier.

(Ichikawa's more developed version includes reference to the basis of the evidence, but this complication need not concern us for present purposes.) The identity claim is that the 'all cases' in the above definition for knowledge and the 'all cases' in the definition for counterfactuals are identical in any given context. Ichikawa offers three reasons to support this: (1) the domains seem to shift together, i.e., the same possibilities can be ignored when it comes to knowledge and counterfactuals, and the same possibilities when introduced into the domain undermine knowledge claims and counterfactuals alike; (2) theoretical simplicity; and (3) treating the domains as identical allows the dissolution of counterexamples to treating safety and sensitivity as necessary conditions on knowledge.

In support of the first point, Ichikawa offers the case of Blanche the professor of abstract science:

Blanche is, and has long been, Professor of Abstract Science. This, as Melissa is well aware, won't change any time soon. So (27) is true:

(27) Melissa knows that Blanche will be Professor of Abstract Science tomorrow.

In the unlikely event that Ida, the principal, abandoned her position tonight, Blanche would leave her post as Professor of Abstract Science and take her place:

(28) If Ida resigned tonight, Blanche would be principal tomorrow.
(2011, p. 299, my numbering of examples)

As Ichikawa points out, the domains for both (27) and (28) in their natural, non-skeptical contexts do not include remote possibilities in which Blanche resigns tonight. Moreover, if the possibility that she resigns tonight is explicitly introduced into the domain, both (27) and (28) are undermined. Ichikawa (2011) writes, "I am unaware of any data suggesting that the two domains should come apart; consideration of particular cases like this one provides some reason for thinking that they will shift together" (p. 300).[11]

In support of the third point, because safety and sensitivity are generally formulated in terms of counterfactuals, and because they are contrapositives of each other, on Ichikawa's semantics for counterfactuals, they are equivalent, necessary conditions on knowledge:

Sensitivity: S knows that p only if $\neg p \; \Box \!\!\rightarrow \neg B(p)$ [on the basis of evidence E]
Safety: S knows that p only if $B(p)$ [on the basis of evidence E] $\Box \!\!\rightarrow p$

In brief, some of the advantages of adopting identity contextualism is that it solves the alleged problem of sensitivity implying the failure of single-premise closure for knowledge claims, because the context shifts between premise and conclusion in the apparent counterexamples. It also resolves various counterexamples that have nothing to do with the failure of closure. For example, consider, as Ichikawa does, Ernie Sosa's garbage chute case.

> **Garbage chute:** Anna throws a trash bag down the chute of her high rise condo. She knows that the bag will soon be in the basement. But in the (incredibly unlikely) case that the bag gets caught in the chute on the way down, she would still believe that the bag would soon be in the basement (based on the same evidence). Thus Anna's belief is insensitive, but seems to constitute knowledge anyhow.
>
> *(Adapted from Sosa 1999, pp. 145–6)*

The counterfactual that establishes sensitivity is *If the bag were not to arrive shortly in the basement, Anna would not believe that the bag would arrive shortly in the basement*. On Ichikawa's identity contextualism, this is *true* in the same context as *Anna knows the bag will arrive shortly in the basement*, since in that context there are no worlds in the domain in which the bag fails to arrive in the basement. Of course, we hear the counterfactual as false, but this is because as soon as it is asserted, it shifts the context so at to include worlds in which the bag doesn't arrive in the basement. In this context, the counterfactual is false, but so is the knowledge claim. It is Ichikawa's contention that all alleged counterexamples can be explained away in this way.[12]

Is identity contextualism right? It certainly is theoretically desirable; we get one contextualism for knowledge and counterfactuals, and it offers an elegant explanation of how sensitivity and safety are necessary conditions on knowledge. But I worry it can't be right. Knowledge claims deal in epistemic possibilities, would-counterfactuals (by most people's lights) in metaphysical ones. By identifying the domains over which they each range, either counterfactuals are more epistemic or knowledge claims more metaphysical than is plausible. Consider the following case. Suppose Kristy and Mary Anne are discussing whether they should take a particular vase off the table before they move the table (since if they move the table with the vase on it, it might fall off). The vase is actually extremely fragile, but they do not know what the vase is made out of, or whether or not it is fragile. Suppose further that the table is 5 feet off the ground, and the floor is marble. In the natural, non-skeptical context the three following sentences are all intuitively true:

(29) If the vase were to drop, it would break.
(30) Kristy doesn't know that if the vase were to drop, it would break.
(31) Kristy doesn't know that the vase is fragile.

For (29) to be true on Ichikawa's semantics, all the worlds in the domain are either ¬drop-worlds or they are drop&break-worlds. In this case, it is trivial that Kristy's evidence rules out

Counterfactuals and knowledge

all drop&¬break-worlds, since there are none in the domain. By the contextualist definition of 'know', Kristy's evidence ruling out all the drop&¬break-worlds in the domain is a sufficient condition for knowledge, thus it follows that Kristy knows that if the vase were to drop, it would break (contra our intuition about [30]). Similarly, assuming that for the vase to be non-fragile means that it can drop without breaking, it is trivial that Kristy's evidence rules out all worlds in which the vase is not fragile, since there are none in the domain. So, contra (31), Kristy does know that the vase is fragile. But this is absurd. The whole set up for the case is that neither Kristy nor Mary Anne know anything about the compositions or dispositions of the vase vis-a-vis its fragility. Now take the case where the domain is such that it makes (30) and (31) true; that is, there are some worlds in the domain (which Kristy's evidence cannot rule out) in which the vase is not fragile, i.e., it drops but does not break. In this case, (29) is straightforwardly false if it ranges over this same domain.[13]

While contextualism may be the right semantic strategy for counterfactuals and knowledge alike (though I want to make no claims about the latter), I have cast doubt on whether the contextualist semantics for the two range over the same domain of possibilities in a given context. It is possible that a more sophisticated contextualism for knowledge or for counterfactuals (or both) could resolve these worries.[14]

Notes

1 For someone who accepts that most counterfactuals are false and adopts an error theory to explain ordinary judgments, see Hájek (ms). For a pragmatic explanation of the data, see Moss (2013).

2 This is equally a problem for Stalnaker, who endorses the uniqueness assumption in his formal semantics, i.e., that there is a unique closest world. In reality, the application of the semantics is often faced with indeterminacy, and ties for equal closeness are represented by the selection function potentially selecting different worlds on different precisifications. For Stalnaker, the problem of counterfactual skepticism as presented by this puzzle is not that most counterfactuals are false, but that most counterfactuals are indeterminate.

3 For arguments against these views see Hawthorne (2005) (against quasi-miracles) and Lewis (2016) (against both).

4 Then again, maybe not. Perhaps the fact that I am uncoordinated just means that there are not *many* worlds among the closest in which I catch the mug, if we think of skill as something like corresponding to how many lottery tickets one has. Thanks to Jonathan Ichikawa (p.c.) for suggesting this. In any case, if this is right, it is only more fuel for counterfactual skepticism and the contextualist solution.

5 See Moss (2012) for a pragmatic account of this data that maintains the traditional Lewis-Stalnaker semantics.

6 In fact, I agree with Ichikawa in that I think a contextualist solution is the best account of this data. See Lewis (Forthcoming) for a full defense of this claim and the account.

7 An exception to this generalization is when the consequent includes much more precise considerations than the sort previously under consideration in the conversation, but this is only applicable here when these rules are combined with substitution of equivalents.

8 Brogaard and Salerno (2008) also argue that apparent counterexamples to antecedent strengthening, contraposition and transitivity are due to shifts in context. It's not clear whether they are using this as an argument in favor of a contextualist strict conditional analysis or not.

9 For a discussion of the metaphysical consequences of embracing either kind of contextualism for the notion of chance, see Emery (2015).

10 For considerations of space, I put aside here the very interesting question of whether there is better or different linguistic evidence for contextualism for one or the other, as well as the question of what alternative options there are for each; e.g. subject-sensitive invariantism is an option for an account of knowledge claims whereas it is not an option for an account of counterfactuals.

11 This example seems like an odd choice in support of the view, since (27) and (28) can't range over the same domain and both be true (unless (28) is trivially true, which is not what I think Ichikawa has in mind). For (28) to be non-trivially true, there are some possibilities in the domain over which it ranges in

which Ida resigns and Blanche is principal tomorrow and so not Professor of Abstract Science. For (27) to be true, there can be no such cases in the domain, since presumably Melissa's evidence doesn't rule out cases in which Ida resigns tonight; rather those cases are properly ignored in the natural, non-skeptical context in which (27) is true. This is just to comment on the oddity of the case in support of identity contextualism, not an objection to identity contextualism itself. Since cases in which Ida resigns are not part of the natural context of (27), there is nothing in Ichikawa's view that requires that these two have the same domain.

12 See Ichikawa (2011) for much more detail on sensitivity and safety.

13 Moving to Ichikawa (2011)'s more sophisticated version of contextualism with basing doesn't help here. On this version, S knows that p just in case, for some evidence E, (i) S believes that p on the basis of E, and (ii) all E cases are p cases (2011: p. 301). The counterexample need only be adjusted to include that Kristy believes that if the vase were to drop, it would break (or that the vase is fragile) based on some intuitively irrelevant or inconclusive evidence (e.g. that it is a vase). Because there are no drop&¬break-worlds in the domain, any evidence, no matter how irrelevant, will trivially eliminate any such worlds.

14 See Ichikawa (2017) for further discussion.

References

Brogaard, Berit & Joe Salerno. 2008. Counterfactuals and Context. *Analysis* 68(297). 39–46.

DeRose, Keith. 1995. Solving the Skeptical Problem. *Philosophical Review* 104(1). 1–52.

DeRose, Keith. 1999. Can It Be That It Would Have Been Even Though It Might Not Have Been? *Noûs, Supplement: Philosophical Perspectives* 33(13). 385–413.

Emery, Nina. 2015. The Metaphysical Consequences of Counterfactual Skepticism. *Philosophy and Phenomenological Research* (Advanced online access: http://dx.doi.org/10.1111/phpr.12254).

Gillies, Thony. 2007. Counterfactual Scorekeeping. *Linguistics and Philosophy* 30. 329–360.

Hájek, Alan. ms. *Most Counterfactuals Are False*. ANU, monograph in progress.

Hawthorne, John. 2004. *Knowledge and Lotteries*. Oxford: Oxford University Press.

Hawthorne, John. 2005. Chance and Counterfactuals. *Philosophy and Phenomenological Research* 70(2). 396–405.

Ichikawa, Jonathan Jenkins. 2011. Quantifiers, Knowledge, and Counterfactuals. *Philosophy and Phenomenological Research* LXXXII(2). 287–313.

Ichikawa, Jonathan Jenkins. 2017. *Contextualising Knowledge*. Oxford: Oxford University Press.

Kratzer, Angelika. 1977. What 'Must' and 'Can' Must and Can Mean. *Linguistics and Philosophy* 1(3). 337–355.

Kratzer, Angelika. 1981. Partition and Revision: The Semantics of Counterfactuals. *Journal of Philosophical Logic* 10(2). 201–216.

Lewis, David. 1973. *Counterfactuals*. Malden, MA: Blackwell.

Lewis, David. 1986. Counterfactual Dependence and Time's Arrow. In *Philosophical Papers Volume II*, chap. 17. Oxford: Oxford University Press, 32–51.

Lewis, Karen. 2016. Elusive Counterfactuals. *Noûs* 50(2). 286–313.

Lewis, Karen. Forthcoming. Counterfactual Discourse in Context. Noûs.

Moss, Sarah. 2012. On the Pragmatics of Counterfactuals. *Noûs* 46. 561–586.

Moss, Sarah. 2013. Subjunctive Credences and Semantic Humility. *Philosophy and Phenomenological Research* LXXXVII(2). 251–278.

Sosa, Ernest. 1999. How to Defeat Opposition to Moore. *Philosophical Perspectives* 13. 141–153.

Stalnaker, Robert. 1968. A Theory of Conditionals. In N. Rescher (ed.), *Studies in Logical Theory*. Oxford: Oxford University Press, 98–112.

Stalnaker, Robert. 1981. A Defense of Conditional Excluded Middle. In W.L. Harper, G.A. Pearce, and R. Stalnaker (eds.), *Ifs: Conditionals, Belief, Decision, Chance, and Time*. Dordrecht: D. Reidel, 87–104.

von Fintel, Kai. 2001. Counterfactuals in a Dynamic Context. In M. Kenstowicz (ed.), *Ken Hale: A Life in Language*. Cambridge, MA: MIT Press, 123–152.

Williams, Robert G. 2008. Chances, Counterfactuals, and Similarity. *Philosophy and Phenomenological Research* 77(2). 385–420.

33

CONTEXTUALISM ABOUT FOUNDATIONS

Daniel Greco

In contemporary philosophical parlance, "contextualism" has a relatively precise meaning. One counts as a contextualist about some sentence just in case one holds that the sentence expresses different propositions when uttered in different contexts. Within epistemology, contextualism about sentences involving "knowledge" and "knows" has been much discussed, as the other essays in this volume illustrate. Contemporary parlance, however, is somewhat recent, and before it came to be established there were other views labeled "contextualist" in epistemology. In the earlier sense I'll focus on in this essay, contextualism was seen as a view about the *structure* of epistemic justification – a kind of middle way between traditional versions of foundationalism on the one hand, and coherentism on the other; on this view, our justified beliefs do rest on a foundation, but *which* foundation they rest on depends, in some sense, on context. While the use of "contextualism" as a label for this view is due mainly to David Annis (1978) and Michael Williams (1991, 2001), the origins of the view itself are often traced to the works of C.S. Peirce, John Dewey, and Ludwig Wittgenstein. Given that contemporary terminology has been relatively securely established, to avoid confusion I won't call this earlier position "contextualism," but will instead refer to it as "flexible foundationalism." I have several aims in this essay. First, I'll present some initial motivations for holding that *something like* flexible foundationalism is attractive as a view about the structure of epistemic justification. Second, I'll show how flexible foundationalism can be developed along different lines, some of which would be classified as contextualist in contemporary parlance, others of which would count as sensitive invariantist, relativist, or even expressivist. Lastly, I'll suggest that flexible foundationalism has fruitful applications to recent epistemological debates, using the internalism/ externalism debate as a case study.

1 Regresses and foundations

Paradox is an engine of progress, at least in philosophy. And while semantic paradoxes drive work in logic, skeptical paradoxes are what animate epistemologists. Flexible foundationalists are no different – in particular, flexible foundationalism can be seen as stemming from dissatisfaction with traditional answers to the regress problem.

425

Daniel Greco

For present purposes, the regress problem can be thought of as a taxonomy for classifying positions on the structure of epistemic justification. The familiar taxonomy is as follows:

Skepticism:	Justification is impossible.
Infinitism:	A belief B must be justified by reason(s) R1, which must be justified by reason(s) R2, which must be justified by . . . The chain of reasons is infinite, and non-repeating.
Coherentism:	A belief B must be justified by reason(s) R1, which must be justified by reason(s) R2, which must be justified by . . . The chain of reasons is infinite, but repeating – at some point we start going in a circle.
Foundationalism:	A belief B must be justified by reason(s) R1 which must be justified by reason(s) R2, which must be justified by . . . reason(s) R*n*. The chain of reasons is finite.

This taxonomy has seemed paradoxical because while it looks to be exhaustive,[1] each of the four positions can seem unattractive. *Very* quickly, it's plausible that we have some justified beliefs, so skepticism is unattractive. Circular reasoning and infinite regresses seem epistemically defective, so coherentism and infinitism face uphill battles. And foundationalism faces the worry that any stopping point in a chain of reasons will be arbitrary. Nevertheless, while each has its defenders, both historically and today most epistemologists have been sympathetic to some form of foundationalism.

Once we're foundationalists, it's very natural to wonder *where* chains of justification come to an end. If there is some class of claims that can provide justification without themselves standing in need of justification, which claims are those, and what makes them so special?

At the risk of oversimplifying centuries of work in epistemology, we can state that this question leads to something of a dilemma for the foundationalist. Traditional, obvious answers to the question have the result that it's very hard for any claims to play a foundational role. Famously, Descartes's project involved looking for indubitable foundations.[2] It's not so hard to see why indubitable claims might be apt to stop regresses. Plausibly, what gives the regress problem its force is that, insofar as I doubt whether P, becoming convinced that P is supported by Q doesn't seem to help resolve my uncertainty if I *also* doubt whether Q.[3] But if I don't doubt that Q, then being shown that Q supports some other proposition P is a natural way to resolve any doubts I might have about whether P.

It's widely accepted that the Cartesian project leads to skepticism; indubitable claims are too few and far between to provide a foundation for the rest of what we ordinarily take ourselves to be justified in believing. Insofar as we want to avoid skepticism, coherentism, and infinitism, a natural response to this failure is to relax the criteria for foundationality. Popular moderate foundationalist views have held, e.g., that beliefs based on perception, or on certain sorts of intuitions, are apt to play a foundational role, even if they're not certain, indubitable, incorrigible, or anything like that.[4] But while this response avoids skepticism, it lacks the internal logic of the Cartesian picture. In the previous paragraph we encountered the idea that any doubted claim won't be apt to play a foundational, doubt-resolving role. If that's right, then insofar as the putative foundations endorsed by the moderate foundationalist are open to doubt, they won't be apt to play that role. The dilemma facing the foundationalist, then, is that if she opts for a well-motivated answer to the question of what makes for foundationality, her view collapses into skepticism. And if she avoids skepticism, she does so at the cost of having an arbitrary, *ad hoc* answer to the question of what it takes to legitimately stop a regress.

Contextualism about foundations

One way of motivating some version of flexible foundationalism is to start by taking the Cartesian idea that freedom from doubt, in *some* sense, really is crucial for a claim to play a foundational role. Rather than entirely giving up on this idea, as moderate foundationalists do, the flexible foundationalist holds that foundational beliefs must be free from doubt *in the local context in which they play a foundational role*, even if they are not in principle indubitable. They needn't be undoubt*able*, but they must be undoubt*ed*. To flesh this out, the flexible foundationalist will have to say something about what it means for claims to be free from doubt in particular contexts, even though they are not in principle indubitable. There are many ways of developing this idea, some of which I'll consider in the following section.

2 Routes to flexible foundationalism

2.1 *Social dimensions of justification*

One way to develop a version of flexible foundationalism is to start by thinking of justification, not as an abstract status a belief might have, but as a *social activity* that we can engage in, perhaps to convince others to adopt our beliefs, or at least to defend ourselves from criticism for holding them.[5] A focus on justification as an activity isn't *incompatible* with belief in justification as a status. But focusing on the activity will influence one's account of the status – e.g., it will be natural to think of a justified belief as one that is *defensible*, via the activity of justification.[6]

Once we think of justification as an activity, some kind of foundationalism becomes very attractive. Infinitism looks unattractive because, given our limited lifespans, we can't go on offering reasons forever; we tend to think that the toddler who keeps asking "why" hasn't fully grasped how the practice of justification works. And coherentism looks unattractive because, in real life, circular arguments are typically rejected as unconvincing. Rather, the real-life activity of justification looks foundationalist – we offer some reasons, but at some point we stop, and at least if the reasons we offered were good ones, a sensible, adult audience will rest content that an adequate justification has been given. But some kind of flexibility is attractive, too. The activity of justification has an audience, and who that audience is – and more importantly, which claims they'll let pass without objection – will vary from context to context. This is the basic idea behind the version of flexible foundationalism offered by David Annis (1978). On his view, "to determine whether S is justified in believing *h* we must consider the actual standards of justification of the community of people to which he belongs" (p. 215). Annis goes on to claim that community standards will determine, in each context, an appropriate "objector-group." In his theory, a justified belief is one that can be defended against the objections the group would raise, and a foundationally justified belief is one that would meet with no objections from the appropriate objector-group.[7]

Perhaps without saying more about how appropriate objector-groups are determined, it's impossible to evaluate Annis's view. Nevertheless, it's easy to worry that, however it's fleshed out, it will be too subjectivist. On Annis's view, if there is nobody in S's community who would object to the claim that P in a certain context, then P will be foundational for S in that context.[8] But couldn't everybody in some community *wrongly* or *inappropriately* take some claim for granted? I don't just mean to say that it's possible for a whole community to take for granted a claim that's false – that, I take it, is uncontroversial.[9] Rather, the claim is that an entire community could make a mistake or violate some genuine epistemic norm in taking some claim for granted – they could treat it as foundationally justified for them, even though it isn't. One might think that Annis's requirement that objector-groups be "appropriate" would give him a way to avoid this objection, but it's not clear that it does; however appropriate objector-groups are determined, if they must

427

be drawn from S's community, and if nobody in S's community would raise any objections to S's belief that P in a certain context, then S's belief that P will be foundational in that context. I'll return to this worry in section 3. For the moment, however, I'll set aside this objection to consider another route by which one might be led to a position similar to Annis's.

2.2 Hinges

In the previous subsection, we saw that a focus on justification as an activity could provide rationales both for foundationalism in general, and more specifically for foundationalism's taking a flexible form. On some interpretations, various of Wittgenstein's remarks in *On Certainty* (1969) can play a similar role. Wittgenstein writes that

> the *questions* that we raise and our *doubts* depend on the fact that some propositions are exempt from doubt, are as it were like hinges on which those turn.
>
> *(section 341, emphasis in original)*

The general idea seems to be that the practice of inquiry – treating questions as both open and amenable to investigation – requires treating *some* questions as closed. He gives the following example to illustrate the point:

> If I ask someone "what colour do you see at the moment?", in order, that is, to learn what colour is there at the moment, I cannot at the same time question whether the person I ask understands English, whether he wants to take me in, whether my own memory is not leaving me in the lurch as to the names of colours, and so on."
>
> *(section 345)*

Here the claims that the interlocutor understands English, that he will cooperate, and that the inquirer's memory is reliable as to color names are all serving as "hinges," in the sense of the earlier remark. They are being taken for granted and not subject to inquiry, in order that a different inquiry – concerning which color is present – may be pursued.

If the preceding thoughts are correct, they can be seen as providing a kind of transcendental argument for something like foundationalism – it's a necessary precondition for inquiry to take place that some claims play a foundational role, providing the framework for justifying other claims without themselves standing in need of justification.[10]

It's also not so hard to see why the form of foundationalism this line of thinking supports will plausibly be flexible, rather than fixed. After all, even if it's true that for any project of inquiry, there must exist some hinge propositions, it's a much stronger claim that there are certain sorts of propositions that must serve as hinges for all inquiries.[11] And in various places, Wittgenstein acknowledges that, over time or from individual to individual, which claims are treated as hinges may vary.[12]

2.3 Knowledge, belief, and flexible foundationalism

In the previous two subsections I discussed routes to flexible foundationalism that have been typically seen as such by their proponents.[13] In this subsection, I'll discuss a different sort of route; it's possible to end up as a flexible foundationalist without *trying*, in a sense I hope to make clear.

Timothy Williamson (2000) famously defends the view that knowledge is evidence; E = K. And he goes on to characterize this view as suggesting "a very modest kind of foundationalism, on which all one's knowledge serves as the foundation for all one's justified beliefs" (p. 186). And Williamson consistently rejects interpretations of his view on which items of knowledge, in order to qualify as such, need to derive support from other beliefs or evidence. Items of knowledge can justify our confidence in further beliefs – e.g., by serving as the data in an inference to the best explanation, as discussed in Williamson (2000, chapter 9) – without themselves standing in need of justification by other beliefs.[14] This seems to amount to the claim that knowledge plays a foundational, regress-stopping role.

Suppose we accept E = K, and the characterization of it as a version of foundationalism. Suppose that in addition, we accept some "flexible" view about the nature of knowledge and/or knowledge attributions, such as contextualism (in the contemporary sense), sensitive invariantism, relativism, or others.[15] We would then end up with a view that is naturally classified, I think, in the same broad family as views discussed in the previous two subsections.[16]

Another, very similar route to such a view would go, not via E = K, but via the "general foundations" theory defended by Gilbert Harman (2001). On Harman's view, *all* beliefs are foundational. On its own, while this may seem like an *odd* version of foundationalism, there isn't obviously anything distinctively flexible about it, in the sense of the theories we've been discussing so far. But it can end up that way, when combined with independently motivated views about the nature of belief. Roger Clarke (2013, 2015), for instance, defends a "sensitivist" view about belief, on which whether a subject believes a proposition will in general depend, quite properly, on various features of her situation not traditionally considered by epistemologists, such as the practical tasks she's engaged in or the conversational context she occupies. I've independently argued that sensitive invariantists about knowledge are committed to similar views about the nature of belief, and have defended the views as plausible.[17] So whether one accepts a foundationalism with knowledge at the base, or with beliefs at the base – neither of which is typically thought of, on its own, as in the same family as the views discussed in the previous two subsections – one can easily end up a flexible foundationalist, if one endorses some further theses about knowledge and/or belief that, while controversial, are far from outlandish.

In the next section, I'll discuss the relationship between flexible foundationalism understood as a family of views about the structure of epistemic justification, and more recent debates between epistemic contextualists, sensitive invariantists, relativists, and expressivists.

3 Relations to recent debates

In this section, I'll sketch how views in the flexible foundationalist family can be developed along contextualist, sensitive invariantist, relativist, and expressivist lines. The case of sensitive invariantism is the most straightforward. Familiar sensitive invariantist views about knowledge hold that whether a subject knows a proposition depends, not just on the sorts of "truth-conducive" factors traditionally considered by epistemologists, but also on a wide range of "contextual" factors, including the practical stakes of the decisions she faces, the conversational context she occupies, and perhaps others.[18] It's relatively straightforward to hold that this dependence on non-traditional factors holds, not just for knowledge, but also for foundationally justified beliefs. Annis's view, as discussed in section 2.1, is most naturally interpreted as a sensitive invariantist view about foundational justification, in which facts about the norms accepted by a subject's community are among the non-traditionally recognized factors nevertheless relevant to epistemic justification. That is, according to that view, whether a subject's belief is foundationally justified depends not just on, e.g., her experiences, background beliefs, and so on, but also on the norms accepted by her community. In this formulation, facts about community norms are playing the same role as facts about practical stakes in the familiar examples used to motivate sensitive invariantism.

We can also develop a sensitive invariantist version of the Wittgensteinian version of flexible foundationalism. We can hold that whether a subject has foundational justification to believe a proposition depends on what inquiries she's engaged in, and whether she must treat that proposition as a hinge – a theoretical fixed point – in order to carry out those inquiries. Since facts about which inquiries a subject is engaged in are, arguably, not among the factors traditionally considered relevant to justification, this would count as a version of sensitive invariantism about foundational justification.

Developing a version of flexible foundationalism along contextualist lines – in the contemporary sense of "contextualist" – is more tricky. The most obvious strategy would be to hold that sentences containing the expression "foundationally justified" express different propositions in different contexts. A contextualist version of Annis's view could hold that when a speaker utters a sentence containing the expression "foundationally justified," which proposition she expresses depends on the norms of her epistemic community. A contextualist version of the Wittgensteinian view might hold, analogously, that which proposition a subject expresses when uttering a sentence containing "foundationally justified" depends on which inquiries the subject is engaged in. But this would, I think, be too quick. Unlike "knows," "justified" and "foundational" are technical terms in philosophy, rarely used – at least in their epistemologically significant senses – by non-philosophers. This both threatens to rob the position of its interest, and makes it hard for the contextualist to appeal to the sort of evidence that more familiar versions of epistemic contextualism are (putatively) supported by; while it's easy to see how one might appeal to empirical linguistic data to adjudicate debates about the semantics of "knows," it's harder to see how similar debates can even get off the ground concerning terms that do not occur in ordinary usage.

However, even if "foundational justification" isn't often directly attributed in natural language, the status it denotes might play an important role in explaining linguistic data. For instance, while we rarely say "that belief is foundationally justified," we may manifest judgments about foundationality in other ways. If I assert "it must be cold outside," it's plausible that I am not only expressing my belief that it's cold outside, but also conveying that I do *not* take this belief to be foundationally justified, but that I instead base it on some inference from other beliefs. If I say that I have a toothache, and you ask me "what makes you think that?" and I respond "Oh come on," it's natural to interpret me as conveying, *inter alia*, that I don't take my belief that I have a toothache to stand in need of justification by further beliefs – that I take it to be foundationally justified (and perhaps obviously so). Taking examples like this as a jumping-off point, a contextualist version of flexible foundationalism might be developed that focused, not on direct attributions of foundationality, but instead on other attributions whose felicity depends on which beliefs are foundationally justified.

It's also possible to develop expressivist and relativist versions of flexible foundationalism. To see why one might find such views attractive, especially in contrast with the sensitive invariantist and contextualist views considered so far, it may help to consider some analogous views in ethics. Consider the view that one is morally obligated to always act in ways approved of by one's community. This view has obvious counterexamples in cases where one's community is morally misguided.[19] However, we can see the sensitive invariantist version of Annis's view as a kind of epistemic analog of this implausible ethical theory. Annis's view implies, roughly, that one is justified in accepting a claim with no further supporting reasons if and only if one's community would raise no objections to the claim. But what if one's community is epistemically misguided? Plausibly, even if my community treats belief in astrology as unobjectionable, that doesn't make it so.

In both the moral and epistemological cases, what these views seem to be missing is space for the idea that the norms of a community might be *wrong*.[20] A contextualist, rather than sensitive invariantist, version of flexible foundationalism might seem better placed to make sense of this idea. To see why, let's start by considering a very simple version of the metaethical view known as "speaker-relativism."[21] This is the view that in calling an action "wrong," I am stating that I disapprove of it. As a speaker-relativist, I can say: ⌜That community thinks that S should ϕ, but they're wrong, S shouldn't ϕ.⌝ In doing so, I'll be stating that I disapprove of S's ϕ-ing. We can define a contextualist version of flexible foundationalism that is, in a way, analogous to speaker-relativism.[22]

This view would have it that, in calling a belief "foundationally justified," I am stating that *I* am committed to treating it as such – e.g., to not asking for further reasons when people express the belief, to being willing to accept its being offered as a reason in support of further beliefs, etc. Given such a view, I could in good conscience say something like the following: ⌜That community thinks that S's belief that P is foundationally justified, but they're wrong – it's not.⌝ The view under consideration would have it that saying something like that amounts to stating that I am committed to *not* treating S's belief that P as foundationally justified.

While this is a significant departure from Annis's more communitarian approach to justification, and gives us *some* of what we want, it's not clear whether it goes far enough. The views discussed in the last paragraph have the following, surprising feature. If someone else, whose norms I don't share, sincerely says that some action(belief) is wrong(foundationally justified), then I may have to admit that what she said was true, even while also holding that the action(belief) is *not* wrong(foundationally justified). This is for essentially the same reason that if I am not hungry, and you are, then when you say, "I am hungry," I should agree that what you said was true, even though I am not hungry. That is, "I am hungry," when uttered by you is about your hunger, while when uttered by me, is about mine. So when you say, "I am hungry," and I say, "I am not hungry," we're not disagreeing; we can both be right. The views in the previous paragraph have it that attributions of moral and epistemic statuses are relevantly like attributions of hunger. When you say ⌜ϕ-ing is wrong⌝ or ⌜The belief that P is foundationally justified⌝ and I say what *looks* like a negation of what you say, we can nevertheless both be right, since you're describing your norms – whether moral or epistemic – and I'm describing mine. But this can seem implausible – if you say an action is right, and I say it is wrong, then it's plausible that we're *disagreeing*, in a way that rules out the possibility that both of us are right.

The challenge raised in the previous paragraph is sometimes referred to as the "problem of disagreement," and the question of whether contextualist and subjectivist views can do justice to it is a live one.[23] Some writers take it to motivate a move from contextualist theories to either expressivist or relativist theories.[24] While the focus in these epistemological debates has been knowledge rather than foundational justification, the issues are very similar. After all, as already mentioned, on some views, relativism and expressivism about knowledge *just are* versions of relativism and expressivism about foundational justification. So the question of whether, if we're going to be *some* kind of flexible foundationalist, we should be contextualists, sensitive invariantists, relativists, or expressivists, looks very much like the analogous question about knowledge, which has been discussed at great length (including in this volume). For this reason, I won't discuss it here. Rather, in the next section, I'll offer a surprising application of flexible foundationalism.

4 An application

4.1 Access and foundationalism

Part of the appeal of flexible foundationalism is the idea that it can accept what's attractive about traditional forms of foundationalism without taking on their burdens.

For example, the flexible foundationalist can agree with the Cartesian claim that doubted claims cannot serve as foundations, without taking on the whole Cartesian project. In this section, I want to discuss what will turn out to be a closely related idea; I'll argue that the flexible foundationalist can accept a version of internalism in epistemology – one which might otherwise have looked indefensibly Cartesian.[25]

Consider the following strong "access internalist" epistemological principle:'[26]

> **(Access)** If S has justification to believe that P, then S has justification to believe that S has justification to believe that P.

There are various ways of providing some *prima facie* motivation for this principle, but I'll offer just one.[27] We saw earlier in the chapter that part of the appeal of the Cartesian version of foundationalism is the idea that there's something unsatisfying about trying to stop a regress with a claim that is itself in doubt. The flexible foundationalist explains this idea by holding that doubted claims cannot be foundational *in the contexts in which they are doubted*, even if they can play a regress-stopping role in other contexts. In what follows, I'll try to argue that this idea that foundational claims cannot themselves be in doubt motivates something like (Access).

Many writers have noted that doubts about "higher-order" epistemological claims – e.g., the claim that one knows that P, or that one is justified in believing that P – very naturally give rise to doubts about "first-order," object-level claims.[28] For instance, if I start to doubt that my evidence supports the claim that organic foods have significant health benefits, I will probably also start doubting the claim that organic foods have significant health benefits. Only somewhat more controversially, it's plausible that this would be good reasoning – it would be a *mistake* to doubt whether one knows or has justification to believe that P, while having no doubts about whether P.[29] This creates an awkward situation for foundationalists who deny (Access). They must admit that there are cases in which some claim is foundationally justified for a subject, but where she lacks justification to believe that she has justification to believe that claim.[30] Why is this awkward? Because if the subject has all the attitudes she has justification to have, and makes no mistakes in reasoning, then she'll treat some claim as a regress-stopper – after all, it's foundationally justified for her – while nevertheless having doubts about its truth (since she will doubt whether she has justification to believe it, which will lead to first-order doubt). We can avoid this result if we hold that subjects always have justification to believe, of those claims that are foundationally justified for them, *that* they are foundationally justified. But that's just a special case of (Access).

However, whatever the *prima facie* motivation for (Access), there are powerful reasons to think that nothing of the sort could be true. The truth of (Access) would be puzzling at best; it would mean that there was a class of facts – facts about what we have justification to believe – such that we always have justification to believe the truth concerning facts in the distinguished class. This is highly unusual – in most if not all other domains, it's always possible that our evidence is misleading. Facts about weather, for example, certainly do *not* have this feature; there can be facts about whether it will rain, snow, or shine, such that we lack justification to believe the truth concerning those facts – perhaps because a meteorologist was mistaken, or just because we have no relevant evidence at all.[31] So if facts about justification are unlike facts about weather, what could explain this difference?

A natural, almost inescapable thought, is the following. (Access) could only be true if there were some distinctive realm of propositions that constituted the supervenience base for facts about what we have justification to believe, such that concerning claims in this distinctive realm, one's evidence is never misleading – whatever one has justification to believe to be true, *is* true.[32] While this might not be *enough* to guarantee the truth of (Access), it seems at least required.

Contextualism about foundations

After all, if the supervenience base for facts about justification lacks this feature, then there will be natural candidates for cases in which we lack justification to believe what is in fact the truth concerning what we have justification to believe. For instance, suppose – obviously falsely – that what we have justification to believe depends on the weather. Then cases in which we lack justification to believe the truth about the weather will be natural candidates for cases in which we lack justification to believe the truth about what we have justification to believe.

In light of such considerations, some defenders of (Access) do endorse strong claims about our epistemic access to the facts on which justification supervenes; Smithies (2012) defends a version of (Access), and holds that the truth of his version of (Access) is explained by the fact that facts about what we are justified in believing supervene on facts about a very special class of mental states. According to Smithies, "The determinants of justification are non-epistemic facts about one's mental states, which are introspectively accessible in the sense that one has introspective justification to believe that those mental facts obtain if and only if they obtain" (2012, p. 297). Smithies goes on to hold that since it is an *a priori* matter which beliefs are justified by which introspectively accessible mental states, one is always in a position to know what one has justification to believe, by a combination of introspection (to find out which introspectively accessible mental states one is in), and *a priori* reflection (to find out what beliefs those mental states justify).

If this is the only sort of strategy available for explaining (Access), however, many philosophers will be inclined to deny the truth of (Access), rather than to accept an inference to the best explanation argument for the existence of a distinctive class of "non-epistemic facts about one's mental states," with the feature that one "has introspective justification to believe that those mental facts obtain if and only if they obtain." After all, to accept the existence of such a class of facts is to accept something very much like a traditional, Cartesian sort of foundationalism. It is to accept that we have what Williamson (2000) has called a "cognitive home." A cognitive home is a realm in which nothing is hidden to us – a class of claims such that, if we pay close enough attention (for Smithies, and arguably for Descartes, this will involve doing careful enough introspection), we will always know which such claims are true, and which are false. Moreover, it is to hold that this cognitive home isn't trivially or uninterestingly small – it doesn't only include, e.g., claims to the effect that we exist – but instead it includes enough to form a supervenience base for all facts about what we have justification to believe.

But there are both general theoretical reasons to doubt that we have any such cognitive home, as well as specific reasons to doubt that claims about our mental states in particular could constitute such a home.[33] Rather than try to rebut these claims, in the next subsection I'll try to argue that explaining (Access) does not require positing the existence of a cognitive home, or at least not one of a traditional sort. Rather, if we adopt flexible foundationalism, we can explain (Access) by appeal to a contextually local cognitive home – in each context, we'll regard some class of facts as constituting a subject's cognitive home, but when doubts about the subject's ability to know facts in the relevant class are raised and taken seriously, the context will shift, and so will the class of facts that we take to constitute the subject's cognitive home; because S's cognitive home is apt to shift its location, we might call it a mobile home.[34]

4.2 Access and flexible foundationalism

The basic strategy that the flexible foundationalist can use to defend (Access) – or rather, a contextualized version of it – is to hold that contexts determine *local* supervenience bases for facts about justification, rather than global ones.[35] Moreover, she can hold that it is a constraint on B's counting as a local supervenience base for facts about what a subject S is justified in believing, that in the context in which B counts as such a supervenience base, S counts as in a position to

433

know the truth concerning B. To see what this amounts to, and how it can help the defender of (Access), it will help to consider an example.

Suppose we're in a context in which the following facts are all taken for granted: Peter is hosting a party, and he has either said to Justine that the party starts at 7:00, or that it starts at 8:00. Whatever Peter said, Justine heard him.

Now someone raises the question of what Justine has justification to believe concerning the time at which the party starts. A natural answer is that Justine should believe whatever Peter told her – if Peter said the party starts at 7:00, that's what Justine has justification to believe. *Mutatis mutandis* if he said the party starts at 8:00. That is, the facts about what Justine has justification to believe locally supervene (given the background presuppositions of our context) on the facts about what Peter said. And because we take it that Justine heard Peter – she knows what Peter said – we'll take it that Justine is in a position to know what she has justification to believe.

To be sure, facts about what Peter said would not make a plausible *global* supervenience base for facts about what Justine has justification to believe concerning the start time of the party. There are certainly contexts in which we would *not* hold that what Peter said fixes what Justine has justification to believe concerning when the party starts. One obvious sort of situation in which we might cease regarding facts about what Peter said as such a supervenience base would be if we were to come to doubt that such facts provide good evidence concerning the start time of the party – if, e.g., Peter had a reputation as a prankster, we might not think that Justine would have justification to trust him. But another reason we might cease regarding facts about what Peter said as a supervenience base for Justine's justification would be if we were to come to doubt that Justine was in a position to know what Peter said.

Suppose, e.g., we come to think that Peter might've mumbled, or that Justine has trouble hearing. If we continued to hold that Justine has justification to believe whatever Peter said, then we would have to regard Justine as not being in a position to know what she has justification to believe. But a more likely response, I think, is that we will change our minds about which facts determine what Justine is justified in believing. Perhaps we'll hold that what she ought to believe about when the party starts depends on when Peter's parties have started in the past (which we take her to remember) or on what Peter's email said (which again, we take her to remember), or just on her best guess as to what Peter said (and we'll take her to be in a position to know what her best guess is), or on some combination of the above sorts of facts.[36] Whatever the new local supervenience base is for facts about what Justine has justification to believe, as long as Justine counts as in a position to know the truth about facts in the new base, there needn't be any obstacle to her being in a position to know what she has justification to believe.

Here's the more general picture into which the above example fits. Each context will determine a local supervenience base for facts about what a subject is justified in believing – a set of propositions B such that, within the local set of worlds taken seriously in the context, there are no differences in what the subject is justified in believing without differences in which propositions in B are true. Moreover, it is a constraint on such bases that if B is a supervenience base for S's justification in context C, then S counts as in a position to know which are the truths in B, relative to context C. This way, we will never say that the facts that determine what a subject has justification to believe are facts that the subject is not in a position to know. We can think of B as a sort of cognitive home – a realm of propositions such that the subject is always in a position to know which are the truths in that realm.[37]

But because we do not believe in cognitive homes of the traditional sort, we'll admit that whatever B is, we *will* be able to raise reasonable doubts about S's ability to know which are the truths in B. To the extent that we take such doubts seriously, the context will shift, and in our new context C', B will not be the local supervenience base for facts about what S has justification

Contextualism about foundations

to believe. Rather, there will be some new supervenience base B', such that S *does* count as in a position to know which are the truths in B'. In each context, we'll count S as having *some* cognitive home (i.e., there will be *some* supervenience base for facts about S's justification, such that S is in a position to know which are the truths in the base), but *which* class of facts constitutes S's home will vary from context to context.

Of course, providing a full defense of this contextualized form of access internalism is well beyond the scope of this chapter. My aim here has been merely to whet the philosophical appetite by sketching an unfamiliar but potentially fruitful application of flexible foundationalism.

5 Conclusion

Flexible foundationalism is the idea that, while the foundationalist answer to the regress problem is correct, which beliefs are apt to play a foundational role in some sense depends on context. In this chapter, I've surveyed a variety of ways different philosophers have been led to this idea, as well as a variety of ways it can be fleshed out, especially in connection with more recent debates about knowledge. Lastly, I argued that it provides the materials necessary to articulate a version of access internalism shorn of Cartesian commitments.

Notes

1 As I've presented it, it's not *quite* exhaustive; it presupposes that justification, if it exists, involves chains of reasons. I won't consider views that reject that presupposition in this essay. On at least some interpretations, however, coherentists, while *technically* represented in the taxonomy, might object that it mischaracterizes their position.

2 See Descartes (2004). For a contemporary analogue, see Chisholm (1966), who holds that foundations must be certain, and takes propositions about one's experiences to fit the bill.

3 This way of seeing the regress problem is especially natural if we take a broadly interactive approach to justification, of a sort inspired by the "argumentative" account of reasoning defended by Mercier and Sperber (2011), or the dialogical account of the normativity of logic defended by Dutilh Novaes (2015); I can't *convince* somebody of P by convincing them that it's supported by Q, unless they're already convinced that Q.

4 See, e.g., Pryor (2000), Huemer (2007).

5 See Dogramaci (2012, 2015), Novaes (2015).

6 That's not to say that someone with a justified belief must be able to *articulate* its justification, just that it must be, in principle, available.

7 Foundationally justified beliefs are trivially justified, since they can be defended against the (nonexistent) objections the group will raise. To be clear, he presents his view as a rejection of foundationalism, rather than a flexible or contextualist version of it, but I take it this amounts to a verbal difference; what I am calling foundationally justified beliefs, he calls "contextually basic" beliefs.

8 This is because the appropriate objector-group is always a subset of S's community. See Annis (1978, p. 215).

9 Perhaps not *entirely* uncontroversial. Richard Rorty famously claimed that "truth is what your contemporaries will let you get away with." On that view, perhaps it's impossible for an entire community to take a false claim for granted. But Rorty's contemporaries didn't let him get away with his claim about truth, so it's self-defeating; if it's true, then it's false. We can safely set it aside.

10 On this interpretation, see Wright (2004). Wright's terminology is somewhat different, however; he says that we have "entitlements" – rather than "justification" – for believing the claims that play this inquiry-enabling role.

11 Formally, it's the difference between a $\forall \exists$ claim, and a $\exists \forall$ claim.

12 For example, remark 98: "Yet this is right: the same proposition may get treated at one time as something to test by experience, at another as a rule of testing."

13 That's not to say that their proponents used the terminology "flexible foundationalism," but just to say that their proponents saw themselves as offering non-traditional answers to questions about the structure of justification.

14 See especially the reply to Brueckner in Pritchard and Greenough (2009).
15 Williamson himself denies such views. See Williamson (2005). But others have combined such views with E = K. See Ichikawa (2013).
16 While the resulting view might seem to have much in common with moderate forms of foundationalism of the sort I raised a worry for in section 1 – namely, that it allows for dubitable beliefs to play a regress-stopping role – I suspect that when combined with "flexible" views about knowledge, this worry can be dealt with. For example, if we are contextualists, in the contemporary sense, we might hold that in any context in which an attributor A takes seriously certain doubts about whether P, which a subject S cannot dispel, then "S knows that P" will be false as uttered by A. Given this view, a belief that is subject to salient, unresolved doubts in the context of a given attributor will never count as knowledge by the standards of that attributor, and so will never be apt, by those standards, to stop regresses.
17 See Greco (2015b).
18 See Hawthorne (2004), Stanley (2005), Fantl and McGrath (2009).
19 See Midgley (2003, ch. 5).
20 That's not to say that Annis isn't aware of this difficulty – see Annis (1978, p. 216) for his attempt to meet it.
21 See Dreier (1990) for a more sophisticated version of the view.
22 The analogy between contextualism in epistemology and speaker-relativism in metaethics is due to Chrisman (2007).
23 See Plunkett and Sundell (2013) for some discussion, generally arguing that the challenge to contextualist and speaker-relativist views has been overstated.
24 See Chrisman (2007) for the former, MacFarlane (2011) for the latter.
25 For some general discussion of the relationship between access internalism on the one hand, and foundationalism on the other, see Smithies (2014), who is sympathetic to both, and argues that they form a coherent package. Though his version of that package is far more Cartesian than the one sketched here.
26 For a discussion of access internalism, and how it differs from other versions of internalism, see Conee and Feldman (2001). Recent work in the internalist tradition tends to shy away from defending anything like (Access). See, e.g., Schellenberg (2013) and Schoenfield (2015) both of whom defend views on which there's something importantly right about internalism, but which specifically avoid commitment to anything like (Access).
27 The *locus classicus* for a defense of access internalism is BonJour (2001).
28 See, e.g., Bergmann (2005). I appeal to this idea to argue that many epistemological debates are not merely verbal in Greco (2015a).
29 See Horowitz (2014) and Way and Whiting (2016) for related discussion.
30 In principle, they might deny this, by endorsing a restricted version of (Access) that holds only for foundationally justified beliefs. But I won't consider this position – well-motivated, internally coherent views on which (Access) doesn't hold in general *also* imply that it doesn't hold in the restricted case of foundationally justified beliefs.
31 See Greco (2014, §1.2) for closely related discussion.
32 Srinivasan (2015) makes this assumption – in particular, she assumes that (Access) would require a kind of privileged, Cartesian knowledge of our own minds.
33 Quine (1951/1953) is probably the most influential critic of the general picture on which all of our knowledge rests on beliefs about matters in a "cognitive home," though in recent years the "anti-luminosity" argument offered by Williamson (2000, ch. 4) has received more discussion. For some reasons to doubt that facts about our phenomenology in particular constitute such a home, see Schwitzgebel (2011).
34 I use this terminology in my (Greco, 2016), which concerns the application of flexible foundationalism to some puzzles concerning epistemic defeat.
35 The distinction between local and global supervenience bases should become clear as this subsection progresses. As an aside, it needn't be an idiosyncratic feature of facts about justification that they only have local supervenience bases. See Rayo (2013) for a "localist" view of representation on which, quite generally, contexts only determine local supervenience bases for facts of most sorts. It is the sort of distinction between "local" and "global" supervenience bases that he is talking about that I mean to be tracking with my terminology; the fact that philosophers of mind use the words "local" and "global" to distinguish between different versions of supervenience is, from the standpoint of the present chapter, an unfortunate coincidence – I do not mean to be tracking the same distinction that they are.

Contextualism about foundations

36 In any of these cases, we might take it that she oughtn't have outright beliefs about the start time of the party, but should instead distribute her confidence over various possibilities. This is compatible with (Access), insofar as we take Justine to be in a position to know how she should distribute her confidence.

37 The view sketched here is very much inspired by similar positions defended by Ram Neta (2002, 2003, 2005). See also Salow (Draft) for a view closely related to one sketched in the text.

Bibliography

Annis, David B. 1978. "A Contextualist Theory of Epistemic Justification." *American Philosophical Quarterly* 15:213–219.

Bergmann, Michael. 2005. "Defeaters and Higher-Level Requirements." *Philosophical Quarterly* 55:419–436.

BonJour, Lawrence. 2001. "Externalist Theories of Empirical Knowledge." In Kornblith, Hilary, editor, *Epistemology: Internalism and Externalism*, pages 10–35. Oxford: Wiley-Blackwell.

Chisholm, Roderick M. 1966. *Theory of Knowledge*. Englewood Cliffs, NJ: Prentice Hall.

Chrisman, Matthew. 2007. "From Epistemic Contextualism to Epistemic Expressivism." *Philosophical Studies* 135:225–254.

Clarke, Roger. 2013. "Belief Is Credence One (In Context)." *Philosophers' Imprint* 13:1–18.

———. 2015. "Preface Writers Are Consistent." *Pacific Philosophical Quarterly* Early View.

Conee, Earl, and Richard Feldman. 2001. "Internalism Defended." In Kornblith, Hilary, editor, *"Epistemology: Internalism and Externalism,"* pages 231–260. Oxford: Blackwell.

Descartes, Rene. 2004. *Meditations on First Philosophy*. Ann Arbor: Caravan Books.

Dogramaci, Sinan. 2012. "Reverse Engineering Epistemic Evaluations." *Philosophy and Phenomenological Research* 84:513–530.

———. 2015. "Communist Conventions for Deductive Reasoning." *Noûs* 49(4): 776–799.

Dreier, James. 1990. "Internalism and Speaker Relativism." *Ethics* 101:6–26.

Fantl, Jeremy, and Matthew McGrath. 2009. *Knowledge in an Uncertain World*. Oxford: Oxford University Press.

Greco, Daniel. 2014. "A Puzzle about Epistemic Akrasia." *Philosophical Studies* 167:201–219.

———. 2015a. "Verbal Debates in Epistemology." *American Philosophical Quarterly* 51:41–55.

———. 2015b. "How I Learned to Stop Worrying and Love Probability 1." *Philosophical Perspectives* 29: 179-201

———. 2016. "Cognitive Mobile Homes." *Mind*.

Harman, Gilbert. 2001. "General Foundations versus Rational Insight." *Philosophy and Phenomenological Research* 63:657–663.

Hawthorne, John. 2004. *Knowledge and Lotteries*. Oxford: Oxford University Press.

Horowitz, Sophie. 2014. "Epistemic Akrasia." *Noûs* 48:718–744.

Huemer, Michael. 2007. "Compassionate Phenomenal Conservatism." *Philosophy and Phenomenological Research* 74:30–55.

Ichikawa, Jonathan Jenkins. 2013. "Basic Knowledge and Contextualist 'E = K'." *Thought: A Journal of Philosophy* 2:282–292.

MacFarlane, John. 2011. "Relativism and Knowledge Attributions." In *Routledge Companion to Epistemology*, pages 536–544. New York and London: Routledge.

Mercier, Hugo, and Dan Sperber. 2011. "Why Do Humans Reason? Arguments for an Argumentative Theory." *Behavioral and Brain Sciences* 34:57.

Midgley, Mary. 2003. *Heart and Mind: The Varieties of Moral Experience*. London and New York: Routledge.

Neta, Ram. 2002. "S Knows That P." *Noûs* 36:663–681.

———. 2003. "Contextualism and the Problem of the External World." *Philosophy and Phenomenological Research* 66:1–8211.

———. 2005. "A Contextualist Solution to the Problem of Easy Knowledge." *Grazer Philosophische Studien* 69:183–206.

Novaes, Catarina Dutilh. 2015. "A Dialogical, MultiAgent Account of the Normativity of Logic." *Dialectica* 69:587–609.

Plunkett, David, and Tim Sundell. 2013. "Disagreement and the Semantics of Normative and Evaluative Terms." *Philosophers' Imprint* 13(3):1–37.

Pritchard, Duncan, and Patrick Greenough, editors. 2009. *Williamson on Knowledge*. Oxford: Oxford University Press.

Pryor, James. 2000. "The Skeptic and the Dogmatist." *Noûs* 34:517–549.

Quine, Willard Van Orman. 1951/1953. "Main Trends in Recent Philosophy: Two Dogmas of Empiricism." *The Philosophical Review* 60:20–43. Reprinted, with alterations, in Quine 1953/1980.

Rayo, Agustín. 2013. "A Plea for Semantic Localism." *Noûs* 47(4):647–679.

Salow, Bernhard. Ms. "Elusive Externalism."

Schellenberg, Susanna. 2013. "Experience and Evidence." *Mind* 122:699–747.

Schoenfield, Miriam. 2015. "Internalism without Luminosity." *Philosophical Issues* 25:252–272.

Schwitzgebel, Eric. 2011. *Perplexities of Consciousness.* Cambridge, MA: MIT Press.

Smithies, Declan. 2012. "Moore's Paradox and the Accessibility of Justification." *Philosophy and Phenomenological Research* 85:273–300.

———. 2014. "Can Foundationalism Solve the Regress Problem?" In Neta, Ram, editor, *Current Controversies in Epistemology*, pages 73–94. London and New York: Routledge.

Srinivasan, Amia. 2015. "Normativity without Cartesian Privilege." *Philosophical Issues* 25(1):273–299.

Stanley, Jason. 2005. *Knowledge and Practical Interests.* Oxford: Oxford University Press.

Way, Jonathan, and Daniel Whiting. 2016. "If You Justifiably Believe That You Ought to Φ, You Ought to Φ." *Philosophical Studies* 173(7):187–189.

Williams, Michael. 1991. *Unnatural Doubts: Epistemological Realism and the Basis of Scepticism.* Princeton: Princeton University Press.

———. 2001. *Problems of Knowledge: A Critical Introduction to Epistemology.* Oxford: Oxford University Press.

Williamson, Timothy. 2000. *Knowledge and Its Limits.* Oxford: Oxford University Press.

———. 2005. "Contextualism, Subject-Sensitive Invariantism and Knowledge of Knowledge." *Philosophical Quarterly* 55:213–235.

Wittgenstein, Ludwig. 1969. *On Certainty.* Oxford: Basil Blackwell.

Wright, Crispin. 2004. "Wittgensteinian Certainties." In McManus, Denis, editor, *Wittgenstein and Scepticism*, pages 22–55. London and New York: Routledge.

PART VIII

Foundational linguistic issues

34

THE SEMANTICS-PRAGMATICS DISTINCTION AND CONTEXT-SENSITIVITY[1]

Maite Ezcurdia

Semantics and pragmatics constitute two areas of study of natural language. Although they are both concerned with empirical issues regarding how natural language works, we ought to be able to draw a principled distinction of the phenomena each studies. On a *standard initial* approximation, we can claim that semantics is concerned with meaning and pragmatics with use. This is not to say much until we understand what meaning and use each is or entails. But it provides a good starting point to explore how the semantics-pragmatics distinction might be drawn.

The use of language involves what speakers *do* with linguistic items such as sentences (what linguistic acts they perform, what and how they communicate), whilst the meaning semantics is concerned with is that associated with linguistic *expressions* and the way they combine to form more complex meanings. So, pragmatics would be concerned with linguistic acts, for example, whether a speaker is making an assertion or expressing a doubt or surprise when he uses a sentence like "John is coming to the party", and what and how he is communicating something (if anything) to his audience upon uttering this sentence. And semantics would be concerned with what the meaning of such a sentence is: how it is obtained from the meanings of the expressions it contains and its syntactic arrangement.

Although this initial standard approximation is clear, it doesn't always indicate whether a linguistic phenomenon ought to be treated by semantics or pragmatics. It does not tell, for example, whether indexicals, that is, expressions that depend on the context in which they are used to obtain a referent, ought to be studied by semantics or by pragmatics. Nor does it tell whether the content(s) of a sentence are the purview of semantics and/or pragmatics.

In what follows, I propose both a principled way of drawing the distinction between semantics and pragmatics and, from it, I develop a methodology that tracks the semantics of expressions and seeks to identify when an expression is context-sensitive. I begin with a rather simple view from which we shall take some lessons in order to arrive at what I take to be the way of drawing the distinction. I end by indicating the sort of evidence that, according to the methodology I propose, the contextualist about "knows" needs to gather in order to support a claim that it is a context-sensitive expression.

441

1 The simple view

Some linguists (Levinson 1983 and Relevance Theorists) have taken it that if a linguistic phenomenon involves an appeal to a context then it is the purview of pragmatics.[2] Context may involve a variety of things: the spatiotemporal location of the speaker, background information or, shared information among participants in a conversation, amongst other things. And theories of communication not only use but characterize what a context is in order to explain how communication in a conversational exchange can succeed. But we should tread carefully here for we have learned from Kaplan's work (1989a, 1989b) on indexicals that a semantic theory can handle context-sensitive expressions. So, we should refrain from making a one-to-one correlation between the need for a context and a pragmatic phenomenon, whilst acknowledging that not every appeal to context ought to be dealt with by a semantic theory.

One could argue that a semantic theory can appeal to context when and only when it determines what is *literally said* by an uttered sentence, whereas pragmatics concerns itself with appeals to context that go beyond what is literally said.[3] The picture that emerges is what I call "the Simple View": pragmatics concerns itself with the general principles that govern linguistic communication, with identifying what a linguistic act is and classifying its different kinds, and with any communicated content that extends beyond what is literally said by an utterance; whilst semantics is concerned with the literal meaning or content said by linguistic utterances.

Suppose that, on the 20th of August, Laura's parents are discussing how to punish her after she has been particularly naughty, and one of them says:

(1) It's Laura's birthday today.

What the utterance of (1) literally says is that the 20th of August is Laura's birthday, but what it communicates goes beyond this, namely, that Laura's punishment should be lenient or postponed due precisely to it being her birthday. The Simple View of the semantics-pragmatics distinction on the content of an uttered sentence holds that a semantic theory explains and identifies what is literally said by an utterance whilst a pragmatic theory explains and determines anything else that gets communicated. Thus, it allows for the contribution of context-sensitive expressions like "today" to be explained by a semantic theory, but it does not allow all context-sensitive content to be explained by a semantic theory. For, on the basis of the conversational context, in particular, of the topic under discussion, and on what was literally said by (1), a pragmatic theory would explain the extra content that is being communicated.[4]

The Simple View takes it that there are phenomena that are clearly the purview of semantics and phenomena that are clearly the purview of pragmatics, and it highlights how semantics and pragmatics can interact in successful communication. Such a clear-cut distinction, however, still needs some justification and refining for it does not yet say why it is all right for a semantic theory to treat context-sensitive expressions nor does it say anything about whether the context-sensitive content of utterances like the following are to be treated semantically or pragmatically:

(2) Laura approached the girls swinging the rope and started jumping.

An utterance of (2) could literally say that Laura approached the girls swinging the rope and started to play jump the rope, or that she approached the girls swinging the rope and just started to jump next to them without playing with them.[5] Which of these constitutes the content literally said appears to depend on specific aspects of a context, namely, on background and shared information of conversational participants as well as the speaker's intentions. However, it is not

The semantics-pragmatics distinction

clear why semantics ought to be concerned with this kind of context. Rather it seems that a theory that deals with the principles of communication and, hence, a pragmatic theory, should determine which is the content that is literally said. Thus, the Simple View, according to which a semantic theory is concerned with what is literally said whilst a pragmatic theory with any other content that depends on context, seems wrong-headed.

Still, the Simple View points us in the right direction for it allows semantics to explain the sort of contribution a context-sensitive expression makes to the literal content of an utterance. Why this is so will get us to a principled way of drawing the distinction. One possible answer is that we are happy to let an indexical like "today" be treated by semantics because the aspects of context that it relies on to explain the contribution it makes to the literal content of an utterance – namely, the spatiotemporal location of the speaker at the time – intrude less into the ground of pragmatics than the initial standard view identified. But I think this is not quite so. The answer, as we shall see next, does not lie in what aspects of context are appealed to but in *how* they are appealed to.

2 Linguistic meaning and context-sensitivity

The standard approximation we began with is right in taking it that semantics studies the meaning of expressions. Speaking this way suggests that it studies a meaning that is *constant* across the different uses an expression might be put to. This constitutes its *linguistic meaning*.

Take the indexical "today" again. "Today" has a level of meaning, namely, reference, which may change depending on the context. But it also has a level of meaning that remains constant at all its uses. "Today" *means*, roughly, the current day or the day of the context.[6] This meaning provides a rule for when "today" refers, viz. an utterance of "today" *refers* to the day of the context. The linguistic meaning of "today" also establishes that the contribution to the literal content of an uttered sentence is not the descriptive content the day of the context, but rather its referent. The linguistic meaning of "today" can be captured by the following:

(T) For any x and for any utterance u of "today": u refers to x relative to context C iff x is the day of C; and x is u's contribution to the literally expressed content.[7]

A subject who is competent in the use of "today" comes to know (T) or something akin to it, and he can exploit this knowledge to use it on different occasions to refer to different objects.

By providing a rule of reference, the linguistic meaning of an indexical constrains when its reference may change. Suppose you have three different contexts in which different utterances of "today" are made. In context $c1$, the speaker is Justine and the day is the 5th of September; in $c2$, the speaker is Fred and the day is the 5th of September; in $c3$, the speaker is Phillippa and the day is the 6th of September. Even though these three contexts are different, in $c1$ and $c2$ utterances of "today" will not differ in reference, but they will with respect to $c3$.

Three things ought to be noted at this stage. Firstly, variation in reference in the case of indexicals, though context-sensitive, is constrained by their linguistic meanings. Secondly, because it is thus constrained, there is *systematicity* to the way in which its reference varies. Utterances of "today" vary in reference if and only if there is a difference in the days of the context; utterances of "I" vary in reference if and only if there is a difference in the utterer; and so on. Thirdly, context comes into play only because the linguistic meanings of indexicals *require* it to come into play to determine their contribution to the content that is literally expressed.

It is this last point that justifies that semantics study the context-sensitivity of indexicals. If studying the linguistic meaning of expressions is within the purview of semantics, in the case

443

of indexicals it must study *how* context comes into play in determining their reference. What we find is that it comes into play in the way required by linguistic meaning. As (T) shows, you cannot tease apart the linguistic meaning of an indexical like "today" from its context-sensitivity. What semantics does do is assume notions that a pragmatic theory should explain: the notions of utterance, context, etc. A pragmatic theory will explain which acts count as utterances, what is involved in a context, and so on. Semantics, on the other hand, will take these notions as primitive and rely on pragmatics to explain them. Thus, (LS) holds:

> (LS) Semantics is *legitimately* concerned with context determining content when and only when the linguistic meaning of an expression *requires* it.

To set things apart, from now on we shall say that the literal content determined by semantics is the literally *expressed* content, whilst the content determined by pragmatics (with some contributions from semantics) is the literally *said* content. The difference is meant to strike a chord with the idea that to say something is to perform a speech act and as such should be studied by pragmatics. The literally expressed content by an uttered sentence may coincide with what is literally said but it needn't do so.

Now, if there is a content that is literally said *or* one that is further communicated[8] by an utterance that requires the intervention of context but that is not owed to the linguistic meaning of an expression, then it is not the purview of semantics. In the case of the utterance of (1) above, because the content that goes beyond what is literally *expressed* by it is not owed to the linguistic meaning of an expression within (1), it is not within the purview of semantics. This is the content that Laura should not be punished on the 20th of August, a content that is *communicated* (though not literally said) to an audience (plausibly, a conversational implicature) and extends beyond the linguistic meaning of (1). Furthermore, no linguistic meaning of any expression within (2) will explain or determine whether an utterance of it literally expresses that Laura approached the girls swinging the rope and just started to play jump rope. Whether it *says* that or that she approached them and just started to jump next to them depends rather on the conversation within which (2) is uttered: its purpose, its topic, the point at which it is made in the course of it, the conversational participants' shared knowledge, the speaker's intentions, amongst others. So determining this aspect of what a literal utterance of (2) says will depend on context, but it will not be a context-sensitivity that will be theorized by semantics but rather by pragmatics.

Although I shall not work out the details here, analogous considerations concerning "today" will apply to all other pure indexicals: "I", "now", "yesterday", etc.[9] However, (LS) also holds with respect to other well-known context-sensitive expressions like demonstratives and contextuals. Unlike pure indexicals, a demonstrative requires that the speaker do something in addition to just uttering an expression in order for it to refer. Merely uttering "this" with an intention of speaking English is not enough to determine a referent in a context. What is needed is for something to be particularly salient or for the speaker to make a gesture like a pointing or his having a particular referential intention.[10] Let us call this extra element "the completer of a demonstrative". The linguistic meaning of "this" can be specified thus:

> (D) For any x and for any utterance u of "this": u refers, if anything, to x relative to a context C iff (i) x is a single entity, (ii) x is sufficiently proximate to the utterer, and (iii) x is the target of the completer; and x is u's contribution to the literally expressed content.[11]

(i) picks up on "this" being singular, (ii) on the contrast with "that", and (iii) is needed for an utterance of a demonstrative to be capable of referring. (D) introduces more elements for

The semantics-pragmatics distinction

pragmatics to explain, which semantics will take as primitive notions. Pragmatics will determine what counts as sufficiently proximate and it will explain what a referential intention, a demonstration, and salience are. Thus, a demonstrative will require different aspects of context than what "today" required. But, just as "today", what it will need will depend on its linguistic meaning, namely, (D). Something similar occurs with contextuals, expressions like "local", "enemy", "immigrant", and "foreigner".

Contextuals are common nouns or adjectives whose linguistic meaning involves a relativization to some parameter that is provided by the context.[12] For example, something is a foreigner or is imported with respect to a place. But that place need not be the place of the utterance, but rather the place determined by aspects of the conversation an utterance of "local" or "imported" is made in. The linguistic meaning of a contextual like "local" will be the following:

(CL) For any x and for any utterance u of "local" in context C: u is satisfied by x iff x is local relative to a place l, where the value of l is determined by C; and being local relative to l is u's contribution to the literally expressed content.

The linguistic meaning of a contextual determines the kind of parameter required (for "local" and "imported" a place, for "foreigner" a nation, for "enemy" a group of people, etc.), but the value of the parameter is determined by the context. What aspects of context determine it are not the spatiotemporal location in which the utterance is made, but rather the intentions of the speaker and the conversation or shared information amongst conversational participants, which exactly will depend on what pragmatics tell us each of these is and which turns out to be better suited given the behavior of contextuals. In any event, the appeal to context in the case of a contextual, as with pure indexicals and demonstratives, is governed by its linguistic meaning. Despite each appealing to different aspects of a context, they all do so conforming to (LS).

We can now settle on the following principled distinction between semantics and pragmatics, a distinction that respects the initial standard approximation according to which semantics is concerned with meanings and pragmatics with use.

Semantics studies the *meanings* of expressions and how they may combine to form more complex meanings according to syntactic arrangement. These meanings include both the linguistic meaning of an expression and its contribution to the content literally expressed by uttered sentences in which it appears. The contribution to such content is either the linguistic meaning itself or it is governed by such linguistic meaning as specified by (LS).

Pragmatics studies the *use* of language, in particular, it studies linguistic acts, the general principles that govern linguistic communication, what a context of use is, and the content of utterances that is obtained from those principles and context. Thus, pragmatics will be concerned with things like what is an utterance, whether it is an assertion or a question, or conversational implicatures, amongst others.

As we have already noted, semantics will assume many notions that a pragmatic theory will explain. However, a pragmatic theory will also assume many things that a semantic theory will deliver: for example, the notion of a linguistic meaning and of a content that is literally expressed (though not the content that is literally said), the specific meanings and literally expressed contents of expressions and uttered sentences, amongst others. These will be useful for a pragmatic theory to derive conversational implicatures and, even, the content of an act of saying, that is, the content literally said by an uttered sentence.[13]

445

3 How can we tell

The principled distinction between semantics and pragmatics we have arrived at is independent of the question of how to determine whether a particular expression is context-sensitive[14] or whether a context-sensitivity associated with certain utterances is pragmatic. What is needed is a methodology for this. Because the linguistic meaning of an expression is what remains constant across all uses and, in the case of context-sensitive expressions, it determines how its contribution to the content expressed may vary, we can devise a methodology that tracks what remains constant across all uses and what is *systematically* obtained from what remains constant. Such methodology will track a semantic rather than a pragmatic fact, and it will help determine whether an expression is context-sensitive.

The methodology I propose assumes that evidence can be gathered from the *intuitions* of rational competent speakers regarding the *truth-values* of utterances of *simple* sentences containing the expression whose context-sensitivity we are testing.[15] Much needs explaining here. Firstly, the sentences in question will be *simple* in order to ensure that the least number of variables need controlling. For example, if we are testing whether "every" is context-sensitive we had better focus on simple sentences rather than on sentences that are under the scope of propositional attitude verbs. It is not that we cannot learn from what happens with such complex sentences, but it is just that it will make it more difficult to determine whether speakers' intuitions are sensitive to the propositional attitude verbs or to "every", the expression we want to test.

Secondly, the intuitions we seek to gather concern truth-values and not what speakers take to be what is expressed by utterances. The reason is that speakers are not sensitive to fine-grained distinctions between what an utterance expresses and what it says or even what it further conveys. So, asking them for intuitions about the expressed content will deliver unreliable results. Furthermore, if we ask for truth-values we can obtain only two answers (at most, three if you allow for truth-value gaps) as opposed to having a wide range of possible answers that may be difficult to handle. If you ask competent speakers whether an utterance of "Lois Lane believed that Superman was not Clark Kent" is true, you can only obtain two (possibly, three) answers (and, most likely, they will converge on its being true). But if you ask them what that utterance expresses, you may get any variety of responses such as: that Lois Lane believed that the man with the superpowers was not the journalist with the glasses, that Lois Lane believed that the man in the red cape was not Clark Kent, that Lois Lane believed that the man named "Superman" is not the man named "Clark Kent", and so on.

Thirdly, as with any attempt at gathering evidence from intuitions, if they are truly to be evidence of anything, they need to be *clear* and *widespread*. For them to be clear they must be put to the test, and for them to be widespread they have to be shared widely amongst the relevant community.

Finally, for the intuitions about the truth-values of utterances to track a semantic fact, they will have to track (i) something that is constant across all uses of the expression in question and/or (ii) something that systematically varies and is obtained from (i). (i) will track linguistic meaning whilst (ii) the systematic variation constrained and determined by linguistic meaning.[16]

The methodology I propose involves five steps and it is best appreciated with examples. But let me first state each step. Let s be a simple sentence that contains e, the expression whose context-sensitivity you wish to test:

Step One: Take a literal and sincere utterance u of s containing e.
Step Two: Ask whether there is a clear and widespread intuition regarding u's truth-value.
 In particular, (a) put the intuition to the test and (b) consider whether it is widely shared.

The semantics-pragmatics distinction

Step Three: Generalize to other literal and sincere utterances of *s*, that is, consider other utterances of the same sentence in *relevantly* different contexts, and repeat Step Two. (Contexts will be relevantly different if they differ at the point at which we take the expression to be context-sensitive.)

Step Four: Consider the consequences of denying the context-sensitivity of *e*. In particular, consider whether denying it would render most of what competent speakers express with literal and sincere utterances of *s* as having a different truth-value from what the clear and widespread intuition says.

Step Five: Generalize further. Take other simple sentences that contain *e*, and run Steps One, Two, Three, and Four for them.

The end result is a methodology that, depending on the results for each of the steps, will allow us to gather very strong but defeasible evidence of whether the expression being put to the test is context-sensitive or not. The evidence is defeasible for two reasons: because the generalization we make in Step Five will not include all sentences in the language that contain *e*; and because, as with any empirical study, other kinds of evidence could come to light that defeat the evidence just gathered.

Two examples will illustrate how the methodology is supposed to work and will show why this methodology tracks the semantics of expressions. The first concerns an expression that is obviously context-sensitive to competent speakers, namely, the indexical "today". Looking at it will serve to show how the methodology would work if "today" were not so obviously context-sensitive. The second example concerns expressions whose context-sensitivity is in dispute, namely, quantifier expressions.

"Today"

Suppose that Laura was born on the 18th of December, 1975, and that John literally and sincerely utters sentence (3) on the 18th of December, 2015:

(3) Laura turns 40 years old today.

Surely, a rational competent speaker (who can add properly!) would say that the utterance of (3) is true. But since we are running our methodology, we need to follow Step Two and consider whether this intuition is clear and widespread. To be sure that it is clear the intuition needs to be put to the test; it needs to be pulled in different directions to see if speakers change their minds about its truth-value. In order to do so, we maintain the original situation, hence, the context, in which the utterance is made and try to point out other facts about the world that could affect its truth-value. In the case of (3) it is difficult to see how we could do so, but as we shall see below with quantifier expressions this is possible. If we cannot put the intuition to the test in this way or the intuition holds up against such a test, then the intuition will be clear. We need to run this sort of test not for one but for many competent speakers to see if the intuition holds up and is widespread.

Step Three requires us to consider other relevantly different utterances of (3). These are utterances made in contexts that differ at the point at which we take the expression to be context-sensitive. In this case, they will be utterances made on different days.[17] We can then posit a context in which again Laura was born on the 18th of December, 1975, but we take a literal and sincere utterance of sentence (3) made on the 20th of January, 2016. And we consider whether the intuition that this new utterance of (3) is false is clear and widespread. If the intuitions of competent

447

speakers converge completely or for the most part, we are then able to consider whether there is a systematic variation in the truth-values of (3) that corresponds to a systematic variation in the reference of "today". If they do, we would have good evidence that "today" is context-sensitive. But our job would not be done yet.

Step Four requires us to consider the consequences of denying that "today" is context-sensitive, in particular, whether denying its context-sensitivity renders the truth-values of the different utterances of (3) different from what the clear and widespread intuition says. If they do then, at this point, we have evidence that "today" is a context-sensitive expression. The rationale for this lies in two considerations: (a) competent speakers of a language know the linguistic meanings of the expressions of their language, and (b) the linguistic meaning of an expression is shaped by the use speakers make of it. Given this, if there is a general or systematic mismatch between the truth-values speakers assign to utterances of sentences and what a theory claims such truth-values to be, then the theory will be mistaken. More specifically, if there is such a mismatch between the truth-values competent speakers clearly and widely assign to utterances of sentences containing "today" and those that are assigned by a semantic theory that denies the context-sensitivity of "today", then we have good reason to think the theory must be wrong, for that theory will not be tracking the linguistic meaning shaped by the use speakers make of it.[18]

Finally, if following Step Five, that is, running Steps Two to Four for other sentences containing "today", provides the same results, then this makes our evidence for the context-sensitivity of "today" even stronger.

Quantifier expressions

Suppose that Paul has had a party at our house in Auckland, and there is no more wine left. He is taking stock whilst he is on the phone to me in my flat in Mexico City. And suppose that he sincerely and literally utters sentence (4):

(4) There is no wine.

A rational competent speaker's intuition will likely be that Paul's utterance is true. But whether it is or not needs to be actually tested amongst speakers. Moreover, the intuition will require testing for its clarity. To that end, we maintain the original situation and point out facts about the world that could render it false. For example, we can point out that there is no scarcity of wine in the world or in Auckland. If this makes the competent speaker withdraw his initial intuition and claim that Paul's utterance is false, then the original intuition about its truth is not clear. If, on the other hand, it does not lead him to withdraw it, then it is clear.

The next stage involves considering the intuitions of other competent speakers regarding the truth-value of Paul's utterance. If the intuition is *not* widely shared, then the likelihood is that no systematicity is to be found in the influence of context that mirrors the linguistic meaning of the quantifier expression and, hence, that the context-sensitivity of the utterance in question is not semantic. However, if the intuitions converge completely or for the most part, then the intuition is widely shared. We are then able to proceed to Step Three and generalize to other relevantly different utterances of (4). One such utterance would be one made by Paul when he is in a wine shop that has just been stocked. Would there be a clear and widespread intuition that Paul's utterance is false? If so, then we can detect that there is some systematicity between the truth-values assigned to utterances of (4) and how the domain of the quantifier is constrained by context.

However, in order to garner more solid evidence we need to consider what would happen if we denied that the domain of the quantifier isn't constrained by context (Step Four). If the truth-values assigned clearly and widely by competent speakers mismatch those which a theory that denies the context-sensitivity of "there is no", then we have good reason to think the theory is wrong.

Further evidence for the context-sensitivity of "there is no" would be gathered if similar results are obtained for other sentences containing it (Step Five).

I acknowledge that the semantics-tracking methodology I am proposing supposes an onerous empirical enterprise, for it aims at gathering intuitions from competent speakers and testing them. This may be collected from corpora of "real-world" written texts and speech. But it will also involve experimental work, especially if the intuitions are to be tested as set out in Steps Two and Three.

Contextualists have claimed that there are many more context-sensitive expressions in language than the obvious ones, than pure indexicals, demonstratives, and contextuals. This may well be so. But in order to justify that claim they need to ensure that the intuitions they appeal to are clear and widespread, and for that empirical work is necessary.[19] My proposal suggests the kind of empirical work that needs to be done. The next section explores the work that has been done by contextualists about "knows", and the work that remains to be done according to the methodology I am advocating.

4 Evidence for epistemic contextualism

Epistemic contextualism[20] makes an empirical claim about the semantics of "knows". It claims that "knows" is a context-sensitive expression, whose linguistic meaning involves attributing knowledge to a certain standard and the standard is set by the context in which the knowledge-ascription is made.[21] It can be captured, roughly, thus:

(EC) For any x and for any utterance u of "knows that p" in context C: u is satisfied by x iff x knows that p relative to standard e, where the value of e is determined by C; and knowing that p relative to e is u's contribution to the literally expressed content.

Epistemic contextualism claims as its *advantages* that it can allow for speakers' intuitions about the truth-values of knowledge-ascriptions in everyday life whilst granting the pull of skeptical arguments. In everyday life, the standards for knowledge do not tend to be as high as the skeptic demands. This is because – according to the contextualist – the context in which the ascription is made does not require such high standards. When considering skepticism, however, the standards are raised to its highest level, and so knowledge-ascriptions will have to answer to them.

Now, the *evidence* that epistemic contextualism claims in its favor lies in what ordinary competent speakers count as knowledge (DeRose 2005: 72). The contextualist gathers this evidence by considering the intuitions that competent speakers have about truth-values of utterances that ascribe knowledge set in different scenarios. The best set ups so far involve third-personal knowledge-ascriptions made in two scenarios that differ just in one respect: in one the standards for knowledge are low whilst in the other they are high. The upshot is that competent speakers will make different judgments in these different scenarios: in the low standards case they will take it that the utterance that ascribes knowledge is true whilst in the high standards case what is true is the utterance that denies knowledge.

However, for the contextualist to be able to claim this as evidence in her favor, she must make sure that what determines the standard for knowing is the context in which the ascriptions are made – the context of use or utterance. This has not always been the case with the original setups where the context of ascription was mixed up with the situation of the subject of knowledge, specifically, with how much is at stake for the subject to whom knowledge is ascribed. Cases in which there is a mismatch between how much is at stake for the subject of knowledge and the level of the standards in the context of ascription would better serve as evidence for contextualism. Such cases can be extracted from DeRose's example of Thelma and Louise (2005: 186–7, 196–7).[22]

Thelma Low Standards

Thelma is talking to Karen and is curious as to how much time her co-workers spend at their offices. She can see that John is in his office, and she is considering whether Louise would be a good source of information. Thelma hears Louise say that John is in his office and knows that Louise has seen his car in the parking lot and the lights on in his office. As she talks to Karen, she utters (5).

(5) Louise knows that John is in his office.

Thelma High Standards

Thelma is talking to the police and can see that John in his office. The police are interested in finding out who would be a good source of information about the whereabouts of Thelma's co-workers. Thelma hears Louise say that John is in his office and knows that Louise has seen his car in the parking lot and the lights on in his office. But she also knows that Louise hasn't checked John's office to see if he hasn't left with a friend. As she talks to the police, she utters (6).

(6) Louise doesn't know that John is in his office.

These cases involve different standards for knowledge but do not say anything about what is at stake for the subject of knowledge, that is, for Louise. The contextualists' prediction is that competent speakers will have the intuition that Thelma's utterances are both true. Much empirical work has been done recently to test if indeed the intuitions that contextualists claim competent speakers have are the intuitions they actually have. The strategies by contextualists in gathering evidence and those who seek to debunk such evidence are on the right track according to the methodology I propose.[23] For they are aiming to track actual intuitions about truth-values and whether these are widespread by considering different cases and utterances of different sentences that ascribe knowledge. (So, they conform partially to Steps One, Two, and Five.) But even if the empirical work done used cases like Thelma's above to test speakers' intuitions about truth-values, and these conformed to the contextualist hypothesis,[24] it would still fall short of providing good evidence for it. For it would not make sure that the intuitions gathered were indeed clear.

According to the methodology I propose, competent speakers' intuitions have to be put to the test in each case. To test them (as before), we maintain the original situations and consider whether there are ways in which the intuitions about truth-values could change. If they don't, then speakers' intuitions will be clear. In *Thelma Low Standards* we take the scenario as is, where, most importantly, Thelma's cognitive situation and the context of the ascription does not change. But we introduce new considerations *to the competent speakers* whose intuitions we are testing. This can involve introducing possibilities that have not been taken into account; for example, that Louise has not popped into John's office to double check that he is there. Or it can also involve pointing out to competent speakers that standards for knowledge could vary. How exactly these may be pointed out to the competent speakers being surveyed in actual experimental settings, I

The semantics-pragmatics distinction

leave the experts to sort out. But what we should make sure of is that these issues are pointed out to the competent speakers but are not introduced as part of the context in which the ascription is made. After all, when putting intuitions to the test we don't want to turn *Thelma Low Standards* into *Thelma High Standards*! The experimenter can be more creative than I am and introduce other sorts of considerations to the competent speakers. The aim in introducing them should ultimately be to try to change the standards that competent speakers take into account. If, despite these introductions, competent speakers hold on to their initial intuitions, then their intuitions will be a reliable source of evidence.

By considering two contrasting cases of high and low standards, contextualists are in a way observing Step Three of the methodology. Strictly speaking, however, what ought to be put to the test is an utterance of (5), instead of (6), in *Thelma High Standards* since Step Three requires that an utterance of the same sentence be considered in relevantly different contexts. So we could run *Thelma High Standards* with an utterance by Thelma of (5). The contextualist would then predict that speakers think that this utterance is false. As with *Thelma Low Standards*, the intuitions of the knowledge-ascription need to be put to the test and, as above, the way to do so would be to introduce to the speakers possibilities not taken into account in the original scenario that attempt to raise even further the standards for knowledge, or to point out that the standards for knowledge could vary.

Should the experiments go as the contextualist expects at this point, she will have some evidence towards her view. But to bolster it, she would need to consider the consequences of denying the context-sensitivity of "knows" (Step Four). In particular, she ought to consider whether denying it would mean assigning truth-values to literal and sincere utterances of (5) contrary to those assigned by competent speakers. This is a consideration that traditional invariantists (Rysiew 2007, 2012), subject sensitive invariantists (Hawthorne 2004, Stanley 2005), and semantic relativists (MacFarlane 2005, 2014) address.[25] They deny the context-sensitivity of "knows" and they attempt to show how their own views about the semantics of "knows", the pragmatics of knowledge-ascriptions and/or about knowledge itself, could rescue speakers' intuitions in the cases presented by contextualists or explain away those intuitions. The extent of their individual success would have to be weighed once the results of the experimental work are in.[26] If their views *systematically* contradict speakers' clear and widespread intuitions about many utterances of knowledge-ascriptions, then the contextualist will have good reason to hold her ground. After all, the methodology that has been put forward is meant to track the *semantics* of the expressions in our language. So, even if pragmatic accounts could be given of speakers' intuitions, there would seem to be little reason to believe them.[27]

If all the steps of the methodology are followed and the results go as the contextualist wants, she will have very solid evidence in favor of her view. However, we must remember that the evidence will be defeasible for we are addressing empirical matters and other kinds of evidence could come to light that undermine or affect the conclusions we draw. All this is speculation of what would happen if all goes well for the contextualist when the semantics-tracking methodology I propose is applied. But there is still much work that needs to be done for speakers' intuitions to indeed serve as evidence for the context-sensitivity of "knows" as the contextualist wants.

Notes

1 Some of the ideas in this chapter were presented at the Philogica IV conference in Bogota, Colombia. I am grateful to audience members for discussion, in particular to Jennifer Saul. I am also grateful to Miguel Ángel Fernández, Denis Bühler, Raymundo Morado, Chris Ranalli, and Jonathan Jenkins Ichikawa for comments. Research for this chapter was funded by the projects PAPIIT IN400513 and IN401315 (DGAPA, UNAM).

2 I take a pragmatic phenomenon just to be a linguistic phenomenon that is studied by pragmatics, and a semantic phenomenon a linguistic phenomenon studied by semantics. Whether the distinction I make here further corresponds to cognitive or other ontological categories is a question I leave open.

3 This view finds its inspiration in Grice's theory of conversation (1975), on which what is literally said is assumed rather than explained.

4 On Grice's theory, it would be explained as a conversational implicature where there is an apparent violation of the Maxim of Relevance.

5 These are cases of explicatures. See Carston (2002) for more examples and a Relevance Theoretic treatment. They have been the source of much discussion between minimalists and contextualists. See Cappelen and Lepore (2005) and Recanati (2004).

6 The day of the context in which an utterance is made will generally coincide with the day of utterance. But this need not be so. In a novel or a story with a timeline you may read: "John was thinking of when to send his paper in. What he didn't realize was that today was the deadline." Here "today" does not refer to the day when the writer wrote it but rather to the day of the context, in particular, the day within the timeline of the story.

7 Why the literally expressed content and not what is literally said will become evident shortly.

8 What is communicated or conveyed can extend beyond what is literally said. Conversational implicatures, for example, are part of what is communicated but not of what is said.

9 For a characterization and list of pure indexicals, see Kaplan (1989a). Pure indexicals are indexicals that are not demonstratives.

10 See Kaplan (1989a) for a defense of demonstrations or salience as completers and Kaplan (1989b) for a defense of intentions as completers.

11 See Ezcurdia (forthcoming) for reasons to take (D) as the linguistic meaning of "this".

12 I shall not argue for this treatment of contextuals here. But rather I take on board much of what Vallée (2003) says about them.

13 See the Introduction to Ezcurdia and Stainton (2013) for a discussion of other ways of drawing the semantics-pragmatics distinction.

14 Not all context-sensitive expressions can be identified at first glance. For example, "actual" and "actually" are context-sensitive expressions (see Kaplan 1989a), but it is difficult to say that speakers are aware of this off the cuff.

15 The methodology below is essentially the same I proposed in Ezcurdia (2009), although I didn't fully appreciate the consequences of applying it. A similar methodology is to be found in Dowell (forthcoming).

16 It is worth making explicit the connections, if any, amongst our intuitions about the truth-values of utterances, what is literally *said*, and what is literally *expressed*. When speakers assign truth-values to utterances they are sensitive to many things: to what is literally expressed, to what is literally said, and/or to the content that is further conveyed. So, a single truth-value assignment cannot serve as direct evidence for either the content said or the content expressed by an utterance.

Systematicity in assignments of truth-values as I am suggesting in the methodology above can help to identify what particular expressions contribute to a literally expressed content and what their linguistic meaning is. Hence, it can help identify the literally expressed content, the content that is obtained from the syntactic arrangement of a sentence, the linguistic meaning of the expressions it contains, and the context required by such linguistic meaning.

But the methodology does not help to identify the content that is literally said, for that depends on the speaker's intentions and the conversational context in question. The connection between the evidence we gather from systematicity in the truth-value intuitions that speakers have and the content that is said can run only through the content that is expressed, and it will do so when and only when those contents coincide or overlap and only at the points in which they coincide or overlap.

17 I have simplified things slightly here. Strictly speaking, the point of difference will be the day of the context which can, but needn't, be the day of utterance. See note 6 above.

18 Although the rationale for Step Four in Ezcurdia (2009) is not exactly the same, the spirit of it is.

19 I leave open the question of whether to classify this empirical work within linguistics or experimental philosophy.

20 For the sake of simplicity, the epistemic contextualism I shall be speaking of is based for the most part on DeRose as expressed in his (1992, 1995, 1999, 2005, 2009, and 2011). But what I say should apply *mutatis mutandis* to other forms of epistemic contextualism as long as they are taken as claims about the semantics of "knows". Thus, it will not include Pynn's (2015) pragmatic contextualism.

21 This differs from DeRose's (1992) proposal of the character of "knows" in terms of having a true belief and being in a good enough epistemic position (992). On my version, knowing may involve having a justified/reliable true belief. But this need not show up on the semantics of "knows".

Furthermore, although I shall not argue for this here, my bet is that, if "knows" is context-sensitive, it is more like contextual adjectives and nouns than indexicals (pure or demonstrative), gradable adjectives, or quantifier expressions.

22 What I put forward takes on many elements of DeRose's example, but it doesn't exactly match it. See also Chapter 2 of this volume.

23 See, for example, Chapter 3 of this volume.

24 See DeRose (2011) for discussion of the different empirical studies (directed, primarily, at Schaffer and Knobe 2012). As he notes, much of the empirical work done does not concern speakers' intuitions about truth-values but rather about what was said or about whether the characters in the vignettes know. He also notes that the cases that will tell against contextualism will not be the latter, but rather those in which what is asked about are speakers' truth-value intuitions. I agree with him though not for the same reasons (see section 3 above).

25 See Part IV of this volume.

26 This is not to say that the defenders of these alternative views do not give other theoretical and empirical arguments in favor of their views.

27 Examples of pragmatic accounts are: Jary and Stainton (Chapter 37 of this volume) who give an explanation of knowledge-ascriptions as explicatures within a Relevance Theory, Brown (2006) who accounts for them in terms of the speakers' warrant in making her assertions ascribing knowledge, and Rysiew (2007) within a Gricean framework.

References

Brown, J. (2006) "Contextualism and Warranted Assertibility Manoevres," *Philosophical Studies*, 130/3: 407–435.

Cappelen, H. and E. Lepore (2005) *Insensitive Semantics: A Defense of Semantic Minimalism and Speech Act Pluralism*, Oxford: Blackwell.

Carston, R. (2002) *Thoughts and Utterances: The Pragmatics of Explicit Communication*, Oxford: Blackwell.

DeRose, K. (1992) "Contextualism and Knowledge Attributions," *Philosophy and Phenomenological Research*, 52/4: 913–929.

DeRose, K. (1995) "Solving the Skeptical Problem," *The Philosophical Review*, 104/1: 1–52.

DeRose, K. (1999) "Contextualism: An Explanation and Defense" in J. Greco and E. Sosa (eds.) *The Blackwell Guide to Epistemology*, 185–203, Oxford: Blackwell.

DeRose, K. (2005) "The Ordinary Language Basis for Contextualism and the New Invariantism," *The Philosophical Quarterly*, 55/219: 172–198.

DeRose, K. (2009) *The Case for Contextualism: Knowledge, Skepticism, and Context: Vol. 1*, Oxford: Clarendon Press.

DeRose, K. (2011) "Contextualism, Contrastivism, and X-Phi Surveys," *Philosophical Studies*, 156/1: 81–110.

Dowell, J. L. (forthcoming) "Truth-Assessment Methodology and the Case against the Relativist Case against Contextualism about Deontic Modals".

Ezcurdia, M. (2009) "Motivating Moderate Contextualism," *Manuscrito, Rev. Int. Fil.*, 30/1: 153–199.

Ezcurdia, M. (forthcoming) "Semantic Complexity" in K. Korta and M. Ponte (eds.) *Reference and Representation in Thought and Language*, Oxford: Oxford University Press.

Ezcurdia, M. and R. Stainton, (eds.) (2013) *The Semantics-Pragmatics Boundary in Philosophy*, Calgary: Broadview Press.

Grice, H. P. (1975). "Logic and Conversation" in P. Cole and J. Morgan (eds.) *Syntax and Semantics* Volume 3, 41–58. New York: Academic Press. Reprinted in Grice (1989) *Studies in the Way of Words*, 22–40, Cambridge, MA: Harvard University Press.

Hawthorne, J. (2004) *Knowledge and Lotteries*, Oxford: Oxford University Press.

Kaplan, D. (1989a) "Demonstratives: An Essay on the Semantics, Logic, Metaphysics, and Epistemology of Demonstratives and other Indexicals" in J. Almog, J. Perry, and H. Wettstein (eds.) *Themes from Kaplan*, 481–563, Oxford: Oxford University Press.

Kaplan, D. (1989b) "Afterthoughts" in J. Almog, J. Perry, and H. Wettstein (eds.) *Themes from Kaplan*, 481–563, Oxford: Oxford University Press.

Levinson, S. C. (1983) *Pragmatics*, Cambridge: Cambridge University Press.

MacFarlane, J. (2005) "The Assessment-Sensitivity of Knowledge-Attributions" in T. Szabó Gendler and J. Hawthorne (eds.) *Oxford Studies in Epistemology*, 197–234, Oxford: Oxford University Press.

MacFarlane, J. (2014), *Assessment Sensitivity*, Oxford: Oxford University Press.

Pynn, G. (2015) "Pragmatic Contextualism," *Metaphilosophy*, 46/1: 26–51.

Recanati, F. (2004) *Literal Meaning*, Cambridge: Cambridge University Press.

Rysiew, P. (2007) "Speaking of Knowing," *Noûs*, 41/4: 627–662.

Rysiew, P. (2012) "Epistemic Score-Keeping" in J. Brown and M. Gerken (eds.) *Knowledge Ascriptions*, 130–138, Oxford: Oxford University Press.

Schaffer, J. and J. Knobe (2012) "Contrastive Knowledge Surveyed," *Noûs*, 46/4: 675–708.

Stanley, J. (2005) *Knowledge and Practical Interests*, New York and Oxford: Oxford University Press.

Vallée, R. (2003) "Context-Sensitivity beyond Indexicality," *Dialogue*, 42/1: 79–106.

35

THE MIND-INDEPENDENCE OF CONTEXTS FOR KNOWLEDGE ATTRIBUTIONS

Giovanni Mion and Christopher Gauker

1 Introduction

If we say that the truth of a statement of the form "*S* knows that *p*" depends on the pertinent context, that raises the question, what determines the pertinent context? One answer would be: the speaker. Another would be: the speaker and the hearer jointly somehow. Yet a third answer would be: no one gets to decide; it is a matter of what the conversation is supposed to achieve and how the world really is, and it can happen that all of the interlocutors are mistaken about the pertinent context. In this way, the contexts relevant to knowledge attributions might be mind-independent.

In this chapter, we will explore the consequences of taking contexts to be mind-independent. We will not give a definitive account of what determines the pertinent context, but we will have something to say about it. Our focus will be on pointing out that certain debates that have been conducted in the literature might have a different outcome if the possibility that contexts are mind-independent were clearly on the table.

2 The mind-independence of contexts generally

Suppose that Mary is the chair of a committee at her workplace. The committee is holding a meeting. At the start of the meeting, she looks around to see who is present, and, as a way of getting the meeting started, she declares, "Everyone is present." Her utterance does not express the proposition that everyone in the universe is present. It expresses only a proposition regarding the members of a contextually determined domain: that all of *them* are present. But who is in the contextually determined domain? Is it everyone that Mary thinks is present? No, she might have overlooked someone's absence. Is it everyone who, Mary thinks, is on the committee? That is, does a person belong to the contextually determined domain if and only if Mary thinks that he or she is a member of the committee? No, because she might have some false opinions about who is on the committee. If someone objects, "No, Philip is on the committee, and he is not here," then Mary should reply, "Oh, I didn't know he was on the committee." Or she should dispute that Philip is on the committee. She should not defend her assertion on the ground that she alone gets to decide who "everyone" in this instance refers to. She cannot excuse her error just by saying, "Oh, well, I didn't mean *him*."

What the example of Mary illustrates is that when the truth of an utterance depends on the pertinent context, we do not ordinarily assume that speakers get to decide on their own which context is pertinent. Even if no one at the meeting knows that Philip is on the committee and no one would raise objections to Mary's assertion, her utterance is false, because the domain of discourse for the context pertinent to her utterance is people on the committee, and she does not get to decide who is really on the committee.

Examples of this kind could be multiplied. If the question is who should stand in the back row for a group photo, and the answer is that the *tall* people in the group should stand in the back, then an utterance of the sentence "Sally is tall" will be true only if Sally really is one of the taller people in the group. The speaker cannot make it true just by intending that the pertinent standard of size be the average height of a third-grader.

In order to state the point clearly, it will help to draw some distinctions. First, we need the distinction between *sentences* and *utterances*. Sentences are repeatable types. Utterances are concrete events or inscriptions that occupy a certain location in time and space. So if Mary says, "Everyone is present" and Henry says, "Everyone is present," then they produce different utterances of a single sentence.

Second, we need the distinction between *contexts* and *situations*. For present purposes, a context is a certain sort of formal structure. A context provides values to a number of variables, such as domain of discourse or standard of size, that have to be evaluated in order to assign a truth value to a sentence. The assignment of values to these variables that a given context provides is the *content* of the context. When we define in a general way what it takes for a sentence to be true relative to a context, we will write sentences of the form, "For every context c, a sentence of the form S is true in c if and only if . . . c . . . " The contexts that we quantify over in such sentences will be formal structures of this kind.

A situation, in contrast, is a concrete arrangement of objects and events. An utterance will be an event that, together with other objects and events, forms a situation. For any utterance, there will be some context that *pertains* to the utterance, or to the situation in which the utterance occurs, and that will be the context that we will look to in deciding whether the utterance is true. Quite generally, an *utterance* will be true (simpliciter) if and only if the *sentence uttered* is true relative to the context that *pertains* to that utterance. An utterance may be true or false because of the features of the situation in which it occurs, but its truth value is not *relative* to the situation. Since utterances are not multiply instantiable in different situations, their truth-values do not have to be further relativized to situations or contexts. (We are ignoring here the claim in MacFarlane [2005] that utterances are true or false relative to an assessor.) Something about the situation in which an utterance takes place will determine which context pertains to the utterance, but these decisive features of the situation do not thereby qualify as elements of the context, since they are not the values in terms of which the truth conditions of sentences are defined.

In these terms, we can now ask: what determines which context pertains to a given utterance? Or, more precisely, which features of the situation determine the content of the context that pertains to a given utterance? The position of the *intentionalist* is that the pertinent context is somehow picked out by the interlocutors' intentions or thoughts regarding the pertinent context. Intentionalists may differ amongst themselves with respect to the question what kinds of thoughts do the job and exactly whose thoughts matter. One could hold that the pertinent thoughts are just the intentions of the speaker, or one could allow that the thoughts of the hearer, or an ideal hearer, are somehow constitutive (on their own, or, as King [2005] holds, in conjunction with the thoughts of the speaker). But it is essential to what we are calling *intentionalism* that the thoughts are in some sense thoughts *about* the pertinent context, even though ordinary speakers will not have the concept *pertinent context* as such. *Objectivists*, by contrast, hold that the determinants of the pertinent context are such that the speaker, as well as the other interlocutors, could all be wrong about the content of the pertinent context and could even be wrong if they correctly represent each other's thoughts about the content of the pertinent context.

It is not our objective here to defend objectivism about contexts in general, but just to identify some consequences of adopting an objectivist conception in the debate about knowledge attributions. Nonetheless, here is a list of some starting points on which one might build a defense of objectivism:

- We understand what people are thinking mainly by understanding what they say. So what people say cannot constitutively depend on what they are thinking (Gauker 2008).
- People's thoughts are like spoken sentences in that their contents depend on the content of a pertinent context. But it would be hard to maintain that the contexts pertinent to thoughts are in turn determined by other thoughts (Gauker 1998).
- Close examination of natural-seeming patterns of discourse reveal that people do regard one another as responsible for speaking in accordance with an objectively determined context (Lewis unpublished).

3 Lewis on attention

A tension between intentionalist and objectivist conceptions of context is evident already in David Lewis's early, influential contributions to the subject of the context-relativity of knowledge attributions. In "Scorekeeping in a Language Game" (1979), Lewis describes contexts as mental scoreboards. On the one hand, each interlocutor has his or her own mental scoreboard and "conversational score is, by definition, whatever the mental scoreboards say it is" (p. 346). On the other hand, in order to qualify as a scoreboard, a mental entity has to more or less conform to the rules for updating the score. But even this much objectivity is compromised by the fact that if someone says something that will be true only if the score has a certain value, then it tends to take on that value (p. 347). Lewis calls rules of this type *rules of accommodation*.

This ambivalence is preserved in Lewis's later application of his scorekeeping approach to the context-relativity of knowledge attributions in "Elusive Knowledge" (1996). According to the theory developed in that paper, a sentence of the form "S knows that p" is true in a context if and only if p holds in all of the possible worlds that contain S's evidence and are not properly ignorable in the context in question. The tension between an intentionalist and an objectivist conception of contexts shows up in the list of rules that determine what possibilities are properly ignorable. On the one hand, what is objectively the case must be attended to: The actual world cannot be ignored, and the attributee's beliefs cannot be ignored (which means, apparently, that not all of the worlds in which the attributee's beliefs are true can be ignored, though perhaps some of them can be). On the other hand, if the speaker so much as attends to a possibility, then it cannot be properly ignored, whether or not it otherwise seems relevant. This is Lewis's notorious *rule of attention*.

By appeal to the rule of attention, Lewis explains how the skeptic seems to get the upper hand over the non-skeptic. Once a skeptical possibility has been raised, it cannot simply be dismissed as irrelevant. Otherwise, we will find ourselves saying, "I know that p but I might be wrong." To say this is to endorse what Lewis calls *fallibilism*, which he considers counter-intuitive. So once a skeptical possibility that cannot be ruled out by our evidence is raised, we have to deny that we know anything that is incompatible with it.

But it is not at all obvious that the rule of attention holds. In many situations, a skeptical hypothesis can certainly be dismissed. If I ask someone, "Do you know which way the river is from here?" and he replies, "No, because I might be a brain in vat," the proper reply is: "Cut the philosophical nonsense: Do you know which way the river is or not?" (Compare Blome-Tilman 2009.) In a situation in which we have lost our way and are trying to find our bearings, the possibility that we are brains in vats can be dismissed as objectively irrelevant. More generally, we would like to say, a speaker cannot make a possibility belong to the context just by taking it to belong to the context. To that extent, at least, the intentionalist is mistaken: the context pertinent to a knowledge attribution is not a matter of what the attributor takes it to be.

4 DeRose on disagreement

An important question for epistemic contextualism is: what truth value should we attribute to knowledge ascriptions when two interlocutors insist on evaluating by different standards? If we assume that the content of the context that pertains to our knowledge attributions is "personally indicated", as Keith DeRose likes to put it (2009, p. 133), then if during a conversation speakers *indicate* different epistemic standards, they will not be able to effectively disagree about someone's epistemic status. They would just be talking past each other. On the other hand, an objectivist conception of contexts will answer that the context that really pertains to a conversation does not have to be the one personally indicated by the interlocutors.

In his 2009 book, employing Lewis's scorekeeping terminology, DeRose contemplates the possibility that "the relevant aspect of the truth-conditions of the various speaker's claims is whatever would be the most reasonable score for the speakers to use, no matter what the personally indicated content of the various speakers may actually be" (p. 141). He calls it the "pure reasonableness view". This view seems to entail the possibility of a gap between the content of the relevant context and each speaker's take on it. Accordingly, it seems to allow for the possibility of interlocutors' being mistaken about the content of the context that truly pertains to their conversation. Such an approach might have led to conclusions about disagreement similar to those of the objectivist, but since DeRose lacks a general account of what may *reasonably* determine the content of a context (see section 8 below), he ends up favoring a different sort of gap.

According to DeRose, if two speakers diverge in their personally indicated content, then there is a gap in the truth conditions of their knowledge attributions. Accordingly, where their standards yield formally contrary knowledge attributions, their attributions are neither true nor false (the "gap view"). He claims that the gap view has the *impressive ability* to "simultaneously respect both the sense that our two speakers are contradicting one another and the feeling that the truth conditions of each speaker's assertions should match that speaker's personally indicated content" (p. 145). However, it is not clear why semantic gaps would account for our sense of contradiction. How can "*p* is neither true nor false" account for our sense that *p* and *not-p* contradict one another? Moreover, since disagreements presuppose genuinely contradictory utterances, on DeRose's view, speakers would fail to disagree with each other even when they take themselves to contradict each other. So DeRose fails to secure that sense of disagreement among speakers that he himself set out to preserve.

Be that as it may, in the end, DeRose brushes the issue of disagreement aside: "Are there any *special* problems that arise for contextualism about 'know(s)' in these situations? If not, there doesn't seem to be much of an objection to epistemic contextualism to be found here" (p. 152). DeRose's retreat is explicitly motivated by the assumption that many context-relative expressions generate irresolvable disagreements. But that assumption would be warranted only given an intentionalist conception of contexts. Quite generally, an objectivist will maintain that when interlocutors interpret context-relative expressions differently, then, provided the conversation is not just confused and the interlocutors have roughly the same goals, at least one of them will be wrong, in that he or she is mistaken about the context pertinent to their conversation. In the particular case of knowledge attributions, the objectivist will say that different interlocutors' knowledge attributions will all be governed by the same objective context, provided, again, that the conversation is not just confused and the interlocutors have roughly the same goals. In that case, if one of them says, "S knows that p" and another says, "S does not know that p", then they contradict one another in the sense that not both of their assertions can be true relative to the context that objectively pertains to their conversation. So, the fact that the interlocutors indicate that they have different conceptions of the context pertinent to their conversation does not prevent it from being the case that there is a unique context that objectively pertains to their conversation relative to which their utterances may be evaluated as true or false (Mion 2013a).

5 Stanley on high stakes

Arguments against contextualism can be generated using the following recipe: Two stories are told in which someone says "S knows that p". In one version the attribution seems true; in the other version it seems false. But the mental states of the speakers are in both stories the same. If we assume that contexts have to be determined by the mental states of the interlocutors, then that will seem to show that context is not the relevant variable. The objectivist's answer to this will be that contexts can vary independently of the mental states of the interlocutors.

In his 2005 book on knowledge attributions, Jason Stanley contrasts several versions of a story about Hanna and her wife Sarah. In all versions of the story, a question arises on Friday about whether a bank will be open on Saturday, and in all of them, the bank will in fact be open on Saturday. In the *low stakes* version of the story, Hannah has only a weak reason for believing that the bank will be open, but also nothing very important depends on whether she is right. Hannah says on Friday, "I know that the bank will be open tomorrow," and we accept her assertion as true. In the *ignorant high stakes* version of the story, Hannah's and Sarah's beliefs are exactly the same as in the low stakes version, but in this case, unbeknownst to them, something bad will happen to them if the bank is not open on Saturday. In this case, it is plausible that we will not regard Hannah's assertion as true.

Stanley assumes that the contextualist will agree that the pertinent feature of the context relevant to the evaluation of knowledge attributions is some collection of facts about the mental states of the interlocutors (p. 23), in particular, their "referential intentions" (p. 25). Since Hannah's and Sarah's mental states in the two stories are exactly the same, he concludes, contextualism cannot account for our different evaluations of Hannah's self-attribution of knowledge in the two cases. In place of contextualism, he proposes what he calls *interest-relative invariantism* (chapter 6). According to this, the crucial difference between the two cases is that in the second case, where we judge Hannah's self-attribution of knowledge false, a higher standard of evidence has to be met, because the consequences of being wrong are so much worse.

The objectivist about context has an easy answer to Stanley's critique: the contexts pertinent to Hannah's utterances in the two stories are not in fact the same. Although the thoughts and intentions in the two stories are the same, that does not mean that the contexts pertinent to the two utterances are the same. Precisely because the stakes are higher in the second case, says the objectivist, the standard of justification that has to be met is higher; so high in fact that Hannah's self-attribution of knowledge does not meet it (Mion 2013b).[1]

6 Stanley on "every"

In his 2004 paper and again in his 2005 book, Stanley sets out to show that a linguistic comparison of "knows" to characteristic context-relative expressions does not support epistemic contextualism. We will argue that some of his objections lose their persuasiveness when viewed in the light of an objectivist conception of contexts.

There are at least two variables that might be thought to generate context-relativity in knowledge attributions. According to the *strength of justification* account (e.g., Cohen 1999), the truth of "S knows that p" depends, among other things, on how strong S's justification for believing that p must be according to the context. On this account, the context-relativity of "knows" is comparable to the context-relativity of gradable adjectives like "flat", because both rest on a contextually determined standard. In contrast, according to the *domain of relevant worlds* account (e.g., Lewis 1996), the truth of "S knows that p" depends, among other things, on the set of possible worlds that are relevant according to the context (see section 3 above). On this account, the context-relativity of "knows" is comparable to the context-relativity of "every", because both rest on a contextually determined domain of entities.[2]

Stanley's linguistic critique of epistemic contextualism focuses on the strength of justification account. He argues that "knows" is not comparable to gradable adjectives, because gradable adjectives admit intensification with words like "very" and admit comparative constructions, such as "flatter than"; whereas "knows", when understood as denoting a relation to a proposition, does not admit of such intensification or such comparative constructions.

Stanley has less to say against the domain of relevant worlds account. Against this he has just one linguistic argument. Compare the following two sentences:

(1) Every student is happy and not every student is happy.[3]
(2) If Bill has hands, then Bill knows that he has hands, but Bill does not know that he is not a bodiless brain in a vat.

Stanley thinks (in effect) that sentence (1) is acceptable, but that (2) is not acceptable. Stanley holds that in the case of genuinely context-relative expressions, such as "every", the contextually determined interpretation can vary with different occurrences of the context-relative expression with a single sentence. So (1) can be acceptable and true. But the contextually determined interpretation of "knows" cannot vary across different occurrences of "knows" in a single sentence. So (2) is unacceptable, and not true. This purported difference is supposed to show that "knows" is not context-relative in the way "every" is.

Against this argument, one may object that it is not so obvious that (1) is really acceptable and true. Certainly, someone could mean something true by it. A speaker could manage to make it clear, for instance by pointing to items in a list, that, with the first conjunct, he is talking about the students in one class and, with the second conjunct, he is talking about the students in another class. But in so doing, the speaker is not exploiting the given conventions of language. If someone says,

(3) This is delicious and this is not delicious.

there is no contradiction, because the conventions of English provide for the use of two different occurrences of "this" to refer to two different objects. But if a speaker manages to mean something true by (1), he or she does it not by exploiting the conventions of English, but by getting his or her meaning across in some other way. So there is room to maintain that, literally speaking, (1) cannot be true (Gauker 2010, Mion 2015).

460

Mind-independence of contexts

From the point of view of intentionalism, this objection to (1) will carry little weight. From this point of view, the speaker is free to intend that different occurrences of "every" have to be evaluated with respect to different domains (and to specify those domains by thinking of them) and those intentions determine the proposition expressed. But from an objectivist point of view, this objection to (1) will carry more weight. Among the objective determinants of the content of a context may be linguistic conventions. Since conventions do not provide for the two occurrences of "every" in (1) to be attached to different domains of discourse, the speaker cannot make it the case that the two occurrences of "every" in (1) are attached to different domains just by intending them to be.

7 MacFarlane on retraction

Suppose that speakers are prepared to retract their earlier knowledge attributions when the standards rise. Such cases might appear to contradict contextualism, because the contextualist should say that the knowledge attributions are correctly evaluated relative to the context that pertains to their utterance.[4] Along these lines, John MacFarlane (2005) has argued that sentence-context pairs may be properly evaluated differently relative to what MacFarlane calls *different points of assessment*. We think that some of these retraction cases can be answered on behalf of contextualism by allowing that contexts are objective.

MacFarlane considers the following dialogue (2005, p. 210): Sam is in the courtroom and on December 10 his car was in fact in the driveway.

Judge: Did you know on December 10 that your car was in the driveway?
Sam: Yes, your honor. I knew this.
Judge: Were you in a position to rule out the possibility that your car had been stolen?
Sam: No, I wasn't.
Judge: So you didn't know that your car was in the driveway, did you?
Sam: No, I suppose I didn't, your honor.
Judge: But you just said you did. Didn't you swear an oath to tell the whole truth, and nothing but the truth?

Offhand, this dialogue seems to pose a challenge to the contextualist. At first, Sam is rightly ignoring the possibility that his car had been stolen, so that by a Lewis-like account of the truth-conditions of knowledge attributions, his self-attribution of knowledge was true. Subsequently, the judge raises the possibility that Sam's car has been stolen, at which point, as a contextualist can likewise acknowledge, Sam can no longer truthfully say that he knew that his car was in the driveway. But the judge's mention of this possibility does not change the context pertinent to the earlier self-attribution of knowledge. So, from a contextualist point of view, Sam does not need to go on, as he does, to retract his earlier self-attribution. He should simply explain to the judge that his earlier claim has to be evaluated relative to a different context than the one that the judge has since created. But this is not what happens. MacFarlane's own position, which he calls *relativism*, is that a single utterance has a truth value only relative to the point of view from which it is assessed. From Sam's initial point of view his attribution of knowledge to himself was true; but relative to his subsequent point of view that same attribution was false.

What an objectivist about context can say in defense of contextualism is that, in at least some such retraction cases, there is really only one pertinent context where there might appear to be two. In the story of Sam and the judge, was the possibility that Sam's car was stolen really relevant to the issue facing the court? If so, then Sam was ignorant of the context pertinent to his initial self-attribution of knowledge, and his self-attribution was false. If not, then the judge had no business raising it. Raising it does not impugn Sam's claim to know that his car was parked in his driveway. Either way, there is an error. Either Sam's initial self-attribution of knowledge was in error or his later retraction was in error. However, the error is not what is called in the literature *semantic blindness* (Hawthorne 2004). The error, whichever it is, does not demonstrate that ordinary speakers are oblivious to the fact that the truth of their assertions depends on the pertinent context. It only demonstrates that ordinary speakers can make mistakes about which context pertains to their assertions, which is just what we should expect on an objectivist account of context.

This appeal to the objectivity of contexts is probably at most one prong in what must be a multi-pronged defense of contextualism against the relativist's use of retraction cases. In other cases, it may be clear that between the original assertion and the subsequent retraction there really has been a shift in the pertinent context. For instance, someone might claim to "know that p" in a situation in which very little of importance depends on whether it is true that p (though it is), and then pass to a situation in which a great deal of importance depends on whether it is true that p. In such cases, there may be a variety of other strategies available for defending contextualism. In order to put the appeal to the objectivity of contexts in perspective, we will briefly list some of them:

- Deny the data. It is not obvious that ordinary speakers cannot recognize a shift in context and defend their earlier knowledge attributions on that basis, thus: "Yes, I said I knew, but back then I was not being interrogated by the police." (This is largely the strategy of Marques [2015].)
- Interpret the retraction not as contradicting the earlier assertion but as a *de novo* contemplation of the question. When a speaker appears to be retracting an earlier assertion, what he or she is really doing may be just asking again, "Did S know that p?" and answering according to the demands of the current context, as he or she conceives of it.
- Allow a certain amount of so-called semantic blindness. It is supposed to be a bad thing for a contextualist to have to admit that ordinary speakers do not understand the conditions under which their own assertions are true and false, because the case for contextualism depends on taking seriously ordinary attributions of knowledge. But that does not mean that we cannot afford to allow that ordinary speakers can sometimes be fooled into attributing falsehood to assertions that contextualism would count as true.

8 What determines the content of a context?

The determinants of the contents of the context pertinent to an utterance are multiple and various. For instance, the determinants of the domain of discourse pertinent to the evaluation of the utterance of a quantified sentence may include at least the following factors:

- The goals of the conversation.
- What other sentences have been uttered recently.
- What objects are perceptually salient.
- What would make most of the utterances that make up the conversation true.

For example, if someone says, "Everyone has heard that Smith is stepping down as company president," then the domain could be:

- the employees of the company, if the goal of the conversation is to decide how to prepare the company for the consequences of Smith's decision;
- the attendees at a stockholders meeting, if someone has just uttered the sentence, "The stockholders have just adjourned their meeting";

Mind-independence of contexts

- the people in the room where the conversation is taking place, if a group of activist employees has gathered in the lunch room and all of them are looking at the speaker;
- the management staff of the company, if in fact all of the management staff has heard the news but many other employees have not.

In the case of the utterance of a sentence of the form "S knows that p", the objective factors that can play a role in the determination of the pertinent standard that the putative knower's belief has to meet include the following:

- How important it is to the interlocutors whether it is true that p. (Stanley was on to something here.)
- What other "knows" sentences have been allowed to pass without challenge and what possibilities have been mentioned. (Lewis was on to something here.)
- Who else the interlocutors are prepared to attribute knowledge to. (Standards for S may be lower where knowledge that p is already granted to many of S's peers.)
- Whether the interlocutors have often made errors on matters related to or similar to the question whether it is true that p.
- How low the standards have to be in order that attributions of knowledge that are made in the course of the conversation tend to be true.

With respect to both of these elements of the context – domain of discourse and standards for knowledge – different factors that have a bearing may point in different directions. So the question arises: how do the various factors combine to generate a definite value (a definite domain of discourse or a definite standard)? Certainly we cannot hope for an algorithm that takes various values for the various factors as input and generates a definite value for the element of the context.

Our position is that one has to face the fact that some objective facts are discoverable only by means of an *all-things-considered judgment*. When we choose between two courses of action, the choices will often have different values on different, incomparable scales (e.g., beauty, altruism, time saved). But we do not feel for that reason that there is never a best choice. The best choice is conceived of as accessible only through a judgment to the effect that all things considered it is best. That is not to say that it is always true that the best is that which we judge to be best, all things considered, for our judgment may be mistaken. For instance, when we grade a student paper, we do suppose that there is a correct grade to assign it, but we have no other basis for assigning it than to make a judgment that, in a nonalgorithmic way, takes into account all of the various virtues that a student paper should exhibit.

So it is with respect to the elements of a context. Our supposition as speakers and interpreters is that *there is* a definite context that pertains to an utterance. But we do not suppose we have any other means of finding out what it is than to contemplate the various features of the situation in which the utterance takes place and then to form a judgment that, in the manner characteristic of all-things-considered-judgments, takes them all into account and yields an answer.

Notes

1 In note 4, p. 25, Stanley argues against the possibility of allowing "the subject's interests at the time of knowing" to bear on the truth value of a knowledge attribution. The objectivist's proposal is not this but, rather, the proposal that the objective situation of the attributor, not the subject, bears on the truth value of the utterance.

463

2 See chs. 26 and 27.
3 In his 1995 paper co-authored with Williamson, Stanley seems to admit that a sentence similar to (1) is contradictory. In his 2004 paper, Stanley uses the following examples to argue that in a single sentence different quantifiers can take different domains: "In Syracuse, there are many serial killers and many unemployed men" and "Every sailor waved to every sailor." These are not good examples for his purposes. The first sentence looks like a joke, and in the second sentence the second quantifier is in the scope of the first. In his 2005 book (p. 65) Stanley seems to say that a sentence like (1) can "with no difficulty at all" be taken as true. We take this to be his considered opinion.
4 See ch. 20.

References

Blome-Tilman, M. (2009) "Knowledge and Presupposition", *Mind* 118: 241–294.

Cohen, S. (1999) "Contextualism, Skepticism, and the Structure of Reason" in J. Toberlin (ed.), *Philosophical Perspectives 13: Epistemology*, Oxford: Oxford University Press: 57–89.

DeRose, K. (2009) *The Case for Contextualism: Knowledge, Skepticism, and Context, Vol. 1*, Oxford: Oxford University Press.

Gauker, C. (1998) "What Is a Context of Utterance?", *Philosophical Studies* 91: 149–172.

Gauker, C. (2008) "Zero Tolerance for Pragmatics", *Synthese* 165: 359–371.

Gauker, C. (2010) "Global Domains versus Hidden Indexicals", *Journal of Semantics* 27: 243–270.

Hawthorne, J. (2004) *Knowledge and Lotteries*, Oxford: Oxford University Press.

King, J. (2005) "Speaker Intentions in Context", *Noûs* 48: 219–237.

Lewis, D. (1979) "Scorekeeping in a Language Game", *Journal of Philosophical Logic* 8: 339–359.

Lewis, D. (1996) "Elusive Knowledge", *Australasian Journal of Philosophy* 74: 549–567.

Lewis, K. (unpublished). "The Speaker Authority Problem for Context-Sensitivity (OR: You Can't Always Mean What You Want)."

MacFarlane, J. (2005) "The Assessment Sensitivity of Knowledge Attributions" in T. S. Gendler and J. Hawthorne (eds.), *Oxford Studies in Epistemology 1*, Oxford: Oxford University Press: 197–233.

Marques, T. (2015) "Retractions", Synthese. doi:10.1007/s11229-015-0852-8.

Mion, G. (2013a) "Epistemic Disagreements: A Solution for Contextualists", *Studia Philosophica Estonica* 6: 15–23.

Mion, G. (2013b) "Skepticism and Objective Contexts: A Critique of DeRose", *International Journal for the Study of Skepticism* 3: 119–129.

Mion, G. (2015) "Does *Knowledge* Function like a Quantifier? A Critique of Stanley", *Philosophical Inquiries* 3: 9–16.

Stanley, J. (2004) "On the Linguistic Basis for Contextualism", *Philosophical Studies* 119: 119–146.

Stanley, J. (2005) *Knowledge and Practical Interests*, Oxford: Oxford University Press.

Stanley, J. & T. Williamson (1995) "Quantifiers and Context-dependence", *Analysis* 55: 291–295.

36

INDEX, CONTEXT, AND THE CONTENT OF KNOWLEDGE*

Brian Rabern

The verb 'knows' is often treated as an intensional operator, and the logic of knowledge is often modelled with a modal operator K – a quantifier over ways that things could be compatible with a subject's knowledge (or evidence). 'Knows' is also often taken to be context-sensitive in an interesting way. What 'knows' means seems to be sensitive to the epistemic features of the context, e.g. the epistemic standard in play, the set of relevant alternatives, etc. There are standard model-theoretic semantic frameworks which deal with both intensional operators and context-sensitive expressions. The basic elements of these frameworks were developed by Lewis (1970), Montague (1968), and Scott (1970), and then received more sophisticated renditions and philosophical interpretations in Kaplan (1989a) and Lewis (1980). In this chapter, we provide a brief overview of the various moving parts of these frameworks, the roles of context and index, the need for double indexing, and the relationship between semantic value and content. With the best version of the standard framework explicated we then return at the end to the treatment of 'know' as a context-sensitive intensional operator (contrasting it with an invariantist treatment).

1 The semantics of parameter shifting and sensitivity

Let's begin with intensional model theory. Modal logic and tense logic saw great advances in mid-twentieth century works such as Carnap (1947), Hintikka (1957), Kripke (1959), Montague (1960), and Prior (1956).[1] The general upshot of this work was that the semantics of intensional constructions can be analysed (model-theoretically) in terms of quantification over parameters or "points" of some kind, e.g. possible worlds, times, etc.[2] Where $\square$ is the modal necessity operator and F is the temporal futurity operator, the respective semantic clauses in terms of quantification over such points – worlds w and times t – are standardly given as follows.[3]

> $[\![\square\phi]\!]^w = 1$ iff for all worlds w' (accessible from w), $[\![\phi]\!]^{w'} = 1$.
> $[\![F\phi]\!]^t = 1$ iff there is a time $t' > t$ such that $[\![\phi]\!]^{t'} = 1$.

An interesting feature of these clauses is that a sentence is not just true or false relative to a model (as in e.g. propositional logic) but also relative to a *point of reference* (e.g. a world or a time) within a model.[4] Thus the semantics is "intensional" or non-extensional. This feature, however, isn't

465

altogether novel to modal and tense logic, since the Tarskian semantics for quantification (given relative to a sequence of individuals g) is already "non-extensional" in this sense:[5]

$$\llbracket \forall \alpha \phi \rrbracket^g = 1 \text{ iff for all sequences } g' \text{ (that are } \alpha\text{-variants of } g), \llbracket \phi \rrbracket^{g'} = 1.$$

By the 1960s, theorists began applying the resources of this type of semantics to the study of languages involving "context-sensitivity" or "indexicality" – the phenomenon whereby the *meaning* of an expression depends on the context of use. Richard Montague (in Montague 1968 and Montague 1970a) called such languages "pragmatic languages" and suggested that a systematic treatment could be achieved by extending the tools of possible world semantics:

> It seemed to me desirable that pragmatics should at least initially follow the lead of semantics – or its modern version, model theory, which is primarily concerned with the notions of truth and satisfaction (in a model, or under an interpretation). Pragmatics, then, should employ similar notions, though here we should speak about truth and satisfaction with respect not only to an interpretation but also to a context of use.
>
> *(1970a: 1)*

With this approach in mind early theorists, e.g. Lewis (1970), Montague (1968), and Scott (1970), proposed that we simply expand the points of reference (or "indices") used for languages with modal and tense operators to include the relevant contextual coordinates.[6] For example, Scott advised as follows:

> For more general situations one must not think of the [point of reference] as anything as simple as instants of time or even possible worlds. In general we will have
>
> $i = (w, t, p, a, \ldots)$
>
> where the index i has many coordinates: for example, w is a world, t is a time, $p = (x, y, z)$ is a (3-dimensional) position in the world, a is an agent, etc. All these coordinates can be varied, possibly independently, and thus affect the truth-values of statements which have indirect references to these coordinates.
>
> *(1970: 151)*

Consider a sentence that contains the first-person pronoun.

(1) I am a spiteful man.

Since the truth of this sentence depends crucially on who utters it, truth must be relativised to agents a in addition to worlds w and times t:

$$\llbracket (1) \rrbracket^{w,t,a} = 1 \text{ iff } a \text{ is in the extension of 'spiteful man' at world } w \text{ and time } t.$$

The essential idea was to generalise the techniques of intensional semantics to sentences containing context-sensitive expressions: given that theorists already had the points of reference (i.e. worlds, times, and variable assignments) used for the semantics of modality, tense, and first-order quantification, a straightforward way to incorporate context-sensitivity was to expand the reference points to include various contextual parameters (e.g. speaker, place, addressee, demonstrata,

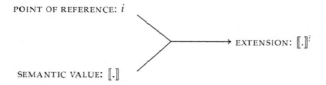

Figure 36.1 Index theory

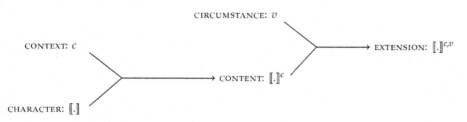

Figure 36.2 Kaplan's two-stage theory

etc.). A model-theory that made use of these expanded indices was thought to afford a formal unified treatment of both intensionality and indexicality (see Figure 36.1). Sentential truth is *sensitive* to a parameter and certain sentential operators *shift* the parameter.

Kaplan (1989a) charged that the notion of a "point of reference" employed by early theorists blurred an important conceptual difference between "context of utterance" and "circumstance of evaluation".[7] He insisted on a two-step semantic procedure, which resolved all context-sensitivity before proceeding, and which distinguished between two kinds of meaning, the *character* and the *content* of an expression. In Kaplan's semantic theory these two aspects of meaning play different roles: the content is the information asserted by means of a particular utterance, whereas the character of an expression encodes what any utterance of the expression would have as content:

- characters $[\![.]\!]$: Contexts → (Circumstances → Extensions)
- contents $[\![.]\!]^c$: Circumstances → Extensions

The general picture is this: the domain of the character function is a set C. Each $c \in C$ is a tuple (or determines a tuple) of content-generating parameters – these tuples are called "contexts of utterance". Character functions map contexts of utterance to contents. The content of an expression is itself a function from a set V to extensions. Each $v \in V$ is also a tuple of parameters, often assumed to be possible worlds (or worlds paired with times, locations, agents, etc.) – these are called "circumstances of evaluation". The resulting Kaplanian picture (Figure 36.2) is as follows:

There are two independent, often conflated, reasons for Kaplan's insistence on this two-step procedure:[8]

- a linguistic motivation stemming from the compositional interaction of intensional operators and indexicals (i.e. double or multiple indexing)
- a pragmatic motivation stemming from the notion of assertoric content ("what is said") and its broader role in communication.

Let's consider each in turn.

Brian Rabern

1.1 Double indexing

The motivation from the compositional interaction of intensional operators and indexicals doesn't actually motivate the character/content distinction. Instead it simply calls for points of reference to be doubly indexed (cf. Lewis 1980). That a semantics for languages with indexicals embedded under intensional operators requires double indexing was first pointed out by Kamp (1971) with regard to tense logic.[9] The following sentences have the same truth-conditions:

(2) It is raining.
(3) It is raining now.

Originally this was taken to motivate a *redundancy* theory of 'now' (Prior 1968b). Letting N be the "now-operator" we could capture the redundancy with the following clause:

$$\llbracket N\phi \rrbracket^t = 1 \text{ iff } \llbracket \phi \rrbracket^t = 1$$

This accounts for the apparent "equivalence" between (2) and (3) but it also raises a difficulty, because (2) and (3) embed differently under other temporal operators:

(4) It will be that case that it is raining.
(5) It will be that case that it is raining now.

These have different truth-conditions, but given the semantics for N above we get the following equivalence (where F is defined as above):

$$\llbracket F \text{ rain} \rrbracket^t = \llbracket F \text{ N rain} \rrbracket^t$$

Kamp showed that a singly-indexed semantics – a semantics that relativises to a point of reference with a single time parameter – cannot accommodate both (i) the data regarding the intuitive equivalence between (2) and (3), and (ii) the difference in embedding behaviour between (2) and (3) – that is, the difference in semantic contribution that (2) and (3) make to more complex sentences such as (4) and (5):

> what we need is not just a definition of the notion: 'ϕ is true at i' but of the more complex notion: 'ϕ is true at i when occurring in a sentence uttered at j'. So our points of reference should be pairs $\langle i, j \rangle$ of moments of time, rather than single moments of time.
> *(Kamp 1967: 2)*

A related way to see the need for double indexing is to consider the following sentence:

(6) Everyone now alive will be dead.

The metalanguage truth-conditions can be represented as such:

$$[\exists t' : t' > t](\forall x(\text{alive}(x, t) \supset \text{dead}(x, t')))$$

And this requires two times in the point of reference, i.e. an assignment of times to *two* distinct temporal variables – for the two temporal variables in the embedded open formula.[10]

Index, context, and content of knowledge

Such considerations – which stem purely from compositionality – motivate double (or multiple) indexing, but don't motivate Kaplan's character/content distinction and the two-step semantics.

1.2 Semantics and "what is said"

The other, more fundamental reason, for Kaplan's insistence on the two-step procedure concerns the relationship between semantics and the contents of assertion. Essential to Kaplan's two-step picture is a particular view about the division of theoretical labor between the components of a point of reference. There's a context, and there's a circumstance. Points of reference are treated as context-circumstance pairs. We need both, according to Kaplan, because we need our semantic theories to be able to capture the two different ways in which, when somebody says (for example), "You are a fool" or "I am a spiteful man," the truth of their utterance depends on the situation in which they say it – roughly, that the situation in which they say it influences both what was said, and whether whatever was said is true. Contexts play a content-generating role – resolving context-dependence in order to determine what's said – and circumstances play a content-evaluating role – they're the things of which what's said is either true or false.

point of reference = ⟨content-generators, content-evaluators⟩

In its content-generating role, the context provides all the various contextual parameters for the resolution of indexicals and other context-sensitive expressions – different people say different things, depending on who's speaking and who's being spoken to, with "You are a fool" and "I am a spiteful man." In its content-evaluating role, the circumstance provides various parameters appealed to in the semantics of intensional constructions. For example, in the evaluation of an utterance of "Necessarily, I am a spiteful man" the modal operator "Necessarily" checks whether, in every circumstance, things are as that particular utterance of "I am a spiteful man" represents things as being. If there is a circumstance of evaluation differing with respect to whether things are as the utterance, in context, represents things as being, then the utterance of the modalized sentence is false (and it's true otherwise).

According to Kaplan the two-step procedure is crucial, since a central task of a semantic theory is to tell us what sentences *say* in various contexts – what propositions or pieces of information do they express in a given context.[11] But contents in Kaplan's framework play an addition role, beyond just being the output of assertion. For Kaplan the content of a sentence also plays a compositional role of being the object of various sentential operators. Thus, contents are constrained depending on the operators of the language, to be the type of semantic entities that enter into compositional relations with those operators. For these reasons, Kaplan is led to endorse temporalism about propositions – the view that propositions can vary in truth value across times.

> If we built the time of evaluation into the contents . . . , it would make no sense to have temporal operators. To put the point another way, if what is said is thought of as incorporating reference to a specific time. . . it is otiose to ask whether what is said would have been true at another time.
>
> *(1989a: 503)*

Lewis insists that the two-step procedure isn't theoretically motivated – he contends that an equally good option is just to evaluate both a context and index in one-step. Lewis emphasises that a theory of the first sort can be easily converted into one of the second, and vice versa, simply by currying or un-currying the functions.

469

The disagreement on this point between Kaplan and Lewis stems from their differing views on the role of assertoric content in the semantic theory. For Kaplan, content has a privileged role in the semantic theory proper: it is both "what is said" and the level of semantic value over which the composition rules can be defined. For Lewis, assertoric content is *post-semantic*. Lewis agrees that "we can assign propositional content to sentences in context" and that "propositions have an independent interest as suitable objects for attitudes such as belief, and [illocutionary acts]" (1980: 37), but he doesn't build into the semantics proper an identification between assertoric content and sets of indices (i.e. semantic values in a context). That is, context and index are playing different roles in the two frameworks for Lewis; in contrast to Kaplan, the "context" is not a sequence of content-generating parameters, and sets of indices are not propositions.

Lewis doesn't equate sets of indices with propositional content, because he doubts that one type of semantic entity can play both roles. In particular, he worries that the parameters that will be required in the indices to provide an adequate compositional semantics might result in sets of indices that are unfit to play the content role. Yalcin provides a nice summary of Lewis' worry as follows:

> It is possible that, owing to the operators the language in question contains, the semantic value of a sentence relative to context must be some complicated intension, variable with respect to an array of parameters – say, parameters for world, time, location, standard of taste, orientation, standard of precision, state of information, etc. The details here will be a contingent matter concerning the particular architecture of the language in question. It has to do with what expressions (if any) are best semantically modeled as intensional operators.
>
> *(2014: 23)*

It was precisely for reasons stemming from "the particular architecture of the language" that Kaplan was led to the conclusion that content is variable with respect to a time parameter – this was due to temporal operators.[12] But since there are potentially further operators that would require further parameters, it seems unlikely that the resulting sets of circumstances will be apt as objects of assertion and the attitudes.

Kaplan's treatment of quantifiers provides a nice example of Lewis's point here (cf. Rabern 2013). The assignment function plays an essential role in the semantics – Tarskian semantics – for the quantifiers. Quantifiers attach to formulas and shift the assignment of values to variables. But if the content of the whole is determined by the content of the parts, then the assignment function is a parameter of the circumstance. Of course, Kaplan doesn't opt for this option, since then contents would be functions from worlds, times, and assignment functions, to truth values.[13] Contents, so conceived, seem ill-suited to play the content role. After all, contents represent what is said, the objects of attitudes such as belief and knowledge, and so forth. What sense does it make to say that what is said, or what is known, is true or false depending on an assignment function? This exemplifies Lewis' point: one type of semantic entity can't play both the compositional and content roles.

Inherent in Lewis's discussion is a dilemma for any view that tries to identify the propositional content of a sentence in a context with the semantic value of a sentence in a context:

1 *First horn*: Let the propositional contents of sentences (in context) be whatever they are according to the preferred account of the representational properties of mental states (belief-desire psychology) and the best account of assertion and communication. Whatever these entities turn out to be, it is very unlikely, given the particular architecture of the language, that they can also serve as the compositional semantic values of sentences.

Index, context, and content of knowledge

2 *Second horn*: Let the semantic values of sentences (in context) be whatever they must be according to our best compositional semantic theory given the particular architecture of the language. Whatever these entities turn out to be, it is very unlikely that they will have independent interest in connection with the representational properties of mental states, and as the objects of assertion, belief, and knowledge.

Of course, someone can wiggle out of the dilemma by either insisting on a (non-standard) syntax/semantics according to which the compositional values are plausibly of independent interest as the objects of assertion or insisting on a theory of assertion and communication such that the entities appealed to there just happen to be the entities apt for compositionality. But Lewis's point is that we have no theoretical reason to expect such correspondence from the outset. Lewis sums up the situation as follows:

> It would be a convenience, nothing more, if we could take the *propositional content* of a sentence in a context as its *semantic value*. But we cannot. The propositional contents of sentences do not obey the composition principle, therefore they are not semantic values.
>
> *(1980: 39)*

If there is no *a priori* constraint on semantic theorizing that a single type of entity plays both of these roles, we should not be worried when the demands of compositional semantics shape "meaning" in a way that is different from our preferred theory of attitude contents. This basic picture of the relationship between compositional semantics and the contents of attitudes has recently been developed and advocated in Ninan (2010), Rabern (2012), and Yalcin (2007). Stanley also endorses such a distinction in terms of Dummett's 'ingredient sense' and 'assertoric content' (Stanley 1997, 2002).[14]

Nevertheless, one might insist that the things we say and the meanings of our words stand in an intimate and theoretically important relationship. After all, we utter words with certain meanings (and certain syntax) in order to say the things we say. Yet, this platitude does not call for the *identification* of the two notions – all it would call for is that the propositional content of a sentence in a context should be systematically *determined* by its semantic value. Lewis states:

> It is enough that the semantic value of a sentence in context should somehow determine the assignment of propositional content. And it does . . . we have the relation: sentence s is true at context c at index i. From that we can define the propositional content of a sentence s in context c as that proposition that is true at world w iff s is true at c at the index i_c^w that results if we take the index ic of the context c and shift its world coordinate to w.
>
> *(1980: 37–38)*

Just as there is a post-semantic definition of *truth-in-a-context* for a sentence given in terms of the sentence's semantic value, there is also a post-semantic definition of the *assertoric-content-in-a-context* of a sentence given in terms of the sentence's semantic value. To demonstrate this point assume that in addition to the context c, extension is relativised to an index consisting of an assignment, a time, and a world – thus points of reference are quadruples $\langle c, g, t, w \rangle$. The compositional semantics will recursively define $[\![.]\!]^{c,g,t,w}$. But we follow Lewis and don't build into the semantics proper an identification between assertoric content and sets of indices.[15] Instead we provide a postsemantic definition of content in terms of semantic values. For example, assuming a classic view of propositions, so that that contents are simply sets of worlds, we can define the content of a sentence ψ in a context c, which we write as $|\psi|^c$, as follows:

Assertoric content: $|\psi|^c = \left\{ w : [\![\psi]\!]^{c, g_c, t_c, w} = 1 \right\}$

2 'Knows': index-shifting and context-sensitivity

The verb 'knows' has been given various semantic analyses in terms of the parameter-sensitive semantic frameworks outlined in the previous sections. In natural language semantics it has been treated as an intensional operator in the manner of Hintikka (1962), and more generally the structure of knowledge has been explored in epistemic modal logic, where knowledge is represented by the modal operator K (see Holliday 2016 for an overview). 'Know' has also been given various analyses where it is sensitive to some contextual parameter, e.g. an epistemic standard, the relevant alternatives, a contrast classes, the question under discussion, etc. (Cohen 1986, DeRose 1995, Lewis 1996, Schaffer 2004). In what follows, we provide an analysis of 'knows' as an intensional operator, and then look at the differences between strict-invariantist, contextualist, and sensitive-invariantist treatments of such an operator.

2.1 'Knows' as an index operator

The idea that attributions of propositional attitudes such as belief, knowledge, memory, desire, etc. can be helpfully analysed as intensional operators goes back to Hintikka:

> an attribution of any propositional attitude to the person in question involves a division of all the possible worlds . . . into two classes: into those possible worlds which are in accordance with the attitude in question and into those which are incompatible with it. The meaning of the division in the case of such attitudes as knowledge, belief, memory, perception, hope, wish, striving, desire, etc. is clear enough. For instance, if what we are speaking of are (say) a's memories, then these possible worlds are all the possible worlds compatible with everything he remembers.
>
> *(1962: 91)*

Hintikka's idea is to treat the semantics of propositional attitudes using off-the-shelf possible world semantics but vary the accessibility relations depending on the attitude. An operator like 'believes' is analysed as follows:

$[\![\alpha \text{ believes } \phi]\!]^{c,w} = 1$ iff for all $w' \in W$ compatible with α's beliefs in w, $[\![\phi]\!]^{c,w'} = 1$

We could also write it in a fashion where it more explicitly appeals to an accessibility relation B^α by letting $B^\alpha(w', w)$ iff w' is compatible with α's beliefs in w. Likewise, 'knows' can be analysed as an intensional operator that quantifies over all the worlds compatible with the agent's *knowledge*, which again we could abbreviate as $K^\alpha(w', w)$:

$[\![\alpha \text{ knows } \phi]\!]^{c,w} = 1$ iff for all $w' \in W$ compatible with α's knows in w, $[\![\phi]\!]^{c,w'} = 1$

Such a clause might not seem very informative − not, at least, to someone interested in the nature of knowledge. But it is not completely uninformative. One could investigate the logical

Index, context, and content of knowledge

properties of the accessibility relation induced by 'knows'. For example, K^α will be reflexive, whereas B^α will not be. One could also unpack the right-hand side in a more informative way in order to reveal the connections to belief, truth, and justification, e.g., as follows:

$[\![\alpha \text{ knows } \phi]\!]^{c,w} = 1$ iff

(i) *Belief*: for all $w' \in W$ compatible with α's beliefs in w, $[\![\phi]\!]^{c,w'} = 1$, and
(ii) *Truth*: $[\![\phi]\!]^{c,w} = 1$, and
(iii) *Justified*: for all $w' \in W$ compatible with α's evidence in w, $[\![\phi]\!]^{c,w'} = 1$.

Of course, this particular semantics seems subject to Gettier counterexamples (Gettier 1963). This is just to demonstrate a way in which 'knows' could be analysed as an intensional operator – Gettier examples are not a special problem for treating 'knows' in such a fashion. For the remaining, we will not worry about adding extra "anti-Gettier" conditions. We will also set aside explicit mention of the belief and factivity conditions,[16] and just focus on the core epistemic feature (with the understanding that the right-hand side really has extra but suppressed sufficient conditions): α knows that ϕ iff α's evidence eliminates every possibility in which not-ϕ and [. . .]. Here we are only interested in certain abstract semantic features concerning the relationship between the meaning of 'knows' and the context of utterance.

2.2 'Knows' as context-sensitive

According to the analyses above 'knows' is an intensional operator, and it is *not* context-sensitive. Consider the simplified clause (let A be a set of worlds, perhaps the set of all worlds):[17]

$[\![\alpha \text{ knows } \phi]\!]^{c,w} = 1$ iff for all $w' \in A$ compatible with α's evidence in w, $[\![\phi]\!]^{c,w'} = 1$

Since "contextualism" is a view about the assertoric content of a sentence in a context, namely the view that the content can vary with context, one can't read "contextualism" off of the semantic clause alone – we also need to appeal to the post-semantic definition of how content is determined by semantic value in a context.[18] Assume a version of the definition of assertoric content from above where the proposition expressed by an utterance of ψ in context c is just the set of worlds in which it is true given c:

$$|\psi|^c = \left\{ w : [\![\psi]\!]^{c,w} = 1 \right\}$$

Contextualism concerns the proposition expressed: does 'α knows ϕ' express the same assertoric content in every context or does the content vary across contexts. The simple clause for 'knows' is clearly not context-sensitive, since for any two contexts c and c', we have (under the assumption that α and ϕ aren't context-sensitive):

$|\alpha \text{ knows } \phi|^c = |\alpha \text{ knows } \phi|^{c'}$

Thus we have a non-contextualist treatment of 'knows'. Call this view "strict invariantism". On this view an utterance of the sentence "α knows ϕ" always expresses the same proposition – in every context it attributes *knowledge* to the agent.[19]

Contextualist views, on the contrary, hold that sentences containing 'knows' can express different propositions in different contexts. What evidence might support this claim? It's the

473

same type of evidence that supports the claim that a sentence such as "I am hungry" (or "Hazel is tall") express different propositions in different contexts: linguistic evidence. It is evidence concerning what we would or wouldn't say, or what would or wouldn't be true, in various situations. (See Part 1 for discussion of Data and Motivations.) In this case, if there are two contexts where utterances of the same sentence seem to have different truth conditions that is some evidence that the knowledge attributions are context-sensitive. For example, consider this situation:

> *Situation 1*. Sam parked his car out front and came into the party. He had a few drinks and mingled with the guests. After a couple of hours we are gossiping with Sam about the party-goers. The conversation turns to the increased number of micro-breweries in the city, and the story of one of our friends who just opened a new brewery in this neighbourhood. Sam suddenly grabs his jacket and heads toward the back door. We interrupt him to remind him that he came in through the front, not the back. Sam replies that he is not leaving he is just going outside to smoke, and then he says

(7) I know that my car is parked out front.

Contrast that with this case:

> *Situation 2*. Sam parked his car out front and came into the party. He had a few drinks and mingled with the guests. After a couple of hours we are gossiping with Sam about the party-goers. The conversation turns to the increased rate of car thefts in the city, and the story of one of our friends who had a car stolen last weekend in this neighbourhood. Sam suddenly grabs his jacket and heads toward the back door. We interrupt him to remind him that he came in through the front, not the back. Sam replies that he is not leaving he is just going outside to smoke, and then he says

(8) I know that my car is parked out front.

Utterance (7) seems unproblematically true. But utterance (8) seems problematic – how can Sam know that his car is parked out front, if he doesn't know that his car hasn't been stolen? It seems that in situation 2, since the prospects of car theft have been made so salient the standards for Sam to count as having knowledge have been raised. There seem to be different epistemic standards operative in the two contexts, in such a way that the proposition expressed varies with the epistemic standard operative in the context.

A very basic kind of contextualism would have it that 'α knows ϕ' is true in c iff α meets the epistemic standard operative in c. An "epistemic standard" is just a placeholder for how good one's epistemic position must be to count as having knowledge – we can construe it in quantitative terms such as the following: the level of justification required or the amount of evidence required. Contextualism doesn't require that *evidence* plays a central role in the account of knowledge, it is compatible with more externalist epistemologies which might cash out the epistemic standard in terms of (e.g.) reliability. The exact nature of the epistemic standard is controversial, and I will remain neutral here. I will simply assume that raising the epistemic standard requires ruling out more possibilities. For example, raising the amount of evidence required for knowledge can be understood as expanding the possibilities that must be ruled out by the evidence. So I will couch the discussion in a way that most resembles the brand of epistemic contextualism found in Lewis (1996) (see Schaffer 2015 for helpful discussion).

Index, context, and content of knowledge

Lewis's gloss on the contextualist semantics was this:

> 'α knows ϕ' is true iff α's evidence eliminates every possibility in which not-ϕ – Psst! – except for those possibilities that we are properly ignoring.

That is, 'α knows ϕ' is true in context c just in case α's evidence eliminates every not-ϕ possibility relevant in c. Since in different contexts different possibilities are relevant, different propositions are expressed. By contrast, on the invariantist view above the set of relevant possibilities A remained constant across contexts. Contrast the invariantist semantics with the contextualist semantics.

STRICT INVARIANTISM:

$[\![\alpha \text{ knows } \phi]\!]^{c,w} = 1$ iff for all $w' \in A$ compatible with α's evidence in w, $[\![\phi]\!]^{c,w'} = 1$

CONTEXTUALISM:

$[\![\alpha \text{ knows } \phi]\!]^{c,w} = 1$ iff for all $w' \in Ac$ compatible with α's evidence in w, $[\![\phi]\!]^{c,w'} = 1$

It is worth pausing here to see the key difference between the contextualist and the invariantist semantics. As I've construed things the difference comes out in a way that might look very insignificant. It comes down to whether or not the set of relevant alternatives A is determined by the context or not. For the invariantist the set of relevant alternatives is invariant – it is always just A,[20] whereas for the contextualist the relevant set of possibilities Ac varies with c. The seemingly insignificant little c subscripted on the A can make a very significant difference: Ac means the set of worlds determined by the context c. Thus, 'knows' requires ruling out all the possibilities in Ac, where this set varies with c – the worlds outside of Ac are "properly ignored". Notice that on the invariantist semantics there is no little subscripted c on A, thus A remains the same no matter the context.

In situation 1, the relevant set of alternatives A_{c_1} doesn't include worlds where the rate of car theft in the neighbourhood is significantly high, whereas in the context of situation 2 – where the prospects of car theft have been made so salient – the relevant set of alternatives A_{c_2} has expanded to include worlds where the rate of car theft is significantly high. According to contextualism the variability data concerning knowledge ascriptions can be accounted for by this sensitivity to the contextually variable epistemic standards.

There is also a brand of invariantism that purports to handle the variability data by appealing to other varying factors that the knowledge attributions are sensitive to.[21] Proponents of this view insist that it isn't the context of the knowledge attributions that matter – the relevant set of worlds doesn't depend on the context – instead what might vary is various factors concerning the agent of the attribution.[22] In this way the relevant set of words is sensitive to the alleged knower's situation – these factors can include things like her presuppositions or what error-possibilities she is considering and further factors that are often described as "non-epistemic" features such as "stakes" or "practical interests" (see e.g. Hawthorne 2004, Stanley 2005, and Chapter 19).

SENSITIVE INVARIANTISM:

$[\![\alpha \text{ knows } \phi]\!]^{c,w} = 1$ iff for all $w' \in A_w^{\alpha}$ compatible with α's evidence in w, $[\![\phi]\!]^{c,w'} = 1$

For situation 1 the set of relevant alternative will be the set $A_{w_1}^{\alpha}$ which depends on Sam's particular situation in w_1, whereas for situation 2, the set of relevant alternatives will be the distinct set $A_{w_2}^{\alpha}$ which depends on Sam's situation in w_2 (where he has just been considering certain theft possibilities, etc.). In this way, the sensitive invariantist claims to account for the variability data in a way that is similar to the contextualist, but while retaining invariantism.

In the case of first-person knowledge ascriptions, contextualism and sensitive invariantism are difficult to tease apart. But the views will make very different predictions about third-person knowledge reports. For example, if we are watching Sam (who is oblivious to the recent increased theft rate) from afar it seems that the truth of our utterance of (9) can vary depending on what is salient in our context of attribution, e.g. the truth of our utterance of (9) can vary depending on whether or not *we* are discussing the recent increased theft rate:

(9) Sam knows that his car is parked out front.

This has been taken to support contextualism over sensitive invariantism. This is not the place to assess contextualism versus sensitive invariantism, but these are the types of cases where the views make different predictions.

Another place where contextualism and subject sensitive invariantism might come apart is with respect to embeddings under various intensional operators, since for the invariantist, but not for the contextualist, shifts of the world can shift the set of relevant alternatives (cf. Stanley 2005: 106–116). For example, take some attribution 'α knows ϕ' that is true according to sensitive invariantism, since the stakes for α in w are so low. Embedding into the consequent of a counterfactual whose antecedent shifts to worlds with higher stakes, however, is predicted to vary the truth value of 'α knows ϕ'. In other words, a counterfactual such as the following is predicted (counterintuitively) to be true.[23]

(10) If the stakes had been higher, then α wouldn't have known ϕ.

In such cases, and further cases involving temporal embeddings, our judgments don't seem to vary in the way the sensitive invariantist predicts. If so, that would be a reason to have the relevant alternatives tied to the context of utterance, instead of the world of the index. See Blome-Tillman (2009), Stanley (2005), and MacFarlane (2014: Chapter 8) for detailed discussion.

Notes

* Thanks to Adam Carter and Derek Ball for helpful comments.

1 See Copeland (2002) for a detailed account of the genesis of possible world semantics.

2 A further important feature of this general approach to intensional semantics is the inclusion of a binary *accessibility relation* on the space of points.

3 Following the notational convention of Dana Scott, we let the equation $\llbracket \phi \rrbracket_{\mathfrak{A}}^{i} = 1$ mean "ϕ is true at point i relative to model $\mathfrak{A}$", but we suppress the model henceforth. See Rabern (2016) and Scott (1970: 150–151).

4 Scott (1970) suggests, "One could call [them] *points of reference* because to determine the truth of an expression the point of reference must be established . . . Maybe *index* is just as good a term, though it seems to me to make them sound rather insignificant" (150).

5 First-order logic is just a modal logic – it's a multi-dimensional modal logic. See discussion in Blackburn et al. (2001).

6 Davidson (1967) also suggested that for natural language semantics, truth should be relativised to times and persons in order to accommodate tense and demonstratives (see Davidson 1967: 319–320). Also notable in this regard is the "egocentric logic" developed in Prior (1968a):

> If I say, not "Brown is ill" but "I am ill", the truth of this depends not only on when it is said but on who says it. It has been suggested, e.g. by Donald Davidson (1967) that just as the former dependence has not prevented the development of a systematic logic of tenses, so the latter should not prevent the development of a systematic logic of personal pronouns.
>
> (193)

Index, context, and content of knowledge

7 Montague, however, seems to have kept a division between the elements of the point of reference that were part of what he called the "context of use" and the element that was the "possible world" (see 1970b: 379–380; Cf. Israel and Perry 1996: 7–8). It is unclear what role, if any, this distinction actually played in Montague's semantic theory – but one might read into it a proto-character/content distinction because Montague seems to identify intensions with Fregean senses.

8 See Stalnaker (forthcoming) for a nice discussion of this point. Cf. Rabern (2012).

9 The ancestor to the 1971 paper on 'now' is Kamp (1967) "The treatment of 'now' as a 1-place sentential operator", which is eight pages of hand-written notes that Kamp presented to Montague's seminar on "pragmatics" at UCLA in 1967. These are stored in the Prior Archives at the Bodleian Library Oxford (Box 15). A copy is also available here: http://semanticsarchive.net/Archive/Tk3ZmEyN/

10 Vlach (1973) upped the ante by focusing on sentences such as the "past tense" version of (6): "Once everyone then alive would be dead." We can represent the logical form of this as follows: $[\exists t' : t' < t][\exists t'' : t'' > t'](\forall x(alive(x, t') \supset dead(x, t'')))$. Given the three temporal variables in the syntax this requires *three* times in the point of reference. With increasingly complex sentences involving further temporal embedding there is a need for further temporal parameters. See Cresswell (1990) for a detailed discussion.

11 "The idea of Content – the what-is-said on a particular occasion – is central to my account" (Kaplan 1989a: 568).

12 Kaplan does notice that there is a tension between the functional notion of content in terms of compositionality and the traditional notion in terms of assertoric content; he says:

> This functional notion of the content of a sentence in a context may not, because of the neutrality of content with respect to time and place, say, exactly correspond to the classical conception of a proposition. But the classical conception can be introduced by adding the demonstratives 'now' and 'here' to the sentence and taking the content of the result. I will continue to refer to the content of a sentence as a proposition, ignoring the classical use.
>
> (1989a: 504)

He does not, however, seem to appreciate the implications of the gap between assertoric content and compositional value.

13 For Kaplan the assignment function is a parameter of context (cf. 1989b: 591). He defines the content of ϕ in the context c under the assignment f, which he symbolises with $\{\phi\}^{c,f}$, as follows (546): $\{\phi\}^{c,f} = \{(w, t) \mid [\![\phi]\!]^{c,f,t,w} = 1\}$. The problem with this option is that it is inconsistent with Kaplan's ban on monsters – quantifiers are monsters (Rabern 2013).

14 For background to Dummett's ingredient sense/assertoric content see Davies and Humberstone (1980), Dummett (1973), and Evans (1979). For more recent discussion of Lewis's semantic value/content distinction see Yalcin (2014).

15 Arguably, linguists tend to follow Lewis in this regard. See Heim and Kratzer (1998) for some basic background, and Von Fintel and Heim (2011) for an extension of the framework to treatments of intensionality.

16 Note that I'm not assuming that knowledge can be analysed into constituent components such as justification, truth, and belief – the discussion is intended to be compatible with Williamson's 'knowledge-first' project (Williamson 2002).

17 We define 'knows' syncategorimatically for ease of presentation and to avoid various issues with the internal syntax and compositional semantics of knowledge attributions.

18 Not that there is complete convergence and agreement on the terminology, but I think the way I've set things up captures what is really at issue in the core debates. An extreme case worth considering is this: assume one insisted that the assertoric content of a sentence was always the diagonal, then content would never vary with context, no matter what semantics one proposed for 'knows' – is this compatible with contextualism?

19 Note that this is not to say that 'knows' is *completely* context invariant. A knowledge attribution might express different propositions at different contexts due to various other (non-epistemic) factors that we are currently ignoring. Stanley (2005) agrees:

> As is standard, I assume that knowledge attributions, like other sentences, express propositions about particular times. One and the same knowledge attribution may express different propositions at different times because the temporal element in the knowledge attribution is

assigned different times in different contexts of use. So, knowledge attributions are context-sensitive, on my view, in the sense that different knowledge attributions are about different times. But this is a relatively innocuous sense of contextualism; it is true of all verbs that they are associated with temporal elements that receive different values at different times. On the semantic clause I have just given, there is no specifically epistemological sense in which knowledge attributions are context-sensitive.

20 One might assume that A is identical to the set of all worlds W, but this is not an assumption that the invariantist *per se* is committed to. In particular, an invariantist might insist that there are certain "hinge propositions" – perhaps there are possibilities outside of A but it is never required that our evidence rule out these possibilities; instead we have a special *entitlement* for these (see, e.g. Wright 2004).

21 There is another important option – the "relativist" option – but I will suppress it in the main text in order to simplify the presentation. The relativist (see MacFarlane 2014: 187–190) will add to the index a parameter A for a set of relevant possibilities, and provide the following clause: $[\![\alpha \text{ knows } \phi]\!]^{c,w,A} = 1$ iff for all $w' \in A$ compatible with α's evidence in w, $[\![\phi]\!]^{c,w',A} = 1$. Without a view about how one moves from the compositional semantics to assertoric content, this clause is compatible with strict invariantism $(|\psi|^c = \{w : [\![\psi]\!]^{c,w,A} = 1\})$, contextualism $(|\psi|^c = \{w : [\psi]^{c,w,A_c} = 1\})$, and sensitive invariantism $(|\psi|^c = \{w : [\psi]^{c,w,A_w} = 1\})$. The real difference comes with the post-semantic definitions of truth and content. MacFarlane takes the "contents of attitudes to be 'relevant-alternatives-neutral' – that is, to have truth values that vary not just with the state of the world but with the relevant alternatives" (189). Thus, we get this relativist definition of content: $|\psi|^c = \{(w,A) : [\![\psi]\!]^{c,w,A} = 1\}$. MacFarlane explains as follows: "On this view, the relation 'knows' expresses does not vary with the context – there is just a single knowing relation – but the extension of that relation varies across relevant alternatives. As a result, it makes sense to ask about the extension of 'knows' only relative to both a context of use (which fixes the world and time) and a context of assessment (which fixes the relevant alternatives)" (189). The relativist definition of truth is relativized to both an utterance context c and an assessment content c' : ψ is true in c and c' iff $[\psi]^{c,w_c,A_{c'}} = 1$.

22 Sometimes the distinction between sensitive-invariantism and contextualism is made by using the misleading terminology "subject contextualism" versus "attributor contextualism", but only the latter is a genuine form of *contextualism* as we have defined things here.

23 Imagine Hannah in a low stakes situation (in the scenario of Stanley 2005) saying, "I know the bank is open, but if I had a bill coming due, then I wouldn't know."

References

Blackburn, P., de Rijke, M. and Venema, Y.: 2001, *Modal Logic*, Cambridge: Cambridge University Press.

Blome-Tillman, M.: 2009, Contextualism, subject-sensitive invariantism, and the interaction of 'knowledge'-ascriptions with modal and temporal operators, *Philosophy and Phenomenological Research* **79**(2), 315–331.

Carnap, R.: 1947, *Meaning and Necessity: A Study in Semantics and Modal Logic*, Chicago: University of Chicago Press.

Cohen, S.: 1986, Knowledge and context, *Journal of Philosophy* **83**(10), 574–583.

Copeland, B.: 2002, The genesis of possible worlds semantics, *Journal of Philosophical Logic* **31**(2), 99–137.

Cresswell, M.: 1990, *Entities and Indices*, Dordrecht: Kluwer Academic.

Davidson, D.: 1967, Truth and meaning, *Synthese* **17**(1), 304–323.

Davies, M. and Humberstone, L.: 1980, Two notions of necessity, *Philosophical Studies* **38**(1), 1–31.

DeRose, K.: 1995, Solving the skeptical problem, *Philosophical Review* **104**(1), 1–52.

Dummett, M.: 1973, *Frege: Philosophy of Language*, London: Gerald Duckworth.

Evans, G.: 1979, Reference and contingency, *The Monist* **62**, 161–189.

Gettier, E. L.: 1963, Is justified true belief knowledge?, *Analysis* **23**(6), 121–123.

Hawthorne, J.: 2004, *Knowledge and Lotteries*, Oxford: Oxford University Press.

Heim, I. and Kratzer, A.: 1998, *Semantics in Generative Grammar*, Oxford: Blackwell Publishers.

Hintikka, J.: 1957, Modality as referential multiplicity, *Ajatus* **20**, 49–64.

Hintikka, J.: 1962, *Knowledge and Belief: An Introduction to the Logic of the Two Notions*, Ithaca, NY: Cornell University Press.

Holliday, W. H.: 2016, Epistemic logic and epistemology, *in* S. Hansson and V. Hendricks (eds), *The Handbook of Formal Philosophy*, Dordrecht: Springer.

Israel, D. and Perry, J.: 1996, Where monsters dwell, *in* J. Seligman and D. Westerståhl (eds), *Logic, Language and Computation*, Vol. 1, Stanford: CSLI Publications.

Kamp, H.: 1967, The treatment of 'now' as a 1-place sentential operator, *Multilith*, University of California in Los Angeles.

Kamp, H.: 1971, Formal properties of 'now', *Theoria* **37**, 227–274.

Kaplan, D.: 1989a, Demonstratives, *in* J. Almog, J. Perry and H. Wettstein (eds), *Themes from Kaplan*, Oxford: Oxford University Press, pp. 481–563.

Kaplan, D.: 1989b, Afterthoughts, *in* J. Almog, J. Perry and H. Wettstein (eds), *Themes from Kaplan*, Oxford: Oxford University Press, pp. 565–614.

Kripke, S.: 1959, A completeness theorem in modal logic, *The Journal of Symbolic Logic* **24**(1), 1–14.

Lewis, D.: 1970, General semantics, *Synthese* **22**(1), 18–67.

Lewis, D.: 1980, Index, context and content, *in* S. Kanger and S. Ohman (eds), *Philosophy and Grammar*, Amsterdam: Reidel, pp. 79–100.

Lewis, D.: 1996, Elusive knowledge, *Australasian Journal of Philosophy* **74**(4), 549–567.

MacFarlane, J.: 2014, *Assessment Sensitivity: Relative Truth and Its Applications*, Oxford: Oxford University Press.

Montague, R.: 1960, Logical necessity, physical necessity, ethics, and quantifiers, *Inquiry* **3**(1), 259–269.

Montague, R.: 1968, Pragmatics, *in* R. Klibansky (ed), *Contemporary Philosophy: A Survey*, Vol. 1, Florence: La Nuova Italia Editrice, pp. 102–22. Reprinted in *Formal Philosophy: Selected Papers of Richard Montague*, 1974.

Montague, R.: 1970a, Pragmatics and intensional logic, *Synthese* **22**(1), 68–94.

Montague, R.: 1970b, Universal grammar, *Theoria* **36**(3), 373–398.

Ninan, D.: 2010, Semantics and the objects of assertion, *Linguistics and Philosophy* **33**(5), 335–380.

Prior, A.: 1956, Modality and quantification in S5, *The Journal of Symbolic Logic* **21**(1), 60–62.

Prior, A.: 1968a, Egocentric logic, *Nous* **2**(3), 191–207.

Prior, A.: 1968b, Now, *Nous* **2**(2), 101–119.

Rabern, B.: 2012, Against the identification of assertoric content with compositional value, *Synthese* **189**(1), 75–96.

Rabern, B.: 2013, Monsters in Kaplan's logic of demonstratives, *Philosophical Studies* **164**(2), 393–404.

Rabern, B.: 2016, The history of the use of $[.]$-notation in natural language semantics, *Semantics and Pragmatics* **9**(12): 1–9.

Schaffer, J.: 2004, From contextualism to contrastivism, *Philosophical Studies* **119**(1), 73–103.

Schaffer, J.: 2015, Lewis on knowledge ascriptions, *A Companion to David Lewis* **57**, 473.

Scott, D.: 1970, Advice on modal logic, *in* K. Lambert (ed), *Philosophical Problems in Logic: Some Recent Developments*, Dordrecht: D. Reidel, pp. 143–173.

Stalnaker, R.: forthcoming, David Lewis on context, *in* D. Ball and B. Rabern (eds), *The Science of Meaning*, Oxford: Oxford University Press.

Stanley, J.: 1997, Names and rigid designation, *in* B. Hale and C. Wright (eds), *A Companion to the Philosophy of Language*, Oxford: Blackwell Press, pp. 555–585.

Stanley, J.: 2002, Modality and what is said, *Noûs* **36**(s16), 321–344.

Stanley, J.: 2005, *Knowledge and Practical Interests*, Oxford: Oxford University Press.

Vlach, F.: 1973, *'Now' and 'Then': A Formal Study in the Logic of Tense Anaphora*, PhD thesis, UCLA.

von Fintel, K. and Heim, I.: 2011, *Lecture Notes on Intensional Semantics*, Cambridge, MA: MIT Press.

Williamson, T.: 2002, *Knowledge and Its Limits*, Oxford: Oxford University Press.

Wright, C.: 2004, Warrant for nothing (and foundations for free)?, *Aristotelian Society Supplementary Volume* **78**, 167–212.

Yalcin, S.: 2007, Epistemic modals, *Mind* **116**(464), 983–1026.

Yalcin, S.: 2014, Semantics and metasemantics in the context of generative grammar, *in* A. Burgess and B. Sherman (eds), *Metasemantics: New Essays on the Foundations of Meaning*, Oxford: Oxford University Press, pp. 17–54.

37

CONTEXTUALISM IN EPISTEMOLOGY AND RELEVANCE THEORY[1]

Mark Jary and Robert J. Stainton

I Introduction

In the context of this volume, we will assume that readers already have a reasonable understanding of what Contextualism in Epistemology says, and what work it does in the theory of knowledge. By way of a briefest reminder, and very crudely, one can read it as the conjunction of two clauses: (i) knowledge attributions may shift their truth conditions according to the standards at play in the utterance context; and as a result, (ii) one can reconcile the allure of skeptical arguments with ordinary intuition by holding that there is cross-talk. Goes the idea, the skeptic, who says we almost never know, and the anti-skeptic, who says we very frequently know, are not really disagreeing, but talking past each other because they state different things with 'know'. Granting that this would be a happy result for epistemology, notice that Contextualism encompasses a descriptive empirical claim about linguistic meaning in context: they are not making a point (directly) about knowledge, but about the word 'know'.

The point can be illustrated with example (1), to which we will frequently recur. Ajay is renowned for boasting about his hometown of London, Ontario: it used to have a Guy Lombardo museum; its junior hockey team, the Knights, regularly wins the Division Trophy; and it is located only two hours from Toronto. Suppose that Ajay is part of a group of students on the very first day of their very first philosophy class. The instructor asks whether one should say, of Ajay over there, that he knows that he lives in London, Ontario. The unsuspecting students agree that one should definitely assent to:

(1) Ajay knows that he lives in London, Ontario.

The instructor then floats a variety of bizarre doubt-inducing scenarios: Descartes's Evil Genius thought experiment, worries about dreams and brains in vats, "the impenetrable veil of perception", etc. She asks again whether it remains correct to attribute to Ajay the knowledge that he lives in London, Ontario – and many students now respond, very plausibly, in the negative. For instance, they may suppose that Ajay lacks therein sufficient justification for the belief that he lives in London, or that he cannot rule out defeater alternatives. Now suppose that right after class, Ajay trips in the hallway, hitting his head. Paramedics arrive, and one administers tests of Ajay's cognitive faculties. He not only successfully answers the question 'Where do you live?', but gives

Contextualism and Relevance Theory

evidence for it: that he grew up in London, his family home is still there, etc. The paramedic thus reports to her colleague that Ajay knows that he lives in London, Ontario.

Contextualism in Epistemology has this to say about the example. It does seem that attribution of knowledge goes from true to false and back to true. Yet this does not seem to arise from Ajay's evidence going down and then up again: he didn't, e.g., learn relevant new facts as he left the classroom. Must philosophers hold that (at least) one of the speakings was mistaken? No, says the Contextualist, because there is a linguistic illusion at play: the changing standards in the utterance contexts yield only *seeming* disagreement. In fact, there isn't one attribution which changes truth values; instead, there are different contents, two of which are true of the (constant and unchanging) epistemic situation, one of which is not.

Having briefly rehearsed the view, the remainder of our chapter will address a linguistic dilemma facing it. We first explain the dilemma, and then provide a response which draws on Relevance Theory and its notion of explicature (Sperber and Wilson 1986).

II A linguistic dilemma for Contextualism in Epistemology

To explain the dilemma, we need to introduce twin terms of art. Both trace to H. Paul Grice (1975) and his famous contrast between what a speaker says versus what she conversationally implicates. However, we employ our own coinage to evade distracting issues of exegesis. Simplifying for now, let us contrast two kinds of meaning: *what is said by a sentence at a context* and *what the speaker merely conveys* in addition. The former, by our stipulative definition, is arrived at by taking the standing-content of the sentence in the language, resolving ambiguities where necessary, and assigning reference to any context-sensitive indexicals such as 'I', 'there', 'now', 'today', etc. The latter kind of meaning is anything which the speaker means which extends beyond that. For example, suppose that it is July 4th, 2016. Bruce, a Seattleite, has recently broken up with his girlfriend Corinne, and she has moved away. A bit distraught and lonely, he calls Corinne's old cell phone number, reaches her, and asks whether she might consider getting back together. After some pleasantries, Corinne eventually utters the words:

(2) I live in New York now.

What is said by the sentence would be that *Corinne* lives in *New York City* on *July 4th, 2016* – taking 'New York' to designate the city rather than the state, and assigning contextually-fixed reference to 'I', 'now', and the present-tense-marker on 'live'. In addition, however, Corinne conveys-without-saying that it's not feasible to revive their romantic relationship.

Given this terminology, the central focus of the chapter can be couched in three simple premises:

> **P1**: Appeal to *what is said by a sentence at a context* cannot underwrite the required shift in the truth conditions of knowledge attributions.
>
> **P2**: Appeal to *what the speaker merely conveys* cannot underwrite the required shift in the truth conditions of knowledge attributions.
>
> **P3**: If P1 and P2 are true, then nothing can underwrite the required shift in the truth conditions of knowledge attributions.

We will not undertake to defend P1 and P2. Their plausibility is debated in detail elsewhere in this volume. Instead, we will try to underscore what they mean by noting the kind of evidence which supports them. We begin with P1.

Given how we have defined 'what is said by a sentence at a context', it could underwrite a shift in truth conditions in exactly two ways, namely, if 'know' is ambiguous or if 'know' is an indexical. Now, there does seem to be a certain kind of ambiguity which infects English's 'know'. It has at least a propositional and an objectual use: 'know *that* chickens lay eggs' versus 'know Denis'. In discussing the viability of Contextualism, the issue is whether the former itself admits of an "ordinary standards" versus "skeptical standards" ambiguity. To be clear, what is meant by "the word 'know' is ambiguous" herein is not that knowledge comes in degrees (as wealth and youth do); nor that there are different kinds of propositional knowledge (as there are different kinds of love and food). The issue, as we stressed at the outset, is about the word 'know'. More specifically, to use the nomenclature of theoretical linguistics, P1 pertains to whether there is *homophony* at work: one sound corresponding to two or more words. The terms 'lock', 'bank', and 'mine' really are homophonous in just this way: rather than there being one term which applies to a variety of things, there are various terms which just happen to be pronounced /la:k/, /bæŋk/, and /maɪn/, respectively. (Think also of 'to', 'two', and 'too': this is another case of three distinct words, three homonyms – which also happen, nowadays, to have different spellings.) In this strict sense of the term, the hearer's job, when faced with an ambiguous sound, is to discover which linguistic item was actually produced.

Is propositional 'know' ambiguous in this sense? One piece of evidence that it is not is that homophony is accidental. It is thus not repeated across unrelated languages. (For instance, the words for clump-of-hair and door-fastener are not pronounced the same cross-linguistically. This provides evidence that English's 'lock' really is homophonous.) In contrast, the alleged accident of "ordinary standards" and "skeptical standards" being encoded in the same term is widespread across human tongues. Another bit of evidence is this: there are not two standards, but many; and, as Peter Unger (1986) stressed, they vary along a range of axes. Variation might pertain to: degree of felt certainty required; how reliable the relevant epistemic mechanism needs to be; how discriminating/sensitive the informational state must be to the environmental circumstances; the kind of evidence demanded; the alternatives to be rejected; the practical interests at play; etc. So, there would be not two lexical items corresponding to the one sound /noʊ/, but a massive number. (Compare here the propositional versus objectual uses of English 'know'. Only two terms for the one sound are required, and the accident is not replicated cross-linguistically. In other languages, there *are* two words: 'saber' vs. 'conocer' in Spanish; 'savoir' vs. 'connaitre' in French; 'vissen' vs. 'kennen' in German.)

Further evidence for P1, this time pertaining to both (alleged) ambiguity and indexicality, is that, as Stephen Schiffer (1996) has stressed, people tend to notice when truth-conditions shift because of these. If Corinne says, 'I live near a bank', referring to Chase-Manhattan, hearers are not tricked into supposing that 'I don't live near a bank', said by our Seattleite Bruce about the Duwamish River, will be inconsistent with what Corinne stated. Indeed, we all recognize right off that conjunctions whose sound pattern is of the form "p, but not p" can be unproblematically true when the sentence p contains either an indexical or a homonym. Patently, 'know' behaves very differently: it certainly doesn't seem to the skeptic and the anti-skeptic that they are talking past one another.[2] (Readers may be thinking that there are other "kinds of ambiguity" or "kinds of indexicality" which might rescue Contextualism. Quite right. We will revisit the issue in the final section of the chapter.)

Consider now P2, recalling the twin clauses of Contextualism with which we began. The first says that different knowledge attributions are made as the utterance context changes, while the second say that, as a result, there is no real disagreement regarding the attribution. Thus, both the skeptic's and the dogmatist's attributions can be true. It is essential to recognize that these are not merely two conjuncts of a philosophical view. They are interdependent. In particular, and emphasizing the word 'required' in the linguistic dilemma, what the Contextualist needs is for knowledge attributions to shift their so-called *strict and literal truth conditions* according to the standards at play in the utterance context. This is to be sharply contrasted, for instance, with the proposal that (most) knowledge attributions are strictly speaking false (as per skepticism), but that ordinary people often convey-without-saying a range of truths – such as that the attributee has reasonable grounds for believing, would not be blameworthy for acting on the belief, can be relied upon in practice as an authority, etc. Such a proposal would not reconcile the philosophical skeptic and the ordinary person. It would grant total victory to the skeptic, while offering a "pragmatic consolation prize" to common sense. (Following Keith DeRose [1995], this sort of proposal is often denigrated as a "warranted assertability maneuver".) Yet what the speaker merely conveys precisely cannot deliver a difference in the "fully on-the-record", "full-blown stated", truth conditions.[3]

The remainder of the chapter will focus on P3. We will introduce Relevance Theory, a cognitive-representational, modular, and intention-oriented approach to linguistic communication. We will explain its notion of explicature, urging that it is an empirically supported level of meaning in between what is said by a sentence at a context and what a speaker merely conveys in addition. The existence of explicatures, we will claim, offers a way out of the linguistic dilemma. We end by clarifying the Relevance Theoretic proposal by contrasting it with other ways to resist P3.

III Overview of Relevance Theory

Relevance Theory, originally developed by Dan Sperber and Deirdre Wilson in the early 1980s, may be thought of as lying at the confluence of two 20th century philosophical traditions. Drawing on H. Paul Grice, it emphasizes meaning intentions and their recognition in communication. Human linguistic interaction is a species of 'ostensive-inferential communication': ostensive in that the speaker *overtly* produces a stimulus ('to ostend' means to exhibit, to show, e.g., by intentionally pointing); inferential in that the hearer uses the fact that this stimulus has been overtly produced as the basis on which to *surmise* the underlying reasons for speaking, thereby identifying the speaker's intended meaning. Drawing on Noam Chomsky and Jerry Fodor, Relevance Theory takes its task to be the empirical description of the actual linguistic and psychological mechanisms at work in human communication; and the description it favours posits unconscious mental operations over representations, some of these performed in a modular way by a special-purpose language faculty. The output of that faculty is a schematic mental representation (rather than a worldly entity) which grossly underdetermines what the utterance means. This lexically encoded content, the schematic mental representation, is itself associated with other conceptual representations; and it is by means of this association that the linguistic form serves as a stimulus, activating encyclopaedic information stored at those conceptual addresses. Thus decoding, on this view, is not a method of accessing the whole intended message, but merely a means of activating, via an interaction effect of various mental modules, propositions which will serve as premises in the inferential process of identifying the speaker's intended meaning.

Relevance Theory sets itself in opposition to the *Code Model* of linguistic communication. According to the latter, linguistic communication is achieved by the encoding of a thought, a precise message by a speaker, and its subsequent decoding by a hearer who shares that code. In contrast, Relevance Theory holds that linguistic understanding is an interaction effect, with inference always at play. Now, a wink, a shrug, or an intentionally produced grimace could serve as a stimulus in ostensive-inferential communication. But in the case of linguistic communication, the ostensive stimulus is an act of producing a token of a natural language expression, e.g., a sentence of English, Swahili, or Urdu. In such cases, Relevance Theorists do indeed take the linguistic signals to be decoded, yielding some communality with the Code Model. However, decoding is far from sufficient.

There are any number of ways to integrate a Gricean perspective with the sort of cognitive scientific picture found in Chomsky and Fodor. One feature which sets Relevance Theory apart is its emphasis on cognitive efficiency. This is essential because of a pressing issue, namely how the addressee arrives at the correct interpretation, if not by a preset code. Partly, the answer involves denying the presupposition that correct interpretation always involves finding the one precise message meant. Still, how does Relevance Theory ensure that the open-ended inferences drawn are appropriate ones? This coordination problem is solved by first making a simple assumption about human cognition, and then exploiting it in the model of communication. The assumption is that human cognition is geared towards *maximising relevance* (in a technical sense of those words) by balancing cognitive benefit and effort: for any given level of effort, the greater the cognitive benefit, the greater the relevance; for any given level of cognitive benefit, the lower the effort involved in achieving that benefit, the greater the relevance. (Cognitive benefit is to be understood in terms of various sorts of improvements in the individual's representation of the world: e.g., a brand new belief may be added, or its strength may be increased; an old belief may be discarded, or its credence level decreased.) This tendency to balance benefit and effort is referred to as 'The Cognitive Principle of Relevance'. This extremely general principle about the efficiency of human cognition gets applied specifically to cognition about interlocutors. The idea is that every act of ostensive-inferential communication conveys a presumption of its own optimal relevance. This justifies the hearer in seeking to balance benefit and effort by following a path of least effort in interpreting the utterance, until he reaches a level of benefit that merits the effort taken. Once this level has been achieved, he should stop – or at least he should not assume that any further benefits derived are intended by the communicator. The assumption that each act of ostensive communication conveys a presumption of its own optimal relevance is known as 'The Communicative Principle of Relevance'.

IV Explicature and the linguistic dilemma

Our brief overview of Relevance Theory has already hinted at two levels of meaning therein, namely the decoded content and total conveyed content, i.e., the overall result of the hearer's inferences. Neither, however, will serve the purposes of refuting P3. For that, we require another crucial contrast from Relevance Theory, a distinction between two kinds of conveyed content: that which is *explicitly* conveyed and that which is *implicitly* conveyed. Relevance Theory draws this contrast in terms of propositional contents which are derived by *developing* the linguistically encoded meaning of the utterance (roughly, modulating the elements within the mental representation as decoded) versus contents which cannot be so derived. The former is called an *explicature*; any other communicated proposition is then an *implicature*. This contrast is well illustrated by an example from Robyn Carston (1988: 261):

(3) *Denis*: How is Jane feeling after her first year at university?
   Ebrahim: She didn't get enough units and can't continue.

What Ebrahim's utterance encodes is something along the lines of the mental representation in (4):

(4) IDENTIFY A CERTAIN SALIENT FEMALE *F.* IDENTIFY UNITS OF A CERTAIN SALIENT KIND *U.* IDENTIFY A CERTAIN SALIENT ACTIVITY *A.* IDENTIFY A

CERTAIN MODULATION *AND** OF CONJUNCTION. THE SPEAKER IS SAYING
THAT *F* FAILED TO OBTAIN SUFFICIENT *U*'S AND* *F* IS UNABLE TO CON-
TINUE *A*.

Ebrahim conveys explicitly (5), while what he conveys implicitly is (6):

(5) JANE DID NOT PASS ENOUGH UNIVERSITY COURSE UNITS TO QUALIFY FOR
     ADMISSION TO SECOND YEAR STUDY AND, AS A RESULT, JANE CANNOT
     CONTINUE WITH UNIVERSITY STUDY.
(6) JANE IS NOT FEELING VERY HAPPY.[4]

Although the schema in (4) falls a long way short of anything Ebrahim conveys, (5) is much closer
to (4) than (6) is. According to Relevance Theory, (5) is a development of (4): that is, we can get
from (4) to (5) by specifying various more precise contents. In contrast, to arrive at (6), it is not
enough to modulate the elements within (4). So, (6) is an implicature.

   How does development of the explicature work? A key idea in recent research is *lexical adjustment* of encoded conceptual content: the encoded meaning of a lexical item can be inferentially
modified in the interpretation process so that its denotation is broadened or narrowed. These
processes are said to result in a thought that contains an *ad hoc* concept. Importantly for us, this *ad
hoc* concept contributes towards the strictly stated truth conditions of the utterance, rather than
merely contributing to what the speaker got across.

   Here is an example of broadening from Deirdre Wilson (2003: 276):

(7) The water is boiling.

The sentence in (7) might be used to claim that the water is at exactly 100 degrees centigrade,
that it is at approximately 100 degrees centigrade, that it is too hot to bathe in (without any commitment to its specific temperature), or that it is behaving like boiling water in that it is bubbling
ferociously. These would be, respectively, exact, approximate, hyperbolic, and metaphoric uses of
'boiling', and in each case the denotation of the term would be broader than in the previous.
Now consider a case of narrowing (Wilson 2003: 278):

(8) Churchill was a man.

An utterance of (8) might be a claim that Churchill was a male human being, but it is more likely
to be a claim that he was a special type, or perhaps typical type, thereof. In these latter cases, the
denotation of 'man' is narrowed, so as to exclude some male humans.[5] Crucially, the strictly stated
truth conditions of the utterance will be distinct in each case.

   This is a very powerful account, and, to a large degree, its plausibility rests on how the process
of lexical adjustment is constrained – so that, e.g., a speaker cannot use (1) to assert that *Queen
Elizabeth fears that she'll be crushed by an asteroid*, with 'Ajay', 'know', 'live', etc., merely being
"adjusted". We must therefore say a word about what constrains it. The first has been mentioned
already: something is an explicature only if it traces to the decoded mental representation, so that
wholly novel additions do not count. That is why (6) is not a candidate explicature. Second, the
mere activation of thoughts by a linguistic stimulus is insufficient reason for the hearer to take
these as intended by the hearer, and the Communicative Principle of Relevance requires them
to have been so intended to be conveyed, explicitly or implicitly. Third, this principle holds
not merely that the act is relevant, but that it is the most relevant stimulus available given the

communicator's abilities and preferences. (This very important point is often missed by critics.) These first three will resonate immediately with those who know Grice or have ever encountered Relevance Theory. A fourth is this: the process is constrained by the need for a development of the linguistically encoded meaning of the utterance to provide *warrant* for the implicatures of the utterance, i.e., for the explicature of the utterance to imply the implicatures. The adjustment of lexically encoded material is an outcome of this need for warrant. To return to one of our examples, consider a child uttering (7) in a complaint that her bath water is too hot for her to get in. Her use of 'boiling', predicated of water and in the scenario described, will give rise to thoughts about the discomfort and scalding associated with immersion in very hot water. This will lead to further thoughts such as *The child does not want to enter the water*. In order to get warrant to ascribe this thought the status of an implicature, the hearer need only assume that the child intends the weaker claim that the water is too hot to bathe in, rather than the stronger claim that it is at 100 degrees. Thus, despite being hyperbolic, this is the thought the hearer will treat as being strictly stated by the child's utterance, and he will accuse the child of asserting an untruth only if the water is patently not too hot to bathe in. The question of whether it is at exactly 100 degrees will not arise.[6]

In brief, the overall pattern, which keeps explicatures from "over-generating", is this: thoughts activated by the decoding of a linguistic stimulus are *candidates* for things meant by the utterance, but, the theory has it, mere activation does not warrant them as intended by the speaker; rather, warrant must be sought by developing the linguistically encoded meaning of the utterance until it implies those thoughts activated by decoding, thereby conferring on them speaker-intended status:

> the hearer's expectations of relevance warrant the assumption that the speaker's explicit meaning will contextually imply a range of specific consequences (made easily accessible, though not yet implied, by the linguistically encoded sentence meaning). Having identified these consequences, he may then, by a process of backwards inference, enrich his interpretation of the speaker's explicit meaning to a point where it does carry these implications.
>
> *(Wilson and Sperber 2002: 616)*

The upshot of this section is that, within Relevance Theory, there exists a three-way contrast among kinds of content. There is the linguistically encoded meaning of the utterance. This is a highly schematic mental representation which typically will not express a proposition. (In itself, it does not represent part of the communicated content of the utterance.) There are the implicatures of the utterance: any communicated propositions which are not arrived at by modulating the elements in the utterance's linguistically encoded meaning. Finally, there is the explicature: an explicitly conveyed proposition which is a development of what is decoded. The essential point of our chapter is that, given this three-way contrast, Contextualism in Epistemology may be rescued from the linguistic dilemma by taking the explicature to be what shifts across utterance contexts. For this gambit to succeed, the explicature must be sharply contrasted with the notion of what is said by the sentence at the context. To reinforce their dissimilarity, notice that what is said by sentence (5) at the context will not include what kind of units Jane failed to receive, and which activity she cannot continue. Or again, consider what Relevance Theory would say about (2) above, 'I live in New York now.' Yes, the explicature of Corinne's utterance has to do with her present domicile, while the implicature pertains to the end of a romantic relationship. This is, we agree, similar to the terminological contrast introduced on P2. However, according to Relevance Theory, the explicature of Corrine's utterance of sentence (2) will extend well beyond what results from assigning reference to 'I' and 'now' and disambiguating 'New York'. For instance, the

Contextualism and Relevance Theory

in-context use of the linguistic expression 'in __ now' will, for the Relevance Theorist, yield a specific modulation: what satisfies IN and NOW is different for LIVE IN NEW YORK NOW as opposed to BE IN BANKRUPTCY NOW or BE SINGING IN FRENCH NOW.

V Compare and contrast

We end by contrasting this Relevance Theoretic proposal to other means of rejecting P3. This will both reinforce certain points made above, and fill in some gaps.

Relevance Theory maintains that linguistic communication is inevitably modular. In particular, even fixing the explicature is an interaction effect, because an *ad hoc* concept must be developed from the decoded content. A certain kind of "context sensitivity" will thus prove ubiquitous, occurring with lexical items generally. (For instance, what counts as a satisfier of 'weapon', 'dog', or 'water' will vary according to context: if a son kills his mother with a knitting needle, and it is placed in a city's museum, does that mean that the museum allows weapons on its grounds? Does a taxidermied wolf count as a dog? When you order water at the bar, would it satisfy your request for the barkeep to bring just an ice cube on a saucer?) An important result is that Relevance Theory can treat 'know' as a plain-old lexical item. It need not be in any respect morphosyntactically or semantically peculiar. To the contrary, if the statements/claims that can be performed with 'know' were not pragmatically flexible, that would be an extraordinary exception.

This contrasts with the means of rejecting P3 which grant that 'know' in its propositional use isn't homophonous, and grant that it is unlike 'I' or 'now', but maintain that 'know' is special in that it somehow "triggers" context – specifically, it triggers a search for a standard in the context of utterance. Sub-varieties of this gambit include taking 'know' to be a degree-theoretical word, comparable to 'tall' or 'flat'; taking it to be a "contextual" along the lines of 'enemy' or 'neighbor'; or taking it to be implicitly modal like 'must' or 'can'.[7]

A closely related feature of Relevance Theory is that it embraces a Mentalistic "idea theory" of meaning. Semantics involves not assignment of worldly referents, but rather translation from a natural language expression to a corresponding mental representation. Indeed, this is precisely what modular decoding achieves. An upshot of this is that meanings are mere schemata, and partly procedural ones at that. Hence, though for a much more general reason, the word 'know' itself, the type, no more has an extension than 'enough' or 'appropriate' do: it is only the contextually-modulated *ad hoc* concept which does so. Turning to sentences, in general they are not truth-evaluable – not even relative to a limited set of contextual parameters. Thus, sentences of the form "S knows that p", even after resolving ambiguities and assigning reference to indexicals, do not express propositions – they certainly do not "divide the space of worlds" into those which satisfy the sentence and those which fail to.

This contrasts with attempts to rebut P3 according to which a sentence of the form "S knows that p" semantically encodes a standard, loose or strict, though context can escalate/reduce that standard in such a way as to change what is "full-blown stated". This would be a variant on Minimalism about the semantics of 'know', conjoined with Speech Act Pluralism regarding what 'know' can be used to assert/claim/state. Another competitor idea is that instances of "S knows that p" typically do express propositions, but assigning an actual truth value requires a (varying) context of assessment for the proposition. This would be Relativism about knowledge attributions.[8]

The final contrast we wish to highlight concerns the degree of psychological commitment in play. Relevance Theory understands semantics and pragmatics to be part of cognitive psychology. It thus reads clause (i) of Contextualism as a claim in cognitive science, such that verifying

487

it requires empirical investigation of actual neurocognitive mechanisms, drawing on whatever evidence one can find. As we have stressed, Relevance Theory also takes a strong and specific empirical stance. Knowledge attributions may indeed shift their truth conditions according to the standards in the utterance context, because of: activation of concepts linked to the decoded mental schema; the unconscious and automatic development thereof, via the maximization of relevance, constrained by backwards inference from what would be implicated.

An overarching alternative is to de-psychologize. A moderate sub-option, which tempts one of the co-authors (namely, Jary), is to rebut P3 along broadly Relevance Theoretic lines, but without buying the entire picture. The Relevance Theoretic model outlined above has two elements: one is designed to show that it is reasonable for a hearer to interpret an utterance as he does, given the data made available to him by that act of speaking; the other is to suggest how, as a matter of cognitive psychology, he might reliably reach the intended interpretation (in a seemingly instantaneous and unreflective manner). The first element concerns the relationship between the thoughts activated by decoding the linguistic form of the utterance and the development of this form into a proposition that provides inferential warrant for those thoughts such that they are implied by the utterance. The second element involves the balance of neurocognitive effort and effect that justifies treating the thoughts activated as (being intended by the speaker as) having a role in the interpretation process. It is, we think, the *first* element that does the main work in rebutting P3, even pursuing a broadly Relevance Theoretic approach – for it is this which results in the modulation of the verb's content in the knowledge attribution. What the cautious shopper might do, then, is borrow from Relevance Theory the idea that the explicit content of an utterance is that proposition which is both a development of the linguistically encoded meaning of the utterance and provides warrant for its implicatures. Hence, in analysing an utterance, one would consider its overall import and seek the weakest proposition that (a) can be developed from the linguistically encoded meaning of the utterance and (b) will also warrant those propositions that contribute to the utterance's import that cannot be derived by developing its encoded meaning. Consider how this approach would apply to the various utterances of (1). The variation in the concepts arrived at will trace to warranting potential implicatures. In the skepticism case, what is at issue is whether Ajay is justified in believing that he lives in London in the face of bizarre error-inducing scenarios. In the bang-on-the-head case, it is whether Ajay both believes that he lives in London and can deploy evidence the way that normally functioning people can. Therefore, an implicature of 'Ajay knows that he lives in London' in the skepticism scenario is that Ajay's evidence, degree of certainty, etc., defeat skeptical considerations; whereas this is not an implicature of 'Ajay knows that he lives in London' in the bang-on-the-head case, because it is irrelevant to the concerns of the speakers. Rather, the implicature is that Ajay's mental faculties are functioning normally.

A more radical de-psychologizing alternative, consonant with Stainton (2016), would be to urge that Contextualism hardly owes debts in empirical cognitive science at all. What matters is *whether* pragmatics can impact upon what is stated with 'know', not *how*. And one can show that it does, without addressing linguistico-cognitive mechanisms, by taking the notion of the literal truth conditions of knowledge attributions to pertain to the kind/degree of *commitment* the attributor undertakes. This amounts to recasting the Relevance Theoretic contrast between content conveyed explicitly versus implicitly in forensic/normative terms. A shift in truth conditions is explicit, goes the idea, if it is lie-prone rather than merely misleading-prone. Consider an example. Corinne, having moved to New York, and having struggled to find a job, is on trial for attempting to rob a bank. She was caught with a loaded gun in her purse as she entered the nearby Chase-Manhattan branch, and was arrested immediately. In an attempt to convince

Contextualism and Relevance Theory

the grand jury that there was a giant misunderstanding, an embarrassing oversight on her part, Corinne says on the witness stand:

(9) I didn't know that there was a gun in my purse.

Suppose further that Corinne placed the firearm in her purse just a minute before entering the bank, even double-checking to make sure that it was loaded. Could she show that she did not commit perjury with (9), because an Evil Demon might have tricked her, sensory perception is always fraught, etc.? Insofar as the answer is 'No', that alone establishes that "ordinary standards" are built into the content of what Corinne *stated* with (9). Hence, even if we don't understand the mechanisms, additional empirical work in cognitive science is not required to resolve the "whether issue".

On the one hand, this thoroughly agnostic approach to the "how issue" can claim the advantage of consistency with the truth of the "cautious shopper's" view: it's simply non-committal about it. Indeed, this radical option is consistent with the truth of any of the foregoing defenses of Contextualism in Epistemology, including the full-blown Relevance Theoretic one. On the other hand, a disadvantage is that an independently motivated, detailed account of how the shift in truth conditions occurs makes it more plausible that P3 really is false. Another disadvantage of de-psychologizing, whether moderately or radically, is that one forfeits a promising reply to Schiffer's objection, viz., that interlocutors would notice the (alleged) meaning-shift. When speakers are talking past each other with indexicals and homophones, they recognize this quite quickly. Not so with "knows that __". In embracing the full Relevance Theoretic picture, one has an easy time explaining one aspect of this: as stressed above, Relevance Theory simply does not take 'know' to belong to a special class of ambiguous or context-sensitive lexical items. One does face the issue of why the interlocutors do not readily recognize that they are *lexically adjusting* in different ways. Even here, however, Relevance Theory has advantages. Development, as explained, is a modular, unconscious process which occurs automatically and rapidly. Not being a matter of personal-level reflection, it is more plausible that interlocutors might, under the right circumstances, become "blind" to it. The tricky and unnoticed shift of standards in terms of whether a use of (1) is true would be more comparable, say, to a shift wherein a jeweler, informed by a passionate youth that he simply must buy his boyfriend a gemstone ring despite limited funds is first shown a large and lovely cubic zirconia. Having laid the trap, the salesperson then suggests that cubic zirconias "aren't really gemstones", and induces the young lover to buy a diamond. The decoded content GEMSTONE gets different lexical adjustments across the discourse, without the buyer noticing.

VI Conclusion

To sum up, we introduced the twin clauses of Contexualism in Epistemology: one says that there is a shift in truth conditions, one says that a philosophical reconciliation can be achieved as a result. We then presented a linguistic dilemma which it faces, to the effect that one cannot satisfy the first clause consistent with both the empirical facts and the philosophical demands of the second clause. Without defending them in detail, we sketched the kind of evidence in favour of two key premises of that dilemma, and then proposed a means of rejecting its third premise by drawing on Relevance Theory. Specifically, we characterized a kind of truth-conditional content, the explicature, which is both strictly stated yet modulated in a novel pragmatic way. We ended by contrasting this approach with three other strategies for resisting P3: appealing to another kind of special context-sensitivity for 'know'; assigning minimal truth conditions to knowledge-attributing sentences while denying that they are the (only) ones asserted; and welcoming some of Relevance Theory's insights, all the while de-psychologizing them to a lesser or greater degree. The general lesson is that the linguistic dilemma can indeed be overcome.

Notes

1 A draft of this chapter was presented to Linguistic Talks at Western, in London, Ontario, on October 23rd, 2015. We are grateful to the audience members for discussion. We also thank Jonathan Jenkins Ichikawa, Martin Montminy, Ram Neta, Geoff Pynn, Patrick Rysiew, John Turri, and Deirdre Wilson for helpful comments. The project was supported by grants from: Research Project: Lexical Meaning and Concepts, FFI2014-52196-P, funded by the Spanish Ministry of Economy and Competitiveness, via Mark Jary; and Linguistic Pluralism, funded by the Social Sciences and Humanities Research Council of Canada, via Robert Stainton.
2 For additional linguistic evidence relevant to P1, see Pynn (2015a, section 5). It affords an excellent overview. For some of the original sources, see: Cappelen and Lepore (2005), Hawthorne (2004), and Stanley (2004). (Interestingly, both Cappelen and Hawthorne ultimately change their minds about how compelling some of the linguistic data is. See their 2009 book.) See also Ludlow (2005) for a novel corpus-based defense of context sensitivity of knowledge attributions.
3 Here is another way at the main points, in terms of our recurring example. According to the Contextualist, though Ajay's epistemic state remains constant, the attributions using (1) go from true (as said by the students at the outset of the philosophy class) to false (after the introduction by the instructor of the skeptical scenarios) and back to true (as said by the paramedic in the hallway), because the relevant standards in the utterance context have risen and then dropped again. Thus, continues the idea, the dogmatic philosopher who says that all the attributions are true, and the skeptical philosopher who says that all are false, are equally mistaken. This middle-path is to be achieved by having the truth conditions of the knowledge-attribution shift. The problem posed by the dilemma is about how this can occur. P1 says, in effect, that standards cannot enter in at the level of what is said by the sentence 'Ajay knows that he lives in London, Ontario.' That's because the English word 'know' simply does not function as required: the only two linguistic mechanisms for shifting that kind of meaning, namely ambiguity and indexicality, seem to be blocked with respect to 'know'. P2 says, in effect, that standards cannot enter in at the level of what the speaker merely conveys. That's because, though this might be empirically plausible, it would not actually yield the result that the Contextualist wants. Granting that there are no other options, nothing can underwrite the required shift. Hence Contextualism as a whole is false.
4 To understand Relevance Theory, it is very important to distinguish representations within a spoken natural language from representations inside the mind. A central plank of the theory is that these need not correspond closely to one another. To reflect this important contrast, we here follow the usual notational custom of using lowercase letters for expressions of natural language and uppercase ones for mental representations. Thus, what the typefaces mean here is that Ebrahim spoke the English sentence 'She didn't get enough units and can't continue,' meaning to get across the content that Jane did not pass enough university course units to qualify for admission to second year study and, as a result, Jane cannot continue with university study.
5 Narrowing and broadening are not mutually exclusive. Consider 'Jane is a real princess,' which might be uttered to claim that Jane is royalty, but might also be uttered to claim that she is high maintenance, given to tantrums, and so on, without also claiming that she is blue-blooded. In the latter case, the denotation of the English word 'princess' is both broadened to include non-royalty, but also narrowed to exclude temperamentally well-balanced princesses (Carston 2002: 347).
6 To mention another much-discussed example, suppose Georgina asks Henri whether he is hungry. Henri replies, 'I have had breakfast.' Here, Georgina does not first arrive definitively at the explicature, find something amiss with it, and then seek out an implicature. Rather, the explicature is mutually adjusted with potential implicatures, by a "backwards inference". The potential implicature that Henri is not in fact hungry would not be licensed by the explicature HENRI HAS EATEN BREAKFAST AT SOME TIME IN HIS LIFE. That is why this explicature would be rejected.
7 Theorists who have been tempted to treat 'know' as context-sensitive in a special way include Cohen (1999) and Lewis (1996). Other theorists who, with Relevance Theorists, countenance full-bore, non-triggered "pragmatic determinants of literal speech act content", "free pragmatic enrichment"

Contextualism and Relevance Theory

of assertions/statements, or something along these lines include: Bach (1994), Bezuidenhout (1997), Moravcsik (1998), Perry (1986), Pietroski (2005), Recanati (2002), Searle (1978), and Travis (1985).

8   For the general framework of Semantic Minimalism plus Speech Act Pluralism, see Borg (2004) and Cappelen and Lepore (2004, 2005). For a very clever and detailed application of the general framework to Contextualism in Epistemology, see Pynn (2015b). The Relativist approach to pragmatic enrichment has been developed in Brogaard (2008) and MacFarlane (2009). See also Montiny (2007) and Rysiew (2011). As an aside, consider a line of argument which merits mention. If 'knows' has an extension, then it seems that there is something which the skeptic and the dogmatist cannot agree upon. Returning to (1) as our example, if 'knows' expresses a relation between agents and propositions, say, then across all three contexts either <Ajay, that Ajay lives in London, Ontario> is in its extension or it isn't. Continues the argument: pragmatics be damned, this issue is such that either the skeptic is right about it (i.e., the pair lies outside the extension in all three cases) or the dogmatist is (i.e., the pair is uniformly inside the extension of 'knows'). So, with respect to this question, either the skeptic or the dogmatist is correct – and no appeal to pragmatics-based cross-talk is available to "split the difference". Obviously Relevance Theorists have a ready answer: for them 'knows' encodes a mental schema which, as in the usual case, simply does not have an extension. But what of other colleagues who defend P3 yet accept the antecedent of the above if-then? Following Stainton (2010), they too have a ready response. Even if there is "something that the camps cannot agree on", the debate has never been about that something. It has always been about knowledge attributions – assertions, claims and statements about what is known – not about some recherché construct of the formal semanticist, viz., which ordered pairs fall in the extension of a transitive verb. Returning to the very outset of the paper, and eschewing Relevance Theoretic terminology, the key point is this: insofar as it's worth caring about, Contextualism pertains to the strict and literal content of speech acts using 'know'; and whether such contents can vary with the standards in the utterance context, so as to reconcile seeming philosophical conflicts. Regardless of whether 'knows' has an extension, the answer to this question can easily be 'Yes'.

References

Bach, Kent. 1994. "Conversational Impliciture". *Mind and Language* 9: 124–162.

Bezuidenhout, Anne. 1997. "Pragmatics, Semantic Underdetermination and the Referential/Attributive Distinction". *Mind* 106: 375–409.

Borg, Emma. 2004. *Minimal Semantics.* Oxford: Oxford University Press.

Brogaard, Berit. 2008. "In Defense of a Perspectival Semantics for 'Know'". *Australasian Journal of Philosophy* 86(3): 439–459.

Cappelen, Herman and John Hawthorne. 2009. *Relativism and Monadic Truth.* Oxford: Oxford University Press.

Cappelen, Herman and Ernie Lepore. 2004. "A Tall Tale: In Defense of Semantic Minimalism and Speech Act Pluralism". In M. Ezcurdia, R. J. Stainton and C. Viger (eds.) *New Essays in the Philosophy of Language and Mind.* Calgary: University of Calgary Press, pp. 3–28.

———. 2005. *Insensitive Semantics.* Oxford: Blackwell.

Carston, Robyn. 1988. "Implicature, Explicature and Truth-Theoretic Semantics". In R. Kempson (ed.) *Mental Representations: The Interface between Language and Reality.* Cambridge: Cambridge University Press, pp. 155–181.Reprinted in M. Ezcurdia and R. J. Stainton (eds.) (2013) *The Semantics-Pragmatics Boundary in Philosophy.* Peterborough, ON: Broadview Press, pp. 261–283.

———. 2002. *Thoughts and Utterances.* Oxford: Blackwell.

Cohen, Stewart. 1999. "Contextualism, Skepticism, and the Structure of Reasons". *Philosophical Perspectives* 13: 57–89.

DeRose, Keith. 1995. "Solving the Skeptical Problem". *Philosophical Review* 104: 1–52.

Grice, H. Paul. 1975. "Logic and Conversation". In P. Cole (ed.) *Syntax and Semantics, Vol. 3: Speech Acts.* New York: Academic, pp. 41–58.

Hawthorne, John. 2004. *Knowledge and Lotteries.* Oxford: Oxford University Press.

Lewis, David. 1996. "Elusive Knowledge". *Australasian Journal of Philosophy* 74(4): 549–567.

Ludlow, Peter. 2005. "Contextualism and the New Linguistic Turn in Epistemology". In G. Preyer and G. Peters (eds.) *Contextualism in Philosophy: Knowledge, Meaning and Truth.* Oxford: Oxford University Press, pp. 11–50.

MacFarlane, John. 2009. "Nonindexical Contextualism". *Synthese* 166(2): 231–250.

Montminy, Martin. 2007. "Epistemic Contextualism and the Semantics-Pragmatics Distinction". *Synthese* 155(1): 99–125.

Moravcsik, Julius M. 1998. *Meaning, Creativity, and the Partial Inscrutability of the Human Mind*. Chicago: University of Chicago Press.

Perry, John. 1986. "Thought without Representation". *Proceedings of the Aristotelian Society* 60: 137–152.

Pietroski, Paul. 2005. "Meaning before Truth". In G. Preyer and G. Peters (eds.) *Contexualism in Philosophy*. Oxford: Oxford University Press, pp. 253–300.

Pynn, Geoff. 2015a. "Pragmatic Contextualism". *Metaphilosophy* 46(1): 26–51.

———. 2015b. "Contextualism in Epistemology". *Oxford Handbooks Online*. New York: Oxford University Press. <http://www.oxfordhandbooks.com/view/10.1093/oxfordhb/9780199935314.001.0001/oxfordhb-9780199935314-e-12>

Recanati, François. 2002. "Unarticulated Constituents". *Linguistics and Philosophy* 25: 299–345.

Rysiew, Patrick. 2011. "Epistemic Contextualism". In E. Zalta (ed.) *The Stanford Encyclopedia of Philosophy*. <http://plato.stanford.edu/entries/contextualism-epistemology/>

———. 2001. "The Context-Sensitivity of Knowledge Attributions". *Nous* 35: 477–514.

Schiffer, Stephen. 1996. "Contextualist Solutions to Skepticism". *Proceedings of the Aristotelian Society* 96: 317–333.

Searle, John. 1978. "Literal Meaning". *Erkenntnis* 13: 207–224.

Sperber, Dan and Deirdre Wilson. 1986. *Relevance*. Cambridge, MA: Harvard University Press.

Stainton, Robert. 2010. "Contextualism in Epistemology and the Context Sensitivity of 'Knows'". In M. O'Rourke and H. Silverstein (eds.) *Knowledge and Skepticism*. Cambridge, MA: MIT Press, pp. 113–139.

———. 2016. "Full-On Stating". *Mind and Language* 31(4), 395–413.

Stanley, Jason. 2004. "On the Linguistic Basis for Contextualism". *Philosophical Studies* 119: 119–146.

Travis, Charles. 1985. "On What Is Strictly Speaking True". *Canadian Journal of Philosophy* 15(2): 187–229.

Unger, Peter. 1986. "The Cone Model of Knowledge". *Philosophical Topics* 14(1):125–178.

Wilson, Deirdre. 2003. "Relevance and Lexical Pragmatics". *Italian Journal of Linguistics* 15: 273–292.

Wilson, Deirdre and Dan Sperber. 2002. "Truthfulness and Relevance". *Mind* 111: 583–632.

INDEX

abominable conjunctions 6, 133, 160, 317, 339–42, 421

access principle: defenders of 433; described 432; flexible foundationalism and 433–5; foundationalism and 431–3; *prima facie* motivation for 432

agreement: as activity 272; as state 272–3; *see also* disagreement

Airport Cases 207, 208–9

Albritton, R. 150

Alexander, J. 100

ambitious contextualism 306; Cartesian Scepticism and 306–7; Semantic Error Problem for 308–9

Anderson, E. 59

Annis, D. 59, 425, 427, 430–1

anti-intellectualism 39

Antony, L. 61–2

applied ethics 128

A-quantifiers 23, 342–4

ascriber contextualism 16

assertoric-content 471–2

assessment-indexical 283; knowledge ascriptions and 285

assessment-sensitive 283; epistemic modal claims 287–8; knowledge ascriptions 285; semantics for knowledge attributions master argument 295

attention, Lewis on 457–8

attitudes, disagreement and individual 274–6; conflicting beliefs and 274–6; context and 278–80

attributor contextualism 71–2, 75; conversational contextualism and 321, 323; disagreement and 262; feminist epistemologists and 58; Gettier cases and 191–2, 195–6, 198; Ichikawa's endorsement of 421, 422; indexical contextualism and 308; interest-relative invariantism and 240, 242; as knowledge

ascription 45, 71, 131–2, 169–71, 335, 396; lost disagreement and 283–7; metalinguistic analysis of 71, 72; methodology of straightforward and 83–6; modest contextualism and 306; objections of 211–12; pragmatic invariantism and 315; psychological context of 94; Relevance Theory and 487; Semantic Error Problem and 305; skepticism and 133–4, 237; truth of 57–8

Austin, J. L. 150, 361

automatic indexicals 354–6

availability heuristic 99–100

Bach, K. 38, 206, 402

background conditions, ERAs and 381–2

Bank case 15, 33–9, 45–51, 207, 208–9, 212–13, 218, 241, 262, 292, 321, 364, 370, 407, 459

Barn Facade Gettier case 191, 194; contextualism about 198–200; Greco and 198–9

belief ascriptions 400–8; context-sensitive accounts of 405–6; flexible foundationalism and 428–9; full/partial belief 400–1; interest-relative invariantism and 247–8; options and, shifting 403–4; overview of 400; partitions and, shifting 402–3; phenomenal, dispositional account 406–7; presuppositions and, shifting 404–5; situation-sensitive accounts of 402–5; threshholds and, shifting 402; Truman case 407–8

belief variation 218–27; epistemology case 226–7; hyperbole and 220–1; irony and 220–1; loose use and 225–7; overview of 218; semantic theories and 218–20; strong/weak semantics 223–5

bias paradox, relativism as 61–2

Blackburn, S. 275, 361

Blome-Tillmann, M. 84, 136, 209–10, 213, 312, 322, –325, 334, 352, 355, 476; on Sosa 125–6

Boghossian, P, 293–4

Index

Borg, E. 111, 211, 230
Boyd, K. 249–50
brain-in-a-vat skeptic's argument 2, 52–4, 124,
132–6, 157–9, 226–7, 307, 335, 339, 341, 458
Braun, D. 108
Brister, E. 65
Brogaard, B. 195–6, 423, 491
Brown, J. 37–8, 187, 208–13, 224, 242–3, 245,
249, 315
Brueckner, A. 140
Buchak, L. 401, 405
Buckwalter, W. 35, 46, 243, 249
Burgess, A. 76

Canary case 196
Cappelen, H. 115, 230, 234–8, 250–1, 272, 279,
280, 372
careless use 225; *see also* loose use
Carnap, R. 465
Carston, R. 206, 484–5
character 74, 106–10, 131, 346, 354, 365, 453, 467
character representation 106; from Meaning
Perspective 107–10; psychology rules
perspective 111; on Simple Strategy 108, 109;
sociology rules perspective 113
Chemla, E. 35
Chomsky, N. 36, 111, 113, 211, 483
Clarke, R. 404–5, 429
closure 156–64; accrual of risk and 161–4;
formulating 156–7; knowledge and 156; lottery
knowledge and 159–61; meta-linguistic single
premise 157; multi-premise 157; overview of
156; single-premise 156; skeptical paradoxes and
158–9
cognitive home 433
Cognitive Principle of Relevance, The 484
Cohen, S. 15, 16, 34, 59, 84–5, 132, 145–7, 171,
207, 232, 313, 322; Canary case and 196;
critique of Lewis 194–8; Sheep on a Hill case
and 195
common ground 141–2, 184, 259–61, 324–7,
389–93, 405; *see also* conversational score
conceptual ethics, epistemic contextualism
and 71–8; disagreement and metalinguistic
reply 74–7; disagreement at level of
thoughts objection 78; introduction to
71–2; non-linguistic disagreement objection
77–8; normative terms, disagreement and
metalinguistic reply 72–4
conceptual synthesis 86; genealogical stages of 86–8
concrete situation 107
conflicting attitudes: in belief 274–6; disagreement
and 276–8; rationality and 277; satisfaction and
277–8, 279
content articulation thesis 311
content of knowledge 465–76; double indexing
and 468–9; 'knows' as context-sensitive and

473–6; 'knows' as index operator and 472–3;
overview of 465; parameter shifting, sensitivity
and 465–7; "what is said," semantics and
469–72
contents of context, determinants of 462–3
context: of assessment 294; of attitudes,
disagreement and 278–80; components of 106;
contents of 462–3; defined 131; of use 294
context representation 106; from Meaning
Perspective 107–10; relativist view 115; Rules
Perspective-Revealing Strategy 112; Simple
Strategy and 108–9; straightforward 109, 110
context-sensitive expressions 1, 3; intention-based
view of 322
context sensitivity, theorizing about 105–16;
character and context representation 107–10;
context shifting 113–14; indices and 114–15;
Meaning Perspective 106–7; overview of 105;
presuppositions of 105–6; psychology rules
perspective 110–12; sociology rules perspective
113
contexts: defined 456; mind-independence of
455–7
contextual empiricism 59; endorses value relativism
60, 61–3; implies dogmatism 60–1; lacks
justification 60–1
contextualism: about knows 1, 257, 332; ascriber
16; attributor 71–2; classical (flexible) 22;
closure and (*see* closure); contextualists beg the
question objection 140; for counterfactuals
416–20; data/motivations for (*see* data/
motivations for contextualism); defined 131;
experimental philosophy challenges to 88–90;
fallibilism and 146; felted 59; feminism and (*see*
feminism, contextualism and); foundational
linguistic issues (*see* foundational linguistic
issues, contextualism); gate-keeping 87;
Gettier cases and (*see* Gettier cases); intuitive
basis for 32–41; irrelevant to epistemology
objection 137–8; knowledge norms and (*see*
knowledge norms); knowledge types and 2–3;
Lewis's articulation of 3–4; lotteries/prefaces
and (*see* lotteries and preface scenarios);
mention and 3–4; as metaepistemology
127–9; methodological disputes and (*see*
methodological disputes, contextualism and);
methodological issues for (*see* methodological
issues for contextualism); mischaracterize
skepticism objection 138–40; non-indexical
17, 20, 22; psychological context of (*see*
psychological context of contextualism);
semantic implementations for (*see* semantic
implementations for contextualism); skepticism
and (*see* skepticism); too skeptic-friendly
objection 134–7; toy 2, 4; use and 3–4; *see also*
epistemic contextualism
contextualism as metaepistemology 127–9

494

Index

"Contextualism in Feminist Epistemology and Philosophy of Science" (Rolin) 59–60

contextualism is epistemology objection 125–7; Blome-Tillman on Sosa 125–6; DeRose on Kornblith 127; DeRose on Sosa 126–7

contextualism is not epistemology objection 122–5; philosophy of language and 122–3; skepticism objection and 123–5

contextualism outside knows: belief ascriptions 400–8; counterfactuals 411–23; epistemic modals 388–98; flexible foundationalism 425–35; moral *vs.* epistemic contextualism 361–73; normative epistemic reasons ascriptions(ERAs) 375–85; overview of 8–9; *see also individual headings*

contextualist fallacy, defined 122–3

contextualist solution to skepticism 133–4; objections to 134–40

conversational contextualism 322, 323–9; problems for 325–7; responses to argument against 327–9; rules for 323

conversational kinematics 321–9; conversational contextualism and 323–9; introduction to 321–3

conversational score 131, 322; *see also* common ground

Co-operative Principle (CP) 206–7

counterfactuals 411–23; contextualism for 416–20; introduction to 411–12; knowledge and 420–3; motivations for 412–15; semantics for 411; skepticism about 412

Craig, E. 86–8

Crasnow, S. 60, 61

Cresswell, M. 110

critical contextual empiricism 328

cross-contextual assessments 40–1

Curley, E. 139

data/motivations for contextualism: feminism and 57–66; intuitive basis 32–41; linguistic behavior and 44–55; overview of 5; variability of knows 13–29; *see also individual headings*

Daukas, N. 62–3

Davis, W. 38

debunking arguments, against interest-relative invariantism 248–50

defective context 325

defective justification, of belief 223

deflationism about knows 28–9

DeRose, K. 15, 16, 29, 32, 52, 57, 59, 64, 65, 75, 82–4, 89, 90, 96, 98, 122, 125, 132–3, 136–9, 171, 180, 207, 212, 224–5, 233, 237, 241, 243, 267, 310, 364, 370, 412, 415, 421; argument from knowledge norms for contextualism 182–4; on disagreement 458–9; on Kornblith 127; Low-High pair from 33–4; on Sosa 126–7; Thelma and Louise Cases 39–40;

Truth and 34–5; warranted assertability manoeuvre 208

Descartes, R. 124, 132, 139, 249, 426, 480

Dever, J. 235

Dewey, J. 425

Dietz, R. 287

disagreement 272–80; about knowledge ascription 282–9; boundaries of discussion of 272–3; challenge to contextualism 257–67; conflicting attitudes and 276–8; conflicting beliefs and 274–6; context of attitudes and 278–80; defined 282; DeRose on 458–9; individual attitudes and 274–6; non-doxastic attitudes and 275; overview of 272; as psychological phenomenon 273–4

disagreement challenge to contextualism 257–67; described 258; hypothesis about disagreement 259–60; knowledge ascription case of 257–8; motivation behind argument 258–60; overview of 257–8; refining 260–2; schematic argument 258; strong disagreement, resisting 263–4; strong disagreement hypothesis 261–2, 264–7

domain of relevant worlds 460

Doris, J. M. 250

double indexing 468–9

Dreier, J. 276, 277

dual process theory 95–6, 101–2, 316

Eaton, D. 250

"Elusive Knowledge" (Lewis) 3–4, 85, 135, 145, 170, 171, 190, 192–4, 283, 321, 323, 334, 457

Emotional Construction of Morals, The (Prinz) 128

encoded conceptual content, lexical adjustment of 485, 489

epistemic egocentrism theory 53, 316

epistemic focal bias 101–2

epistemic intuitions 98–9

epistemic modals 287, 289, 388–98; coffee shop-that case example 389–93; flexible contextualism/relativism about 389–94; knowledge-attributions and 396–8; Mastermind case example 397–8; methodology used 388–9; non-factualism about 394–6; overview of 388; raincoat case example 395; windowless office case example 395–6

epistemic primitivism 13–14

epistemic responsibility, criteria for 60

epistemological implications of contextualism: closure and 156–64; fallibilism and 145–53; Gettier cases and 190–200; knowledge norms and 177–86; lotteries and preface scenarios 168–74; overview of 6; shifting the question objection and 121–9; skepticism and 131–41; *see also individual headings*

ERAs *see* normative epistemic reasons ascriptions (ERAs)

error salience, as contextual feature 44, 45–7; research on 53

495

Index

error theory about disagreement intuitions 263
Evans, G. 297
experimental philosophy challenges to
  contextualism 88–90
explanatory claims of ERAs 383–4
explicatures 206; defined 484
expressives 361
extensions 107, 108

fallibilism 145–53, 457; GC- 148; infallibilist's
  tensions and 150–3; intuitive 145–6; overview
  of 145
Fantl, J. 57, 243, 245, 402, 404
Fate of Knowledge, The (Longino) 59
Feldman, R. 135, 138
felted contextualism 59
Feltz, A. 35, 45
feminism, contextualism and 57–66; connections/
  gaps between 65–6; features of 58; justification
  and 58–61; overview of 57–8; relativism and
  61–3; situated knowing and 58–9; skepticism
  and 64–5; subject-sensitive invariantism and
  57–8
Feyerabend, P. 292
Fintel, K. von 397, 415
flexible foundationalism 425–35; access and 431–3,
  433–5; debates concerning 429–31; justification
  and 427–8; knowledge/belief and 428–9;
  overview of 425; regresses and 425–7; routes to
  427–9; Wittgenstein and 428
flexible relativism 288, 289
focal bias theory 53, 101–2
Fodor, J. 483
Fogelin, R. 135
Foley, R. 401
forked-tongue test 23–4
foundational linguistic issues, contextualism
  439–92; content of knowledge 465–76;
  Contextualism in Epistemology 480–3; mind-
  independent knowledge attributions 455–63;
  overview of 9; Relevance Theory 483–96;
  semantics-pragmatics distinction 441–51; *see also
  individual headings*
free shifting within discourse critique 338–42;
  Ichikawa reply to 340–1; Mion reply to 341–2
Frege, G. 287
Frege-Geach problem 361–2
Fricker, M. 61
full belief: credences and 401, 405–6; defined 400;
  logical coherence and 401; options and 401,
  403–4; partitions and 401, 402–3; threshold for
  401, 402
Full Blooded Skepticism (FBS) 124, 138–9
Fumerton, R. 128

Ganson, D. 402
Garcia-Carpintero, M. 210

gate-keeping contextualism 87
Gauker, C. 342
Gerken, M. 38, 101–2, 316
Gettier cases 190–200; Barn Facade 191, 194,
  198–200; Cohen's critique of Lewis and
  194–8; Evidence without Belief 191–2;
  Lewis's contextualist treatment of 192–4; lousy
  definition of knowledge and 191, 192; overview
  of 190; Sheep on a Hill 191, 195; Someone
  Owns a Ford 190, 194
Gibbard, A. 275
Gillies, A. 397, 415
Glanzberg, M. 326
global context-sensitivity error 308
global indexical error 308, 309
global/partial defence of IRI 246–7
global semantic error objection 311–13; initial
  response to 311–12; responding to strengthened
  312–13; strengthened 312
global *vs.* local semantic error 306, 307–8
Gonnerman, C. 100
gradability, knowledge and 348–56; automatic
  indexicals and 354–6; clarification techniques
  and 352–4; gradable adjectives and 348–9;
  overview of 348; quantifier view 351–2;
  Stanley's objection to 349–51
Gradability Constraint (GC) 350
gradable adjectives 1, 23, 84–6, 232, 453, 460; scalar
  analyses of 348–9
Greco, D. 405
Greco, J. 198; Barn Facade case and 199; Tax
  Collector case and 199; Working Farm case and
  199
Grice, H. P. 205–7, 213, 481, 483; cancellability
  test 211
Grimm, S. R. 249

Hacking, I. 292
Hájek, A. 413, 415, 418
Hannon, M. 87
Hansen, N. 35
Harman, G. 158, 429
Haslanger, S. 76
Hawthorne, J. 14, 16, 57, 99, 100, 172, 234, 241,
  243, 272, 279, 280, 316, 337, 348, 352–3, 372,
  421; argument from knowledge norms against
  contextualism 180–2
Heikes, D. 61
Heim, I. 415
Henderson, D. 87
Henning, T. 379–80
Hicks, D. 61
High Standards Skepticism (HSS) 124, 138–40
Hintikka, J. 465, 472
homophonic reporting 336
"How to Be a Fallibilist" (Cohen) 134, 145–6, 171,
  283

Index

Hume, D. 14, 16, 33
Huvenes, T. 326
hyperbole: conversational implicatures and 220; irony and 220–1; loose use and 221–3

Ichikawa, J. J. 196–7, 247, 249, 250, 328, 334, 340–1, 352, 411, 415, 418–22
identity contextualism 421
ignorant assessors 288
implicature rejection 260
implicatures 206, 220; defined 484
impurism 39
in-between believing 407
index ignorance 315
index theory 467
indexical contextualism 308, 365, 366, 368, 371
indexical contextualism, knowledge ascriptions and 283–4; problem of lost disagreement and 284, 288
indices context sensitivity and 114–15
infallibilism 146–7
infallibilist's tensions, handling 150–3
information, ERAs sensitivity to 379–80
inhabitives 361
insensitive invariantism 219
intensions 107, 108
intention-based view 75
intentional indexicals 354
intentionalism, context and 456
interest-relative invariantism (IRI) 16–18, 38, 57, 240–51, 459; beliefs and 247–8; debunking arguments against 248–50; direct arguments against 250–1; global/partial versions of 246–7; interest types and 245–6; introduction to 240–1; justification and 248; knowledge-ascriptions and 21; motivations for 241–3; odds/stakes and 243–5; ugly conjunction and 22
intuitive, defined 32
intuition, philosophy role in 35–7
intuitive basis for contextualism 32–41; cross-contextual assessments and 40–1; invariantists and 37–40; Low-High pairs and 33–5; overview of 32; propriety challenge 37–8; Truth and 35–7; truth challenge 38–9
intuitive capacity: epistemic 98–9; mindreading as 97–8; relying on, difficulty in 98
intuitive fallibilism 145–6; characterizing 146–8; characterizing, in micro-terms 148–50; contextualism's relation to 146; described 145
intuitively seems, defined 32
intuitive (Type 1) thinking 95
invariantism 28; about knows 257; classical 219; interest-relative 16, 17–18, 20; subject-sensitive 57–8
invariantists: contextualism and 37–40; epistemic standards and 37; moderate 37; skeptical 37
irony: hyperbole and 220–1; loose use and 221–3

Jackson, F. 273
Jarvis, B. 247, 249, 250
justification: contextual empiricism and lack of 60; contextualism as theory of 59; feminism and 58–61; flexible foundationalism and 427–8; scientific reasoning and 59, 60–1; Williams' account of contextualist 59–60

Kamp, H. 468
Kaplan, D. 106, 107, 113–14, 283, 322, 354, 365, 368, 442, 465; two-stage theory 467–72
Kaplan, M. 401
Kasaki, M. 249
Khoo, J. 266, 267
Kim, B. 243
Kindermann, D. 315
K-Nec principle 243
Knobe, J. 35, 88–9, 266, 267
knowing, feminism and 58–9
knowledge: attributor contextualism and 71–2; closure under competent deduction 156; closure under entailment 156; contextualism and types of 2–3; counterfactuals and 420–3; flexible foundationalism and 428–9; high-standards 2, 4; lousy definition of 191, 192; low-standards 2, 4; meaning of 71, 74 (see also conceptual ethics, epistemic contextualism and); relevant alternatives approach to 170; safety theories of 199–200; use of term 78
knowledge, pragmatics and 205–14; contextualism and 207–11; introduction to 205–7; objections to 211–14; utterances and 205–6
knowledge ascription, disagreement about 282–9; indexical contextualist semantics and 283–4; introduction to 282–3; lost substantial disagreement, epistemic relativism and 286–8; nonindexical contextualism, epistemic relativism and 284–6
Knowledge Ascription Absolutism 294, 298
knowledge attributions, mind-independent 455–63
knowledge-evidence equivalence 295–6
knowledge/know truth-conditions 169–71
knowledge norm of assertion (KNA) 177–9; as constitutive of assertion 178; Doubly-Relativized 181–2; Relativized 179–80, 182–4
knowledge norms 177–86; arguments for/against contextualism from 180–4; of assertion 177–9; contextualist suspicion of, reasons for 184–6; data offered in favor of 178–9; defined 177; DeRose's argument for 182–4; Hawthorne's argument against 180–2; introduction to 177–9; relativize, contextualists need to 179–80
knows: A-quantifiers and 342–4; as context-sensitive 473–6; contextualism about 257, 332; critiques of, as universal quantifier 335–40; deflationism about 28–9; disagreement and 336–7; free shifting within discourse and

497

338–42; homophonic reporting and 336; as index operator 472–3; invariantism about 257; nominal expression and 338; quantifiers and 332–44; replies to critiques of 340–4; semantic ignorance and 337–8; stability and 234; as universal quantifier 332–5; variability of (*see* variability of knows)

"know(s) that" ascriptions, semantics for: Cohen and 171; DeRose and 171; Lewis and 170–1

Kornblith, H. 85, 121–2, 138–40; DeRose on 127; skepticism objection 124

Kratzer, A. 388, 411

Kripke, S. 465

K-Suff principle 242–3; direct objections to 249–50

Kusch, M. 86

Kyburg, H. 401, 402

Lackey, J. 121, 249

Larson, R. 106

Leitgeb, H. 402–3

Lena cases 98–9

Lepore, E. 230, 236, 250–1

Levi, I. 405

Lewis, D. 2–4, 59, 84, 85, 105, 108, 110, 113, 131, 135, 136, 145, 170, 233, 267, 278, 322, 323, 334–5, 351–2, 382, 411, 414, 415, 465, 466, 470–1, 474–5; on attention 457–8; Cohen's critique of 194–8; knowledge ascriptions and 170–1, 193–4; Poor Bill case 194; Rule of Resemblance 196–7; skepticism and 193; treatment of Gettier cases 192–4

Lewis, K. 411, 416

linguistic analogies, contextualism and 84–6

linguistic behavior, epistemic contextualism and 44–55; error salience studies of 44, 45–7, 48; features of 44; introduction to 44–5; knowledge ascription studies of 47–9; mixed evidence of motivation for 45–9; rival theories of, acceptance of 50–2; skeptical judgments and 52–3; theoretical advantage of 52–4

linguistic meaning, context-sensitivity and 443–5

local semantic error objection regimented 309–10; contextualism response to 310–11

location question 17–18

Longino, H. 59–60, 61, 62, 328–9

loose use 221–3; belief variation and 225–7; coffee case 221; irony and 221–3; overview of 218

lost substantial disagreement, epistemic relativism and 286–8

lotteries and preface scenarios 168–74; introduction to 168–9; knowledge/know truth-conditions and 169–71; lotteries example 171–3; prefaces example 173–4

lotteries case: Hawthorne and 172–3; hyperbole and 220; Lewis's rules and 171–2

lottery knowledge, closure and 159–61

Low-High pairs 33–5

Low vignette, described 33

Ludlow, P. 265–6

MacFarlane, J. 16, 85, 230, 273–5, 277–9, 283–6, 293–5, 297, 313–15, 337, 390–3, 397–8, 476; on retraction 461–2

McGrath, M. 57, 243, 245, 402, 404

McKenna, R. 60

Maher, P. 401

Marques, T. 277

Meaning Perspective 106–7; character and context from 107–10; character representation 109; context representation 109; Simple Strategy and 108–9

Medina, J. 59

mention, contextualism and 3–4; quotation marks and 3

Metaepistemology and Skepticism (Fumerton) 128

metaethics 128

metalinguistic analysis 71, 72; normative terms, disagreement and 72–4

meta-linguistic single premise closure (MSPC) 157

method of cases, methodology of straightforward and 82–4

methodological disputes, contextualism and 81–90; conceptual genealogies, functional roles and 86–8; experimental philosophy challenges 88–90; introduction to 81; linguistic analogies of 84–6; method of cases and 82–4; questions surrounding 81–2

methodological issues for contextualism: conceptual ethics and 71–8; context sensitivity and, theorizing about 105–16; methodological disputes and 81–90; overview of 5–6; psychological context of 94–103; *see also individual headings*

micro-bumps 149–50

mind-independent knowledge attributions 455–63; contents of context, determinants of 462–3; of contexts 455–7; DeRose on disagreement 458–9; introduction to 455; Lewis on attention 457–8; MacFarlane on retraction 461–2; Stanley on "every" 460–1; Stanley on high stakes 459

mindreading: described 97; egocentric bias and 98–9, 100; as intuitive capacity 97–8

minimalistic pluralism 235, 236

Mion, G. 340, 341–2

modal expressions *see* epistemic modals

moderate invariantists 37

modest contextualism 306

monsters 113–14

Montague, R. 105, 465, 466

Montminy, M. 41, 136, 315

Moore, G. E. 128, 207

moral retraction case 369–70

Index

moral *vs.* epistemic contextualism 361–73; bank cases and 364; contextualist semantics and 364–6; disagreement arguments 370–2; Frege-Geach problem for 361–2; functions of 362–4; introduction to 361–2; moral retraction case for 369–70; retraction case for 366–9

Moss, S. 415

multi-premise closure (MPC) principle 157, 169; accrual of risk and 161–2; prefaces and 173–4

Nagel, J. 36, 38, 49, 89, 247, 316

neutrality constraint 389

new epistemic relativism 294–5

Ninan, D. 471

nominal expression 338

noncotenability of attitudes 277

non-doxastic attitudes 275

non-factualism about epistemic modals 394–6

non-indexical contextualism 17, 20, 22, 365, 366, 368, 371–2; epistemic relativism and 284–6; problem of lost disagreement and 284–6, 288; ugly conjunctions and 22

normative epistemic reasons ascriptions (ERAs) 375–85; background conditions and 381–2; context-sensitivity of 376–83; described 375; explanatory claims of 383–4; information and 379–80; introduction to 375–6; normative facts and 375; questions and 378–9; relevant alternatives and 376–8; as representatives 382–3; standards/thresholds and 380–1

normative epistemology 128

normative ethics 128

normative non-absolutism 297

Nozick, R. 405

Nunberg, G. 112

objectivism, context and 456–7

occurrences 107

O'Connor, P. 59

odds, interest-relative invariantism and 243–5

On Certainty (Wittgenstein) 428

parameter shifting, sensitivity and 465–7

Parfit, D. 274

Partee, B. 342

partial belief: defined 400; options and 401, 403–4; partitions and 401, 402–3; probabilistic coherence and 401

Peirce, C.S. 425

Perry, J. 354

pertinent context 456–7

Pettit, P. 273

phenomenal, dispositional view of belief 406–7

philosophy: intuitions role in 35–7; of language 122–3

Pickavance, T. 250

Pinillos, Á. 89, 241

Plunkett, D. 72–7, 265, 266

polyphonic contextualism 59

practical consequences, as contextual feature 44

pragmatic invariantist accounts, error in 315–16

pragmatic languages 466

pragmatic presupposition 325

pragmatics: contextualism and 207–11; described 205, 445; Grice's letter of recommendation example 205–6; knowledge and 205–14

Presuppositional Epistemic Contextualism (PEC) 355, 356

Preyer, G. 230

primitivism, epistemic 13–14

Principia Ethica (Moore) 128

Prinz, J. 128

Prior, A. 283, 465

Pritchard, D. 297

protoknowledge concept 86–7

psychological context of contextualism 94–103; dual process theory 95–6; future research for 102–3; introduction to 94–5; mindreading, egocentric bias and 97–9; psychological research, applications of 99–102; search termination 96–7

psychological error theories 314, 316

psychological phenomenon of disagreement 273–4

pure indexicals 354

Pust, J. 35

quantifier expressions 1, 448–9

questions, ERAs sensitivity to 378–9

Rabern, B. 471

rationality, conflicting attitudes and 277

Reading-No Enslavement 178

reasonable reliability constraint 389

Recanati, F. 206, 368

redundancy theory of 'now' 468

Reed, B. 122, 249–50; skepticism objection 124–5

reflective (Type 2) thinking 95

regresses, flexible foundationalism and 425–7

relativism 22; about epistemic modals 389–94; about "knows" 292–4; as the bias paradox 61–2; described 283; disagreement and 2, 255; epistemic, relativism about "knows" and 292–4; epistemic contextualism and 282–301; epistemological implications of 292–8; equivalence/reduction and 295–6; feminism and 61–3; flexible 288, 289; implications of 295–7; Index Error 314–15; knowledge 16, 27–8; lost disagreement and; new epistemic 294–5; normativity/value and 296–7; overview of 7–8; truth-value 283, 284–5; wider epistemological implications of new 298

Relativism and Monadic Truth (Cappelen and Hawthorne) 372

Relevance Theory 483–96; contrasts/comparisons with other rejection means 487–9; linguistic

Index

dilemma, explicature and 484–7; overview of 483–4

relevant alternatives, ERAs sensitivity to 376–8

representatives, ERAs as 382–3

Retraction Case for 'Know' 366–9

retractions 24; of knowledge 25–8; MacFarlane on 461–2

Revealing Strategy 112

Richard, M. 74–5

Richardson, A. 60

risk: multi-premise closure and 161–2; single-premise closure and 162–4

Rolin, K. 59–61, 62, 65

Rooth, M. 377–8

Rorty, R. 292

Ross, J. 401, 405

Rubin, K. 247, 249, 250

rules: of accommodation 457; of actuality 323, 416; of attention 323, 417, 457–8; of belief 323; of pragmatic presupposition 325; of resemblance 323

Russell, G. 250

Ryle, G. 296

Rysiew, P. 152, 208–9, 211, 213, 224, 225, 315

safety theories of knowledge 199–200

Salmon, N. 230

satisfaction, conflicting attitudes and 277–8, 279

"satisficing" principle 101

Saul, J. 207

Schaffer, J. 23, 35, 38, 88–9, 233, 243, 263, 311, 312, 332, 335–8, 340, 342–4, 352, 384

Schiffer, S. 132, 308, 309, 337–8, 482; global semantic error objection 311–13; local semantic error objection regimented 309–10

Schroeder, M. 401, 405

Schwitzgebel, E. 406–7

Science as Social Knowledge (Longino) 59

scientific reasoning, justification and 59, 60–1

"Scorekeeping in a Language Game" (Lewis) 457

Scott, D. 465, 466

search termination 96–7

Searle, John 361

Segal, G. 106

self-undermining objection 313–14; responding to 314

semantic blindness 462; *see also* semantic error

semantic error 305–17; ambitious contextualism, Cartesian Scepticism and 306–7; for ambitious contextualism 308–9; contextualism response to 310–11; for epistemic contextualism 305–6; introduction to 305; local and global 307–8; modest *vs.* ambitious contextualism 306; pragmatic invariantist accounts, error in 315–16; preliminary distinctions of 306; psychological error theories 316; relativism's Index Error and 314–15; Schiffer's global semantic error

objection 311–13; Schiffer's local semantic error objection 309–10; self-undermining objection 313–14; *vs.* semantic ignorance 306

semantic ignorance 337–8

semantic implementations for contextualism: conversational kinematics and 321–9; gradability, knowledge and 348–56; knows, quantifiers and 332–44; overview of 8; Semantic Error Problem 305–17; *see also individual headings*

semantic minimalism/speech act pluralism (SM+SAP) 230–8; minimalistic pluralism and 236; motivation for 230–1; overview of 230; responses to stability/variability tensions 234–6; skepticism and, defense of 237–8; speech act pluralism and 235–6; stability data 233–4; variability data 231–3

semantic theories: bank case 218; belief variation and 218–20; insensitive-invariant 219–20; parking case 218; strong/weak 223–5; subject-sensitive invariantism and 219; truth-independent factors 219

semantic thesis 122

semantic values 106

semantics: approaches to 106–7; described 445; psychology rules perspective, context sensitivity and 110–12; sociology rules perspective, context sensitivity and 113

semantics-pragmatics distinction, context-sensitivity and 441–51; determining factors 446–7; epistemic contextualism and 449–51; linguistic meaning and 443–5; overview of 441; quantifier expressions example 448–9; simple view of 442–3; "today" example 447–8

sensitive invariantism 38, 475–6; *see also* interest-relative invariantism (IRI)

sentence nonliterality 206

sentences, defined 456

sentences-in-contexts 107

Sheep on a Hill Gettier case 191

shifting-options view of belief 403–4

shifting-partition view of belief 402–3

shifting-presuppositions view of belief 404–5

shifting the question objection 121–9; contextualism as metaepistemology 127–9; contextualism is epistemology 125–7; contextualism is not epistemology 122–5; overview of 121–2; *see also individual objections*

shifting-threshold view of belief 402

Sibley, D. A. 408

Simple Lottery Case 192, 194

Simple Strategy 108–9; character representation 109; context representation 109; objections to 109–10

Simple Threshold 400–1; views of belief; quantifiers in 402; *see also* belief ascriptions

Simpson, S. 89

single-premise closure (SPC) 156; accrual of risk and 162–4
situations, defined 456
skeptical invariantists 37; *see also* loose use; skepticism
skepticism 131–41; Cartesian 58, 132–3; closure and 158–9; contextualism irrelevant to epistemology objection 137–8; contextualism mischaracterize, objection 138–40; contextualism too skeptic-friendly objection 134–7; contextualist solution to 133–4; contextualists beg the question objection 140; epistemic contextualism and 123–5, 131–2; fallibilism and 146; feminism and 64–5; introduction to 131; linguistic behavior and 52–3; and paradox 133, 134; semantic minimalism and speech act pluralism in defense of 237–8
SM+SAP *see* semantic minimalism/speech act pluralism (SM+SAP)
Smithies, D. 433
Smith's stolen car case 99–102
Soames, S. 230
Sobel sequence 415, 418
Solomon, M. 60
Someone Owns a Ford Gettier case 190, 194
Sosa, E. 121, 422; Blome-Tillman on 125–6; DeRose on 126–7; epistemic contextualist objection 122–3
source-content bias theory 53–4
speech act pluralism 235–6
Sperber, D. 206, 207, 213, 483
stability data 231, 233–4; knows and 234
Stainton, R. 488
stakes-based version of IRI 243–5; *see also* interest-relative invariantism (IRI)
standards and thresholds, ERAs sensitivity to 380–1
Stanley, J. 16, 20, 23, 40, 57, 63, 75, 241, 243, 246, 247, 296, 321–2, 332, 335–6, 338–41, 348, 355, 471, 476; on "every" 460–1; gradability objection of 349–51; on high stakes 459
Stanovich, K. 95
Stevenson, C. L. 275–6
Stine, G. 3, 152, 380–1
Stokke, Andreas 326
straightforward, methodology of 82–4, 109, 110
strength of justification 460
strength of one's epistemic position (SEP) 124–5
strengthenings of sentence meanings 206
Strevens, M. 383
strict invariantism 473, 475; *see also* invariantism
strong disagreement hypothesis 261–2; resisting 263–7
Sturgeon, S. 402
subject-sensitive invariantism 57–8, 219, 241; *see also* interest-relative invariantism (IRI)
Sundell, T. 72–7, 265, 266
surface-contradictory claims 37

Swanson, E. 382
systematic vs non-systematic semantic error 306
Szabó, Z. G. 23, 263, 311, 312, 332, 335–8, 340, 342–4, 352

Tax Collector case 199
Timmons, M. 128
toy contextualism 2, 4
true demonstratives 354
Truman case 407–8
Truth, intuitions and 35–7
truth-in-a-context 471
truth-independent factors 219
truth-value relativism 283, 284–5; *see also* relativism
Turri, J. 298
two-stage theory 467–72

ugly conjunctions 21–2; classical (flexible) contextualism 22; interest-relative invariantism and 22; non-indexical contextualism and 22
unenlightened usage 225
Unger, P. 128, 148–9, 225, 482
Unity Thesis 245
universal quantifier, knows as 332–5; critiques of 335–40; disagreement critique 336–7; free shifting within discourse critique 338–42; homophonic reporting critique 336; nominal expression critique 338; semantic ignorance critique 337–8
universal *vs.* individual semantic error 306
use, contextualism and 3–4
use-indexicality 282–3
use-sensitivity 282, 283; epistemic modal claims and 287

value insight 297
variabilism, varieties of 16–17
variability: data 231–3; in reference 231; in truth value 232; in what is said 231–2
variability of knows 13–29; consideration types suggestive of 14–16; context-sensitivity and 22–5; epistemic primitivism and 13–14; hard cases, explain away 18–21; location question 17–18; retraction data and 25–8; ugly conjunctions and 21–2; varieties of variabilism 16–17
views of belief: in-between believing 407; phenomenal, dispositional 406–7; shifting-options 403–4; shifting-partition 402–3; shifting-presuppositions 404–5; shifting-threshold 402
Vogel, J. 99

warranted assertability manoeuvre (WAM) 182, 208, 224, 483
Waterman, J. 100

Index

Weatherson, B. 243, 246, 247, 402, 403–4
what-is-said-monism 235
"what is said" semantics 469–72
Williams, M. 57, 59–62, 64, 425
Williams, R. G. 414, 415
Williamson, T. 13, 38, 99, 100, 129, 147, 224, 295, 296, 298, 316, 428–9, 433
Wilson, D. 206, 207, 213, 483, 485

within-case knowledge ascriptions 89
Wittgenstein, L. 292, 425, 428
Working Farm case 199

Yalcin, S. 394–6, 470, 471

Zagzebski, L. 191
Zarpentine, C. 35, 45